HIROHIKO ARAKI

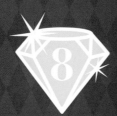

JOJO'S BIZARRE ADVENTURE

PART 4 ★ DIAMOND IS UNBREAKABLE

8

JoJo's
BIZARRE ADVENTURE

PART 4 ★ DIAMOND IS UNBREAKABLE

CONTENTS

CHAPTER 134: Let's Live on a Transmission Tower, Part 2 .... *3*

CHAPTER 135: Let's Live on a Transmission Tower, Part 3 .... *23*

CHAPTER 136: Let's Live on a Transmission Tower, Part 4 .... *43*

CHAPTER 137: Let's Live on a Transmission Tower, Part 5 .... *63*

CHAPTER 138: Let's Live on a Transmission Tower, Part 6 .... *83*

CHAPTER 139: Misterioso, Part 1 .... *103*

CHAPTER 140: Misterioso, Part 2 .... *125*

CHAPTER 141: Misterioso, Part 3 .... *145*

CHAPTER 142: Misterioso, Part 4 .... *165*

CHAPTER 143: Misterioso, Part 5 .... *185*

CHAPTER 144: Misterioso, Part 6 .... *205*

CHAPTER 145: My Dad Is Not My Dad, Part 1 .... *225*

CHAPTER 146: My Dad Is Not My Dad, Part 2 .... *245*

CHAPTER 147: Cheap Trap, Part 1 .... *265*

CHAPTER 148: Cheap Trap, Part 2 .... *285*

CHAPTER 149: Cheap Trap, Part 3 .... *305*

CHAPTER 150: Cheap Trap, Part 4 .... *325*

CHAPTER 151: Cheap Trap, Part 5 .... *345*

CHAPTER 152: Cheap Trap, Part 6 .... *365*

Author's Comments *387*

Credits *390*

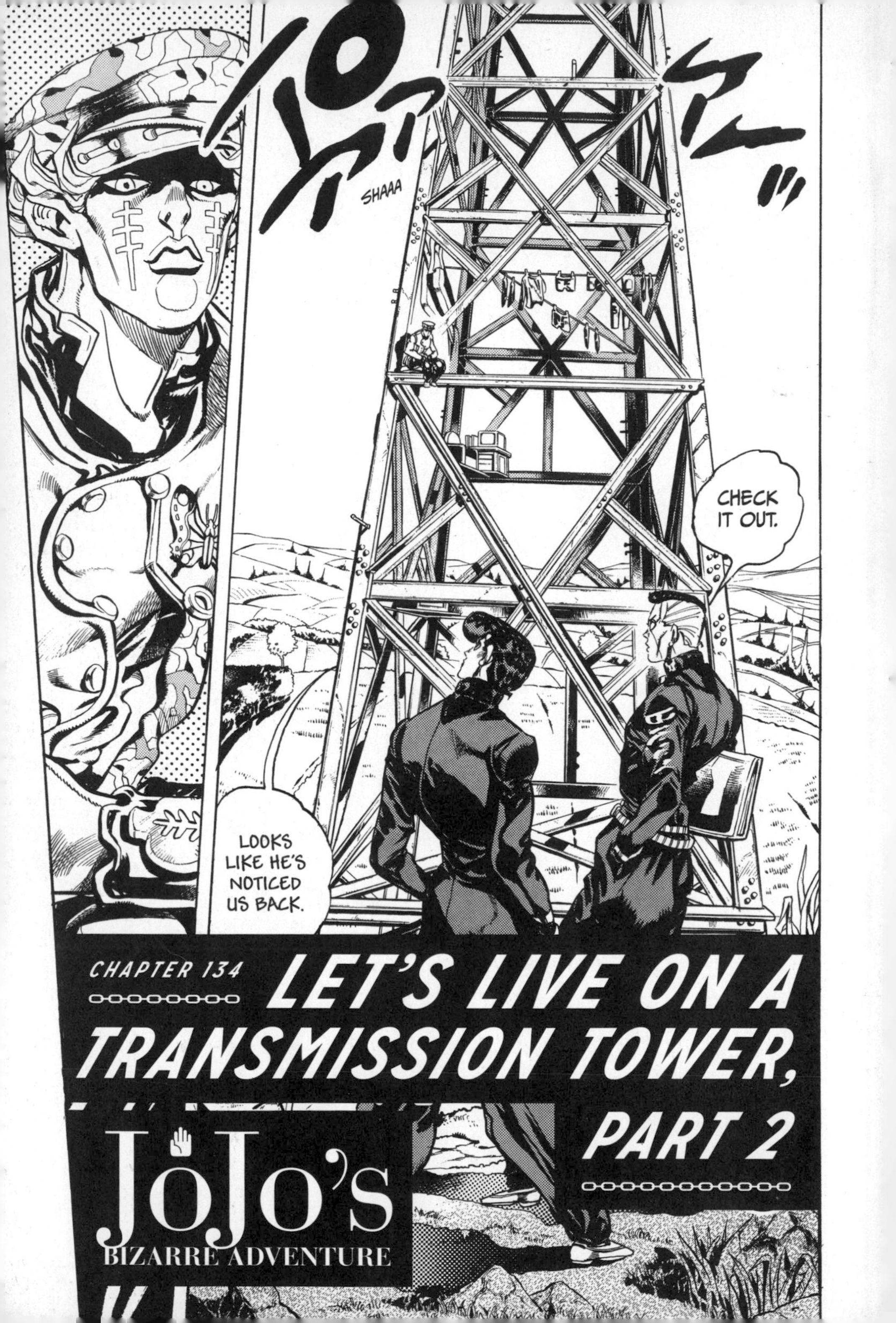
SHAAA
CHECK IT OUT.
LOOKS LIKE HE'S NOTICED US BACK.
CHAPTER 134
LET'S LIVE ON A TRANSMISSION TOWER, PART 2
JoJo's
BIZARRE ADVENTURE

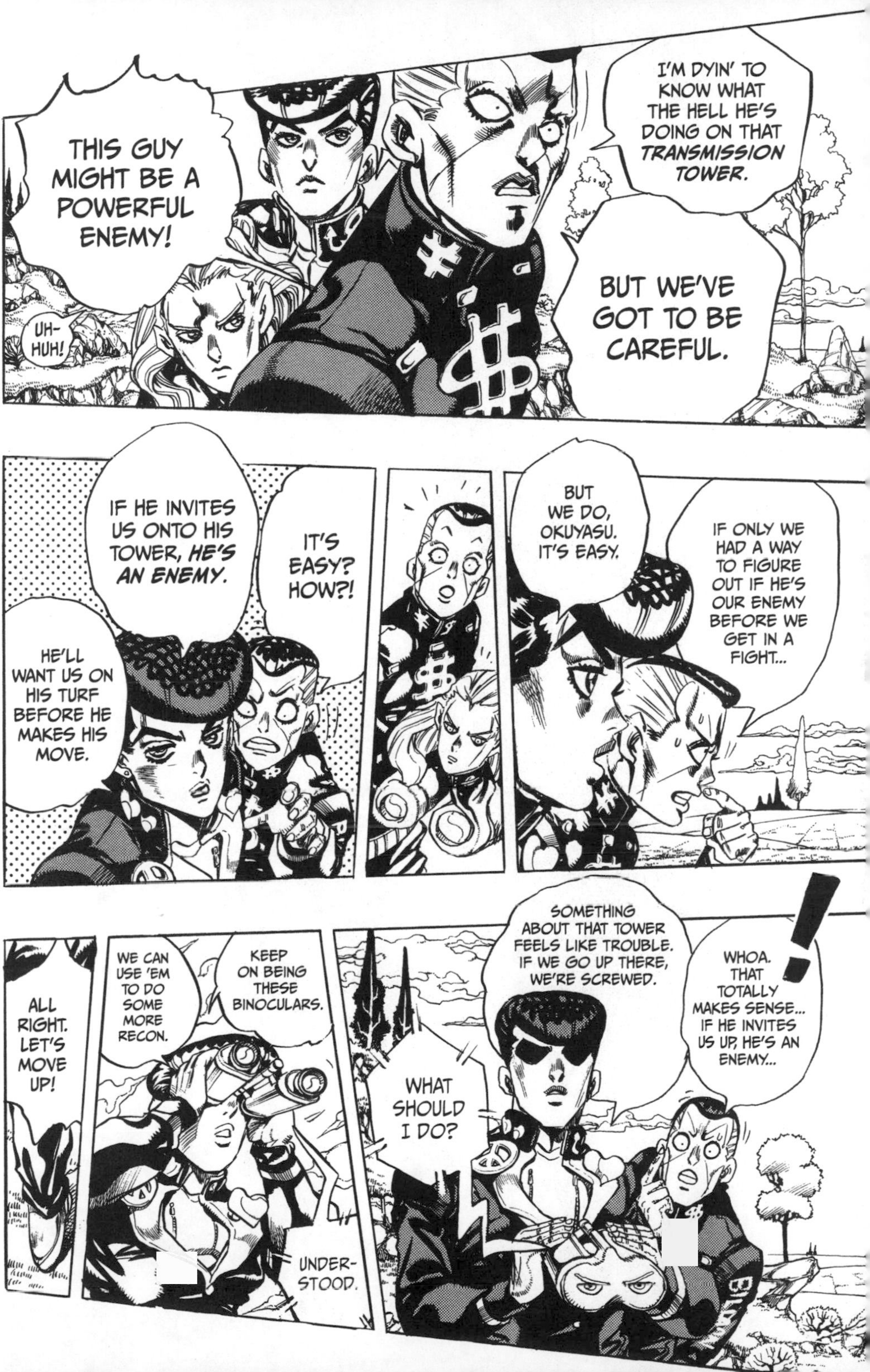
I'M DYIN' TO KNOW WHAT THE HELL HE'S DOING ON THAT *TRANSMISSION TOWER.*
BUT WE'VE GOT TO BE CAREFUL.
THIS GUY MIGHT BE A POWERFUL ENEMY!
UH-HUH!
IF ONLY WE HAD A WAY TO FIGURE OUT IF HE'S OUR ENEMY BEFORE WE GET IN A FIGHT...
BUT WE DO, OKUYASU. IT'S EASY.
IT'S EASY? HOW?!
IF HE INVITES US ONTO HIS TOWER, *HE'S AN ENEMY.*
HE'LL WANT US ON HIS TURF BEFORE HE MAKES HIS MOVE.
WHOA. THAT TOTALLY MAKES SENSE... IF HE INVITES US UP, HE'S AN ENEMY...
SOMETHING ABOUT THAT TOWER FEELS LIKE TROUBLE. IF WE GO UP THERE, WE'RE SCREWED.
WHAT SHOULD I DO?
KEEP ON BEING THESE BINOCULARS.
WE CAN USE 'EM TO DO SOME MORE RECON.
UNDER-STOOD.
ALL RIGHT. LET'S MOVE UP!

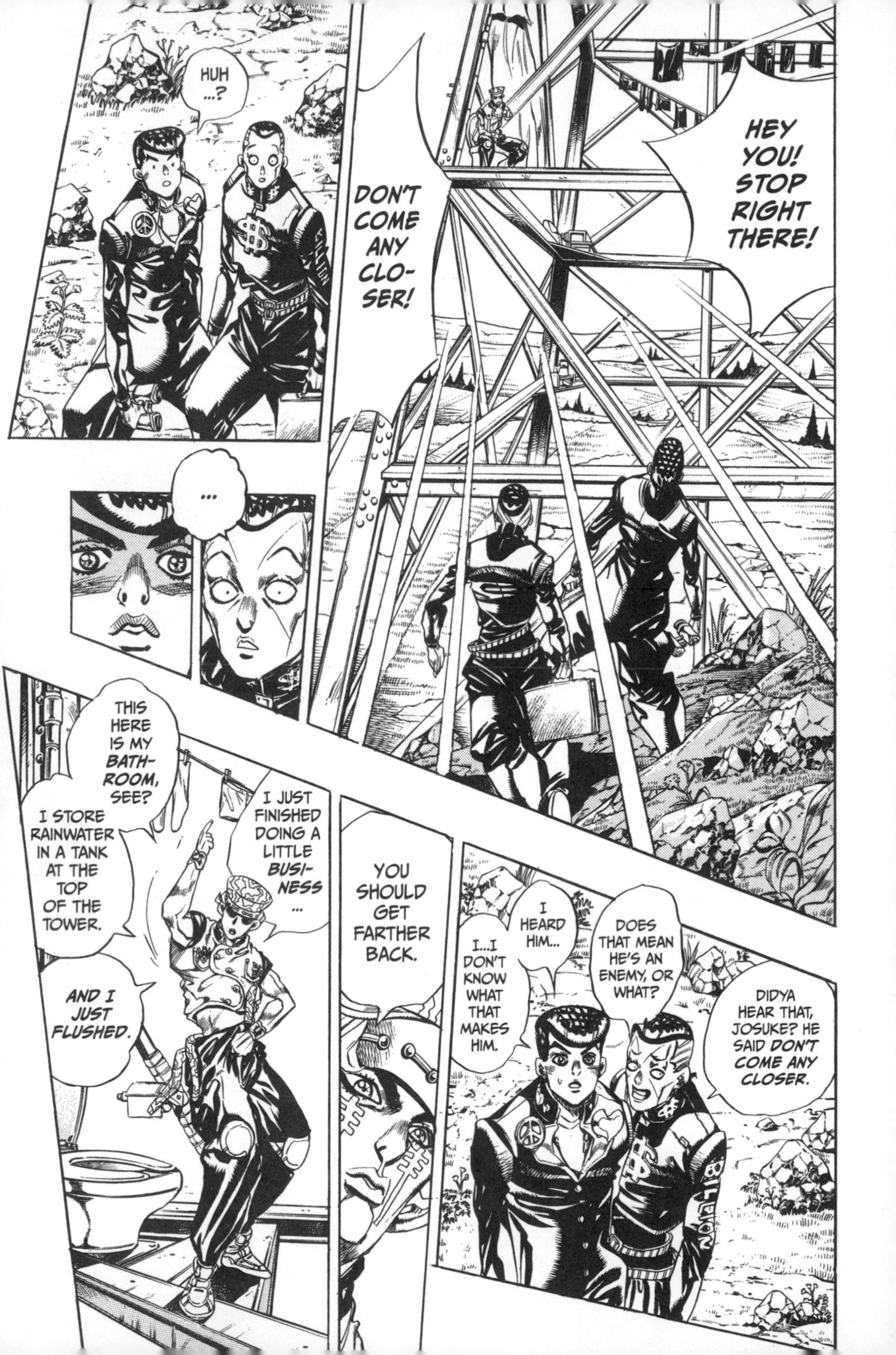
HEY YOU! STOP RIGHT THERE!
DON'T COME ANY CLO-SER!
HUH ...?
...
DIDYA HEAR THAT, JOSUKE? HE SAID DON'T COME ANY CLOSER.
DOES THAT MEAN HE'S AN ENEMY, OR WHAT?
I HEARD HIM...
I...I DON'T KNOW WHAT THAT MAKES HIM.
YOU SHOULD GET FARTHER BACK.
I JUST FINISHED DOING A LITTLE BUSINESS...
THIS HERE IS MY BATHROOM, SEE?
I STORE RAINWATER IN A TANK AT THE TOP OF THE TOWER.
AND I JUST FLUSHED.

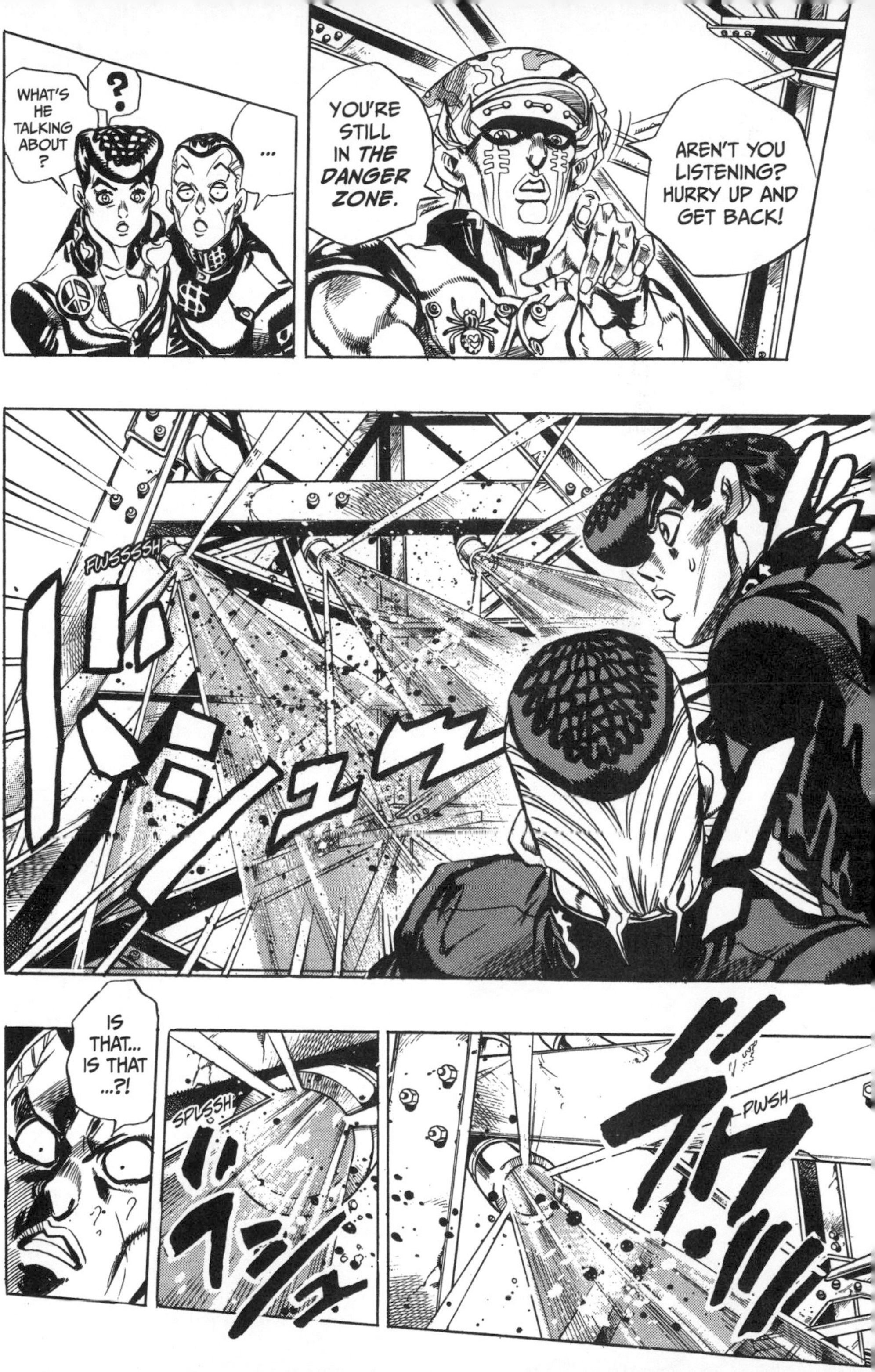
AREN'T YOU LISTENING? HURRY UP AND GET BACK!
YOU'RE STILL IN *THE DANGER ZONE.*
...
?
WHAT'S HE TALKING ABOUT?
FWSSSSH
PWSH
SPLSSH
IS THAT... IS THAT ...?!

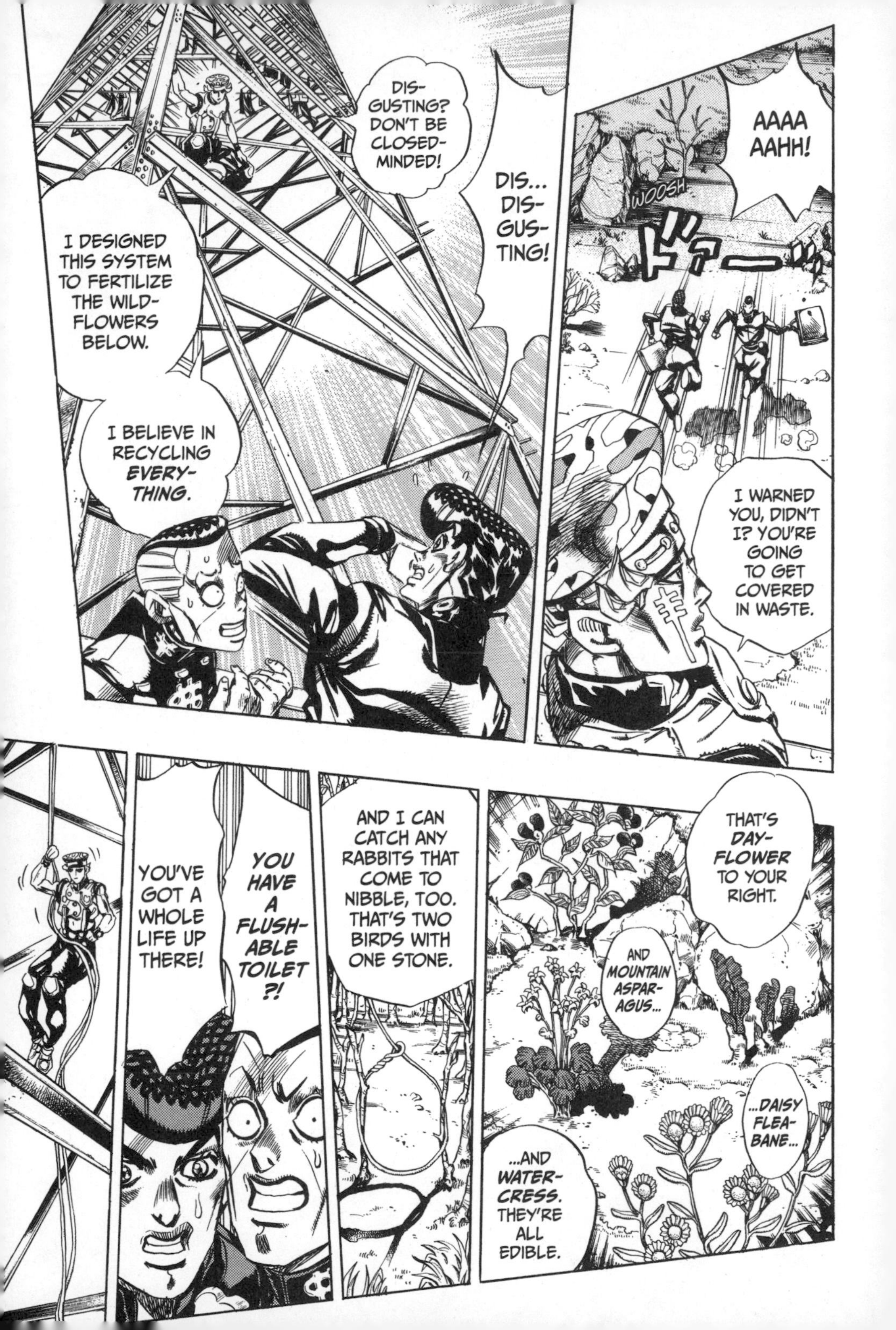
AAAA AAHH!
WOOSH
ドァーーッ
I WARNED YOU, DIDN'T I? YOU'RE GOING TO GET COVERED IN WASTE.
DIS... DIS-GUS-TING!
DIS-GUSTING? DON'T BE CLOSED-MINDED!
I DESIGNED THIS SYSTEM TO FERTILIZE THE WILD-FLOWERS BELOW.
I BELIEVE IN RECYCLING *EVERY-THING.*
THAT'S *DAY-FLOWER* TO YOUR RIGHT.
AND *MOUNTAIN ASPAR-AGUS...*
...DAISY FLEA-BANE...
...AND *WATER-CRESS.* THEY'RE ALL EDIBLE.
AND I CAN CATCH ANY RABBITS THAT COME TO NIBBLE, TOO. THAT'S TWO BIRDS WITH ONE STONE.
YOU HAVE A FLUSH-ABLE TOILET ?!
YOU'VE GOT A WHOLE LIFE UP THERE!

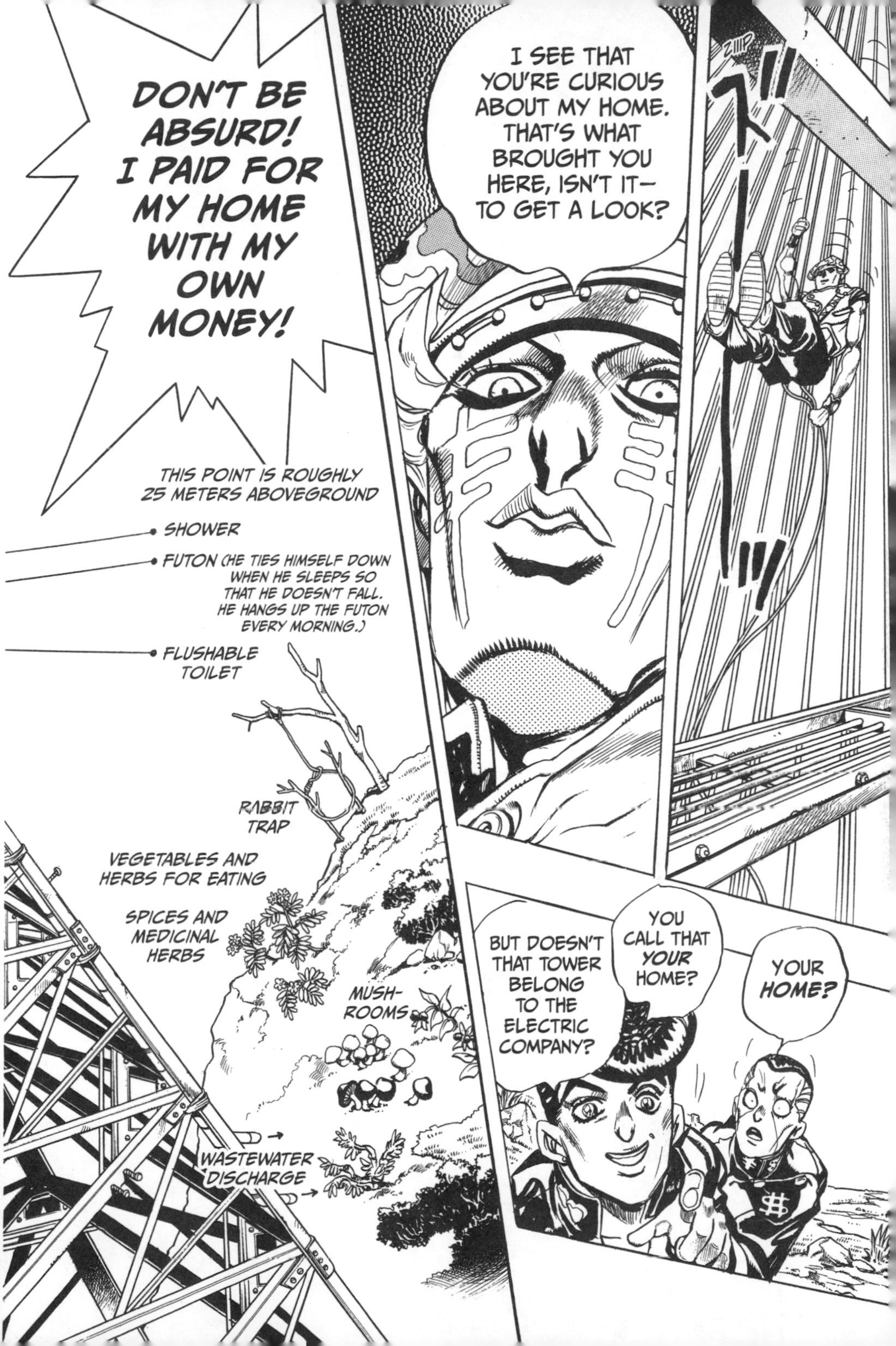
ZIIIP
I SEE THAT YOU'RE CURIOUS ABOUT MY HOME. THAT'S WHAT BROUGHT YOU HERE, ISN'T IT— TO GET A LOOK?
YOUR HOME?
YOU CALL THAT YOUR HOME?
BUT DOESN'T THAT TOWER BELONG TO THE ELECTRIC COMPANY?
DON'T BE ABSURD! I PAID FOR MY HOME WITH MY OWN MONEY!
THIS POINT IS ROUGHLY 25 METERS ABOVEGROUND
SHOWER
FUTON (HE TIES HIMSELF DOWN WHEN HE SLEEPS SO THAT HE DOESN'T FALL. HE HANGS UP THE FUTON EVERY MORNING.)
FLUSHABLE TOILET
RABBIT TRAP
VEGETABLES AND HERBS FOR EATING
SPICES AND MEDICINAL HERBS
MUSH-ROOMS
WASTEWATER DISCHARGE

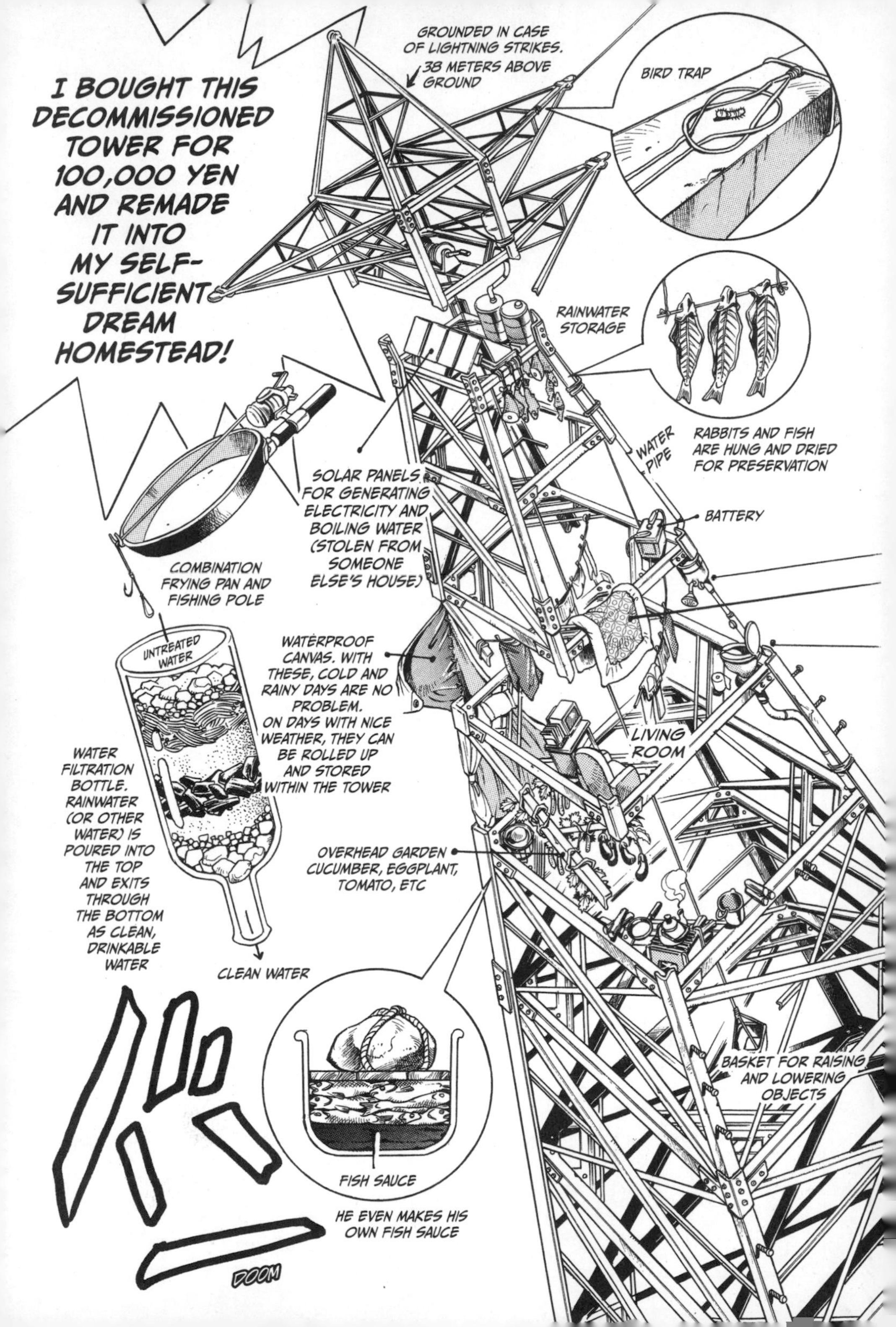
I BOUGHT THIS DECOMMISSIONED TOWER FOR 100,000 YEN AND REMADE IT INTO MY SELF-SUFFICIENT DREAM HOMESTEAD!
GROUNDED IN CASE OF LIGHTNING STRIKES.
38 METERS ABOVE GROUND
BIRD TRAP
RAINWATER STORAGE
RABBITS AND FISH ARE HUNG AND DRIED FOR PRESERVATION
WATER PIPE
SOLAR PANELS FOR GENERATING ELECTRICITY AND BOILING WATER (STOLEN FROM SOMEONE ELSE'S HOUSE)
BATTERY
COMBINATION FRYING PAN AND FISHING POLE
UNTREATED WATER
WATERPROOF CANVAS. WITH THESE, COLD AND RAINY DAYS ARE NO PROBLEM. ON DAYS WITH NICE WEATHER, THEY CAN BE ROLLED UP AND STORED WITHIN THE TOWER
LIVING ROOM
WATER FILTRATION BOTTLE. RAINWATER (OR OTHER WATER) IS POURED INTO THE TOP AND EXITS THROUGH THE BOTTOM AS CLEAN, DRINKABLE WATER
OVERHEAD GARDEN CUCUMBER, EGGPLANT, TOMATO, ETC
CLEAN WATER
BASKET FOR RAISING AND LOWERING OBJECTS
FISH SAUCE
HE EVEN MAKES HIS OWN FISH SAUCE
DOOM

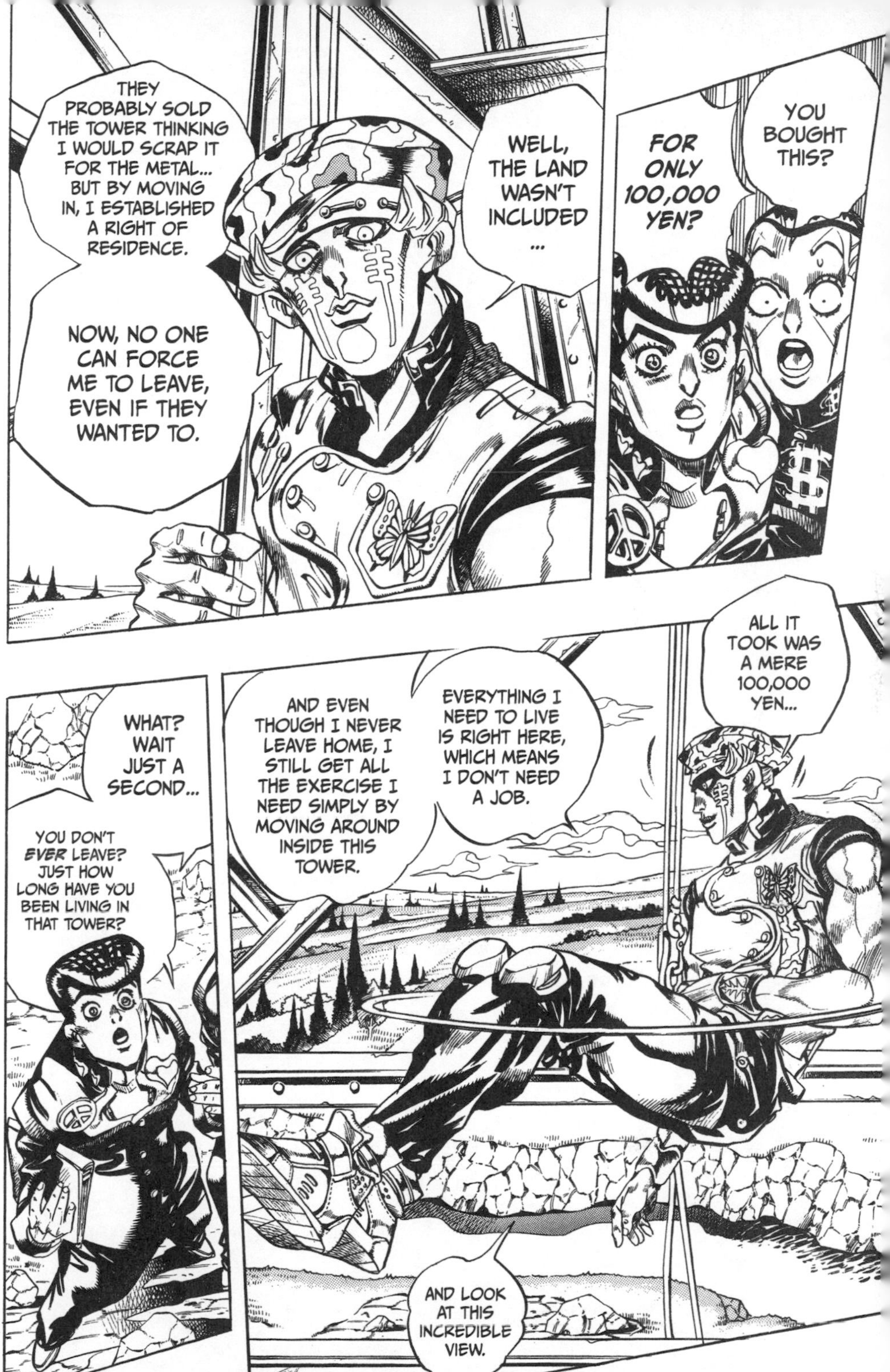
YOU BOUGHT THIS?
FOR ONLY 100,000 YEN?
WELL, THE LAND WASN'T INCLUDED ...
THEY PROBABLY SOLD THE TOWER THINKING I WOULD SCRAP IT FOR THE METAL... BUT BY MOVING IN, I ESTABLISHED A RIGHT OF RESIDENCE.
NOW, NO ONE CAN FORCE ME TO LEAVE, EVEN IF THEY WANTED TO.
ALL IT TOOK WAS A MERE 100,000 YEN...
EVERYTHING I NEED TO LIVE IS RIGHT HERE, WHICH MEANS I DON'T NEED A JOB.
AND EVEN THOUGH I NEVER LEAVE HOME, I STILL GET ALL THE EXERCISE I NEED SIMPLY BY MOVING AROUND INSIDE THIS TOWER.
AND LOOK AT THIS INCREDIBLE VIEW.
WHAT? WAIT JUST A SECOND...
YOU DON'T *EVER* LEAVE? JUST HOW LONG HAVE YOU BEEN LIVING IN THAT TOWER?

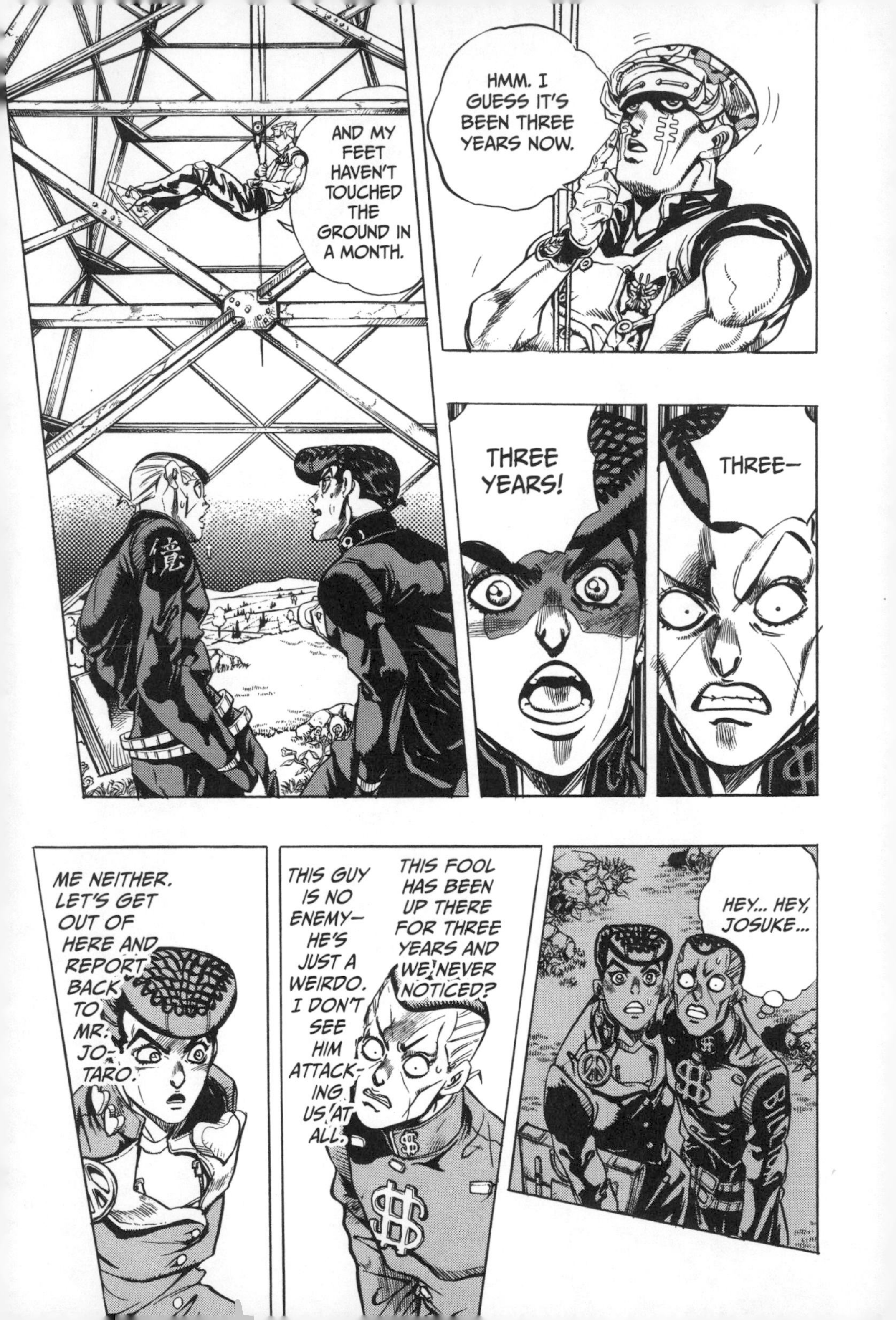

HMM. I GUESS IT'S BEEN THREE YEARS NOW.
THREE—
THREE YEARS!
AND MY FEET HAVEN'T TOUCHED THE GROUND IN A MONTH.
HEY... HEY, JOSUKE...
THIS FOOL HAS BEEN UP THERE FOR THREE YEARS AND WE NEVER NOTICED?
THIS GUY IS NO ENEMY—HE'S JUST A WEIRDO. I DON'T SEE HIM ATTACKING US AT ALL.
ME NEITHER. LET'S GET OUT OF HERE AND REPORT BACK TO MR. JOTARO.

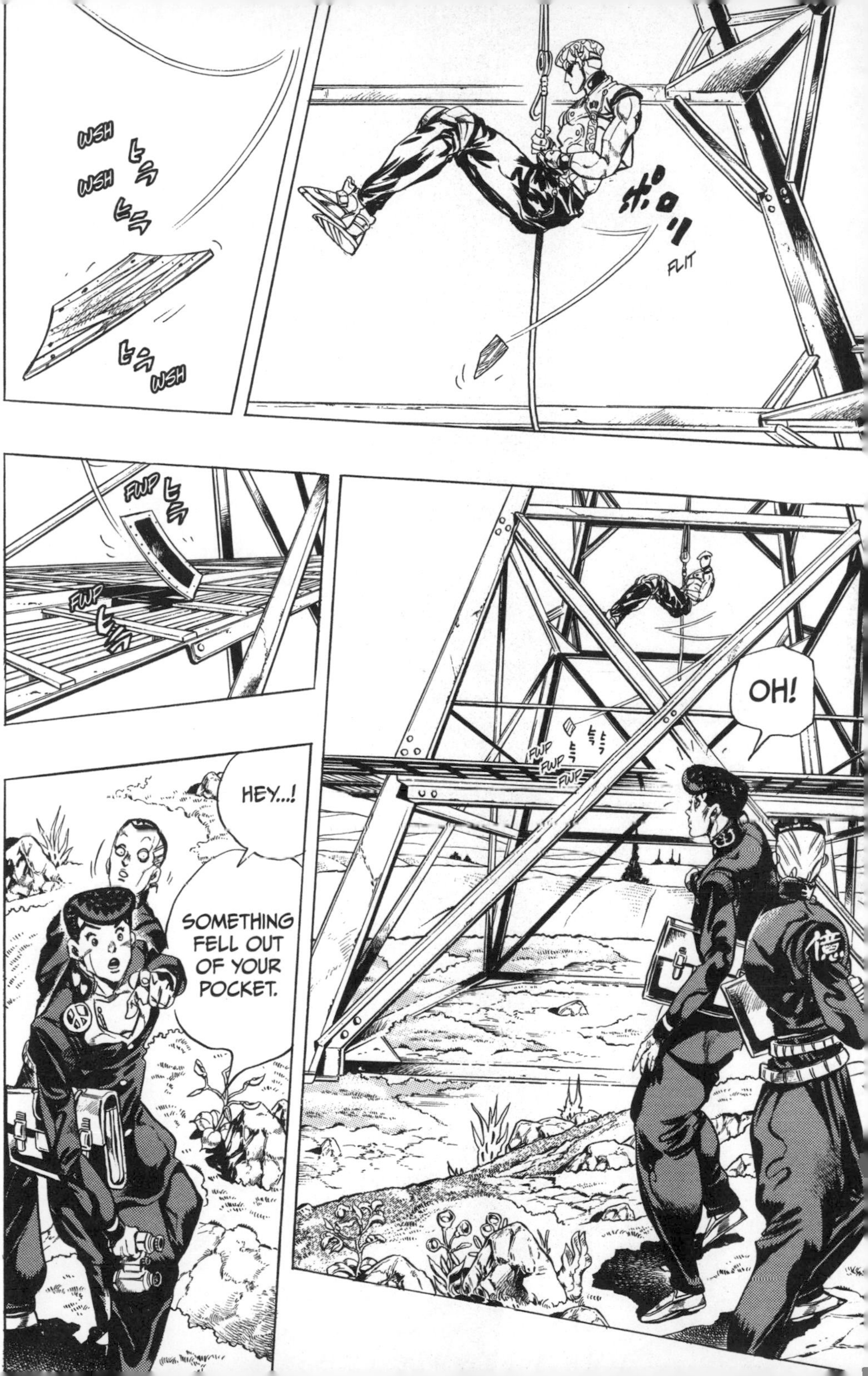
ポロリ
FLIT
WSH ヒラ
WSH ヒラ
ヒラ WSH
OH!
FWP FWP FWP
FWP ヒラ
FWP ヒラ
HEY...!
SOMETHING FELL OUT OF YOUR POCKET.

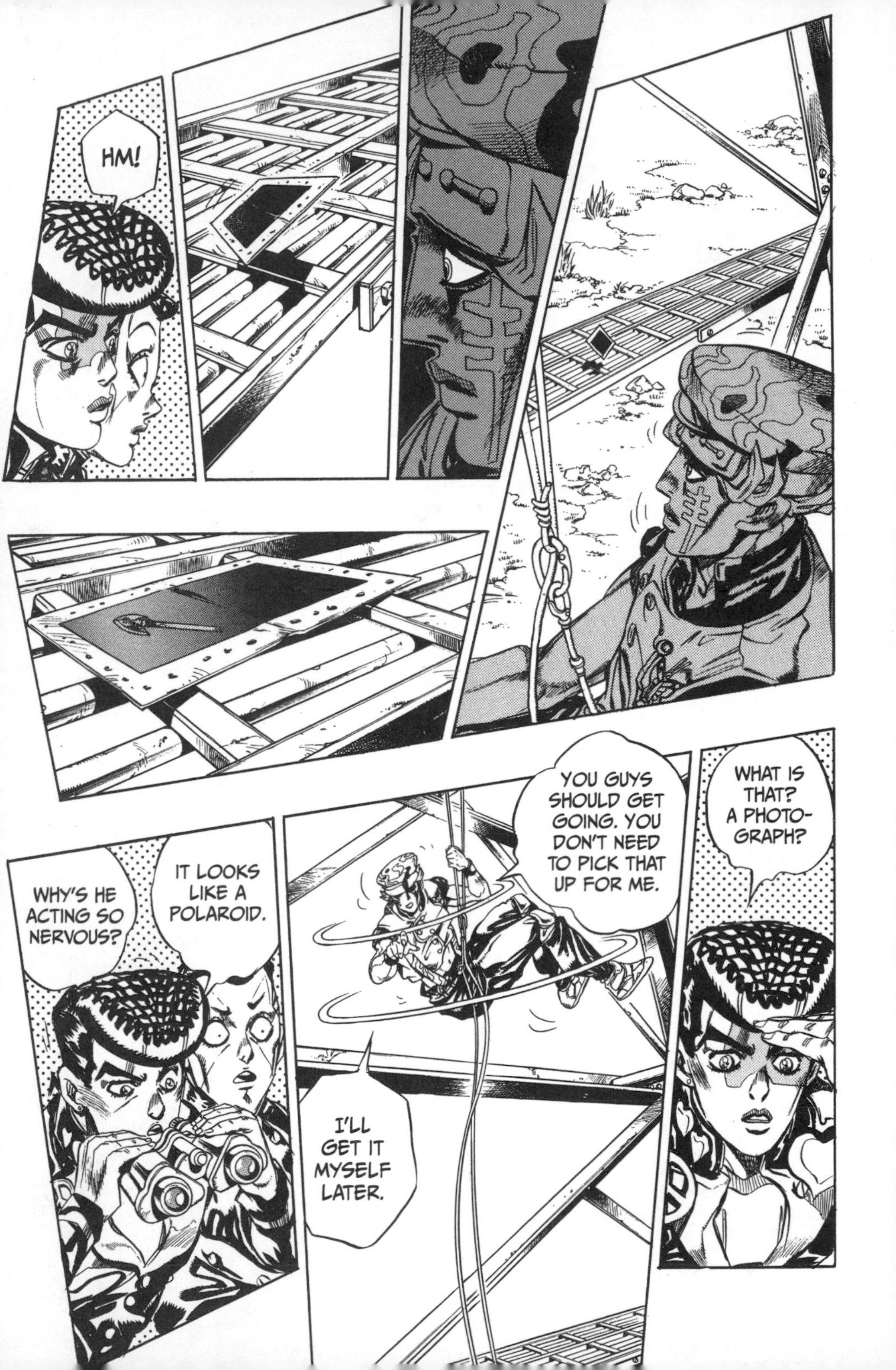
HM!
WHAT IS THAT? A PHOTO-GRAPH?
YOU GUYS SHOULD GET GOING. YOU DON'T NEED TO PICK THAT UP FOR ME.
I'LL GET IT MYSELF LATER.
IT LOOKS LIKE A POLAROID.
WHY'S HE ACTING SO NERVOUS?

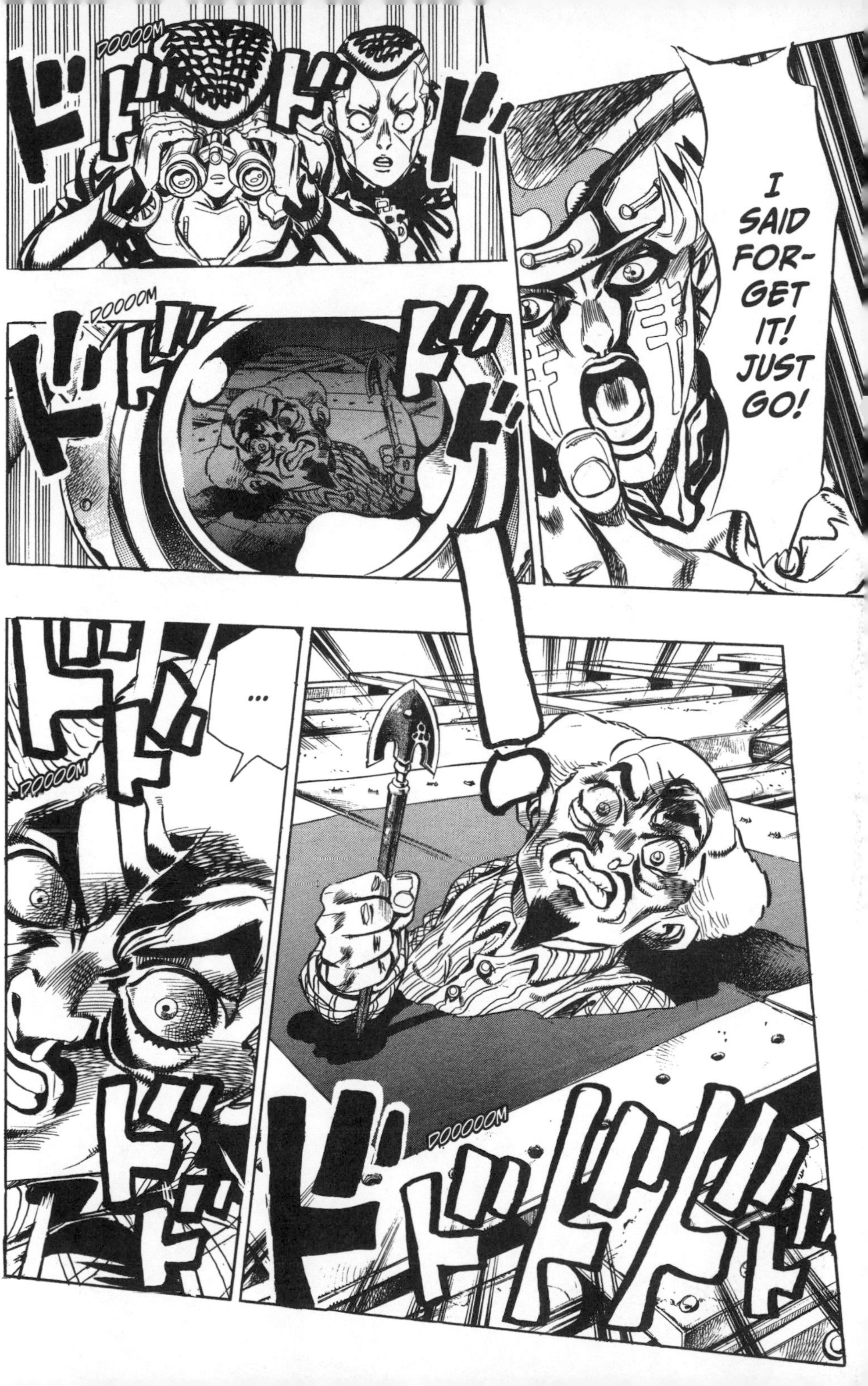
I SAID FOR-GET IT! JUST GO!
DOOOOM
DOOOOM
DOOOOOM
...
DOOOOM

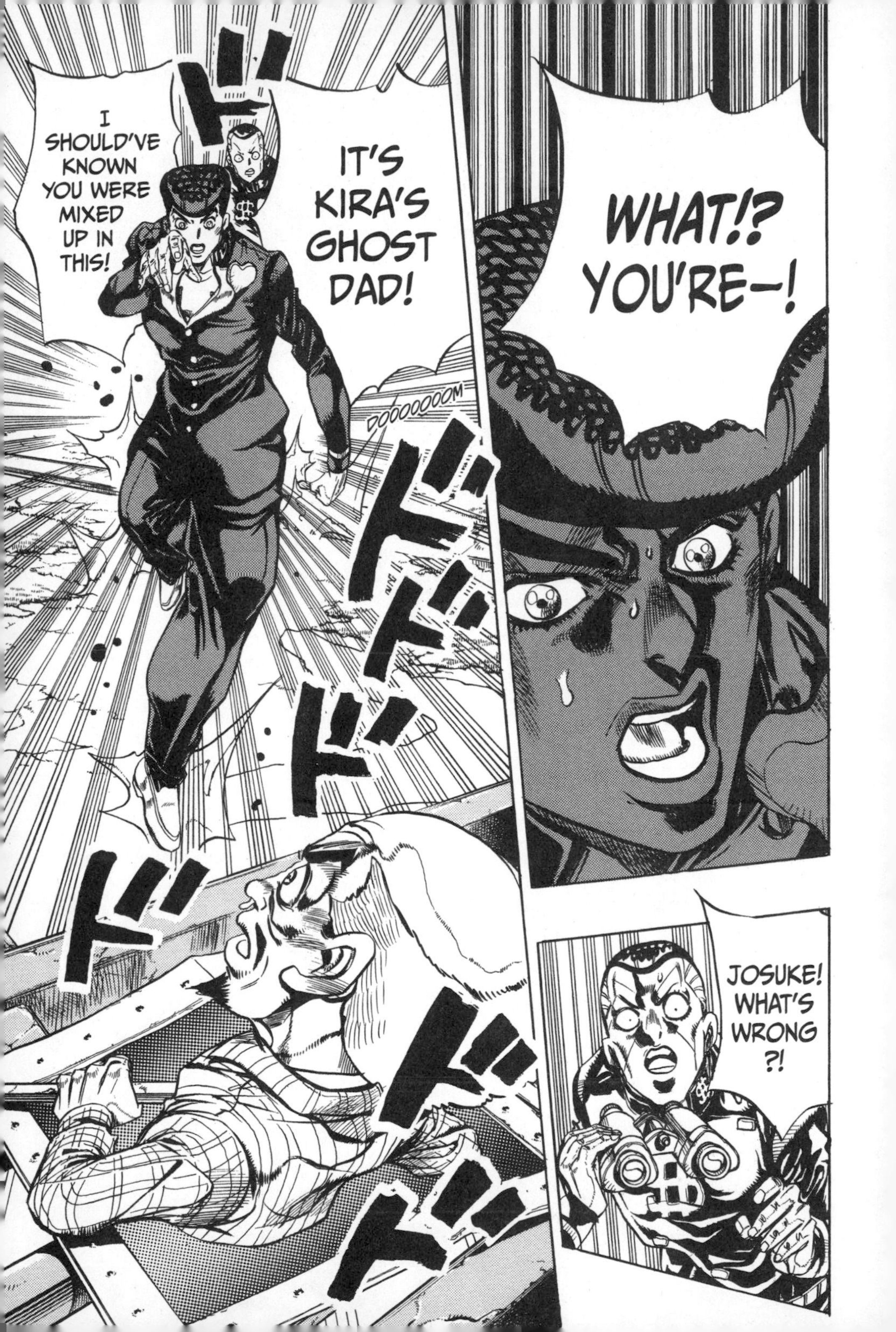
WHAT!? YOU'RE--!
JOSUKE! WHAT'S WRONG ?!
IT'S KIRA'S GHOST DAD!
I SHOULD'VE KNOWN YOU WERE MIXED UP IN THIS!
DOOOOOOOM

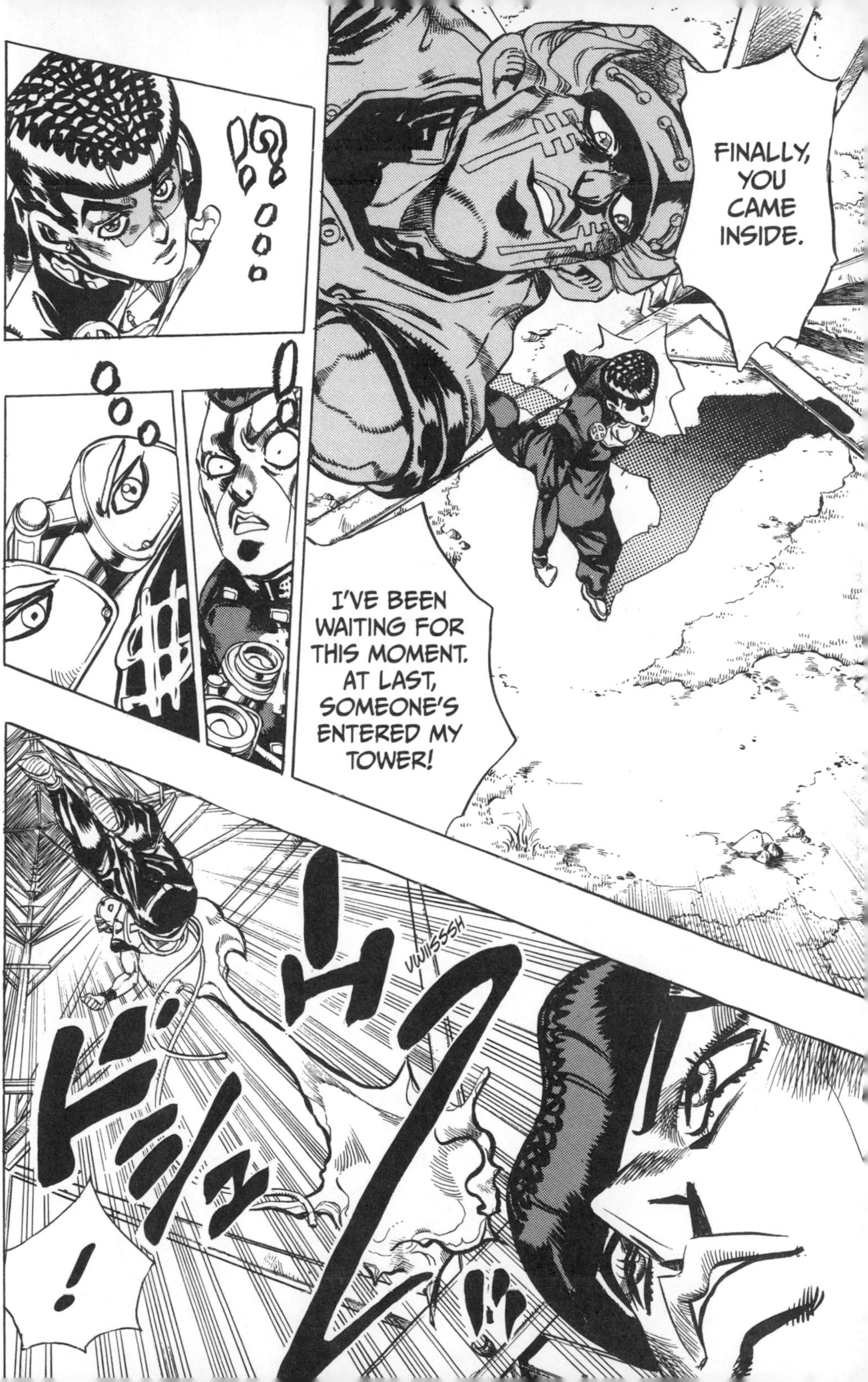
FINALLY, YOU CAME INSIDE.
I'VE BEEN WAITING FOR THIS MOMENT. AT LAST, SOMEONE'S ENTERED MY TOWER!
!?
VWIISSSH
!
!!

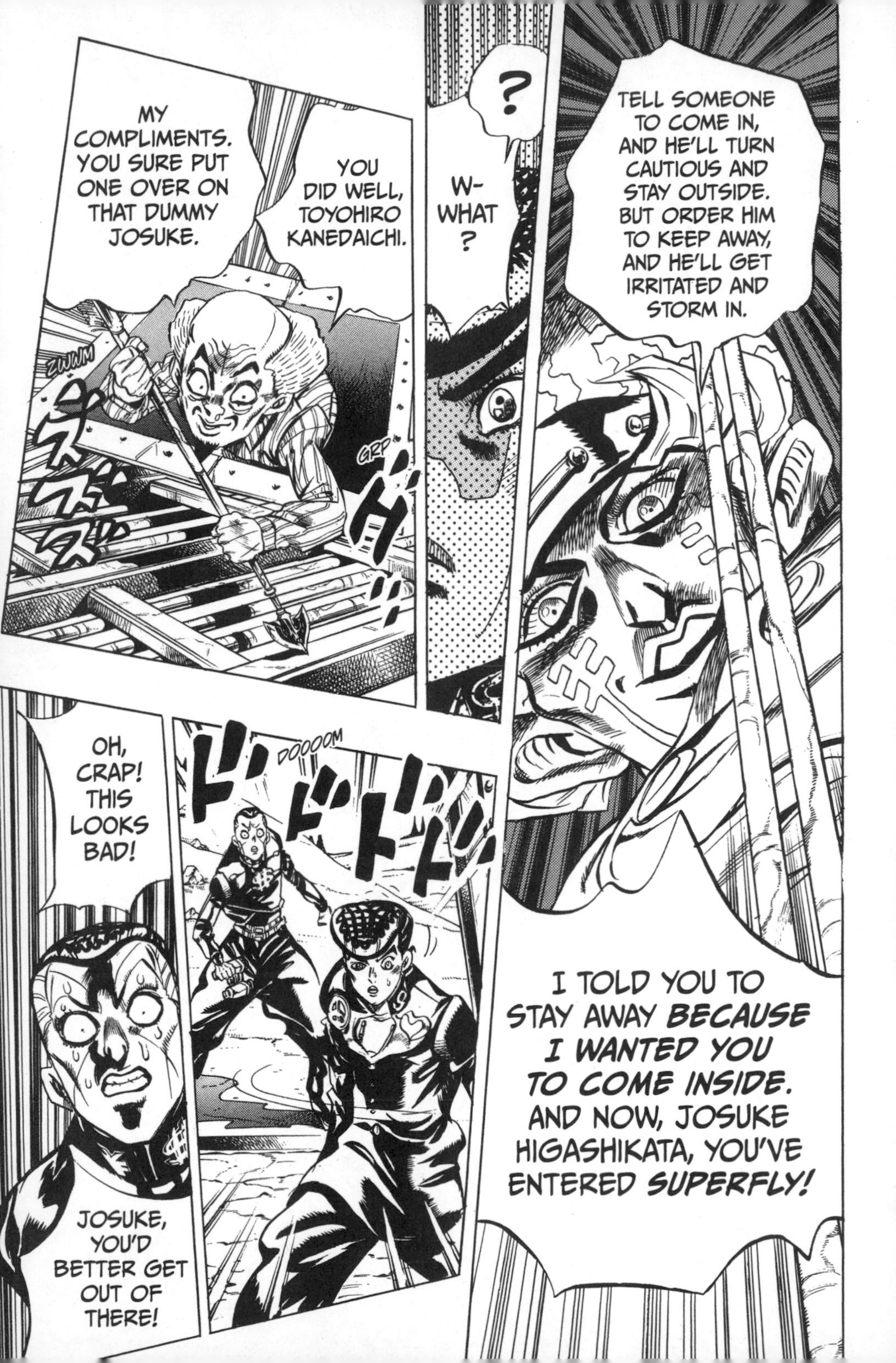
TELL SOMEONE TO COME IN, AND HE'LL TURN CAUTIOUS AND STAY OUTSIDE. BUT ORDER HIM TO KEEP AWAY, AND HE'LL GET IRRITATED AND STORM IN.
I TOLD YOU TO STAY AWAY *BECAUSE I WANTED YOU TO COME INSIDE*. AND NOW, JOSUKE HIGASHIKATA, YOU'VE ENTERED *SUPERFLY!*
?
W- WHAT?
GRP
YOU DID WELL, TOYOHIRO KANEDAICHI.
MY COMPLIMENTS. YOU SURE PUT ONE OVER ON THAT DUMMY JOSUKE.
ZWWM
DOOOOM
OH, CRAP! THIS LOOKS BAD!
JOSUKE, YOU'D BETTER GET OUT OF THERE!

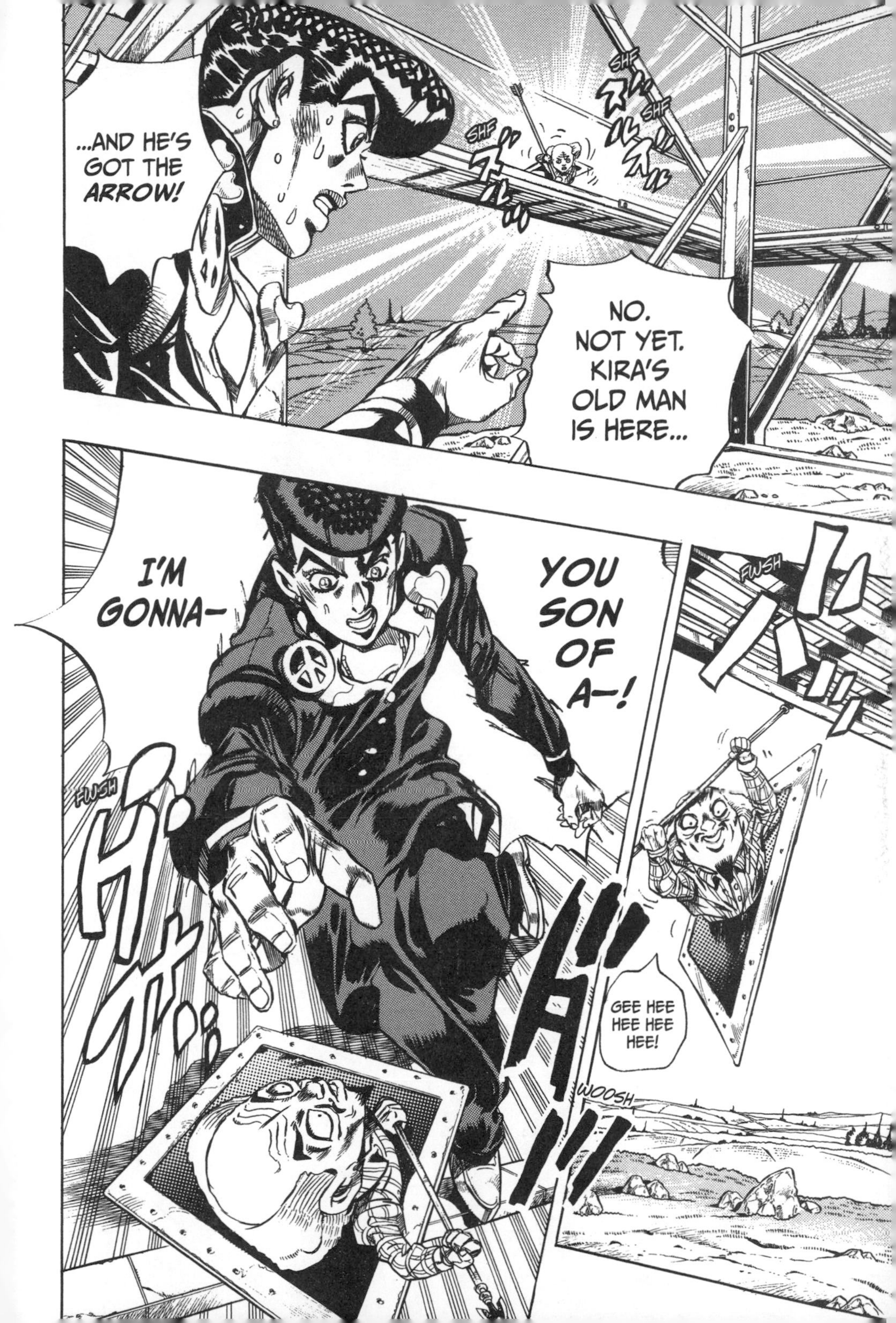
SHF
SHF
SHF
NO. NOT YET. KIRA'S OLD MAN IS HERE...
...AND HE'S GOT THE ARROW!
FWSH
GEE HEE HEE HEE HEE!
WOOSH
YOU SON OF A—!
I'M GONNA—
FWSH

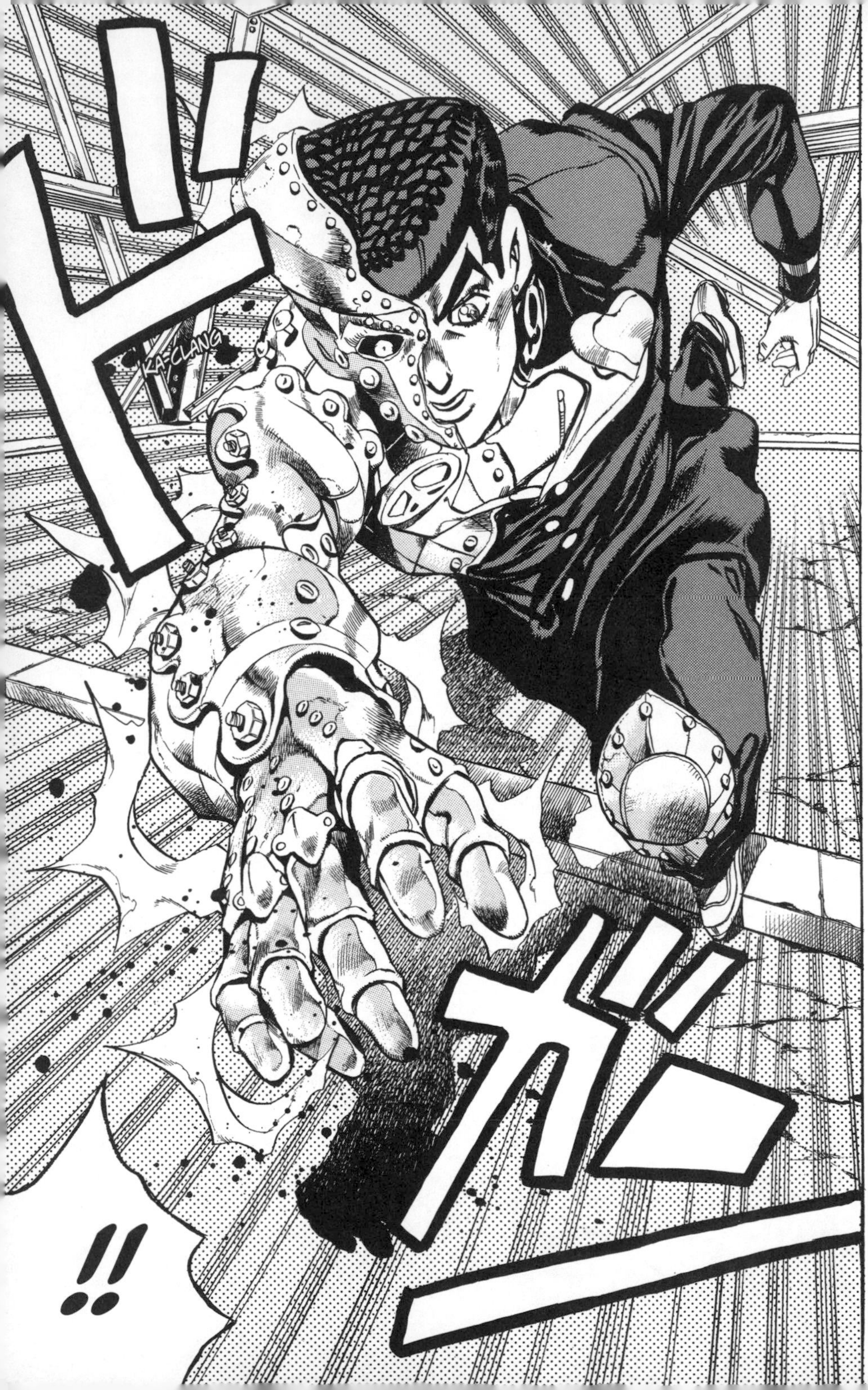
ドド
KA-CLANG
ガン
!!

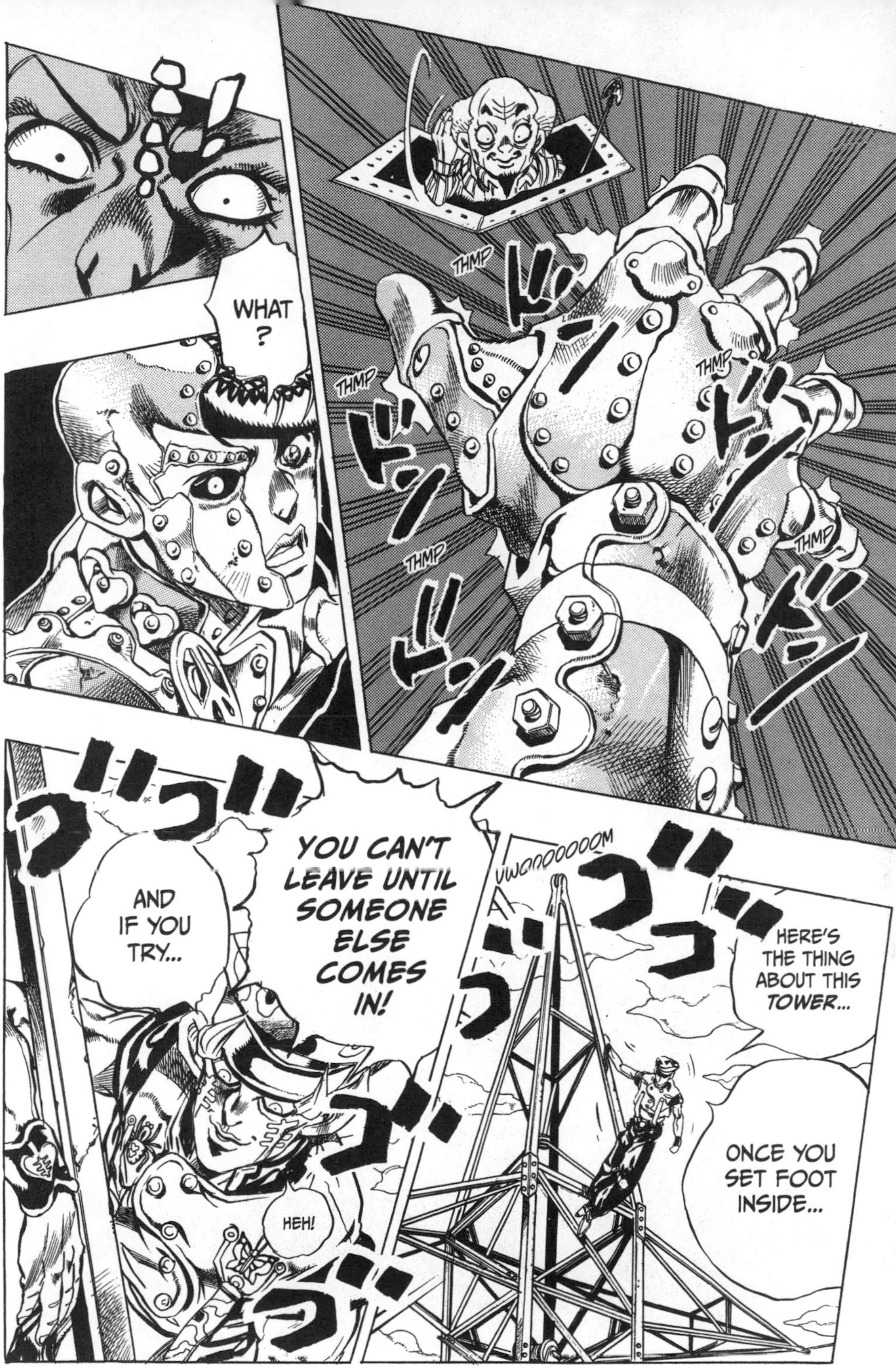
THMP
THMP
THMP
THMP
THMP
WHAT?
VWOOOOOOOM
HERE'S THE THING ABOUT THIS TOWER...
ONCE YOU SET FOOT INSIDE...
YOU CAN'T LEAVE UNTIL SOMEONE ELSE COMES IN!
AND IF YOU TRY...
HEH!

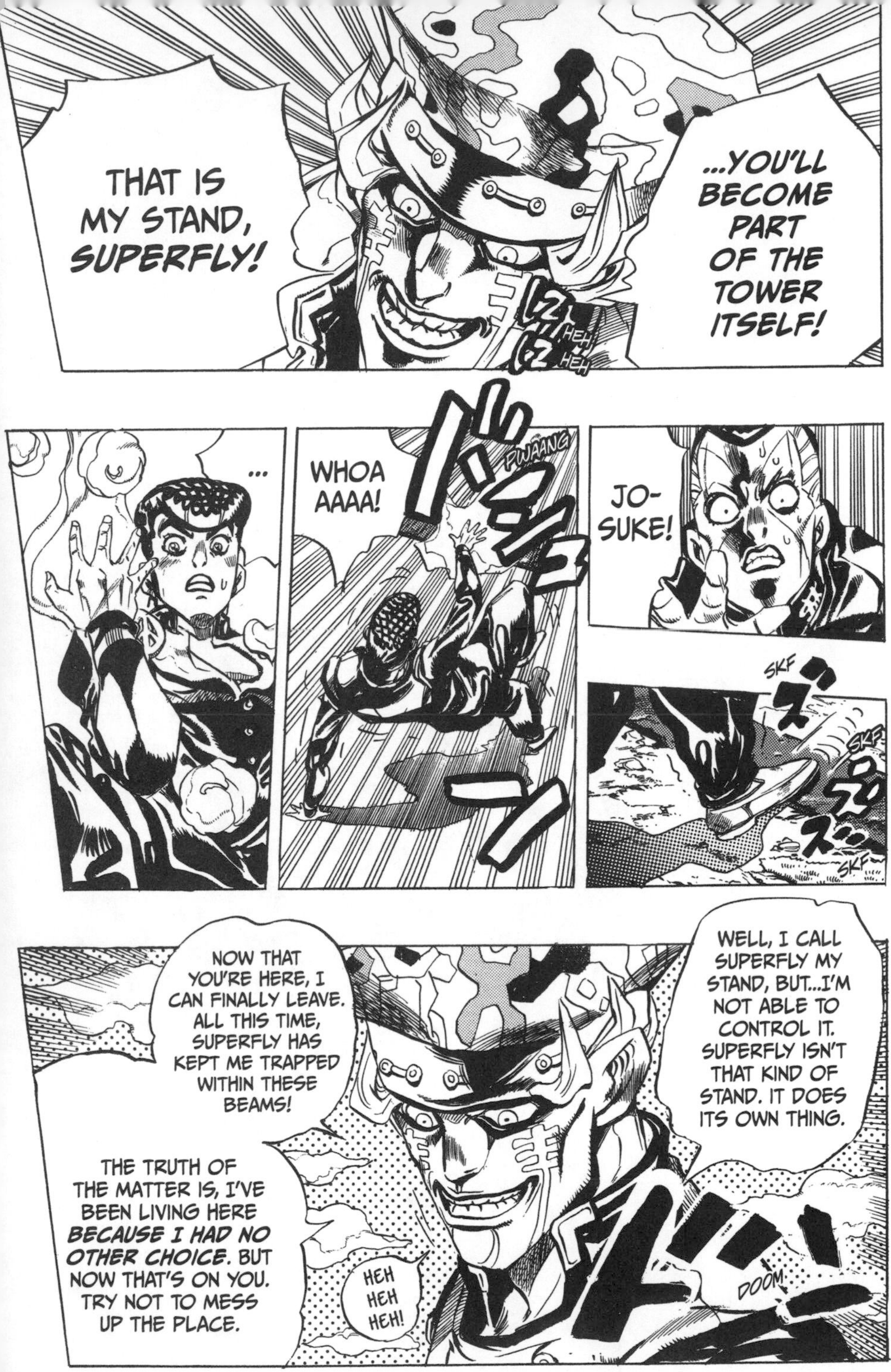
THAT IS MY STAND, SUPERFLY!
...YOU'LL BECOME PART OF THE TOWER ITSELF!
HEH HEH
JO-SUKE!
SKF
SKF
SKF
PWAANG
WHOA AAAA!
...
WELL, I CALL SUPERFLY MY STAND, BUT...I'M NOT ABLE TO CONTROL IT. SUPERFLY ISN'T THAT KIND OF STAND. IT DOES ITS OWN THING.
NOW THAT YOU'RE HERE, I CAN FINALLY LEAVE. ALL THIS TIME, SUPERFLY HAS KEPT ME TRAPPED WITHIN THESE BEAMS!
THE TRUTH OF THE MATTER IS, I'VE BEEN LIVING HERE BECAUSE I HAD NO OTHER CHOICE. BUT NOW THAT'S ON YOU. TRY NOT TO MESS UP THE PLACE.
HEH HEH HEH!
DOOM

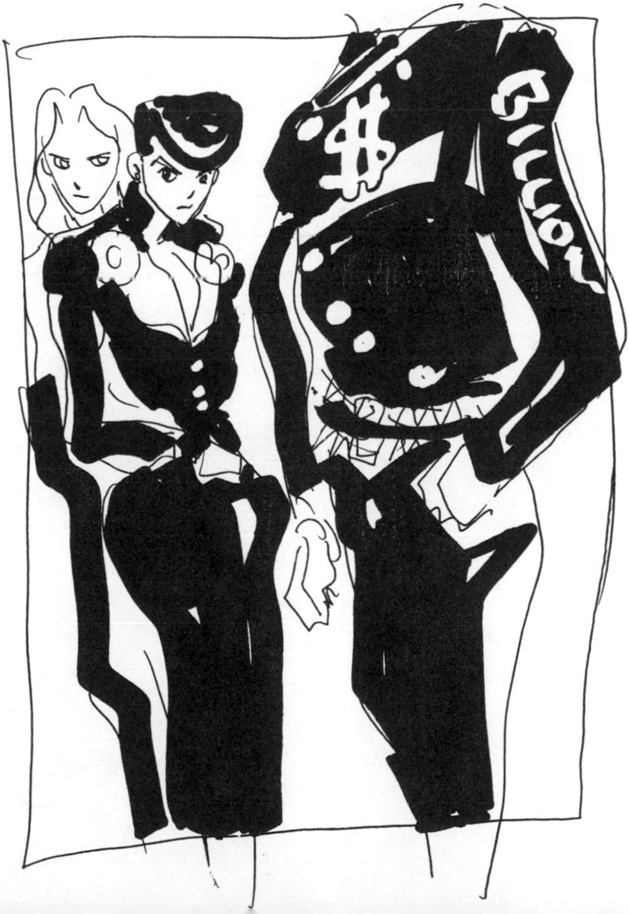
BILLION

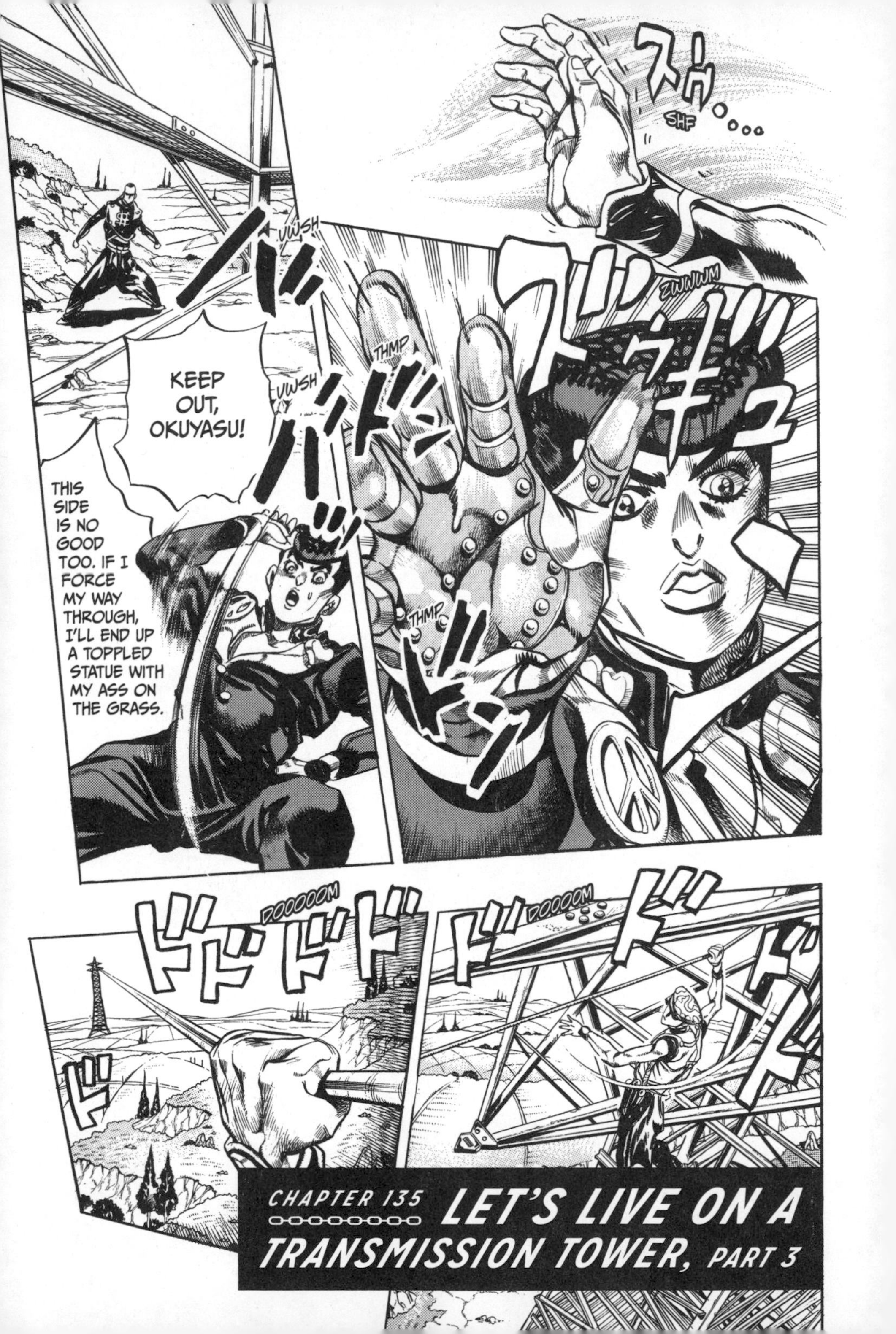
SHF
ZWWWM
THMP
THMP
VWSH
UWSH
KEEP OUT, OKUYASU!
THIS SIDE IS NO GOOD TOO. IF I FORCE MY WAY THROUGH, I'LL END UP A TOPPLED STATUE WITH MY ASS ON THE GRASS.
DOOOOM
DOOOOOM

CHAPTER 135

LET'S LIVE ON A TRANSMISSION TOWER, PART 3

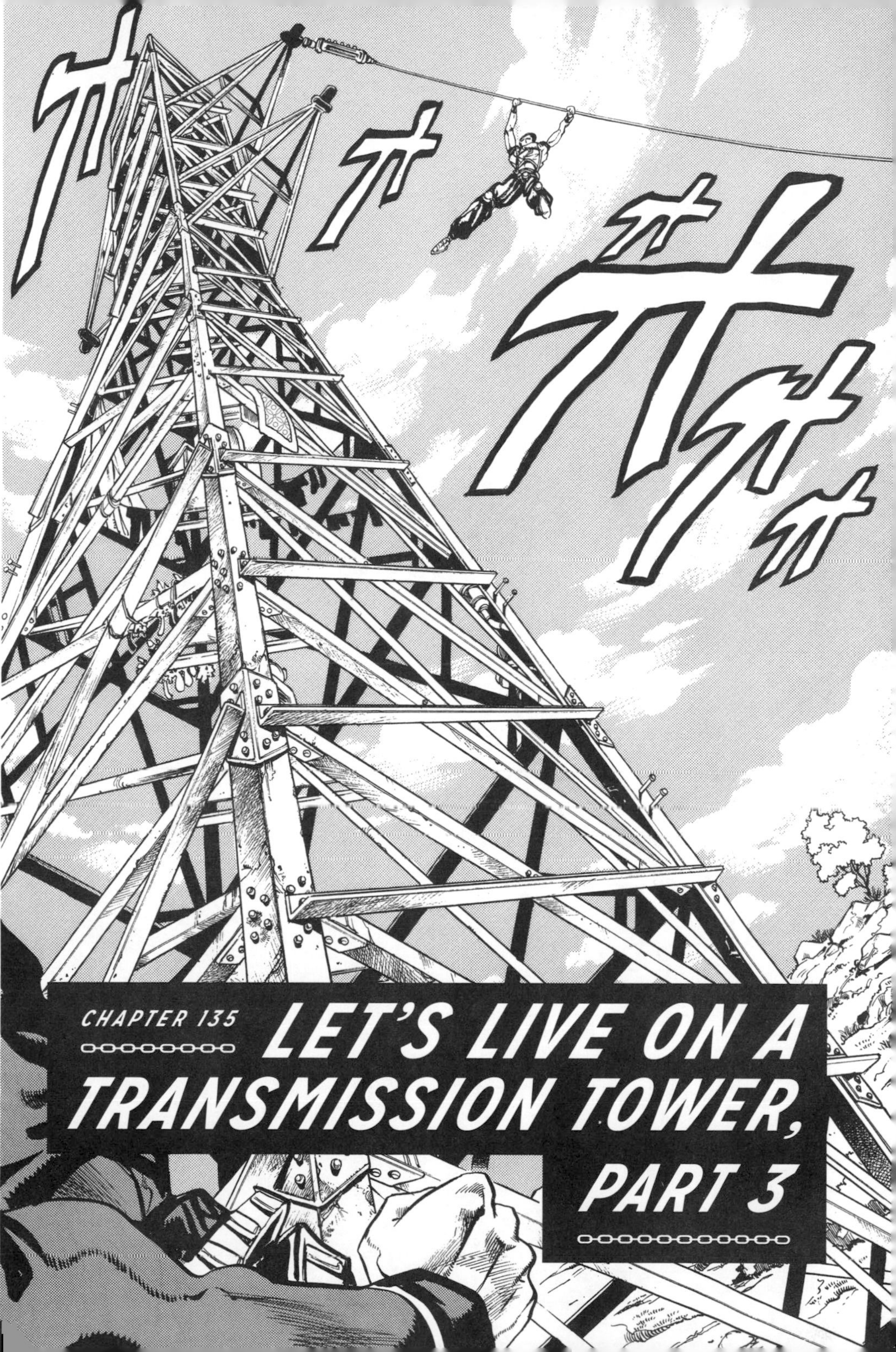
CHAPTER 135
LET'S LIVE ON A TRANSMISSION TOWER, PART 3

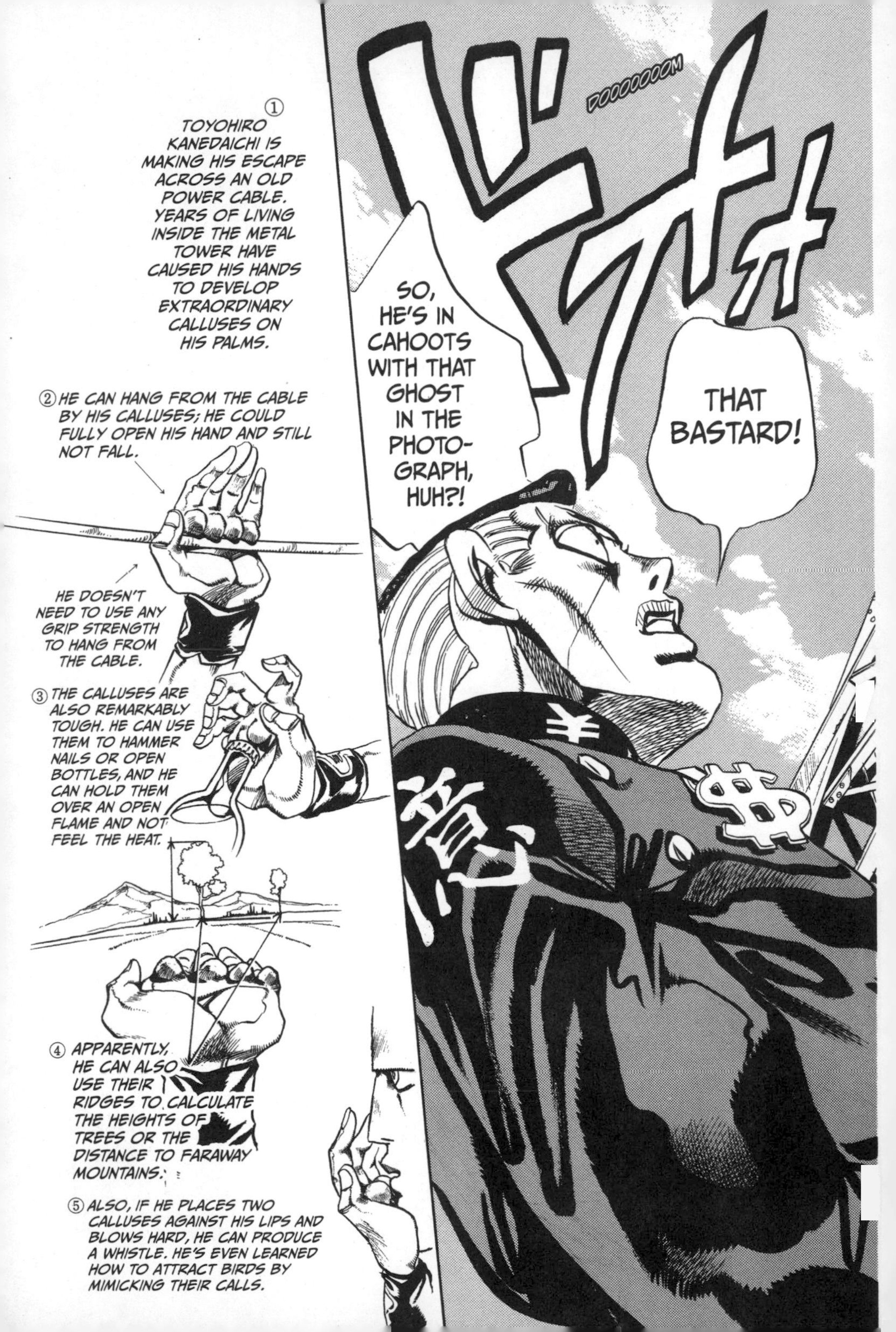
DOOOOOOOM
THAT BASTARD!
SO, HE'S IN CAHOOTS WITH THAT GHOST IN THE PHOTOGRAPH, HUH?!
① TOYOHIRO KANEDAICHI IS MAKING HIS ESCAPE ACROSS AN OLD POWER CABLE. YEARS OF LIVING INSIDE THE METAL TOWER HAVE CAUSED HIS HANDS TO DEVELOP EXTRAORDINARY CALLUSES ON HIS PALMS.
② HE CAN HANG FROM THE CABLE BY HIS CALLUSES; HE COULD FULLY OPEN HIS HAND AND STILL NOT FALL.
HE DOESN'T NEED TO USE ANY GRIP STRENGTH TO HANG FROM THE CABLE.
③ THE CALLUSES ARE ALSO REMARKABLY TOUGH. HE CAN USE THEM TO HAMMER NAILS OR OPEN BOTTLES, AND HE CAN HOLD THEM OVER AN OPEN FLAME AND NOT FEEL THE HEAT.
④ APPARENTLY, HE CAN ALSO USE THEIR RIDGES TO CALCULATE THE HEIGHTS OF TREES OR THE DISTANCE TO FARAWAY MOUNTAINS.
⑤ ALSO, IF HE PLACES TWO CALLUSES AGAINST HIS LIPS AND BLOWS HARD, HE CAN PRODUCE A WHISTLE. HE'S EVEN LEARNED HOW TO ATTRACT BIRDS BY MIMICKING THEIR CALLS.

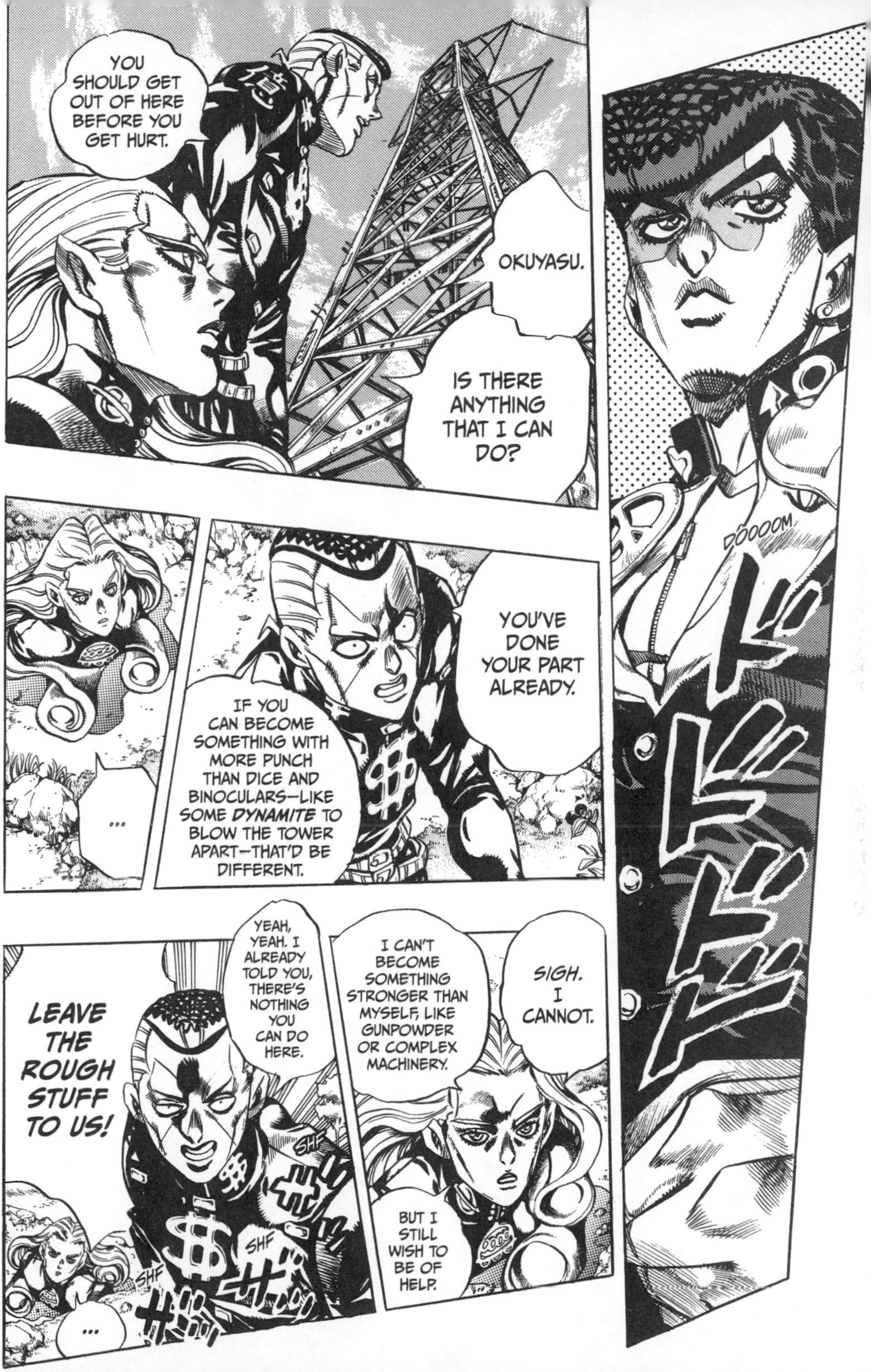
DOOOOM
OKUYASU.
IS THERE ANYTHING THAT I CAN DO?
YOU SHOULD GET OUT OF HERE BEFORE YOU GET HURT.
YOU'VE DONE YOUR PART ALREADY.
IF YOU CAN BECOME SOMETHING WITH MORE PUNCH THAN DICE AND BINOCULARS—LIKE SOME *DYNAMITE* TO BLOW THE TOWER APART—THAT'D BE DIFFERENT.
...
SIGH. I CANNOT.
I CAN'T BECOME SOMETHING STRONGER THAN MYSELF, LIKE GUNPOWDER OR COMPLEX MACHINERY.
BUT I STILL WISH TO BE OF HELP.
YEAH, YEAH. I ALREADY TOLD YOU, THERE'S NOTHING YOU CAN DO HERE.
LEAVE THE ROUGH STUFF TO US!
SHF
SHF
SHF
...

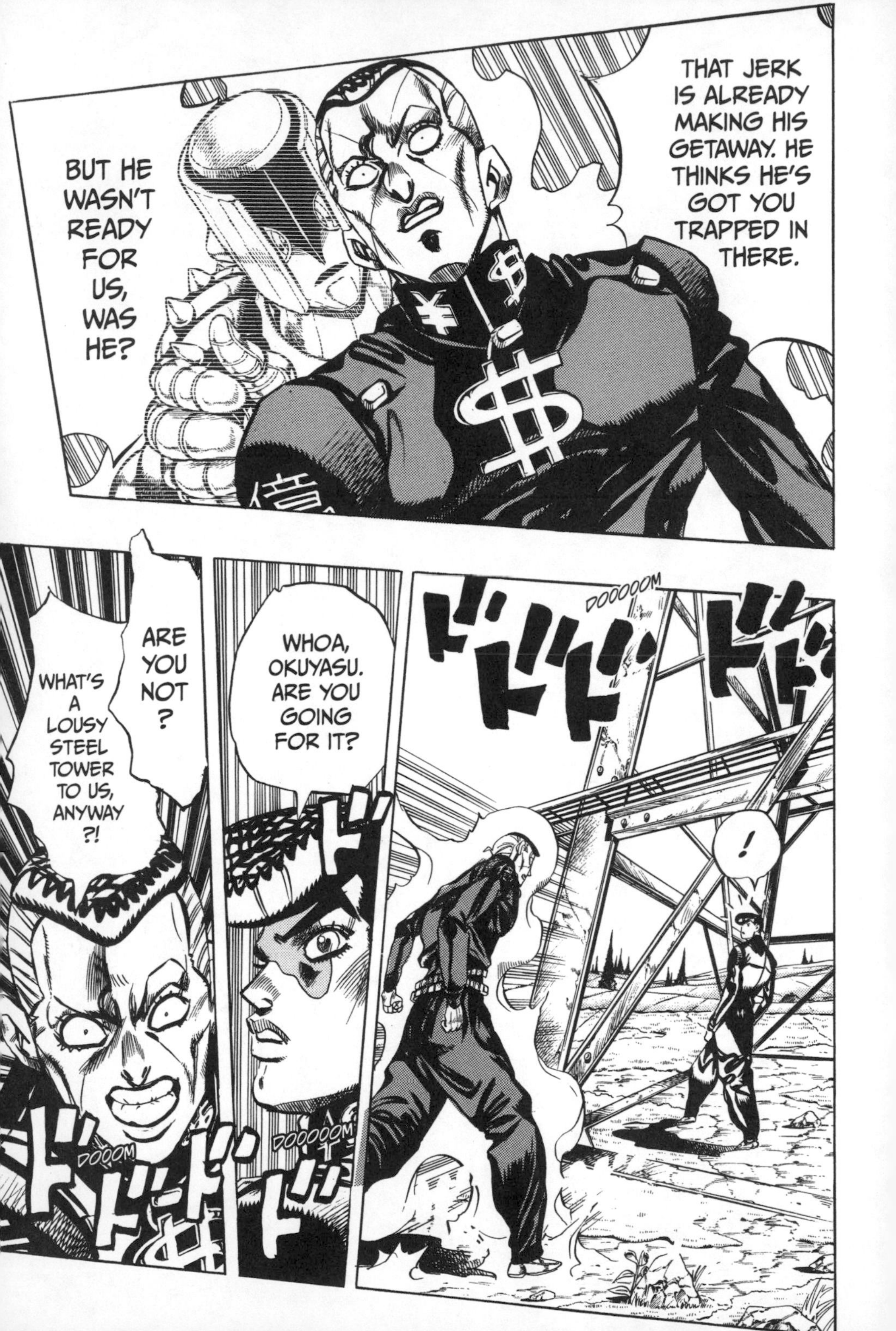
THAT JERK IS ALREADY MAKING HIS GETAWAY. HE THINKS HE'S GOT YOU TRAPPED IN THERE.
BUT HE WASN'T READY FOR US, WAS HE?
DOOOOOM
!
WHOA, OKUYASU. ARE YOU GOING FOR IT?
DOOOOOM
ARE YOU NOT?
WHAT'S A LOUSY STEEL TOWER TO US, ANYWAY?!
DOOOM

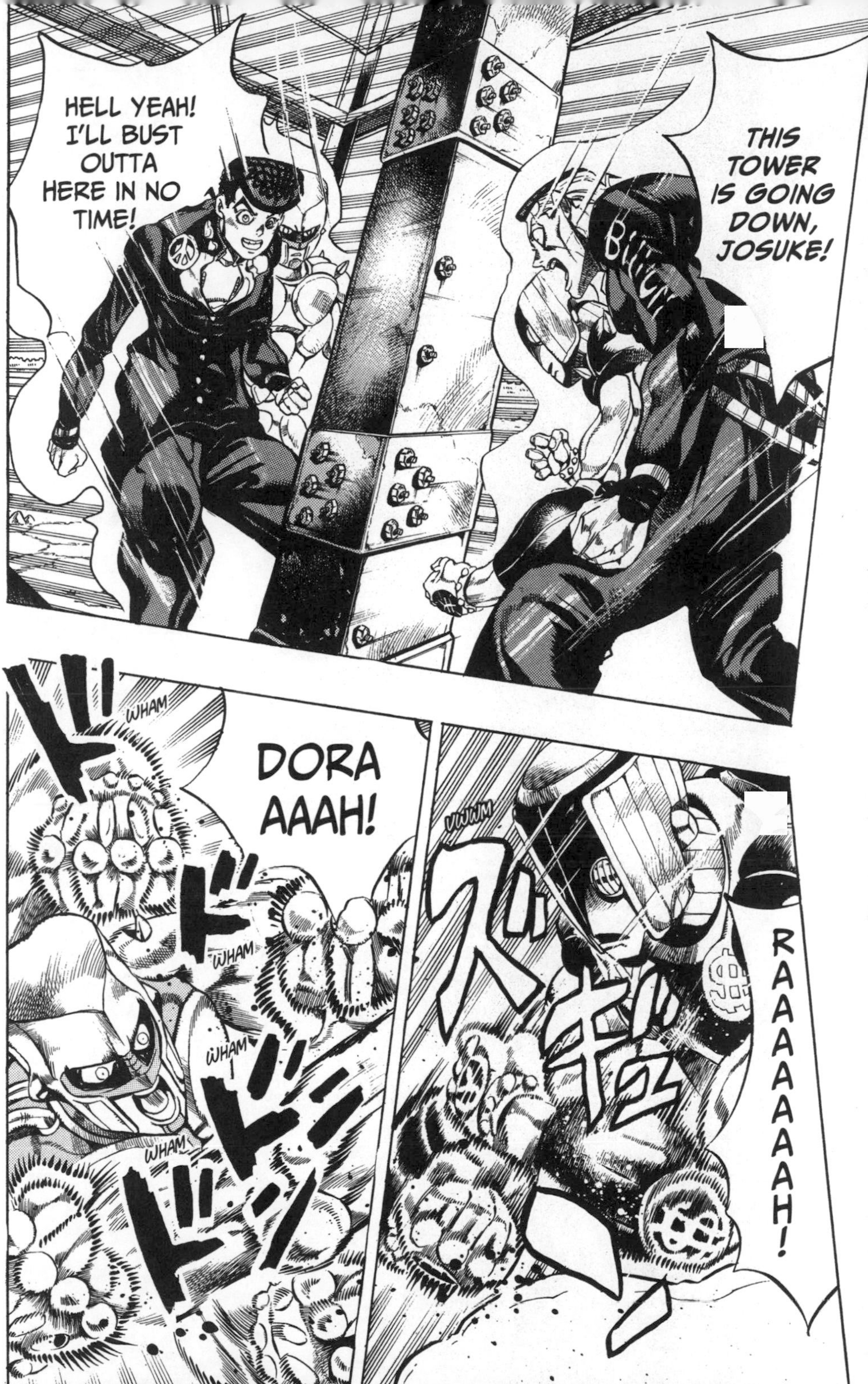
THIS TOWER IS GOING DOWN, JOSUKE!
HELL YEAH! I'LL BUST OUTTA HERE IN NO TIME!
VWWM
RAAAAAAAAAAH!
DORA AAAH!
WHAM
WHAM
WHAM
WHAM

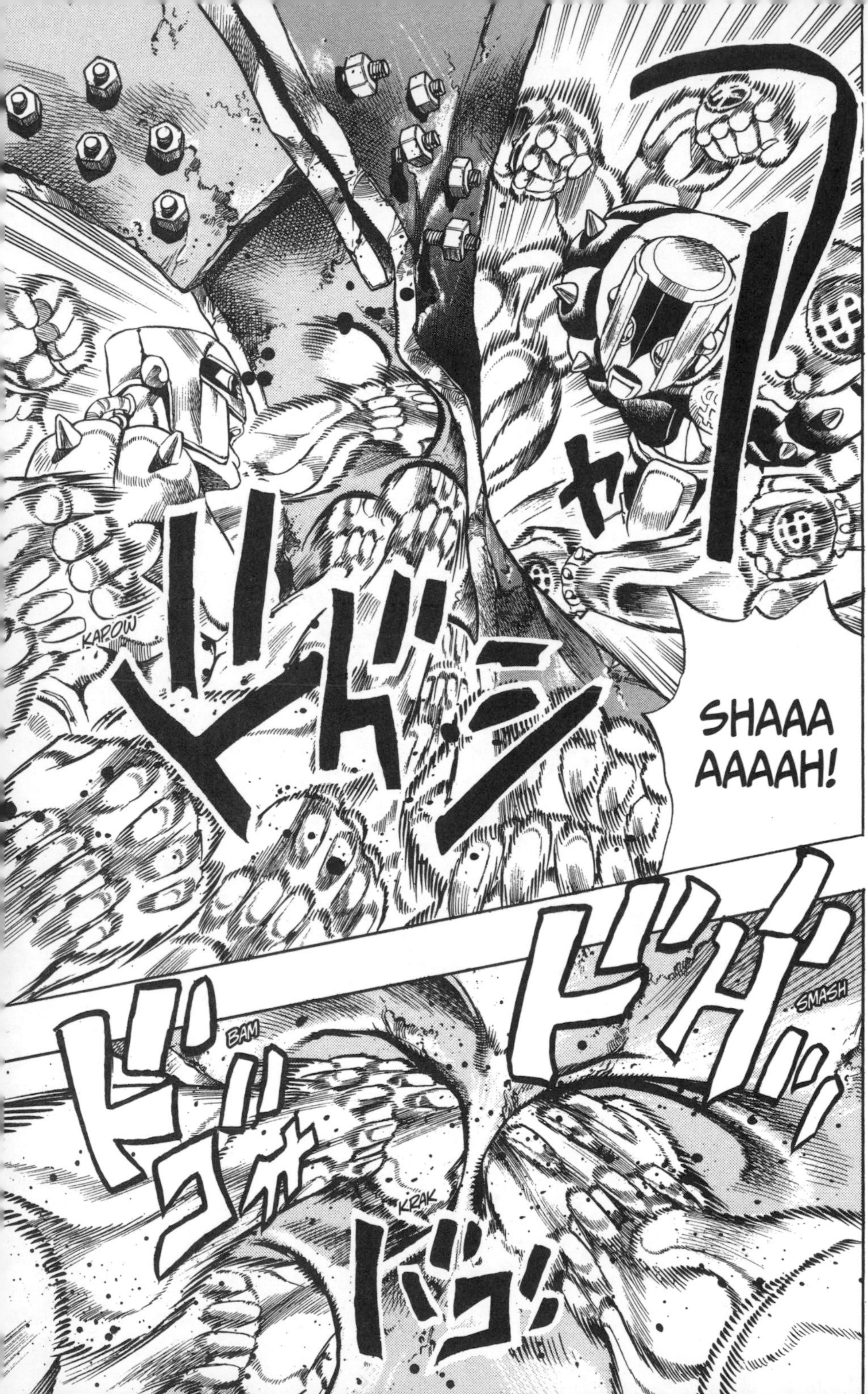
SHAAA
AAAAH!
KAPOW
SMASH
BAM
KRAK

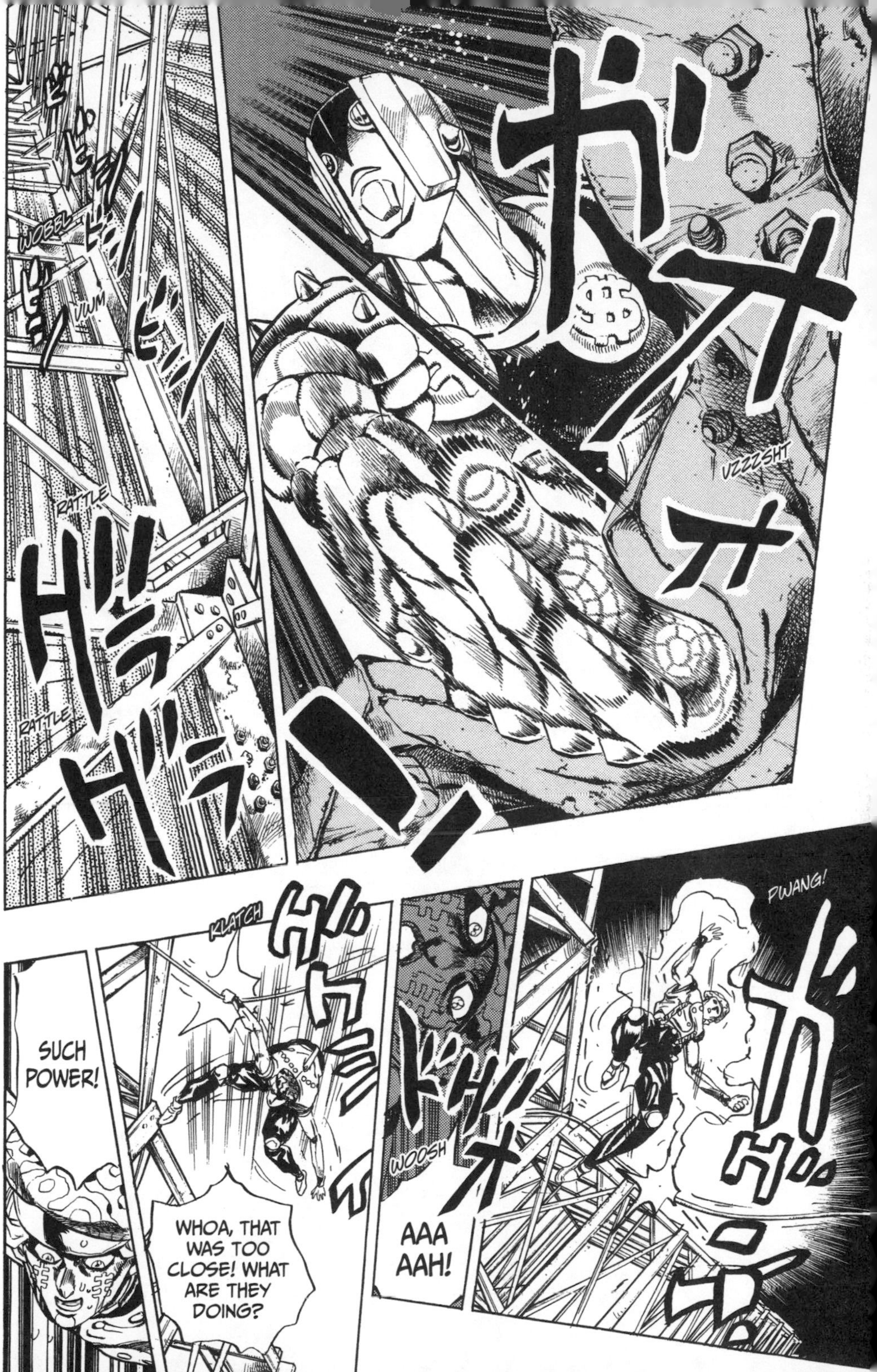
VZZZSHT
WOBBL
VVUM
RATTLE
RATTLE
PWANG!
WOOSH
AAA AAH!
KLATCH
WHOA, THAT WAS TOO CLOSE! WHAT ARE THEY DOING?
SUCH POWER!

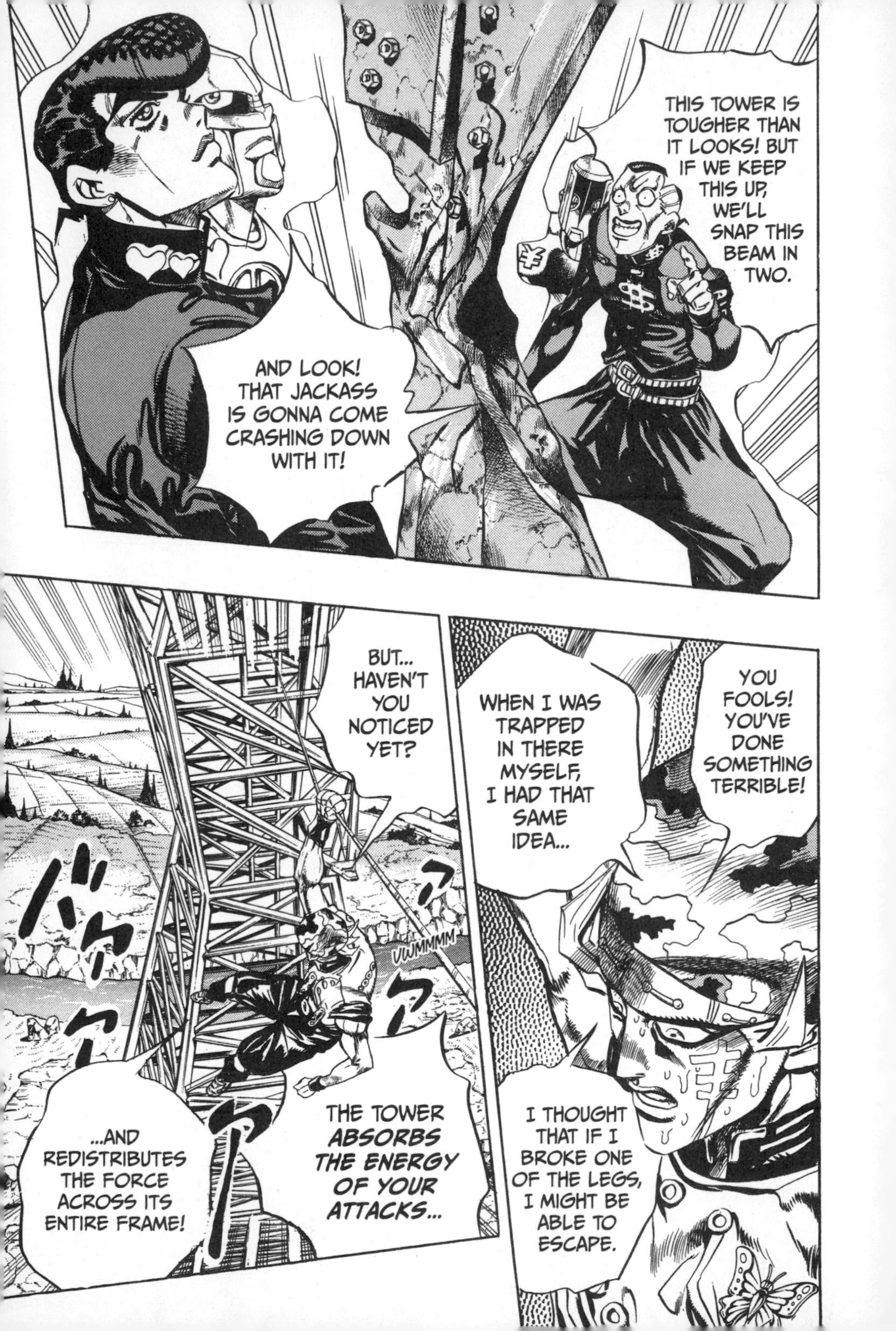
THIS TOWER IS TOUGHER THAN IT LOOKS! BUT IF WE KEEP THIS UP, WE'LL SNAP THIS BEAM IN TWO.
AND LOOK! THAT JACKASS IS GONNA COME CRASHING DOWN WITH IT!
YOU FOOLS! YOU'VE DONE SOMETHING TERRIBLE!
WHEN I WAS TRAPPED IN THERE MYSELF, I HAD THAT SAME IDEA...
I THOUGHT THAT IF I BROKE ONE OF THE LEGS, I MIGHT BE ABLE TO ESCAPE.
BUT... HAVEN'T YOU NOTICED YET?
UWMMMM
THE TOWER ABSORBS THE ENERGY OF YOUR ATTACKS...
...AND REDISTRIBUTES THE FORCE ACROSS ITS ENTIRE FRAME!

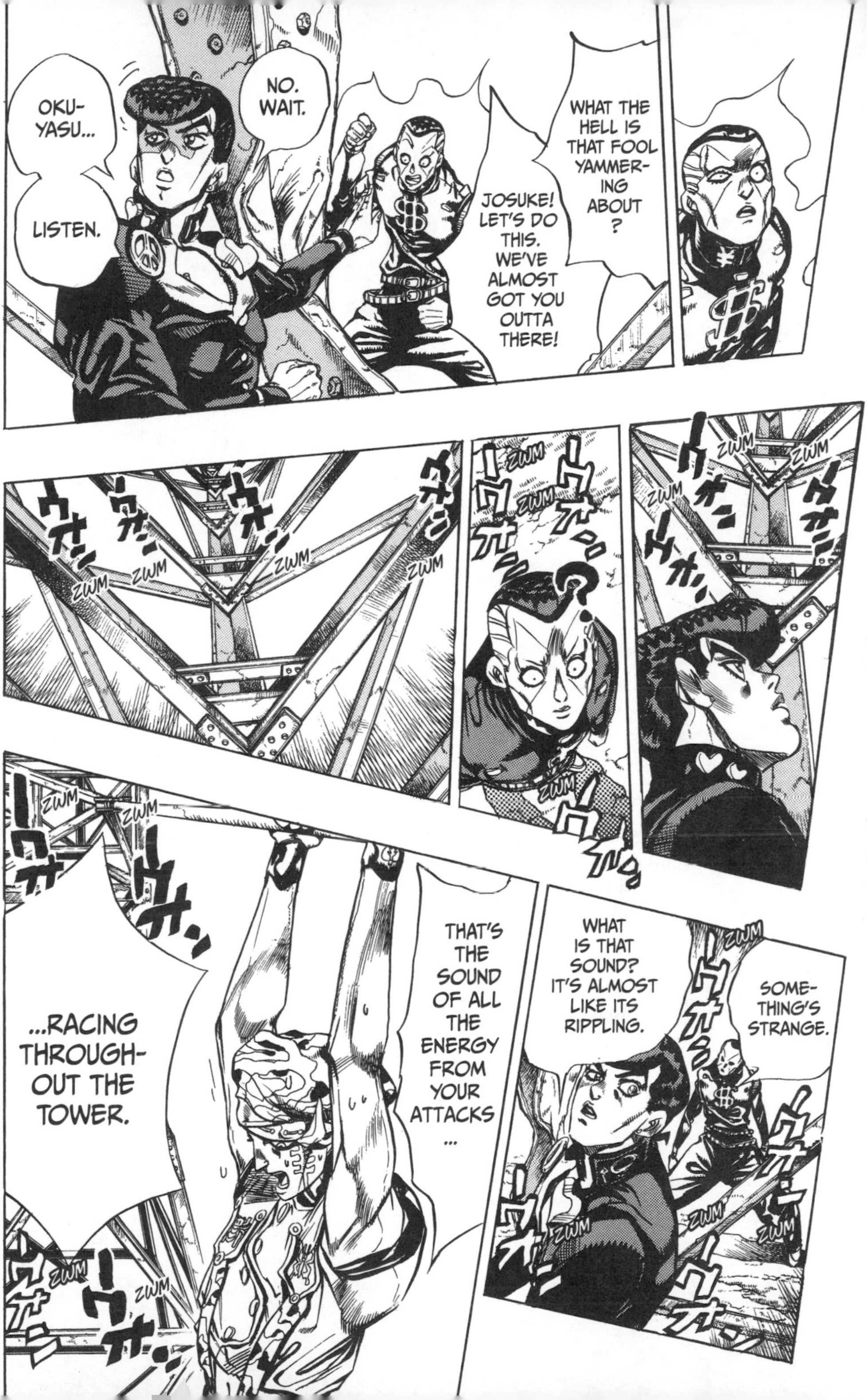
WHAT THE HELL IS THAT FOOL YAMMERING ABOUT ?
NO. WAIT.
JOSUKE! LET'S DO THIS. WE'VE ALMOST GOT YOU OUTTA THERE!
OKU-YASU...
LISTEN.
ZWM ZWM
ZWM ZWM ZWM
ZWM ZWM ZWM ZWM
ZWM ZWM ZWM ZWM
SOME-THING'S STRANGE.
WHAT IS THAT SOUND? IT'S ALMOST LIKE ITS RIPPLING.
ZWM ZWM ZWM ZWM
THAT'S THE SOUND OF ALL THE ENERGY FROM YOUR ATTACKS ...
...RACING THROUGH-OUT THE TOWER.
ZWM ZWM ZWM ZWM

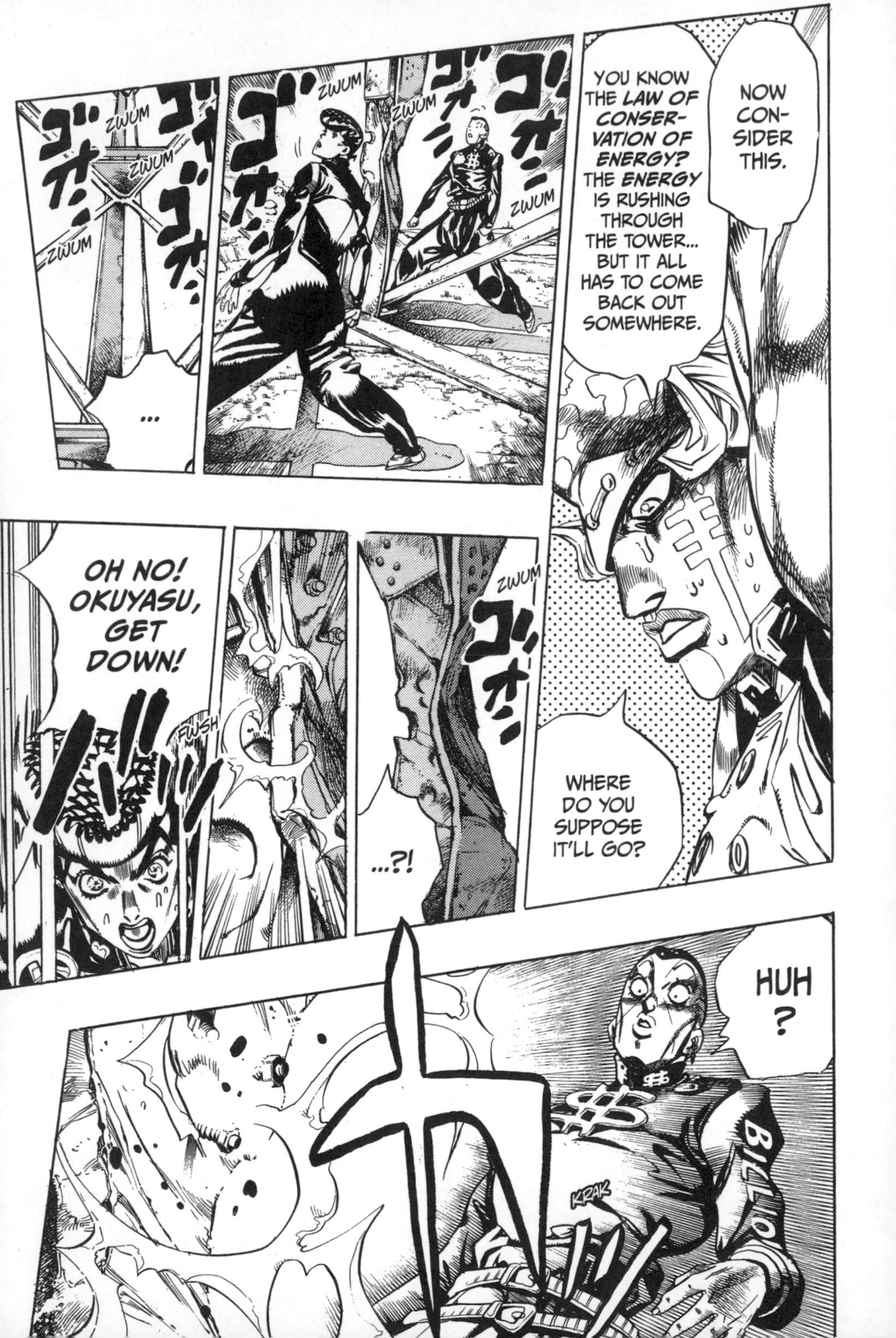
NOW CON- SIDER THIS.
YOU KNOW THE *LAW OF CONSER- VATION OF ENERGY?* THE *ENERGY* IS RUSHING THROUGH THE TOWER... BUT IT ALL HAS TO COME BACK OUT SOMEWHERE.
WHERE DO YOU SUPPOSE IT'LL GO?
ZWUM
ZWUM
ZWUM
ZWUM
ZWUM
ZWUM
ZWUM
...
ZWUM
...?!
FWSH
OH NO! OKUYASU, GET DOWN!
HUH ?
BILLO
KRAK

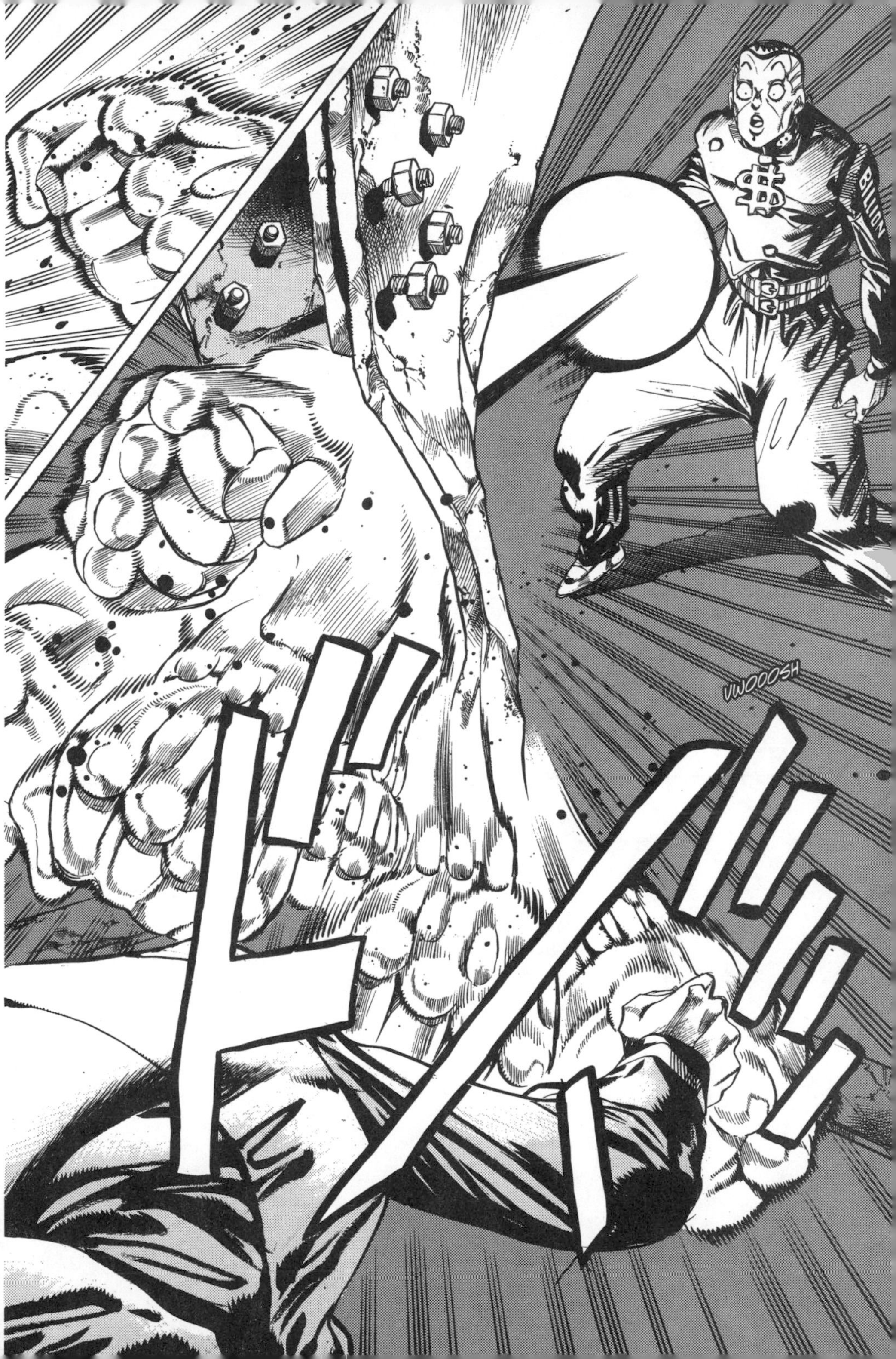
BILLION
VWOOOSH

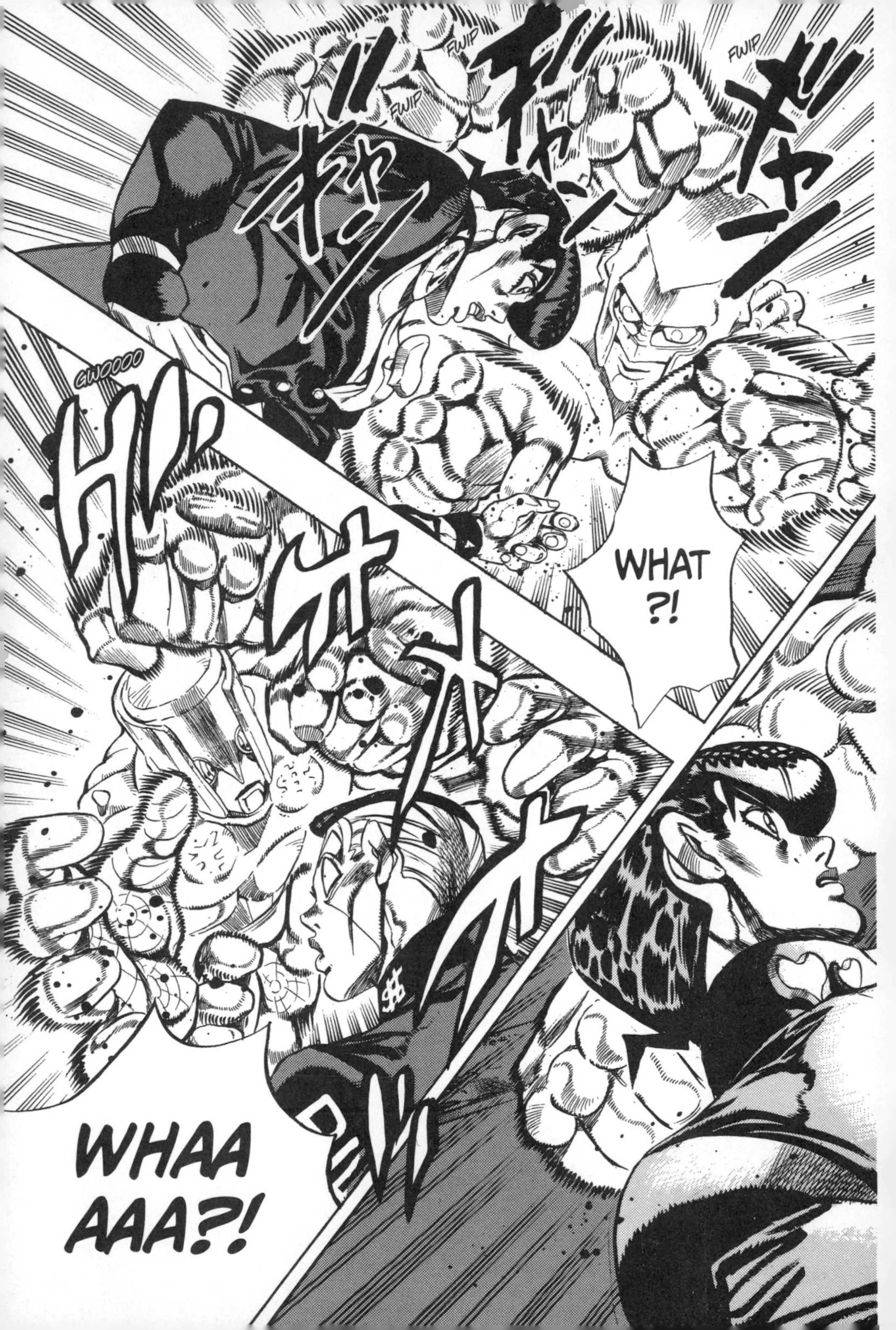
FWIP
FWIP
FWIP
WHAT ?!
GWOOOO
WHAA AAA?!

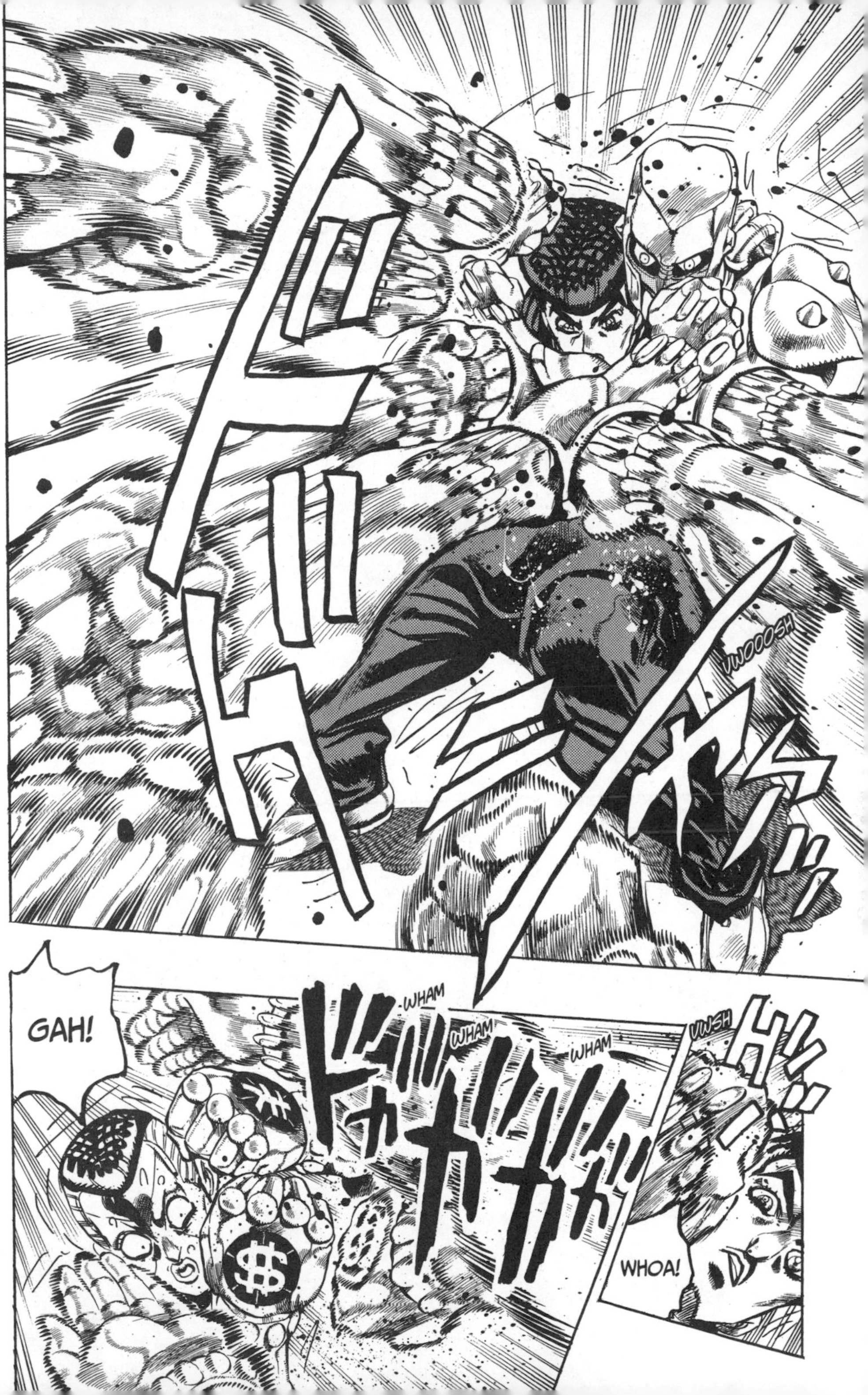
VWOOOSH
VWSH
WHOA!
WHAM
WHAM
WHAM
GAH!

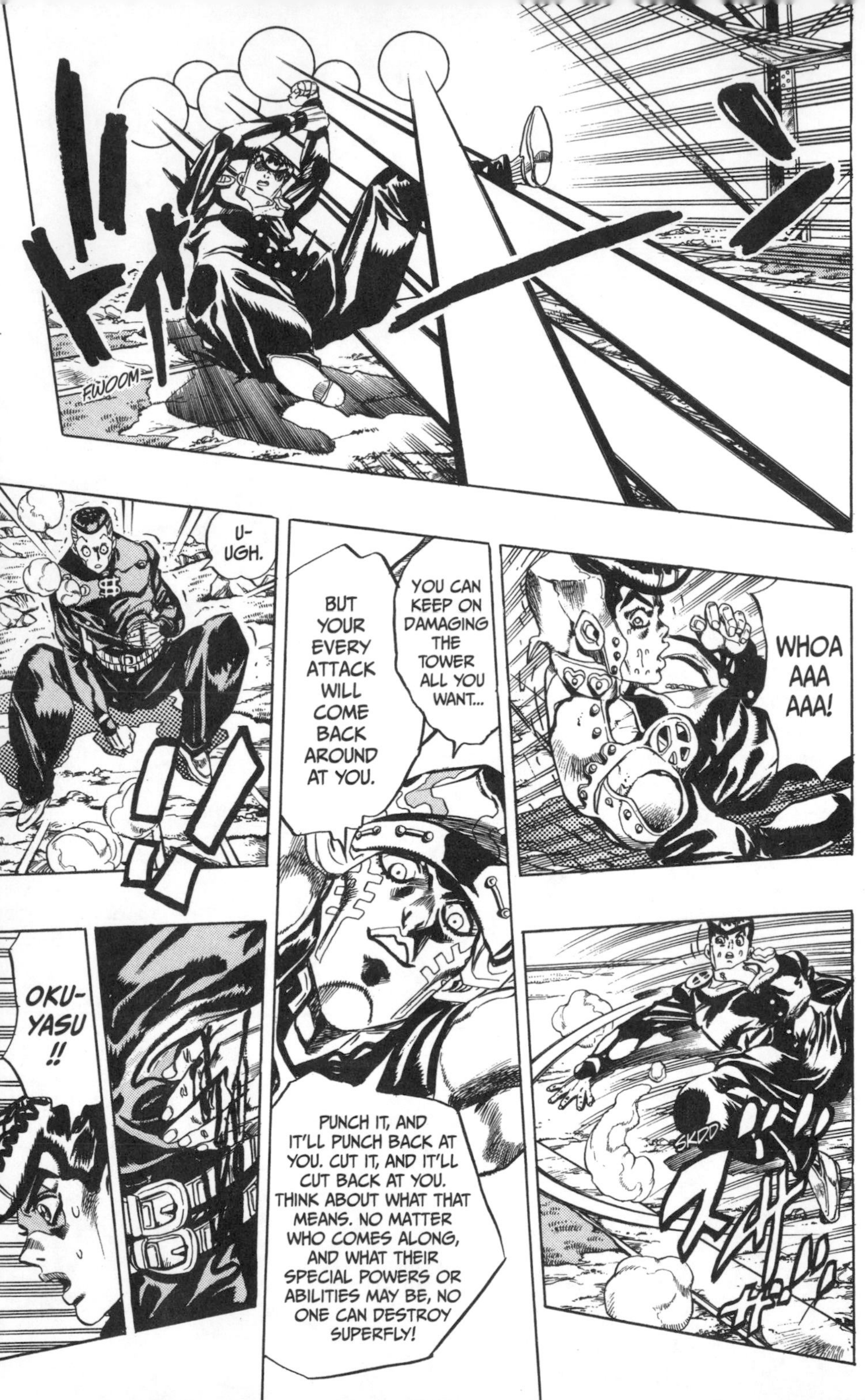
FWOOM
WHOA AAA AAA!
SKDD
YOU CAN KEEP ON DAMAGING THE TOWER ALL YOU WANT...
BUT YOUR EVERY ATTACK WILL COME BACK AROUND AT YOU.
PUNCH IT, AND IT'LL PUNCH BACK AT YOU. CUT IT, AND IT'LL CUT BACK AT YOU. THINK ABOUT WHAT THAT MEANS. NO MATTER WHO COMES ALONG, AND WHAT THEIR SPECIAL POWERS OR ABILITIES MAY BE, NO ONE CAN DESTROY SUPERFLY!
U-UGH.
OKU-YASU !!

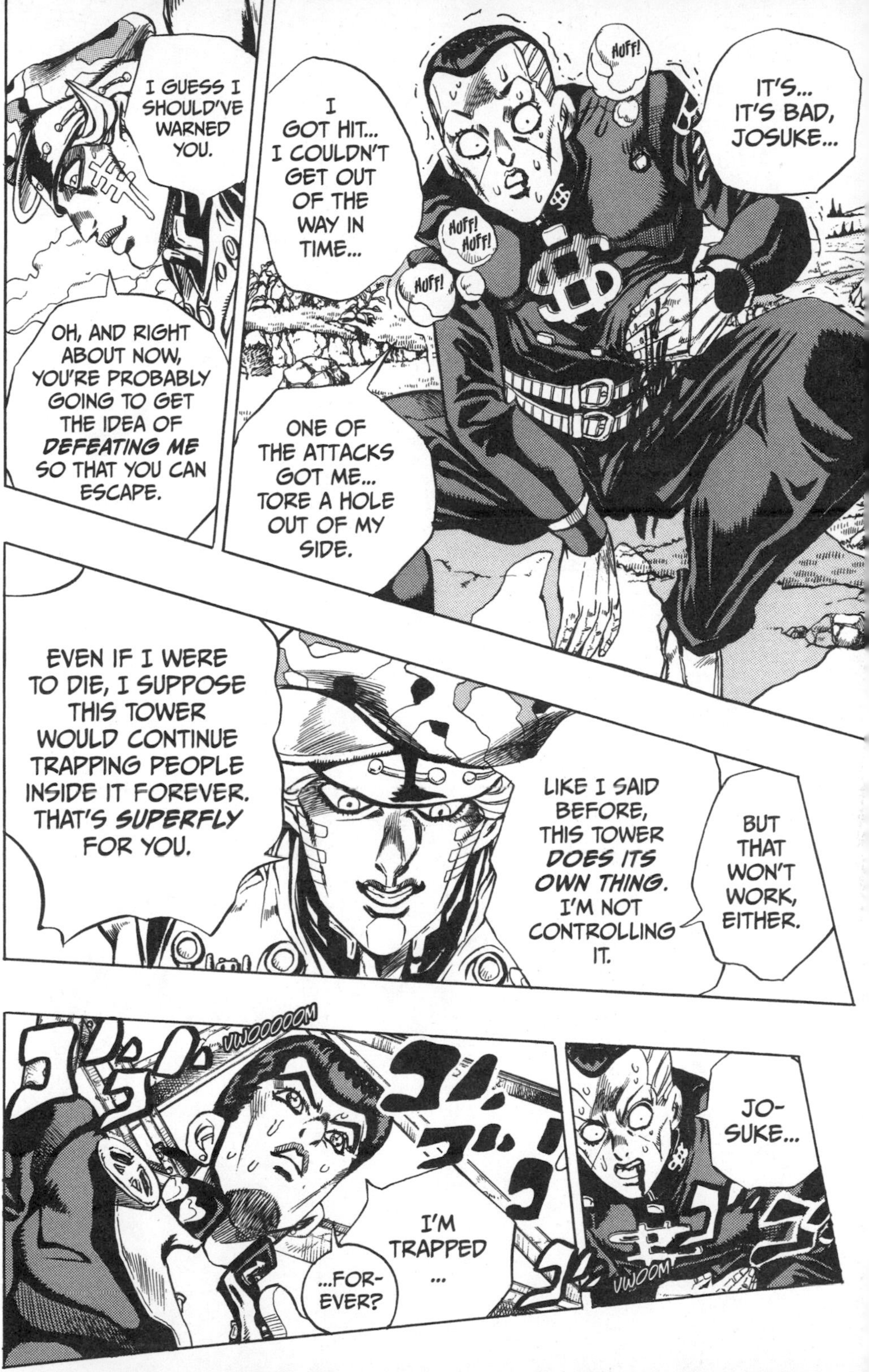
IT'S... IT'S BAD, JOSUKE...
HUFF!
I GOT HIT... I COULDN'T GET OUT OF THE WAY IN TIME...
HUFF! HUFF!
HUFF!
ONE OF THE ATTACKS GOT ME... TORE A HOLE OUT OF MY SIDE.
I GUESS I SHOULD'VE WARNED YOU.
OH, AND RIGHT ABOUT NOW, YOU'RE PROBABLY GOING TO GET THE IDEA OF *DEFEATING ME* SO THAT YOU CAN ESCAPE.
BUT THAT WON'T WORK, EITHER.
LIKE I SAID BEFORE, THIS TOWER *DOES ITS OWN THING*. I'M NOT CONTROLLING IT.
EVEN IF I WERE TO DIE, I SUPPOSE THIS TOWER WOULD CONTINUE TRAPPING PEOPLE INSIDE IT FOREVER. THAT'S *SUPERFLY* FOR YOU.
JO-SUKE...
VWOOM
VWOOOOOM
I'M TRAPPED ...
...FOR-EVER?

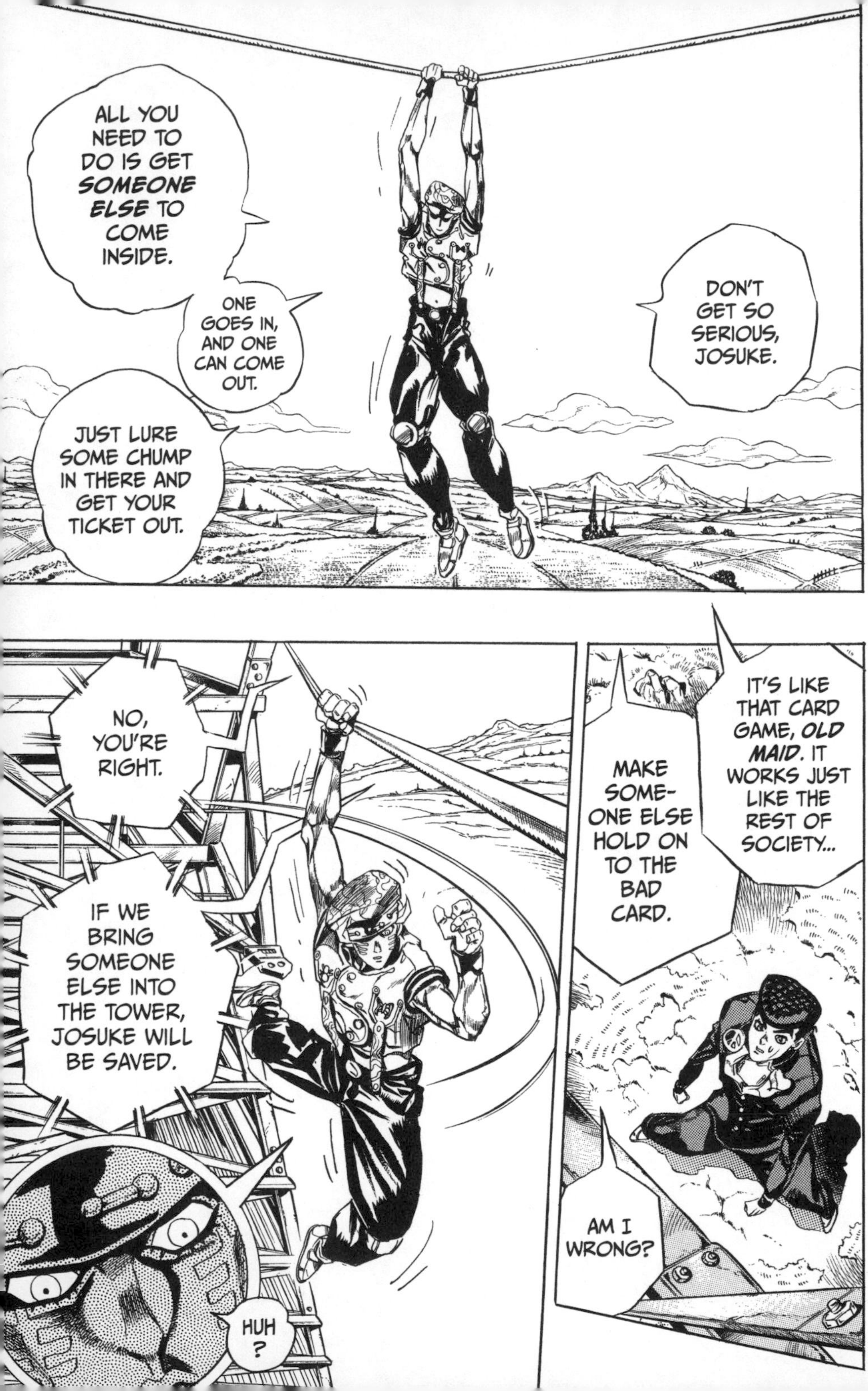
DON'T GET SO SERIOUS, JOSUKE.
ALL YOU NEED TO DO IS GET ***SOMEONE ELSE*** TO COME INSIDE.
ONE GOES IN, AND ONE CAN COME OUT.
JUST LURE SOME CHUMP IN THERE AND GET YOUR TICKET OUT.
IT'S LIKE THAT CARD GAME, ***OLD MAID***. IT WORKS JUST LIKE THE REST OF SOCIETY...
MAKE SOME-ONE ELSE HOLD ON TO THE BAD CARD.
AM I WRONG?
NO, YOU'RE RIGHT.
IF WE BRING SOMEONE ELSE INTO THE TOWER, JOSUKE WILL BE SAVED.
HUH?

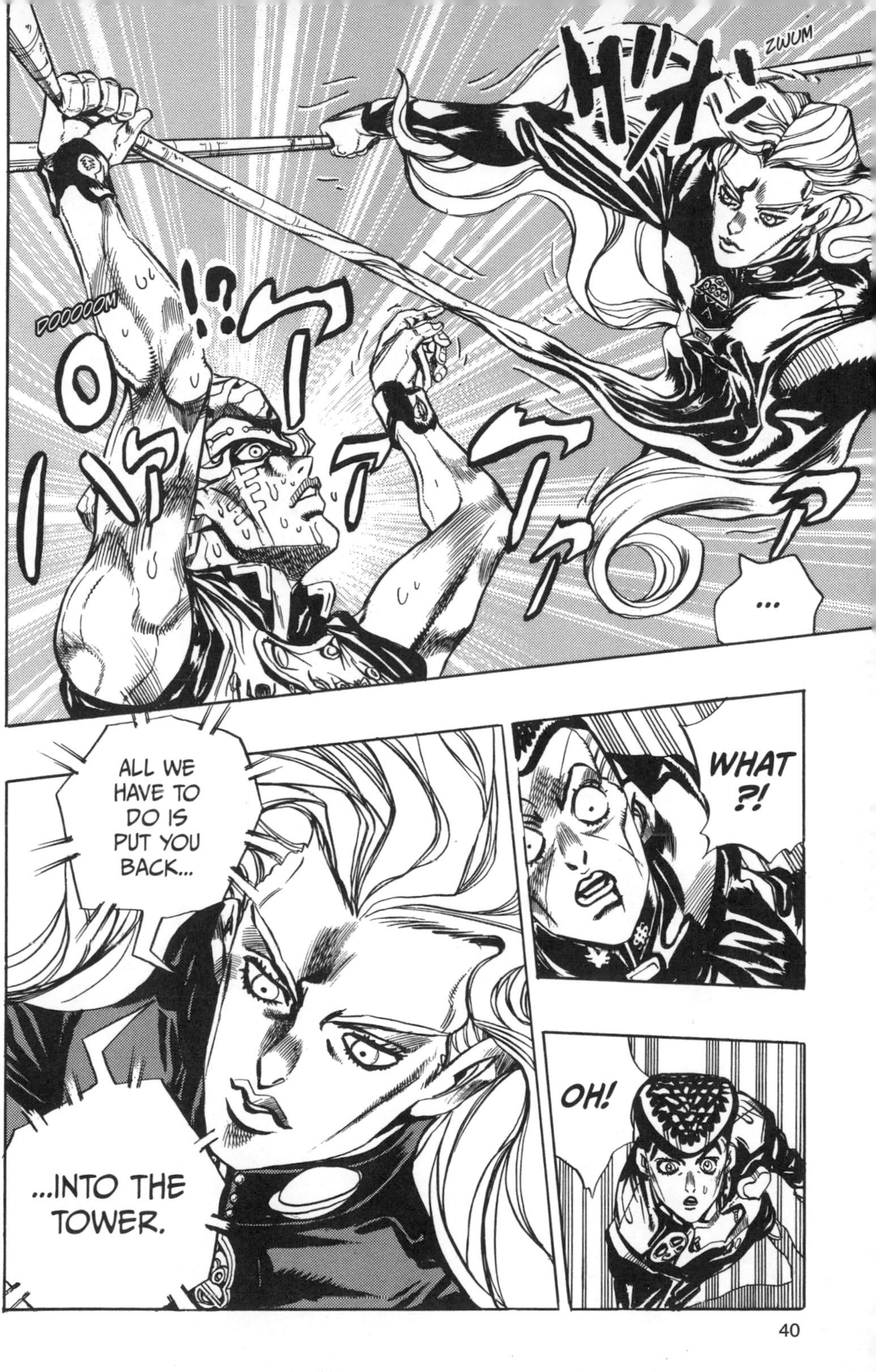
ZWUM
...
DOOOOOM
WHAT ?!
OH!
ALL WE HAVE TO DO IS PUT YOU BACK...
...INTO THE TOWER.

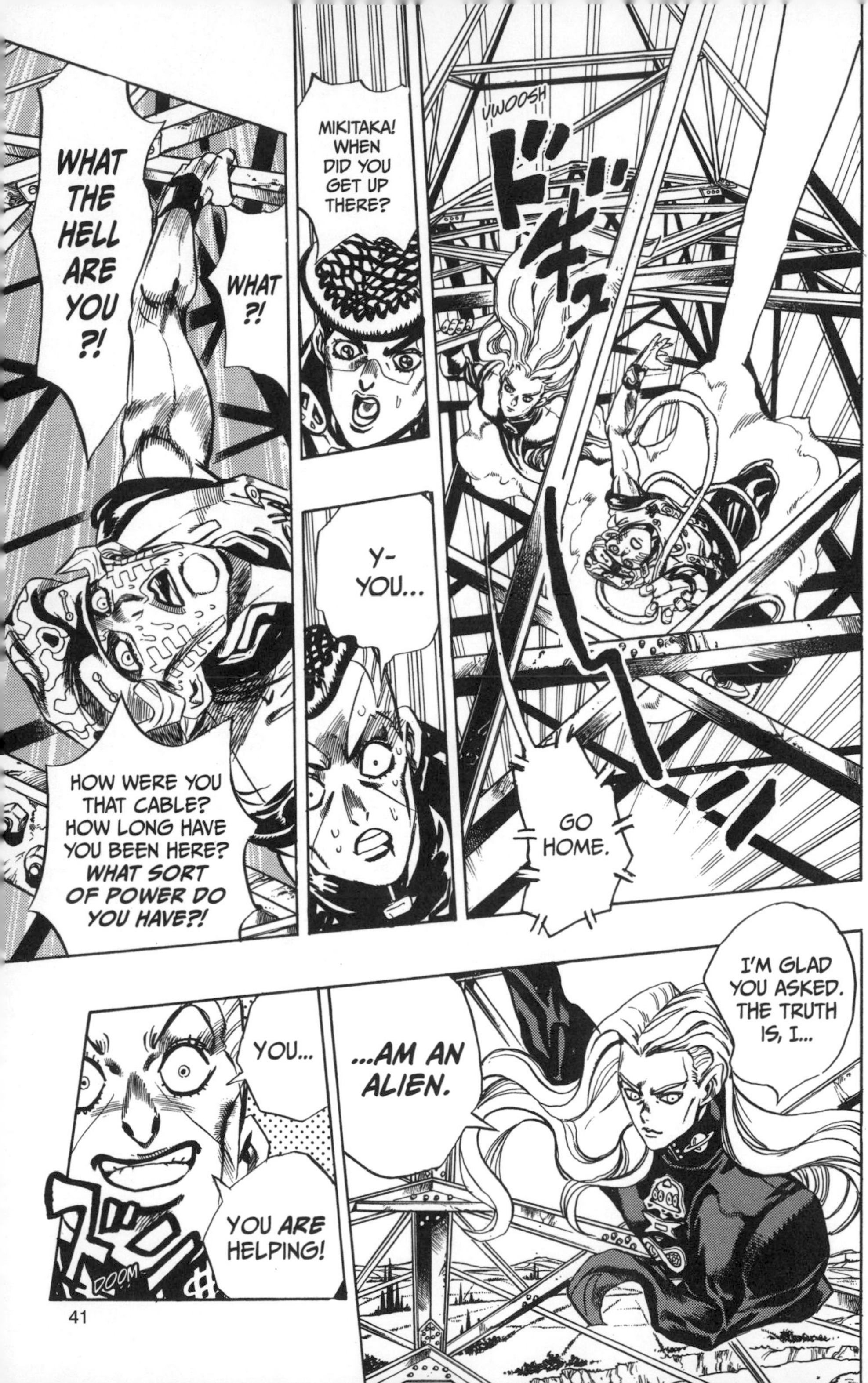
VWOOSH
GO HOME.
MIKITAKA! WHEN DID YOU GET UP THERE?
Y- YOU...
WHAT ?!
WHAT THE HELL ARE YOU ?!
HOW WERE YOU THAT CABLE? HOW LONG HAVE YOU BEEN HERE? WHAT SORT OF POWER DO YOU HAVE?!
I'M GLAD YOU ASKED. THE TRUTH IS, I...
...AM AN ALIEN.
YOU...
YOU ARE HELPING!
DOOM

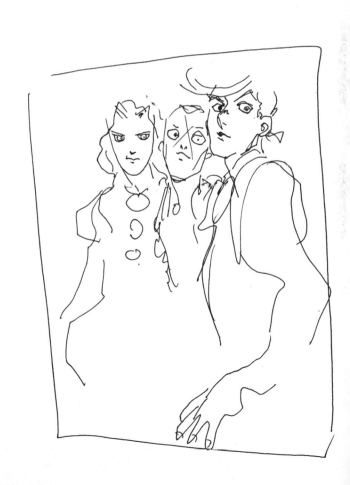

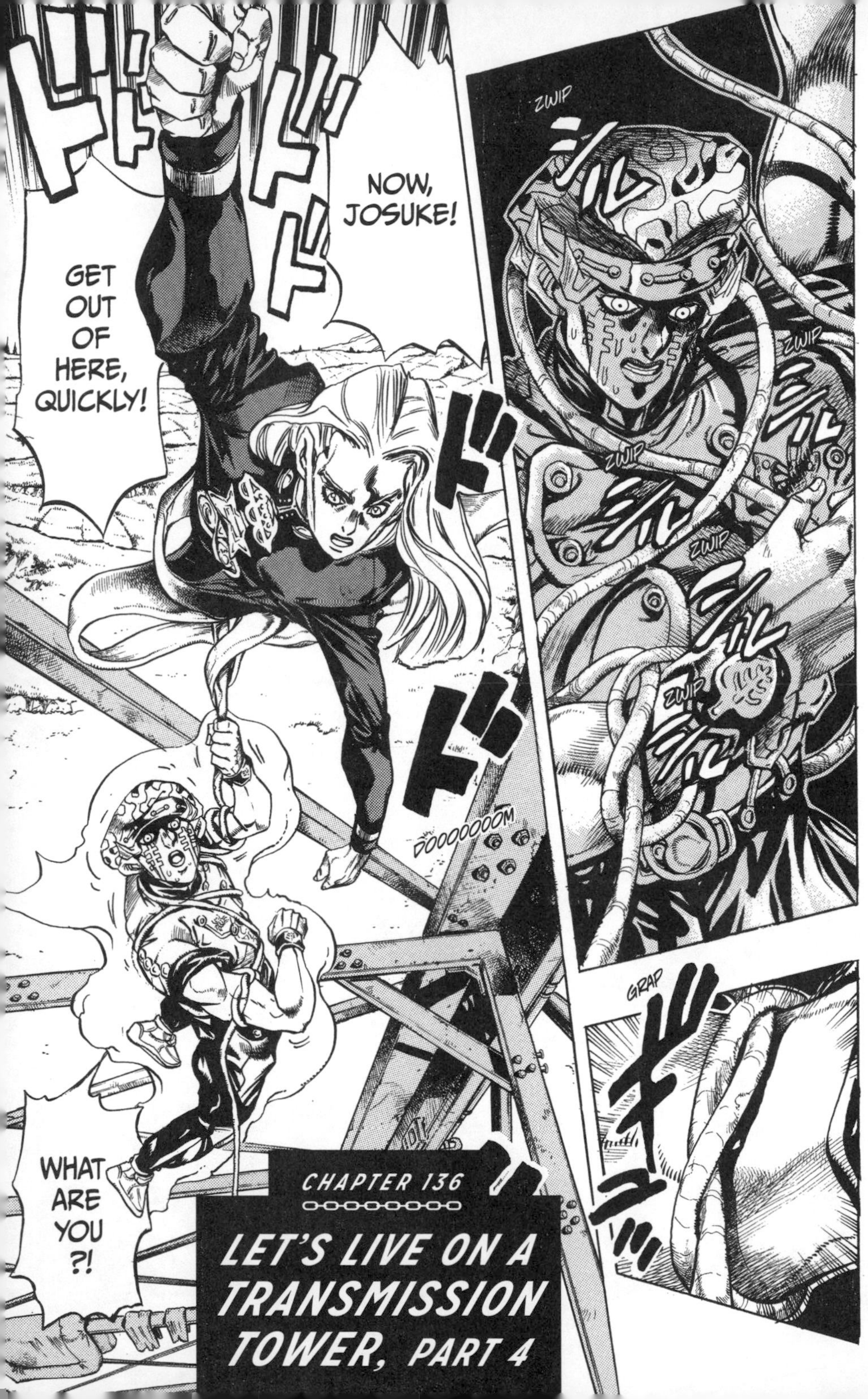
ZWIP
ZWIP
ZWIP
ZWIP
ZWIP
GRAP
NOW, JOSUKE!
GET OUT OF HERE, QUICKLY!
DOOOOOOOOM
WHAT ARE YOU ?!
CHAPTER 136
LET'S LIVE ON A TRANSMISSION TOWER, PART 4

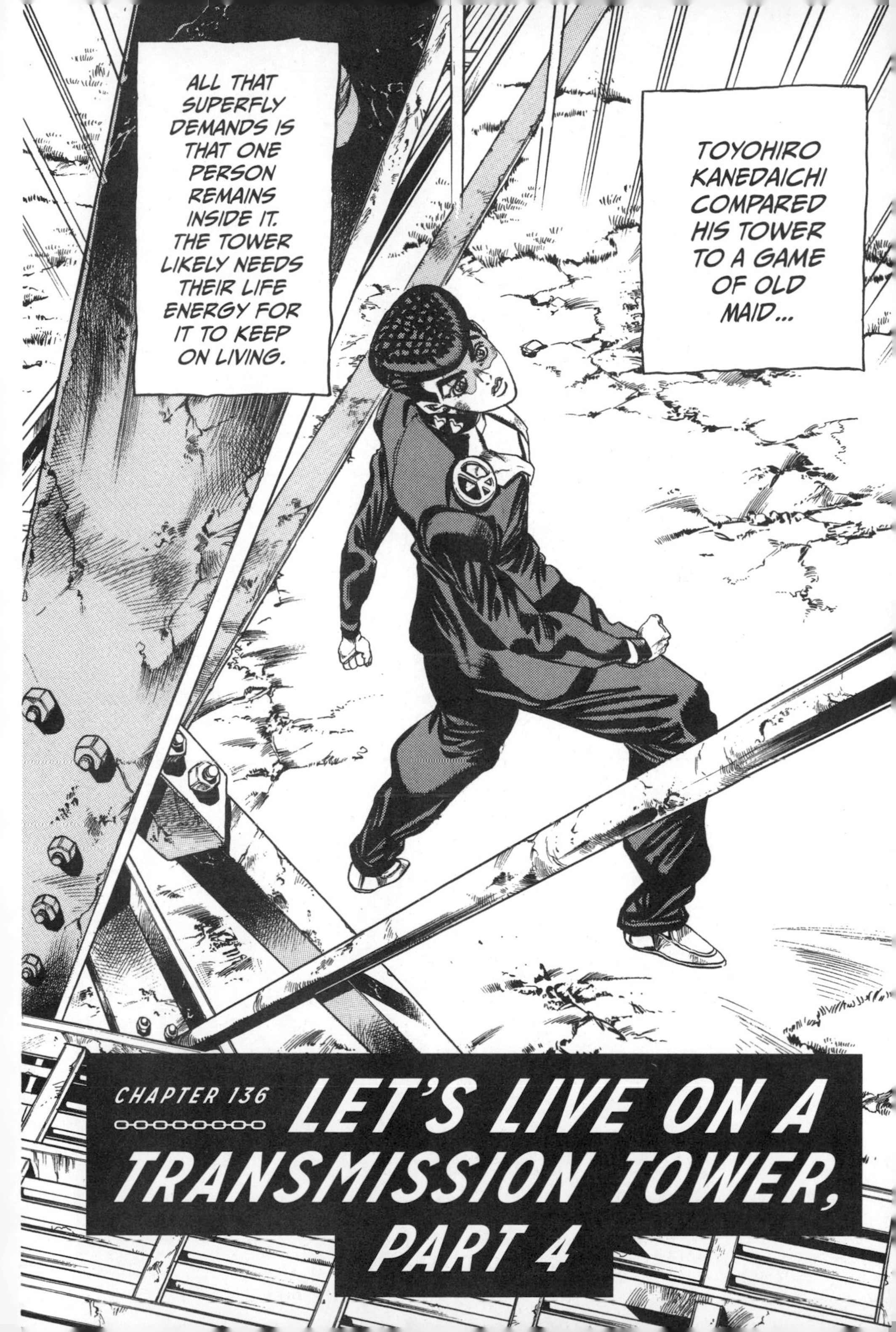
TOYOHIRO KANEDAICHI COMPARED HIS TOWER TO A GAME OF OLD MAID...
ALL THAT SUPERFLY DEMANDS IS THAT ONE PERSON REMAINS INSIDE IT. THE TOWER LIKELY NEEDS THEIR LIFE ENERGY FOR IT TO KEEP ON LIVING.
CHAPTER 136
LET'S LIVE ON A TRANSMISSION TOWER, PART 4

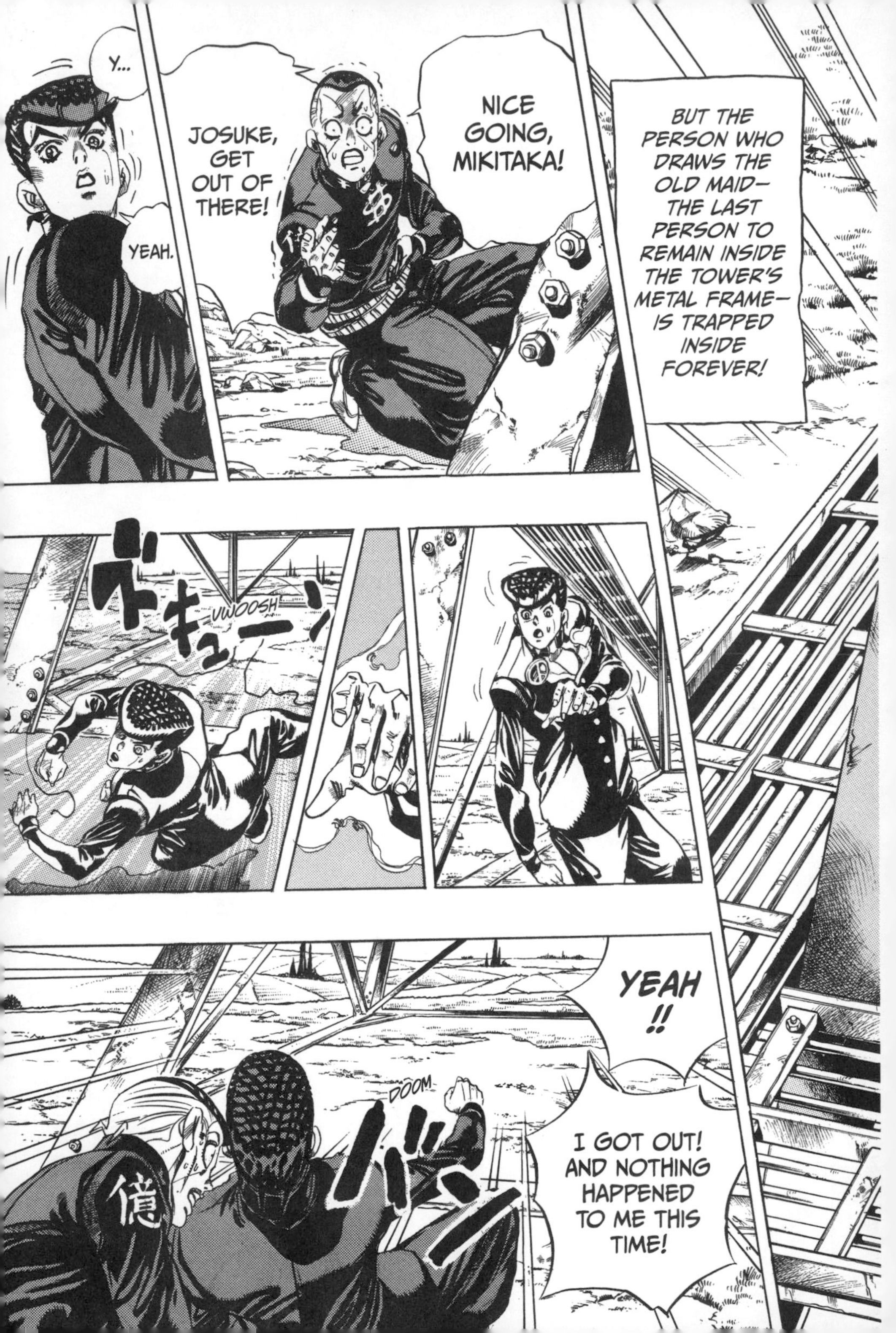
BUT THE PERSON WHO DRAWS THE OLD MAID— THE LAST PERSON TO REMAIN INSIDE THE TOWER'S METAL FRAME— IS TRAPPED INSIDE FOREVER!
NICE GOING, MIKITAKA!
JOSUKE, GET OUT OF THERE!
Y...
YEAH.
UWOOSH
YEAH !!
I GOT OUT! AND NOTHING HAPPENED TO ME THIS TIME!
DOOM

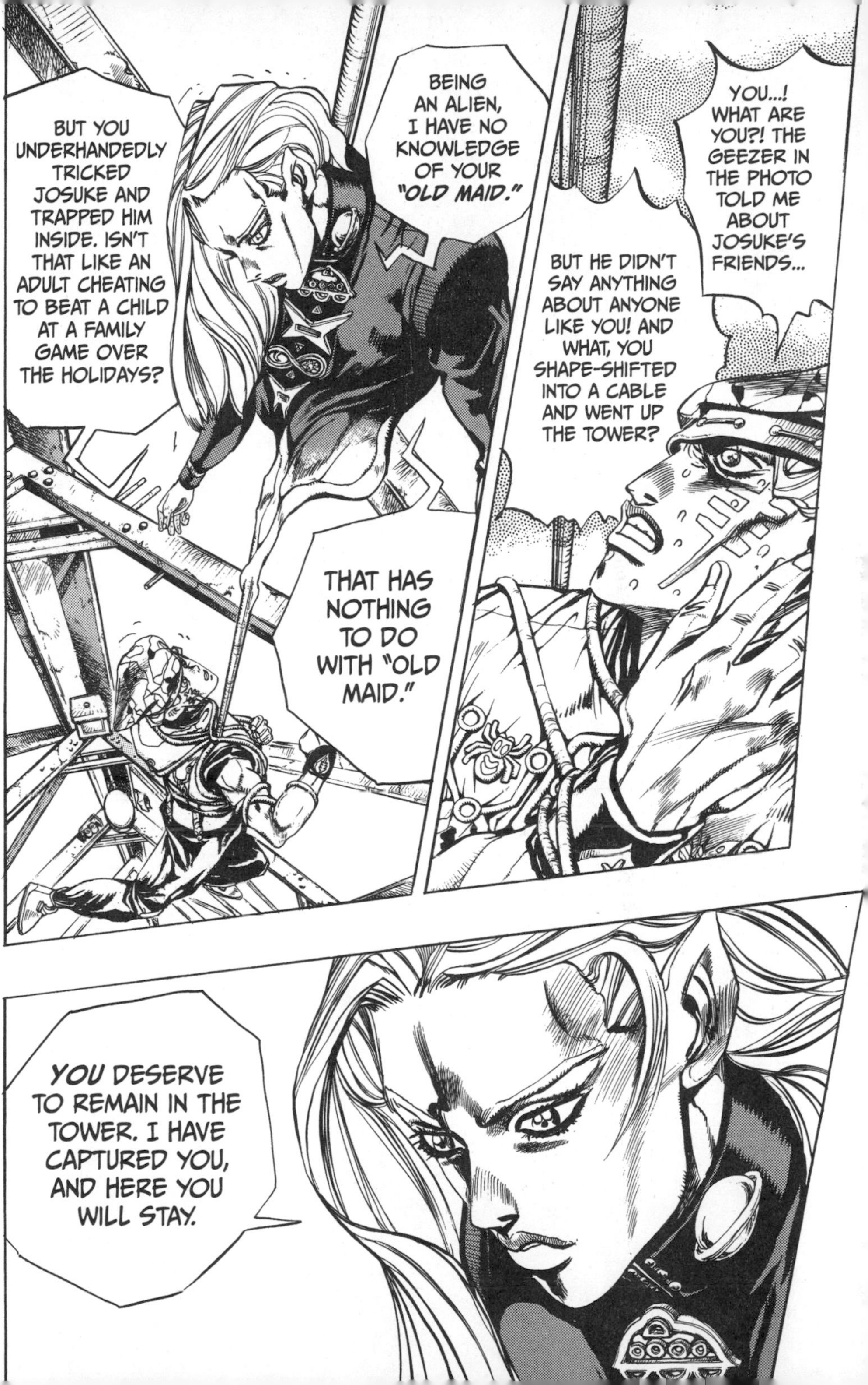
YOU...! WHAT ARE YOU?! THE GEEZER IN THE PHOTO TOLD ME ABOUT JOSUKE'S FRIENDS...
BUT HE DIDN'T SAY ANYTHING ABOUT ANYONE LIKE YOU! AND WHAT, YOU SHAPE-SHIFTED INTO A CABLE AND WENT UP THE TOWER?
BEING AN ALIEN, I HAVE NO KNOWLEDGE OF YOUR *"OLD MAID."*
BUT YOU UNDERHANDEDLY TRICKED JOSUKE AND TRAPPED HIM INSIDE. ISN'T THAT LIKE AN ADULT CHEATING TO BEAT A CHILD AT A FAMILY GAME OVER THE HOLIDAYS?
THAT HAS NOTHING TO DO WITH "OLD MAID."
YOU DESERVE TO REMAIN IN THE TOWER. I HAVE CAPTURED YOU, AND HERE YOU WILL STAY.

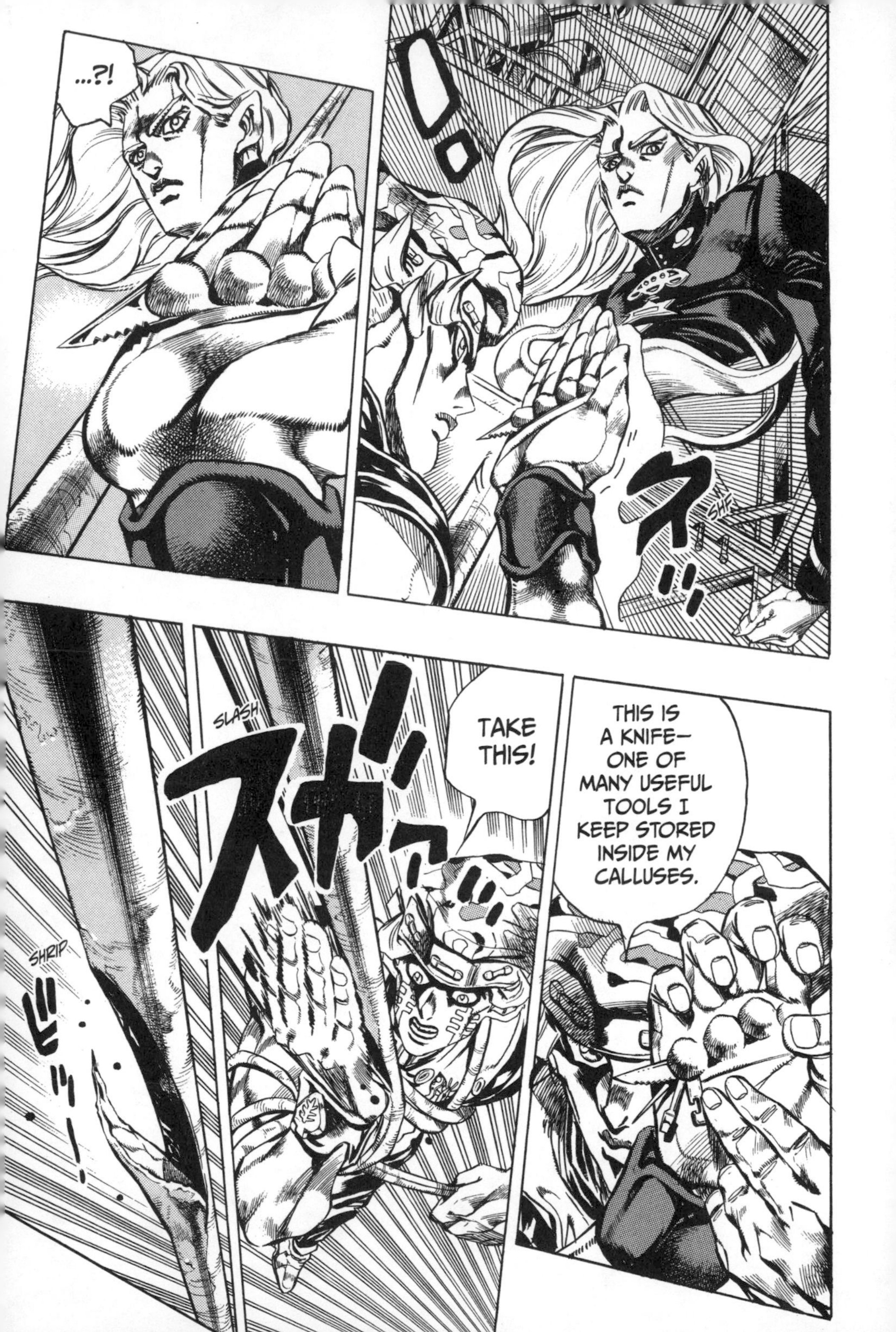
SHF
...?!
THIS IS A KNIFE—ONE OF MANY USEFUL TOOLS I KEEP STORED INSIDE MY CALLUSES.
TAKE THIS!
SLASH
SHRIP

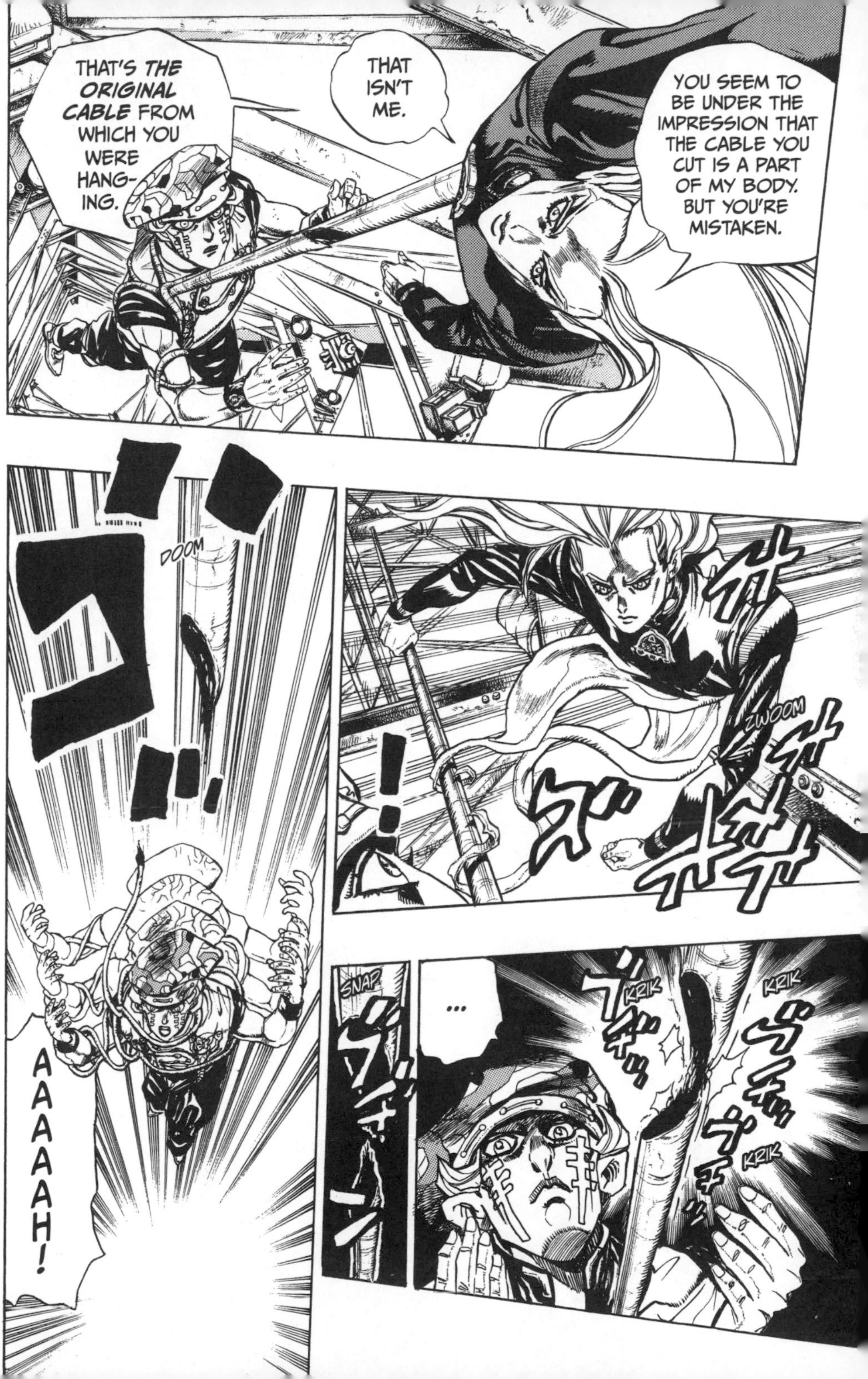
YOU SEEM TO BE UNDER THE IMPRESSION THAT THE CABLE YOU CUT IS A PART OF MY BODY. BUT YOU'RE MISTAKEN.
THAT ISN'T ME.
THAT'S *THE ORIGINAL CABLE* FROM WHICH YOU WERE HANG-ING.
ZWOOM
KRIK
KRIK
KRIK
...
SNAP
DOOM
AAAAAAAH!

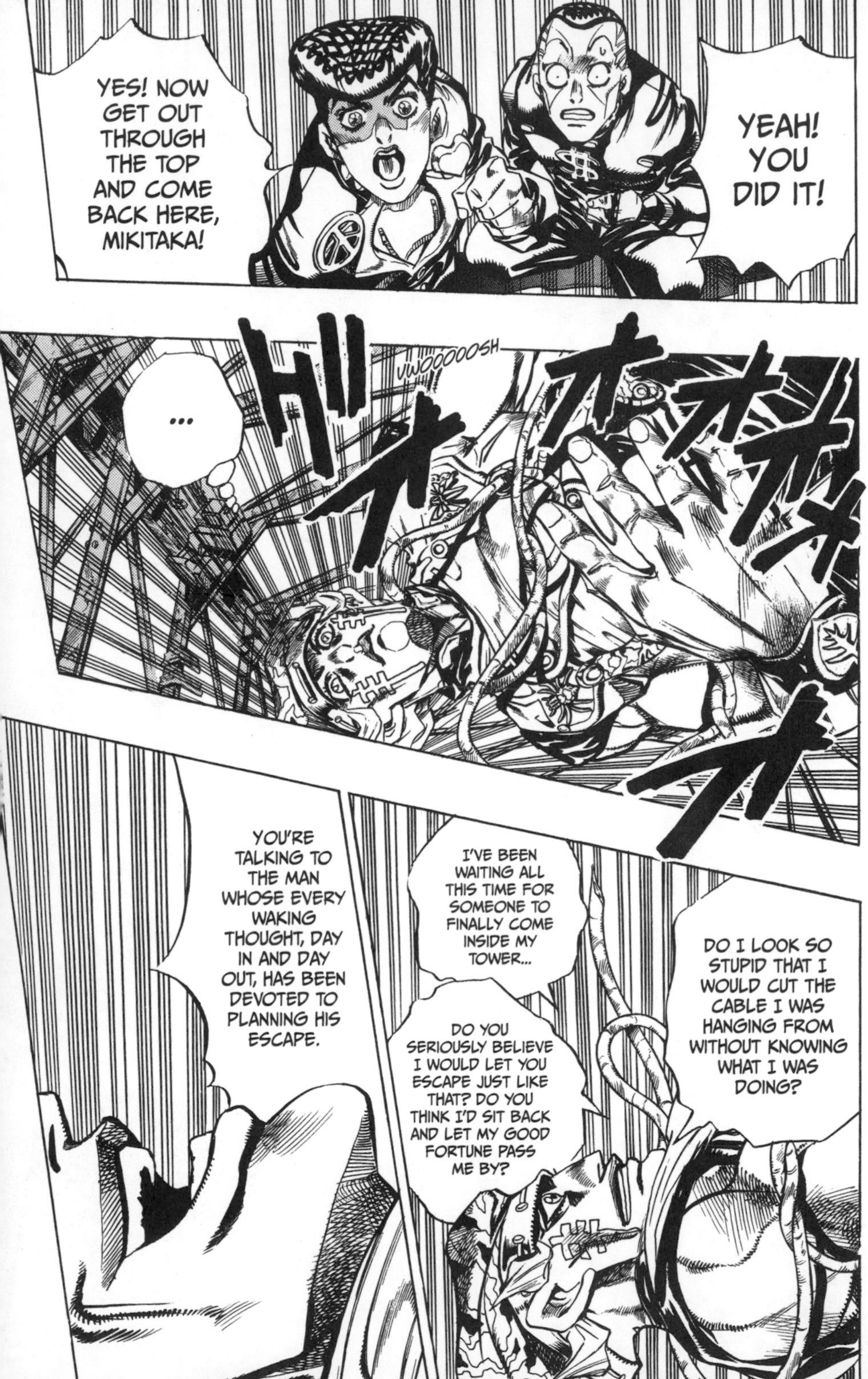

YEAH! YOU DID IT!
YES! NOW GET OUT THROUGH THE TOP AND COME BACK HERE, MIKITAKA!
VWOOOOOSH
...
DO I LOOK SO STUPID THAT I WOULD CUT THE CABLE I WAS HANGING FROM WITHOUT KNOWING WHAT I WAS DOING?
I'VE BEEN WAITING ALL THIS TIME FOR SOMEONE TO FINALLY COME INSIDE MY TOWER...
DO YOU SERIOUSLY BELIEVE I WOULD LET YOU ESCAPE JUST LIKE THAT? DO YOU THINK I'D SIT BACK AND LET MY GOOD FORTUNE PASS ME BY?
YOU'RE TALKING TO THE MAN WHOSE EVERY WAKING THOUGHT, DAY IN AND DAY OUT, HAS BEEN DEVOTED TO PLANNING HIS ESCAPE.

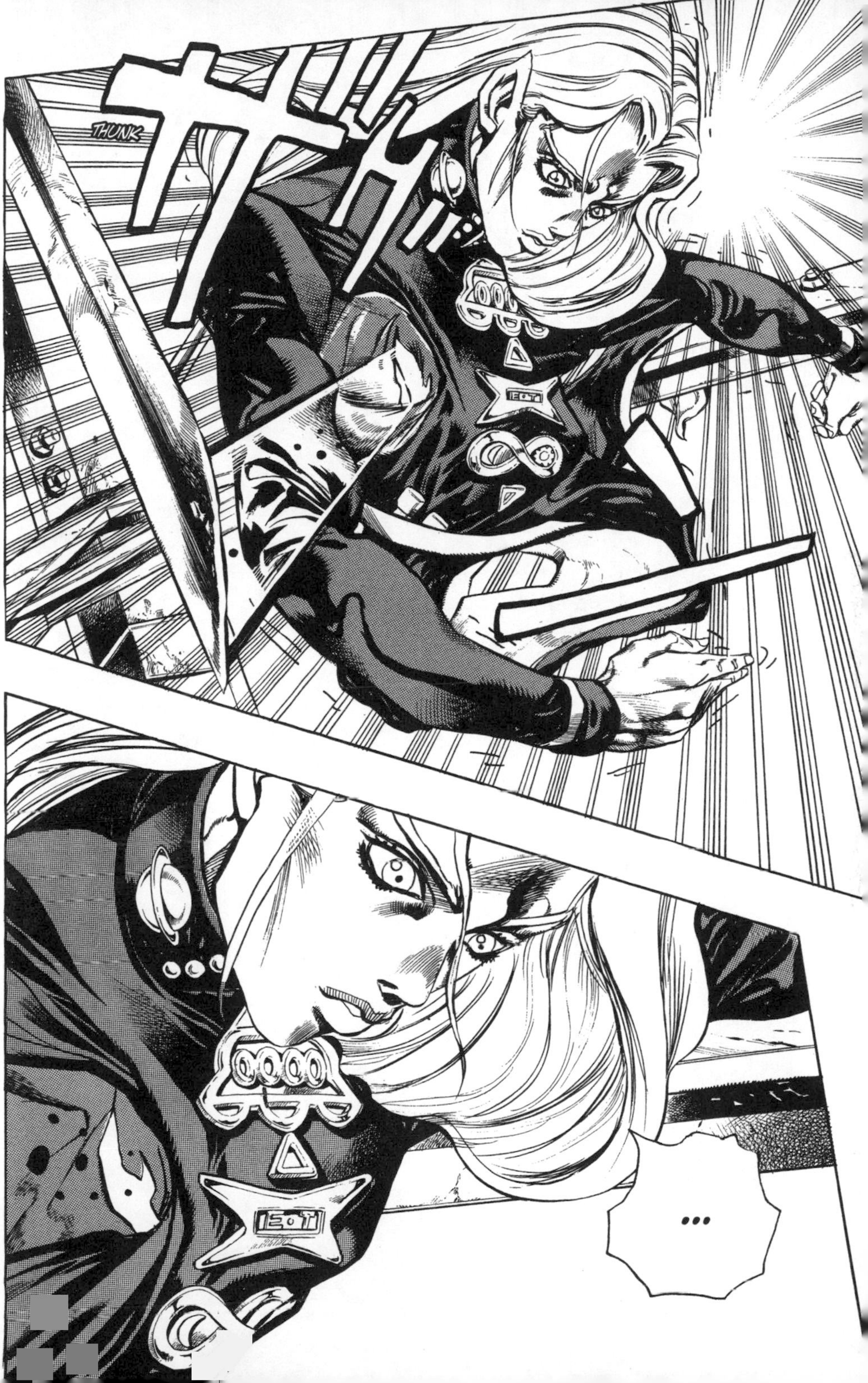
THUNK
...

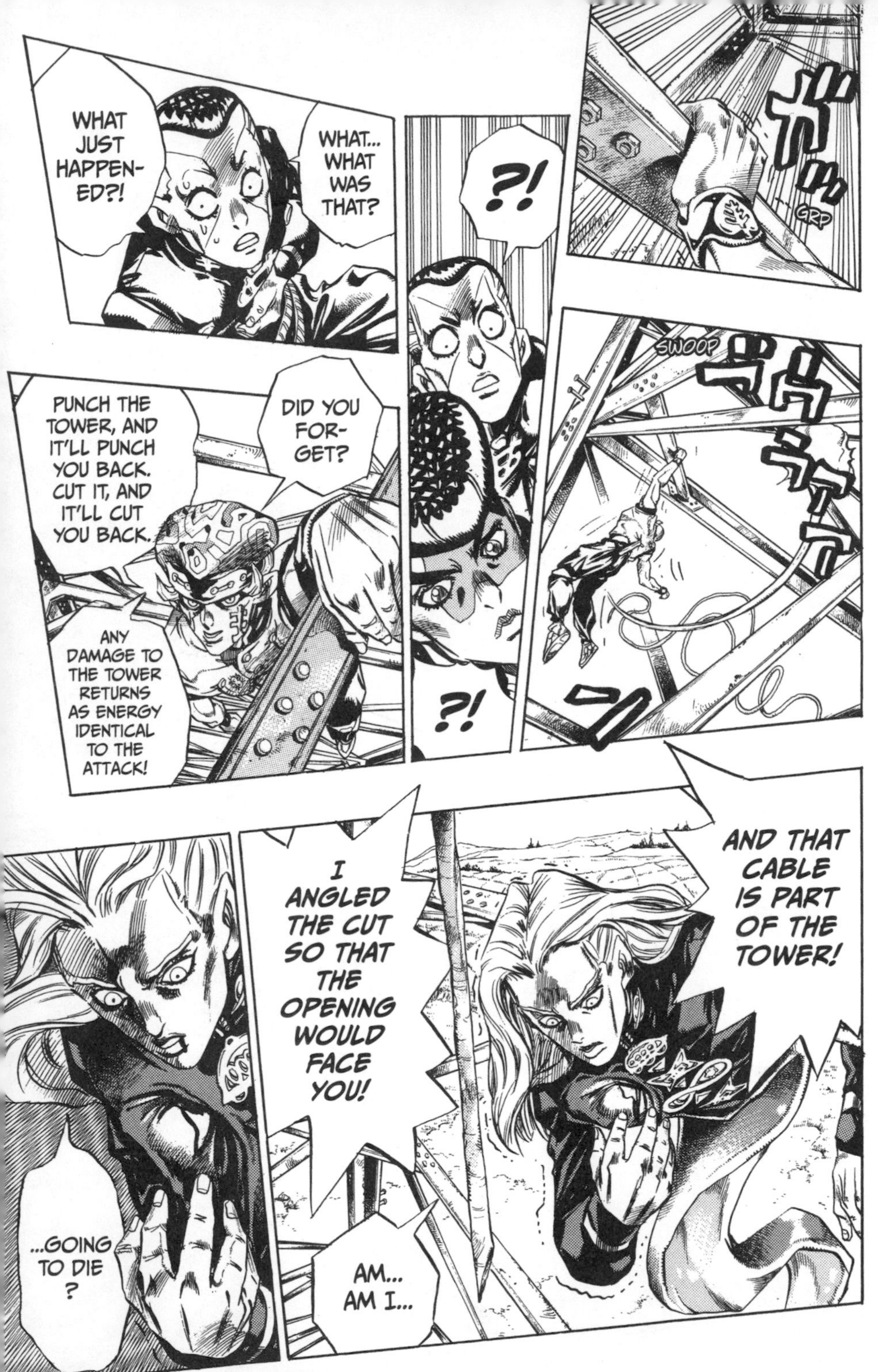
GRP
SWOOP
?!
?!
WHAT... WHAT WAS THAT?
WHAT JUST HAPPEN-ED?!
DID YOU FOR-GET?
PUNCH THE TOWER, AND IT'LL PUNCH YOU BACK. CUT IT, AND IT'LL CUT YOU BACK.
ANY DAMAGE TO THE TOWER RETURNS AS ENERGY IDENTICAL TO THE ATTACK!
AND THAT CABLE IS PART OF THE TOWER!
I ANGLED THE CUT SO THAT THE OPENING WOULD FACE YOU!
AM... AM I...
...GOING TO DIE ?

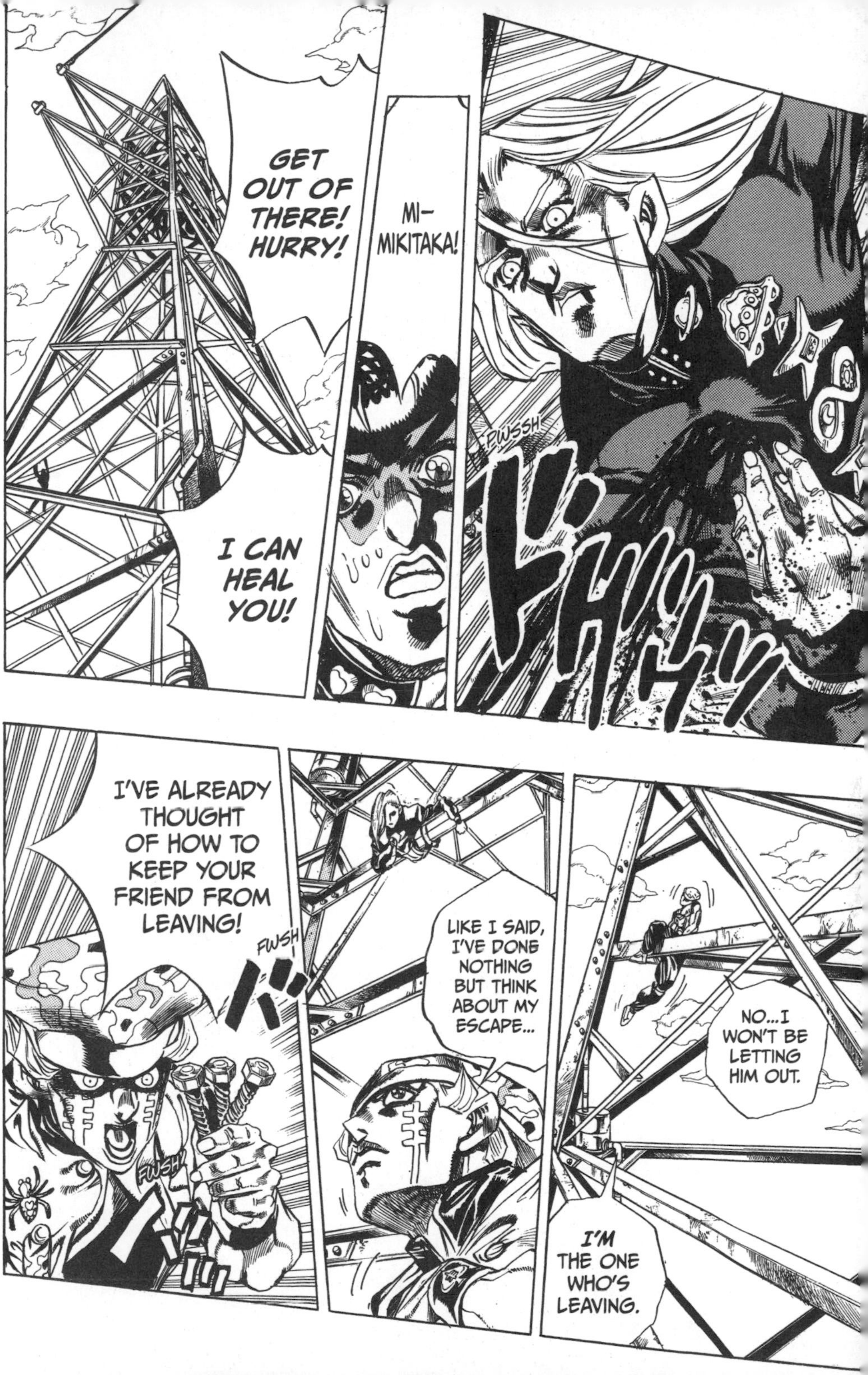
PWSSH
MI-MIKITAKA!
GET OUT OF THERE! HURRY!
I CAN HEAL YOU!
NO...I WON'T BE LETTING HIM OUT.
I'M THE ONE WHO'S LEAVING.
LIKE I SAID, I'VE DONE NOTHING BUT THINK ABOUT MY ESCAPE...
I'VE ALREADY THOUGHT OF HOW TO KEEP YOUR FRIEND FROM LEAVING!
FWSH
FWSH

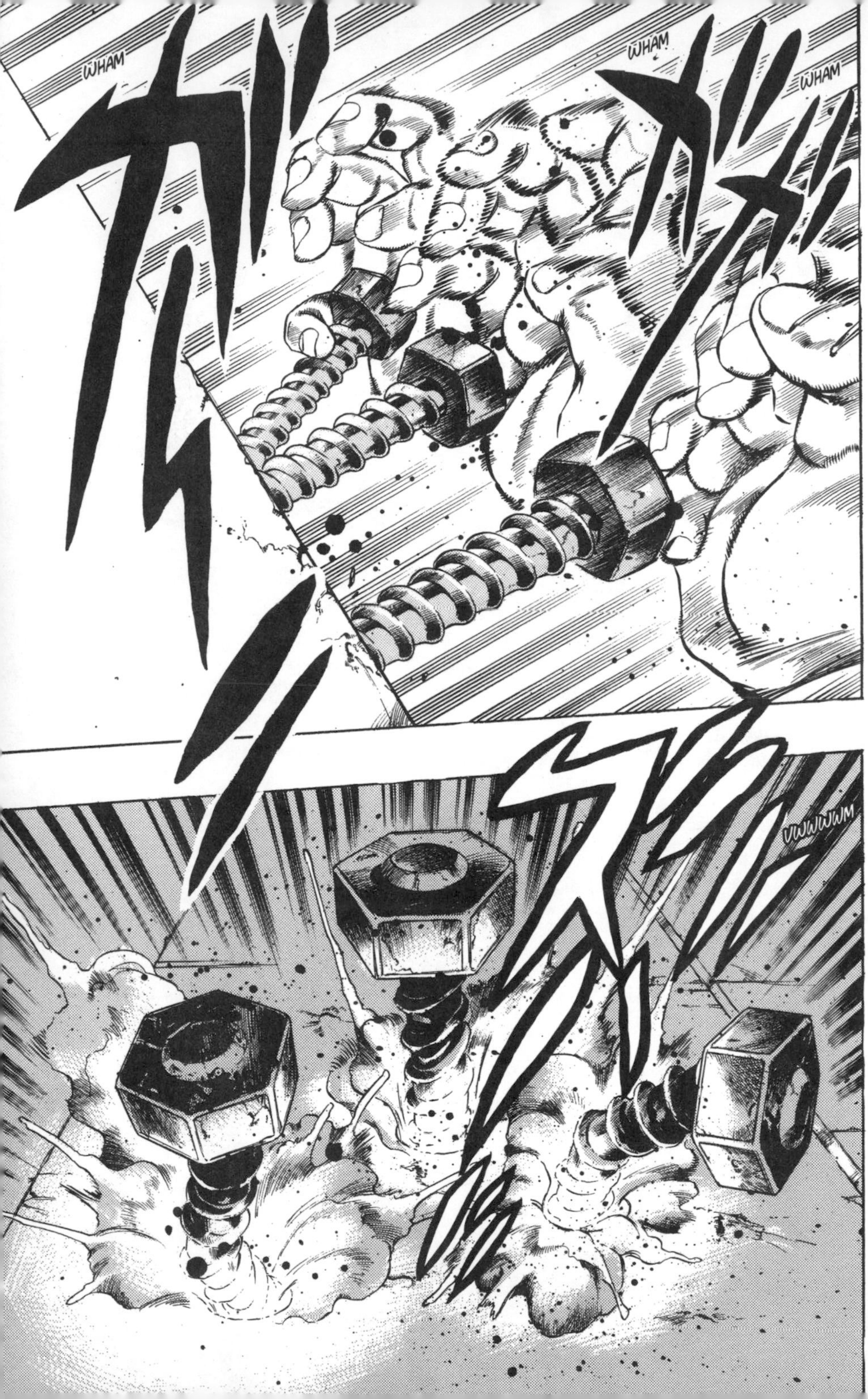
WHAM
WHAM
WHAM
VWWWWM

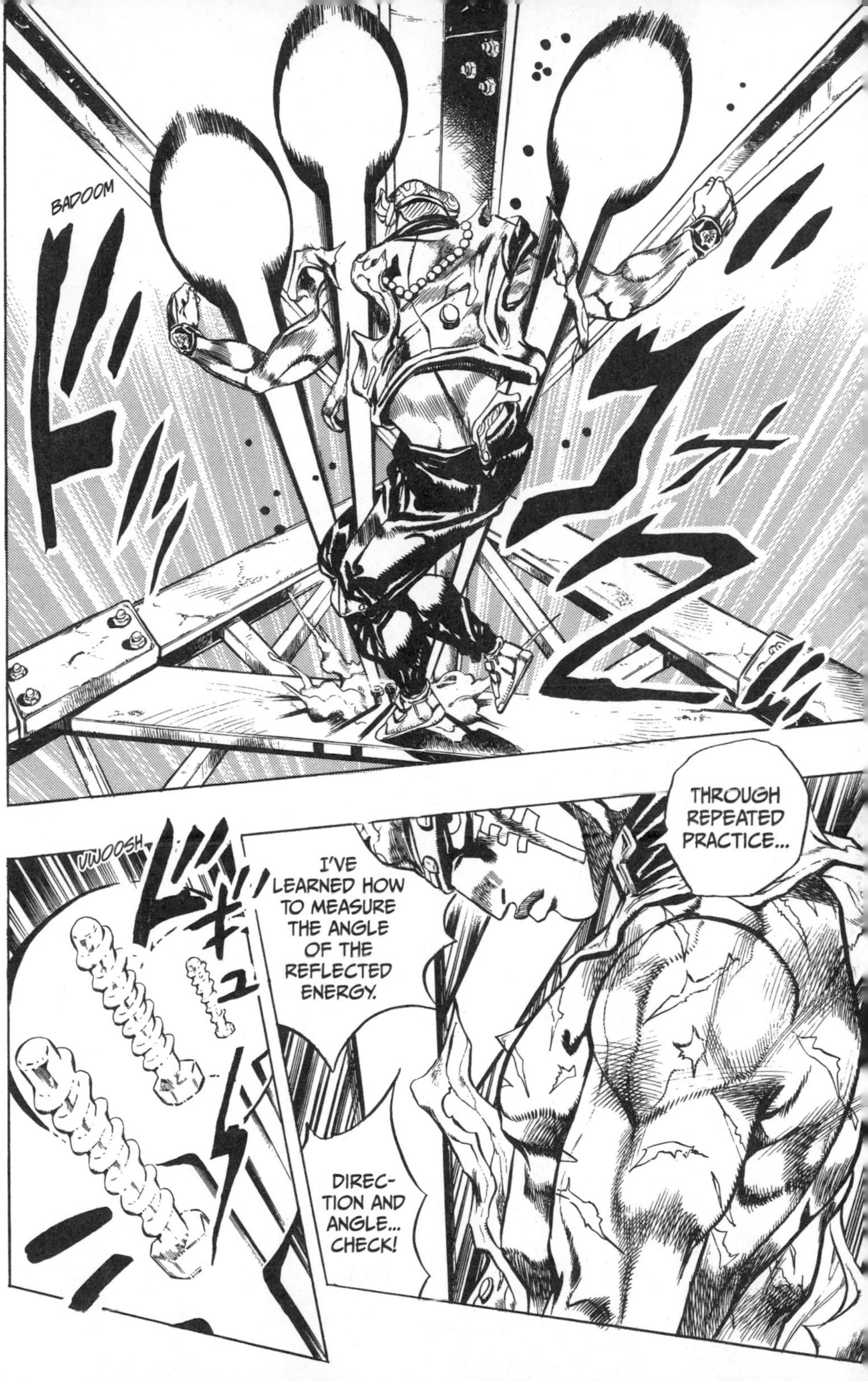
BADOOM
THROUGH REPEATED PRACTICE...
I'VE LEARNED HOW TO MEASURE THE ANGLE OF THE REFLECTED ENERGY.
DIRECTION AND ANGLE... CHECK!
UWOOSH

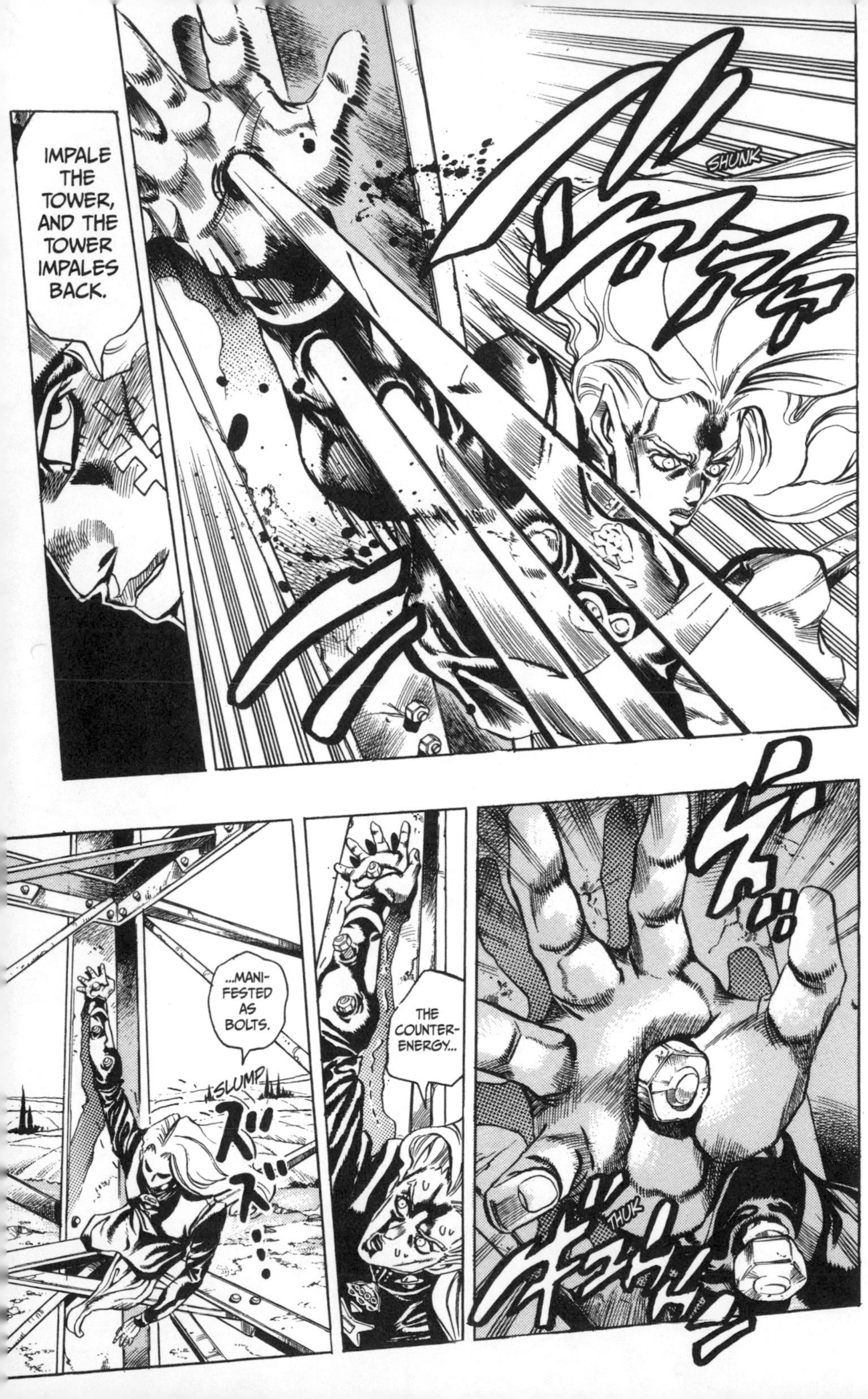
SHUNK
IMPALE THE TOWER, AND THE TOWER IMPALES BACK.
THUK
THE COUNTER-ENERGY...
...MANI-FESTED AS BOLTS.
SLUMP

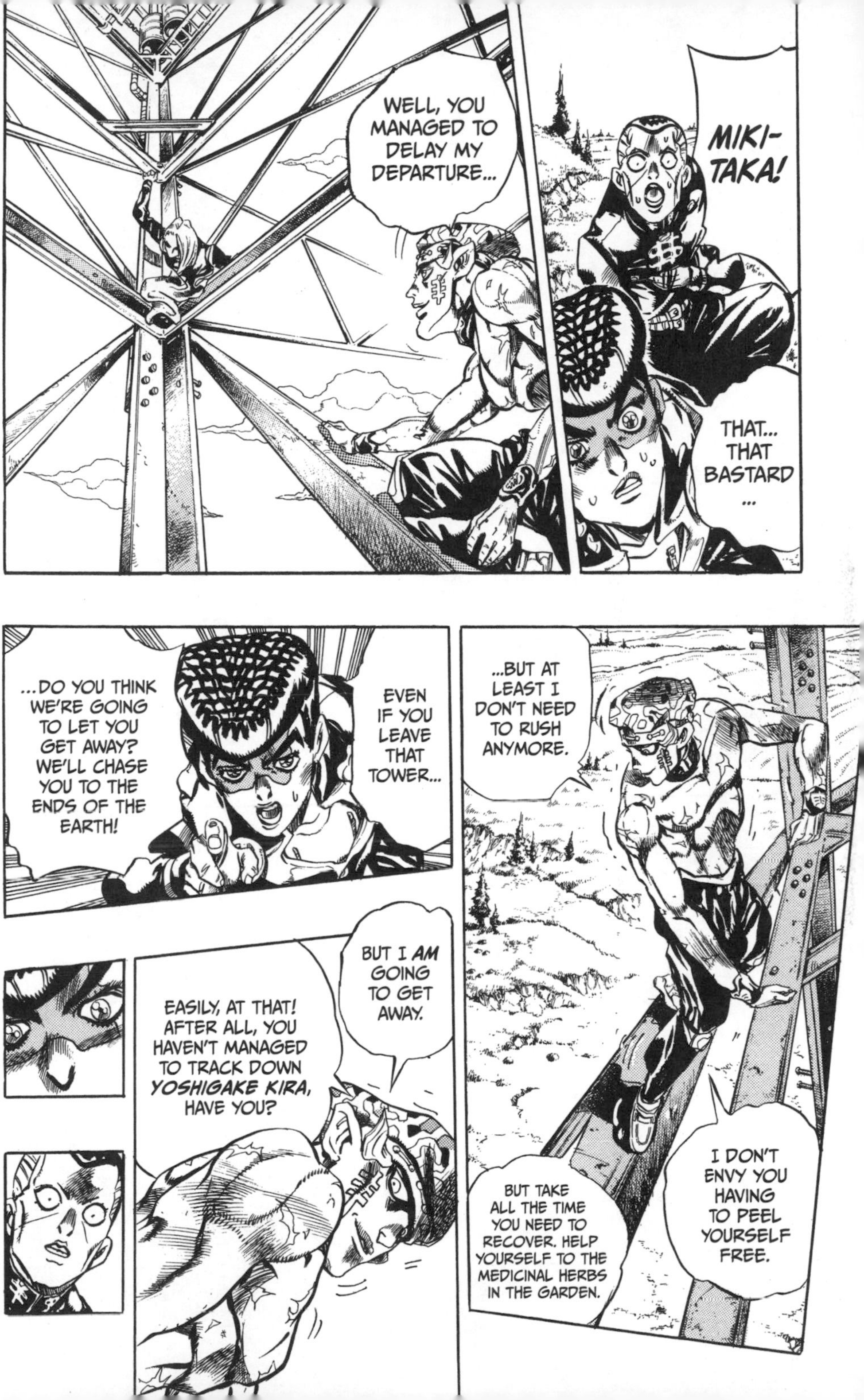

MIKI-TAKA!
WELL, YOU MANAGED TO DELAY MY DEPARTURE...
THAT... THAT BASTARD ...
...BUT AT LEAST I DON'T NEED TO RUSH ANYMORE.
I DON'T ENVY YOU HAVING TO PEEL YOURSELF FREE.
BUT TAKE ALL THE TIME YOU NEED TO RECOVER. HELP YOURSELF TO THE MEDICINAL HERBS IN THE GARDEN.
EVEN IF YOU LEAVE THAT TOWER...
...DO YOU THINK WE'RE GOING TO LET YOU GET AWAY? WE'LL CHASE YOU TO THE ENDS OF THE EARTH!
BUT I *AM* GOING TO GET AWAY.
EASILY, AT THAT! AFTER ALL, YOU HAVEN'T MANAGED TO TRACK DOWN *YOSHIGAKE KIRA*, HAVE YOU?

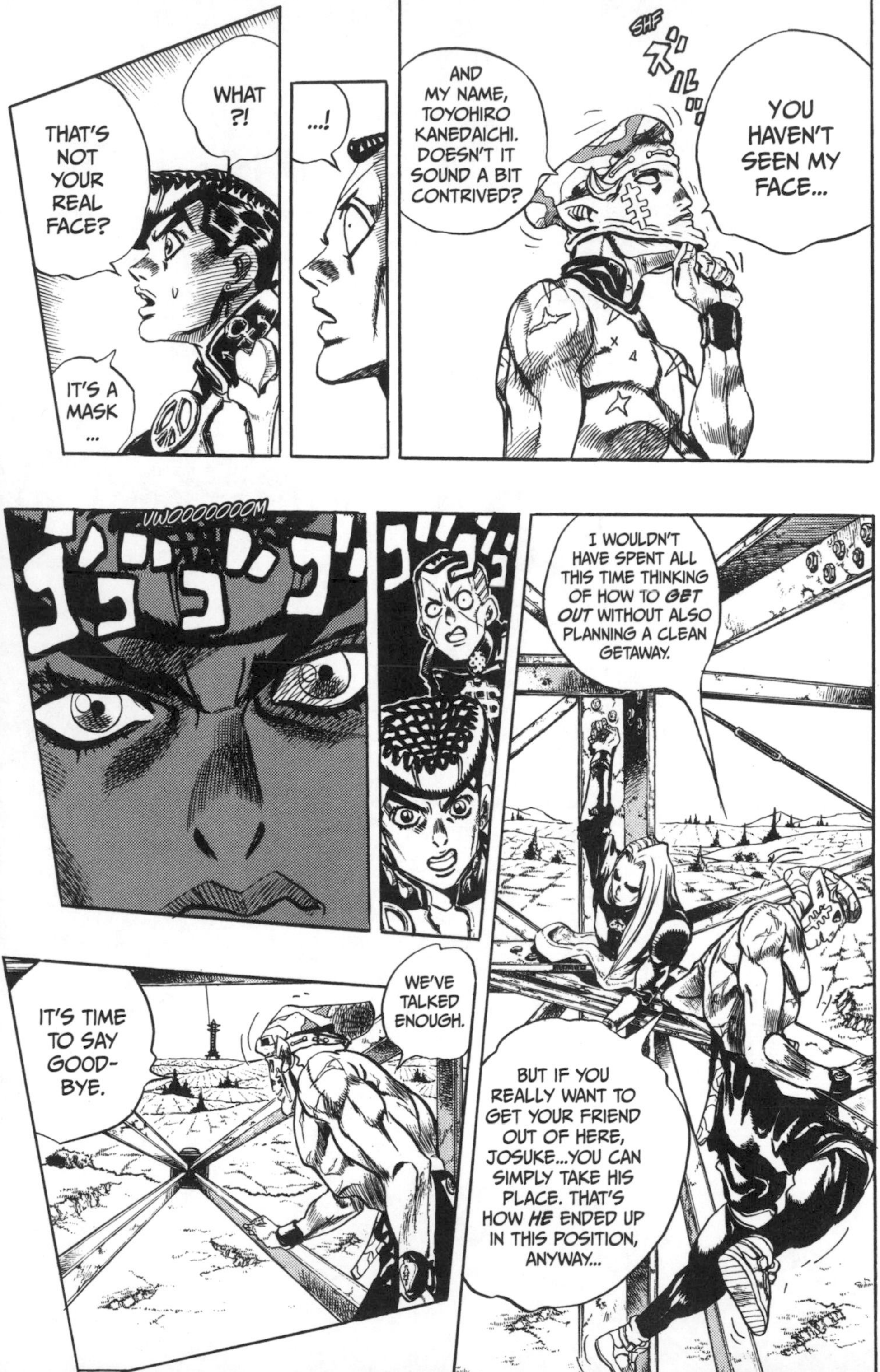
SHF
YOU HAVEN'T SEEN MY FACE...
AND MY NAME, TOYOHIRO KANEDAICHI. DOESN'T IT SOUND A BIT CONTRIVED?
...!
WHAT ?!
THAT'S NOT YOUR REAL FACE?
IT'S A MASK ...
I WOULDN'T HAVE SPENT ALL THIS TIME THINKING OF HOW TO GET OUT WITHOUT ALSO PLANNING A CLEAN GETAWAY.
BUT IF YOU REALLY WANT TO GET YOUR FRIEND OUT OF HERE, JOSUKE...YOU CAN SIMPLY TAKE HIS PLACE. THAT'S HOW HE ENDED UP IN THIS POSITION, ANYWAY...
VWOOOOOOOOM
WE'VE TALKED ENOUGH.
IT'S TIME TO SAY GOOD-BYE.

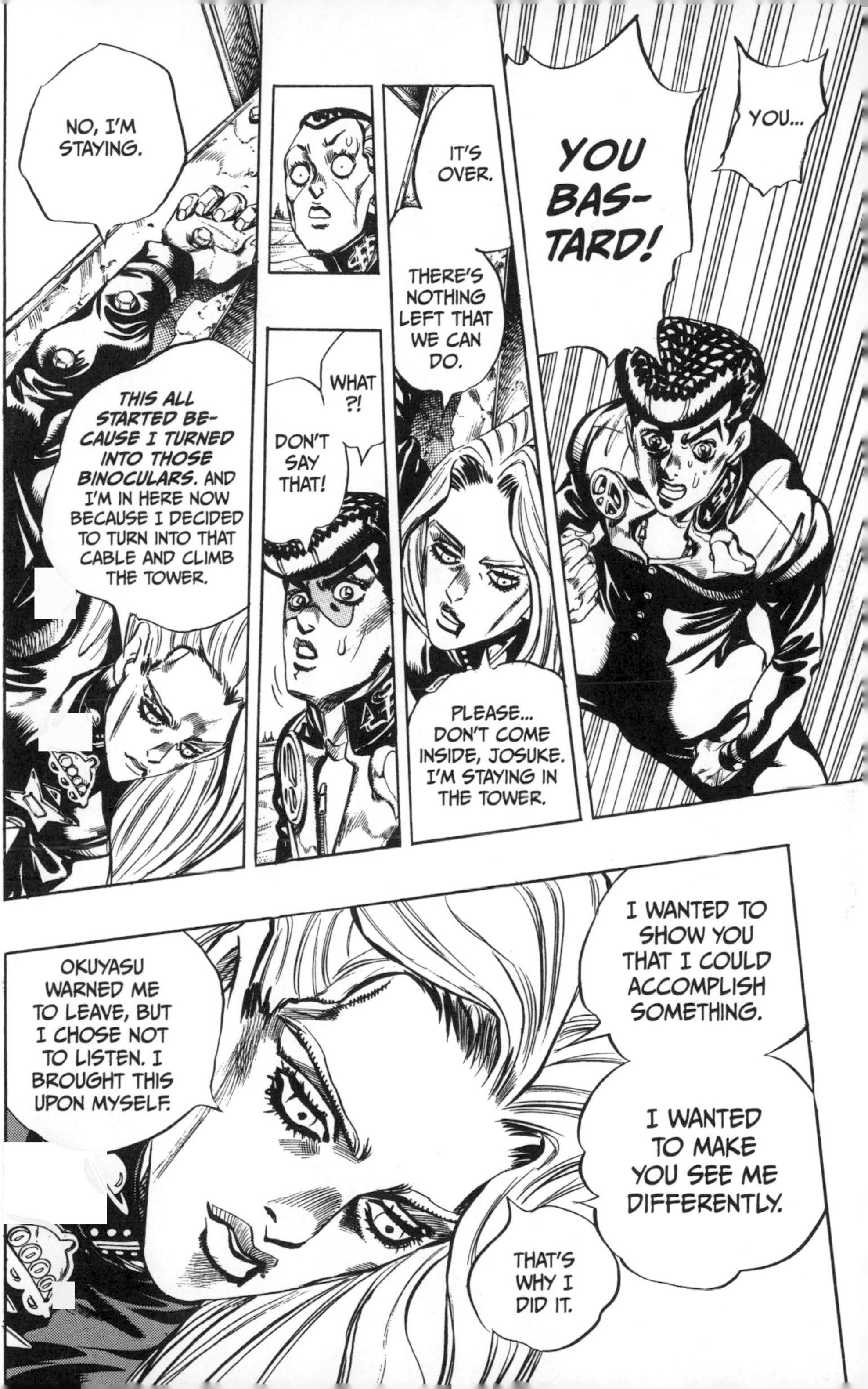
YOU...
YOU BASTARD!
IT'S OVER.
THERE'S NOTHING LEFT THAT WE CAN DO.
PLEASE... DON'T COME INSIDE, JOSUKE. I'M STAYING IN THE TOWER.
WHAT?!
DON'T SAY THAT!
NO, I'M STAYING.
THIS ALL STARTED BECAUSE I TURNED INTO THOSE BINOCULARS. AND I'M IN HERE NOW BECAUSE I DECIDED TO TURN INTO THAT CABLE AND CLIMB THE TOWER.
I WANTED TO SHOW YOU THAT I COULD ACCOMPLISH SOMETHING.
OKUYASU WARNED ME TO LEAVE, BUT I CHOSE NOT TO LISTEN. I BROUGHT THIS UPON MYSELF.
I WANTED TO MAKE YOU SEE ME DIFFERENTLY.
THAT'S WHY I DID IT.

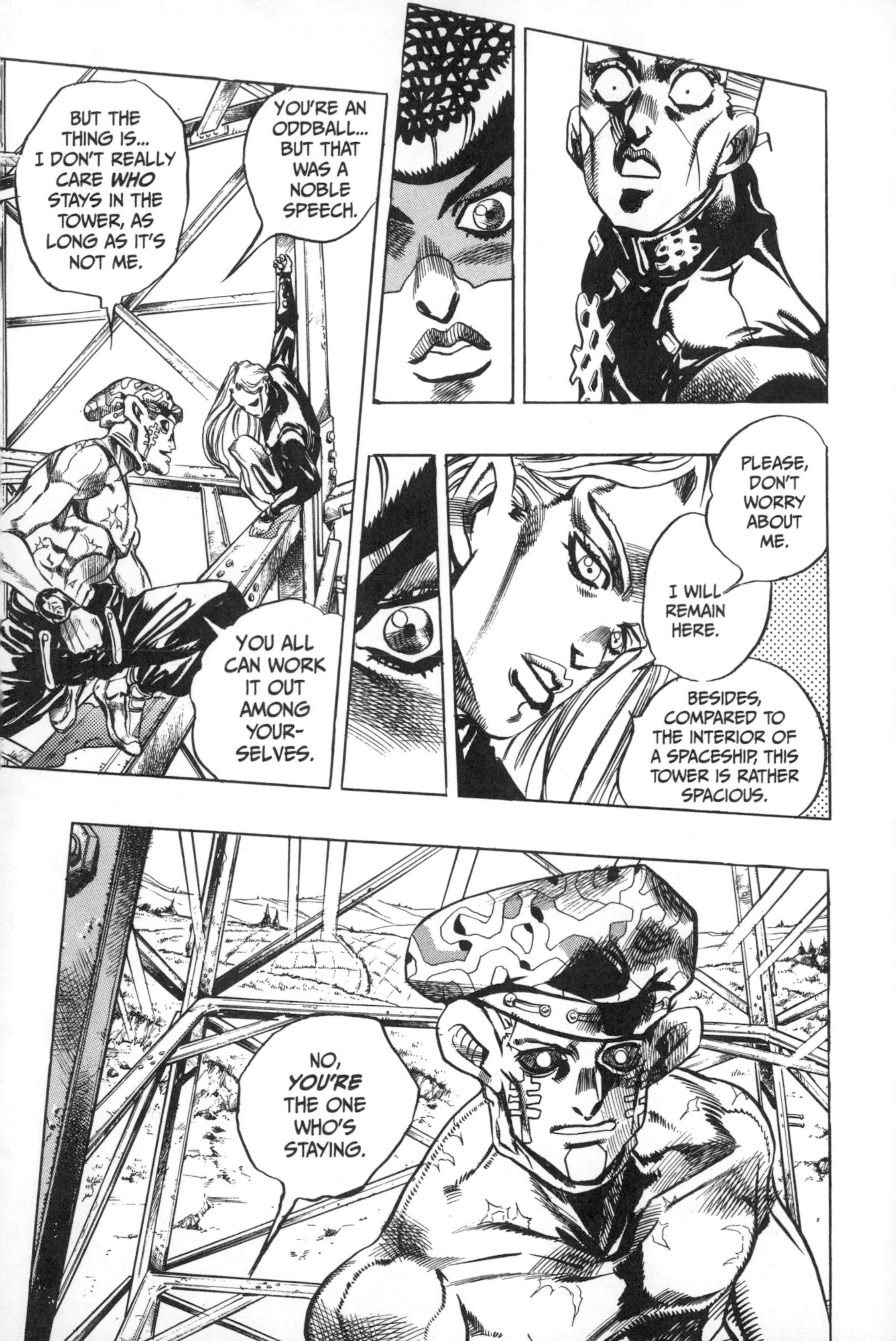

PLEASE, DON'T WORRY ABOUT ME.
I WILL REMAIN HERE.
BESIDES, COMPARED TO THE INTERIOR OF A SPACESHIP, THIS TOWER IS RATHER SPACIOUS.
YOU'RE AN ODDBALL... BUT THAT WAS A NOBLE SPEECH.
BUT THE THING IS... I DON'T REALLY CARE ***WHO*** STAYS IN THE TOWER, AS LONG AS IT'S NOT ME.
YOU ALL CAN WORK IT OUT AMONG YOUR-SELVES.
NO, ***YOU'RE*** THE ONE WHO'S STAYING.

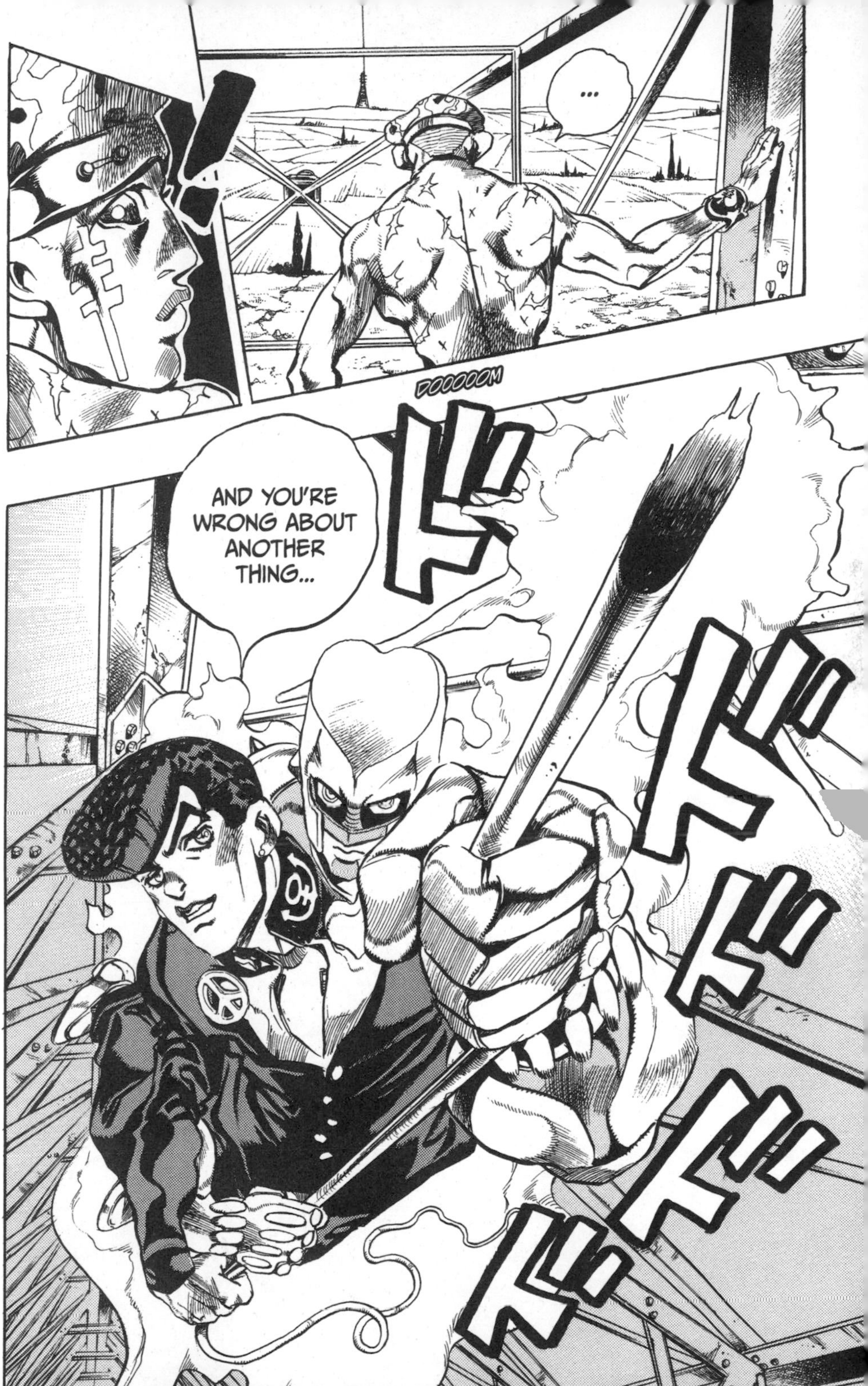
...
DOOOOOM
AND YOU'RE WRONG ABOUT ANOTHER THING...

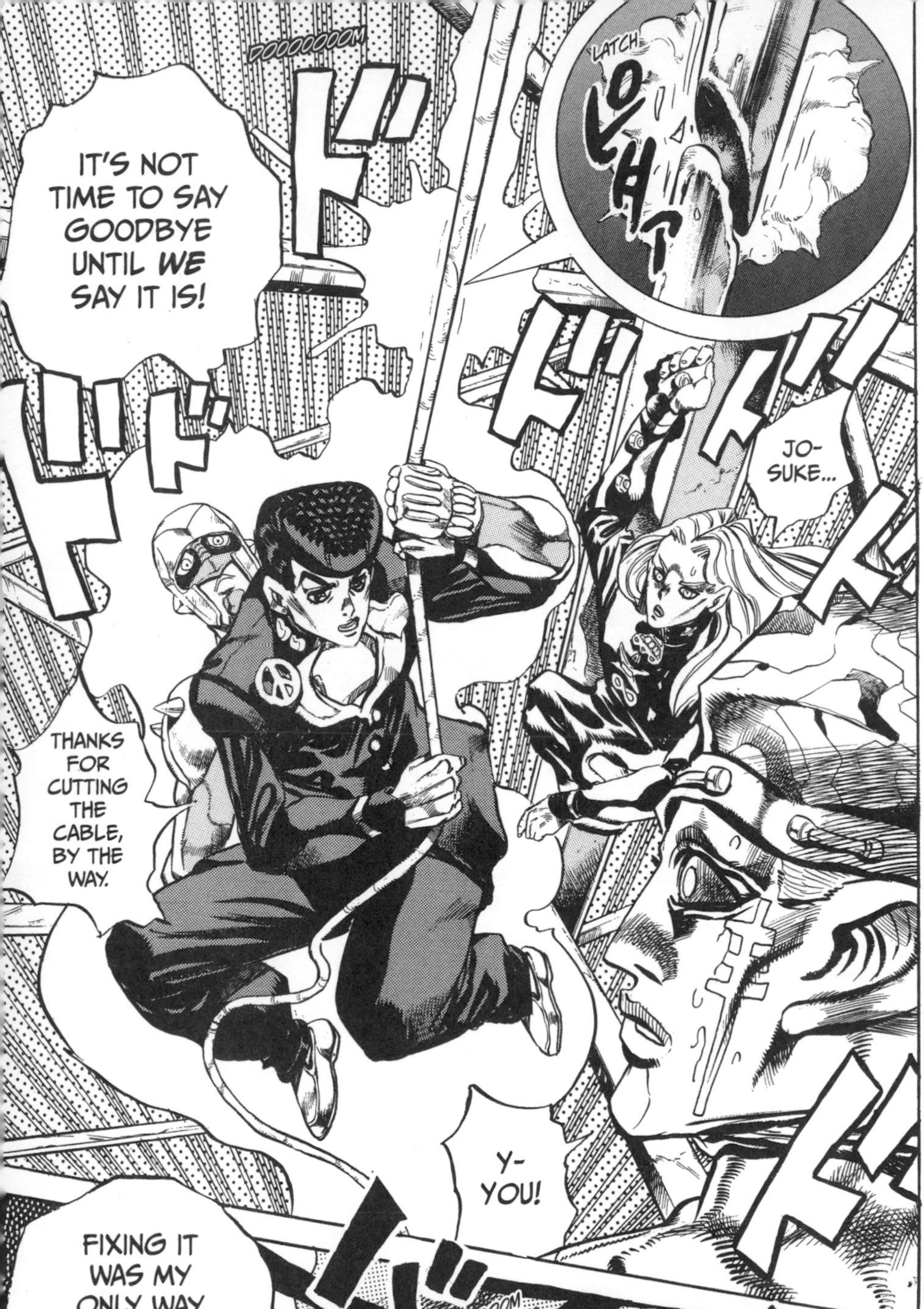
LATCH
DOOOOOOOM
IT'S NOT TIME TO SAY GOODBYE UNTIL WE SAY IT IS!
JO-SUKE...
THANKS FOR CUTTING THE CABLE, BY THE WAY.
Y-YOU!
DOOM
FIXING IT WAS MY ONLY WAY BACK UP HERE!

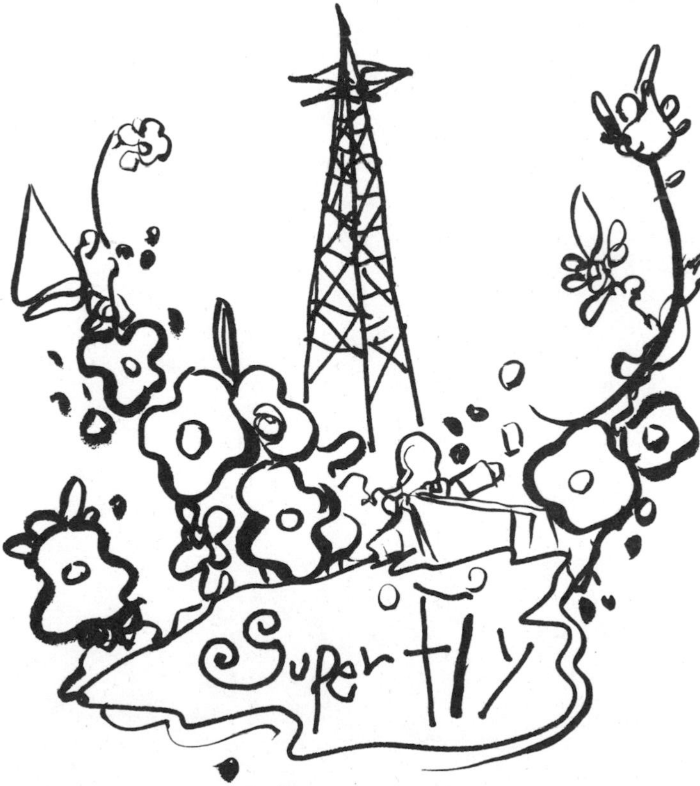
Super fly

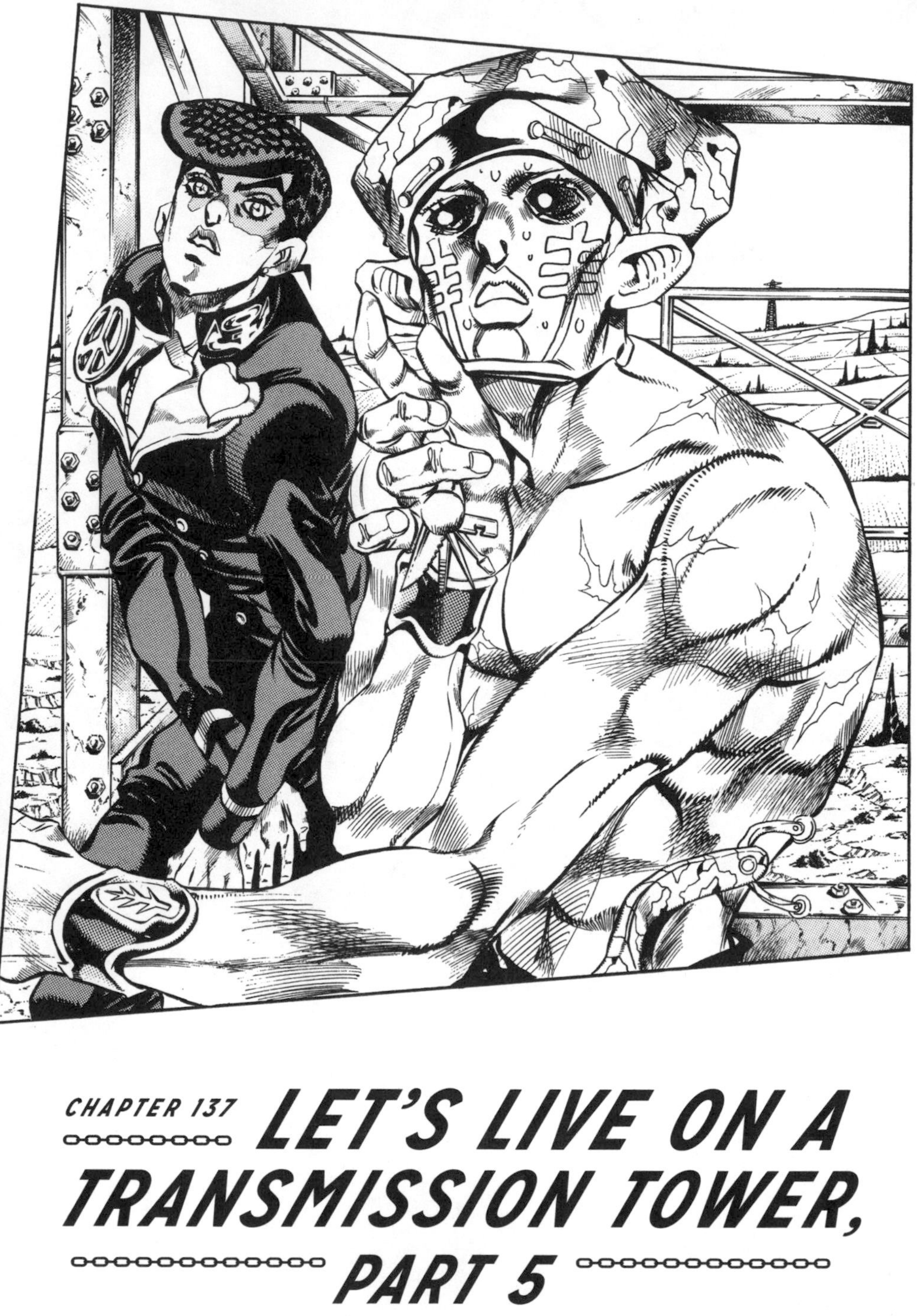

CHAPTER 137 LET'S LIVE ON A TRANSMISSION TOWER, PART 5

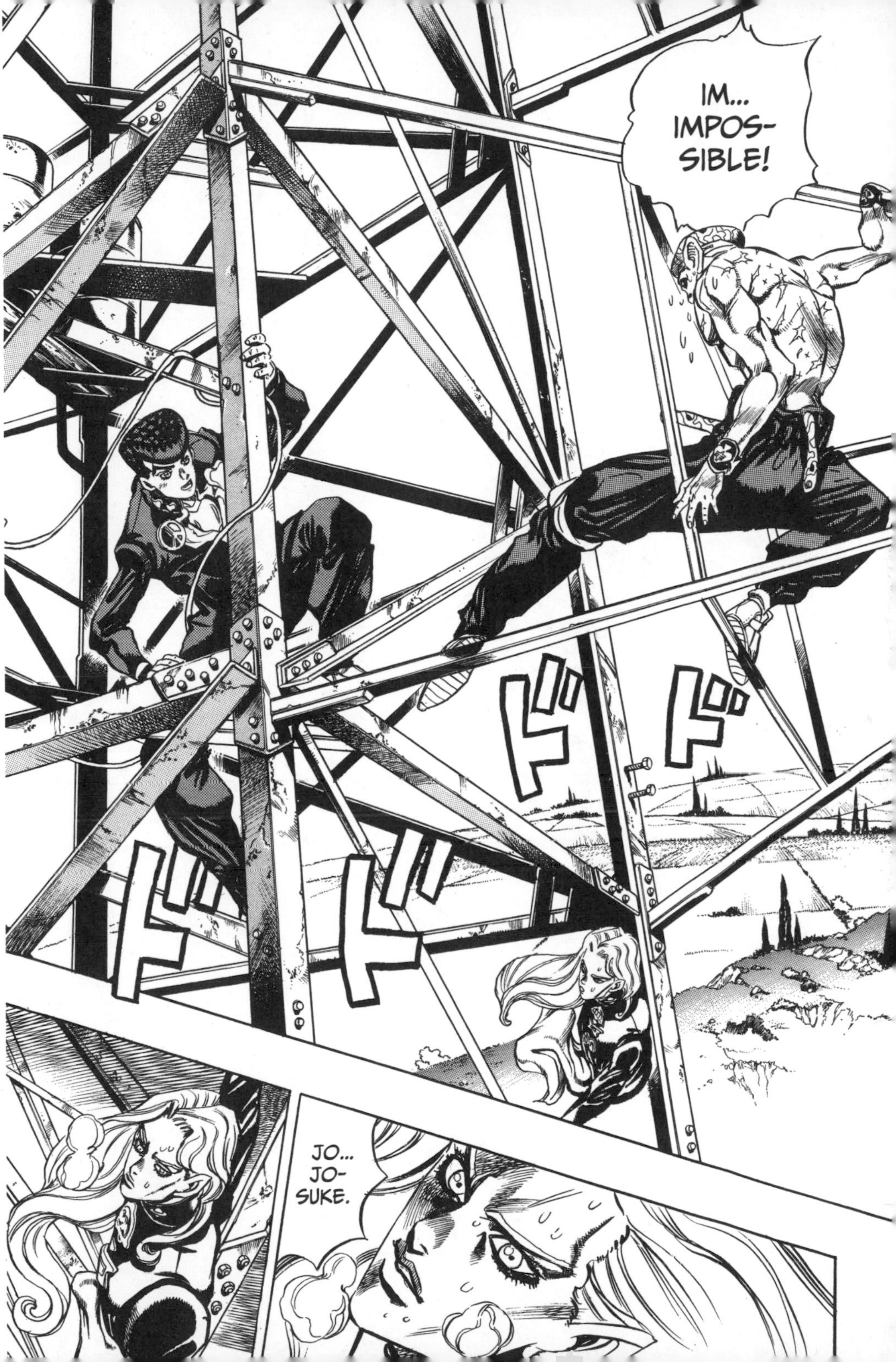
IM... IMPOS-SIBLE!
ドド
ドド
JO... JO-SUKE.

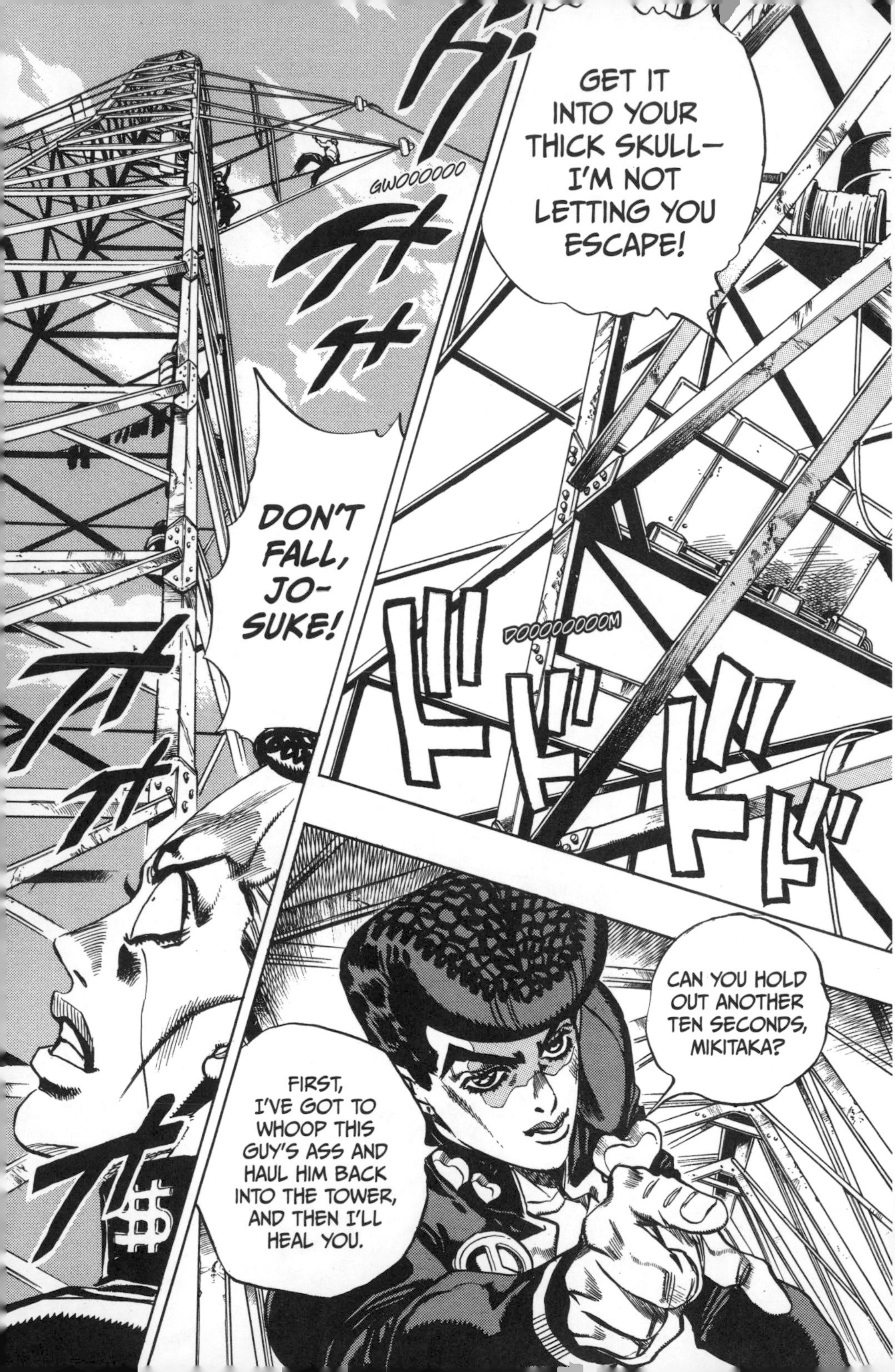
GET IT INTO YOUR THICK SKULL— I'M NOT LETTING YOU ESCAPE!
DOOOOOOOOM
CAN YOU HOLD OUT ANOTHER TEN SECONDS, MIKITAKA?
FIRST, I'VE GOT TO WHOOP THIS GUY'S ASS AND HAUL HIM BACK INTO THE TOWER, AND THEN I'LL HEAL YOU.
GWOOOOOO
DON'T FALL, JO-SUKE!

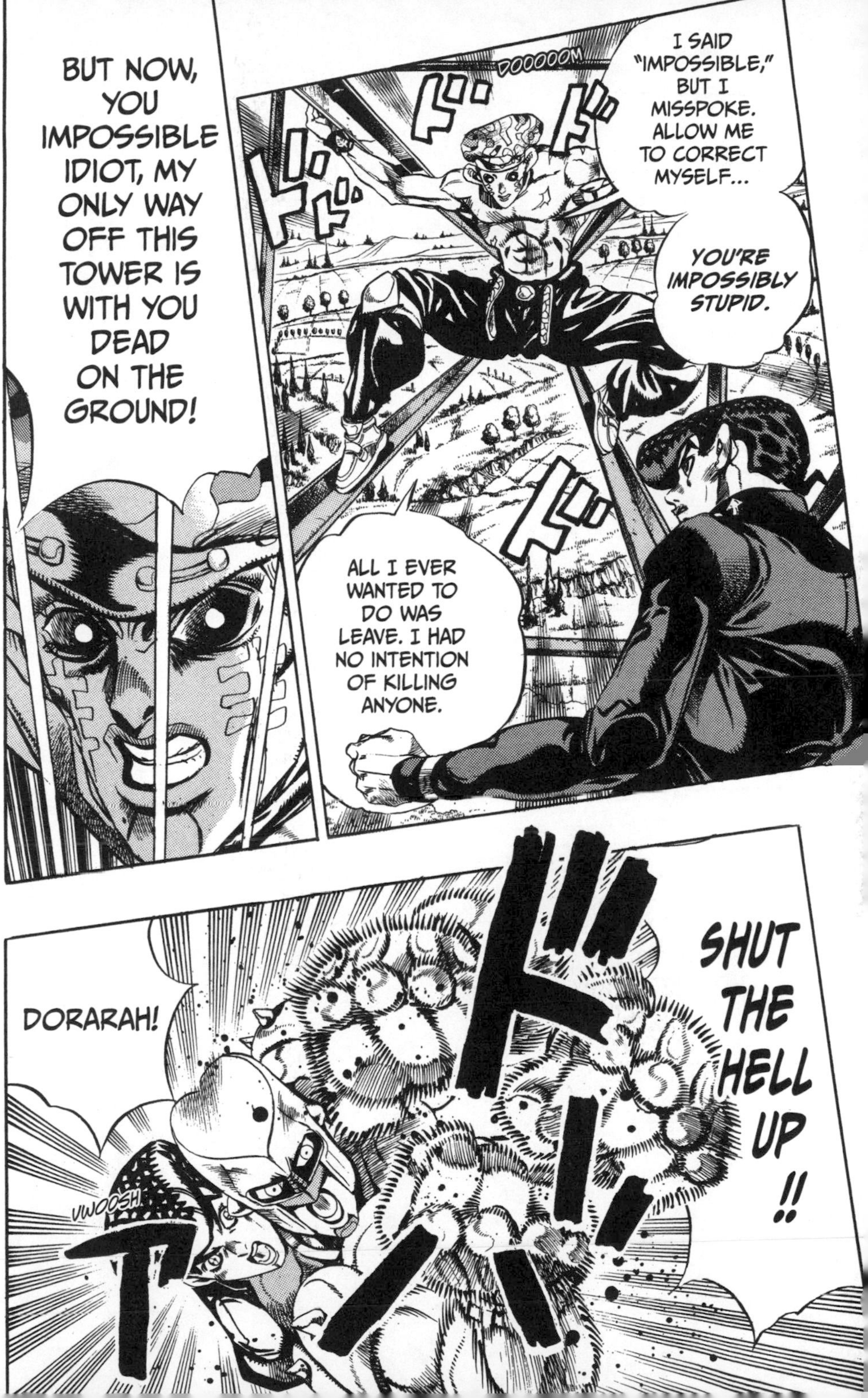
DOOOOOM
I SAID "IMPOSSIBLE," BUT I MISSPOKE. ALLOW ME TO CORRECT MYSELF...
YOU'RE IMPOSSIBLY STUPID.
ALL I EVER WANTED TO DO WAS LEAVE. I HAD NO INTENTION OF KILLING ANYONE.
BUT NOW, YOU IMPOSSIBLE IDIOT, MY ONLY WAY OFF THIS TOWER IS WITH YOU DEAD ON THE GROUND!
SHUT THE HELL UP!!
DORARAH!
VWOOSH

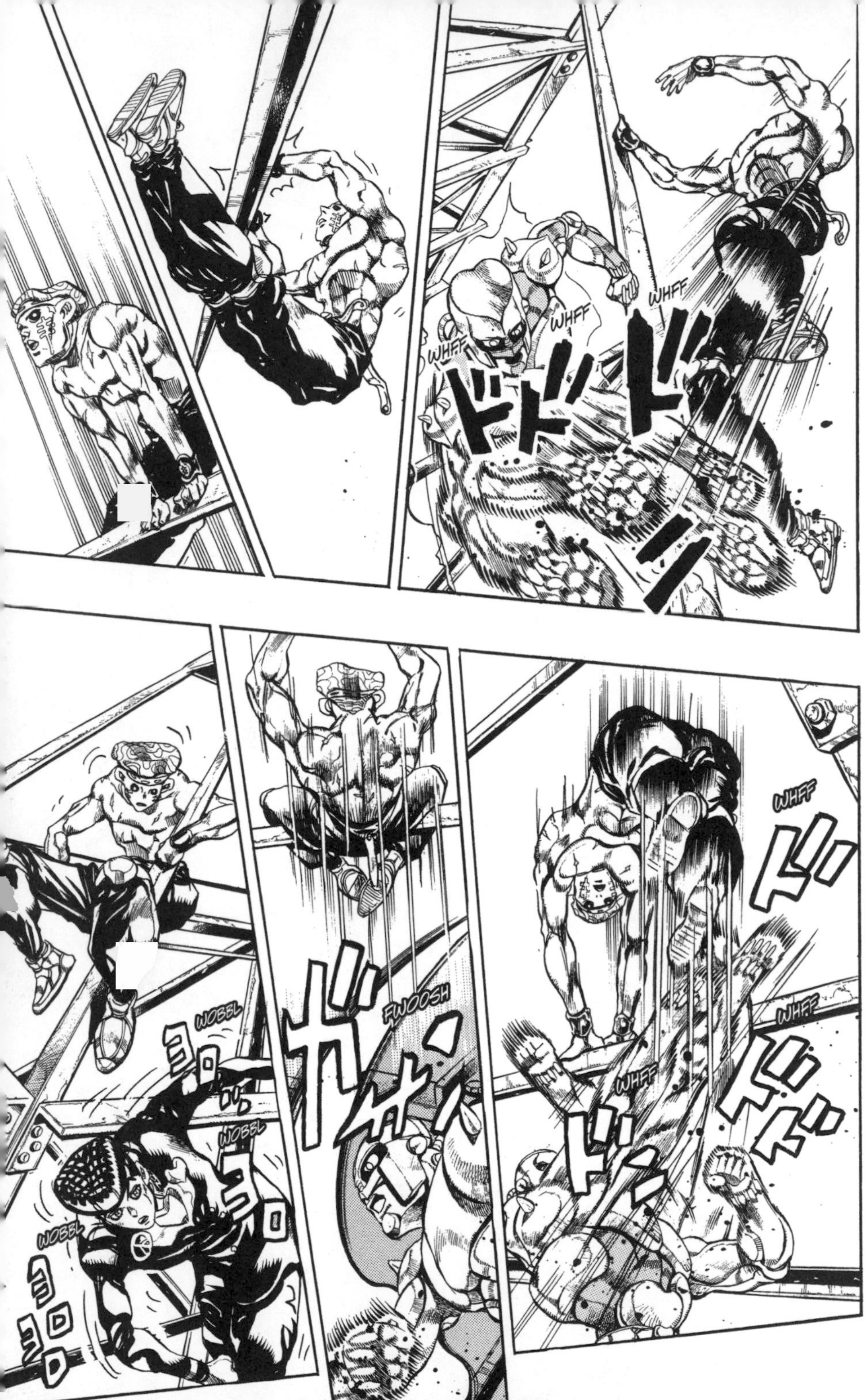
WHFF
WHFF
WHFF
WHFF
WHFF
WHFF
FWOOSH
WOBBL
WOBBL
WOBBL

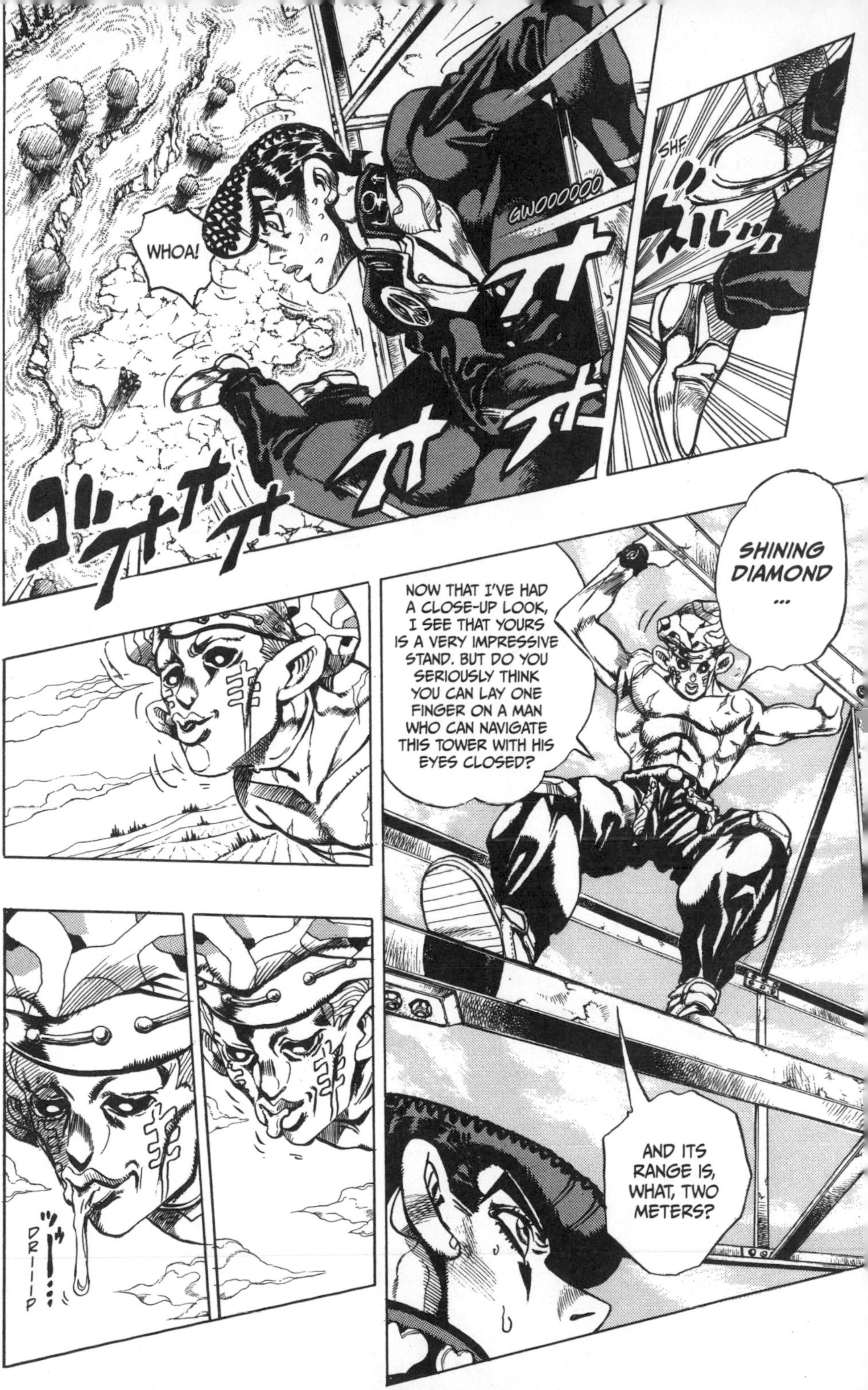
SHF
GWOOOOOO
WHOA!
SHINING DIAMOND ...
NOW THAT I'VE HAD A CLOSE-UP LOOK, I SEE THAT YOURS IS A VERY IMPRESSIVE STAND. BUT DO YOU SERIOUSLY THINK YOU CAN LAY ONE FINGER ON A MAN WHO CAN NAVIGATE THIS TOWER WITH HIS EYES CLOSED?
AND ITS RANGE IS, WHAT, TWO METERS?
DRIIP

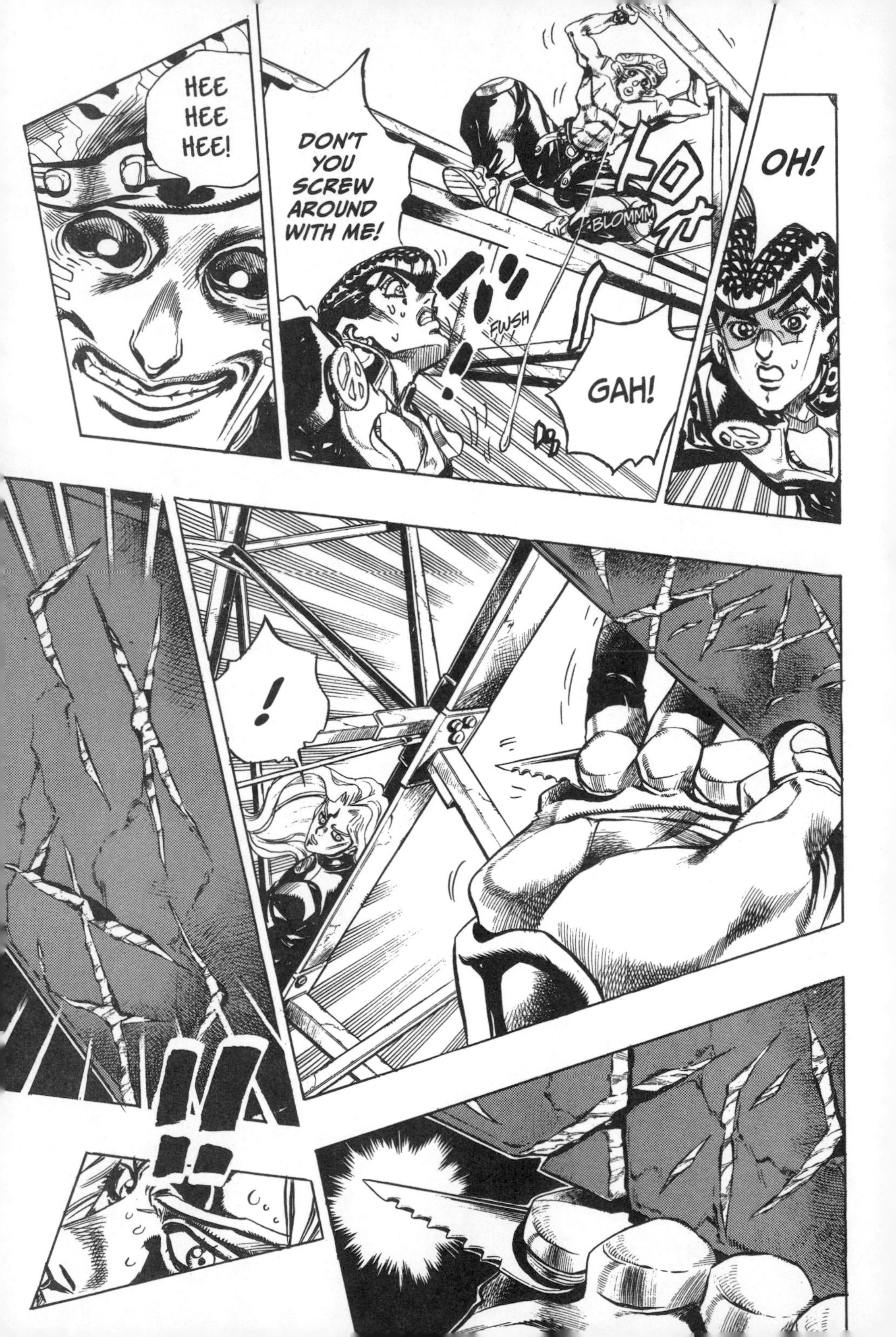
OH!
BLOMMM
DON'T YOU SCREW AROUND WITH ME!
FWSH
GAH!
HEE HEE HEE!
!

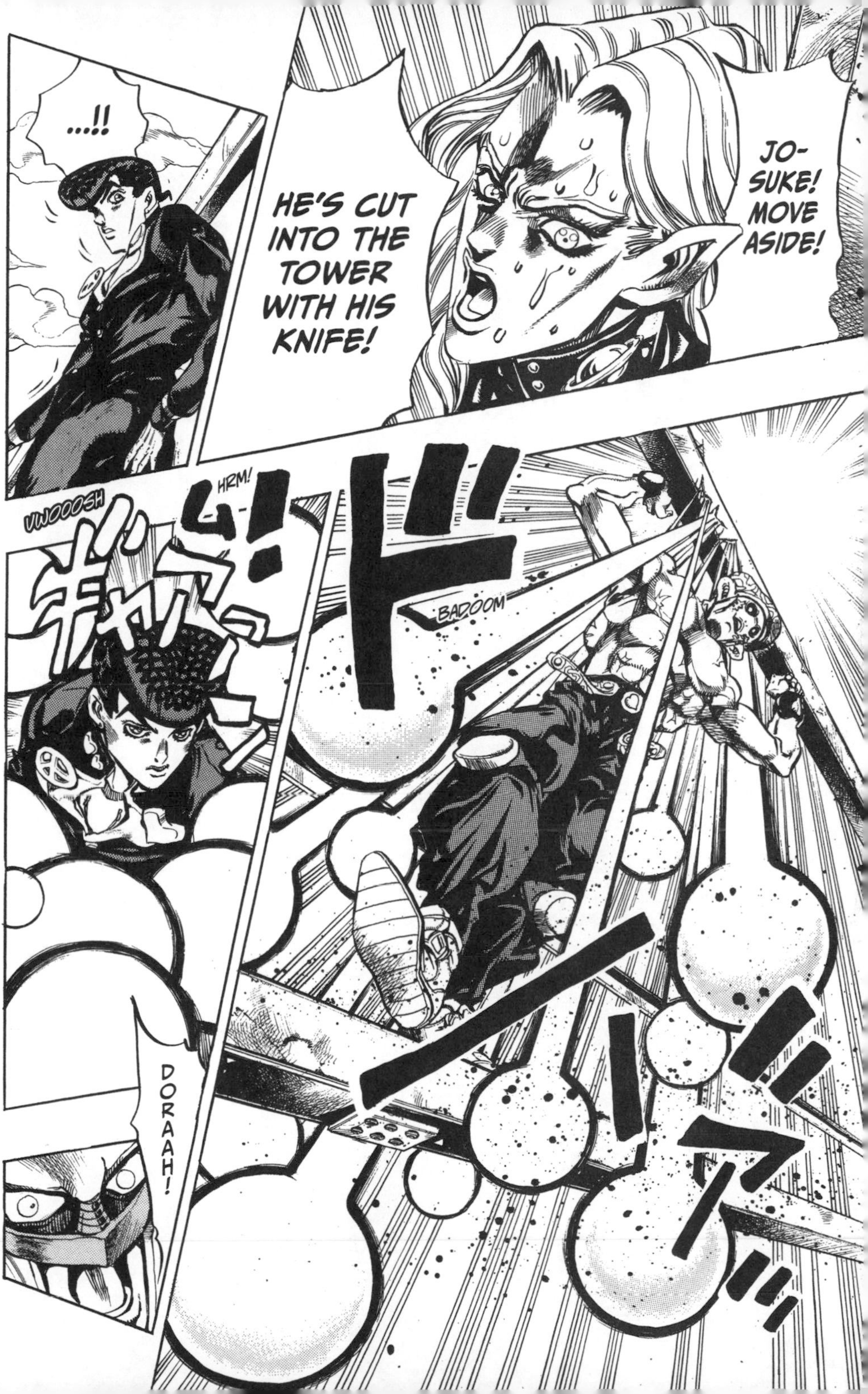
JO-SUKE! MOVE ASIDE!
HE'S CUT INTO THE TOWER WITH HIS KNIFE!
...!!
BADOOM
HRM!
VWOOOSH
DORAAH!

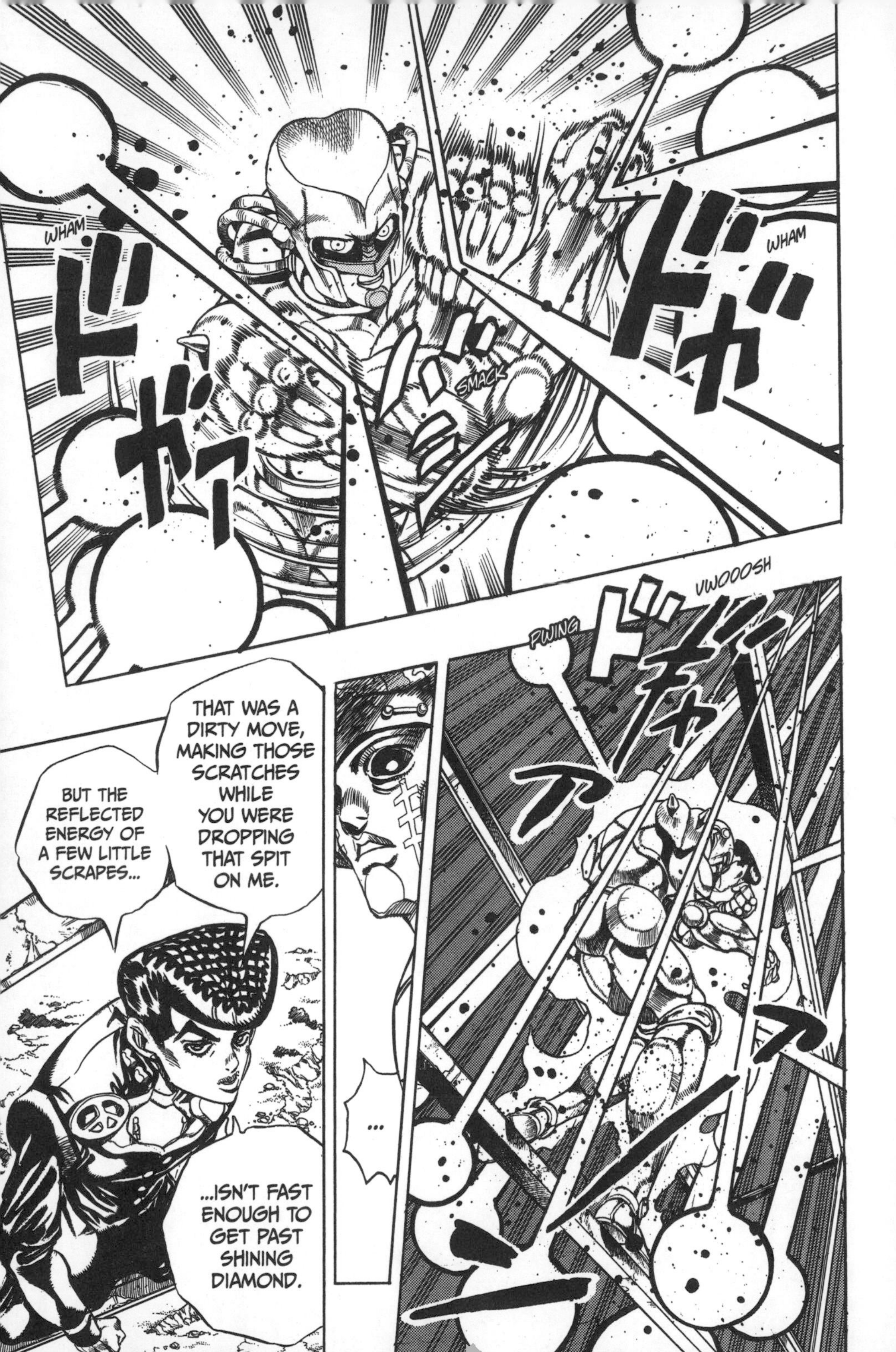
WHAM
SMACK
WHAM
VWOOOSH
PWING
...
THAT WAS A DIRTY MOVE, MAKING THOSE SCRATCHES WHILE YOU WERE DROPPING THAT SPIT ON ME.
BUT THE REFLECTED ENERGY OF A FEW LITTLE SCRAPES...
...ISN'T FAST ENOUGH TO GET PAST SHINING DIAMOND.

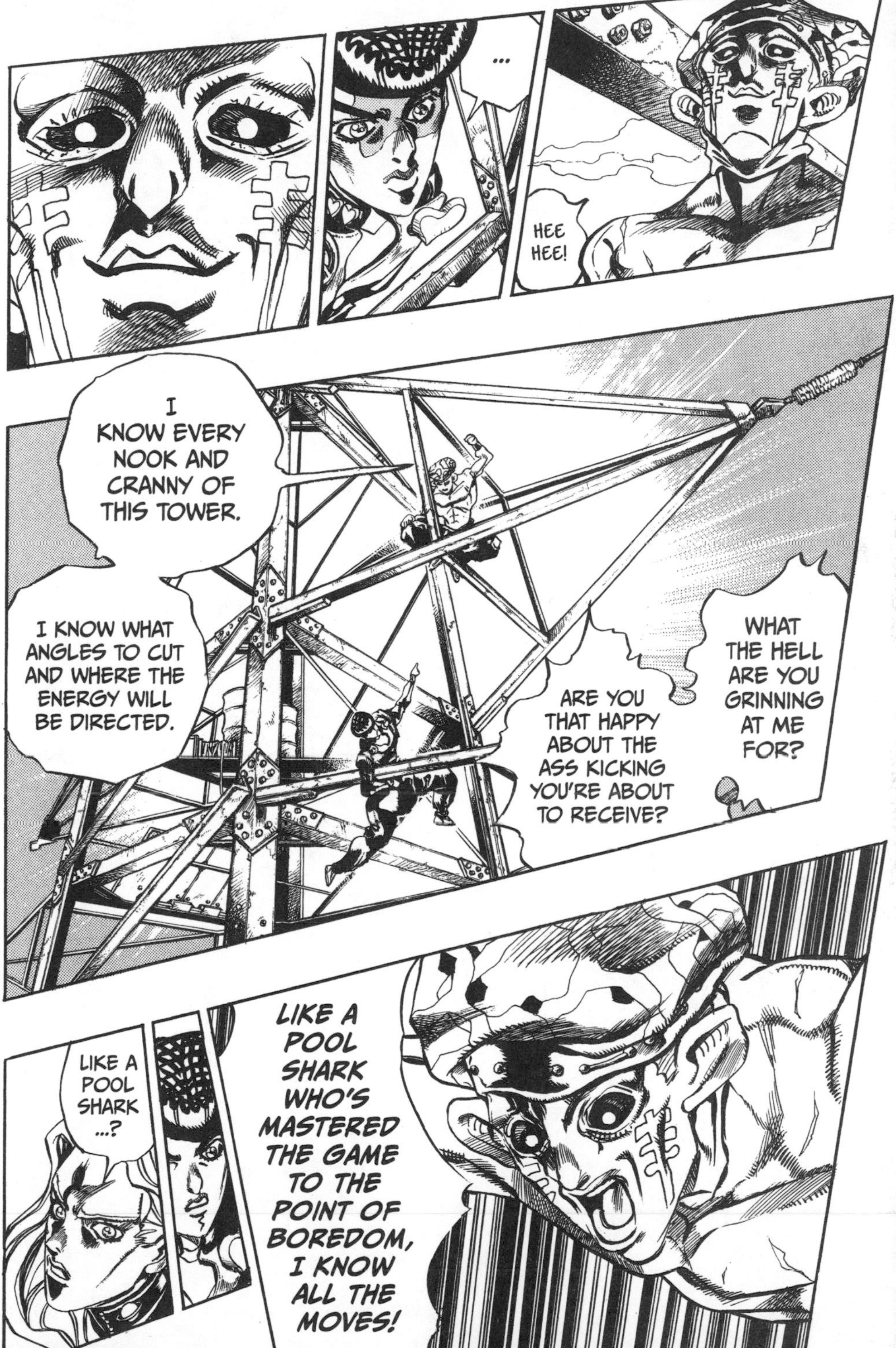
HEE HEE!
...
WHAT THE HELL ARE YOU GRINNING AT ME FOR?
ARE YOU THAT HAPPY ABOUT THE ASS KICKING YOU'RE ABOUT TO RECEIVE?
I KNOW EVERY NOOK AND CRANNY OF THIS TOWER.
I KNOW WHAT ANGLES TO CUT AND WHERE THE ENERGY WILL BE DIRECTED.
LIKE A POOL SHARK WHO'S MASTERED THE GAME TO THE POINT OF BOREDOM, I KNOW ALL THE MOVES!
LIKE A POOL SHARK ...?

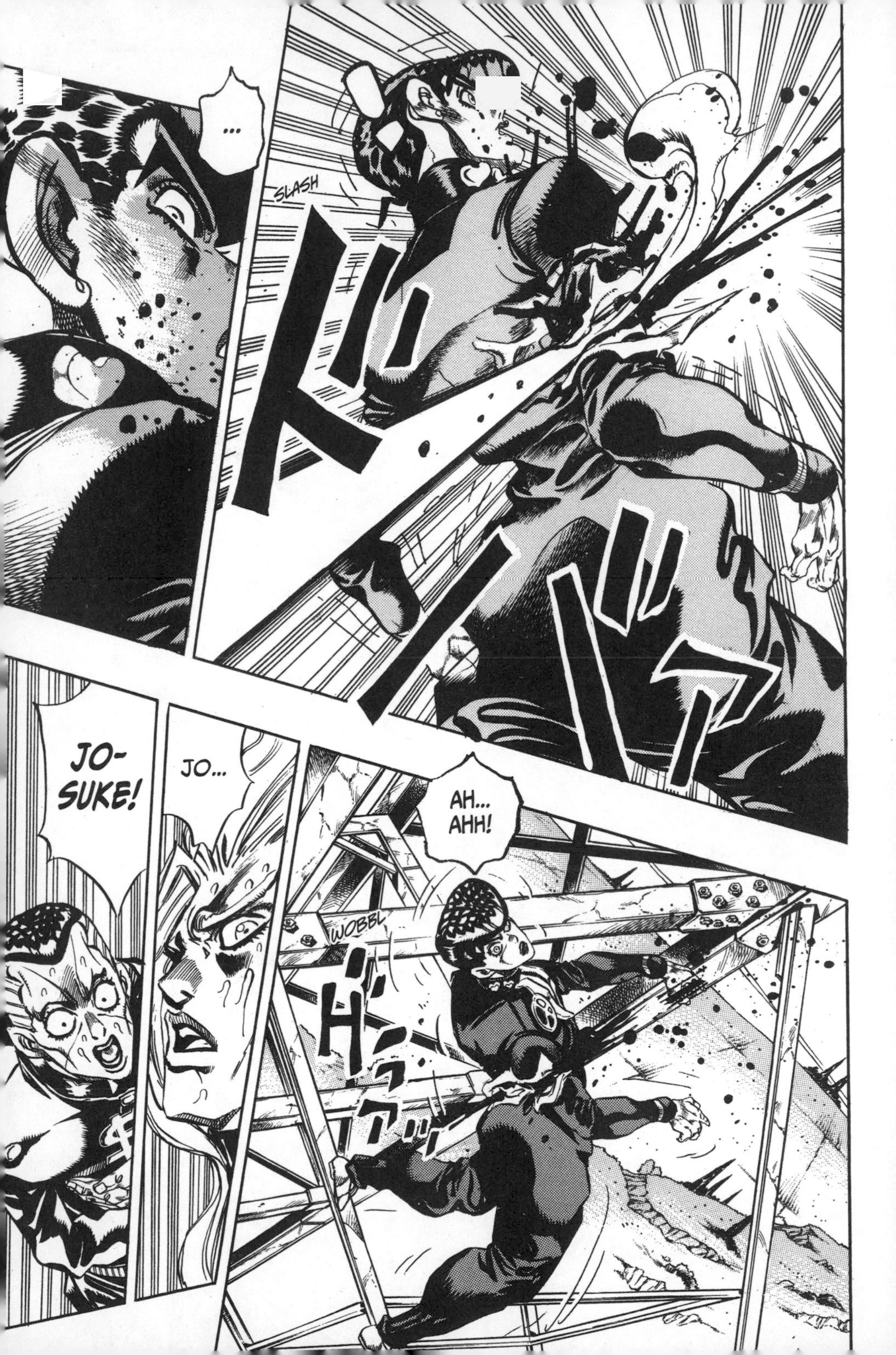
SLASH
...
AH... AHH!
WOBBL
JO...
JO-
SUKE!

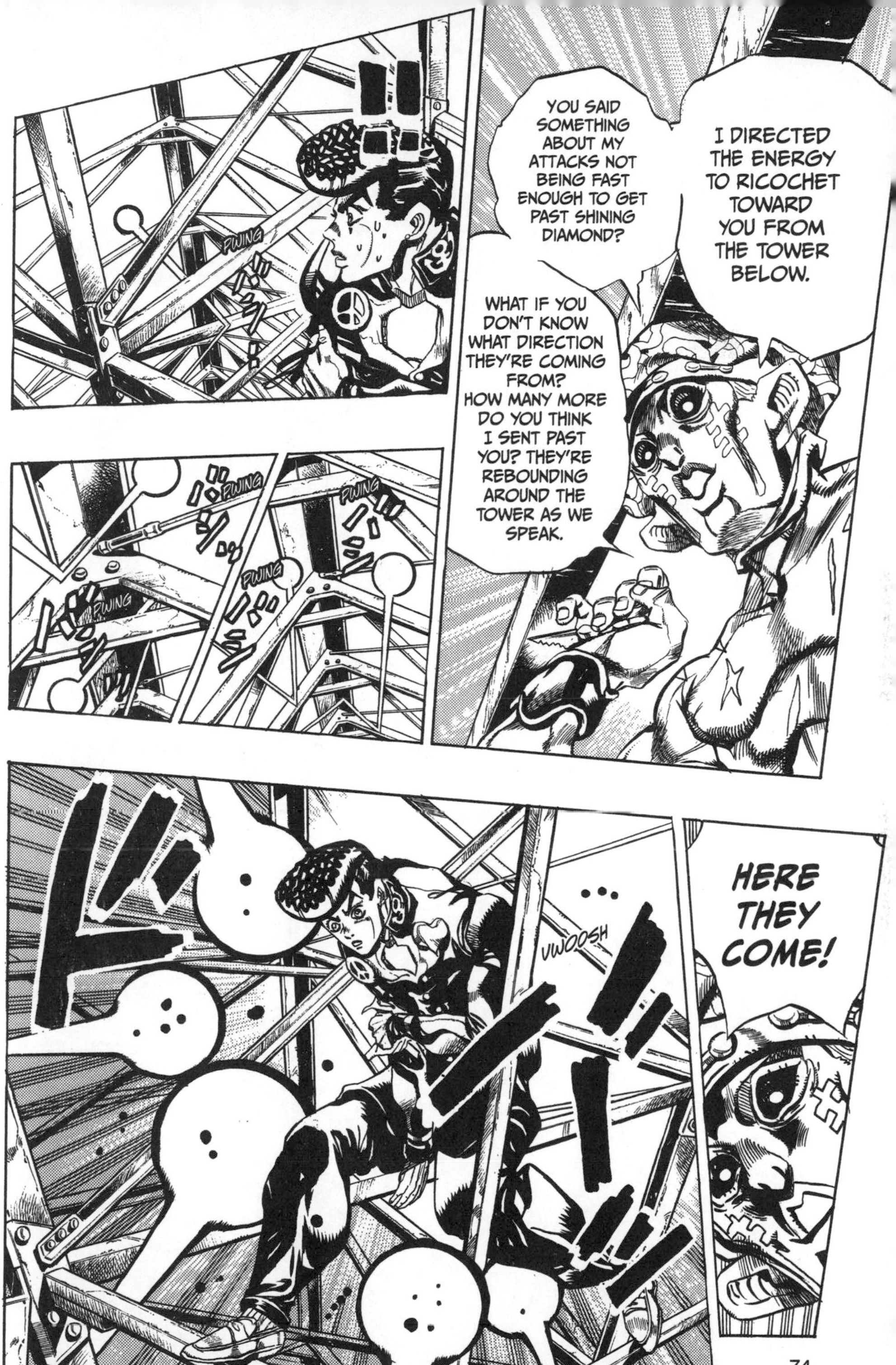
I DIRECTED THE ENERGY TO RICOCHET TOWARD YOU FROM THE TOWER BELOW.
YOU SAID SOMETHING ABOUT MY ATTACKS NOT BEING FAST ENOUGH TO GET PAST SHINING DIAMOND?
WHAT IF YOU DON'T KNOW WHAT DIRECTION THEY'RE COMING FROM?
HOW MANY MORE DO YOU THINK I SENT PAST YOU? THEY'RE REBOUNDING AROUND THE TOWER AS WE SPEAK.
PWING
PWING
PWING
PWING
PWING
HERE THEY COME!
...
VWOOSH

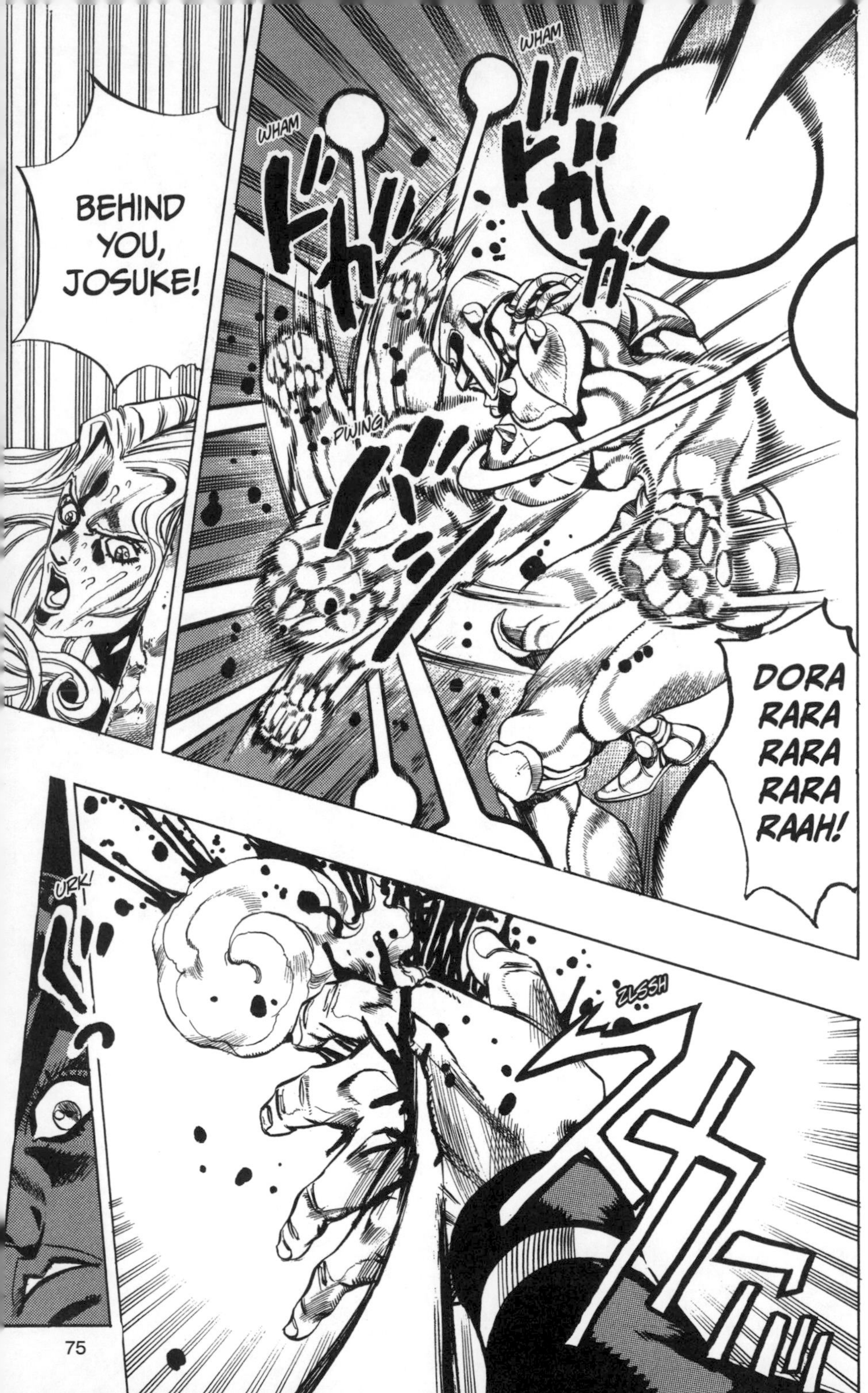
WHAM
WHAM
PWING
DORA RARA RARA RARA RAAH!
BEHIND YOU, JOSUKE!
URK!
ZUSSH

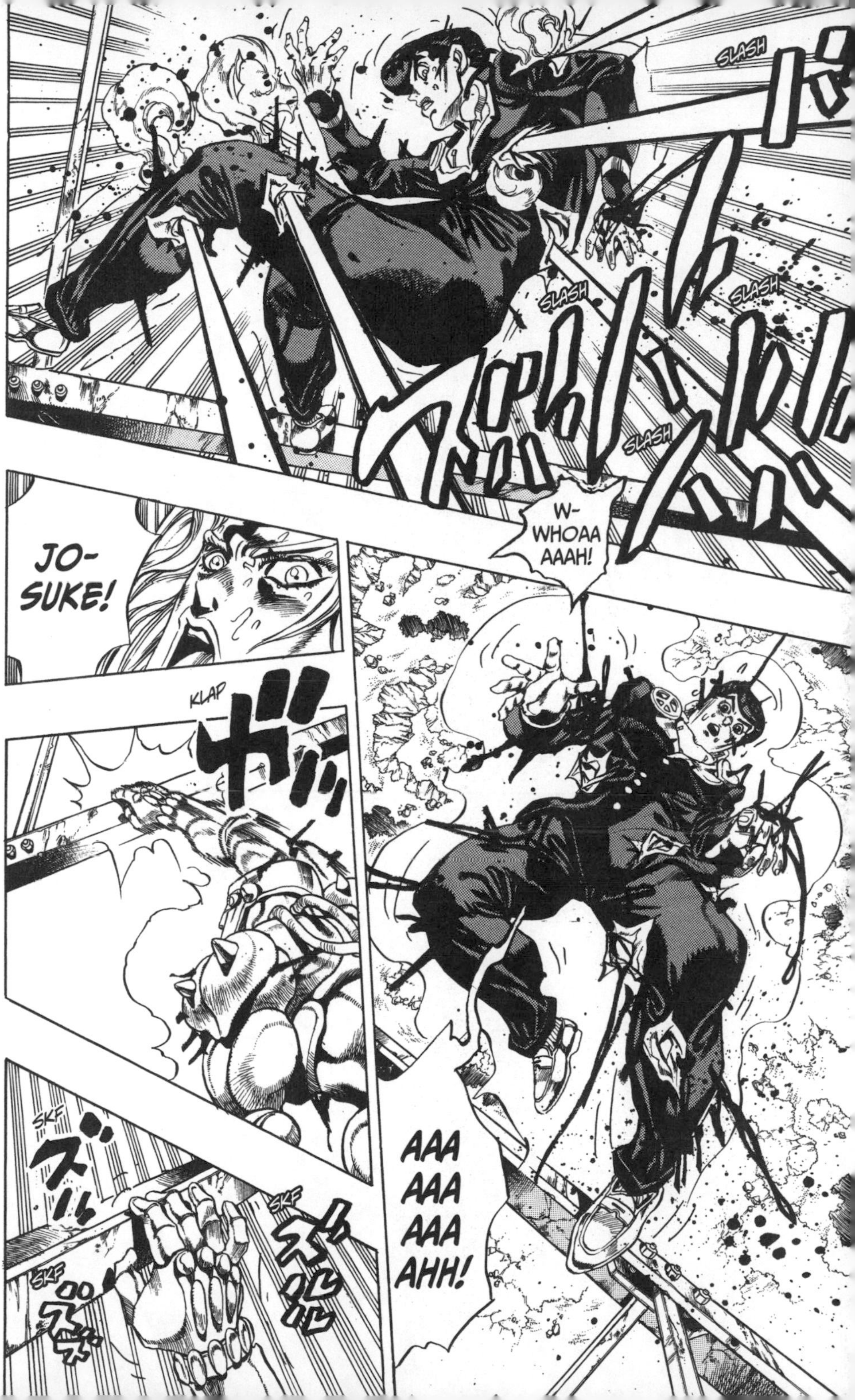
SLASH
SLASH
SLASH
SLASH
W-WHOAA AAAH!
JO-SUKE!
KLAP
AAA AAA AAA AHH!
SKF
SKF
SKF

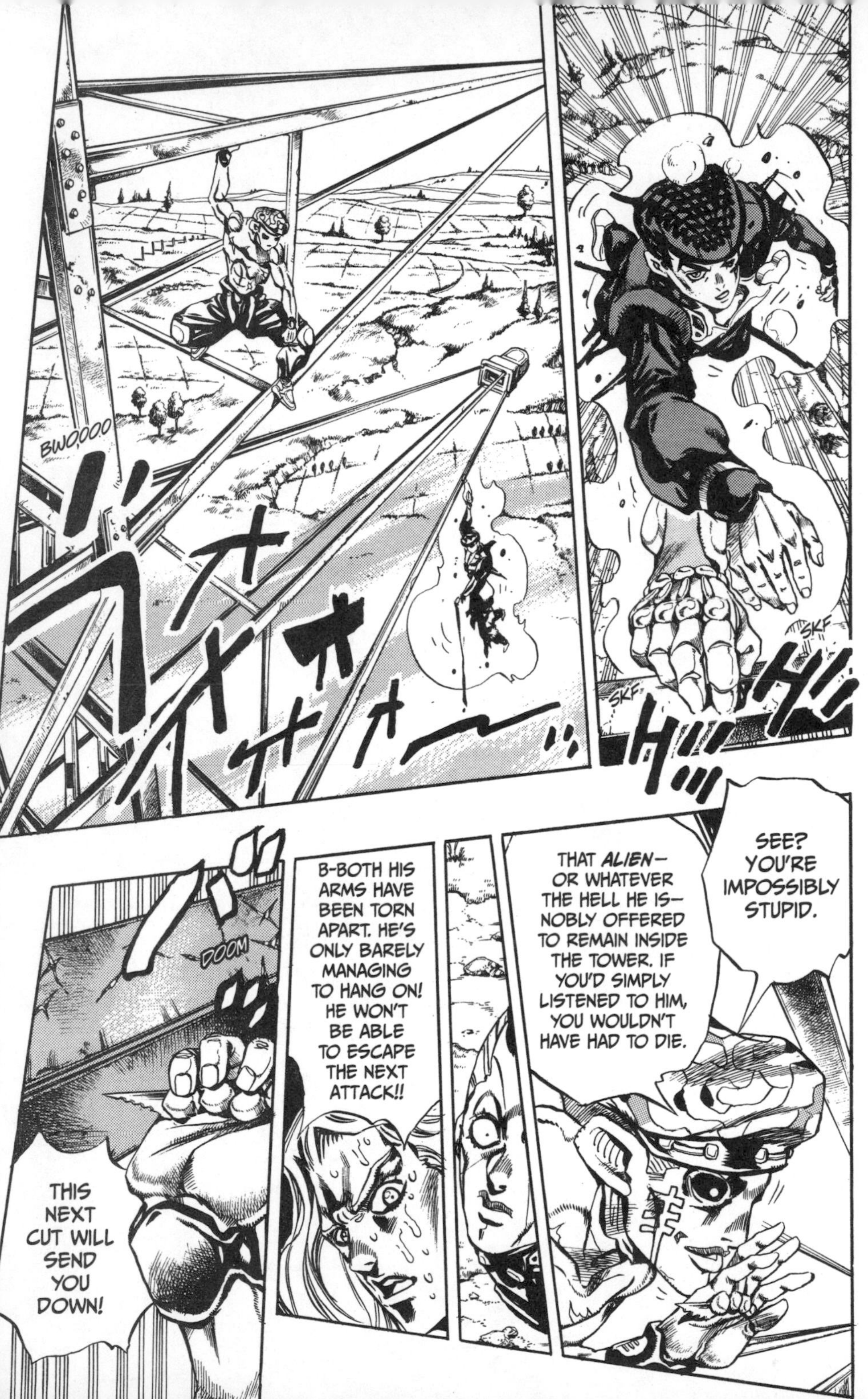
SKF
SKF
BWOOOO
SEE? YOU'RE IMPOSSIBLY STUPID.
THAT ALIEN— OR WHATEVER THE HELL HE IS— NOBLY OFFERED TO REMAIN INSIDE THE TOWER. IF YOU'D SIMPLY LISTENED TO HIM, YOU WOULDN'T HAVE HAD TO DIE.
B-BOTH HIS ARMS HAVE BEEN TORN APART. HE'S ONLY BARELY MANAGING TO HANG ON! HE WON'T BE ABLE TO ESCAPE THE NEXT ATTACK!!
DOOM
THIS NEXT CUT WILL SEND YOU DOWN!

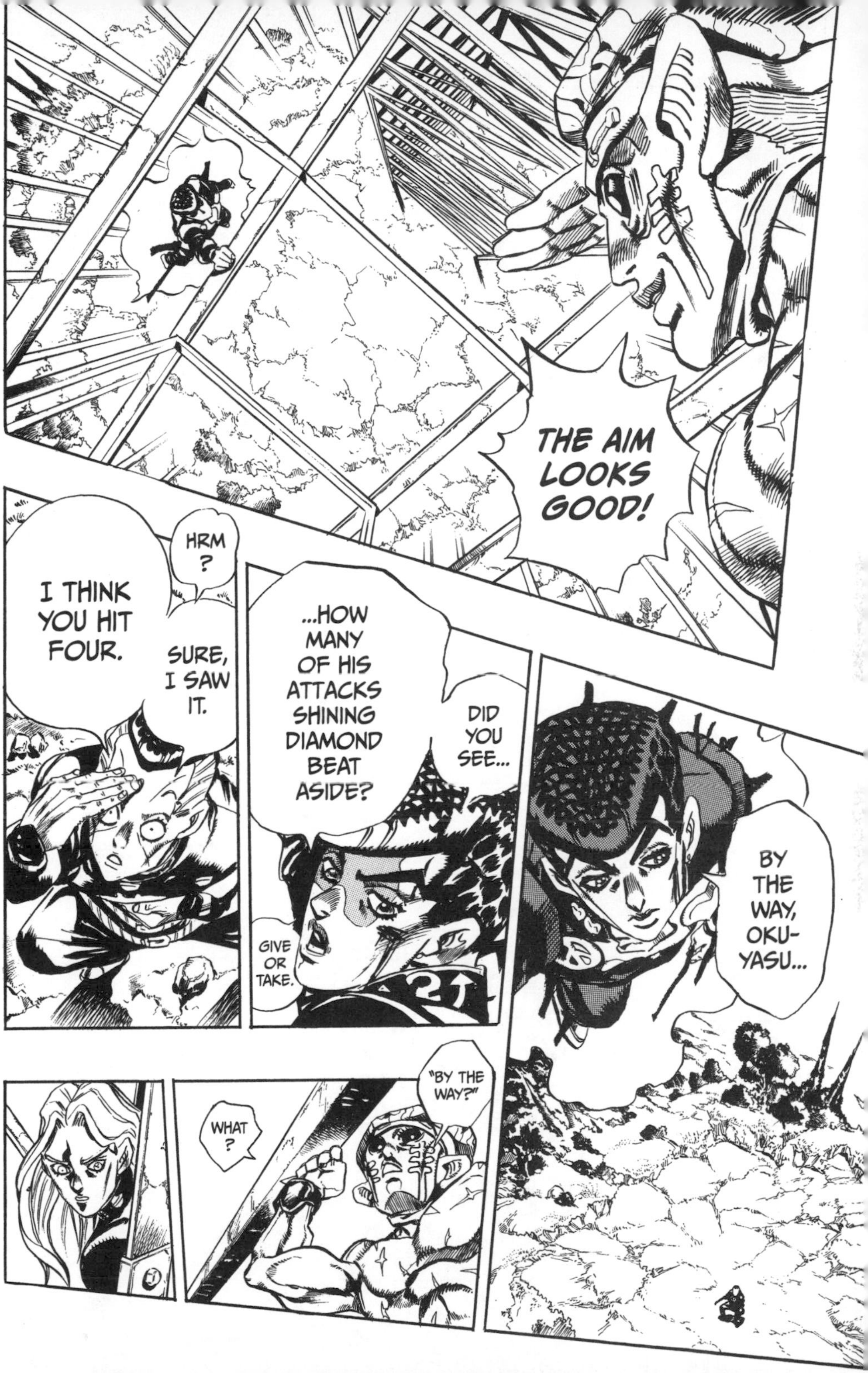
THE AIM LOOKS GOOD!
BY THE WAY, OKU-YASU...
DID YOU SEE...
...HOW MANY OF HIS ATTACKS SHINING DIAMOND BEAT ASIDE?
GIVE OR TAKE.
HRM?
SURE, I SAW IT.
I THINK YOU HIT FOUR.
"BY THE WAY?"
WHAT?

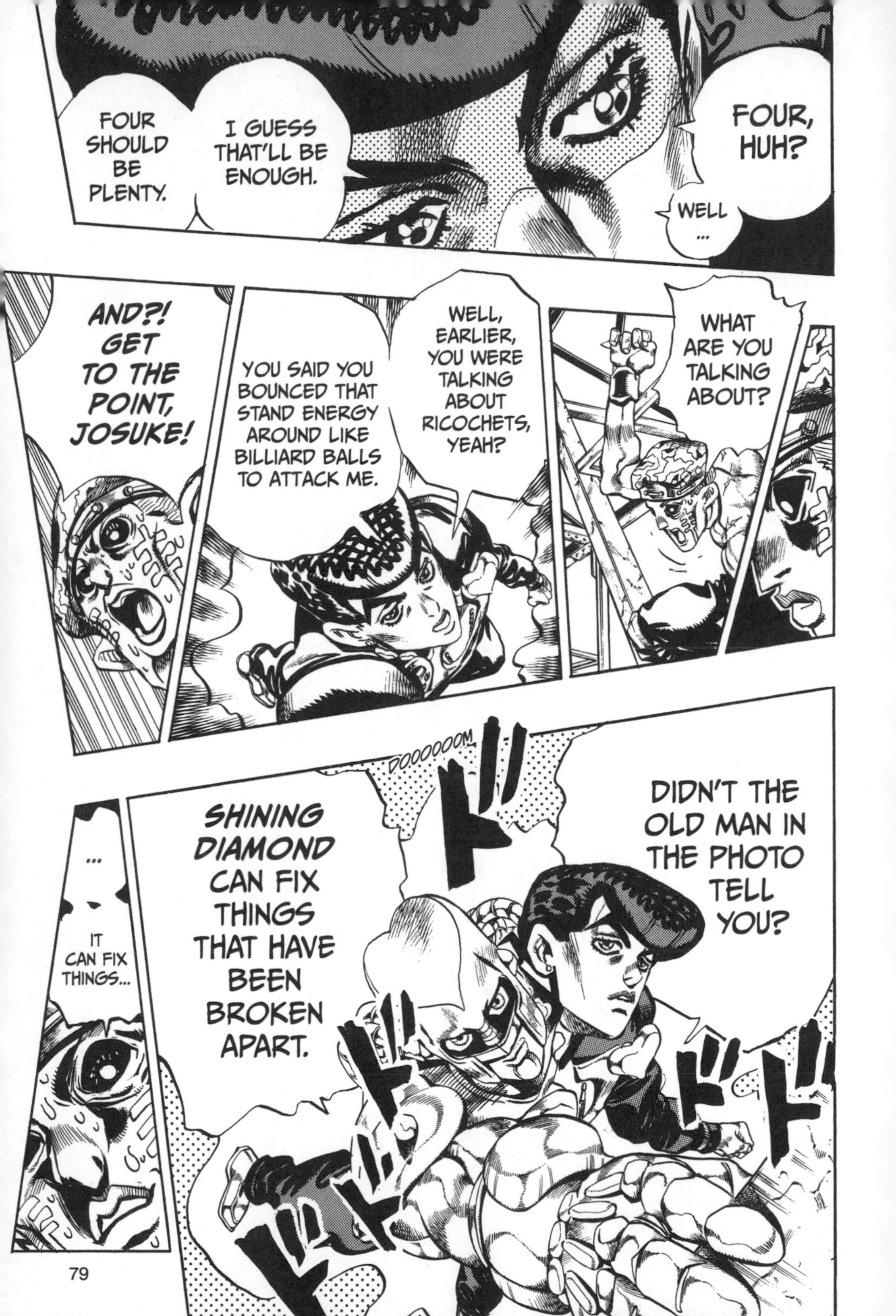
FOUR, HUH?
WELL ...
I GUESS THAT'LL BE ENOUGH.
FOUR SHOULD BE PLENTY.
WHAT ARE YOU TALKING ABOUT?
WELL, EARLIER, YOU WERE TALKING ABOUT RICOCHETS, YEAH?
YOU SAID YOU BOUNCED THAT STAND ENERGY AROUND LIKE BILLIARD BALLS TO ATTACK ME.
AND?! GET TO THE POINT, JOSUKE!
DOOOOOOOM
DIDN'T THE OLD MAN IN THE PHOTO TELL YOU?
SHINING DIAMOND CAN FIX THINGS THAT HAVE BEEN BROKEN APART.
...
IT CAN FIX THINGS...

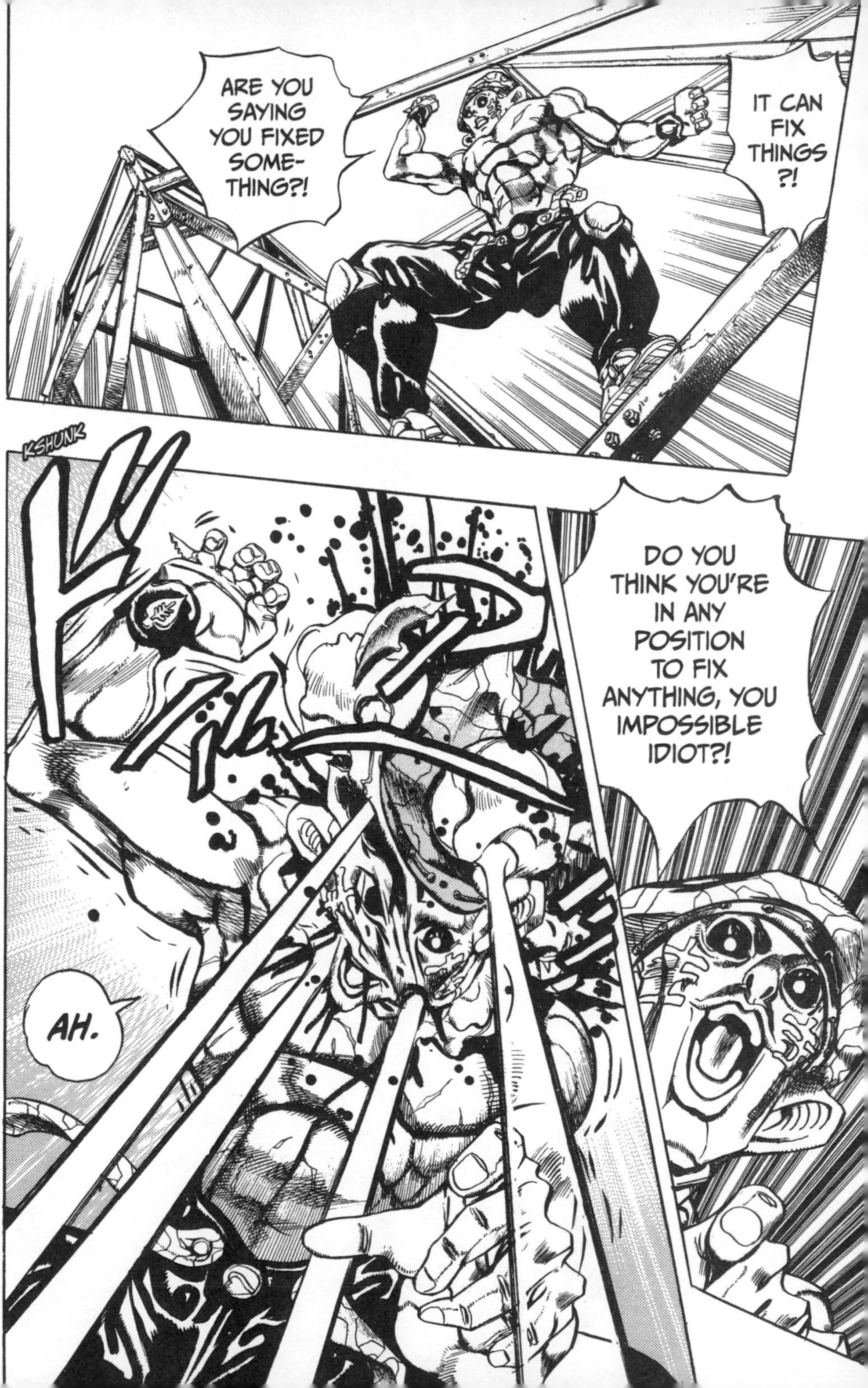
IT CAN FIX THINGS?!
ARE YOU SAYING YOU FIXED SOME-THING?!
DO YOU THINK YOU'RE IN ANY POSITION TO FIX ANYTHING, YOU IMPOSSIBLE IDIOT?!
KSHUNK
AH.

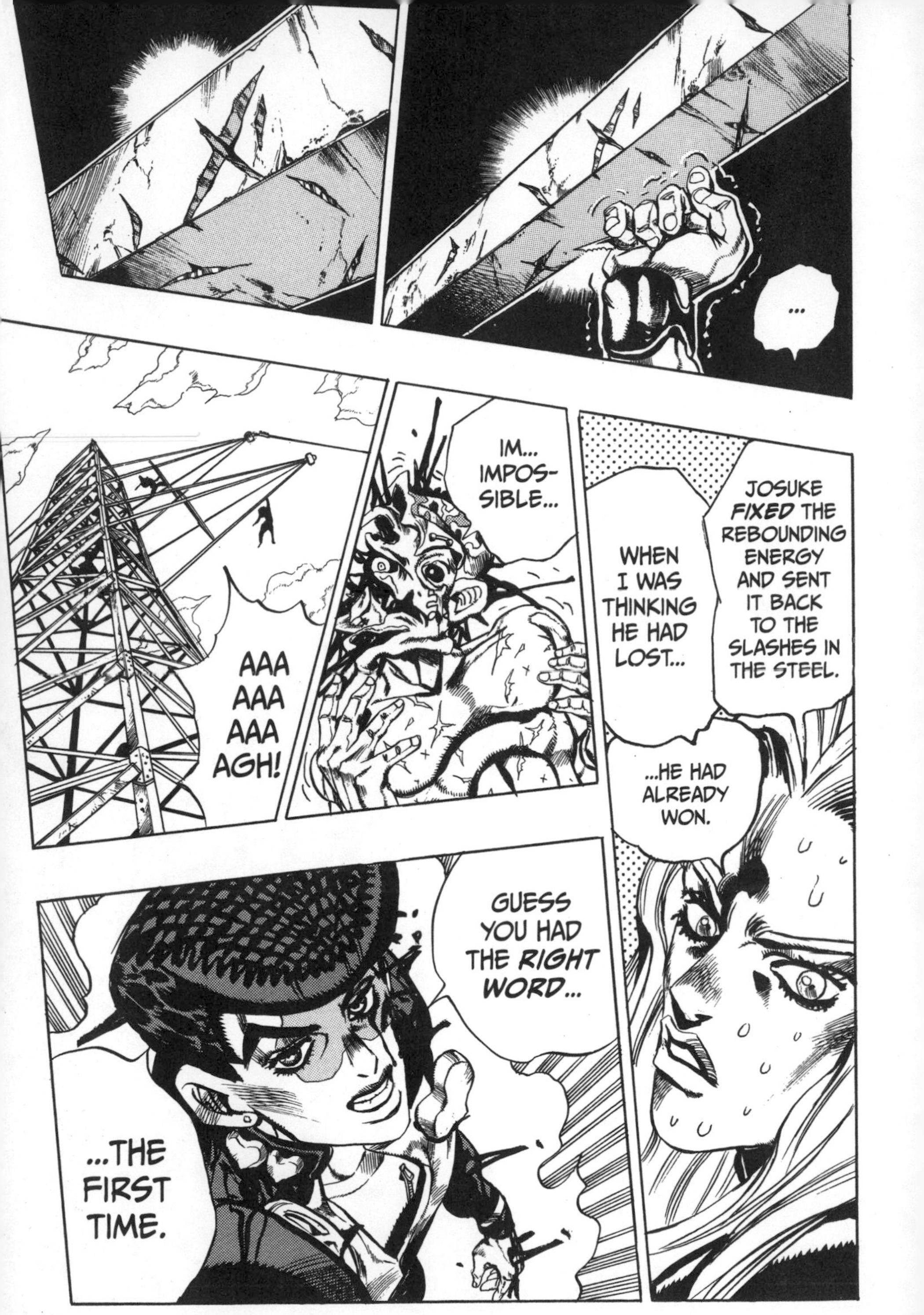
...
JOSUKE FIXED THE REBOUNDING ENERGY AND SENT IT BACK TO THE SLASHES IN THE STEEL.
WHEN I WAS THINKING HE HAD LOST...
...HE HAD ALREADY WON.
IM... IMPOSSIBLE...
AAAAAAAAAAGH!
GUESS YOU HAD THE RIGHT WORD...
...THE FIRST TIME.

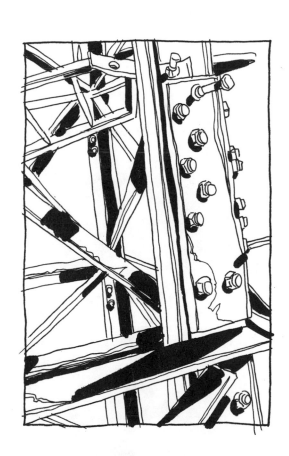

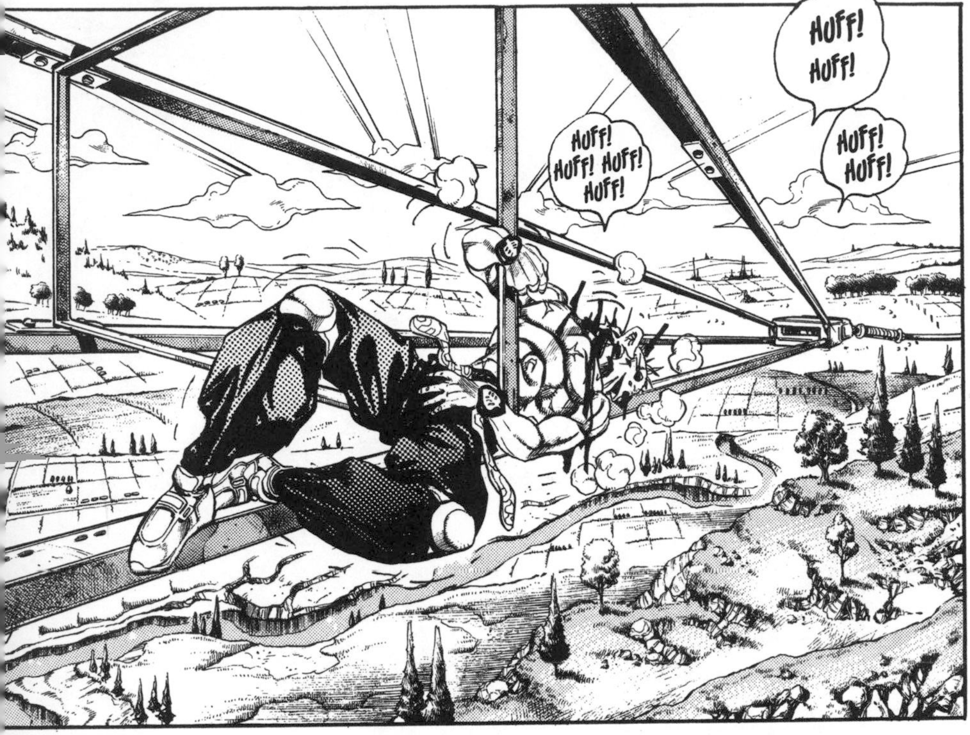
HUFF! HUFF!
HUFF! HUFF!
HUFF! HUFF! HUFF! HUFF!

CHAPTER 138

LET'S LIVE ON A TRANSMISSION TOWER, PART 6

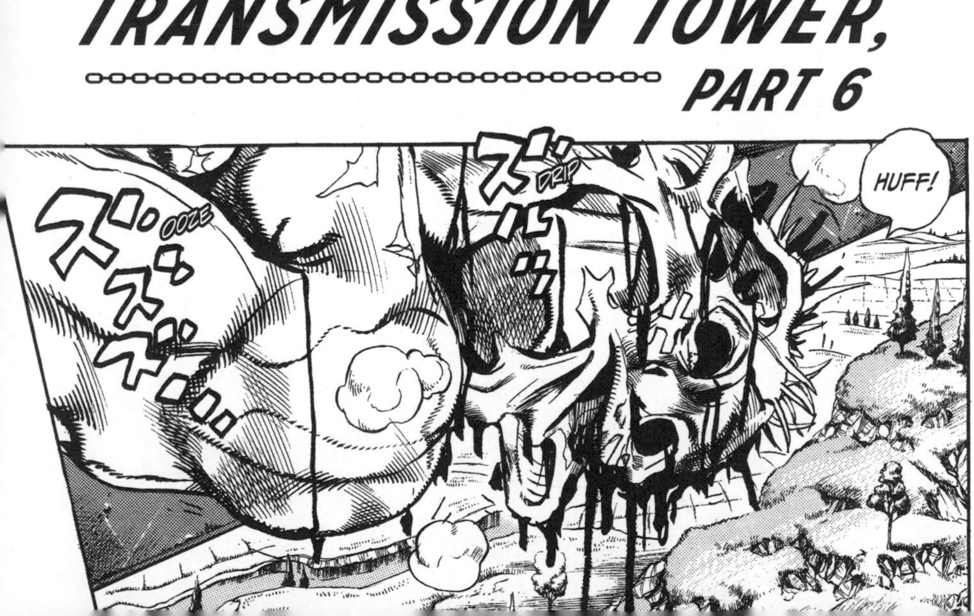
HUFF!
DRIP
OOZE

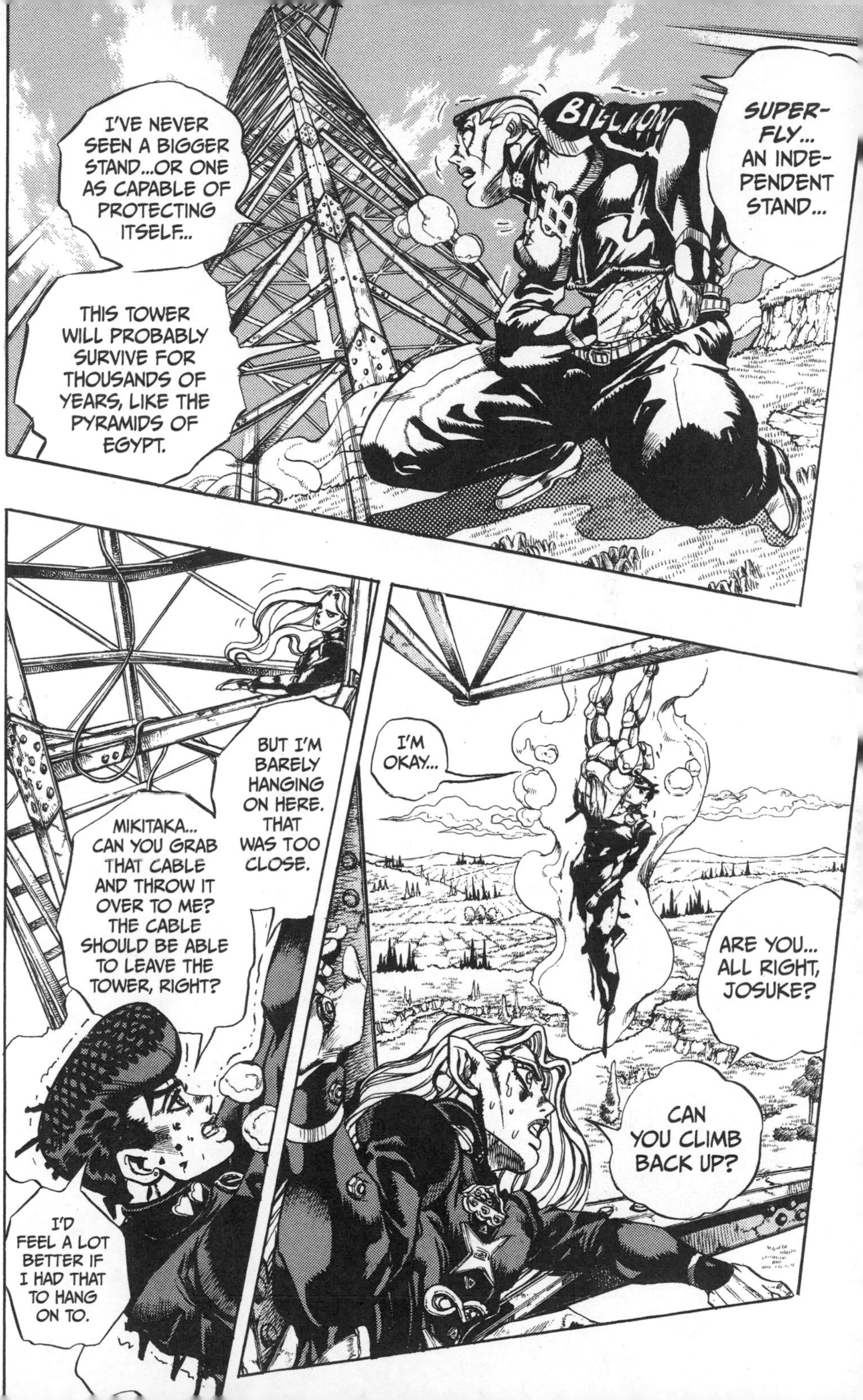
SUPER-FLY... AN INDEPENDENT STAND...
I'VE NEVER SEEN A BIGGER STAND...OR ONE AS CAPABLE OF PROTECTING ITSELF...
THIS TOWER WILL PROBABLY SURVIVE FOR THOUSANDS OF YEARS, LIKE THE PYRAMIDS OF EGYPT.
ARE YOU... ALL RIGHT, JOSUKE?
I'M OKAY...
CAN YOU CLIMB BACK UP?
BUT I'M BARELY HANGING ON HERE. THAT WAS TOO CLOSE.
MIKITAKA... CAN YOU GRAB THAT CABLE AND THROW IT OVER TO ME? THE CABLE SHOULD BE ABLE TO LEAVE THE TOWER, RIGHT?
I'D FEEL A LOT BETTER IF I HAD THAT TO HANG ON TO.

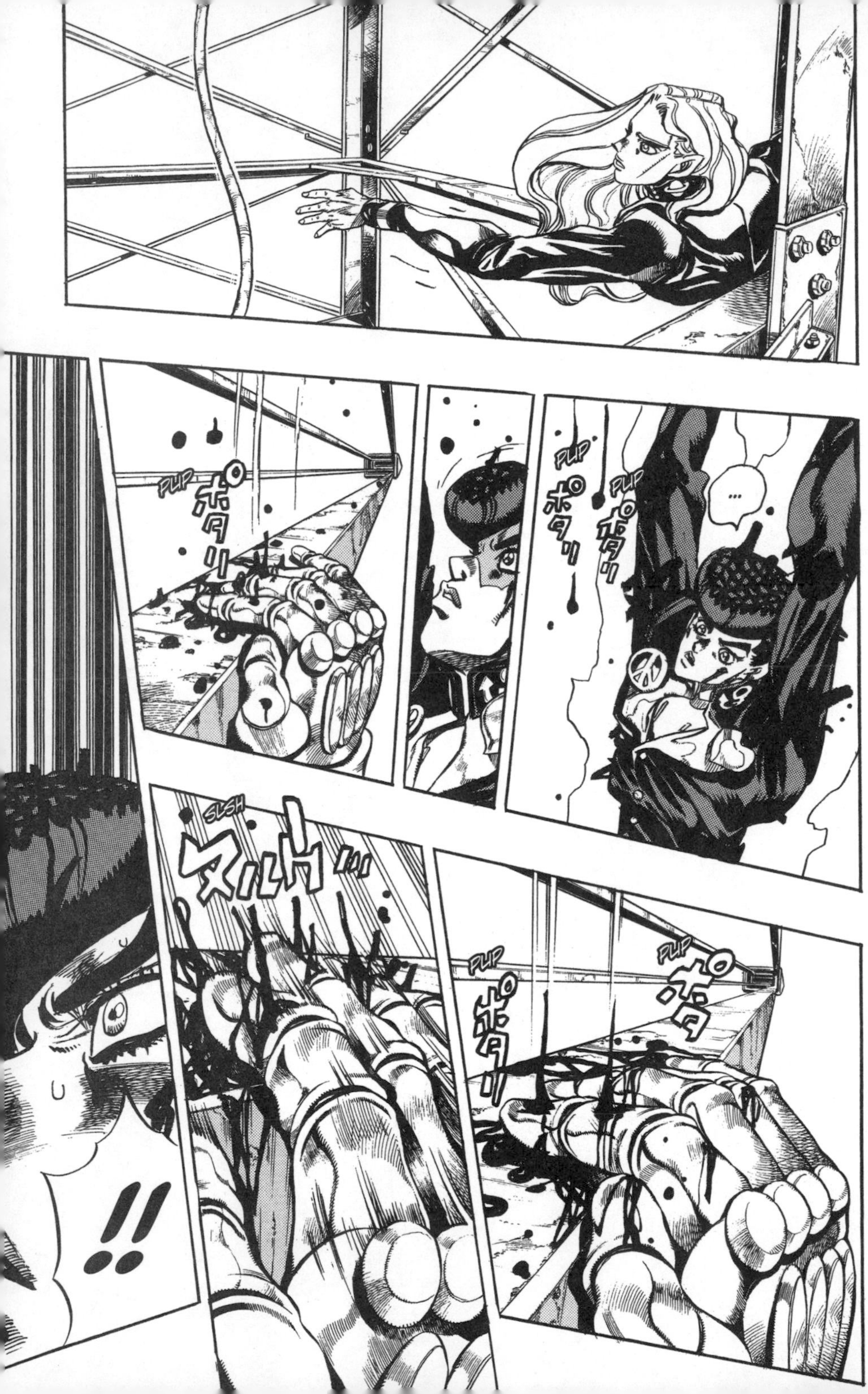

...
PLIP
ポタリ
PLIP
ポタリ
PLIP
ポタリ
PLIP
ポタ
PLIP
ポタリ
SLSH
ズルル…
!!

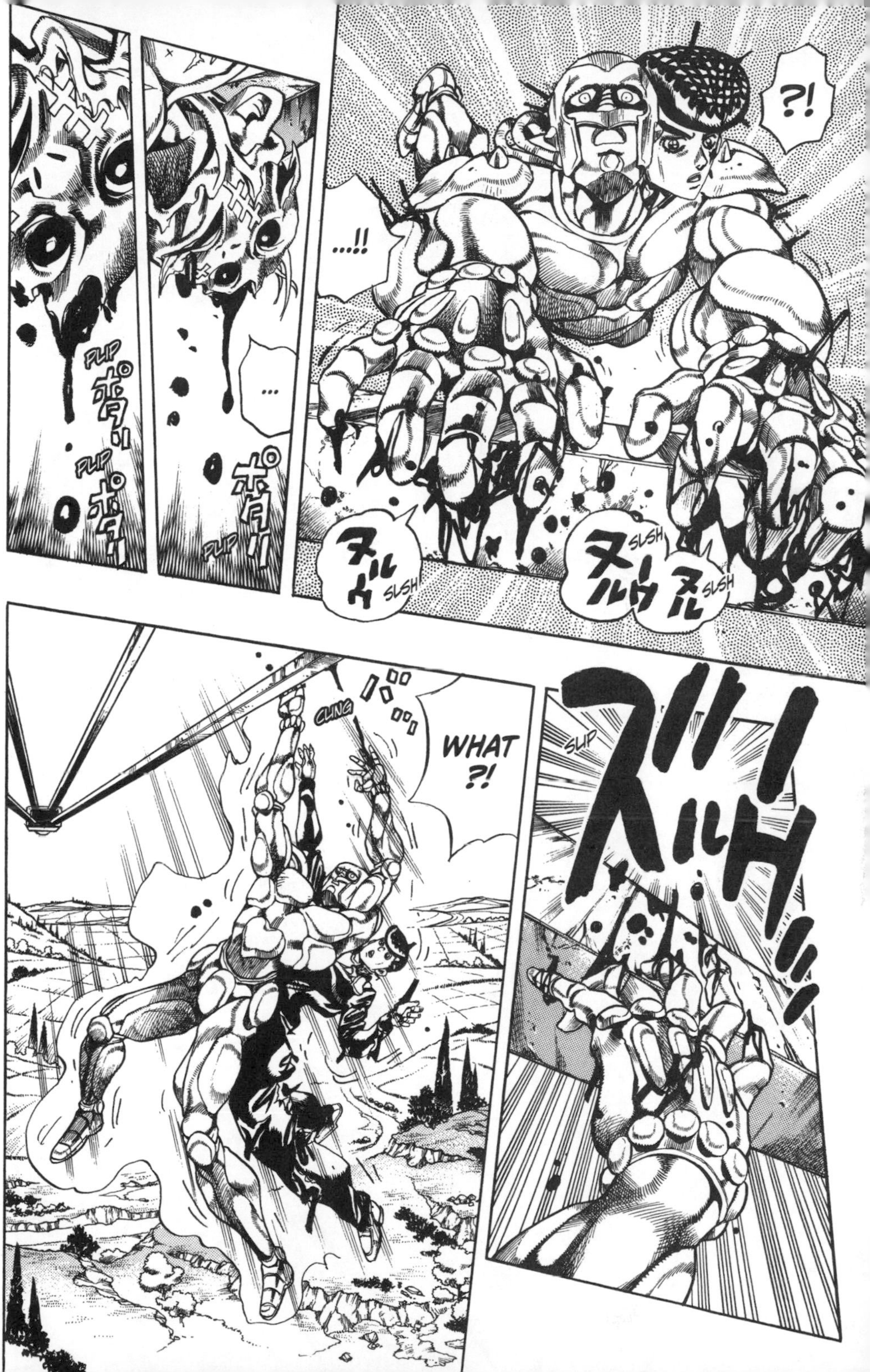

?!
...!!
SLSH
SLSH
SLSH
...
PLIP
PLIP
PLIP
PLIP
SLIP
CLING
WHAT ?!
...

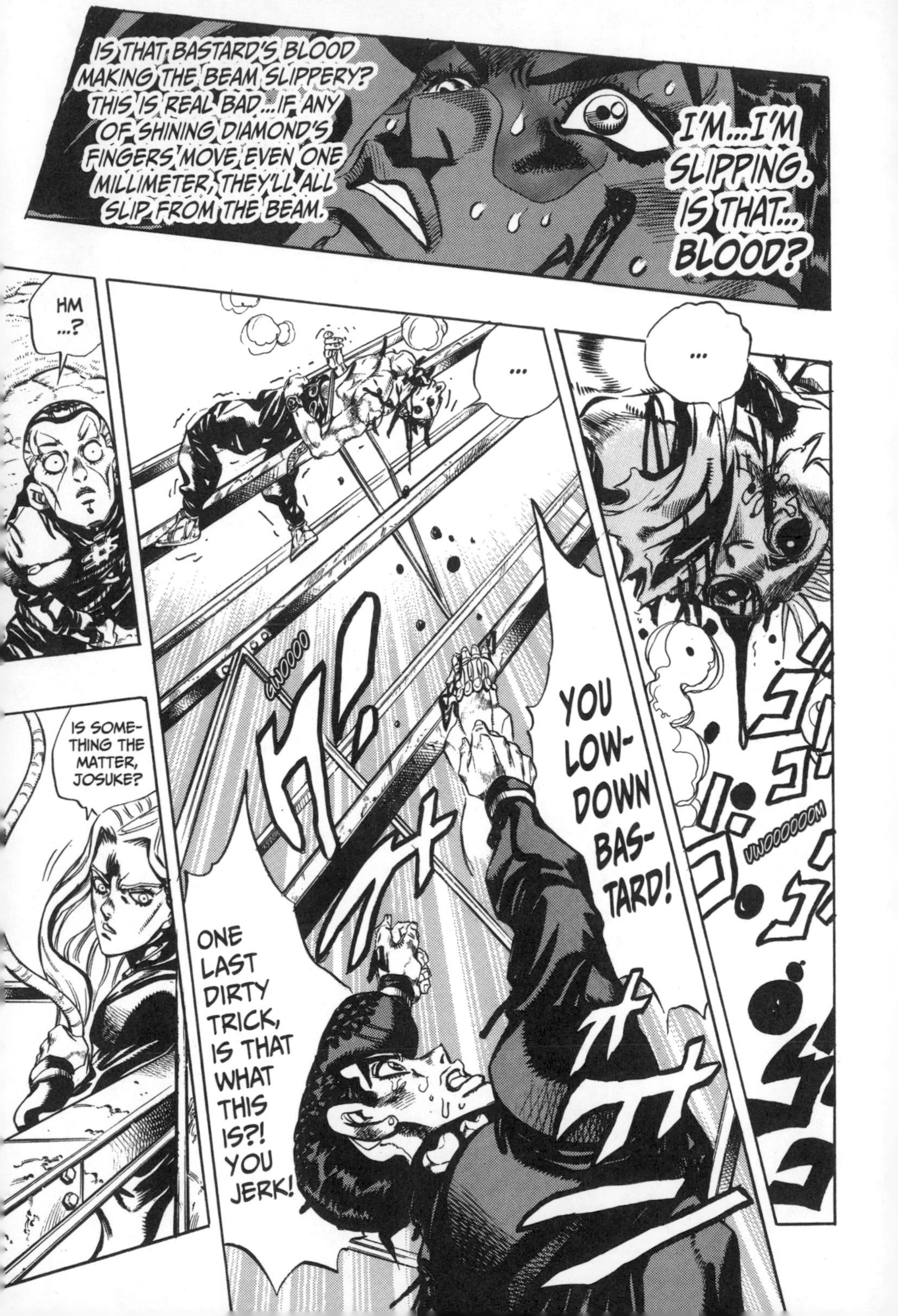
I'M...I'M SLIPPING. IS THAT... BLOOD?
IS THAT BASTARD'S BLOOD MAKING THE BEAM SLIPPERY? THIS IS REAL BAD...IF ANY OF SHINING DIAMOND'S FINGERS MOVE EVEN ONE MILLIMETER, THEY'LL ALL SLIP FROM THE BEAM.
...
VWOOOOOOOM
...
VWOOOO
YOU LOW-DOWN BASTARD!
ONE LAST DIRTY TRICK, IS THAT WHAT THIS IS?! YOU JERK!
HM ...?
IS SOMETHING THE MATTER, JOSUKE?

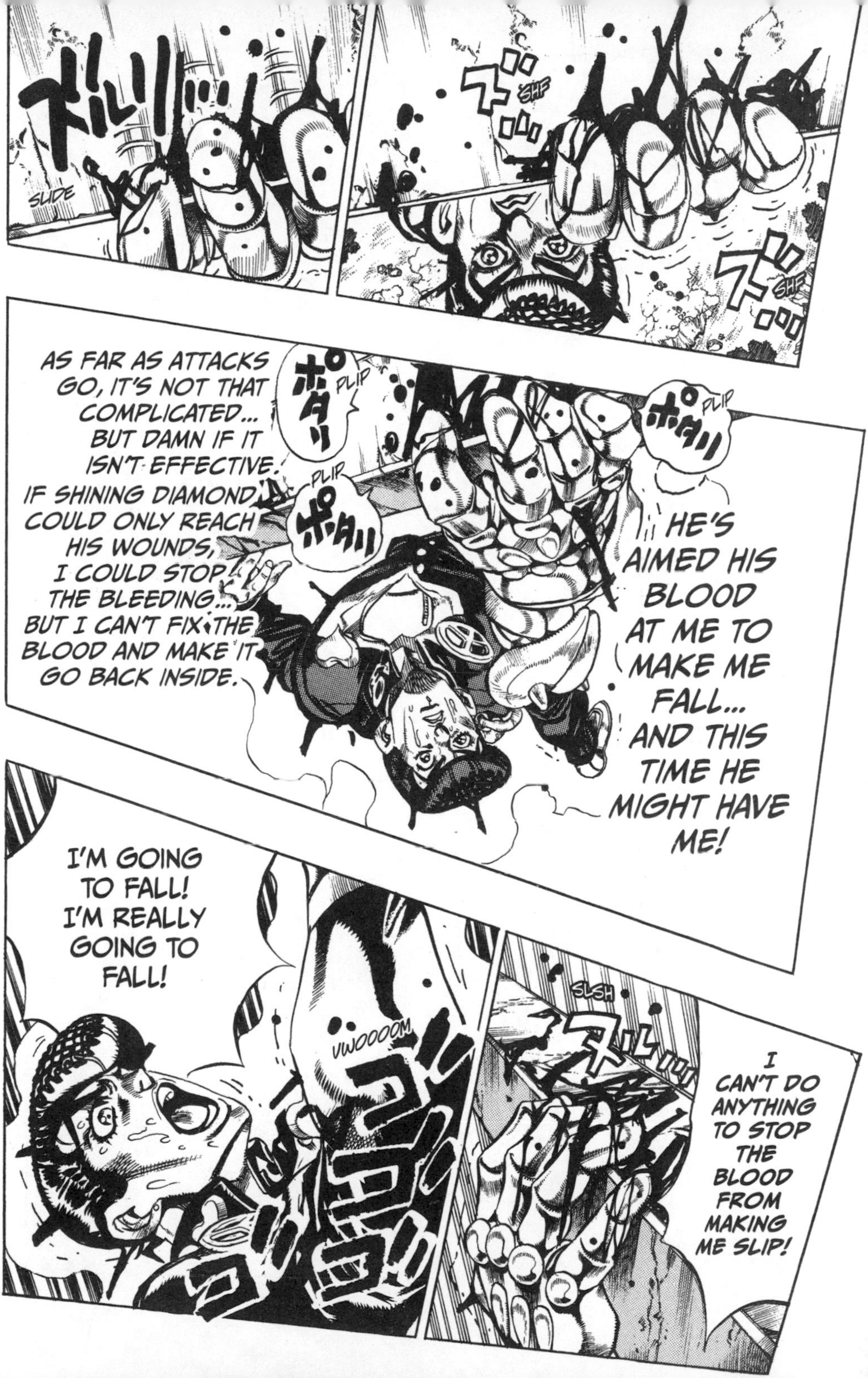
SHF
SHF
SLIDE
PLIP
HE'S AIMED HIS BLOOD AT ME TO MAKE ME FALL... AND THIS TIME HE MIGHT HAVE ME!
PLIP
PLIP
AS FAR AS ATTACKS GO, IT'S NOT THAT COMPLICATED... BUT DAMN IF IT ISN'T EFFECTIVE. IF SHINING DIAMOND COULD ONLY REACH HIS WOUNDS, I COULD STOP THE BLEEDING... BUT I CAN'T FIX THE BLOOD AND MAKE IT GO BACK INSIDE.
SLSH
I CAN'T DO ANYTHING TO STOP THE BLOOD FROM MAKING ME SLIP!
I'M GOING TO FALL! I'M REALLY GOING TO FALL!
VWOOOOM

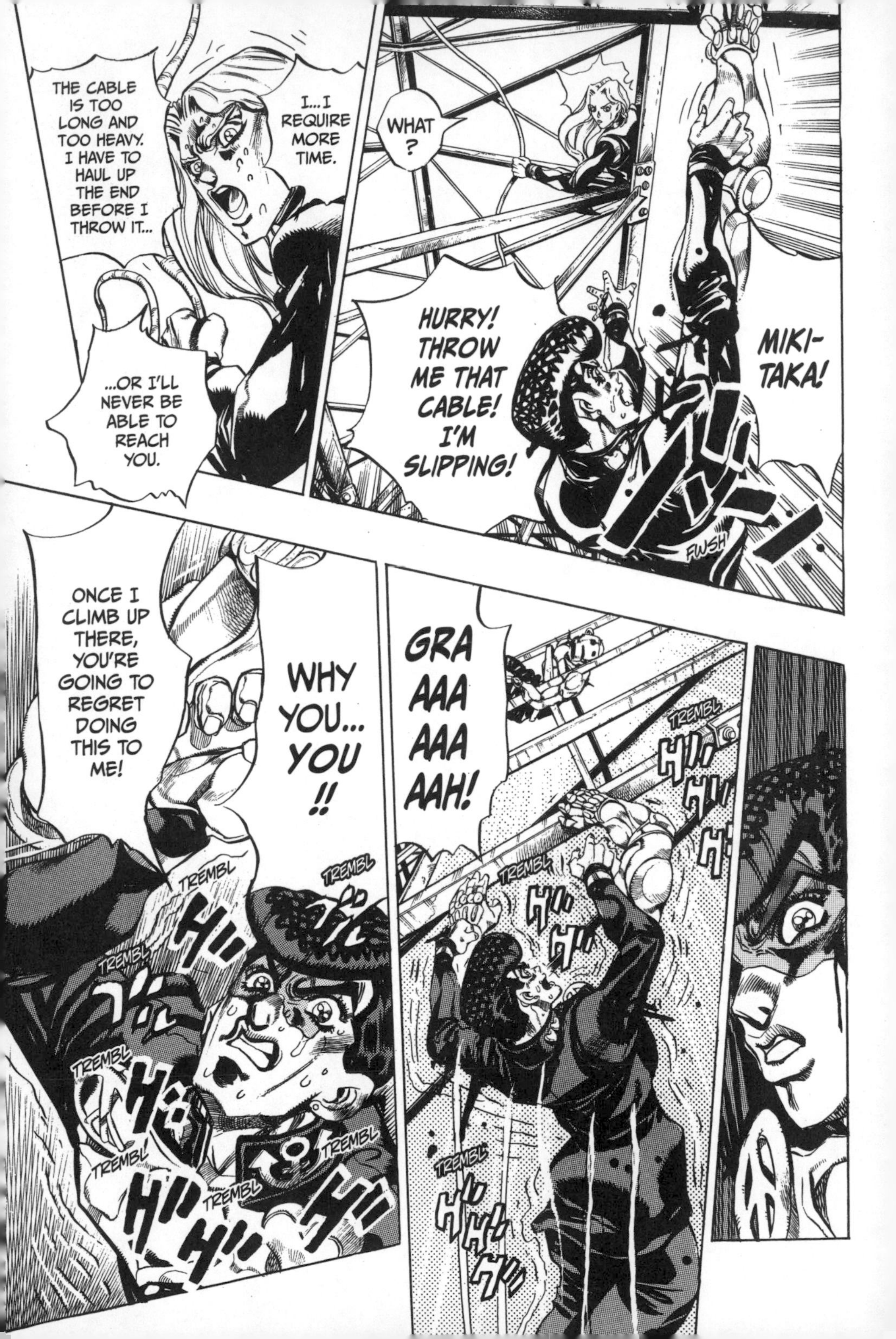
MIKI-TAKA!
HURRY! THROW ME THAT CABLE! I'M SLIPPING!
WHAT?
FWSH
I...I REQUIRE MORE TIME.
THE CABLE IS TOO LONG AND TOO HEAVY. I HAVE TO HAUL UP THE END BEFORE I THROW IT...
...OR I'LL NEVER BE ABLE TO REACH YOU.
GRA AAA AAA AAH!
TREMBL
TREMBL
TREMBL
WHY YOU... YOU !!
ONCE I CLIMB UP THERE, YOU'RE GOING TO REGRET DOING THIS TO ME!
TREMBL
TREMBL
TREMBL
TREMBL
TREMBL
TREMBL
TREMBL

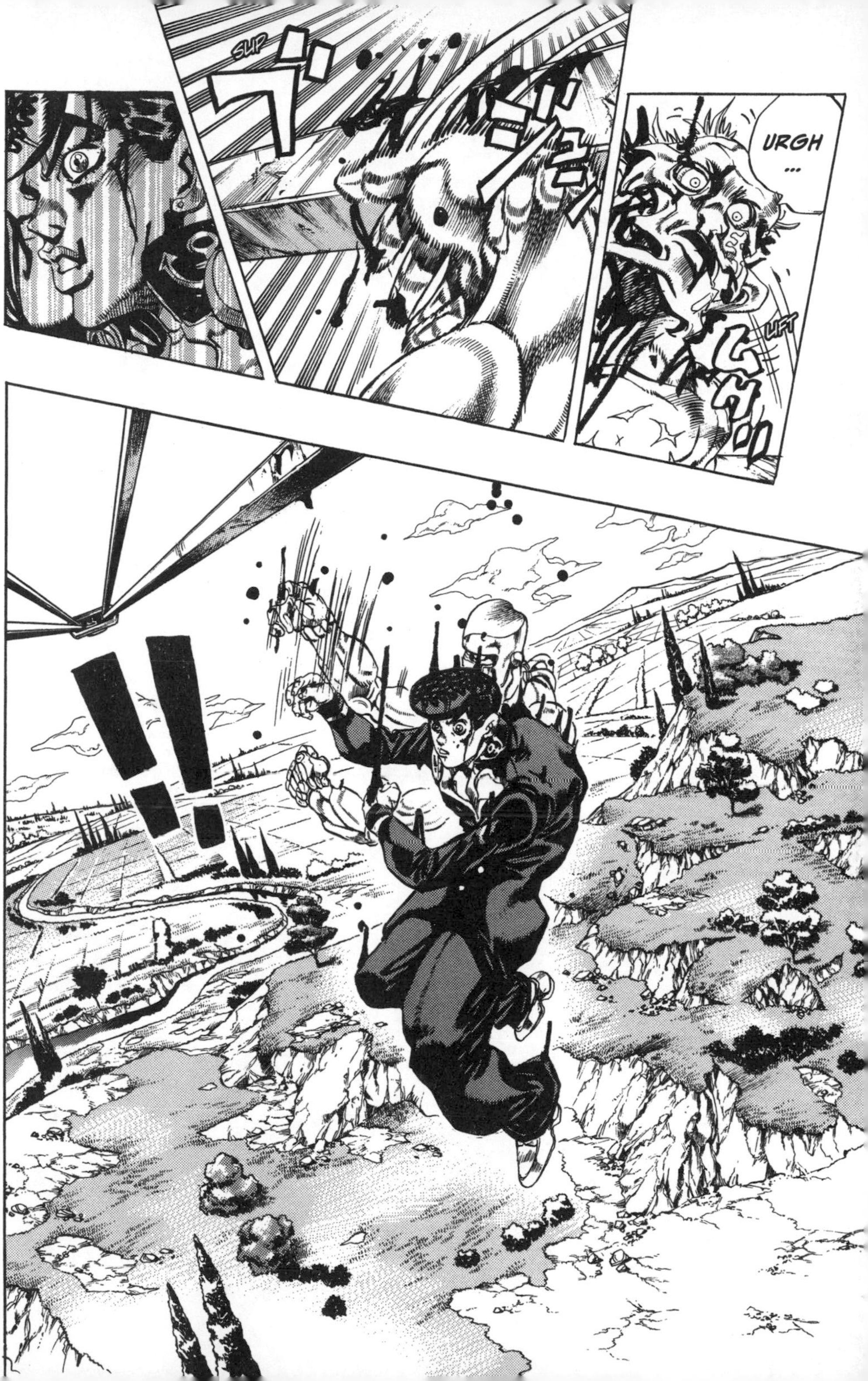
URGH ...
LIFT
SLIP

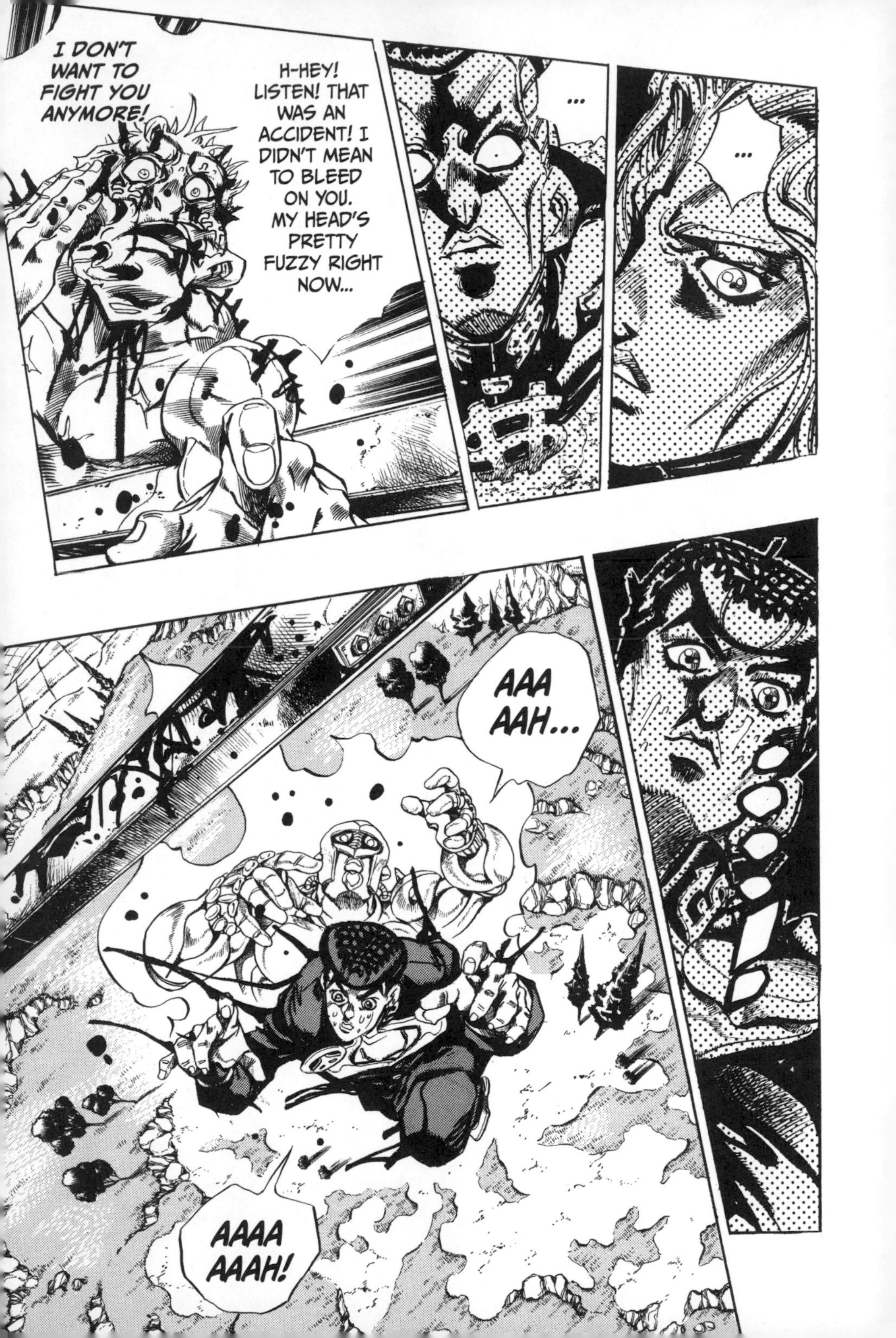
...
...
H-HEY! LISTEN! THAT WAS AN ACCIDENT! I DIDN'T MEAN TO BLEED ON YOU. MY HEAD'S PRETTY FUZZY RIGHT NOW...
I DON'T WANT TO FIGHT YOU ANYMORE!
AAA AAH...
AAAA AAAH!

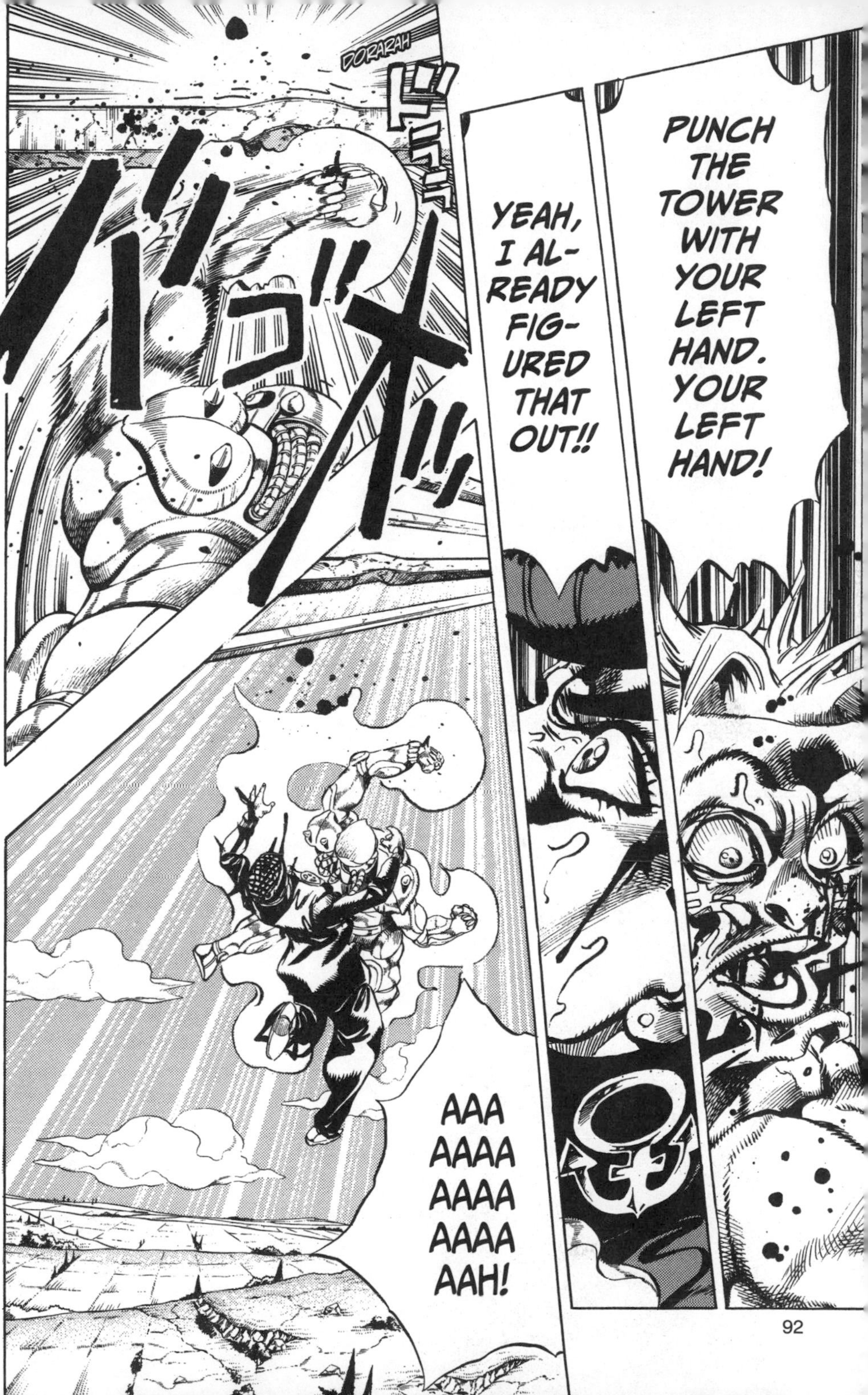
PUNCH THE TOWER WITH YOUR LEFT HAND. YOUR LEFT HAND!
YEAH, I AL-READY FIG-URED THAT OUT!!
DORARAH
AAA AAAA AAAA AAAA AAH!

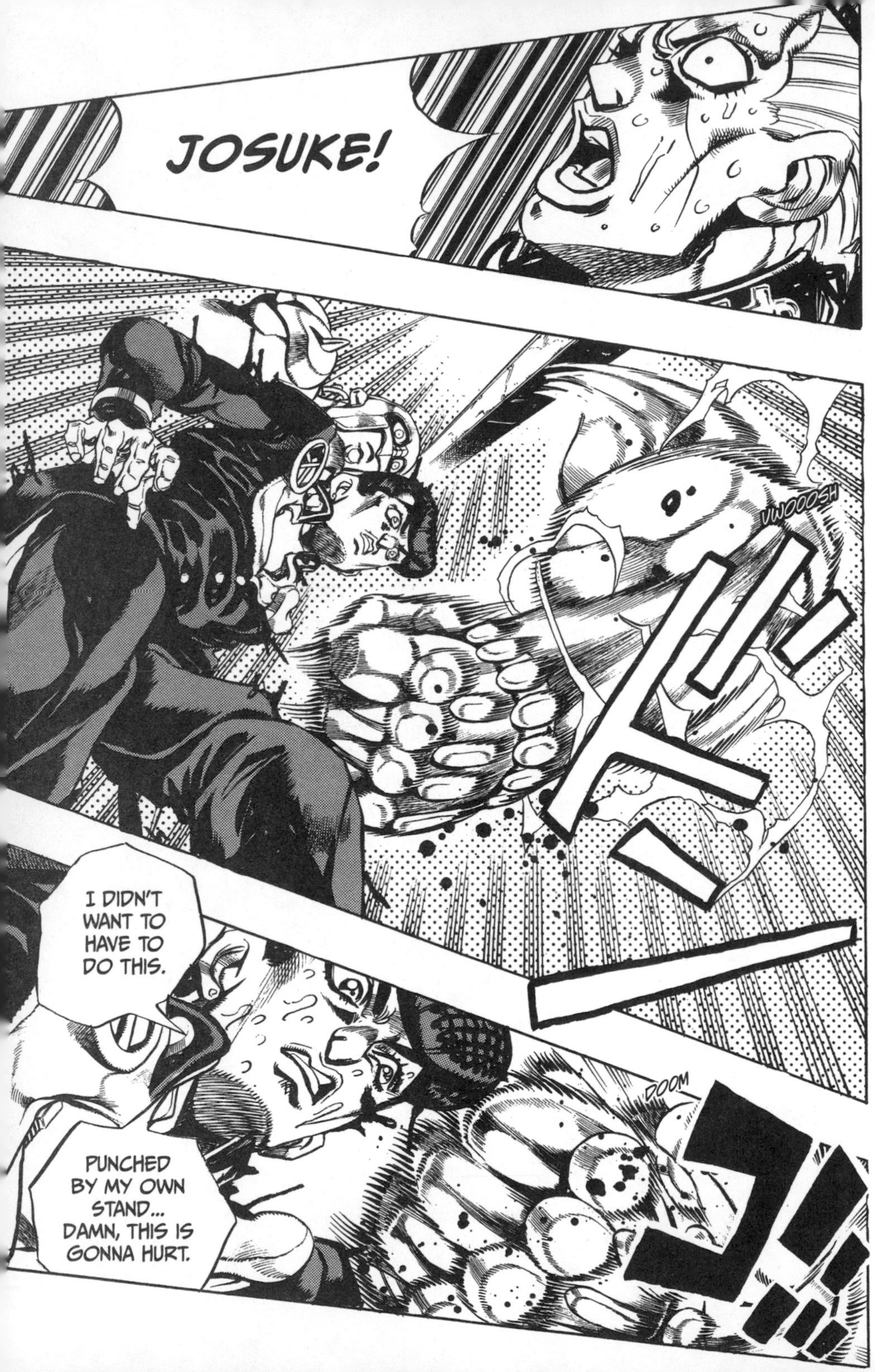
JOSUKE!
VWOOOSH
I DIDN'T WANT TO HAVE TO DO THIS.
DOOM
PUNCHED BY MY OWN STAND... DAMN, THIS IS GONNA HURT.

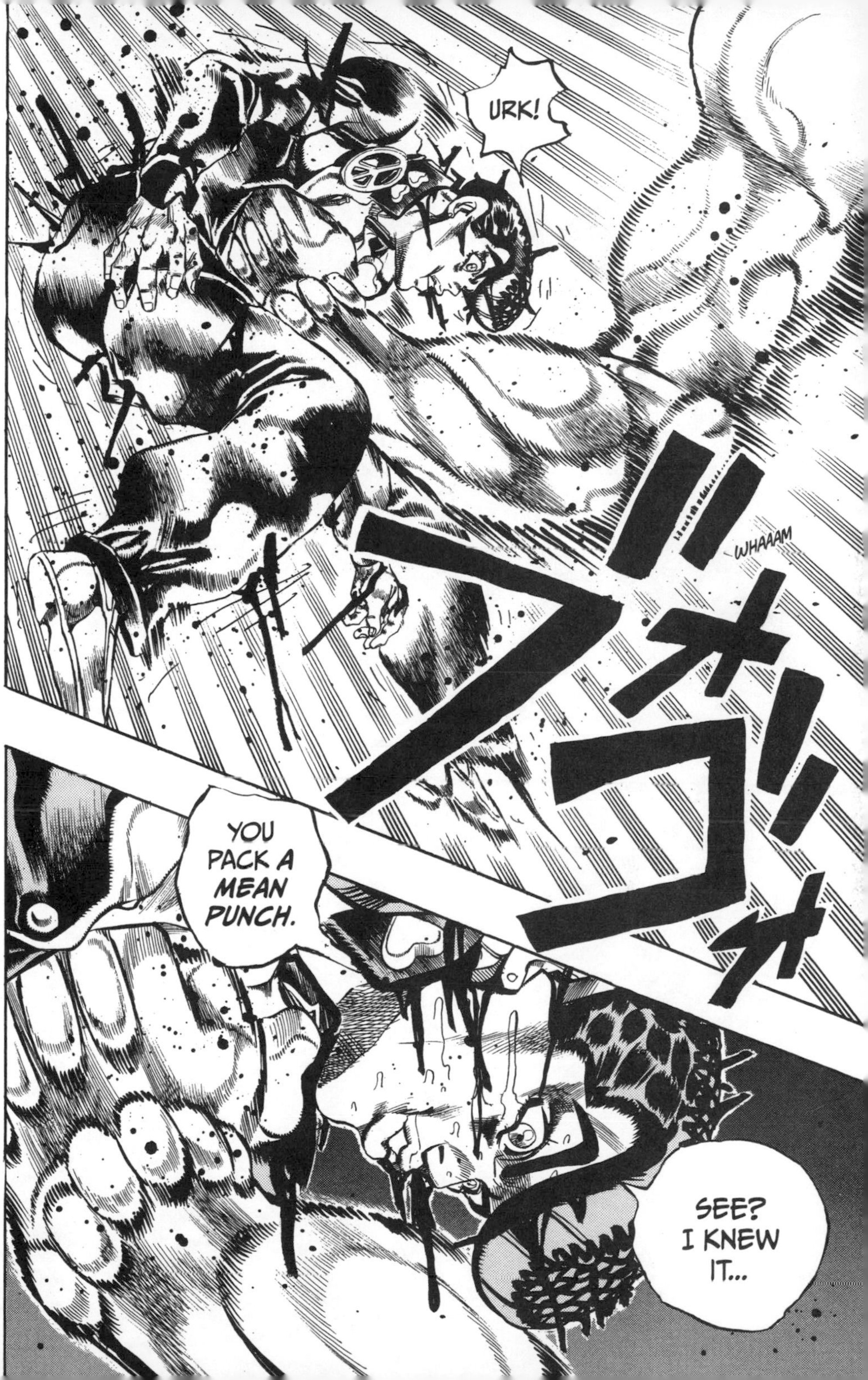
URK!
WHAAAM
YOU PACK A MEAN PUNCH.
SEE? I KNEW IT...

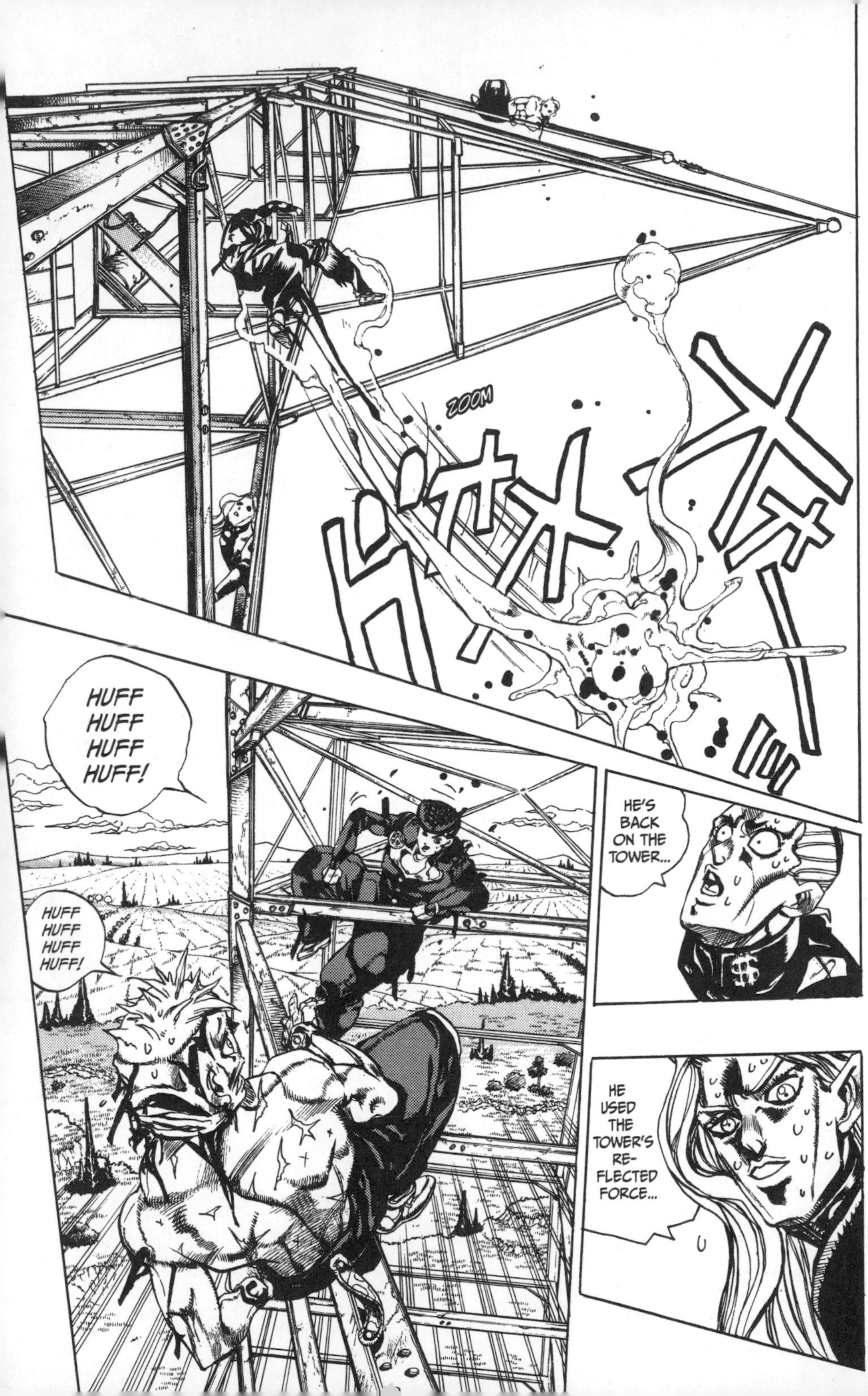
ZOOM
HE'S BACK ON THE TOWER...
HE USED THE TOWER'S RE-FLECTED FORCE...
HUFF HUFF HUFF HUFF!
HUFF HUFF HUFF HUFF!

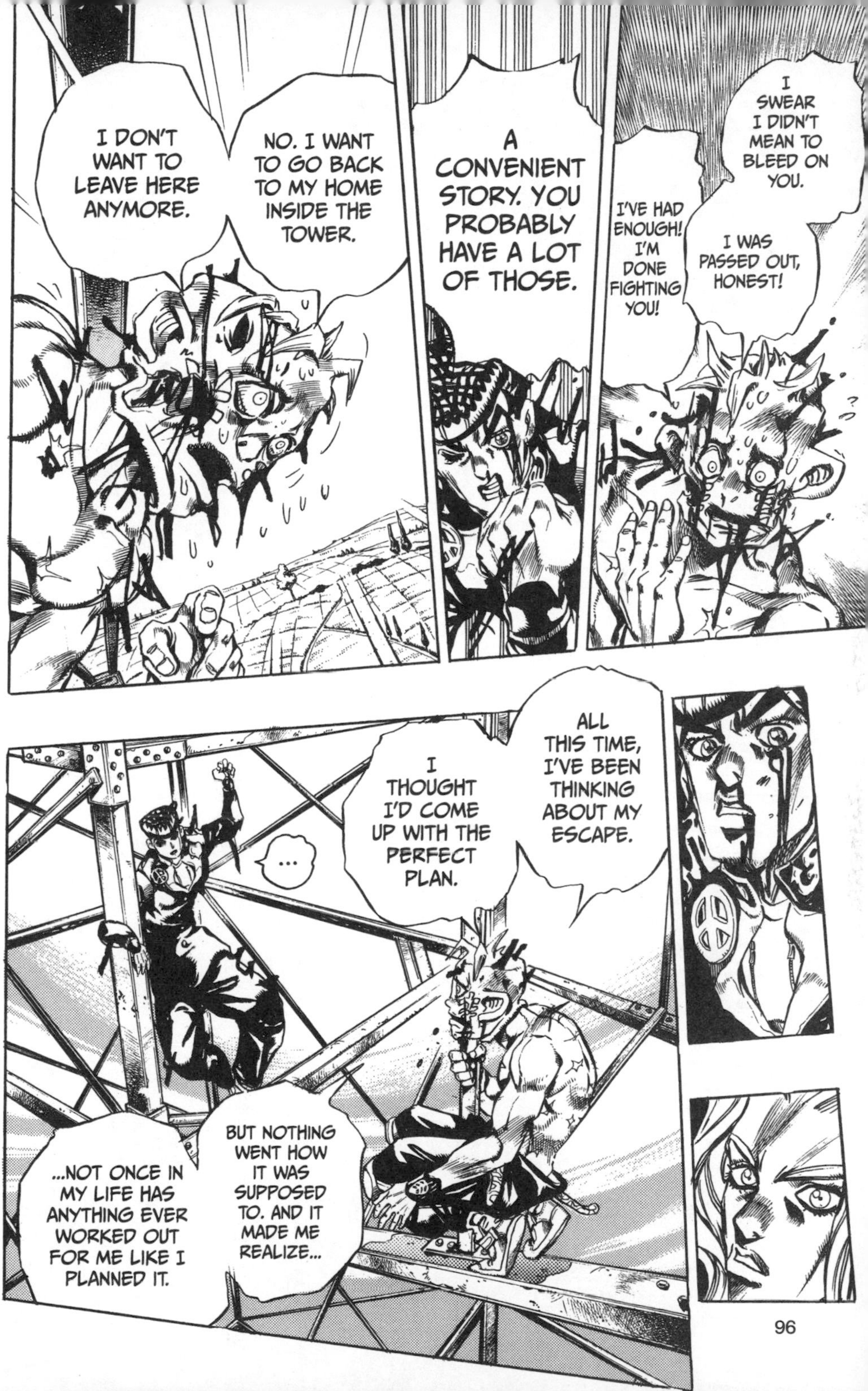
I SWEAR I DIDN'T MEAN TO BLEED ON YOU.
I WAS PASSED OUT, HONEST!
I'VE HAD ENOUGH! I'M DONE FIGHTING YOU!
A CONVENIENT STORY. YOU PROBABLY HAVE A LOT OF THOSE.
NO. I WANT TO GO BACK TO MY HOME INSIDE THE TOWER.
I DON'T WANT TO LEAVE HERE ANYMORE.
ALL THIS TIME, I'VE BEEN THINKING ABOUT MY ESCAPE.
I THOUGHT I'D COME UP WITH THE PERFECT PLAN.
...
BUT NOTHING WENT HOW IT WAS SUPPOSED TO. AND IT MADE ME REALIZE...
...NOT ONCE IN MY LIFE HAS ANYTHING EVER WORKED OUT FOR ME LIKE I PLANNED IT.

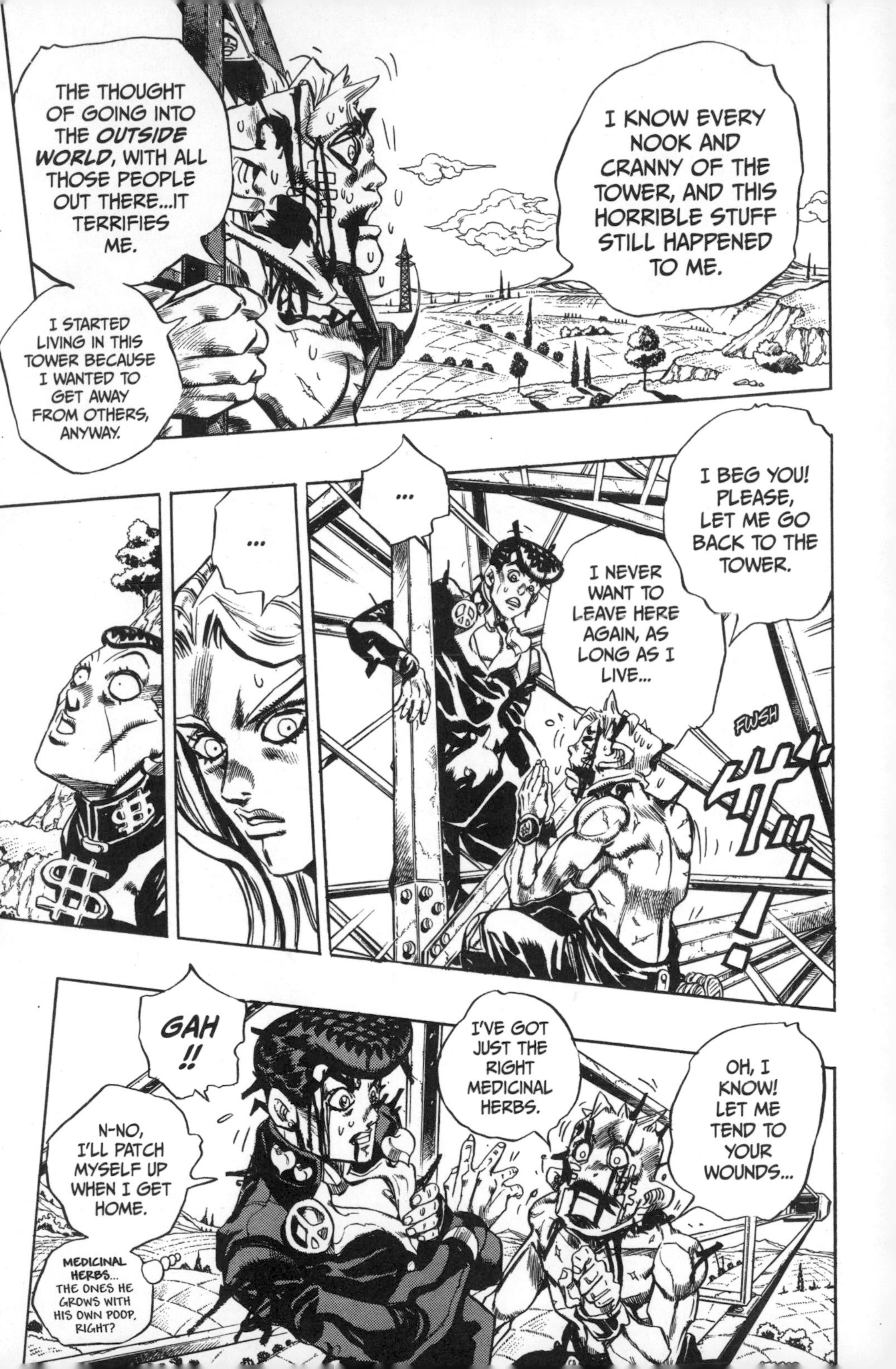
I KNOW EVERY NOOK AND CRANNY OF THE TOWER, AND THIS HORRIBLE STUFF STILL HAPPENED TO ME.
THE THOUGHT OF GOING INTO THE *OUTSIDE WORLD*, WITH ALL THOSE PEOPLE OUT THERE...IT TERRIFIES ME.
I STARTED LIVING IN THIS TOWER BECAUSE I WANTED TO GET AWAY FROM OTHERS, ANYWAY.
I BEG YOU! PLEASE, LET ME GO BACK TO THE TOWER.
I NEVER WANT TO LEAVE HERE AGAIN, AS LONG AS I LIVE...
...
FWSH
...
OH, I KNOW! LET ME TEND TO YOUR WOUNDS...
I'VE GOT JUST THE RIGHT MEDICINAL HERBS.
GAH!!
N-NO, I'LL PATCH MYSELF UP WHEN I GET HOME.
MEDICINAL HERBS... THE ONES HE GROWS WITH HIS OWN POOP, RIGHT?

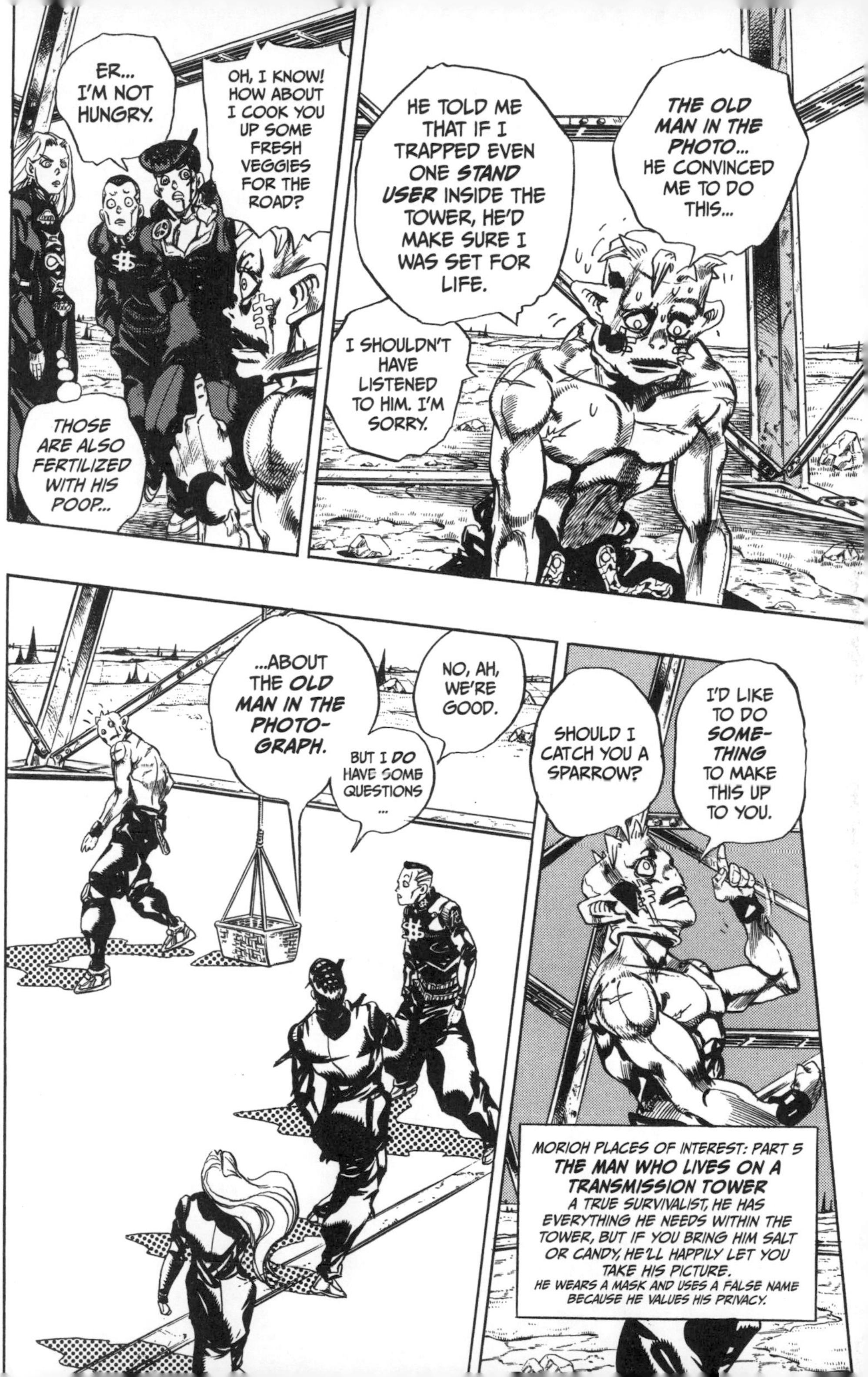
THE OLD MAN IN THE PHOTO... HE CONVINCED ME TO DO THIS...
HE TOLD ME THAT IF I TRAPPED EVEN ONE STAND USER INSIDE THE TOWER, HE'D MAKE SURE I WAS SET FOR LIFE.
I SHOULDN'T HAVE LISTENED TO HIM. I'M SORRY.
OH, I KNOW! HOW ABOUT I COOK YOU UP SOME FRESH VEGGIES FOR THE ROAD?
ER... I'M NOT HUNGRY.
THOSE ARE ALSO FERTILIZED WITH HIS POOP...
I'D LIKE TO DO SOMETHING TO MAKE THIS UP TO YOU.
SHOULD I CATCH YOU A SPARROW?
MORIOH PLACES OF INTEREST: PART 5
THE MAN WHO LIVES ON A TRANSMISSION TOWER
A TRUE SURVIVALIST, HE HAS EVERYTHING HE NEEDS WITHIN THE TOWER, BUT IF YOU BRING HIM SALT OR CANDY, HE'LL HAPPILY LET YOU TAKE HIS PICTURE.
HE WEARS A MASK AND USES A FALSE NAME BECAUSE HE VALUES HIS PRIVACY.
NO, AH, WE'RE GOOD.
BUT I DO HAVE SOME QUESTIONS ...
...ABOUT THE OLD MAN IN THE PHOTOGRAPH.

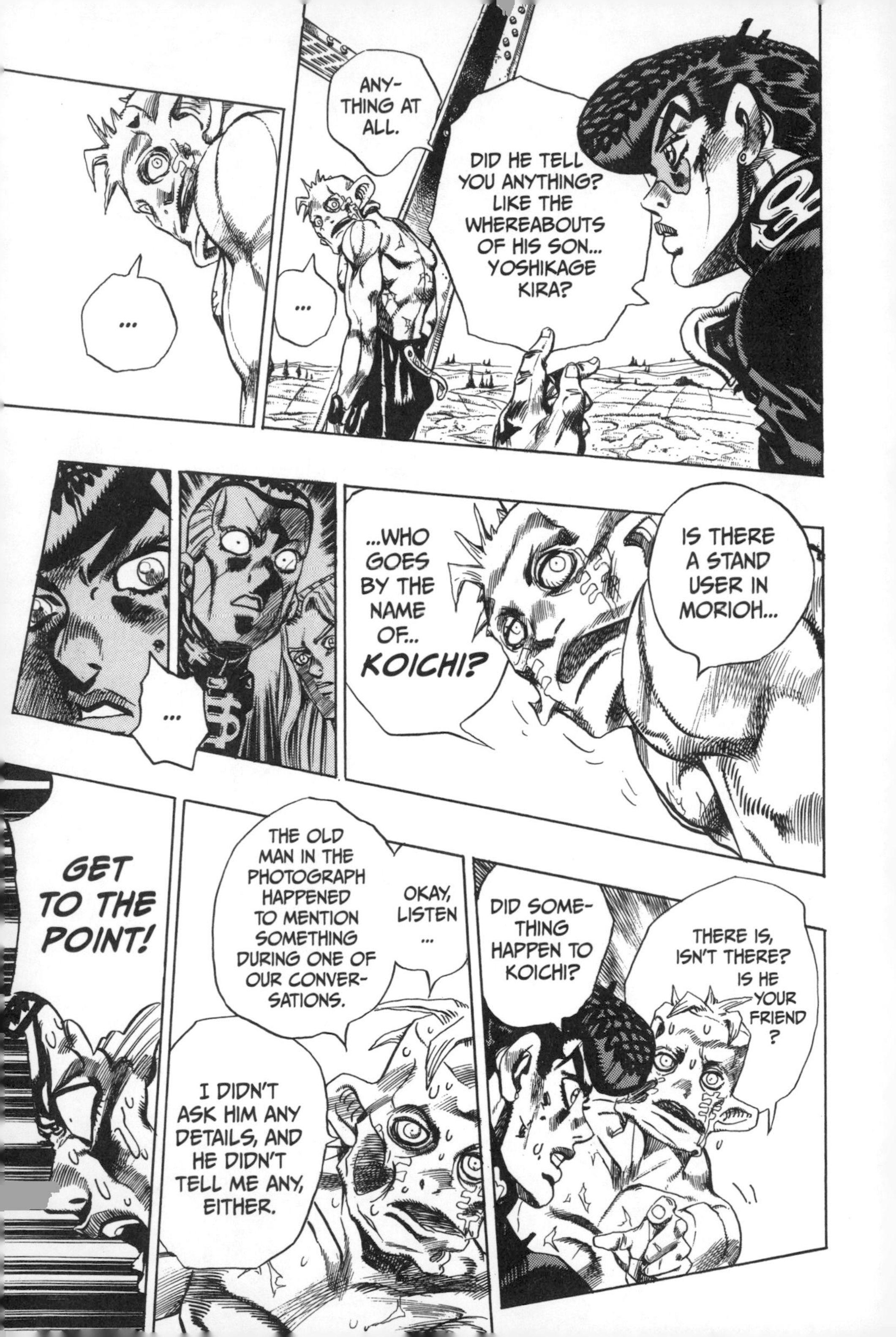
DID HE TELL YOU ANYTHING? LIKE THE WHEREABOUTS OF HIS SON... YOSHIKAGE KIRA?
ANY-THING AT ALL.
...
...
IS THERE A STAND USER IN MORIOH...
...WHO GOES BY THE NAME OF... KOICHI?
...
THERE IS, ISN'T THERE? IS HE YOUR FRIEND?
DID SOME-THING HAPPEN TO KOICHI?
OKAY, LISTEN...
THE OLD MAN IN THE PHOTOGRAPH HAPPENED TO MENTION SOMETHING DURING ONE OF OUR CONVER-SATIONS.
I DIDN'T ASK HIM ANY DETAILS, AND HE DIDN'T TELL ME ANY, EITHER.
GET TO THE POINT!

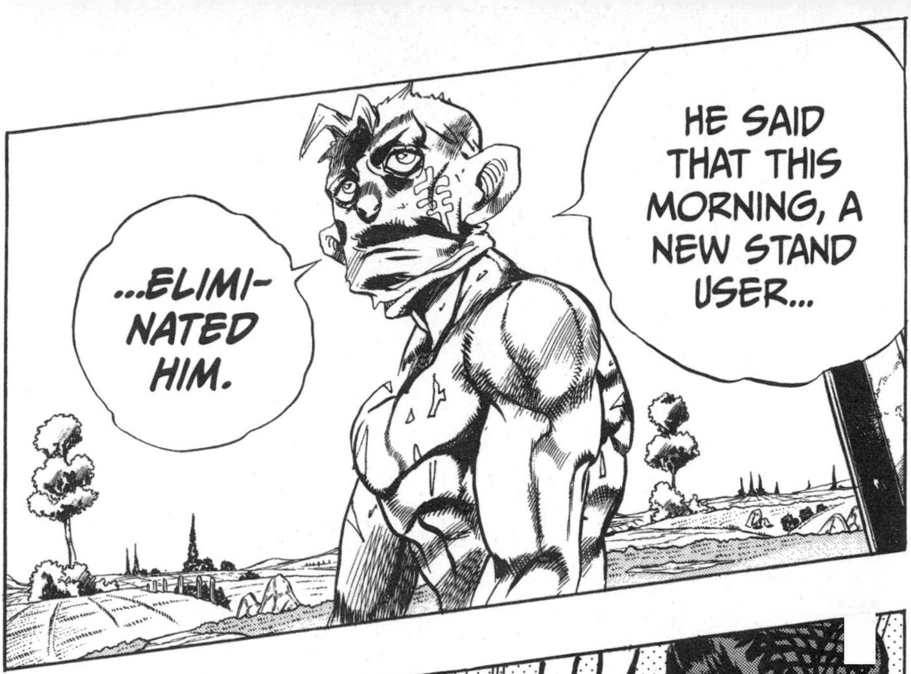
HE SAID THAT THIS MORNING, A NEW STAND USER...
...ELIMI-NATED HIM.
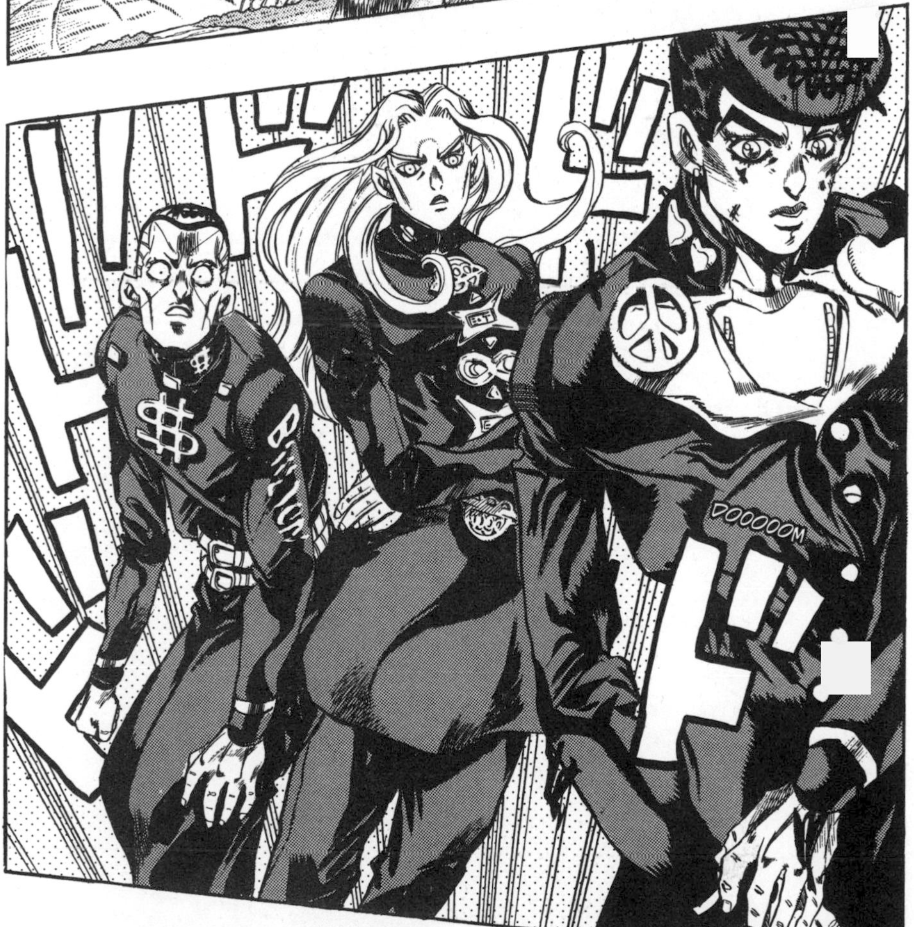
DOOOOOM

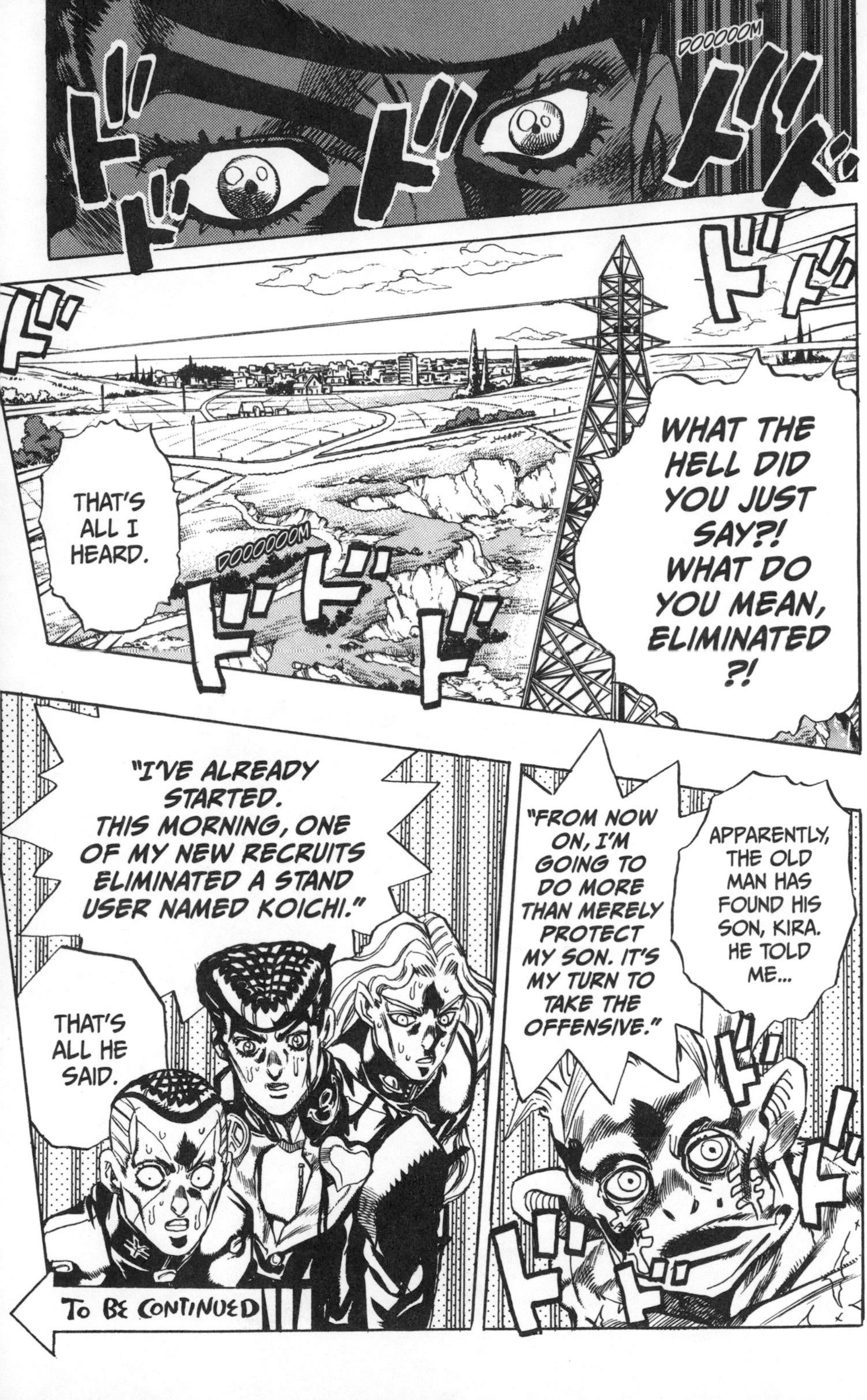

DOOOOOM
WHAT THE HELL DID YOU JUST SAY?! WHAT DO YOU MEAN, ELIMINATED ?!
THAT'S ALL I HEARD.
DOOOOOOM
APPARENTLY, THE OLD MAN HAS FOUND HIS SON, KIRA. HE TOLD ME...
"FROM NOW ON, I'M GOING TO DO MORE THAN MERELY PROTECT MY SON. IT'S MY TURN TO TAKE THE OFFENSIVE."
"I'VE ALREADY STARTED. THIS MORNING, ONE OF MY NEW RECRUITS ELIMINATED A STAND USER NAMED KOICHI."
THAT'S ALL HE SAID.
TO BE CONTINUED

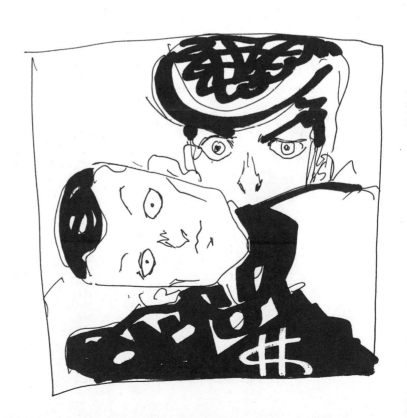

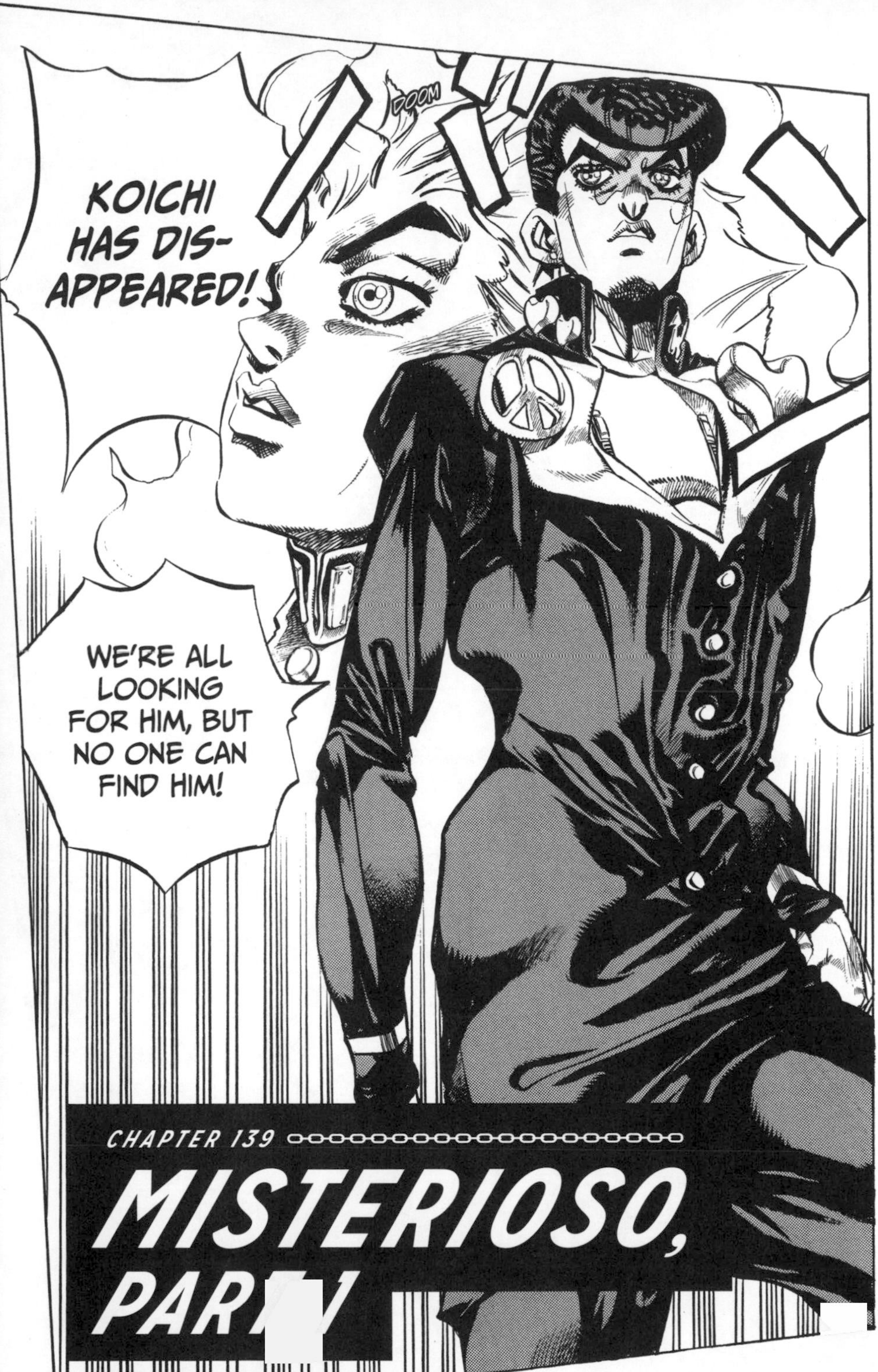
DOOM
KOICHI HAS DIS-APPEARED!
WE'RE ALL LOOKING FOR HIM, BUT NO ONE CAN FIND HIM!
CHAPTER 139
MISTERIOSO,
PAR

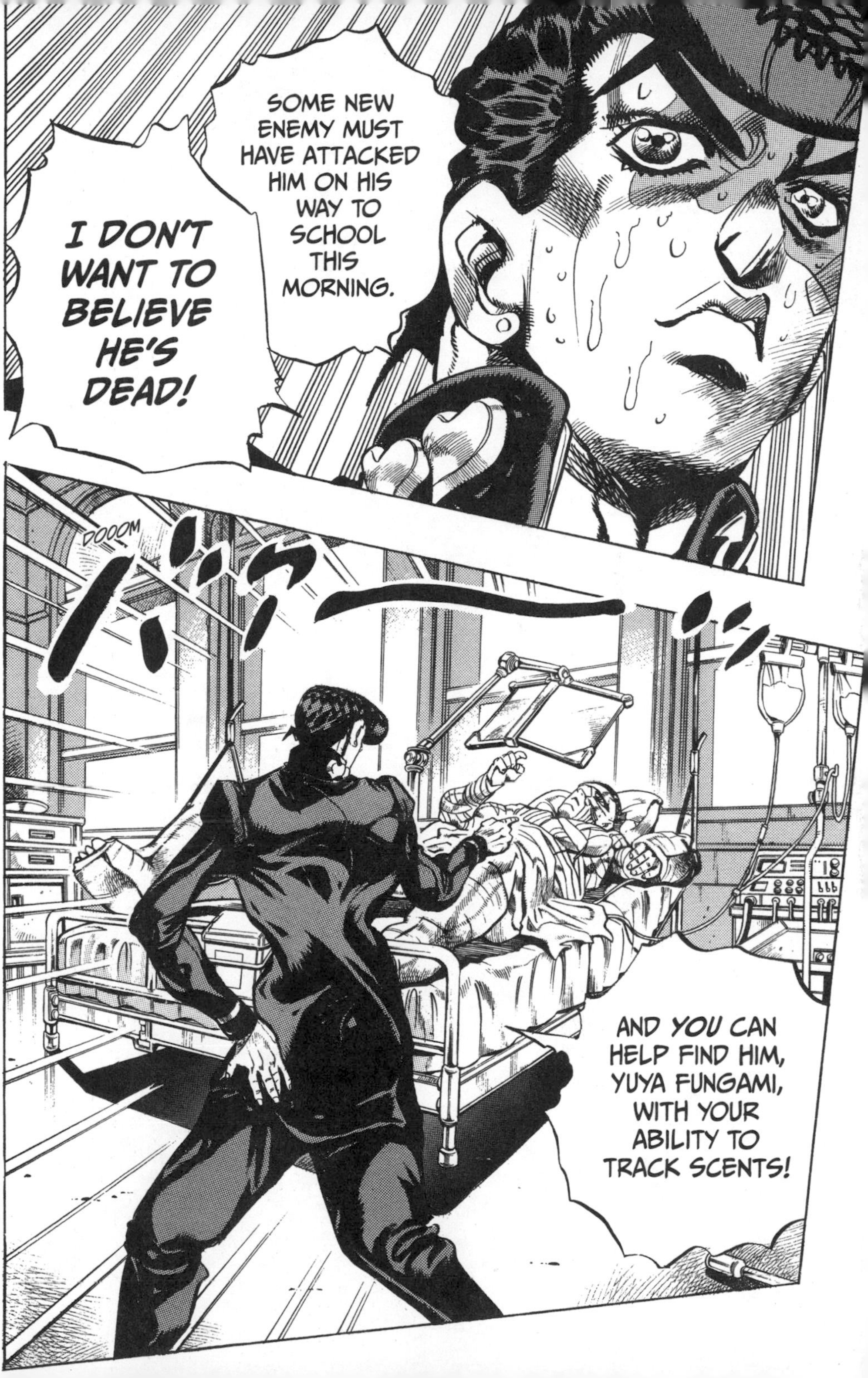
SOME NEW ENEMY MUST HAVE ATTACKED HIM ON HIS WAY TO SCHOOL THIS MORNING.
I DON'T WANT TO BELIEVE HE'S DEAD!
DOOOM
AND YOU CAN HELP FIND HIM, YUYA FUNGAMI, WITH YOUR ABILITY TO TRACK SCENTS!

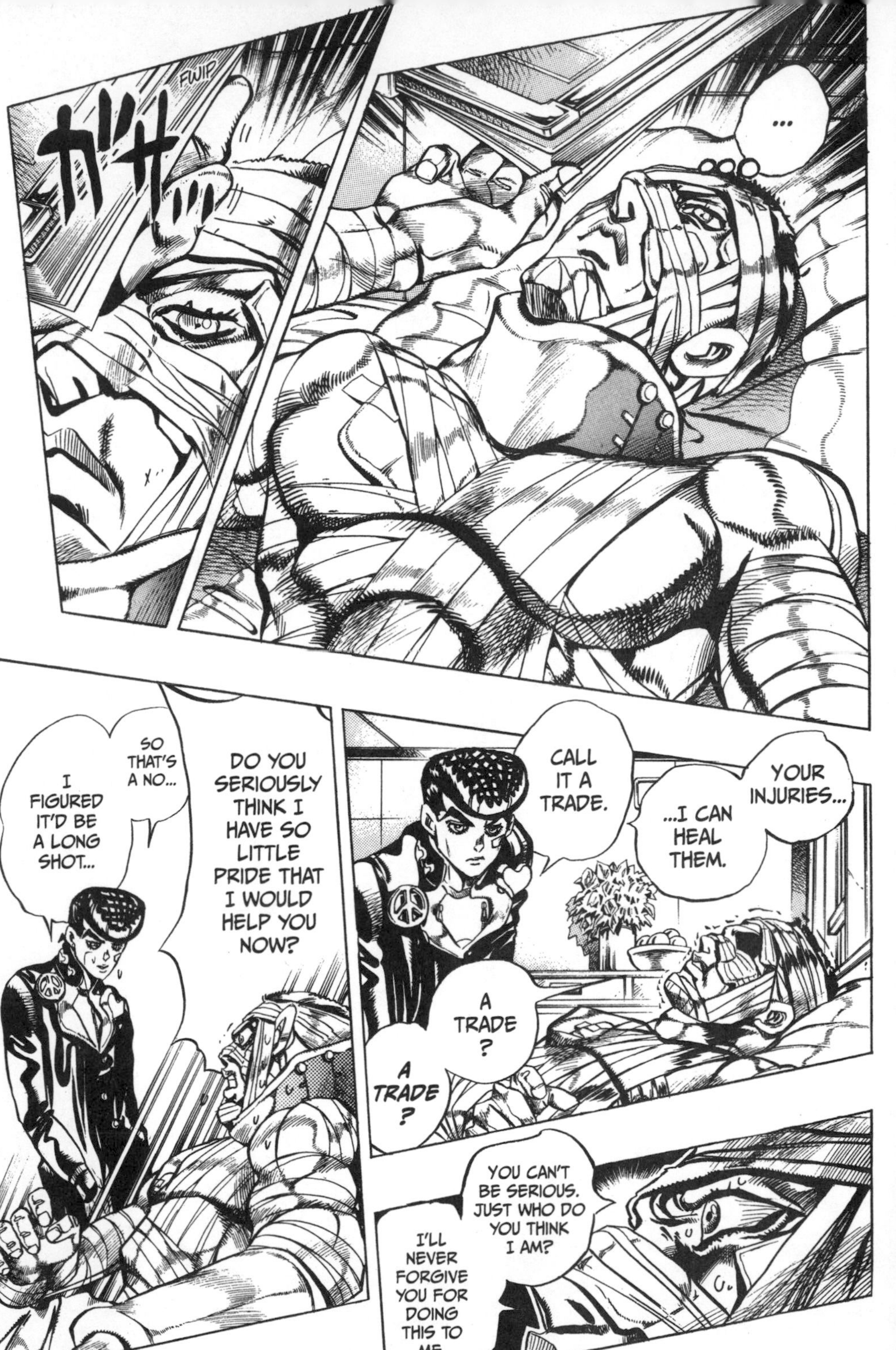
...
FWIP
ガサッ
YOUR INJURIES...
...I CAN HEAL THEM.
CALL IT A TRADE.
A TRADE?
A TRADE?
YOU CAN'T BE SERIOUS. JUST WHO DO YOU THINK I AM?
I'LL NEVER FORGIVE YOU FOR DOING THIS TO ME.
DO YOU SERIOUSLY THINK I HAVE SO LITTLE PRIDE THAT I WOULD HELP YOU NOW?
SO THAT'S A NO...
I FIGURED IT'D BE A LONG SHOT...

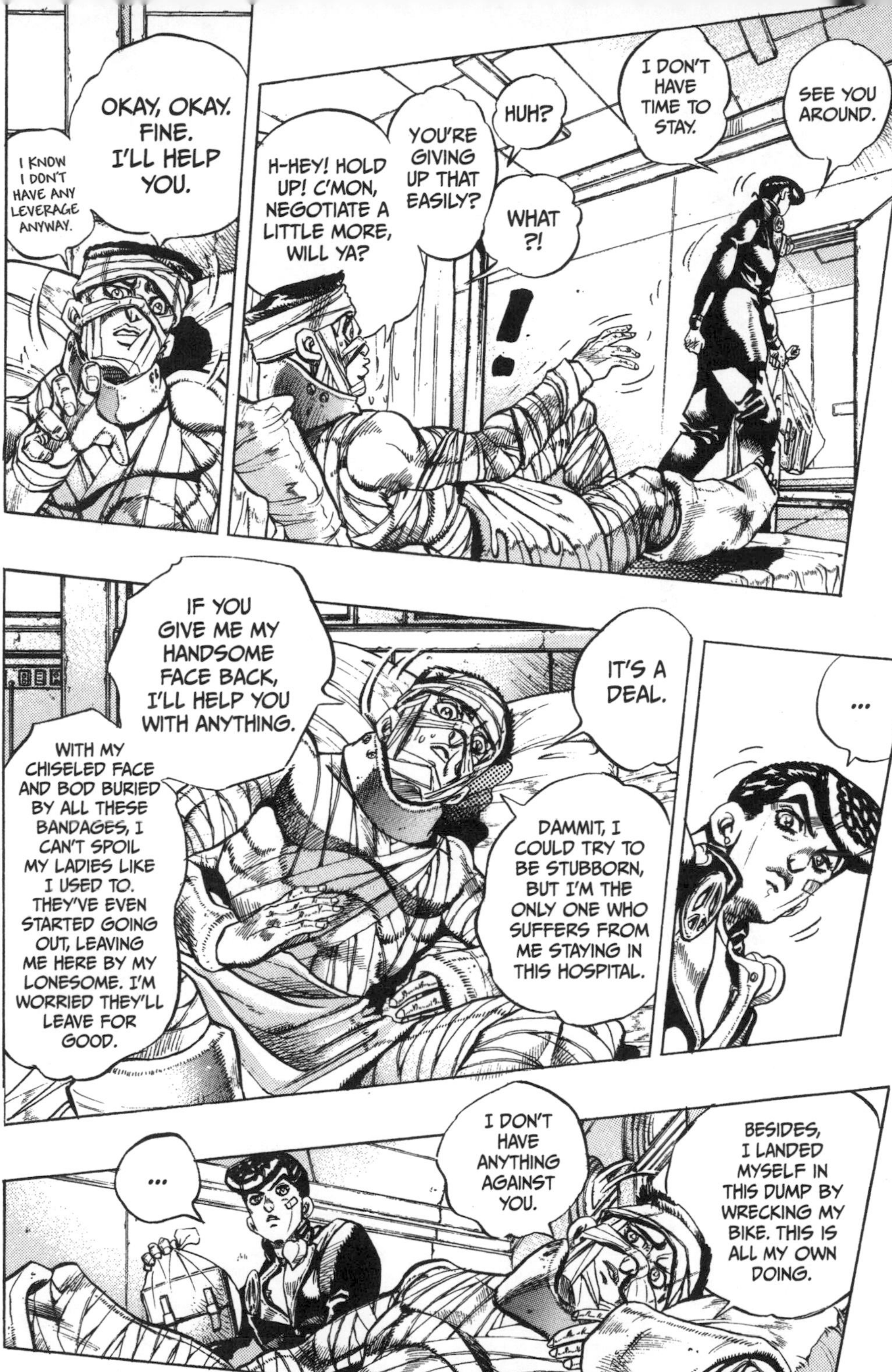
SEE YOU AROUND.
I DON'T HAVE TIME TO STAY.
HUH?
WHAT ?!
YOU'RE GIVING UP THAT EASILY?
H-HEY! HOLD UP! C'MON, NEGOTIATE A LITTLE MORE, WILL YA?
OKAY, OKAY. FINE. I'LL HELP YOU.
I KNOW I DON'T HAVE ANY LEVERAGE ANYWAY.
...
IT'S A DEAL.
IF YOU GIVE ME MY HANDSOME FACE BACK, I'LL HELP YOU WITH ANYTHING.
DAMMIT, I COULD TRY TO BE STUBBORN, BUT I'M THE ONLY ONE WHO SUFFERS FROM ME STAYING IN THIS HOSPITAL.
WITH MY CHISELED FACE AND BOD BURIED BY ALL THESE BANDAGES, I CAN'T SPOIL MY LADIES LIKE I USED TO. THEY'VE EVEN STARTED GOING OUT, LEAVING ME HERE BY MY LONESOME. I'M WORRIED THEY'LL LEAVE FOR GOOD.
BESIDES, I LANDED MYSELF IN THIS DUMP BY WRECKING MY BIKE. THIS IS ALL MY OWN DOING.
I DON'T HAVE ANYTHING AGAINST YOU.
...

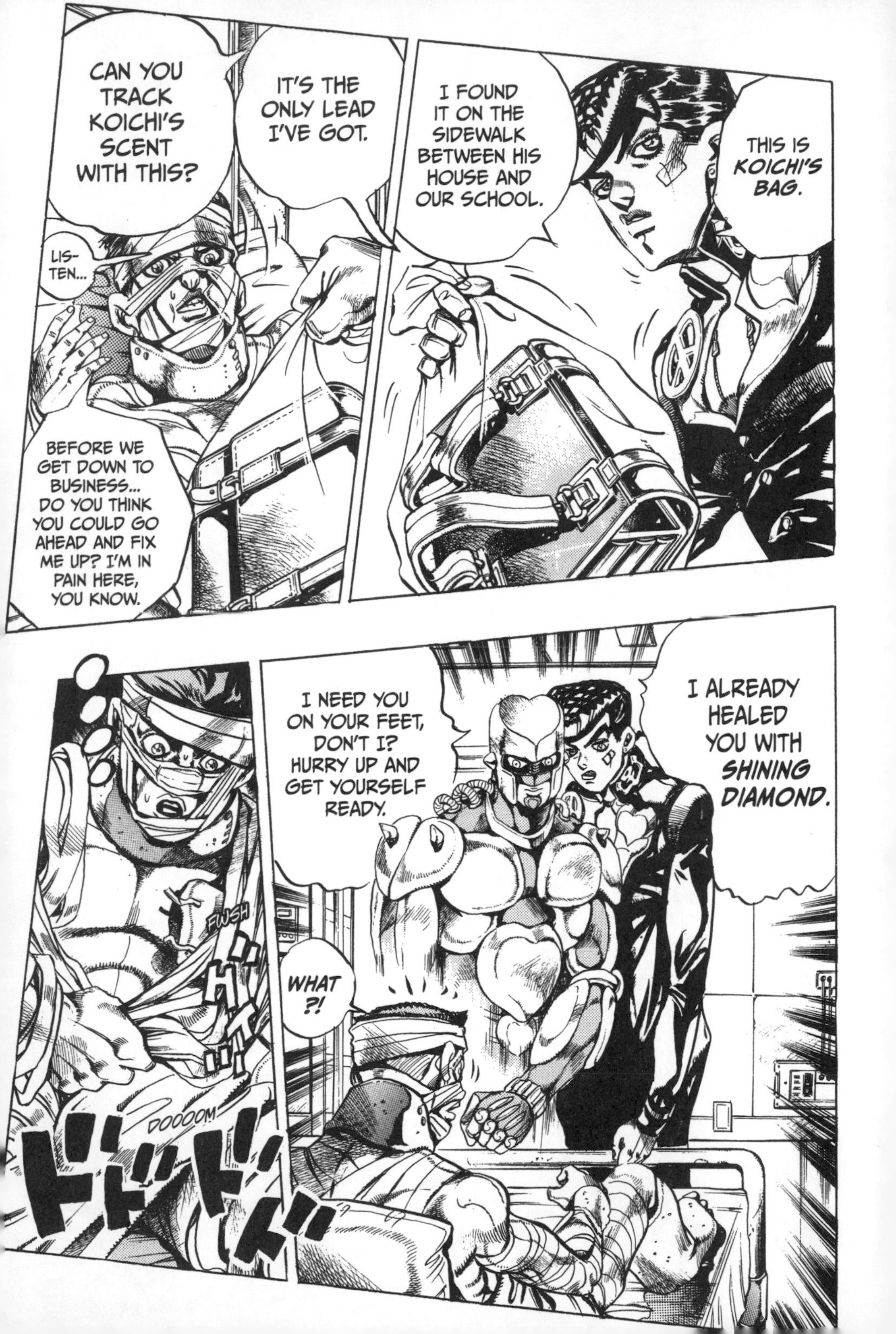
THIS IS KOICHI'S BAG.
I FOUND IT ON THE SIDEWALK BETWEEN HIS HOUSE AND OUR SCHOOL.
IT'S THE ONLY LEAD I'VE GOT.
CAN YOU TRACK KOICHI'S SCENT WITH THIS?
LIS-TEN...
BEFORE WE GET DOWN TO BUSINESS... DO YOU THINK YOU COULD GO AHEAD AND FIX ME UP? I'M IN PAIN HERE, YOU KNOW.
I ALREADY HEALED YOU WITH SHINING DIAMOND.
I NEED YOU ON YOUR FEET, DON'T I? HURRY UP AND GET YOURSELF READY.
WHAT ?!
FWSH
DOOOOM

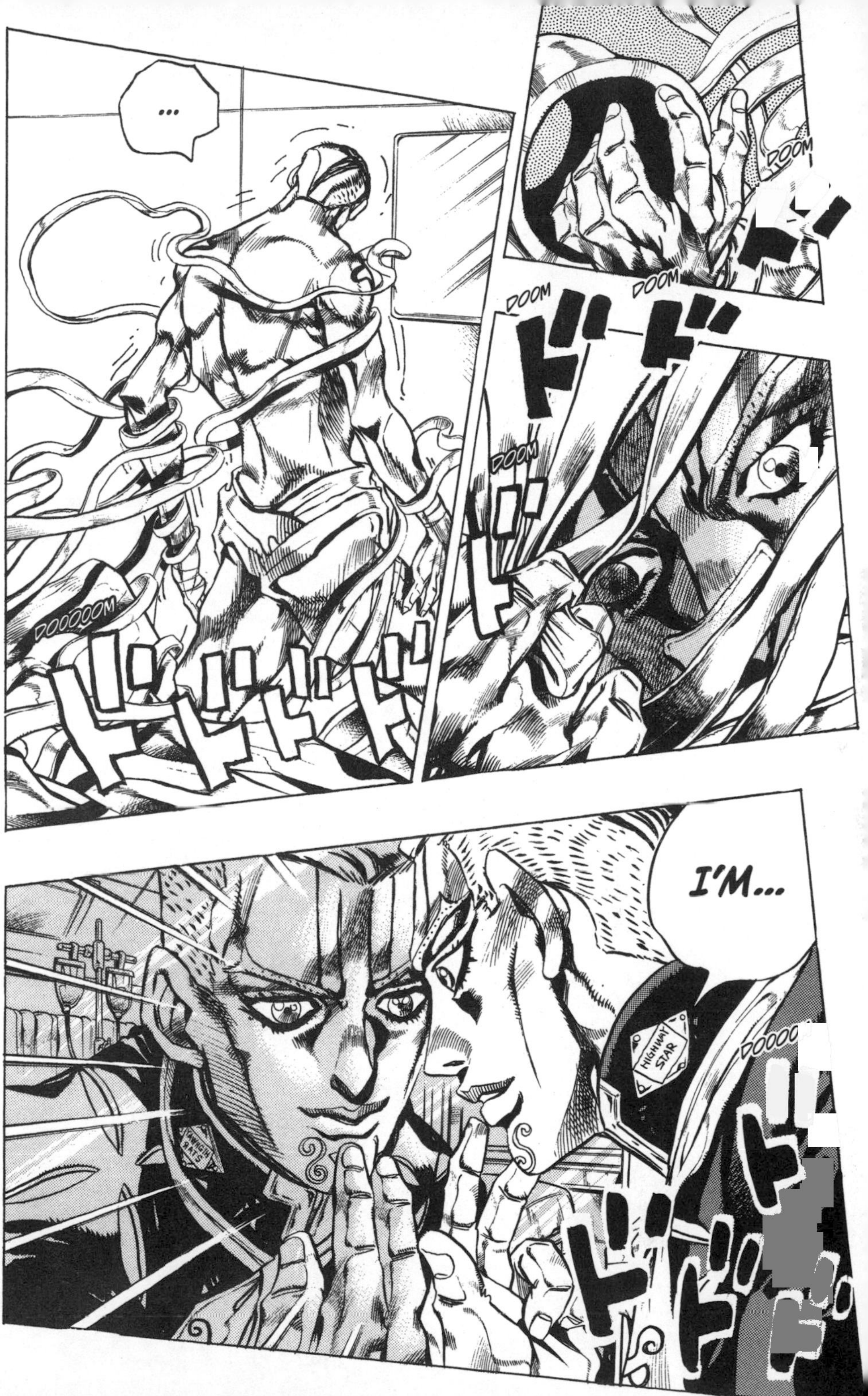
DOOM
DOOM
DOOM
DOOM
...
DOOOOOM
I'M...
HIGHWAY STAR
DOOOO

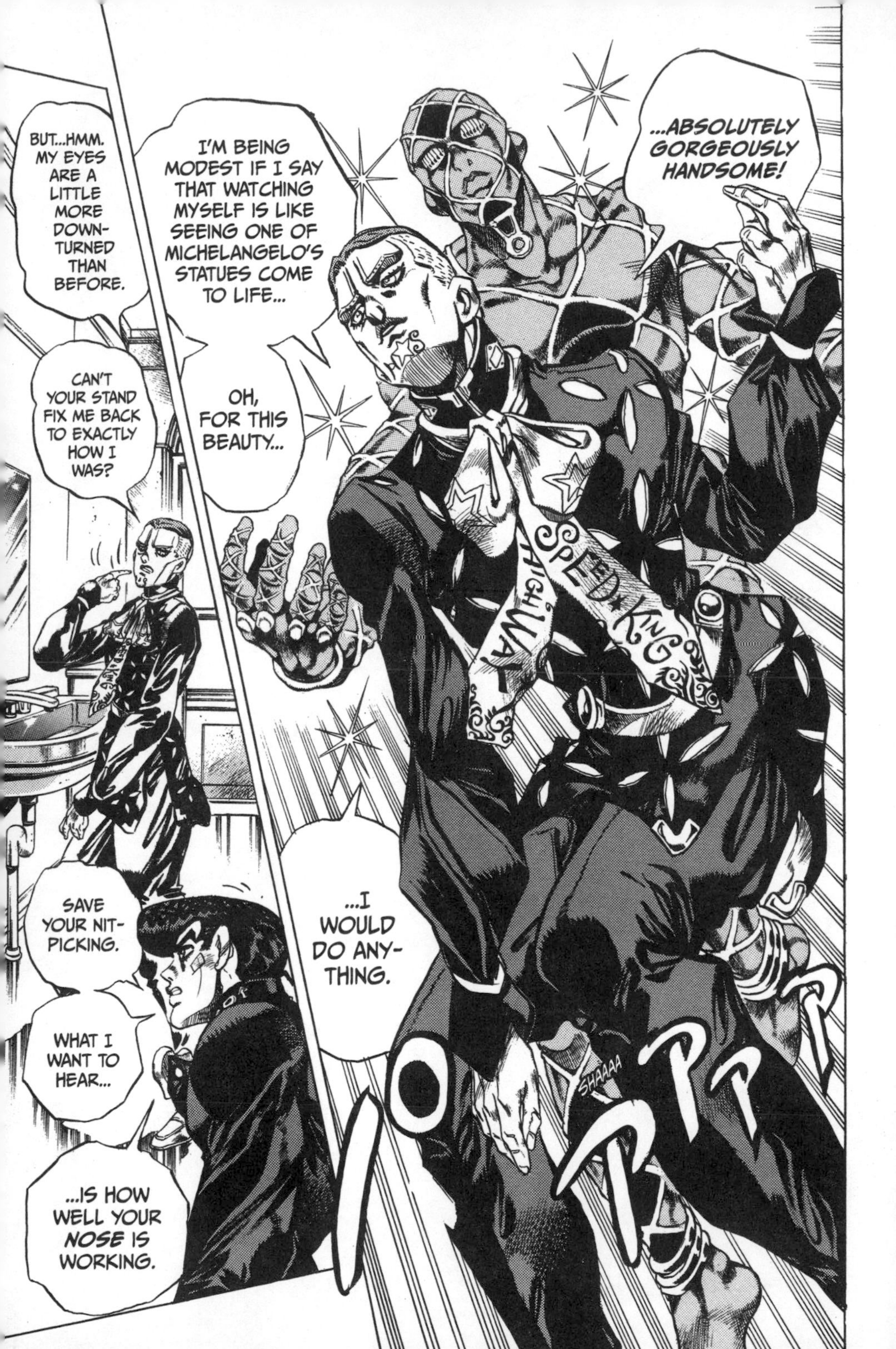
I'M BEING MODEST IF I SAY THAT WATCHING MYSELF IS LIKE SEEING ONE OF MICHELANGELO'S STATUES COME TO LIFE...
...ABSOLUTELY GORGEOUSLY HANDSOME!
SPEED KING
HIGHWAY
OH, FOR THIS BEAUTY...
...I WOULD DO ANY-THING.
SHAAAA
BUT...HMM. MY EYES ARE A LITTLE MORE DOWN-TURNED THAN BEFORE.
CAN'T YOUR STAND FIX ME BACK TO EXACTLY HOW I WAS?
SAVE YOUR NIT-PICKING.
WHAT I WANT TO HEAR...
...IS HOW WELL YOUR *NOSE* IS WORKING.

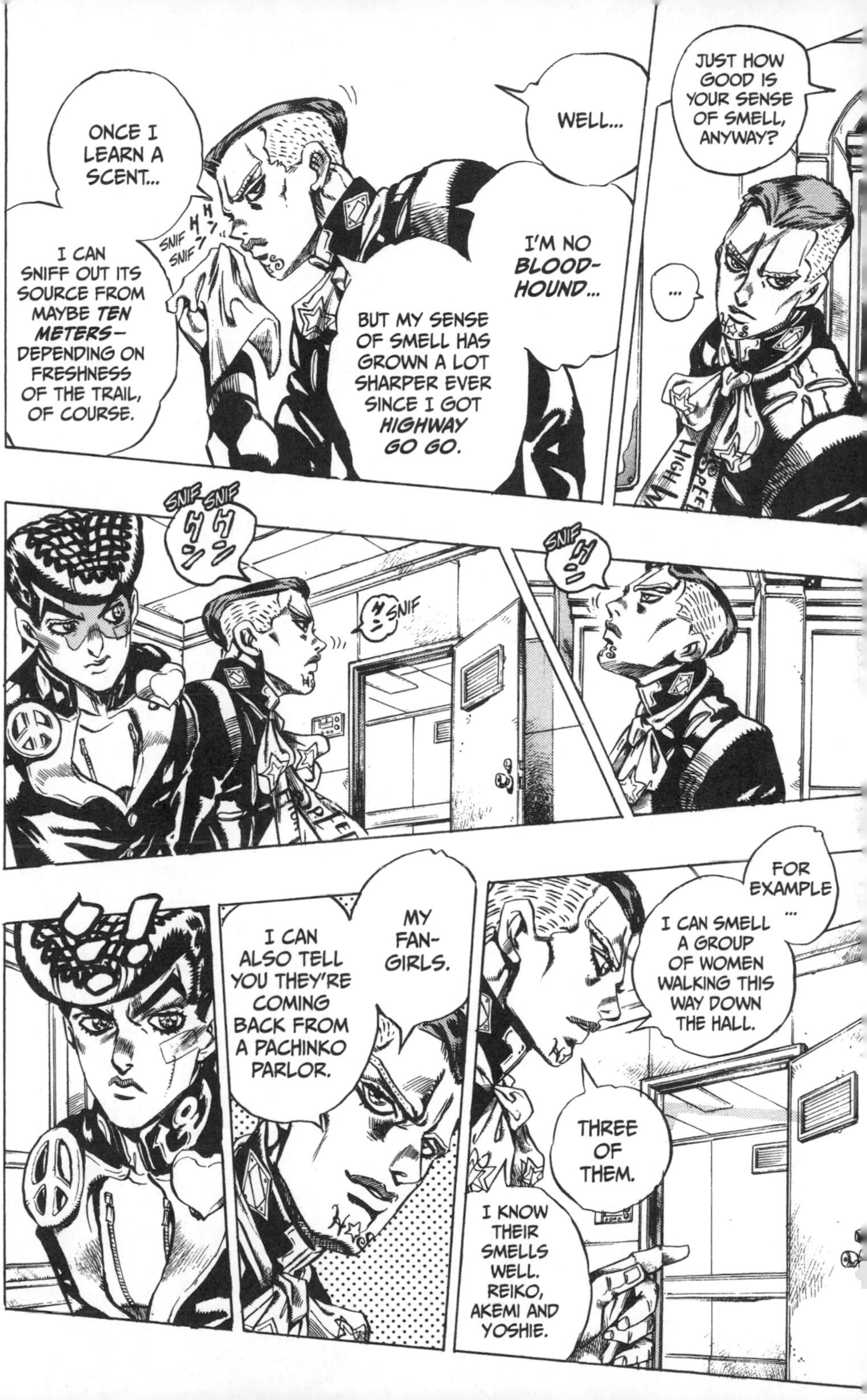
JUST HOW GOOD IS YOUR SENSE OF SMELL, ANYWAY?
...
WELL...
I'M NO *BLOOD-HOUND*...
BUT MY SENSE OF SMELL HAS GROWN A LOT SHARPER EVER SINCE I GOT *HIGHWAY GO GO*.
ONCE I LEARN A SCENT...
SNIF SNIF
I CAN SNIFF OUT ITS SOURCE FROM MAYBE *TEN METERS*— DEPENDING ON FRESHNESS OF THE TRAIL, OF COURSE.
SNIF
SNIF SNIF
SNIF
FOR EXAMPLE...
I CAN SMELL A GROUP OF WOMEN WALKING THIS WAY DOWN THE HALL.
THREE OF THEM.
I KNOW THEIR SMELLS WELL. REIKO, AKEMI AND YOSHIE.
MY FAN-GIRLS.
I CAN ALSO TELL YOU THEY'RE COMING BACK FROM A PACHINKO PARLOR.

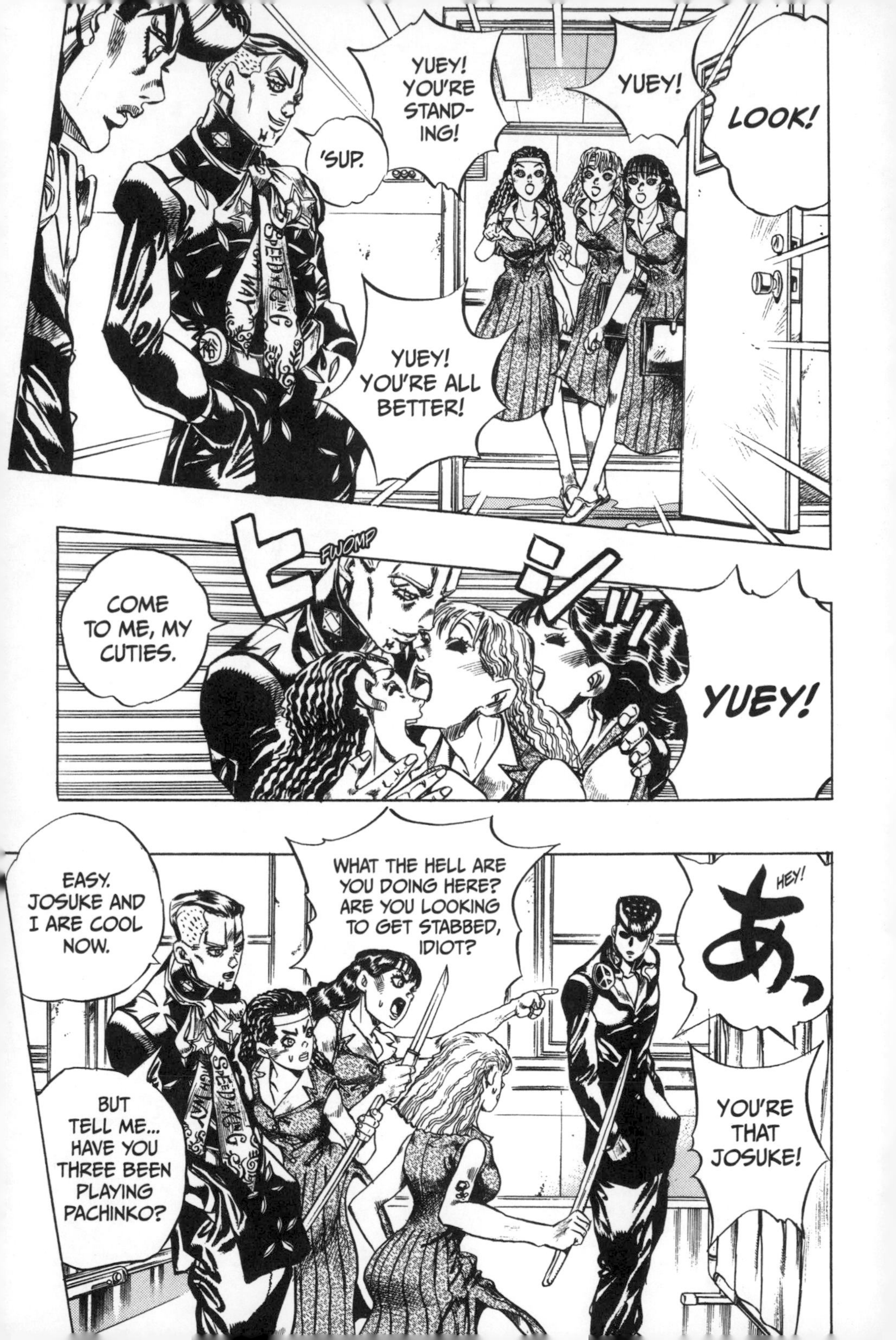
LOOK!
YUEY!
YUEY! YOU'RE STAND-ING!
'SUP.
YUEY! YOU'RE ALL BETTER!
YUEY!
FWOMP
COME TO ME, MY CUTIES.
HEY!
YOU'RE THAT JOSUKE!
WHAT THE HELL ARE YOU DOING HERE? ARE YOU LOOKING TO GET STABBED, IDIOT?
EASY. JOSUKE AND I ARE COOL NOW.
BUT TELL ME... HAVE YOU THREE BEEN PLAYING PACHINKO?

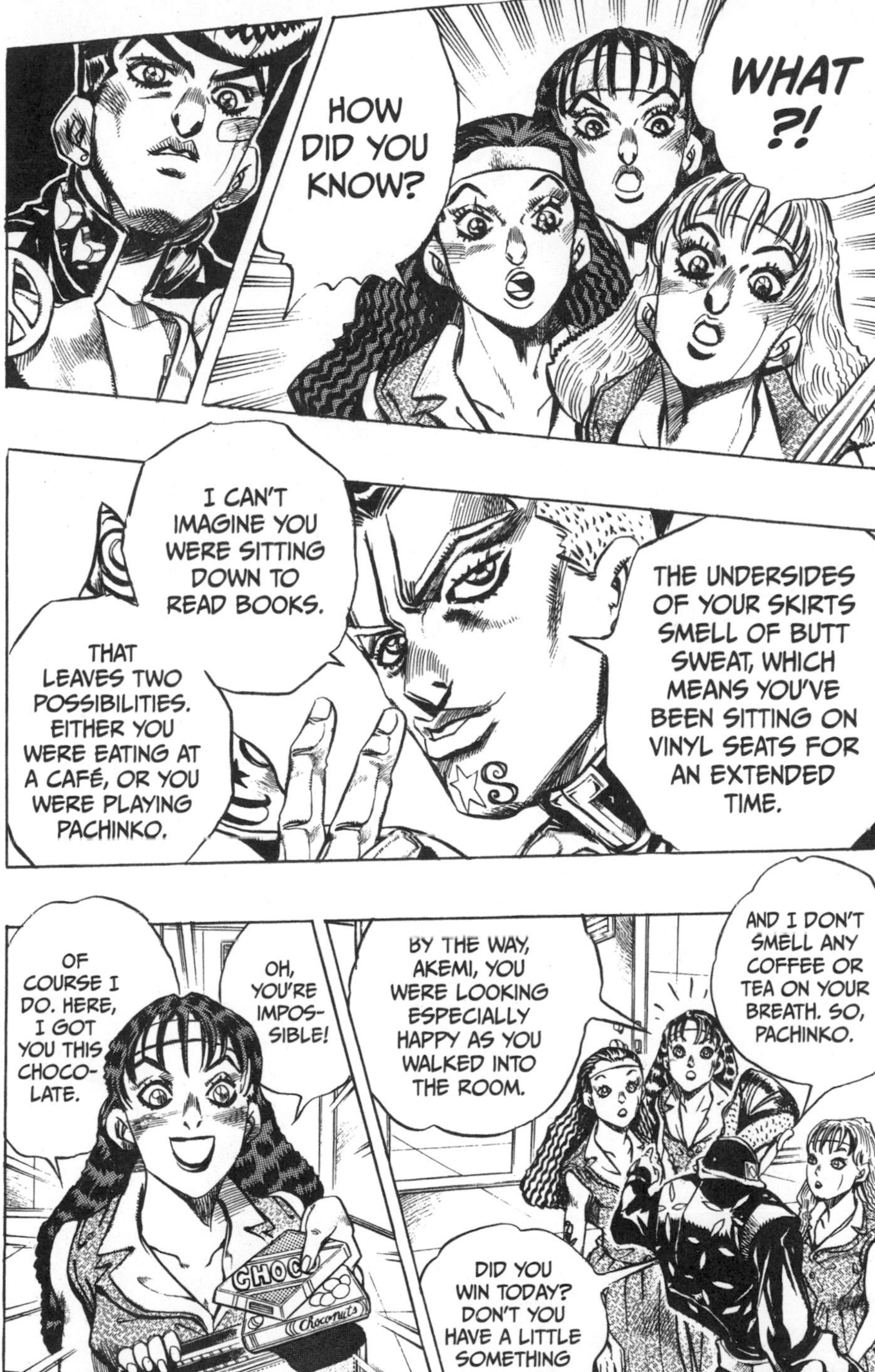
WHAT ?!
HOW DID YOU KNOW?
THE UNDERSIDES OF YOUR SKIRTS SMELL OF BUTT SWEAT, WHICH MEANS YOU'VE BEEN SITTING ON VINYL SEATS FOR AN EXTENDED TIME.
I CAN'T IMAGINE YOU WERE SITTING DOWN TO READ BOOKS.
THAT LEAVES TWO POSSIBILITIES. EITHER YOU WERE EATING AT A CAFÉ, OR YOU WERE PLAYING PACHINKO.
AND I DON'T SMELL ANY COFFEE OR TEA ON YOUR BREATH. SO, PACHINKO.
BY THE WAY, AKEMI, YOU WERE LOOKING ESPECIALLY HAPPY AS YOU WALKED INTO THE ROOM.
DID YOU WIN TODAY? DON'T YOU HAVE A LITTLE SOMETHING FOR ME?
OH, YOU'RE IMPOS-SIBLE!
OF COURSE I DO. HERE, I GOT YOU THIS CHOCO-LATE.
CHOC
Choconuts

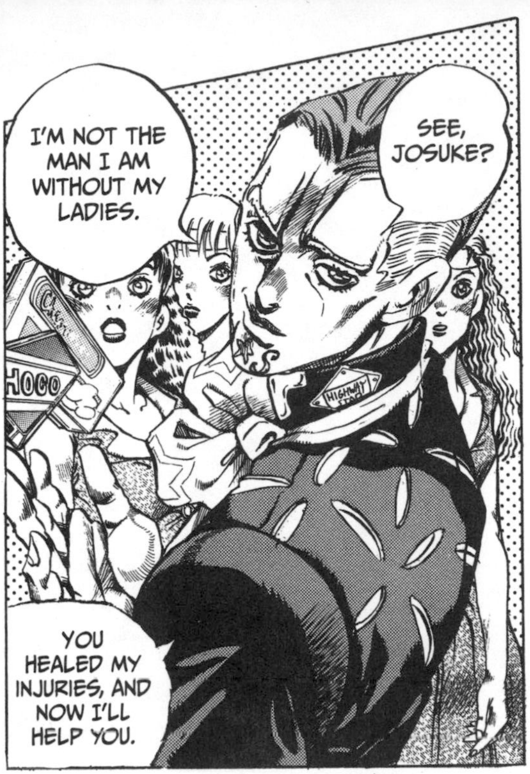
SEE, JOSUKE?
I'M NOT THE MAN I AM WITHOUT MY LADIES.
YOU HEALED MY INJURIES, AND NOW I'LL HELP YOU.
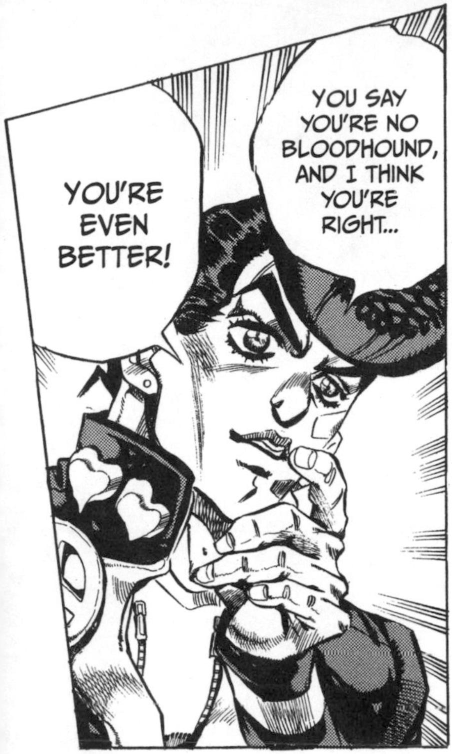
YOU SAY YOU'RE NO BLOODHOUND, AND I THINK YOU'RE RIGHT...
YOU'RE EVEN BETTER!
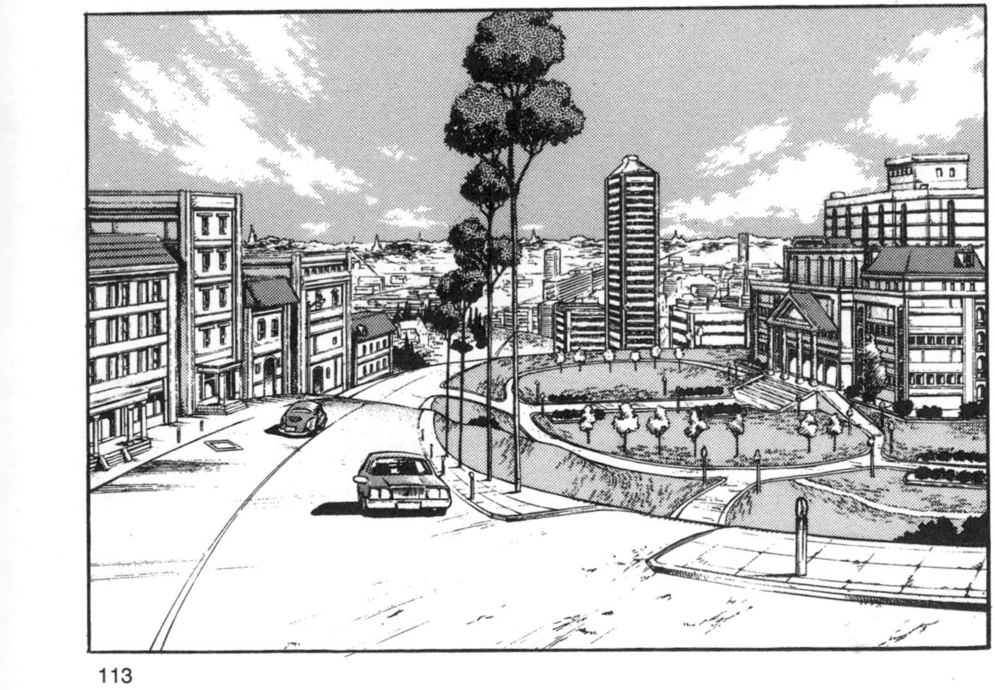

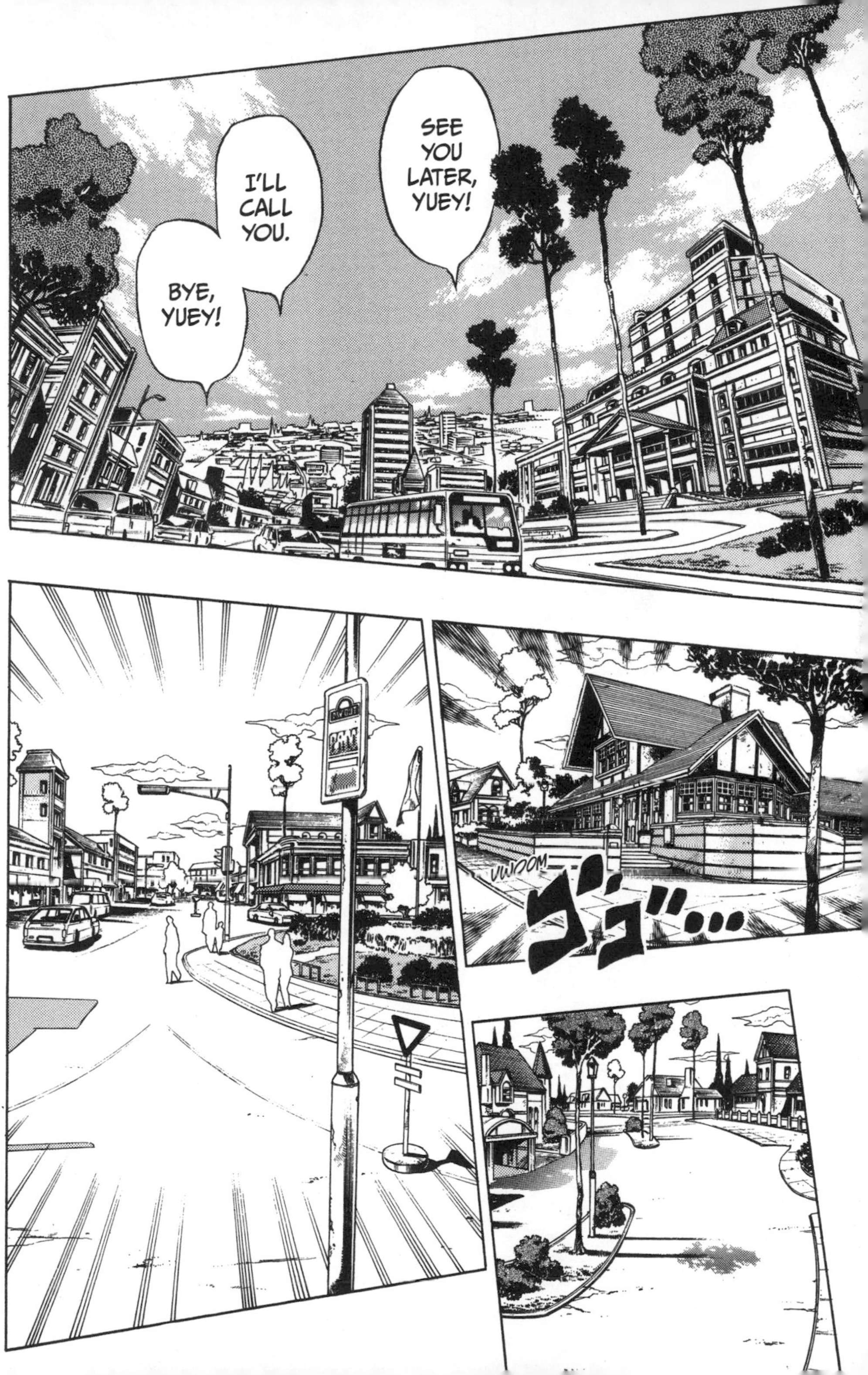
SEE YOU LATER, YUEY!
I'LL CALL YOU.
BYE, YUEY!
VWOOM
ゴゴ…

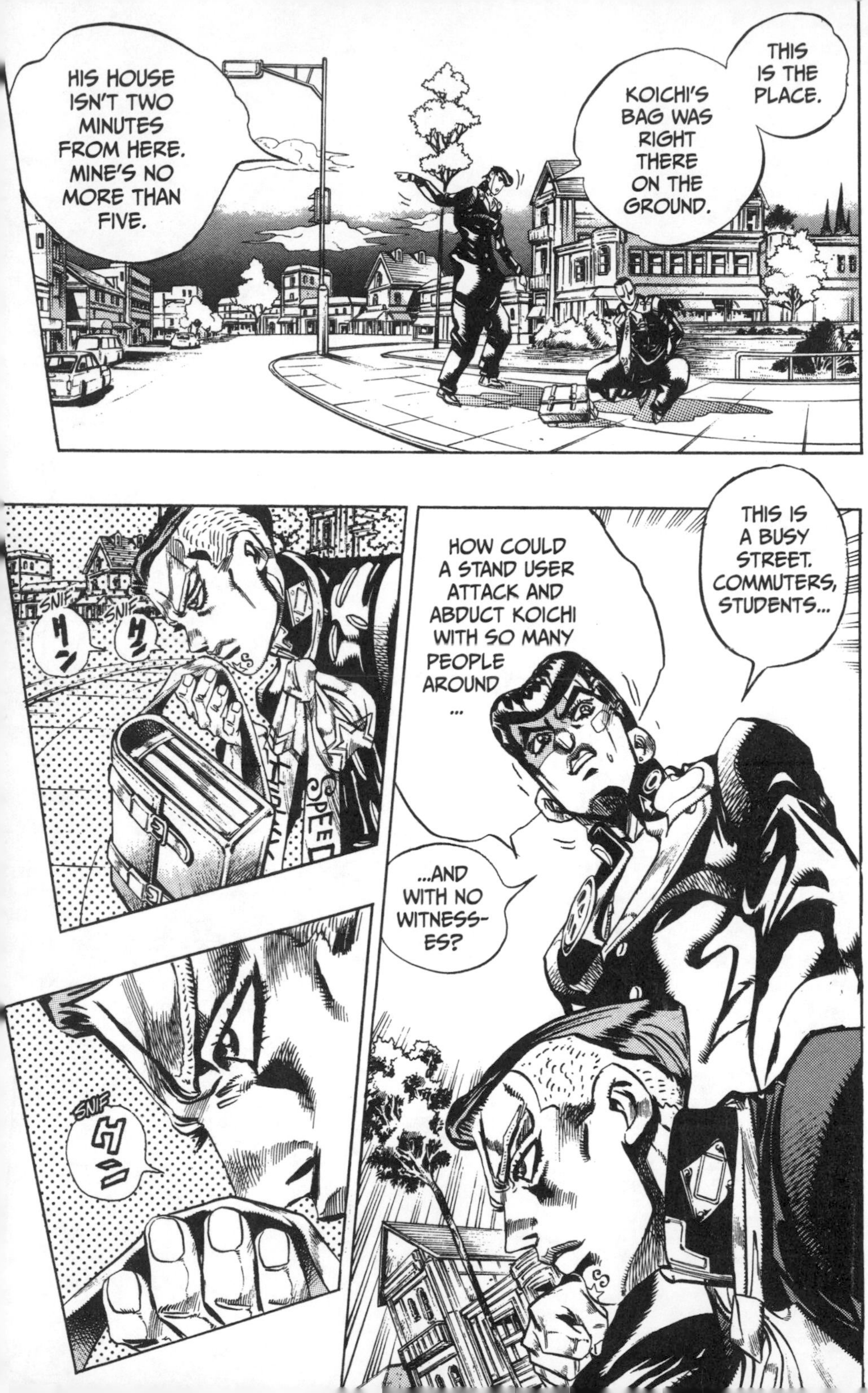
THIS IS THE PLACE.
KOICHI'S BAG WAS RIGHT THERE ON THE GROUND.
HIS HOUSE ISN'T TWO MINUTES FROM HERE. MINE'S NO MORE THAN FIVE.
THIS IS A BUSY STREET. COMMUTERS, STUDENTS...
HOW COULD A STAND USER ATTACK AND ABDUCT KOICHI WITH SO MANY PEOPLE AROUND ...
...AND WITH NO WITNESS-ES?
SNIF
SNIF
SNIF

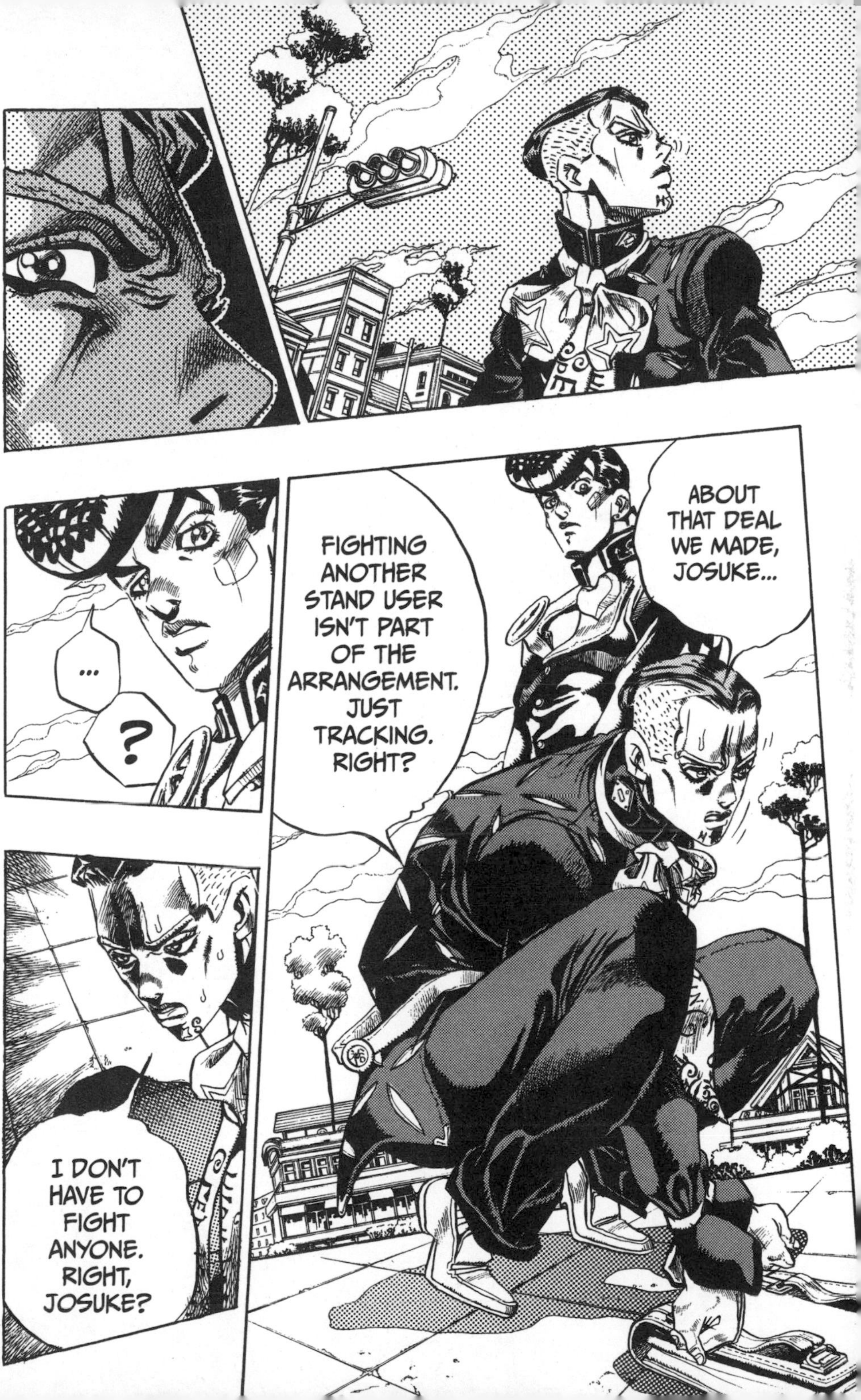
ABOUT THAT DEAL WE MADE, JOSUKE...
FIGHTING ANOTHER STAND USER ISN'T PART OF THE ARRANGEMENT. JUST TRACKING. RIGHT?
...
?
I DON'T HAVE TO FIGHT ANYONE. RIGHT, JOSUKE?

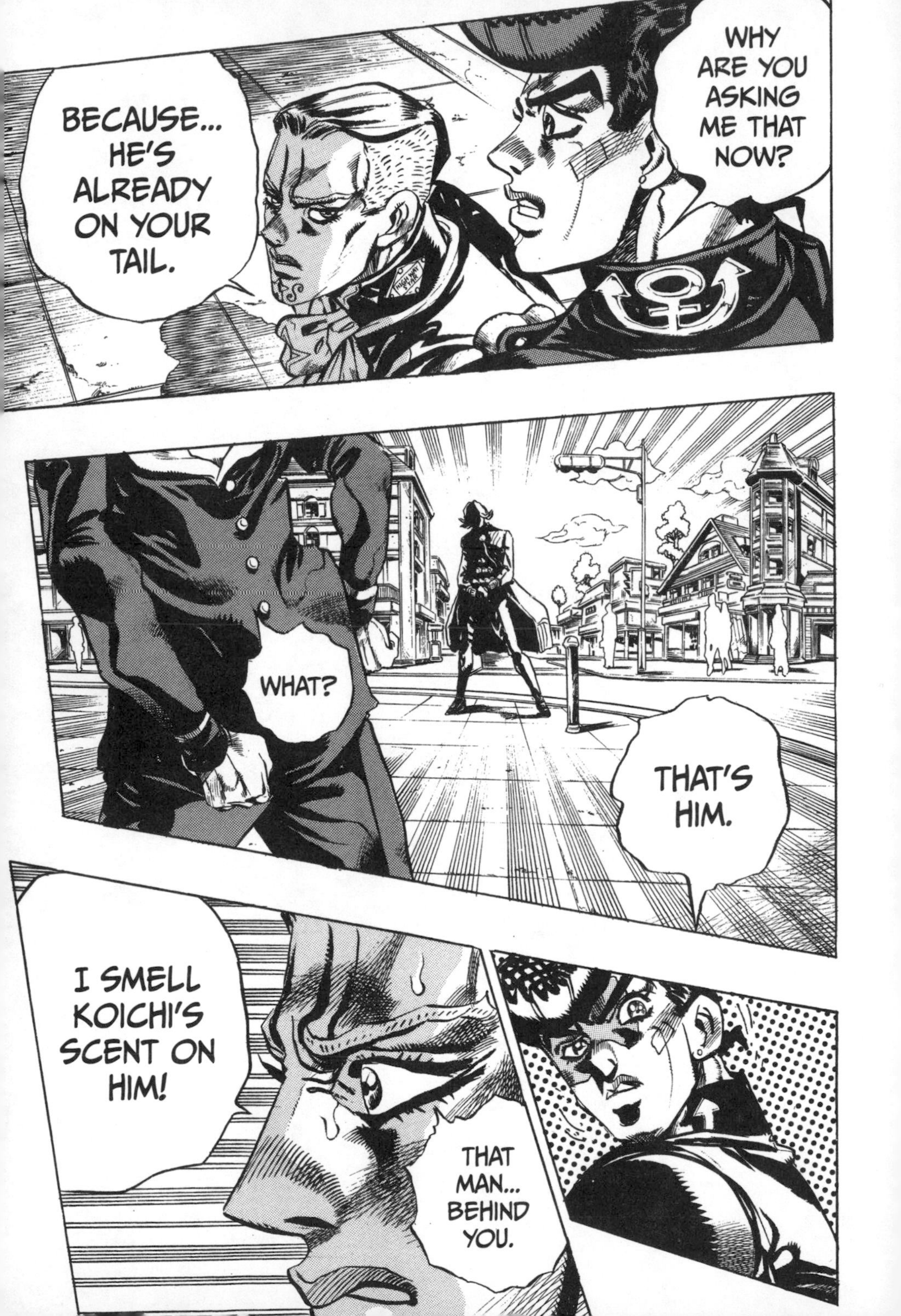
WHY ARE YOU ASKING ME THAT NOW?
BECAUSE... HE'S ALREADY ON YOUR TAIL.
WHAT?
THAT'S HIM.
I SMELL KOICHI'S SCENT ON HIM!
THAT MAN... BEHIND YOU.

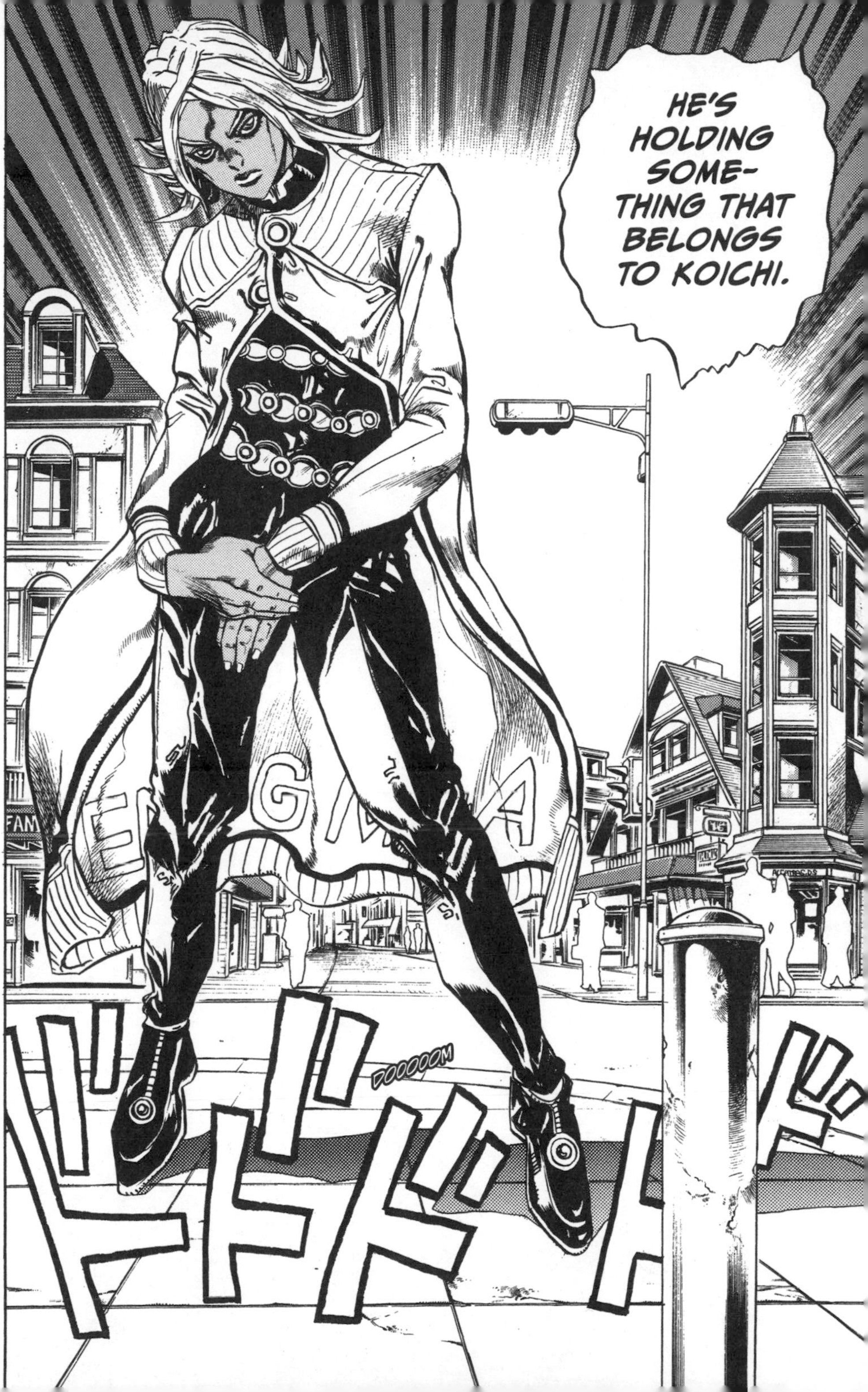
HE'S HOLDING SOME-THING THAT BELONGS TO KOICHI.
DOOOOOM

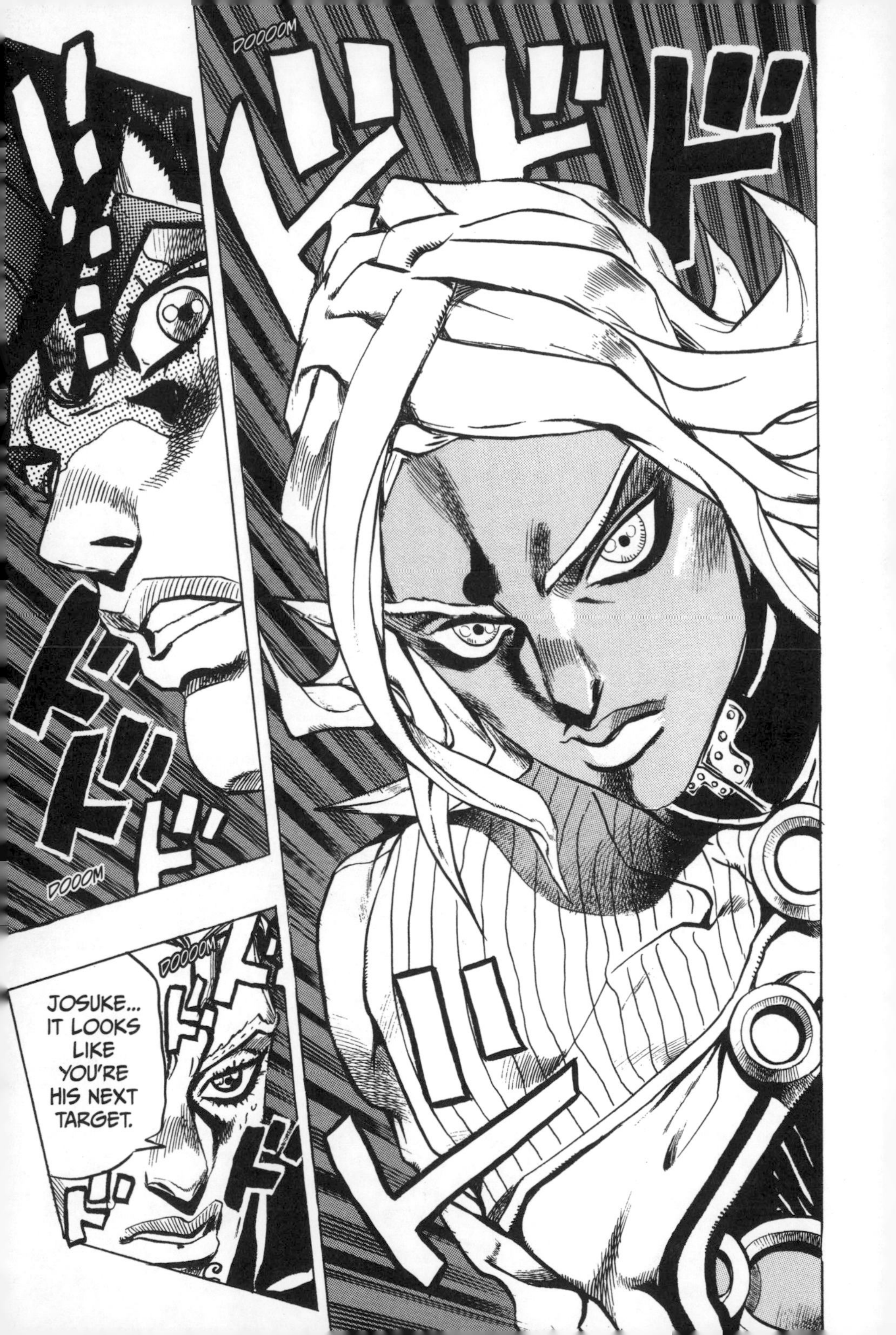
DOOOOM
DOOOM
DOOOOM
JOSUKE... IT LOOKS LIKE YOU'RE HIS NEXT TARGET.

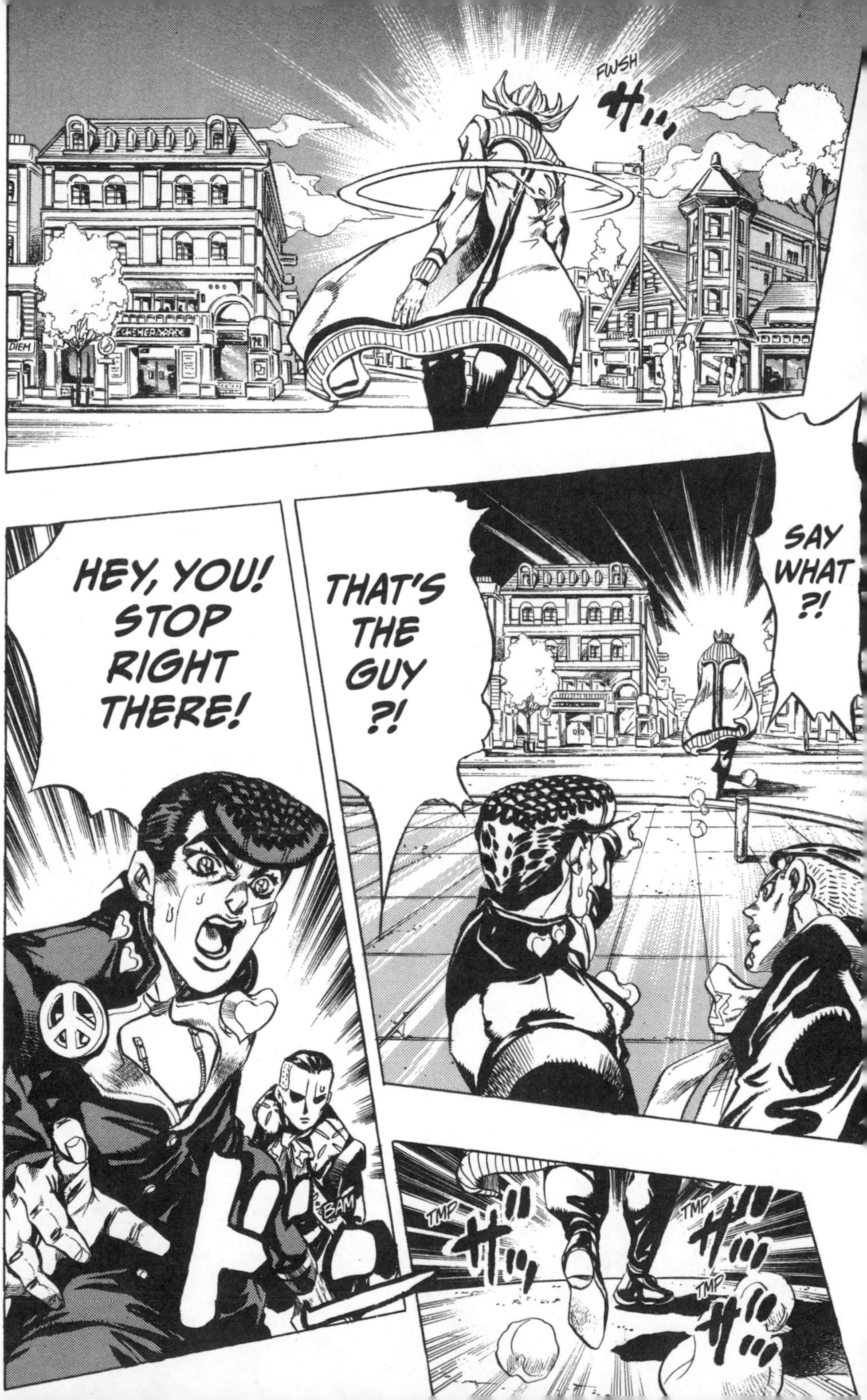
FWSH
SAY WHAT ?!
THAT'S THE GUY ?!
TMP
TMP
TMP
HEY, YOU! STOP RIGHT THERE!
BAM

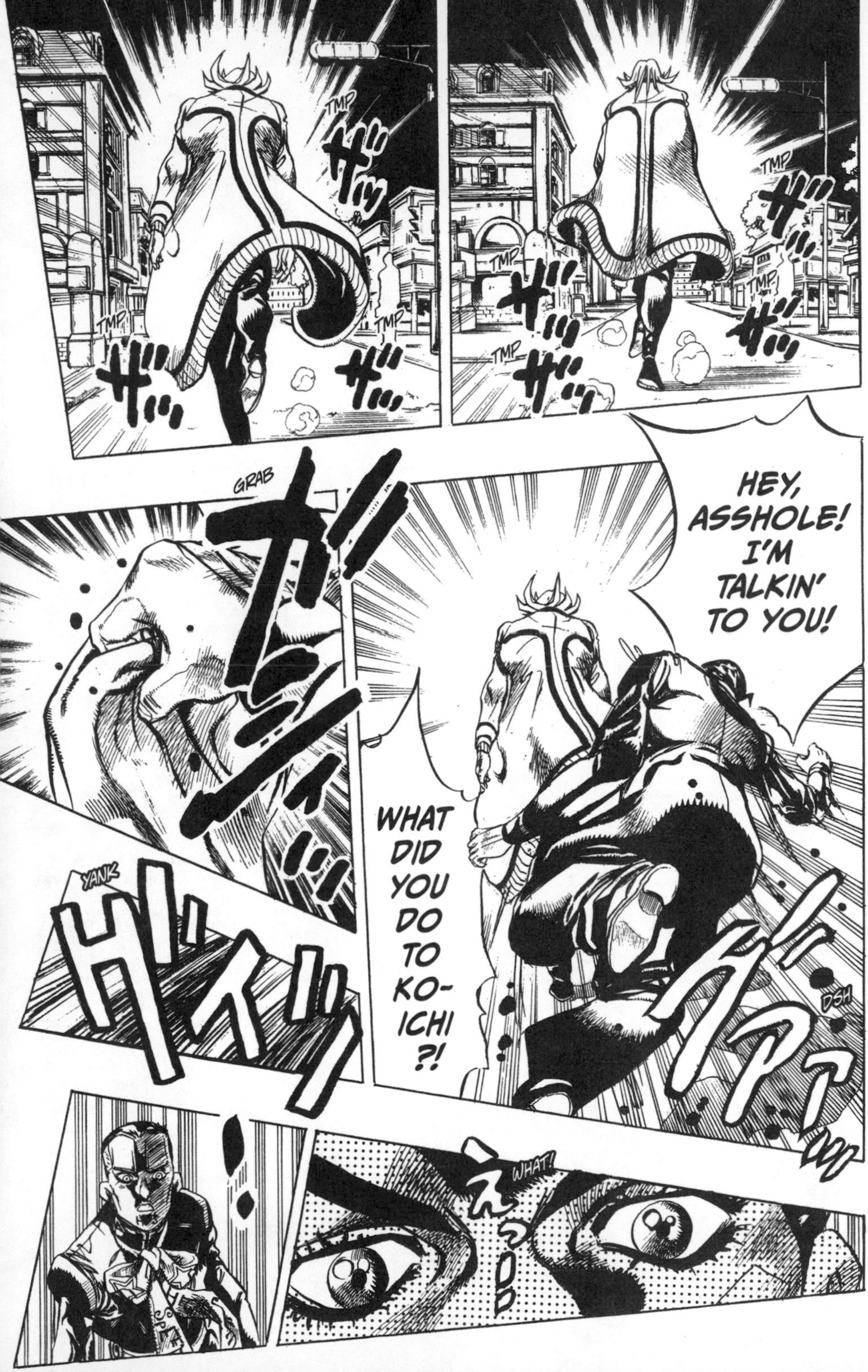
TMP
TMP
TMP
TMP
TMP
TMP
TMP
HEY, ASSHOLE! I'M TALKIN' TO YOU!
WHAT DID YOU DO TO KO-ICHI?!
DSH
GRAB
YANK
WHAT!

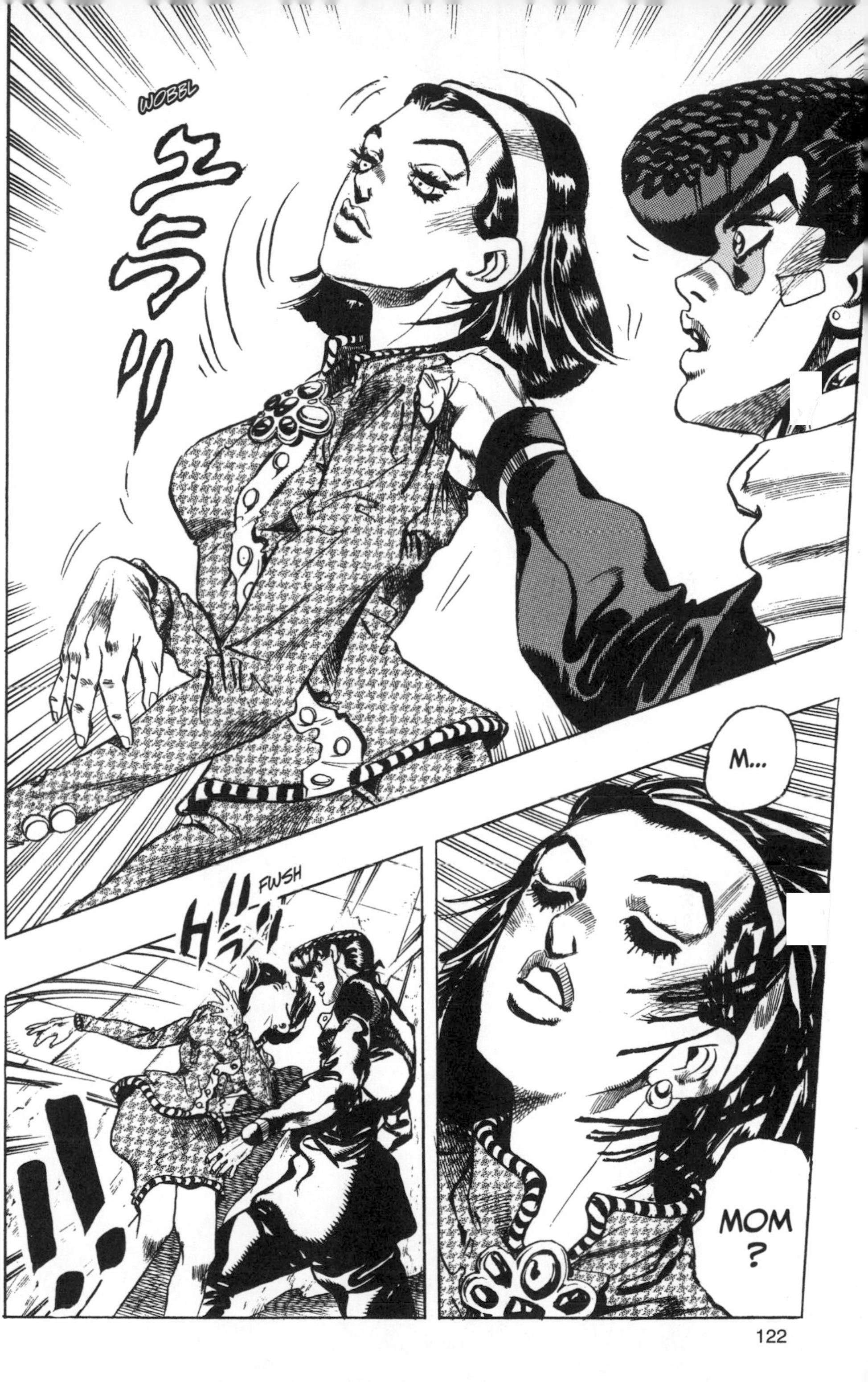
WOBBL
ユラリ
M...
MOM
?
FWSH
!!

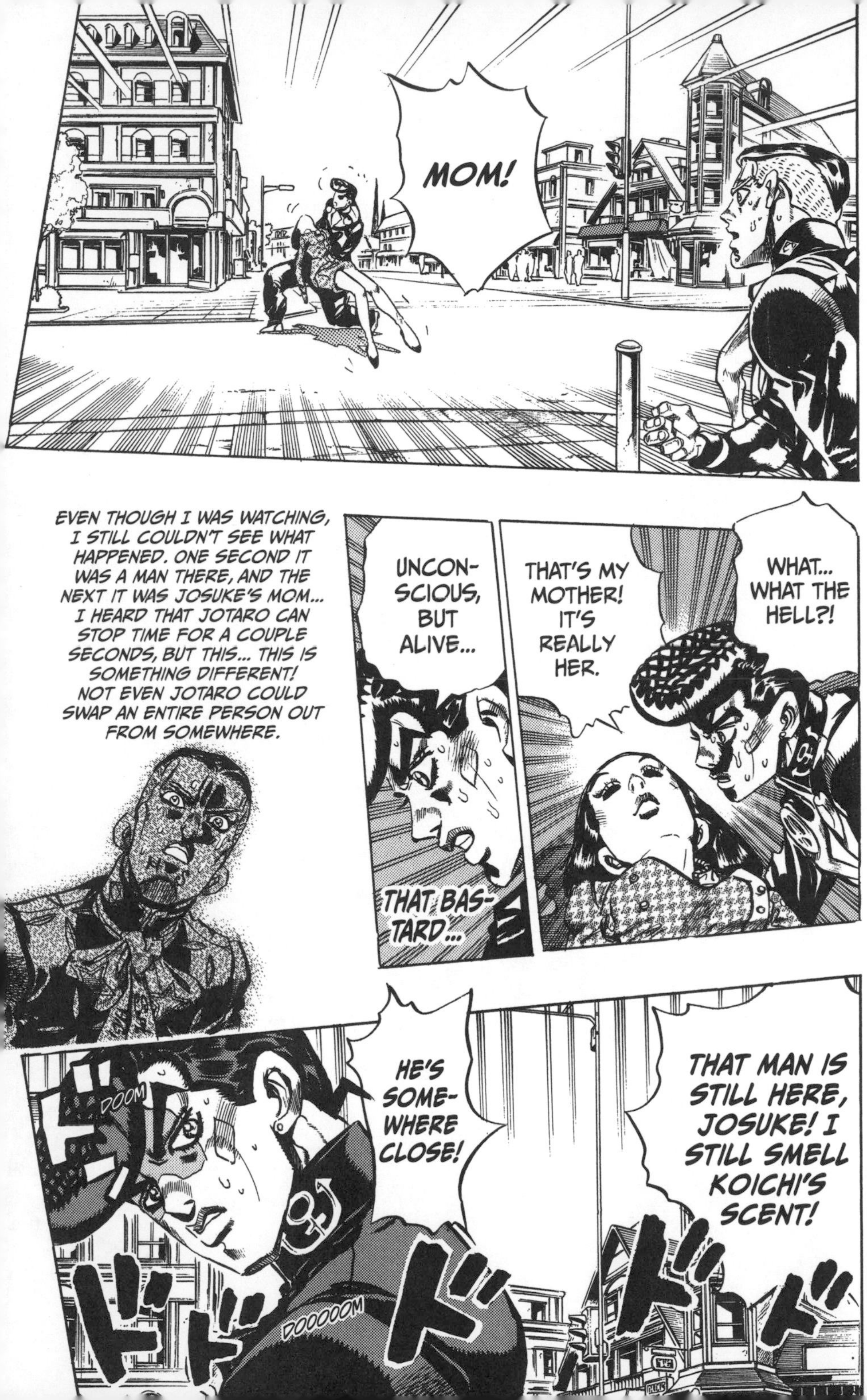
MOM!
WHAT... WHAT THE HELL?!
THAT'S MY MOTHER! IT'S REALLY HER.
UNCON-SCIOUS, BUT ALIVE...
THAT BAS-TARD...
EVEN THOUGH I WAS WATCHING, I STILL COULDN'T SEE WHAT HAPPENED. ONE SECOND IT WAS A MAN THERE, AND THE NEXT IT WAS JOSUKE'S MOM... I HEARD THAT JOTARO CAN STOP TIME FOR A COUPLE SECONDS, BUT THIS... THIS IS SOMETHING DIFFERENT! NOT EVEN JOTARO COULD SWAP AN ENTIRE PERSON OUT FROM SOMEWHERE.
THAT MAN IS STILL HERE, JOSUKE! I STILL SMELL KOICHI'S SCENT!
HE'S SOME-WHERE CLOSE!
DOOM
DOOOOOM

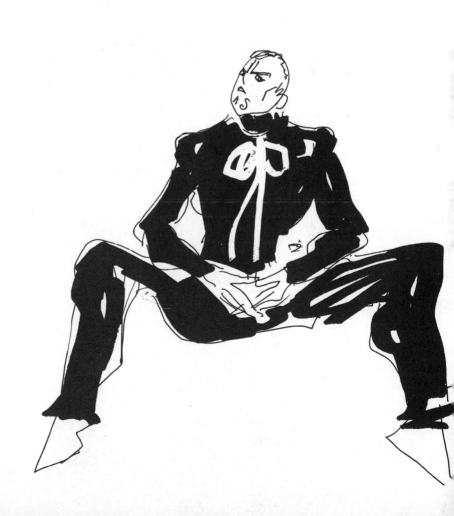

CHAPTER 140
MISTERIOSO, PART 2

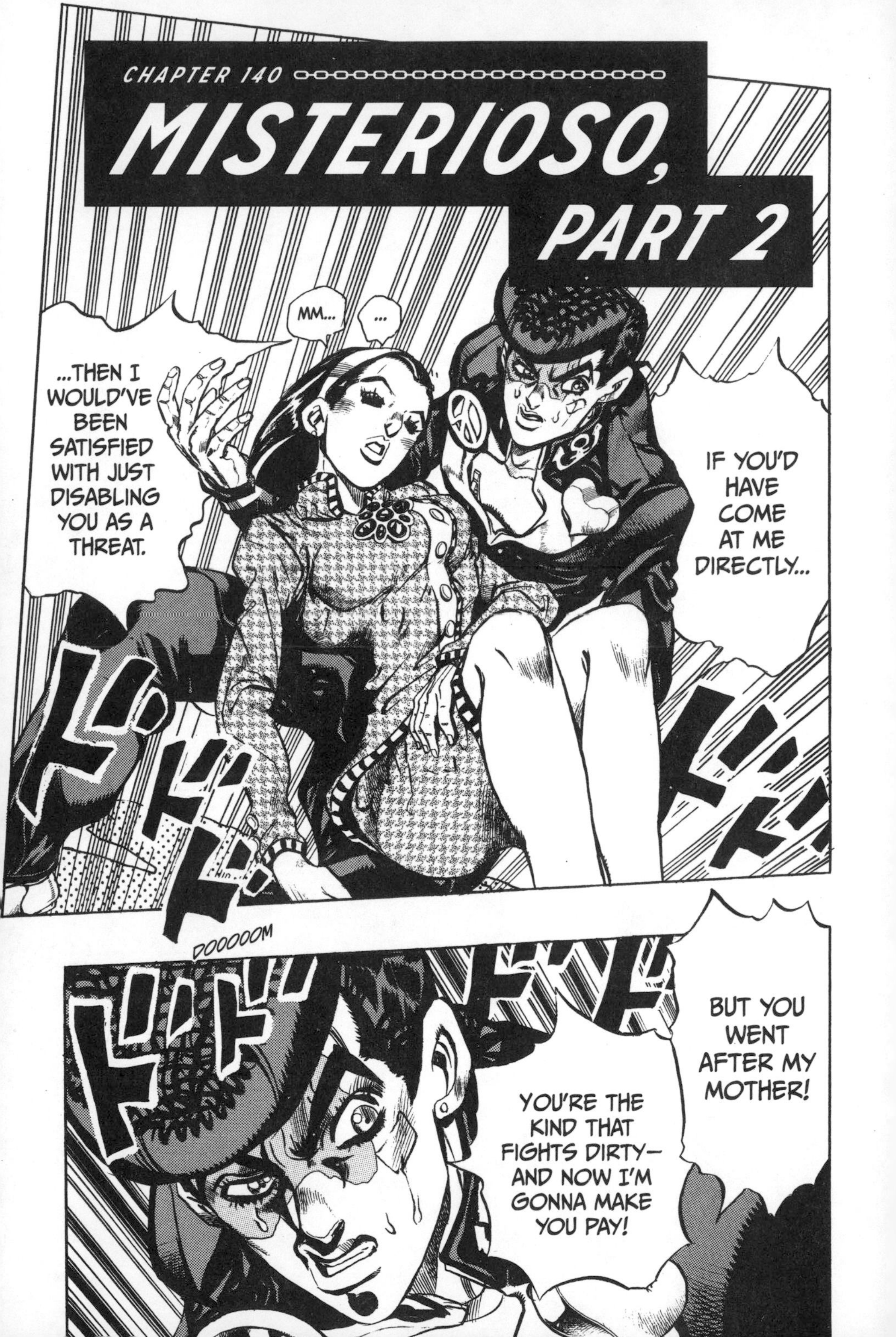
IF YOU'D HAVE COME AT ME DIRECTLY...
...
MM...
...THEN I WOULD'VE BEEN SATISFIED WITH JUST DISABLING YOU AS A THREAT.
DOOOOOM
BUT YOU WENT AFTER MY MOTHER!
YOU'RE THE KIND THAT FIGHTS DIRTY—AND NOW I'M GONNA MAKE YOU PAY!

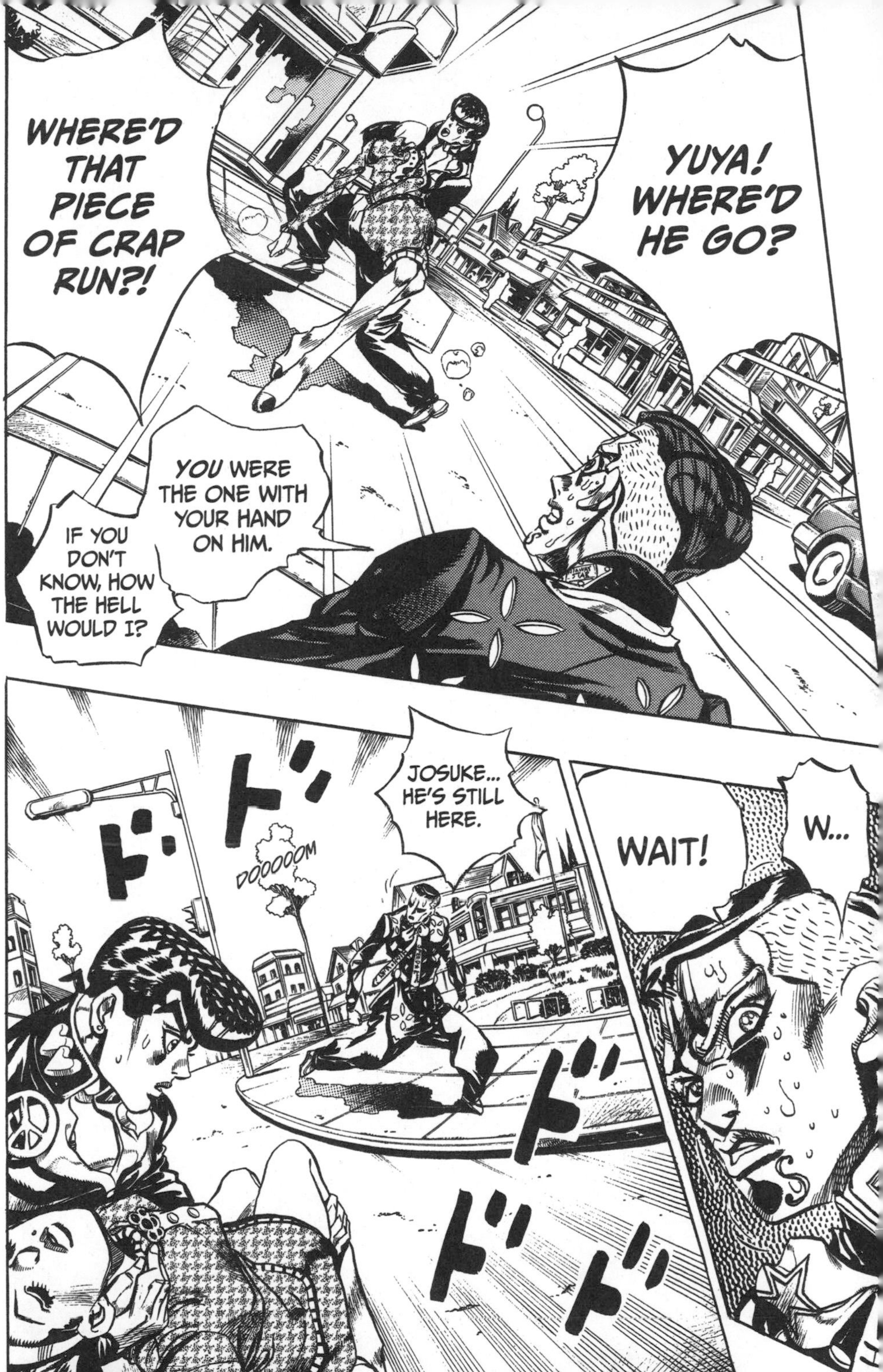
YUYA! WHERE'D HE GO?
WHERE'D THAT PIECE OF CRAP RUN?!
YOU WERE THE ONE WITH YOUR HAND ON HIM.
IF YOU DON'T KNOW, HOW THE HELL WOULD I?
W...
WAIT!
JOSUKE... HE'S STILL HERE.
DOOOOOOM
ドドドドド

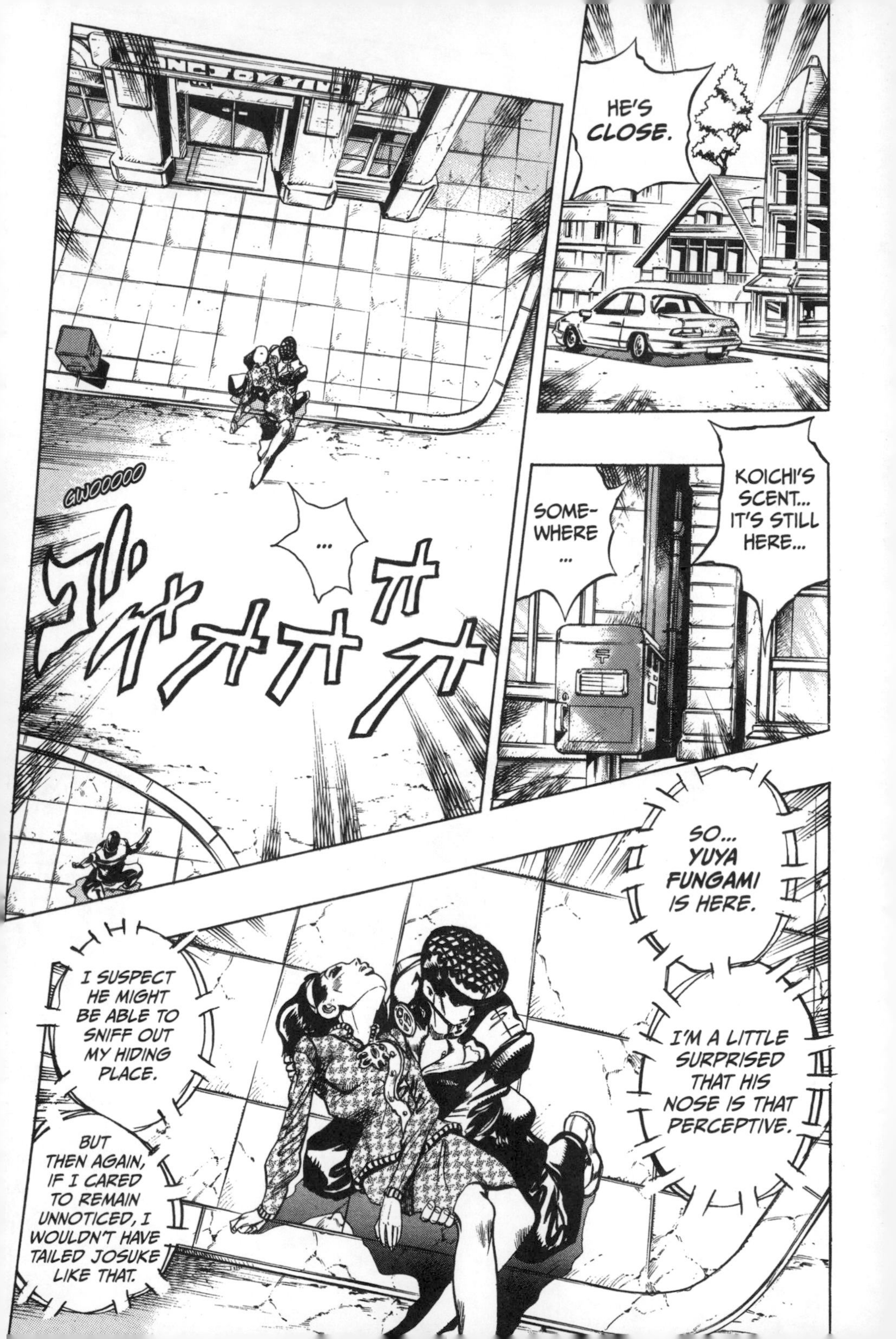
HE'S CLOSE.
KOICHI'S SCENT... IT'S STILL HERE...
SOME-WHERE ...
GWOOOOO
...
SO... YUYA FUNGAMI IS HERE.
I'M A LITTLE SURPRISED THAT HIS NOSE IS THAT PERCEPTIVE.
I SUSPECT HE MIGHT BE ABLE TO SNIFF OUT MY HIDING PLACE.
BUT THEN AGAIN, IF I CARED TO REMAIN UNNOTICED, I WOULDN'T HAVE TAILED JOSUKE LIKE THAT.

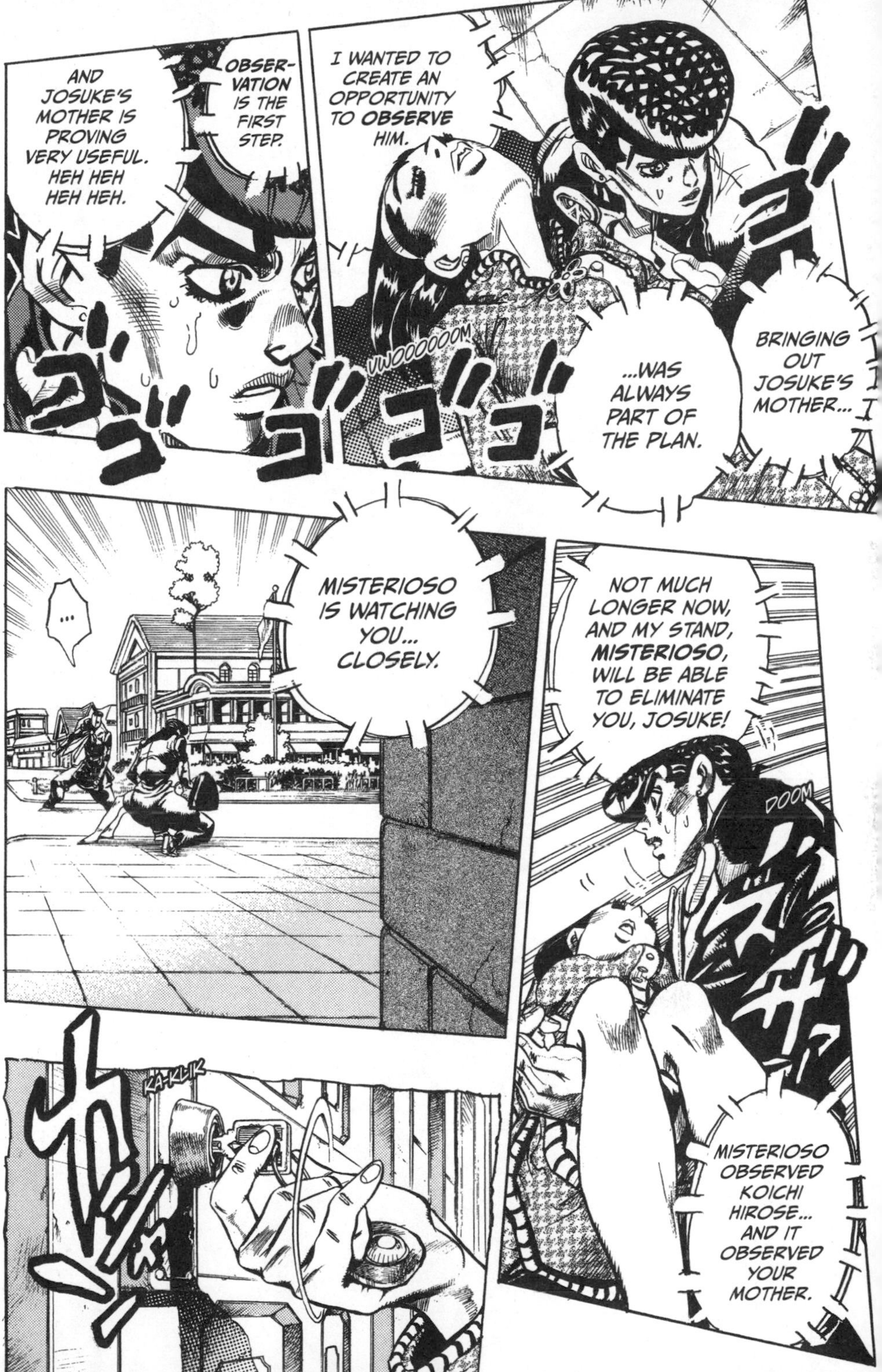
I WANTED TO CREATE AN OPPORTUNITY TO OBSERVE HIM.
BRINGING OUT JOSUKE'S MOTHER...
...WAS ALWAYS PART OF THE PLAN.
VWOOOOOOM
OBSERVATION IS THE FIRST STEP.
AND JOSUKE'S MOTHER IS PROVING VERY USEFUL. HEH HEH HEH HEH.
NOT MUCH LONGER NOW, AND MY STAND, MISTERIOSO, WILL BE ABLE TO ELIMINATE YOU, JOSUKE!
DOOM
MISTERIOSO OBSERVED KOICHI HIROSE... AND IT OBSERVED YOUR MOTHER.
MISTERIOSO IS WATCHING YOU... CLOSELY.
...
KA-KLIK

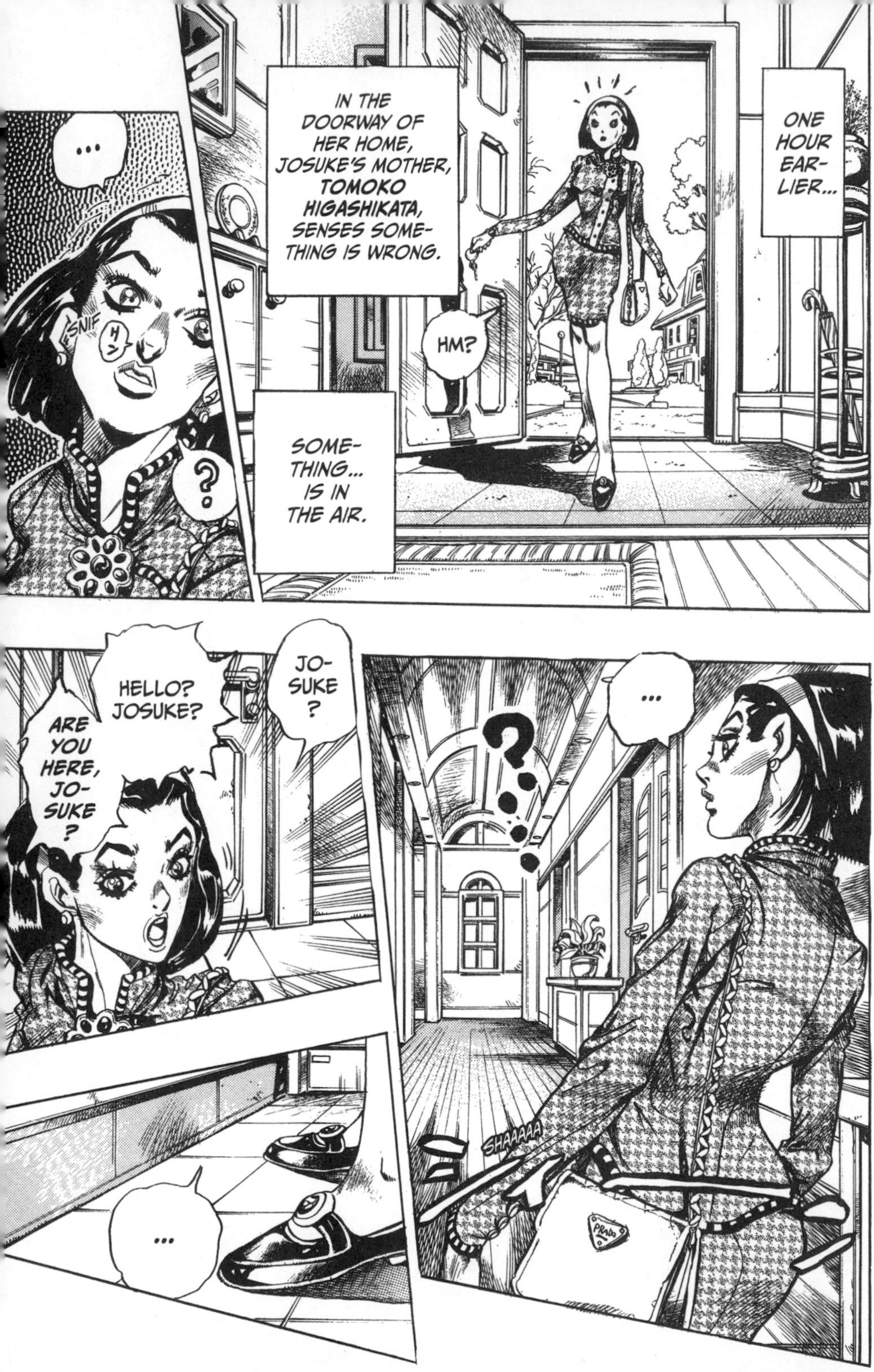
ONE HOUR EARLIER...
IN THE DOORWAY OF HER HOME, JOSUKE'S MOTHER, TOMOKO HIGASHIKATA, SENSES SOMETHING IS WRONG.
HM?
SOMETHING... IS IN THE AIR.
...
SNIF
?
...
?
SHAAAAA
JOSUKE?
HELLO? JOSUKE?
ARE YOU HERE, JOSUKE?
...

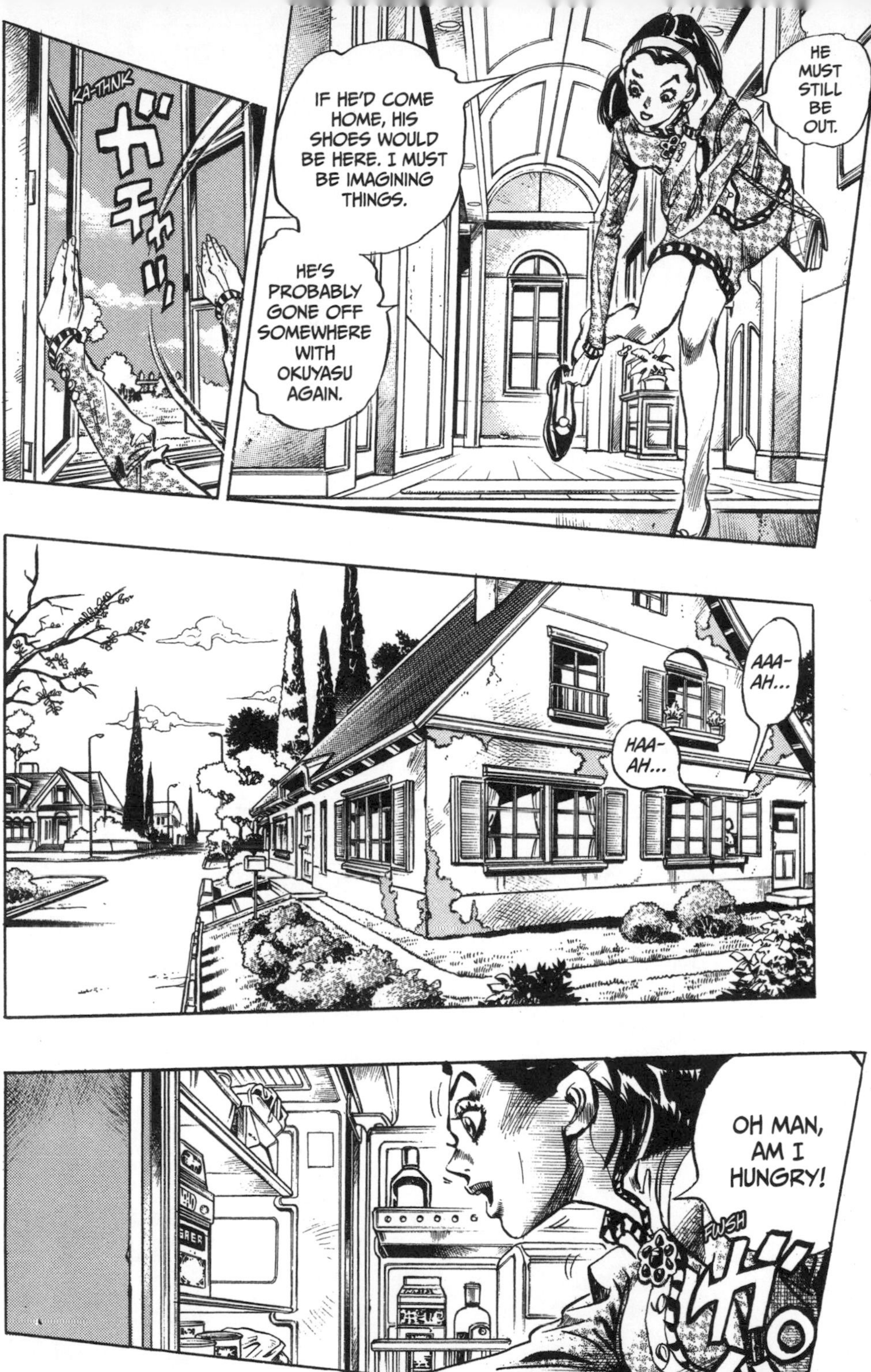
HE MUST STILL BE OUT.
IF HE'D COME HOME, HIS SHOES WOULD BE HERE. I MUST BE IMAGINING THINGS.
HE'S PROBABLY GONE OFF SOMEWHERE WITH OKUYASU AGAIN.
KA-THNK
ガチャッ
AAA-AH...
HAAA-AH...
OH MAN, AM I HUNGRY!
FWISH

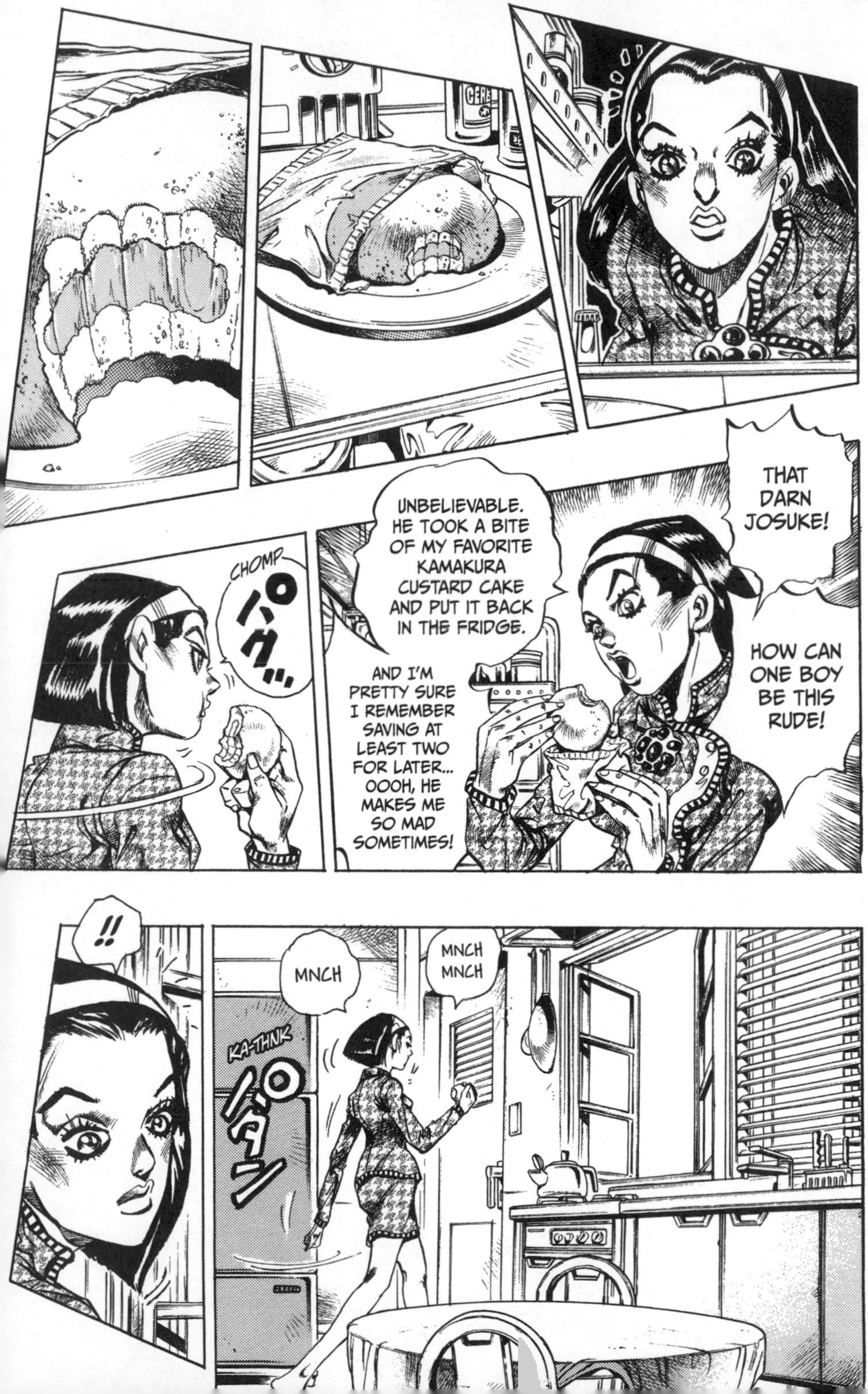
THAT DARN JOSUKE!
UNBELIEVABLE. HE TOOK A BITE OF MY FAVORITE KAMAKURA CUSTARD CAKE AND PUT IT BACK IN THE FRIDGE.
HOW CAN ONE BOY BE THIS RUDE!
AND I'M PRETTY SURE I REMEMBER SAVING AT LEAST TWO FOR LATER... OOOH, HE MAKES ME SO MAD SOMETIMES!
CHOMP
MNCH MNCH
MNCH
KA-THNK
!!

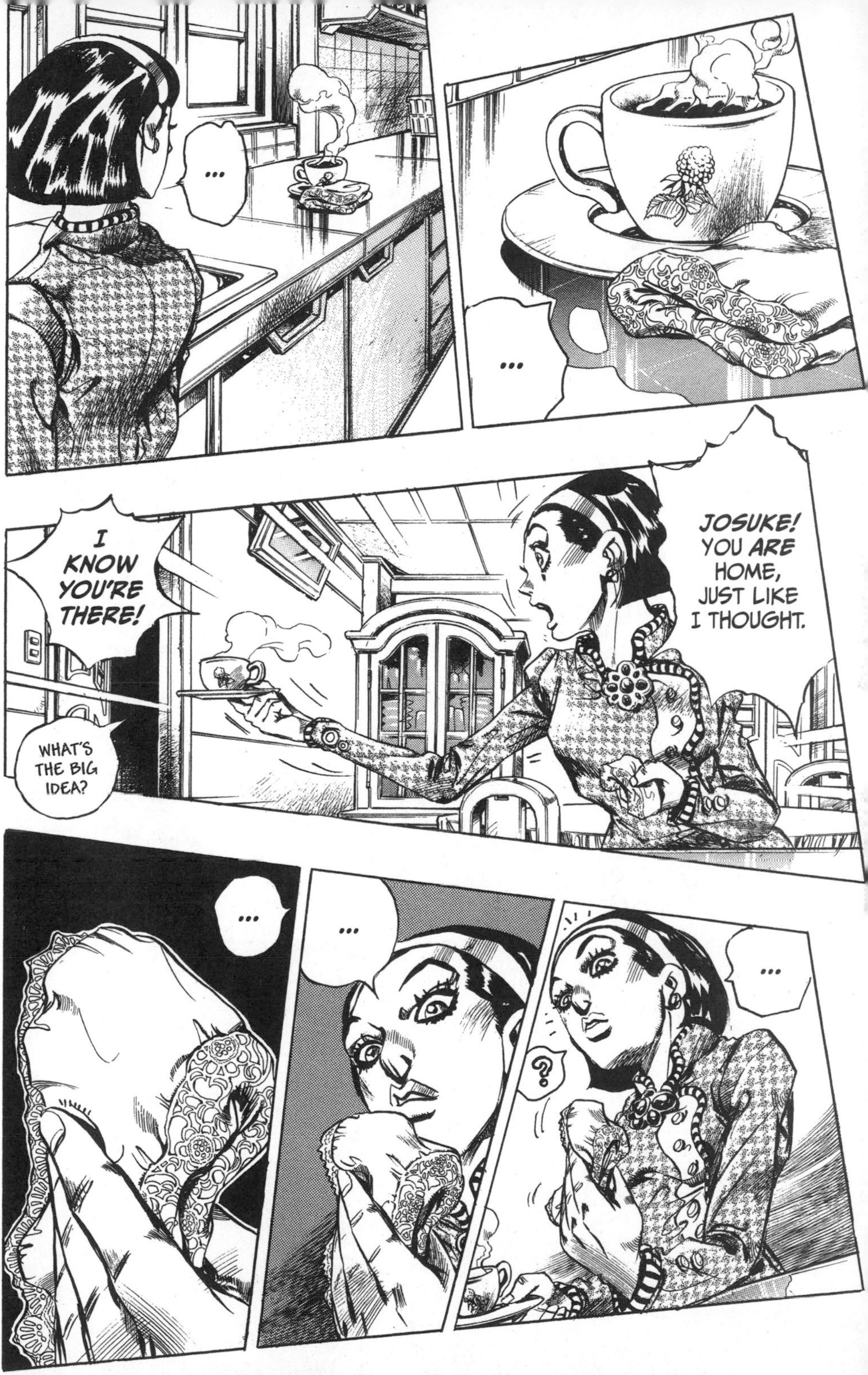
...
...
JOSUKE! YOU ARE HOME, JUST LIKE I THOUGHT.
I KNOW YOU'RE THERE!
WHAT'S THE BIG IDEA?
...
?
...
...

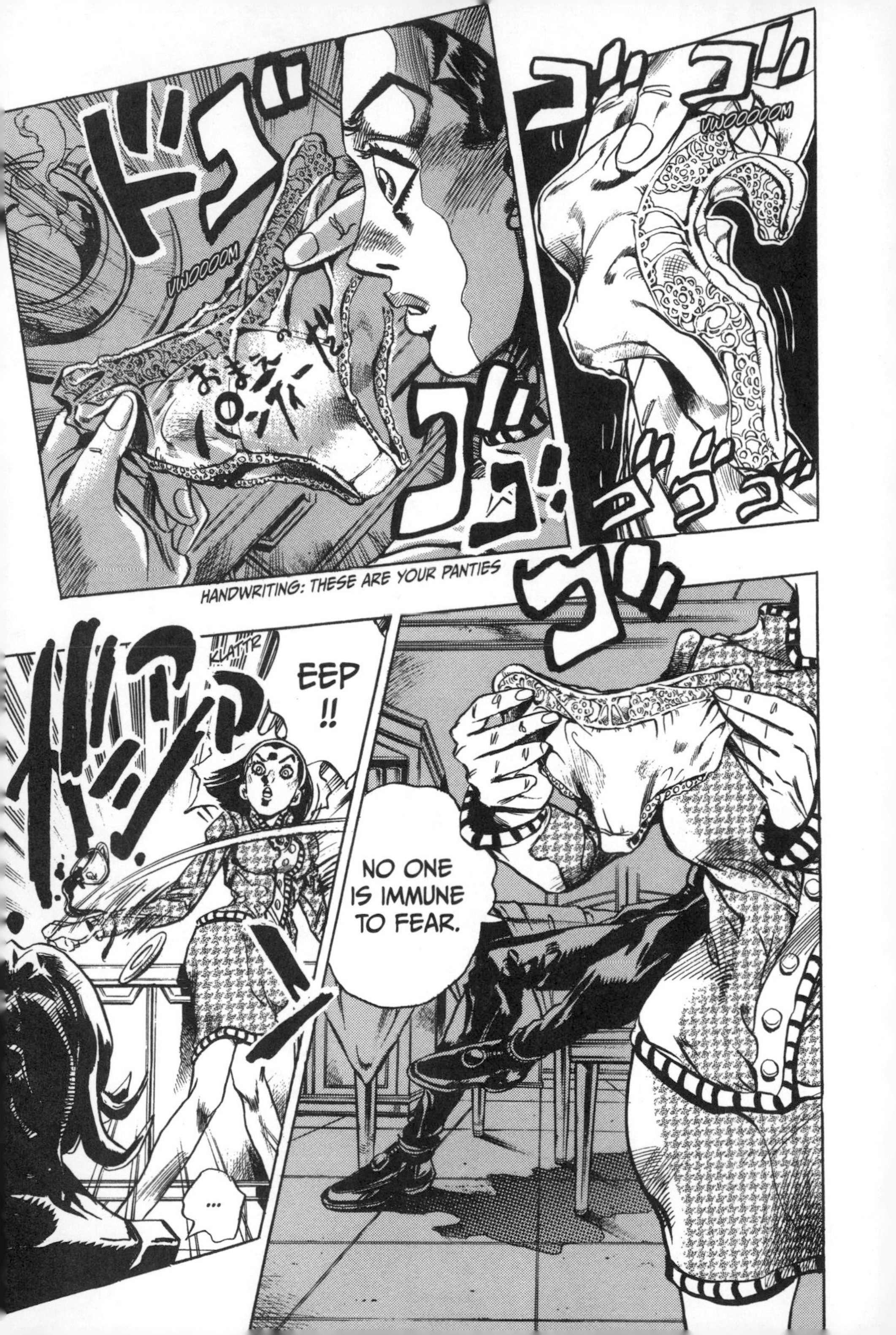
UWOOOOOM
UWOOOOM
HANDWRITING: THESE ARE YOUR PANTIES
NO ONE IS IMMUNE TO FEAR.
KLATTR
EEP !!
...

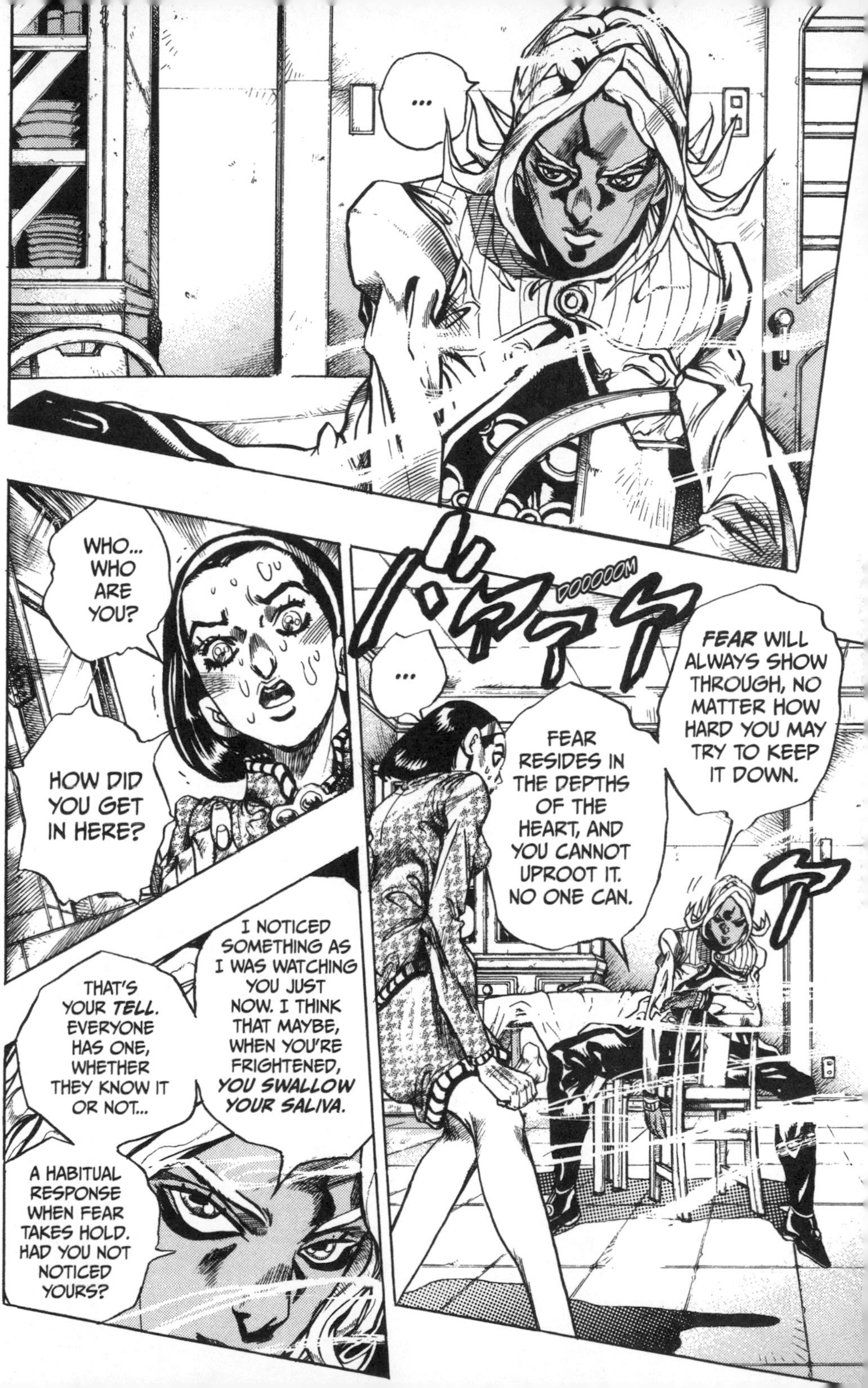
...
DOOOOOM
FEAR WILL ALWAYS SHOW THROUGH, NO MATTER HOW HARD YOU MAY TRY TO KEEP IT DOWN.
...
FEAR RESIDES IN THE DEPTHS OF THE HEART, AND YOU CANNOT UPROOT IT. NO ONE CAN.
WHO... WHO ARE YOU?
HOW DID YOU GET IN HERE?
I NOTICED SOMETHING AS I WAS WATCHING YOU JUST NOW. I THINK THAT MAYBE, WHEN YOU'RE FRIGHTENED, ***YOU SWALLOW YOUR SALIVA***.
THAT'S YOUR ***TELL***. EVERYONE HAS ONE, WHETHER THEY KNOW IT OR NOT...
A HABITUAL RESPONSE WHEN FEAR TAKES HOLD. HAD YOU NOT NOTICED YOURS?

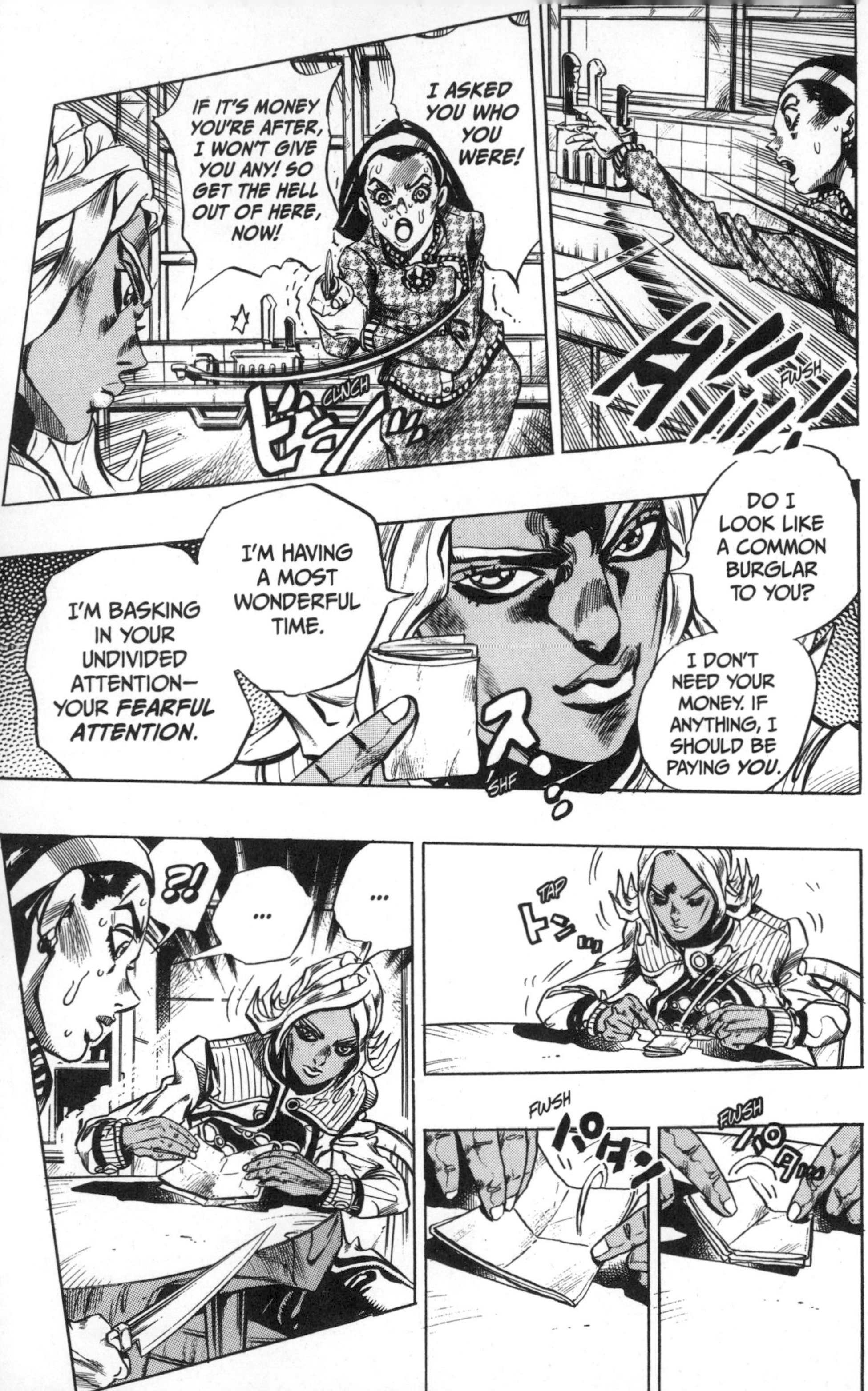
FWSH
I ASKED YOU WHO YOU WERE!
IF IT'S MONEY YOU'RE AFTER, I WON'T GIVE YOU ANY! SO GET THE HELL OUT OF HERE, NOW!
CLINCH
DO I LOOK LIKE A COMMON BURGLAR TO YOU?
I DON'T NEED YOUR MONEY. IF ANYTHING, I SHOULD BE PAYING YOU.
I'M HAVING A MOST WONDERFUL TIME.
I'M BASKING IN YOUR UNDIVIDED ATTENTION—YOUR FEARFUL ATTENTION.
SHF
TAP
FWSH
FWSH
...
...
?!

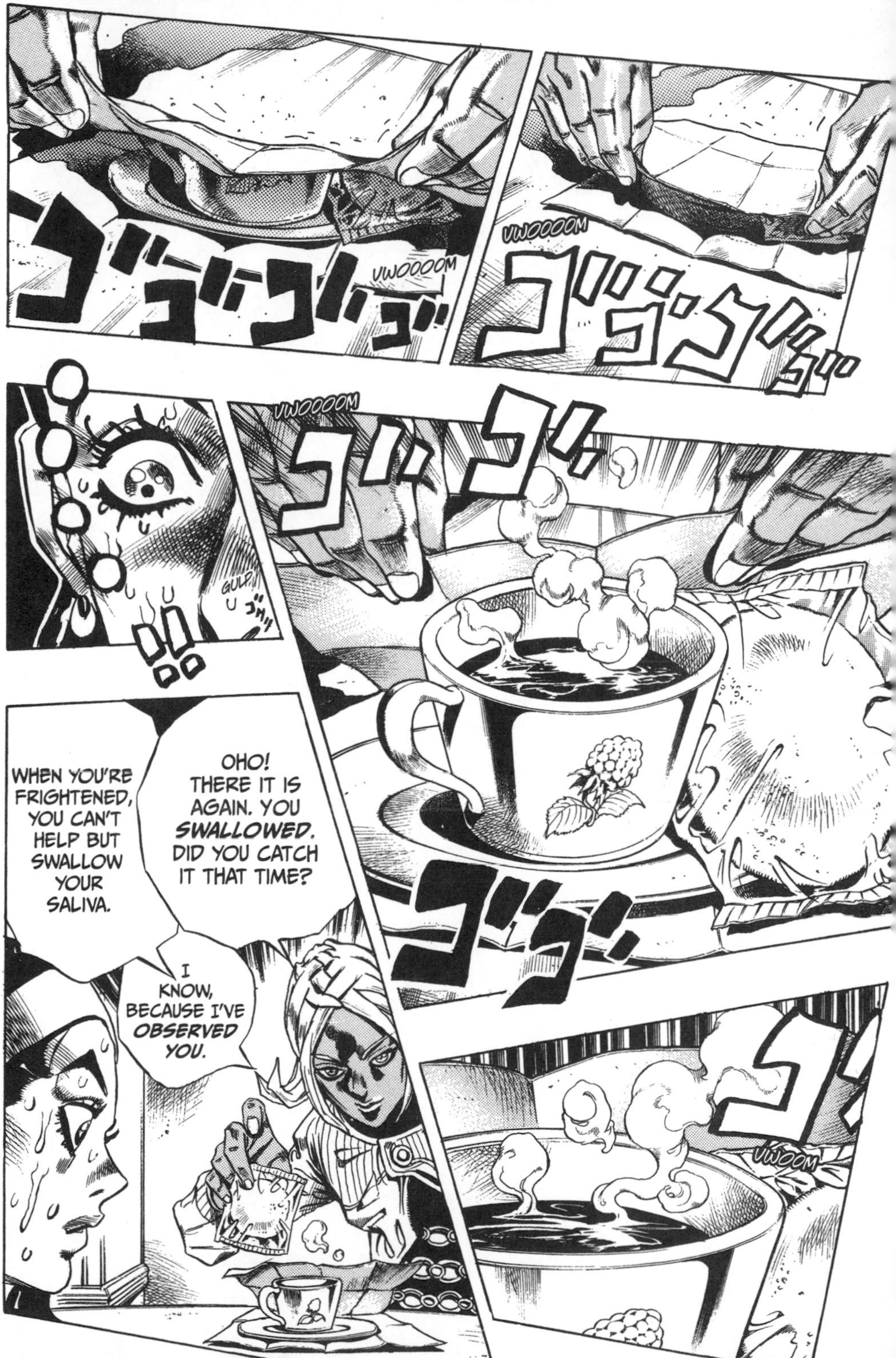
VWOOOOM
VWOOOOM
VWOOOOM
GULP
VWOOM
OHO! THERE IT IS AGAIN. YOU *SWALLOWED*. DID YOU CATCH IT THAT TIME?
WHEN YOU'RE FRIGHTENED, YOU CAN'T HELP BUT SWALLOW YOUR SALIVA.
I KNOW, BECAUSE I'VE *OBSERVED* YOU.

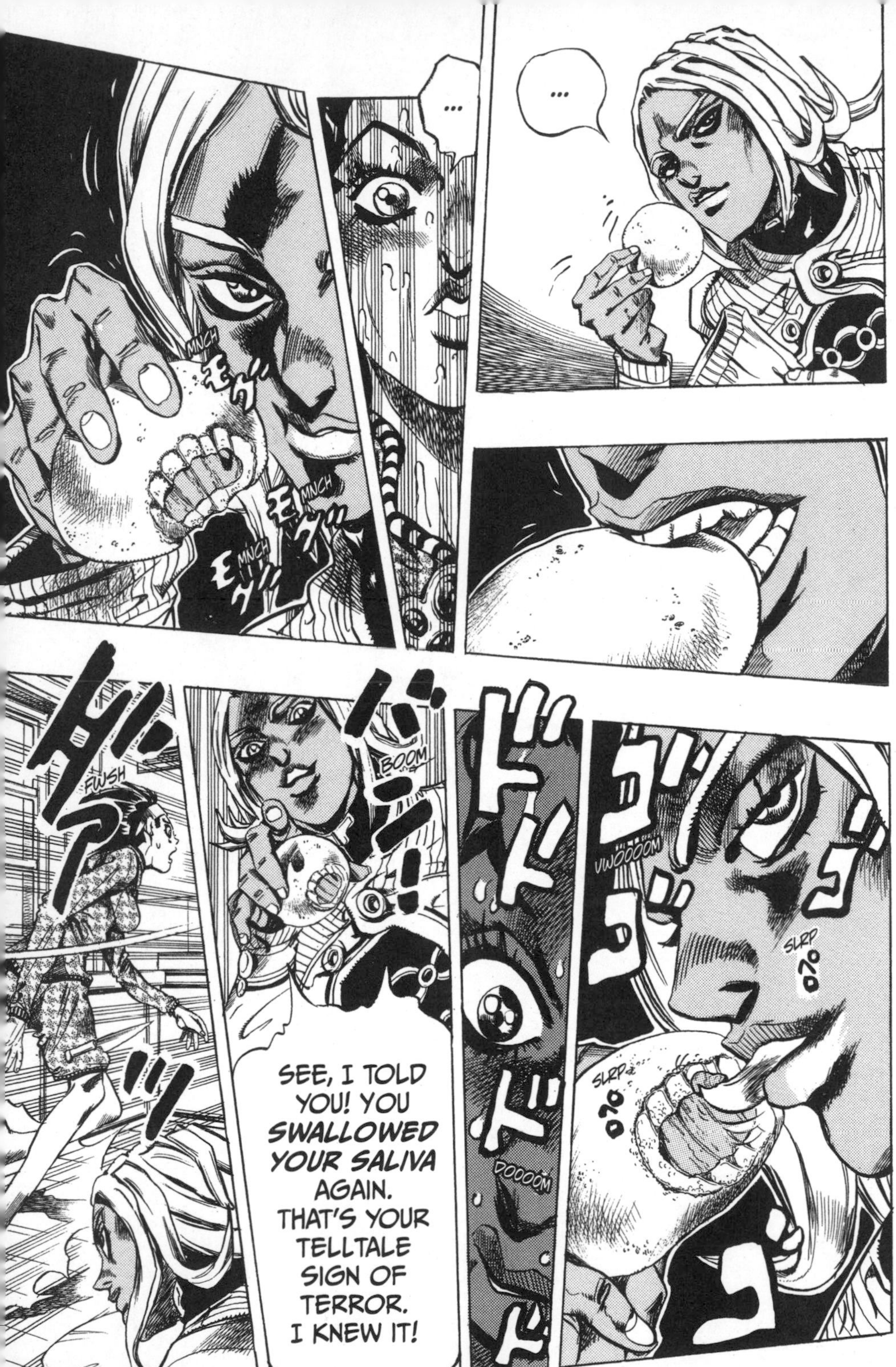
...
...
MNCH
MNCH
MNCH
VWOOOOM
SLRP
SLRP
DOOOOM
BOOM
SEE, I TOLD YOU! YOU *SWALLOWED YOUR SALIVA* AGAIN. THAT'S YOUR TELLTALE SIGN OF TERROR. I KNEW IT!
FWSH

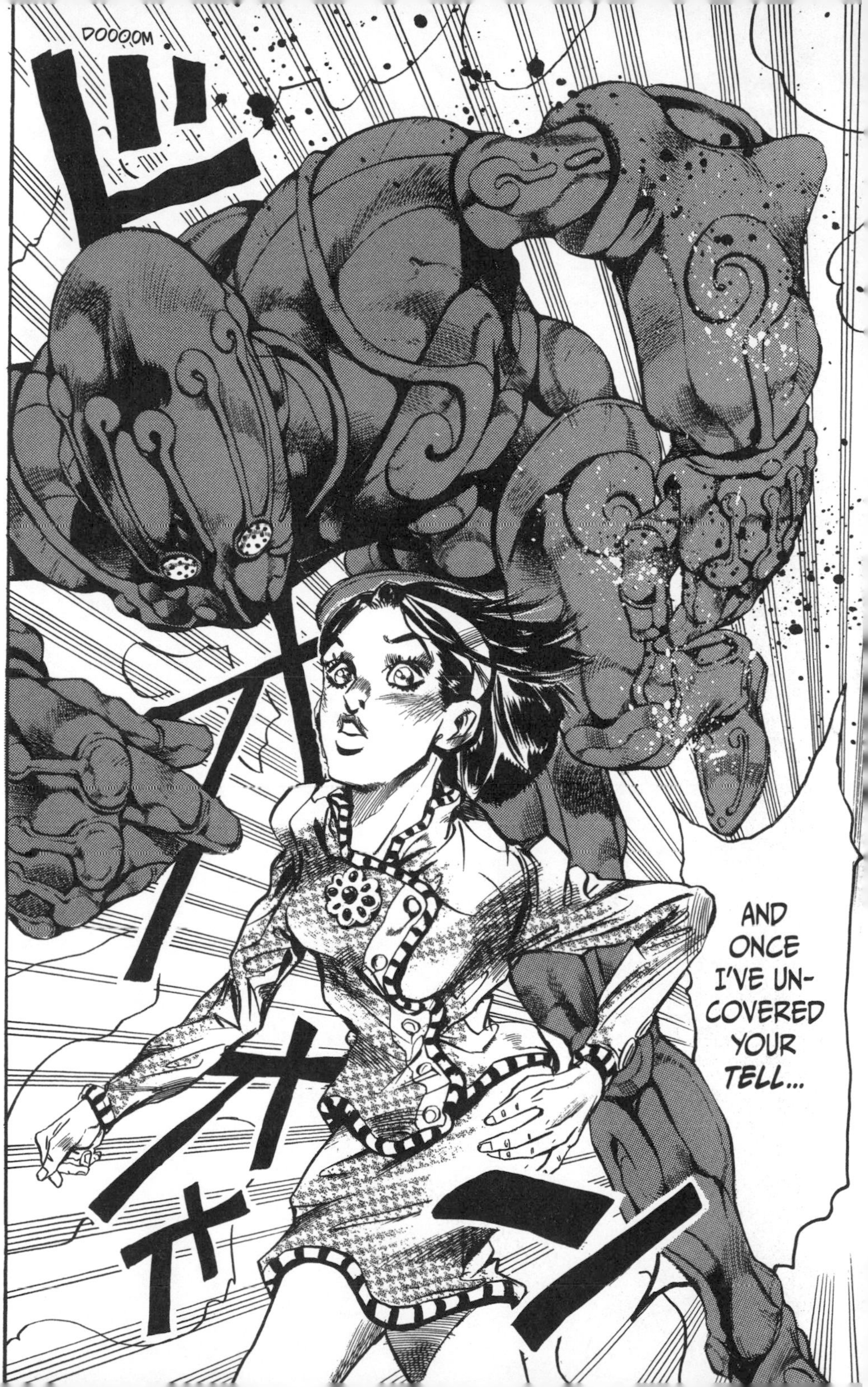
DOOOOM
AND ONCE I'VE UN-COVERED YOUR TELL...

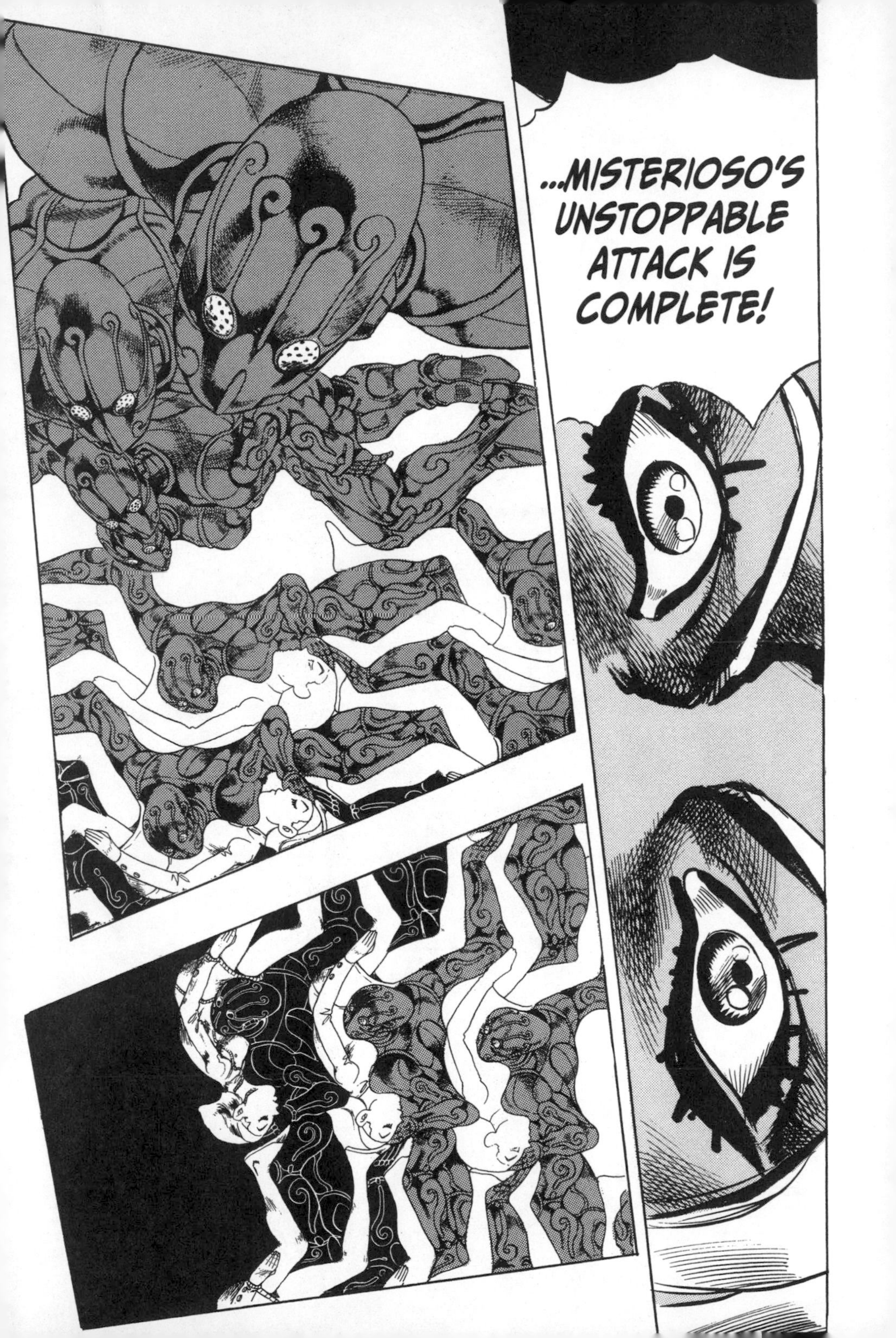
...MISTERIOSO'S UNSTOPPABLE ATTACK IS COMPLETE!

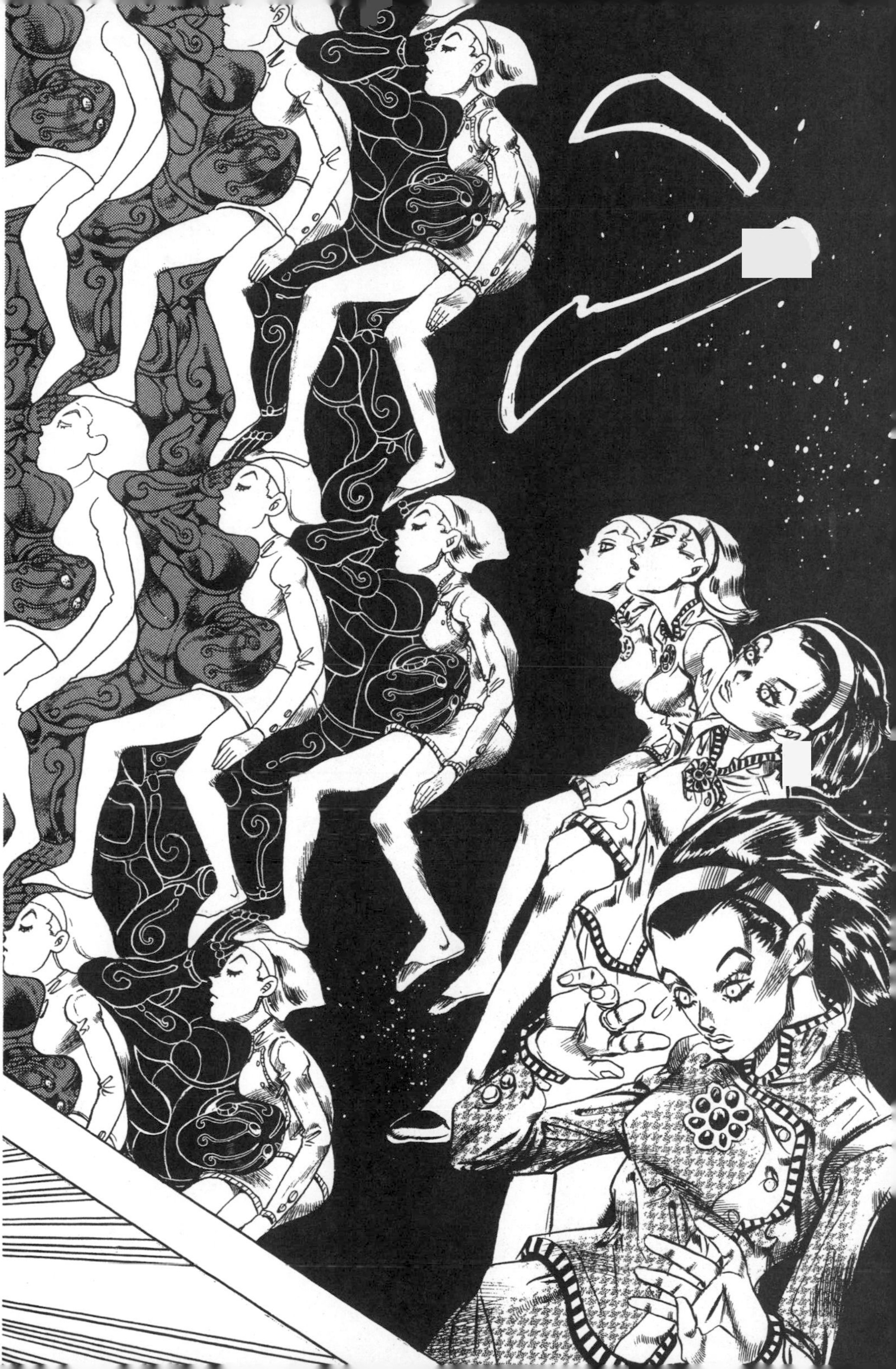

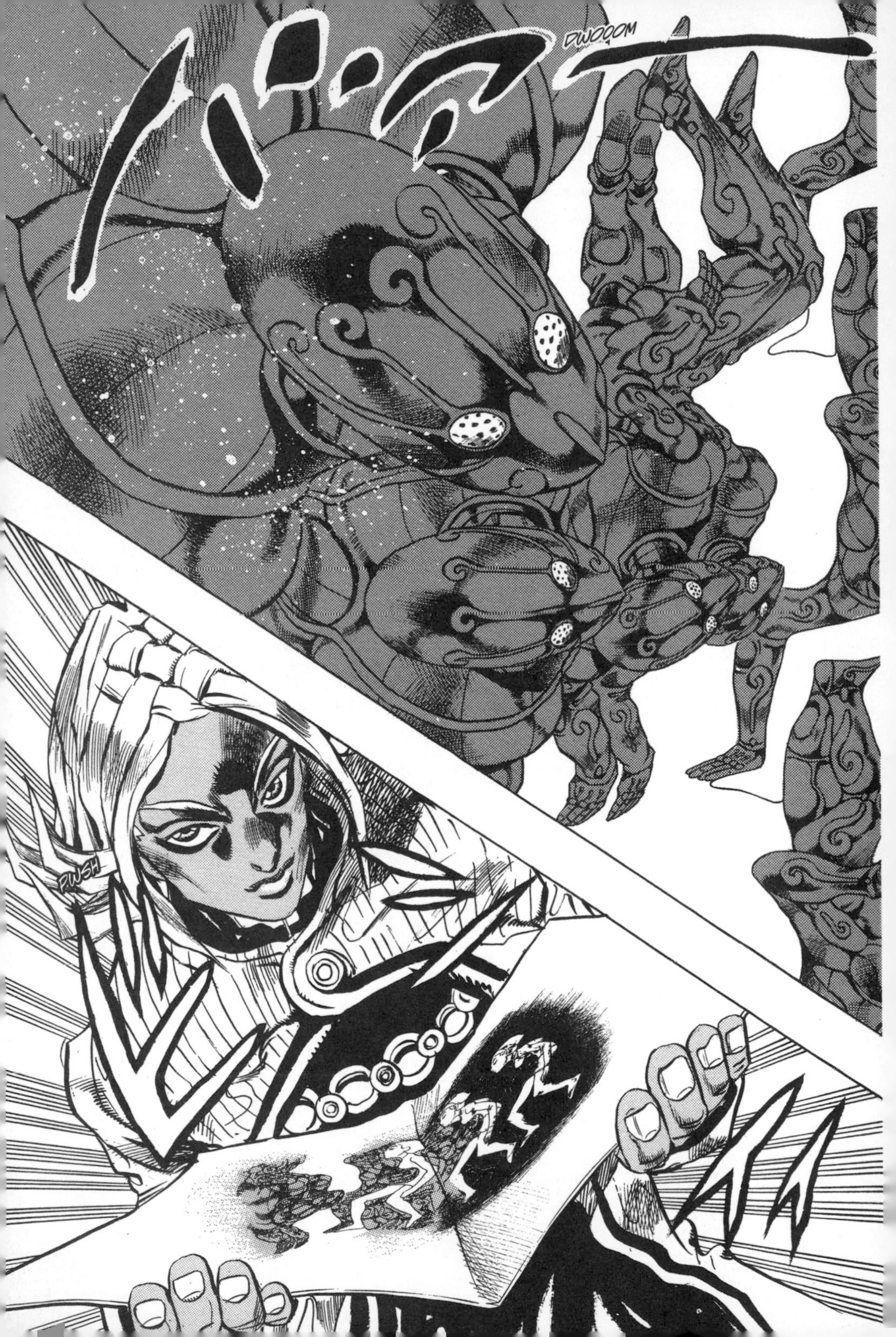
DWOOOM
PUSH

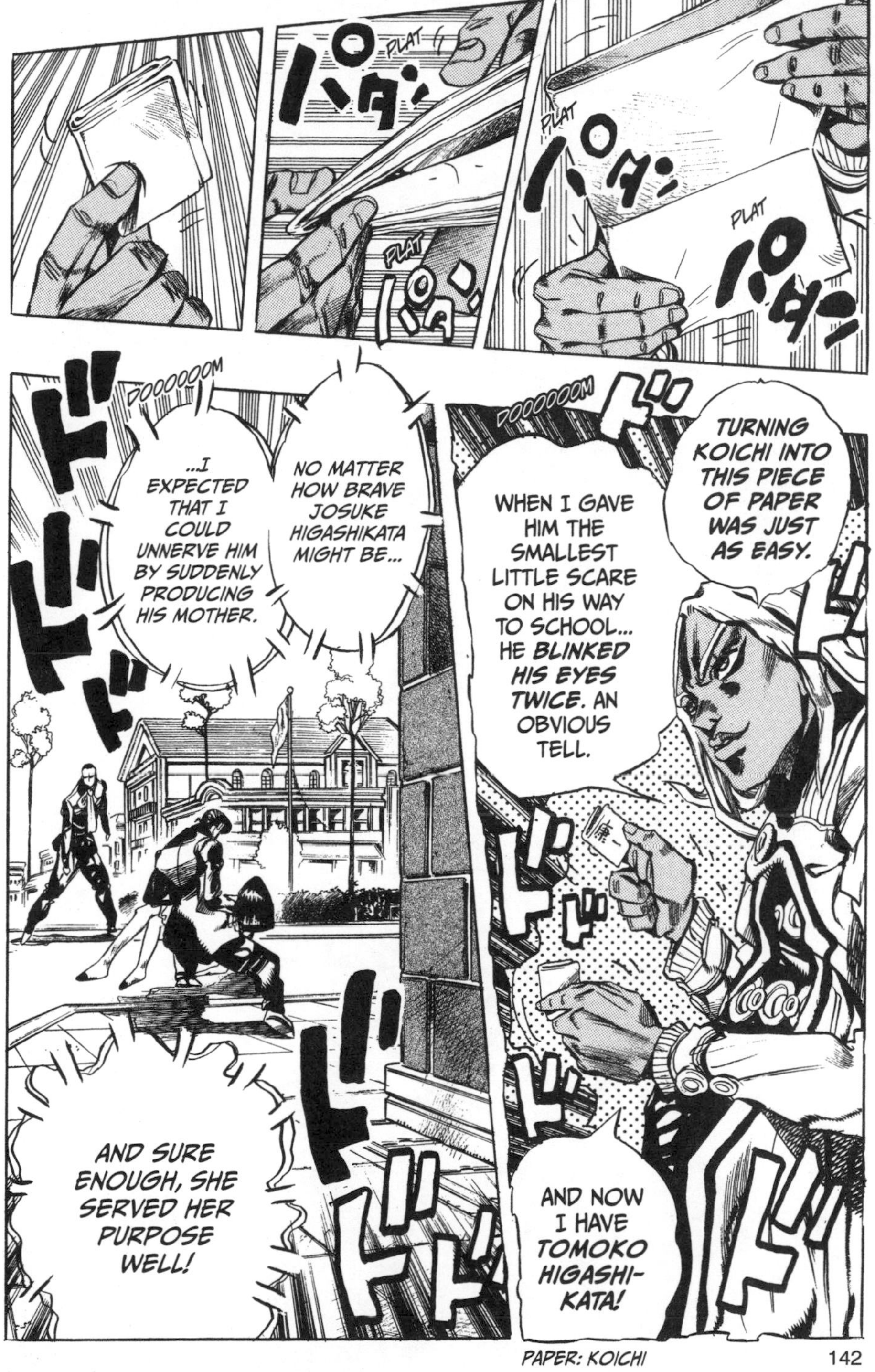
PLAT
PLAT
PLAT
PLAT
DOOOOOOM
TURNING KOICHI INTO THIS PIECE OF PAPER WAS JUST AS EASY.
WHEN I GAVE HIM THE SMALLEST LITTLE SCARE ON HIS WAY TO SCHOOL... HE *BLINKED HIS EYES TWICE*. AN OBVIOUS TELL.
AND NOW I HAVE *TOMOKO HIGASHI-KATA!*
DOOOOOOM
NO MATTER HOW BRAVE JOSUKE HIGASHIKATA MIGHT BE...
...I EXPECTED THAT I COULD UNNERVE HIM BY SUDDENLY PRODUCING HIS MOTHER.
AND SURE ENOUGH, SHE SERVED HER PURPOSE WELL!

PAPER: KOICHI

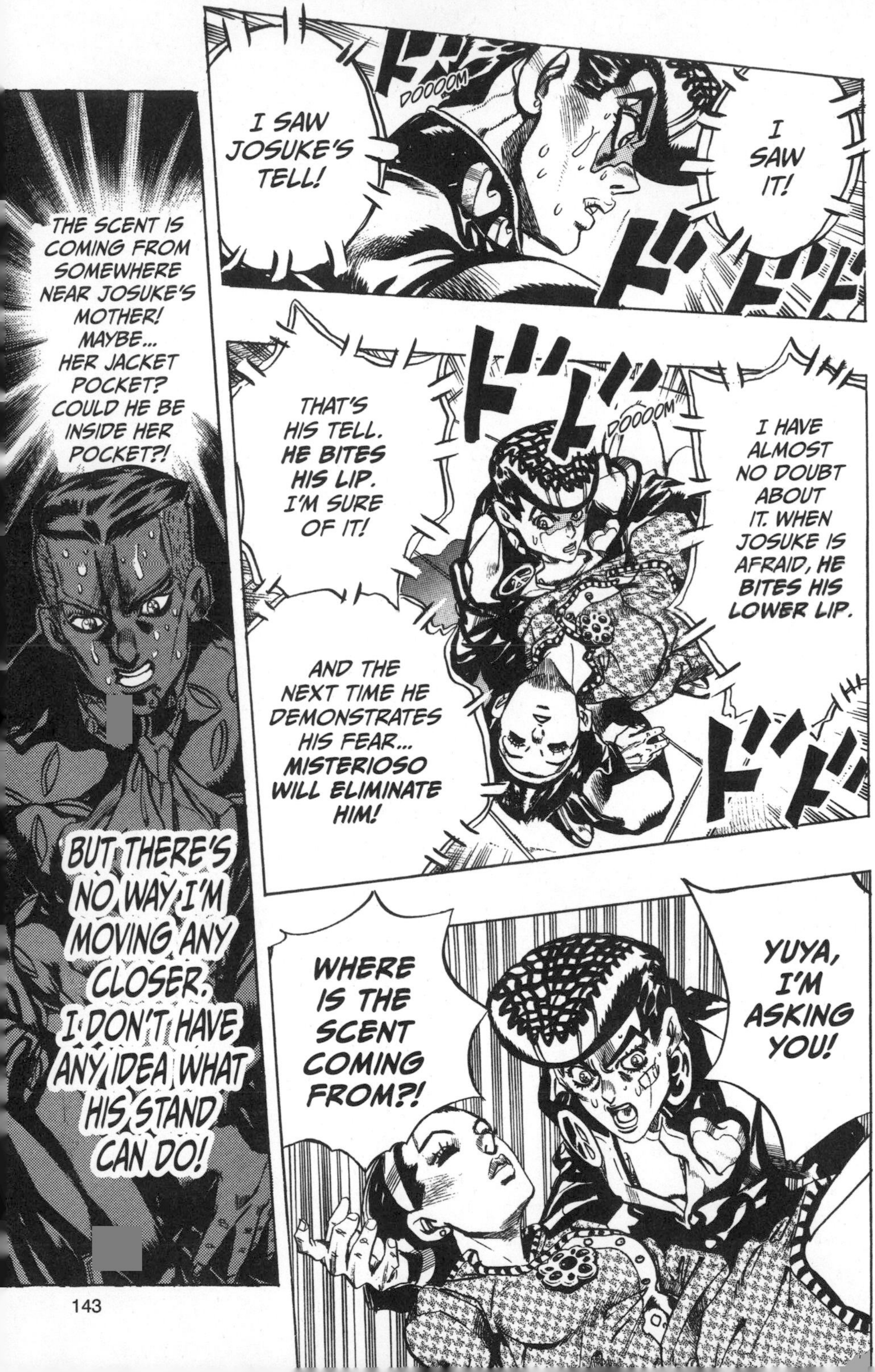
DOOOOM
I SAW IT!
I SAW JOSUKE'S TELL!
I HAVE ALMOST NO DOUBT ABOUT IT. WHEN JOSUKE IS AFRAID, HE BITES HIS LOWER LIP.
DOOOOM
THAT'S HIS TELL. HE BITES HIS LIP. I'M SURE OF IT!
AND THE NEXT TIME HE DEMONSTRATES HIS FEAR... MISTERIOSO WILL ELIMINATE HIM!
YUYA, I'M ASKING YOU!
WHERE IS THE SCENT COMING FROM?!
THE SCENT IS COMING FROM SOMEWHERE NEAR JOSUKE'S MOTHER! MAYBE... HER JACKET POCKET? COULD HE BE INSIDE HER POCKET?!
BUT THERE'S NO WAY I'M MOVING ANY CLOSER. I DON'T HAVE ANY IDEA WHAT HIS STAND CAN DO!

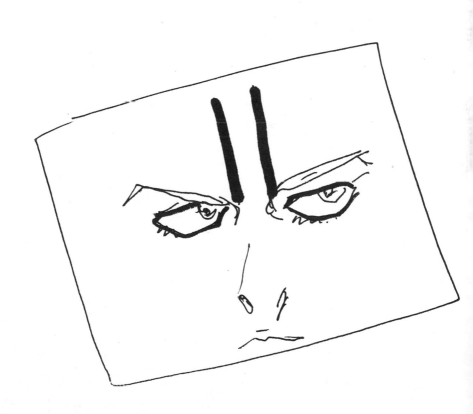

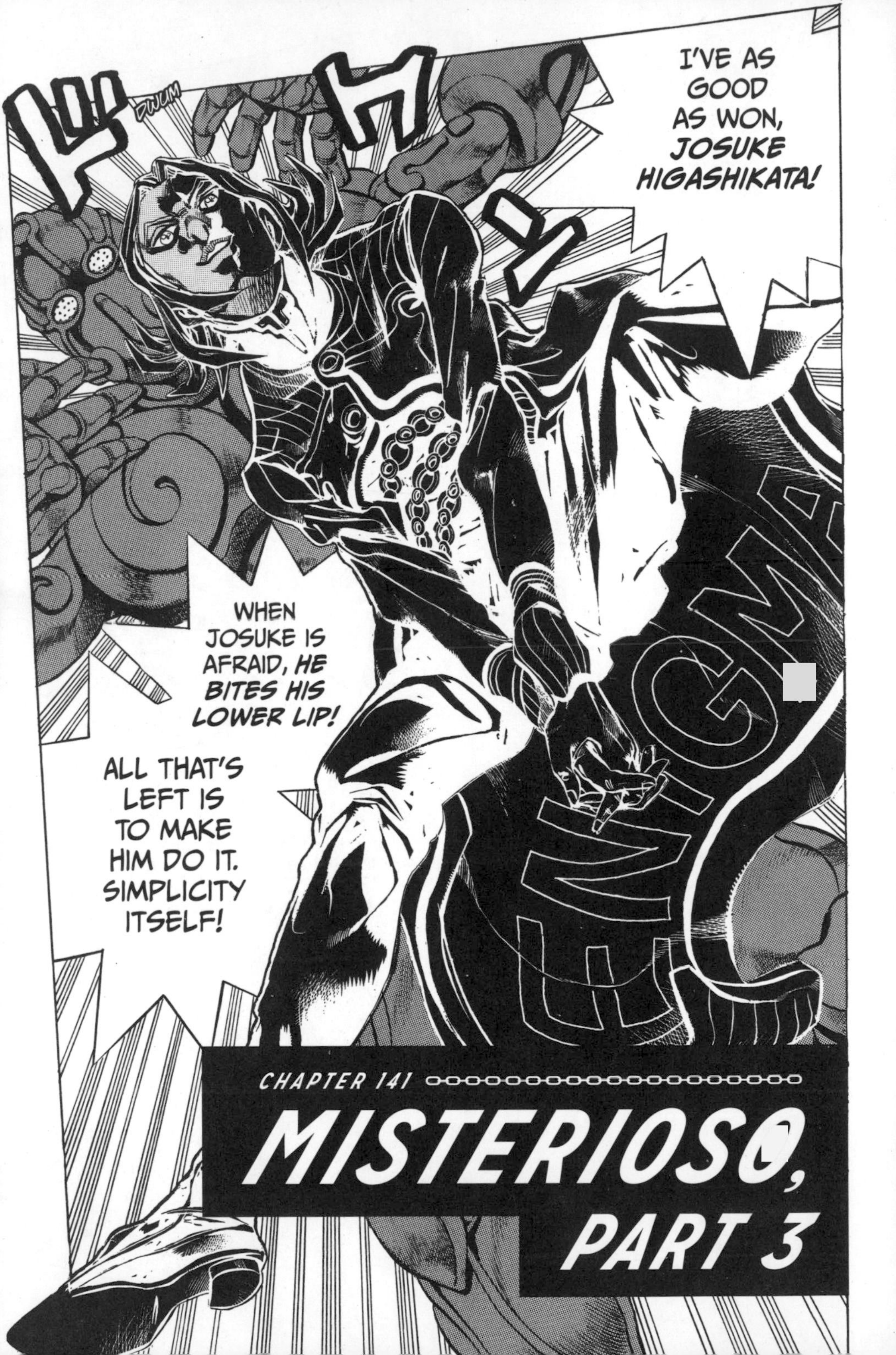
I'VE AS GOOD AS WON, JOSUKE HIGASHIKATA!
DWUM
WHEN JOSUKE IS AFRAID, HE BITES HIS LOWER LIP!
ALL THAT'S LEFT IS TO MAKE HIM DO IT. SIMPLICITY ITSELF!
CHAPTER 141
MISTERIOSO, PART 3

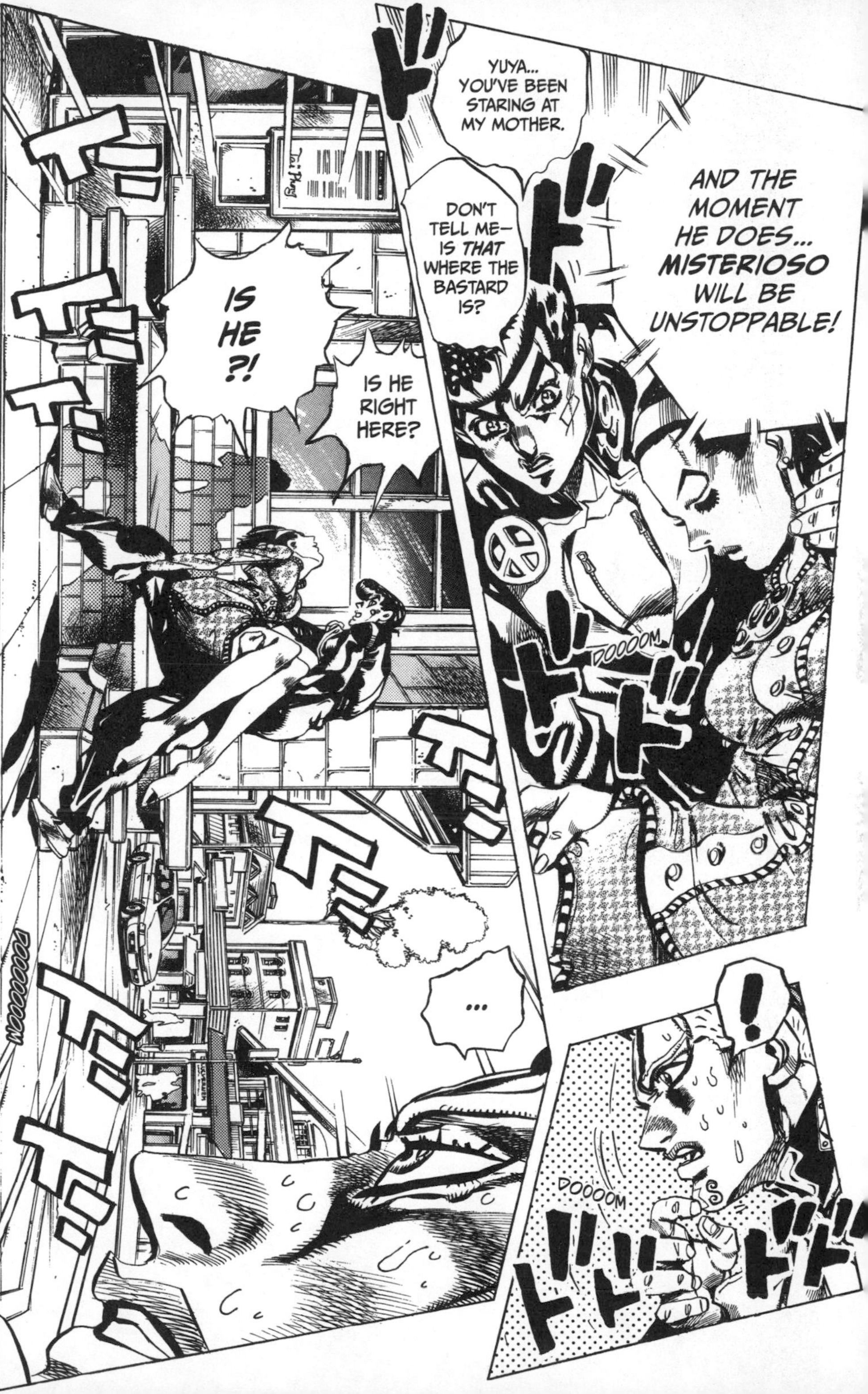
YUYA... YOU'VE BEEN STARING AT MY MOTHER.
DON'T TELL ME— IS *THAT* WHERE THE BASTARD IS?
AND THE MOMENT HE DOES... MISTERIOSO WILL BE UNSTOPPABLE!
DOOOOM
!
DOOOOM
IS HE ?!
IS HE RIGHT HERE?
...
POOOOOOOM

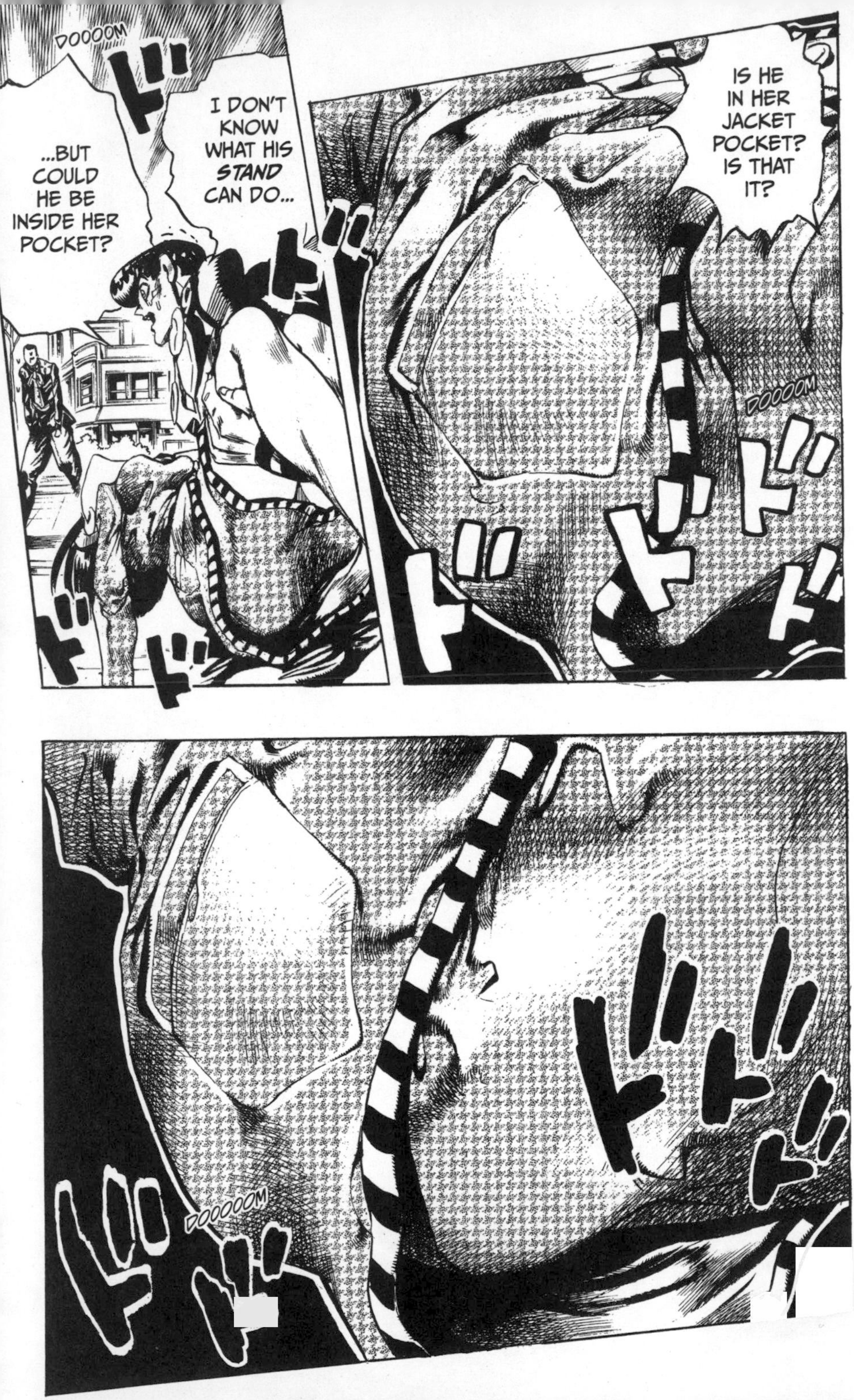
IS HE IN HER JACKET POCKET? IS THAT IT?
DOOOOM
I DON'T KNOW WHAT HIS STAND CAN DO...
...BUT COULD HE BE INSIDE HER POCKET?
DOOOOM
DOOOOOM

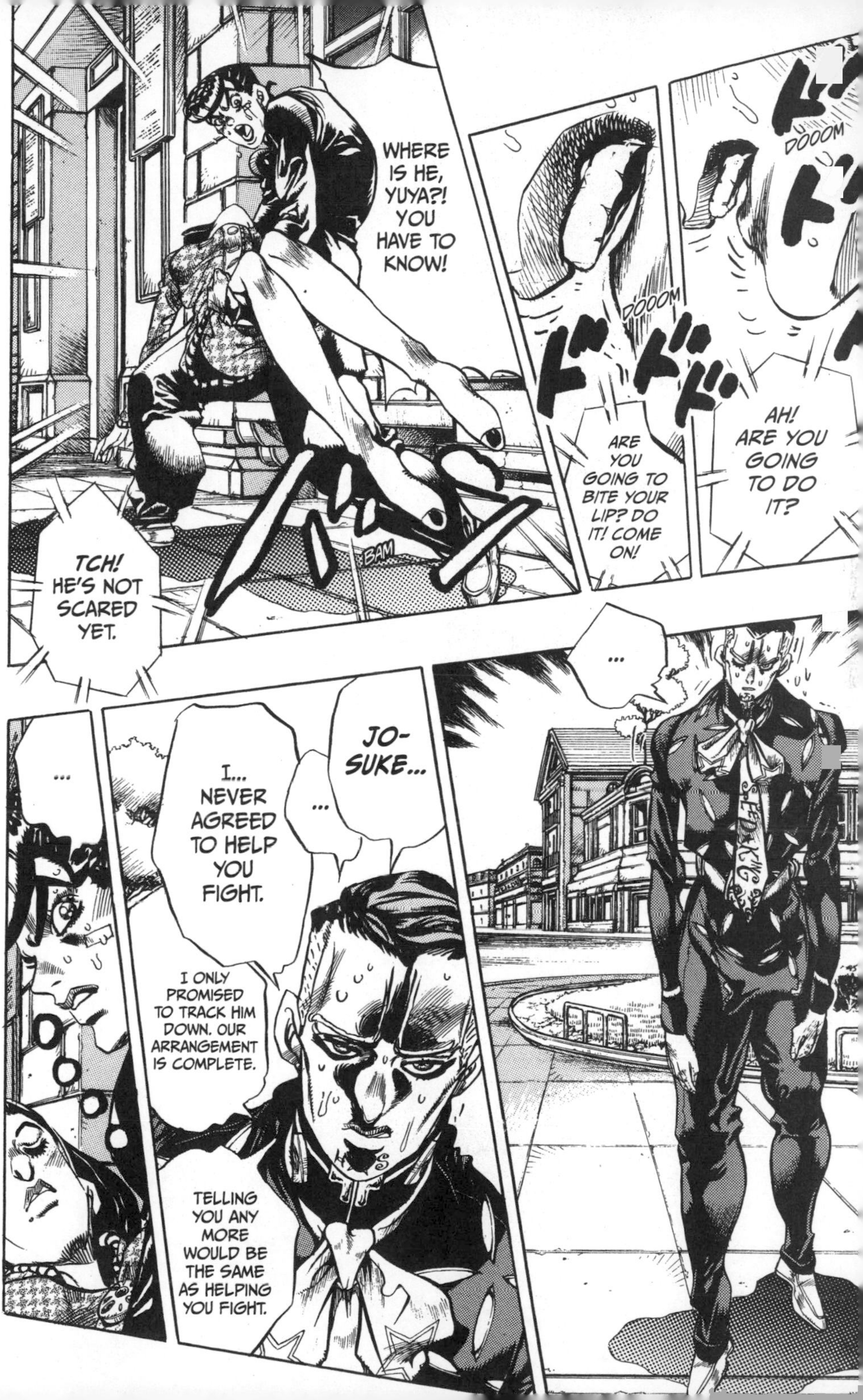
DOOOM
AH! ARE YOU GOING TO DO IT?
DOOOM
ARE YOU GOING TO BITE YOUR LIP? DO IT! COME ON!
WHERE IS HE, YUYA?! YOU HAVE TO KNOW!
BAM
TCH! HE'S NOT SCARED YET.
...
JO-SUKE...
...
I... NEVER AGREED TO HELP YOU FIGHT.
I ONLY PROMISED TO TRACK HIM DOWN. OUR ARRANGEMENT IS COMPLETE.
TELLING YOU ANY MORE WOULD BE THE SAME AS HELPING YOU FIGHT.
...

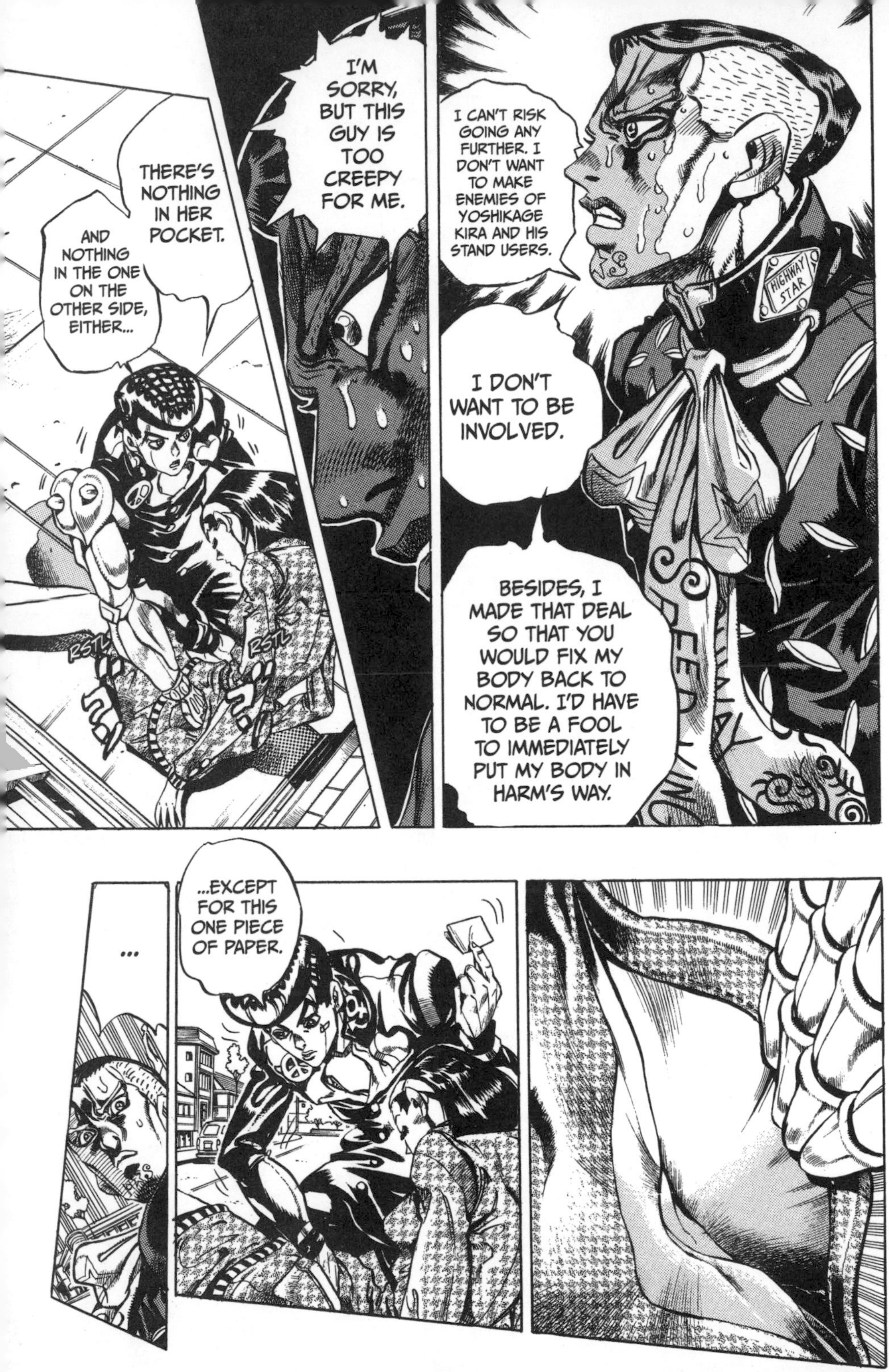
I CAN'T RISK GOING ANY FURTHER. I DON'T WANT TO MAKE ENEMIES OF YOSHIKAGE KIRA AND HIS STAND USERS.
HIGHWAY STAR
I DON'T WANT TO BE INVOLVED.
BESIDES, I MADE THAT DEAL SO THAT YOU WOULD FIX MY BODY BACK TO NORMAL. I'D HAVE TO BE A FOOL TO IMMEDIATELY PUT MY BODY IN HARM'S WAY.
I'M SORRY, BUT THIS GUY IS TOO CREEPY FOR ME.
THERE'S NOTHING IN HER POCKET.
AND NOTHING IN THE ONE ON THE OTHER SIDE, EITHER...
RSTL
RSTL
...EXCEPT FOR THIS ONE PIECE OF PAPER.
...

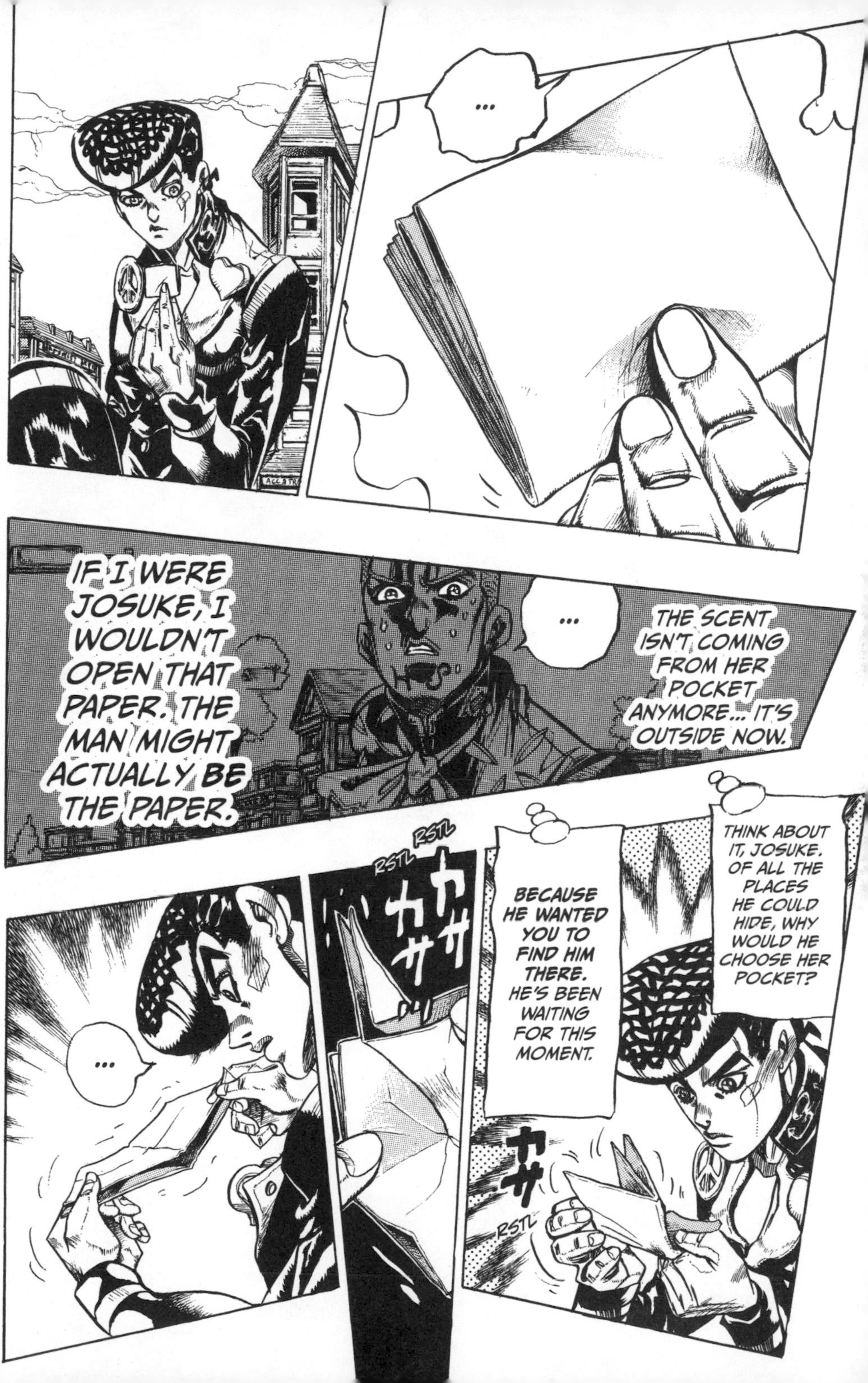
...
THE SCENT ISN'T COMING FROM HER POCKET ANYMORE... IT'S OUTSIDE NOW.
...
IF I WERE JOSUKE, I WOULDN'T OPEN THAT PAPER. THE MAN MIGHT ACTUALLY BE THE PAPER.
THINK ABOUT IT, JOSUKE. OF ALL THE PLACES HE COULD HIDE, WHY WOULD HE CHOOSE HER POCKET?
BECAUSE HE WANTED YOU TO FIND HIM THERE. HE'S BEEN WAITING FOR THIS MOMENT.
カサ
RSTL
カサカサ
RSTL RSTL
...

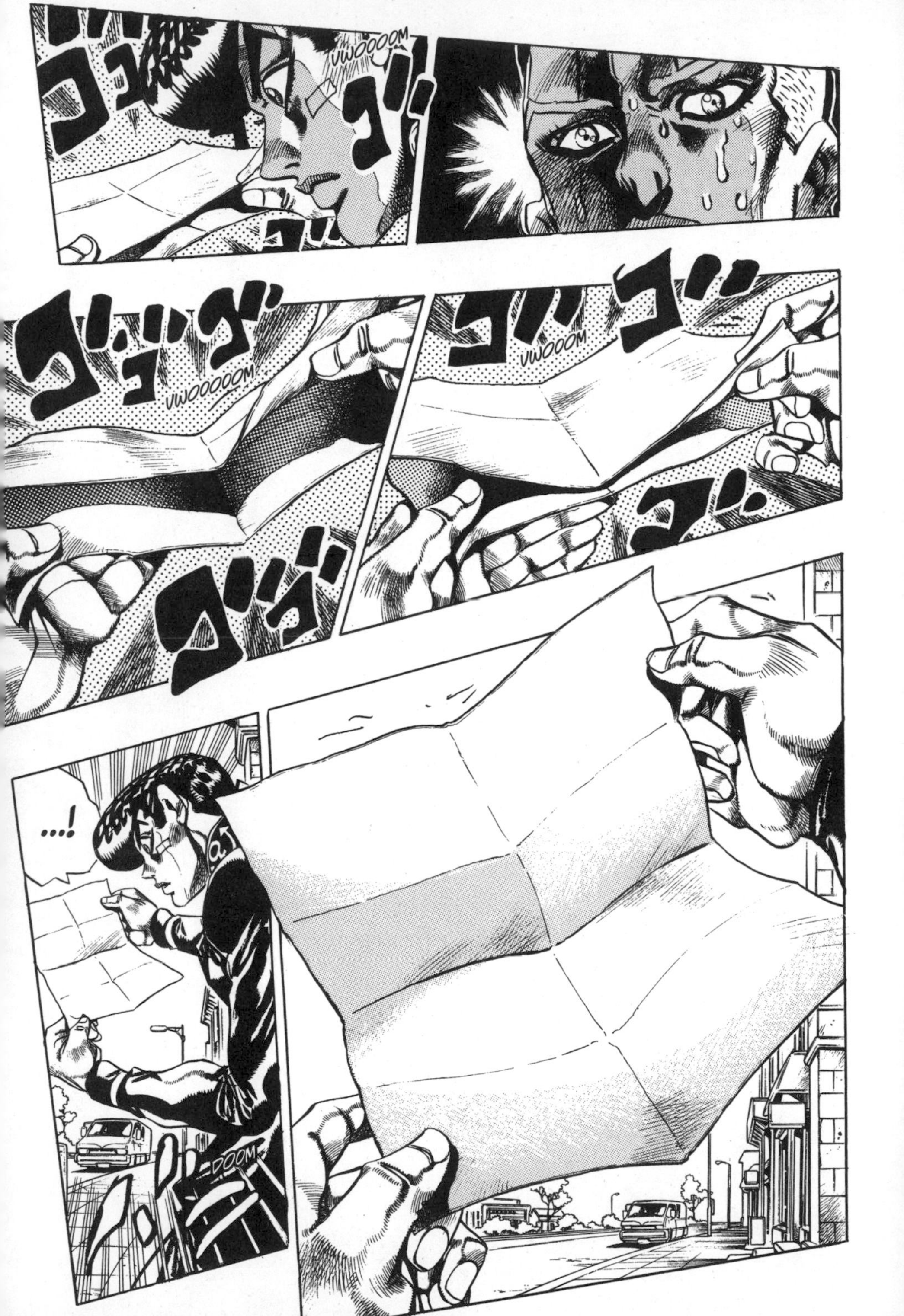
VWOOOOM
VWOOOM
VWOOOOOM
...!
DOOM

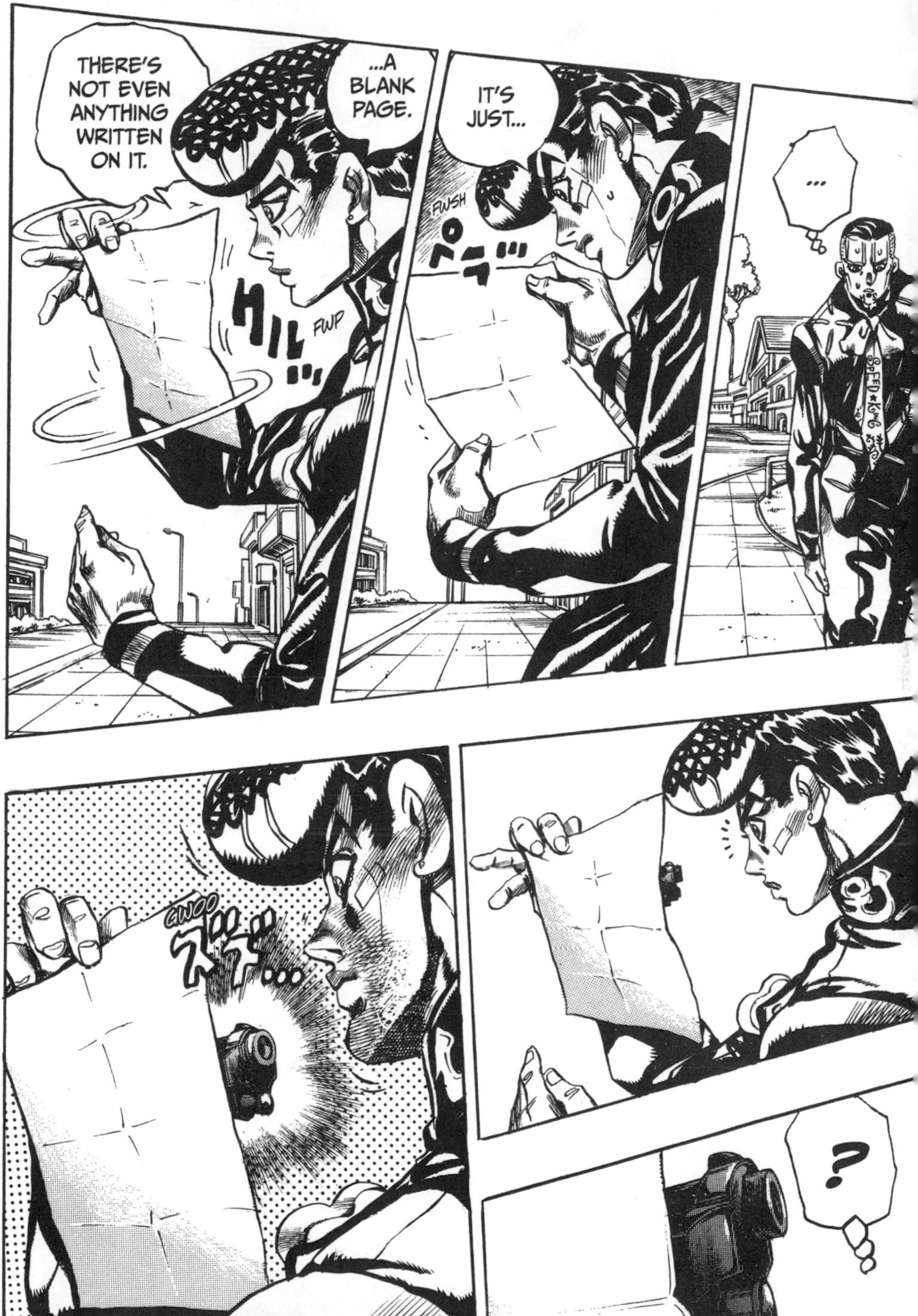
...
FWSH
IT'S JUST...
...A BLANK PAGE.
THERE'S NOT EVEN ANYTHING WRITTEN ON IT.
FWP
?
GWOO

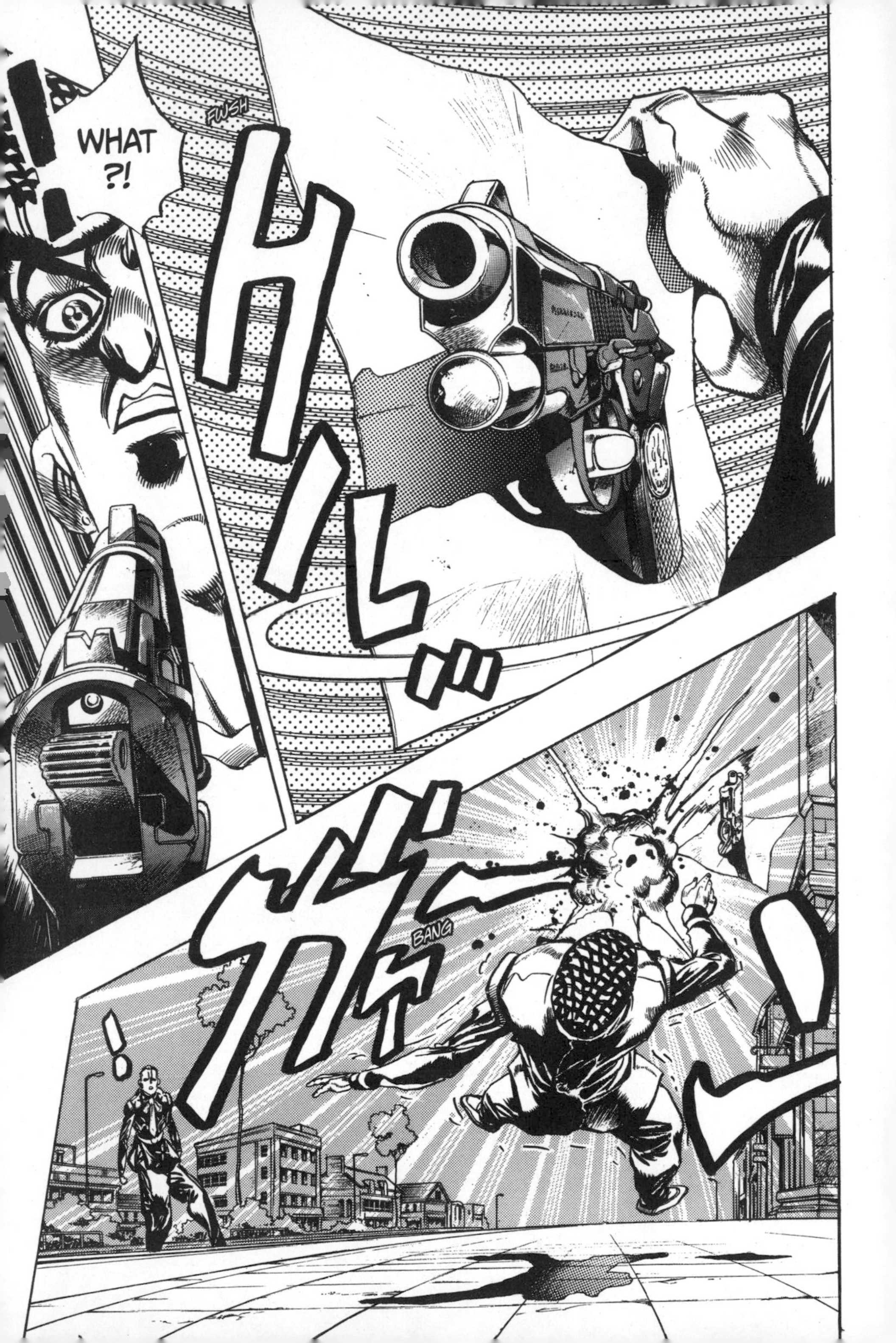
FWSH
WHAT ?!
BANG

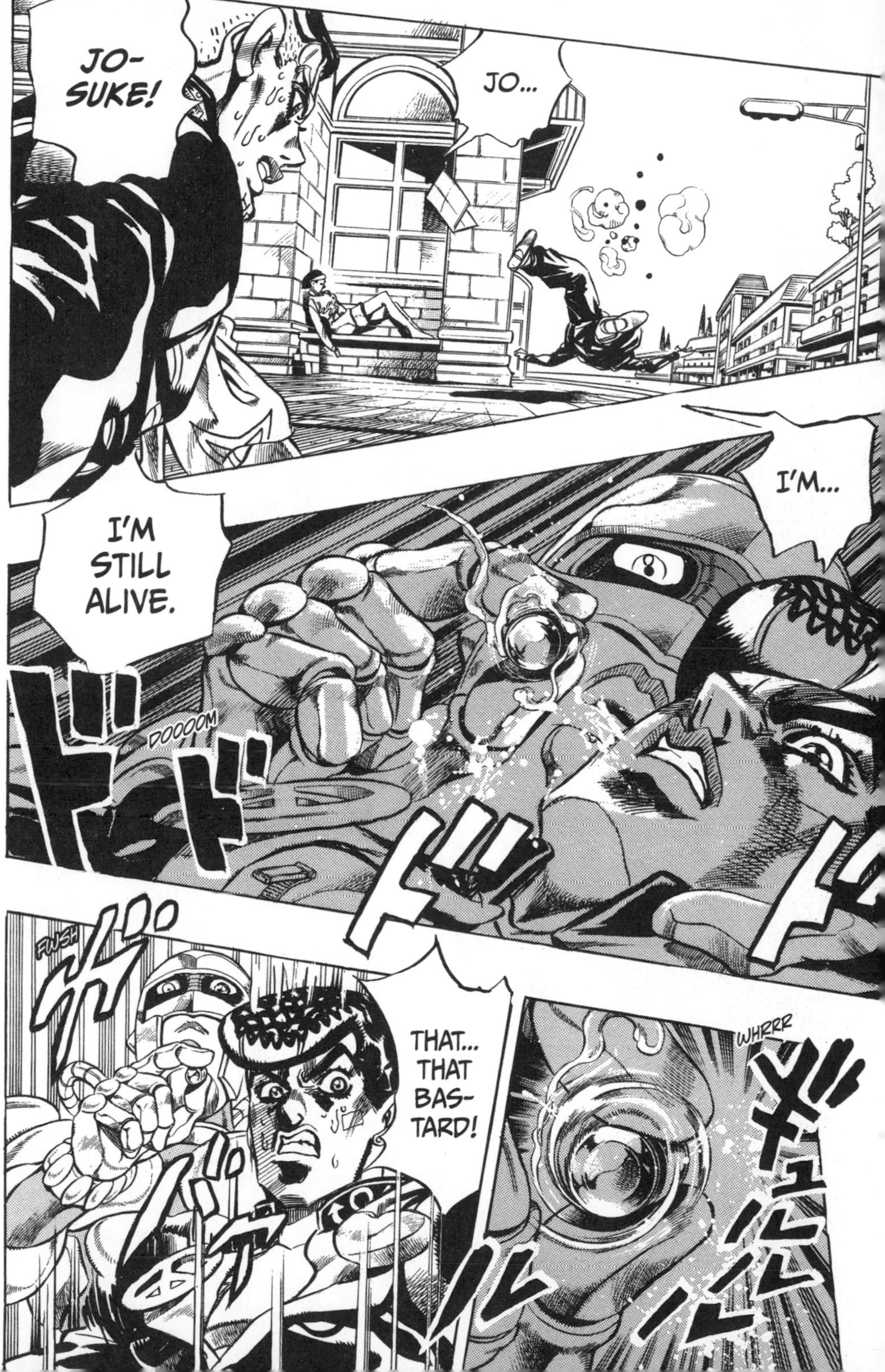
JO...
JO-SUKE!
I'M...
I'M STILL ALIVE.
DOOOOM
WHRRR
THAT... THAT BASTARD!
FWSH

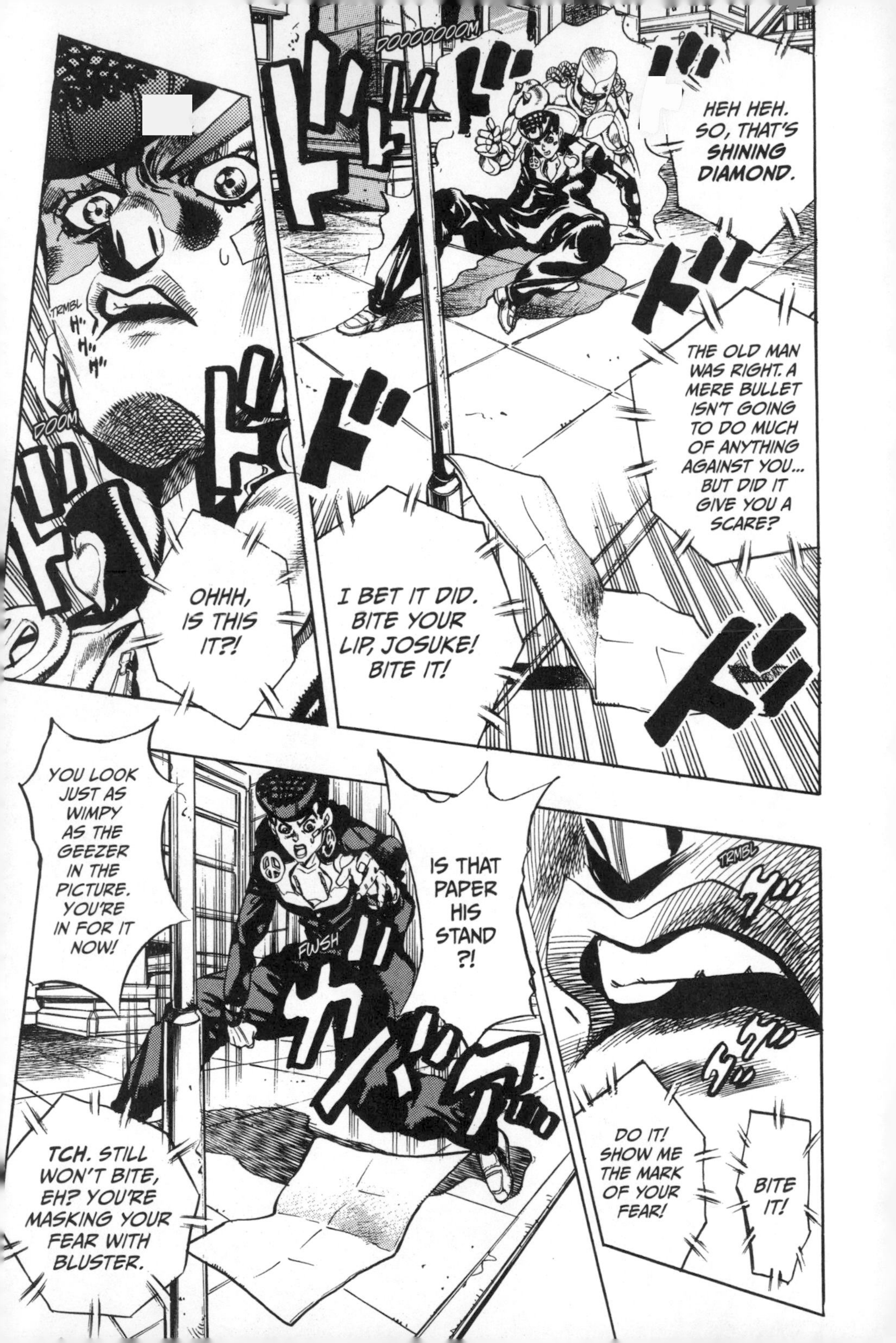
DOOOOOOOOM
HEH HEH. SO, THAT'S SHINING DIAMOND.
THE OLD MAN WAS RIGHT. A MERE BULLET ISN'T GOING TO DO MUCH OF ANYTHING AGAINST YOU... BUT DID IT GIVE YOU A SCARE?
I BET IT DID. BITE YOUR LIP, JOSUKE! BITE IT!
TRMBL
DOOM
OHHH, IS THIS IT?!
TRMBL
DO IT! SHOW ME THE MARK OF YOUR FEAR!
BITE IT!
IS THAT PAPER HIS STAND ?!
YOU LOOK JUST AS WIMPY AS THE GEEZER IN THE PICTURE. YOU'RE IN FOR IT NOW!
FWSH
TCH. STILL WON'T BITE, EH? YOU'RE MASKING YOUR FEAR WITH BLUSTER.

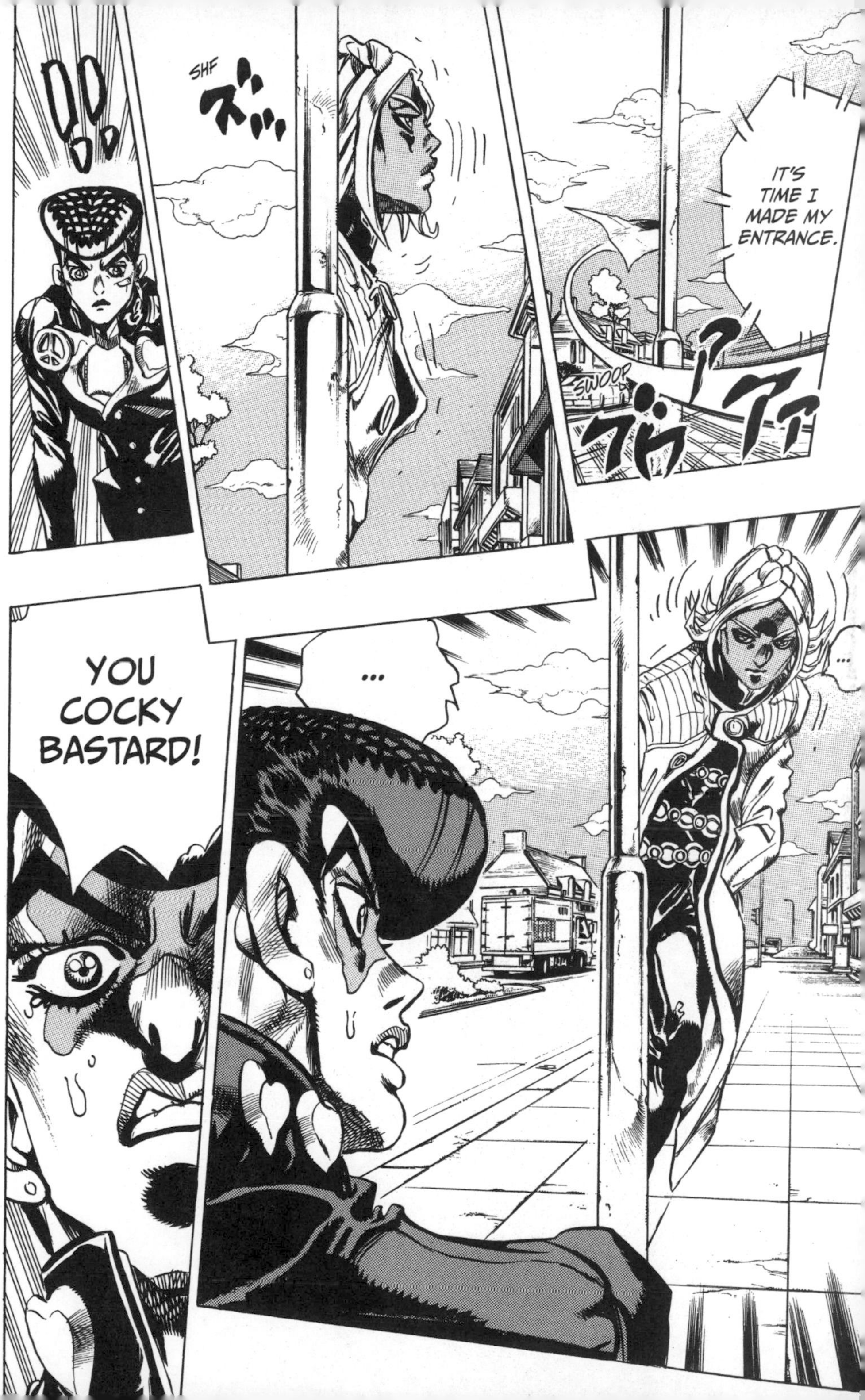
IT'S TIME I MADE MY ENTRANCE.
SWOOP
SHF
...
...
YOU COCKY BASTARD!

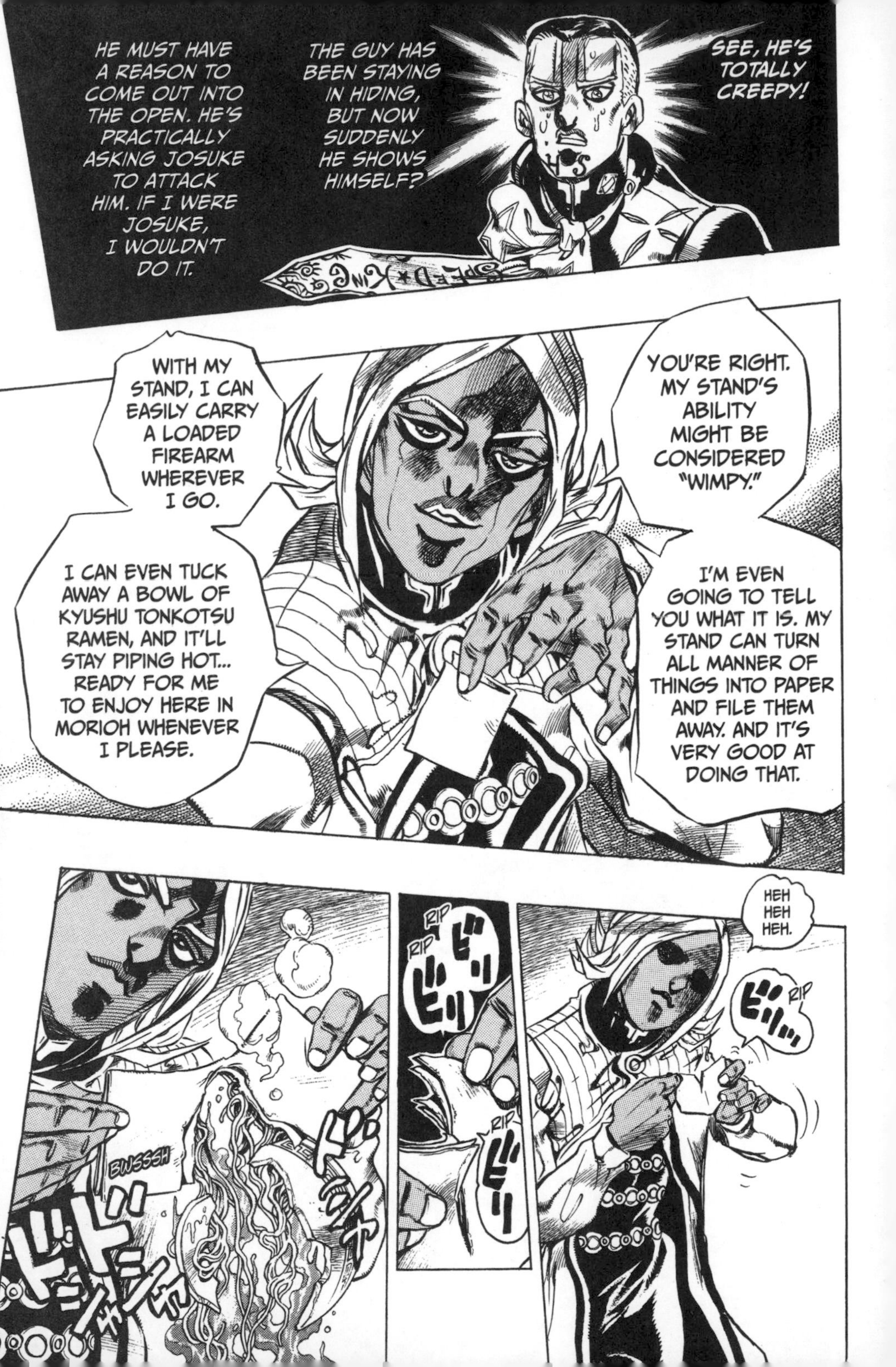
SEE, HE'S TOTALLY CREEPY!
THE GUY HAS BEEN STAYING IN HIDING, BUT NOW SUDDENLY HE SHOWS HIMSELF?
HE MUST HAVE A REASON TO COME OUT INTO THE OPEN. HE'S PRACTICALLY ASKING JOSUKE TO ATTACK HIM. IF I WERE JOSUKE, I WOULDN'T DO IT.
YOU'RE RIGHT. MY STAND'S ABILITY MIGHT BE CONSIDERED "WIMPY."
I'M EVEN GOING TO TELL YOU WHAT IT IS. MY STAND CAN TURN ALL MANNER OF THINGS INTO PAPER AND FILE THEM AWAY. AND IT'S VERY GOOD AT DOING THAT.
WITH MY STAND, I CAN EASILY CARRY A LOADED FIREARM WHEREVER I GO.
I CAN EVEN TUCK AWAY A BOWL OF KYUSHU TONKOTSU RAMEN, AND IT'LL STAY PIPING HOT... READY FOR ME TO ENJOY HERE IN MORIOH WHENEVER I PLEASE.
HEH HEH HEH.
RIP
RIP
RIP
RIP
BWSSSH

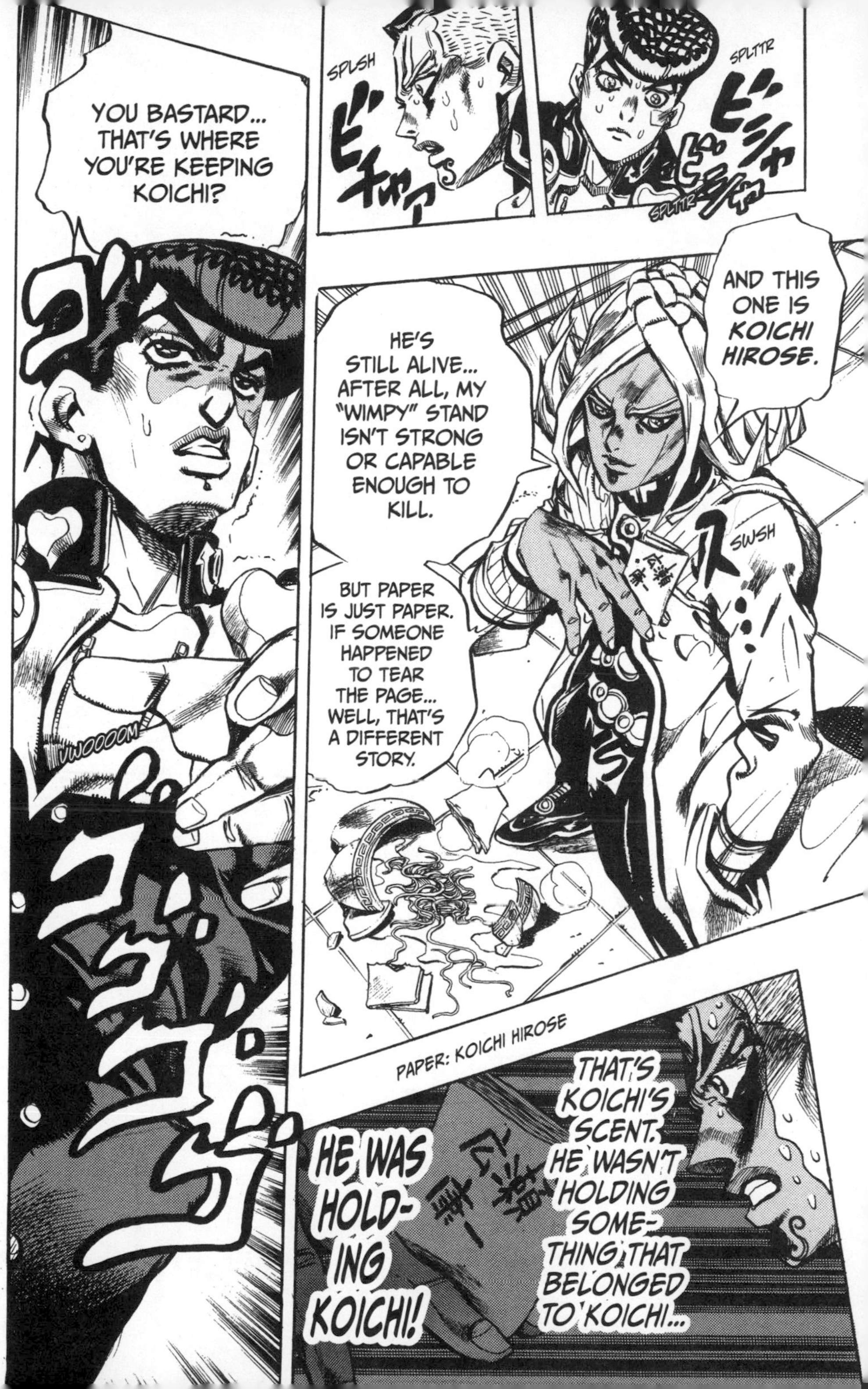
SPLTTR
SPLTTR
SPLSH
AND THIS ONE IS KOICHI HIROSE.
HE'S STILL ALIVE... AFTER ALL, MY "WIMPY" STAND ISN'T STRONG OR CAPABLE ENOUGH TO KILL.
SWSH
BUT PAPER IS JUST PAPER. IF SOMEONE HAPPENED TO TEAR THE PAGE... WELL, THAT'S A DIFFERENT STORY.
PAPER: KOICHI HIROSE
THAT'S KOICHI'S SCENT. HE WASN'T HOLDING SOME-THING THAT BELONGED TO KOICHI...
HE WAS HOLD-ING KOICHI!
YOU BASTARD... THAT'S WHERE YOU'RE KEEPING KOICHI?
UWOOOOM

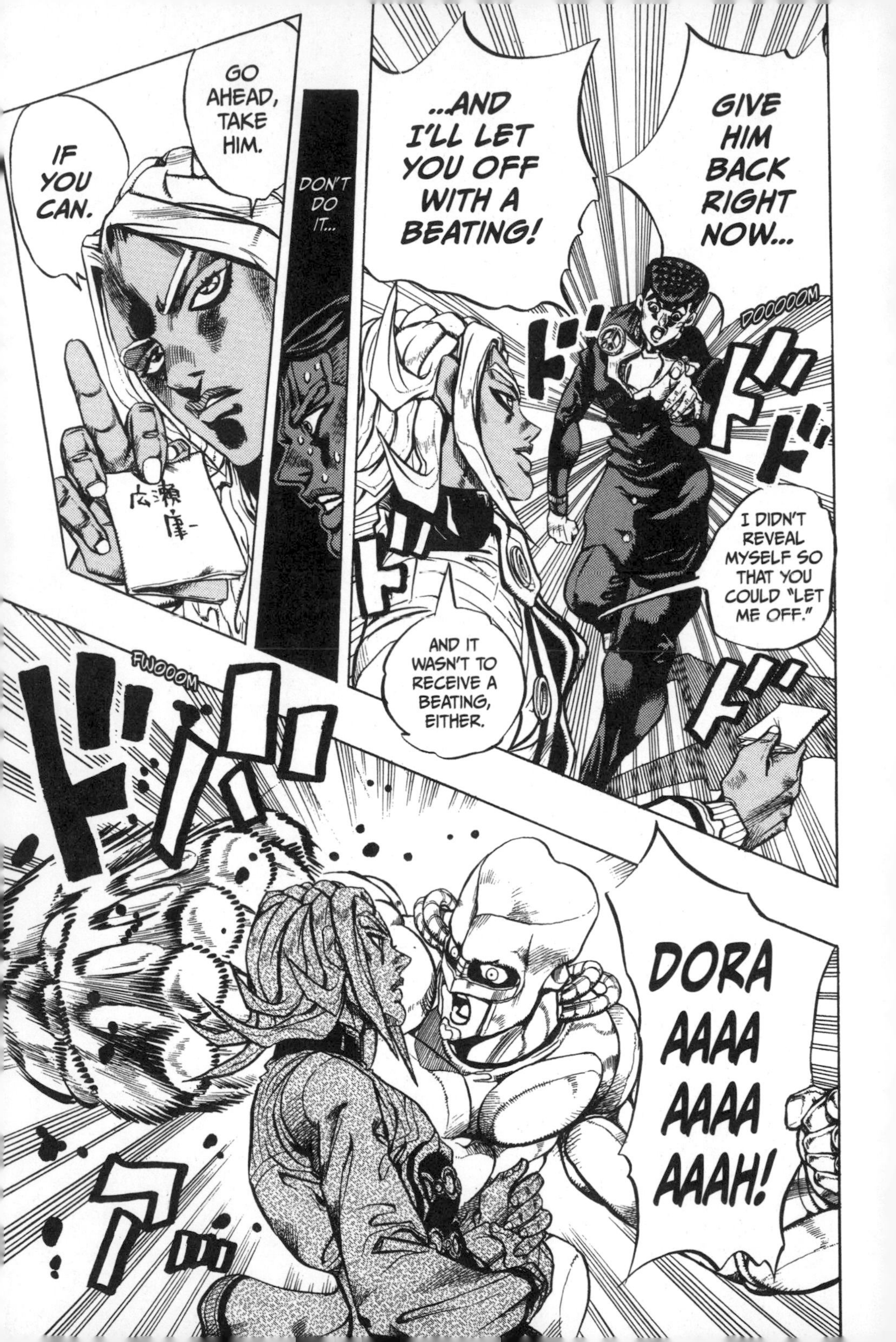
GIVE HIM BACK RIGHT NOW...
...AND I'LL LET YOU OFF WITH A BEATING!
DOOOOOM
I DIDN'T REVEAL MYSELF SO THAT YOU COULD "LET ME OFF."
AND IT WASN'T TO RECEIVE A BEATING, EITHER.
DON'T DO IT...
GO AHEAD, TAKE HIM.
IF YOU CAN.
広瀬康一
DORA AAAA AAAA AAAH!
FWOOOM

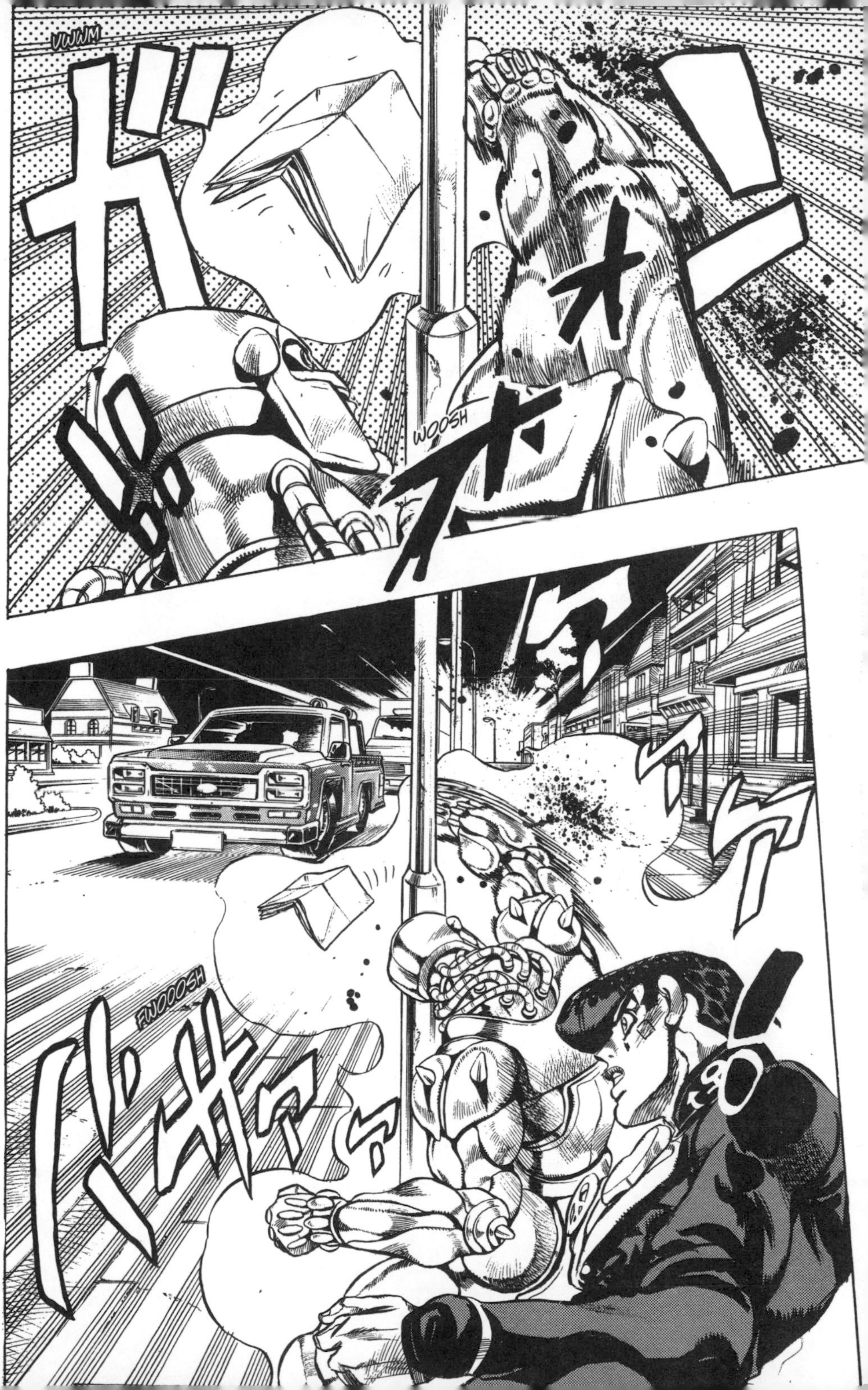
VWWM
WOOSH
FWOOOSH

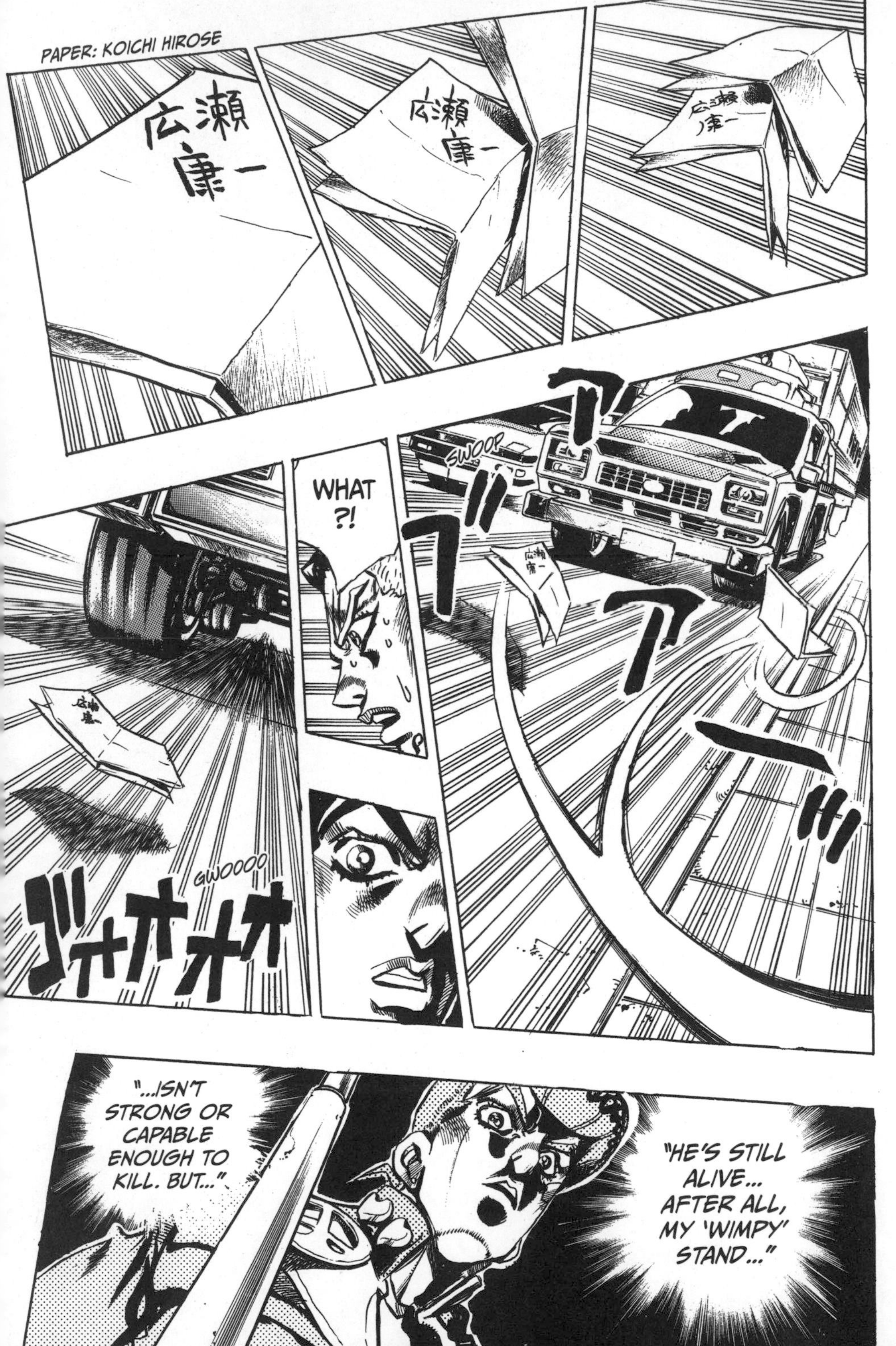
PAPER: KOICHI HIROSE
広瀬康一
広瀬康一
広瀬康一
SWOOP
広瀬康一
WHAT ?!
広瀬康一
GWOOOO
"HE'S STILL ALIVE... AFTER ALL, MY 'WIMPY' STAND..."
"...ISN'T STRONG OR CAPABLE ENOUGH TO KILL. BUT..."

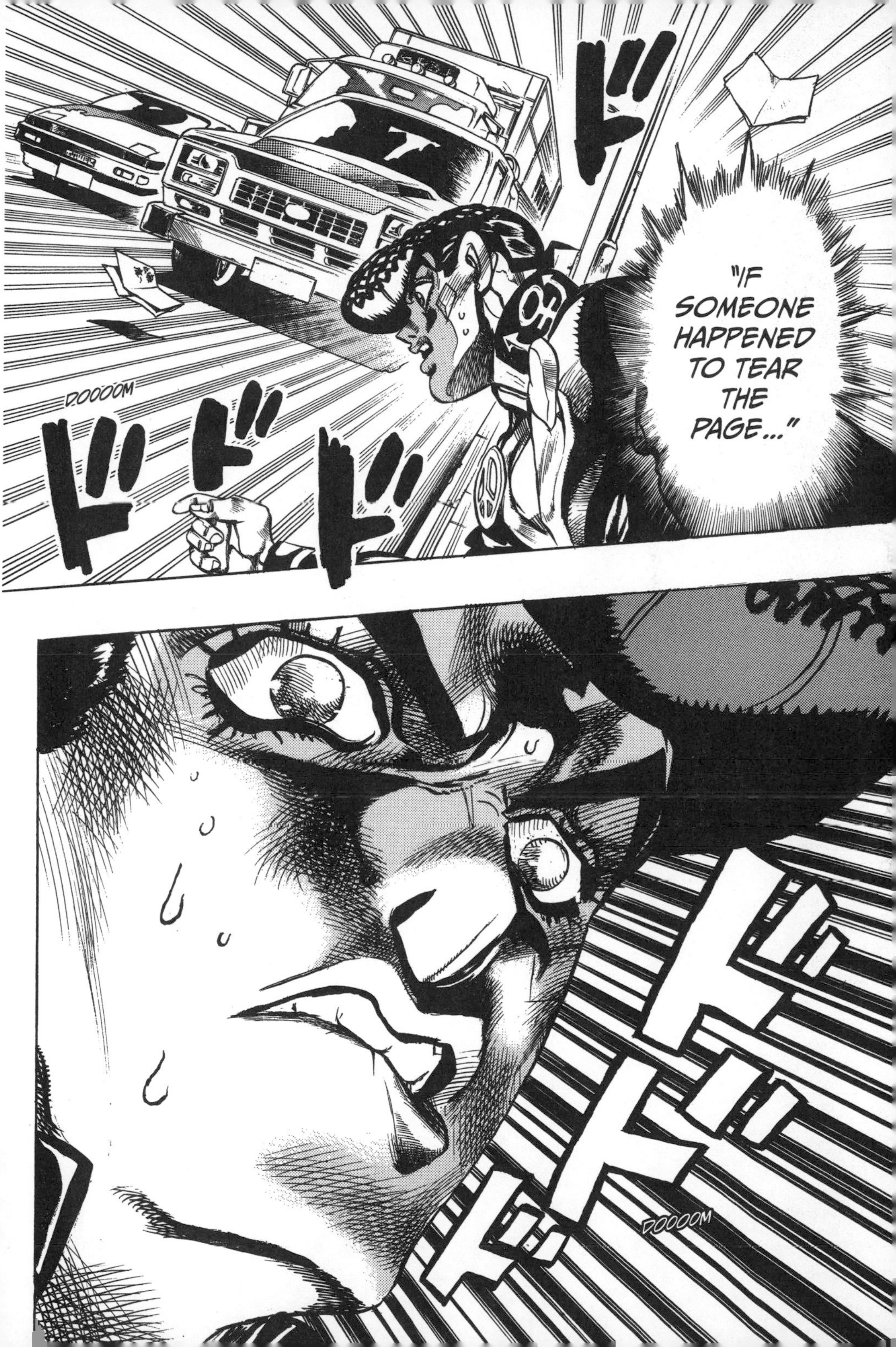
"IF SOMEONE HAPPENED TO TEAR THE PAGE..."
ドドドド
DOOOOM
ドドド
DOOOOM

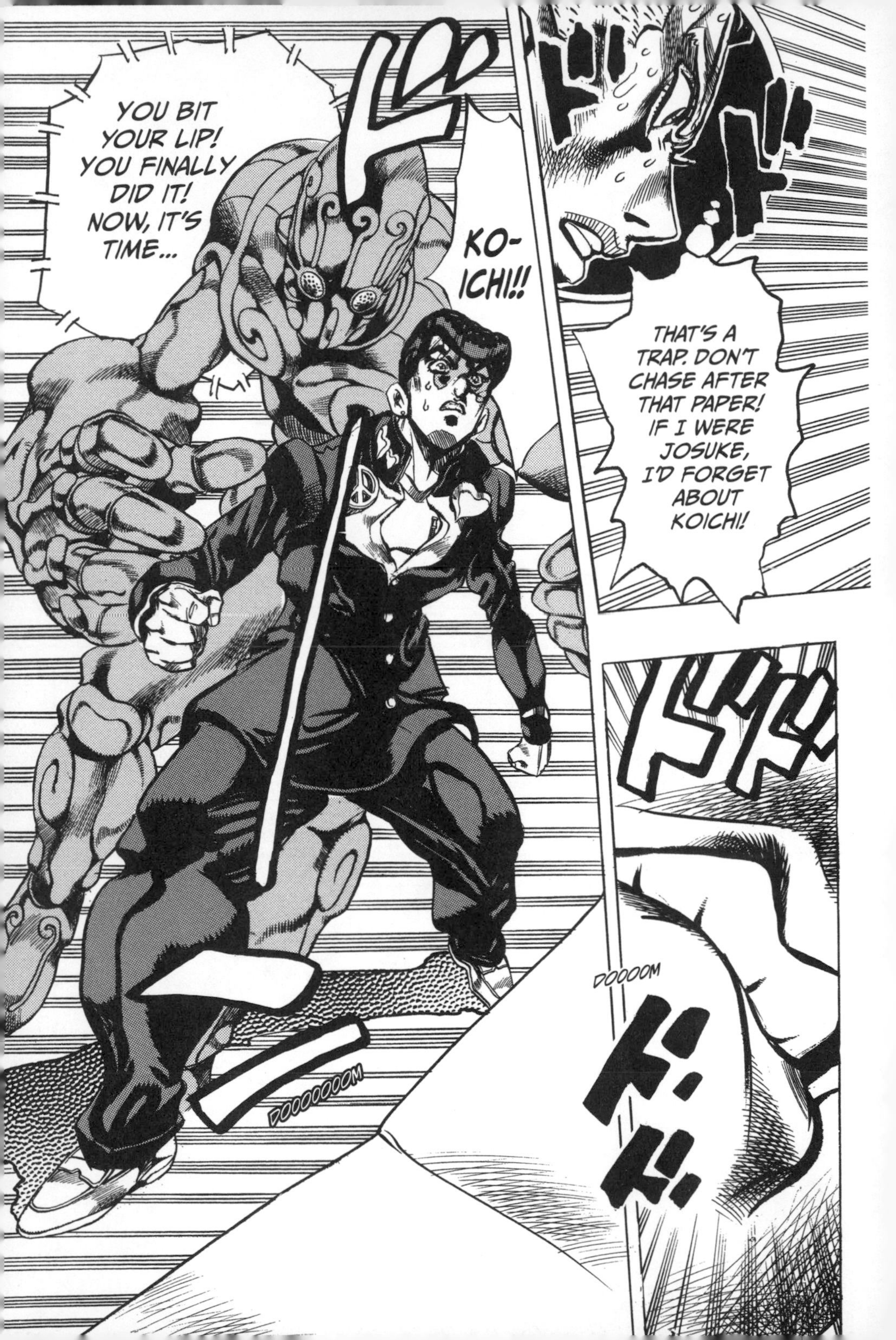
THAT'S A TRAP. DON'T CHASE AFTER THAT PAPER! IF I WERE JOSUKE, I'D FORGET ABOUT KOICHI!
DOOOOM
YOU BIT YOUR LIP! YOU FINALLY DID IT! NOW, IT'S TIME...
KO-ICHI!!
DOOOOOOOM

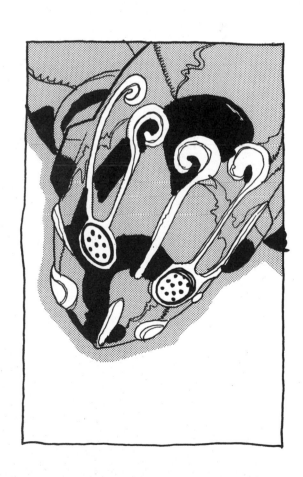

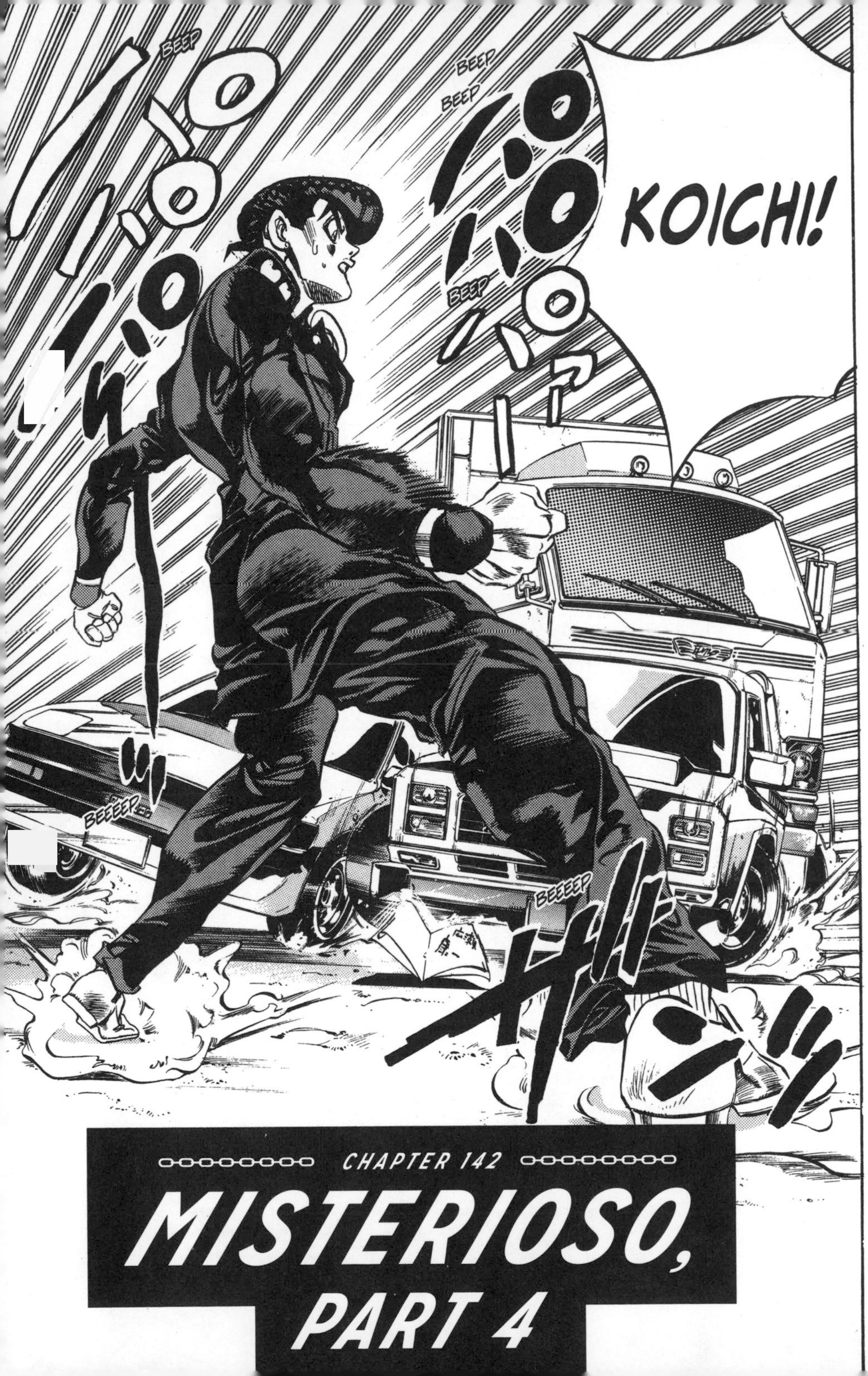
KOICHI!
BEEP
BEEP
BEEP
BEEP
BEEEEP
BEEEEP

CHAPTER 142

MISTERIOSO, PART 4

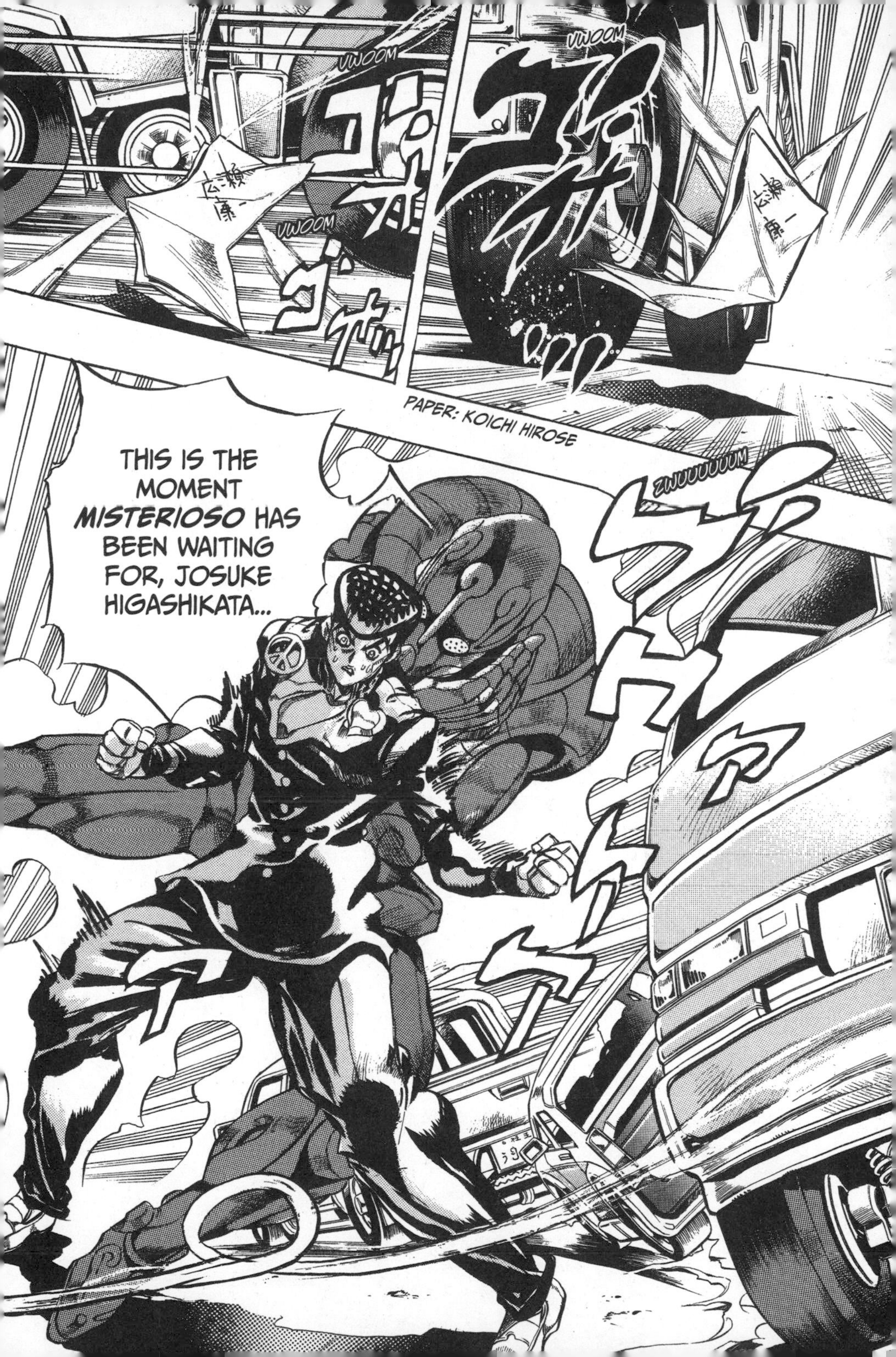
VWOOM
VWOOM
VWOOM
PAPER: KOICHI HIROSE
ZWUUUUUUUM
THIS IS THE MOMENT *MISTERIOSO* HAS BEEN WAITING FOR, JOSUKE HIGASHIKATA...

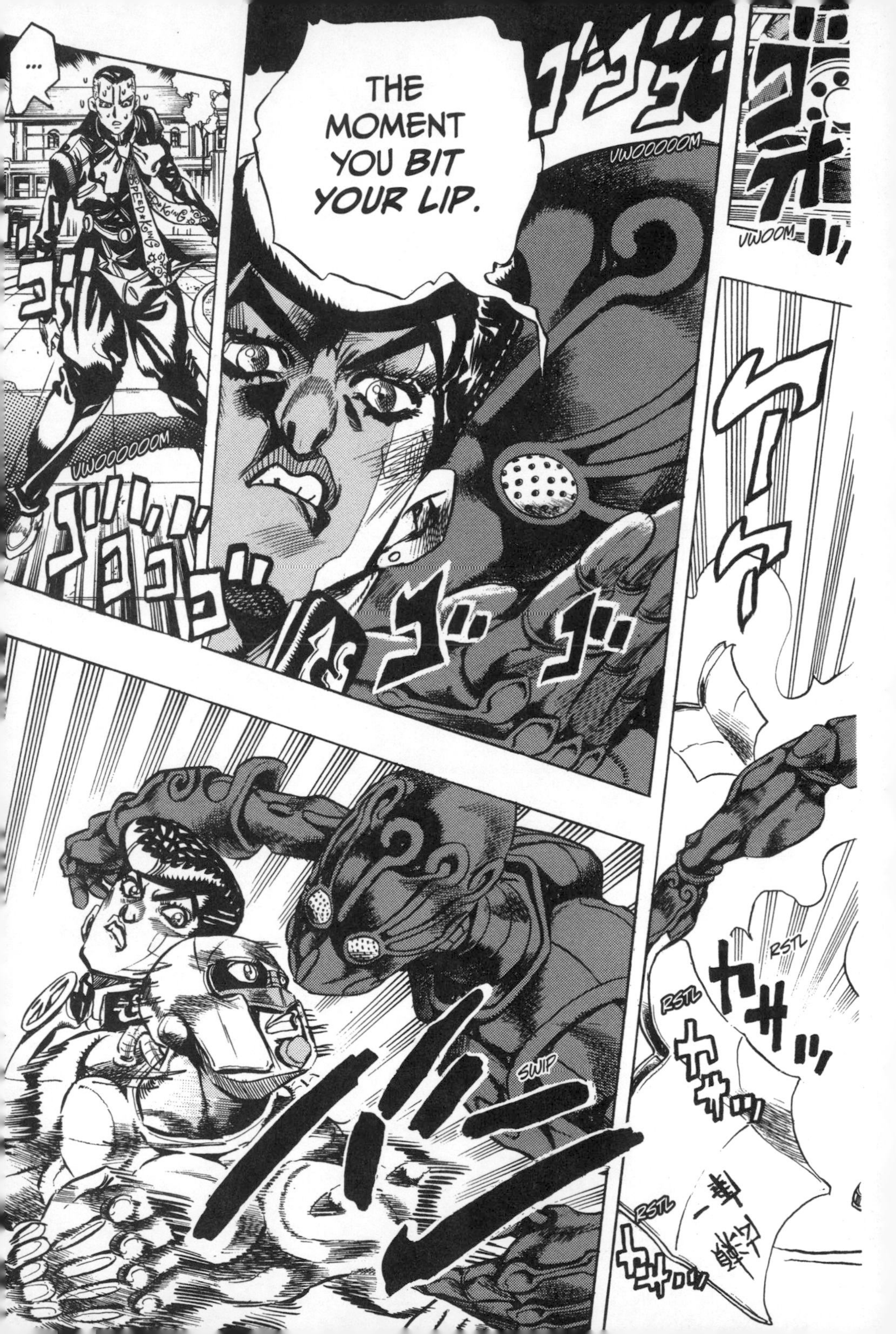
VWOOM
THE MOMENT YOU BIT YOUR LIP.
VWOOOOOM
...
VWOOOOOOM
RSTL
RSTL
RSTL
SWIP

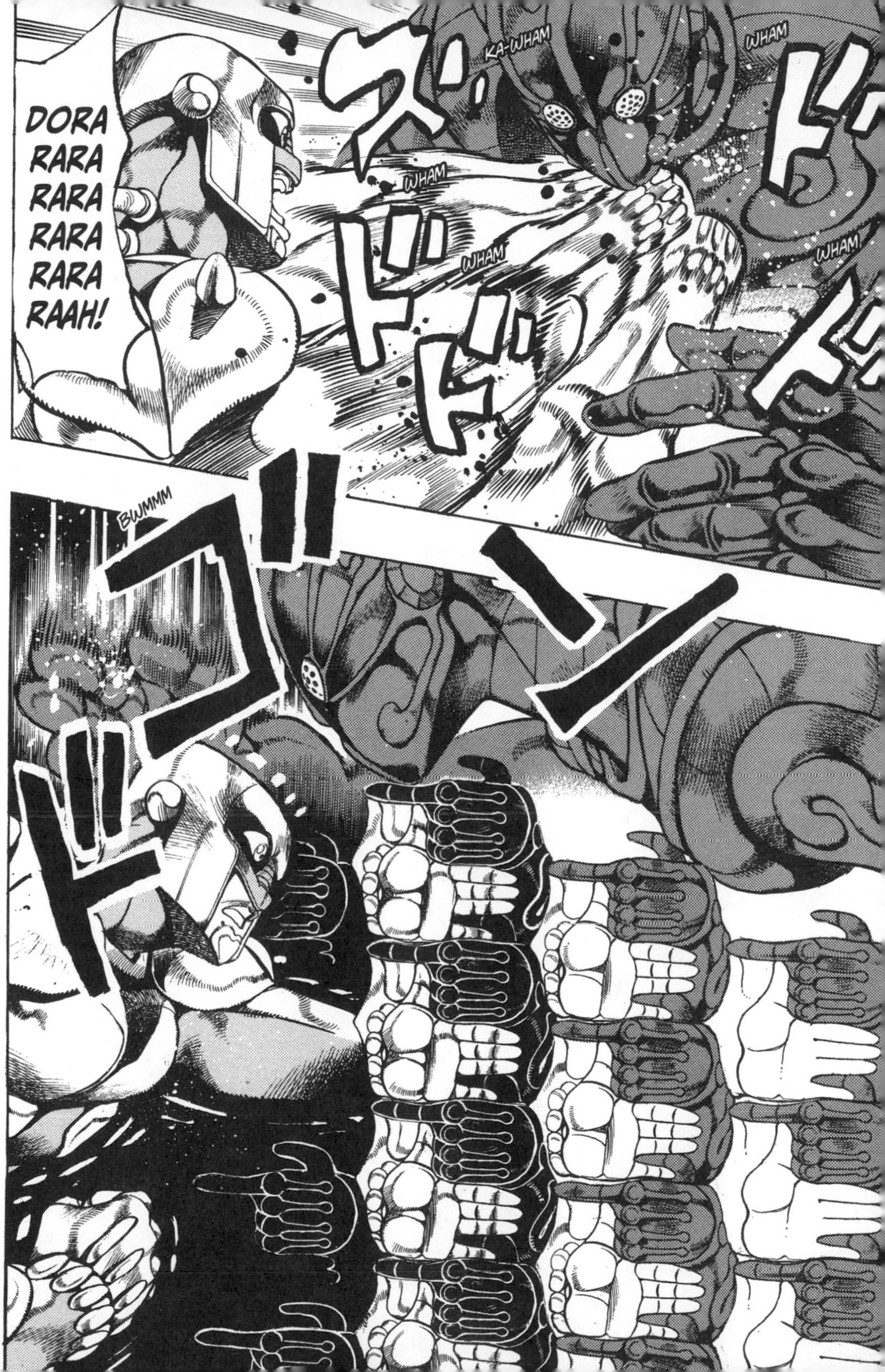
WHAM
KA-WHAM
WHAM
WHAM
WHAM
DORA RARA RARA RARA RARA RAAH!
BWMMM

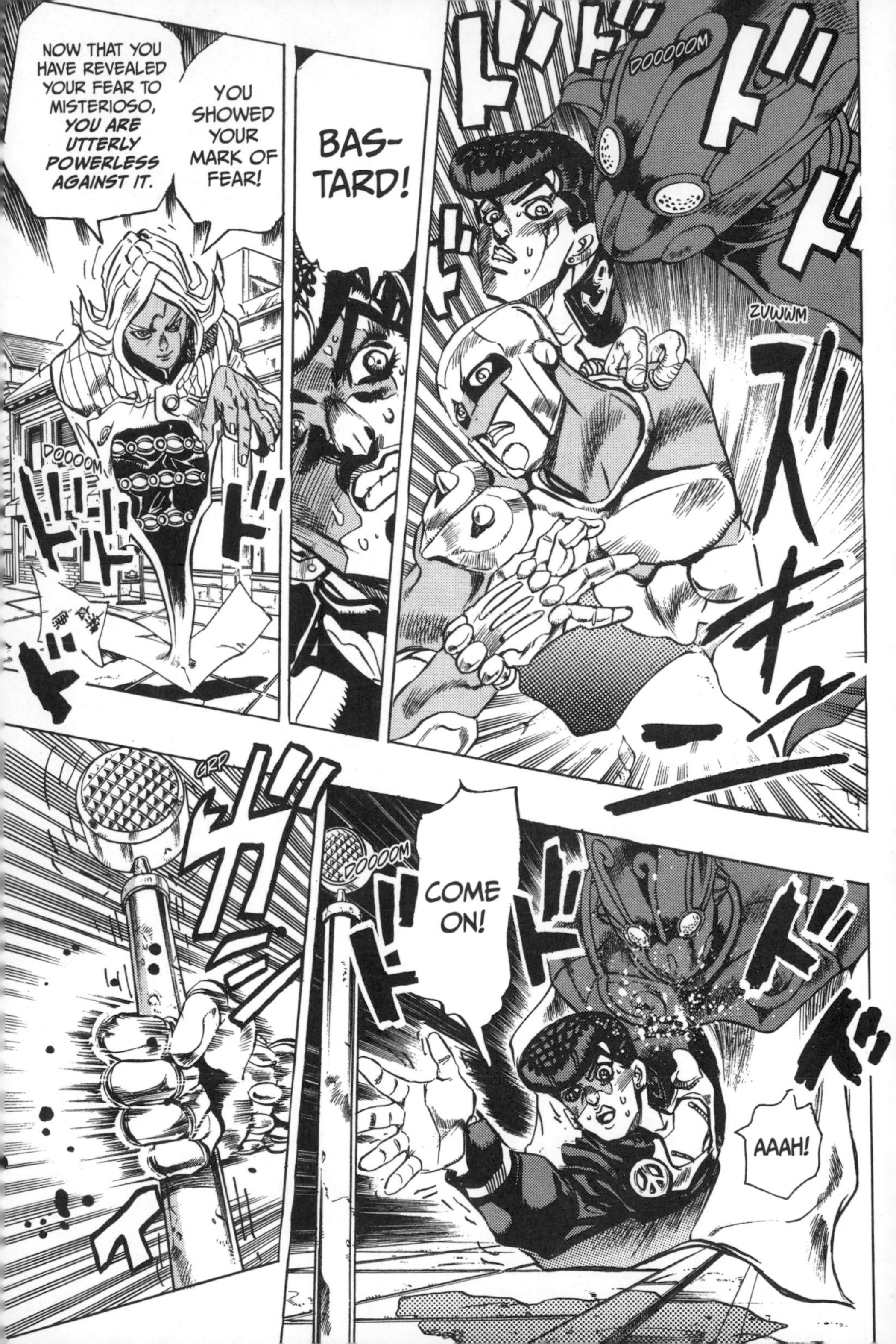
DOOOOOM
ZUWWM
BAS-TARD!
YOU SHOWED YOUR MARK OF FEAR!
NOW THAT YOU HAVE REVEALED YOUR FEAR TO MISTERIOSO, *YOU ARE UTTERLY POWERLESS AGAINST IT.*
DOOOOM
COME ON!
DOOOOM
AAAH!
GRP

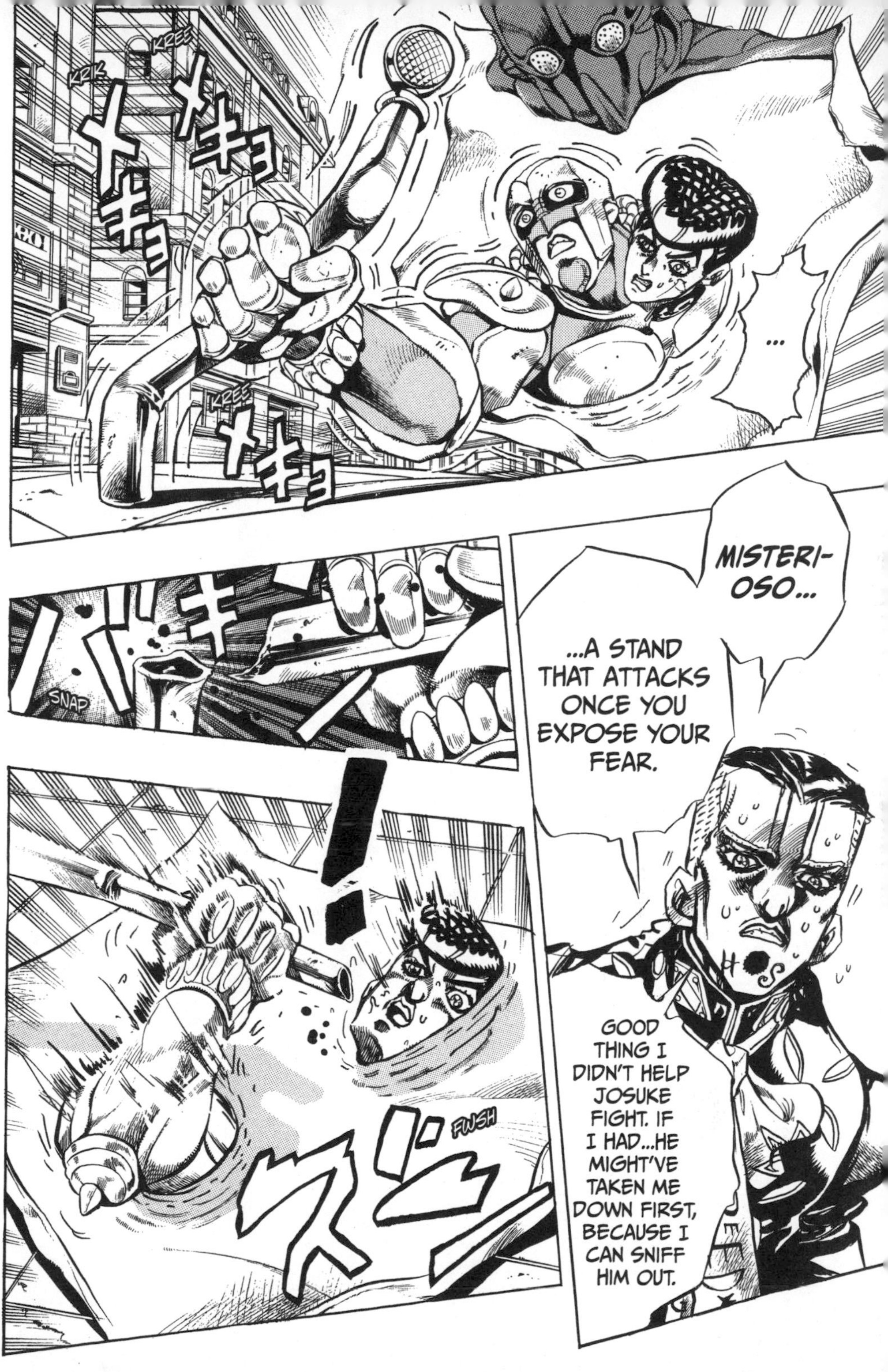
...
KREE
KRIK
KREE
MISTERI-OSO...
...A STAND THAT ATTACKS ONCE YOU EXPOSE YOUR FEAR.
GOOD THING I DIDN'T HELP JOSUKE FIGHT. IF I HAD...HE MIGHT'VE TAKEN ME DOWN FIRST, BECAUSE I CAN SNIFF HIM OUT.
SNAP
FWSH

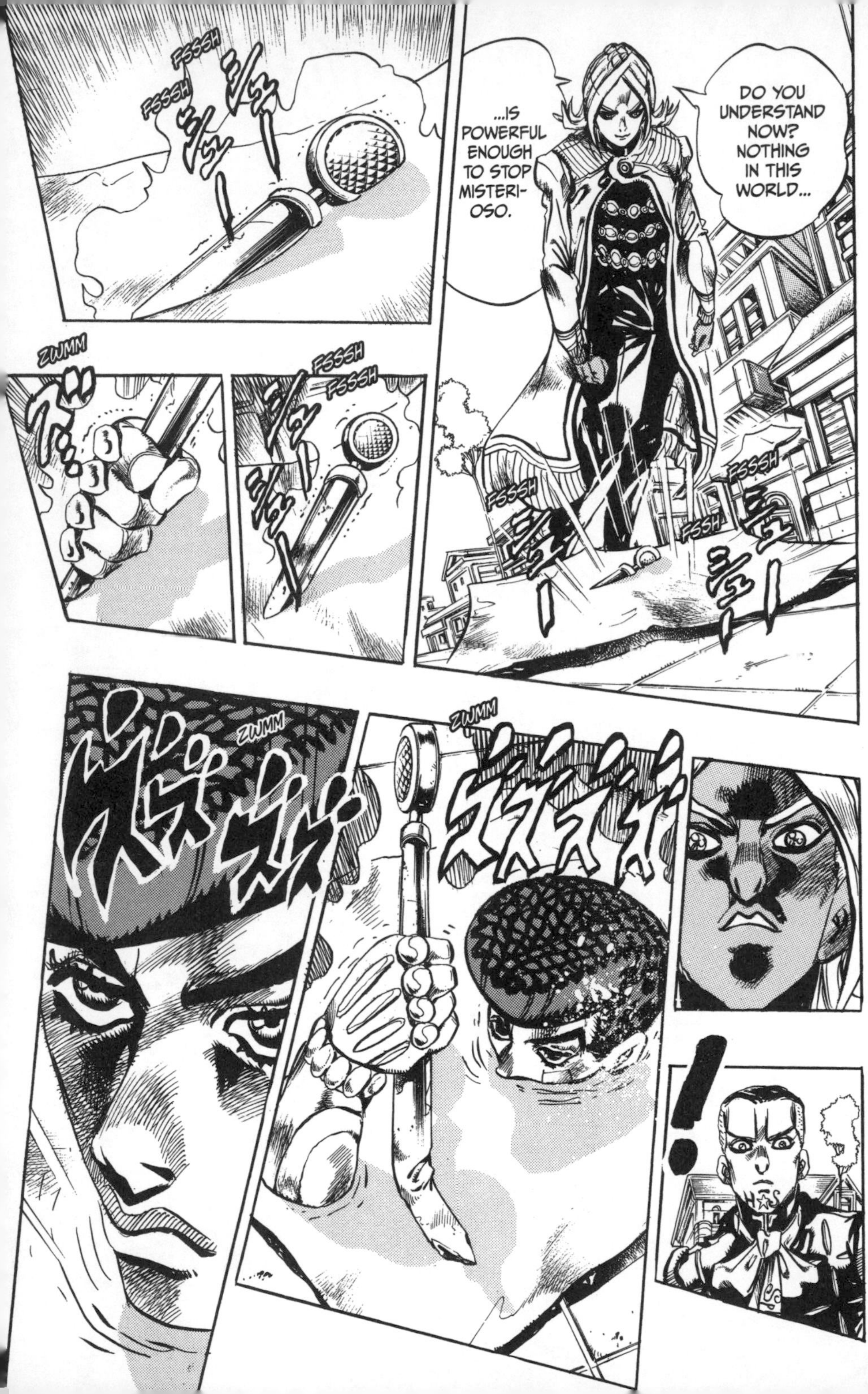
DO YOU UNDERSTAND NOW? NOTHING IN THIS WORLD...
...IS POWERFUL ENOUGH TO STOP MISTERIOSO.
FSSSH
FSSH
FSSSH
FSSSH
FSSSH
FSSSH
FSSSH
ZWMM
!
ZWMM
ZWMM

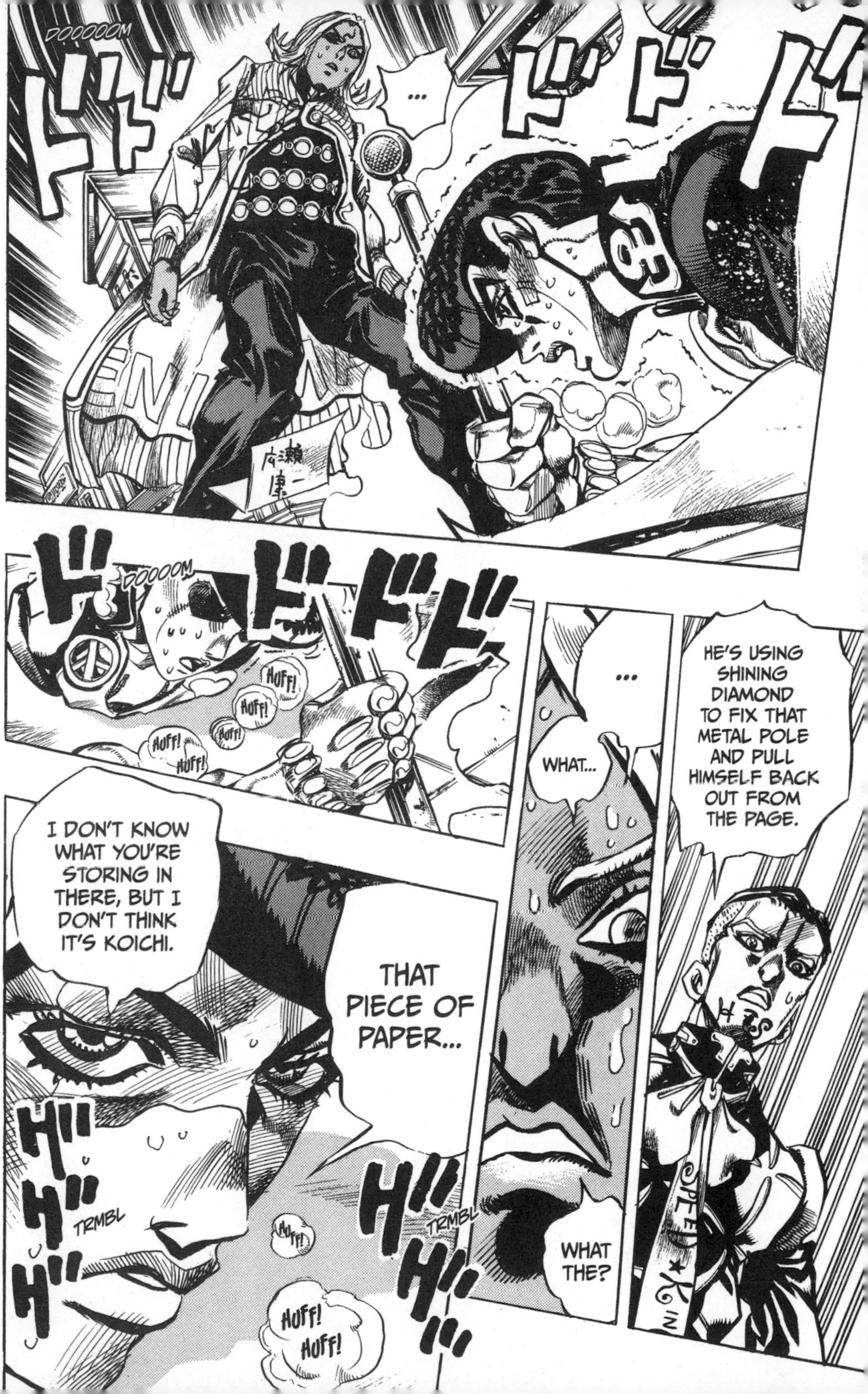
DOOOOOM
...
HE'S USING SHINING DIAMOND TO FIX THAT METAL POLE AND PULL HIMSELF BACK OUT FROM THE PAGE.
...
WHAT...
TRMBL
WHAT THE?
DOOOOM
HUFF! HUFF! HUFF! HUFF! HUFF!
I DON'T KNOW WHAT YOU'RE STORING IN THERE, BUT I DON'T THINK IT'S KOICHI.
THAT PIECE OF PAPER...
TRMBL
HUFF!
HUFF! HUFF!

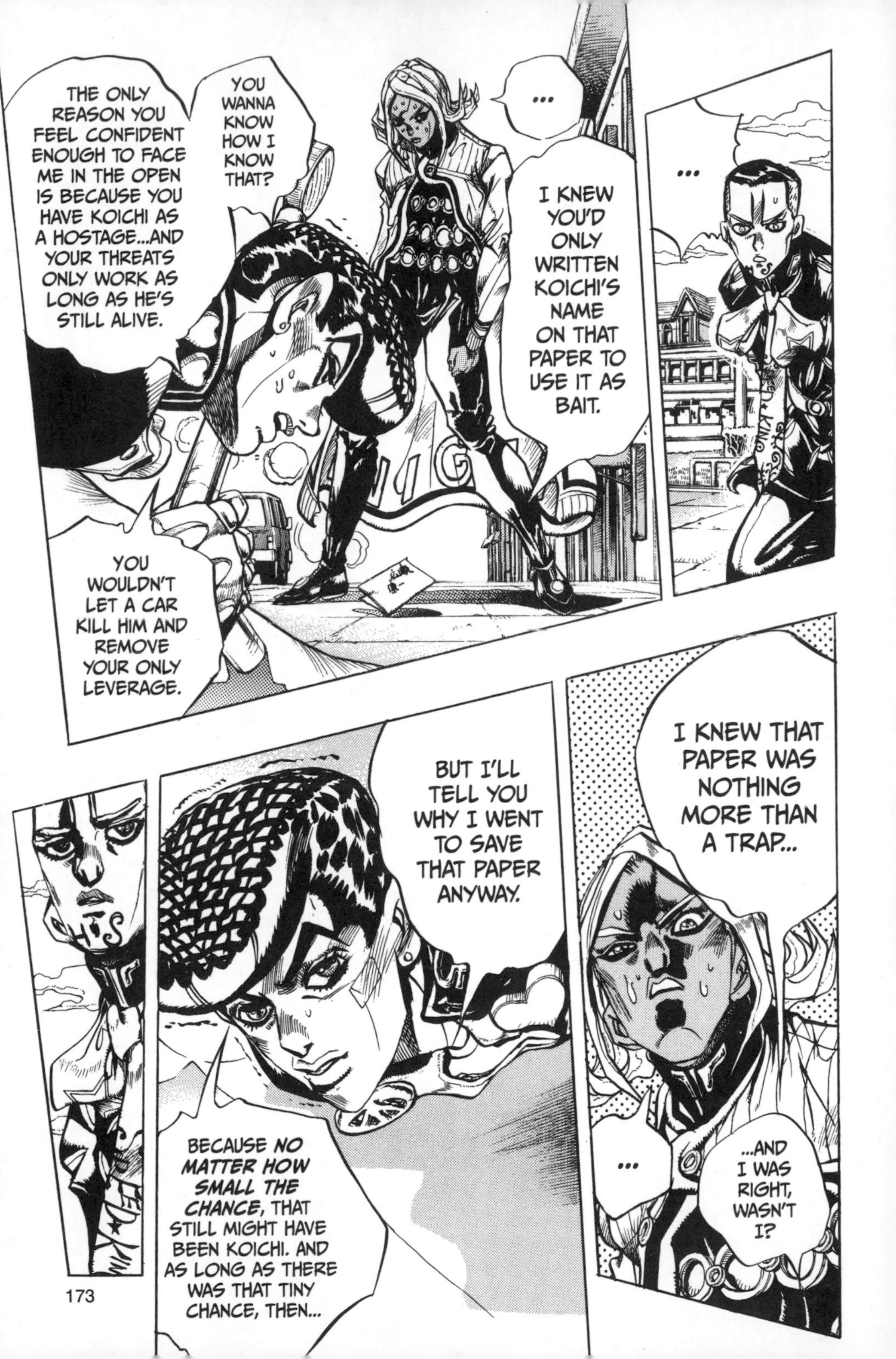
...
...
I KNEW YOU'D ONLY WRITTEN KOICHI'S NAME ON THAT PAPER TO USE IT AS BAIT.
YOU WANNA KNOW HOW I KNOW THAT?
THE ONLY REASON YOU FEEL CONFIDENT ENOUGH TO FACE ME IN THE OPEN IS BECAUSE YOU HAVE KOICHI AS A HOSTAGE...AND YOUR THREATS ONLY WORK AS LONG AS HE'S STILL ALIVE.
YOU WOULDN'T LET A CAR KILL HIM AND REMOVE YOUR ONLY LEVERAGE.
I KNEW THAT PAPER WAS NOTHING MORE THAN A TRAP...
...AND I WAS RIGHT, WASN'T I?
...
BUT I'LL TELL YOU WHY I WENT TO SAVE THAT PAPER ANYWAY.
BECAUSE *NO MATTER HOW SMALL THE CHANCE*, THAT STILL MIGHT HAVE BEEN KOICHI. AND AS LONG AS THERE WAS THAT TINY CHANCE, THEN...

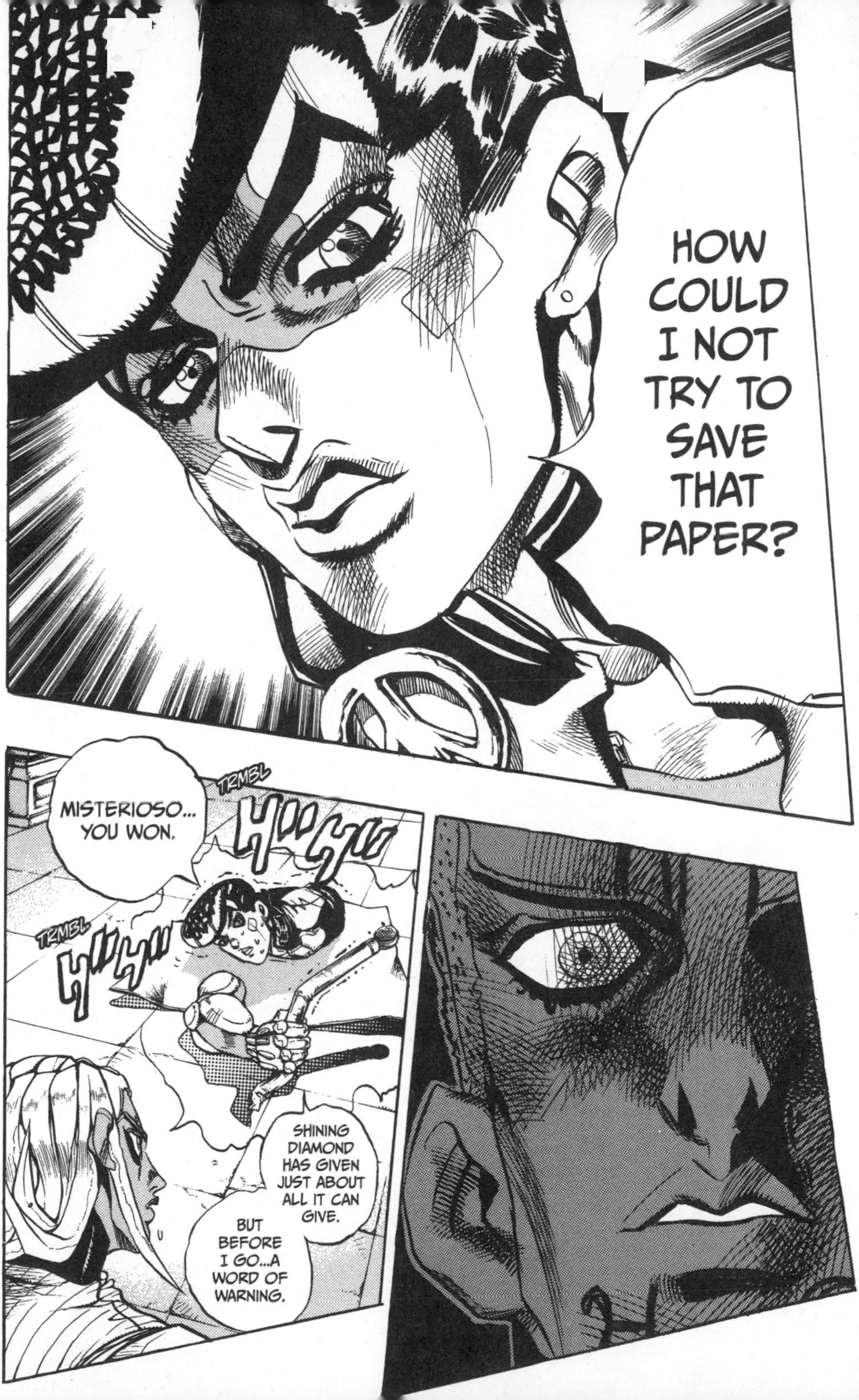
HOW COULD I NOT TRY TO SAVE THAT PAPER?
MISTERIOSO... YOU WON.
TRMBL
TRMBL
SHINING DIAMOND HAS GIVEN JUST ABOUT ALL IT CAN GIVE.
BUT BEFORE I GO...A WORD OF WARNING.

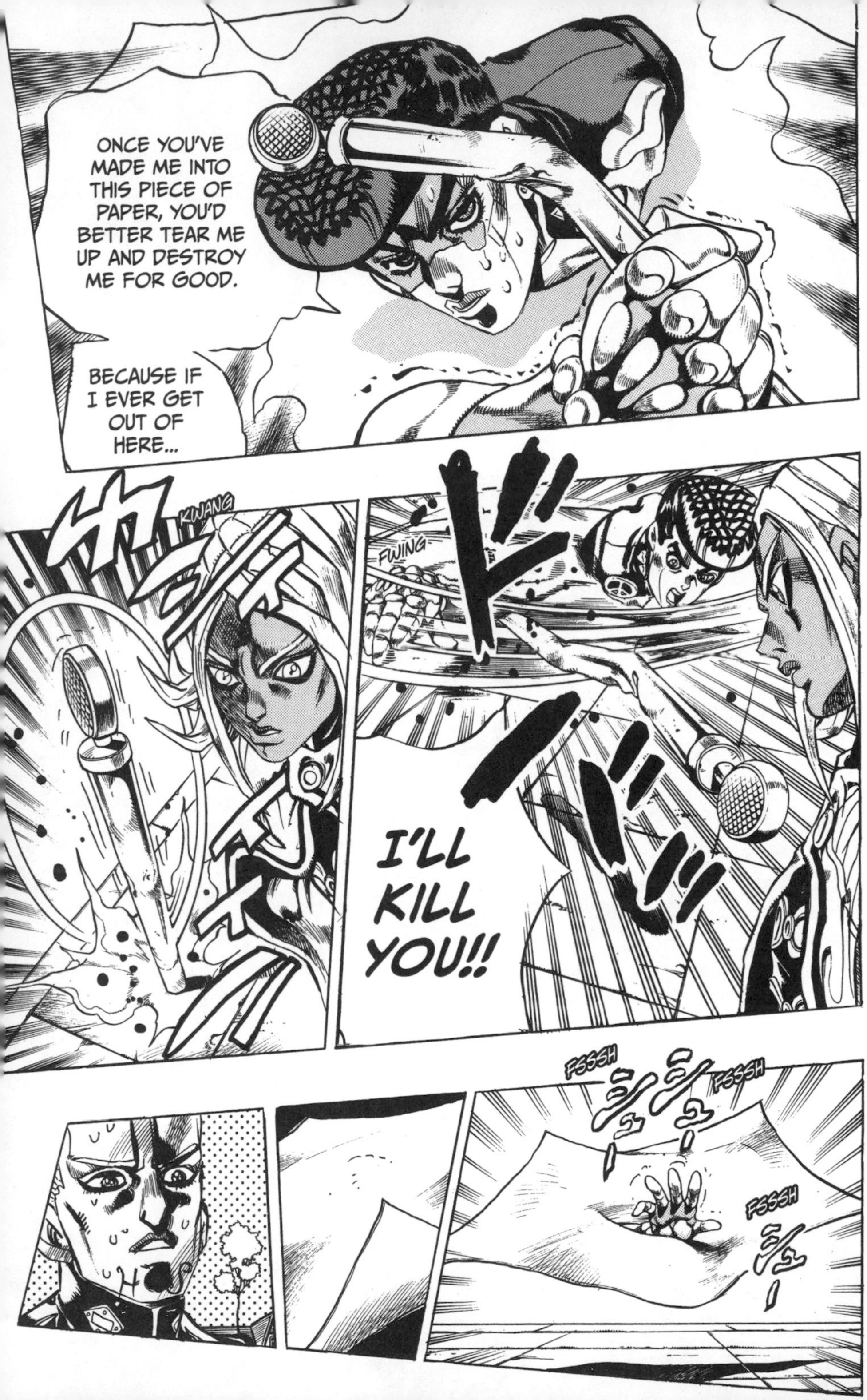
ONCE YOU'VE MADE ME INTO THIS PIECE OF PAPER, YOU'D BETTER TEAR ME UP AND DESTROY ME FOR GOOD.
BECAUSE IF I EVER GET OUT OF HERE...
FWING
I'LL KILL YOU!!
KWANG
FSSSH
FSSSH
FSSSH

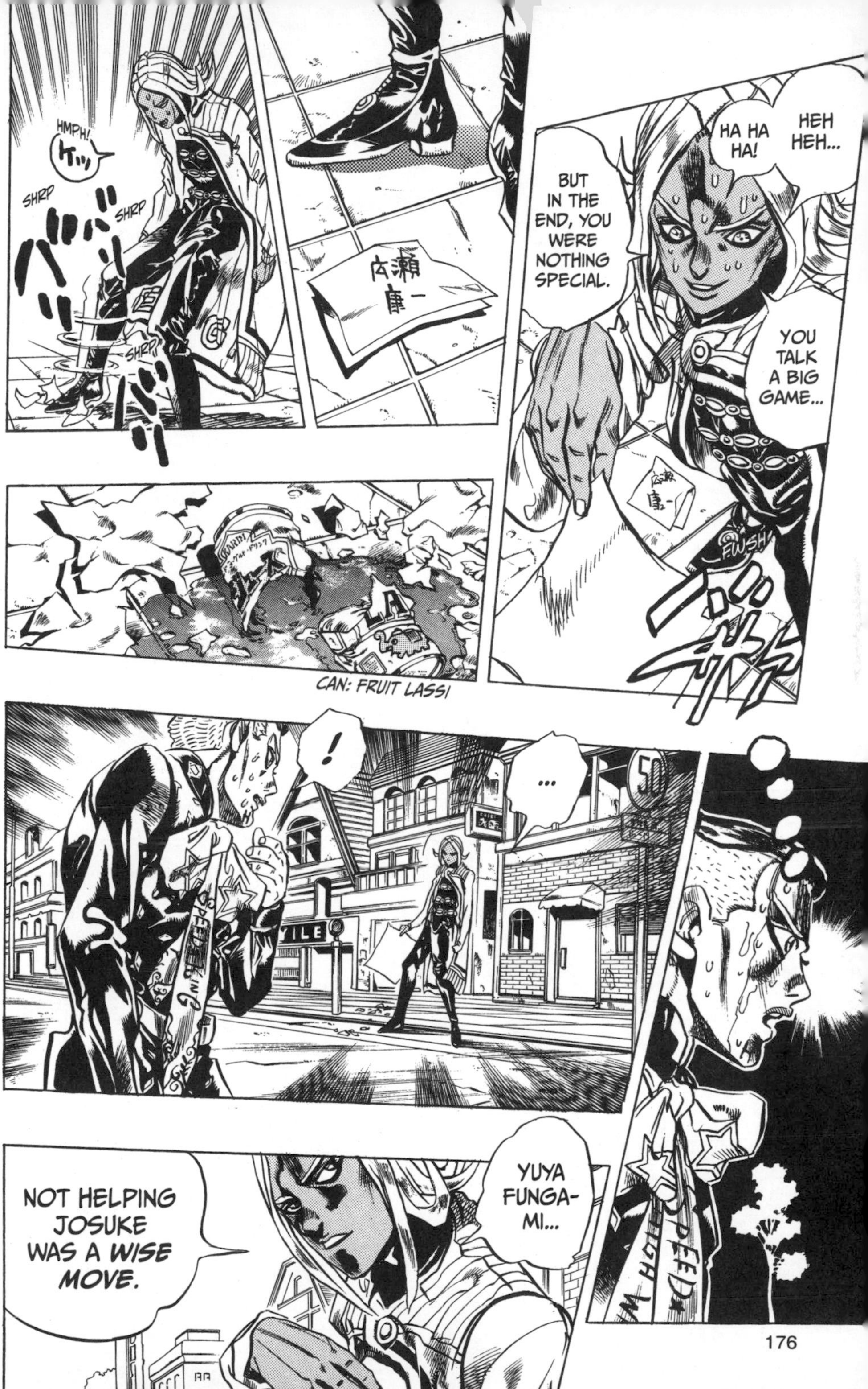
HA HA HA!
HEH HEH...
BUT IN THE END, YOU WERE NOTHING SPECIAL.
YOU TALK A BIG GAME...
FWSH
広瀬 康一
HMPH!
ヒッ
SHRP
SHRP
SHRP
CAN: FRUIT LASSI
...
!
YUYA FUNGAMI...
NOT HELPING JOSUKE WAS A WISE MOVE.

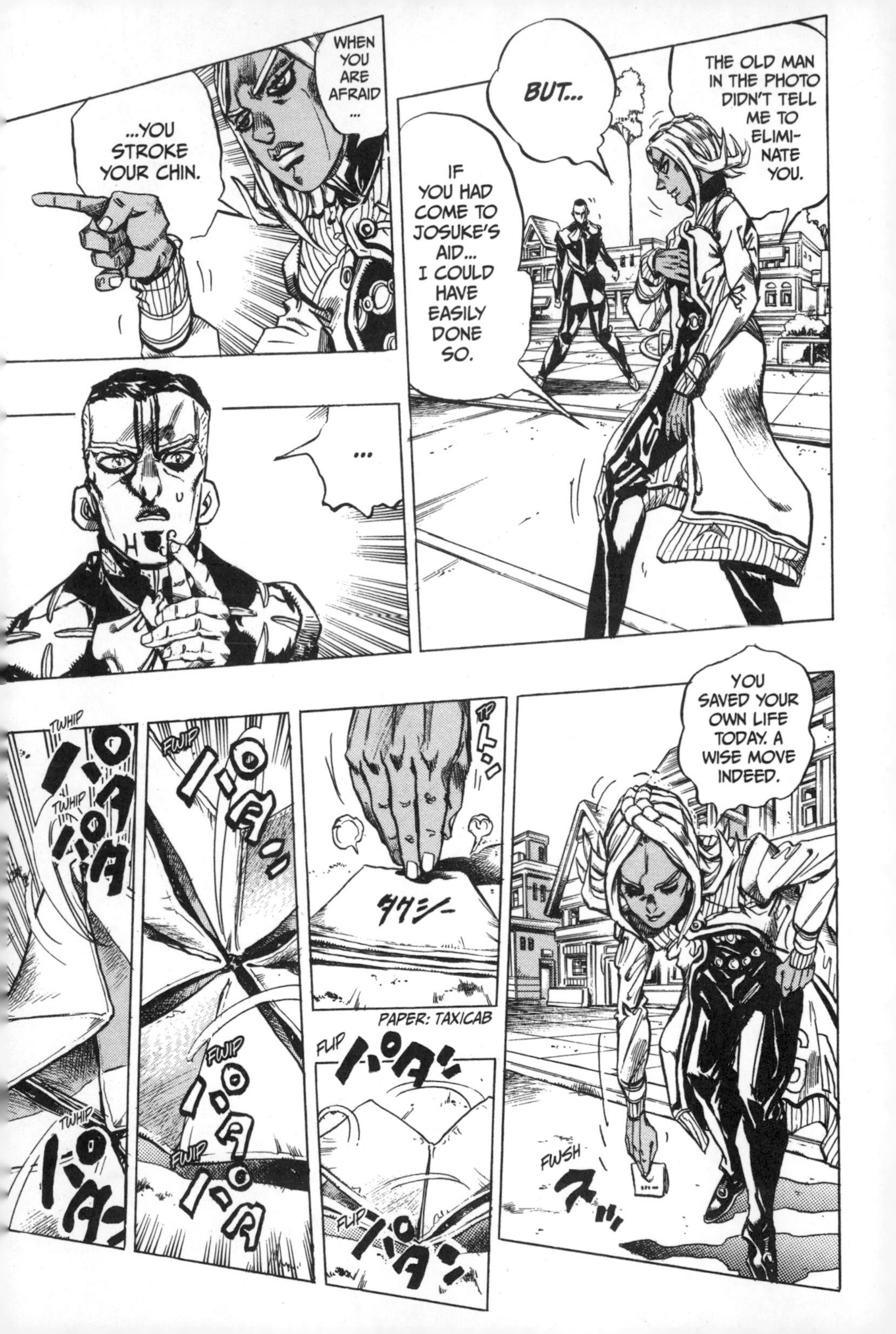

THE OLD MAN IN THE PHOTO DIDN'T TELL ME TO ELIMINATE YOU.
BUT...
IF YOU HAD COME TO JOSUKE'S AID... I COULD HAVE EASILY DONE SO.
WHEN YOU ARE AFRAID...
...YOU STROKE YOUR CHIN.
...
YOU SAVED YOUR OWN LIFE TODAY. A WISE MOVE INDEED.
FWSH
TP
タクシー
PAPER: TAXICAB
FLIP
パタン
FLIP
パタン
FWIP
FWIP
FWIP
TWHIP
TWHIP
TWHIP

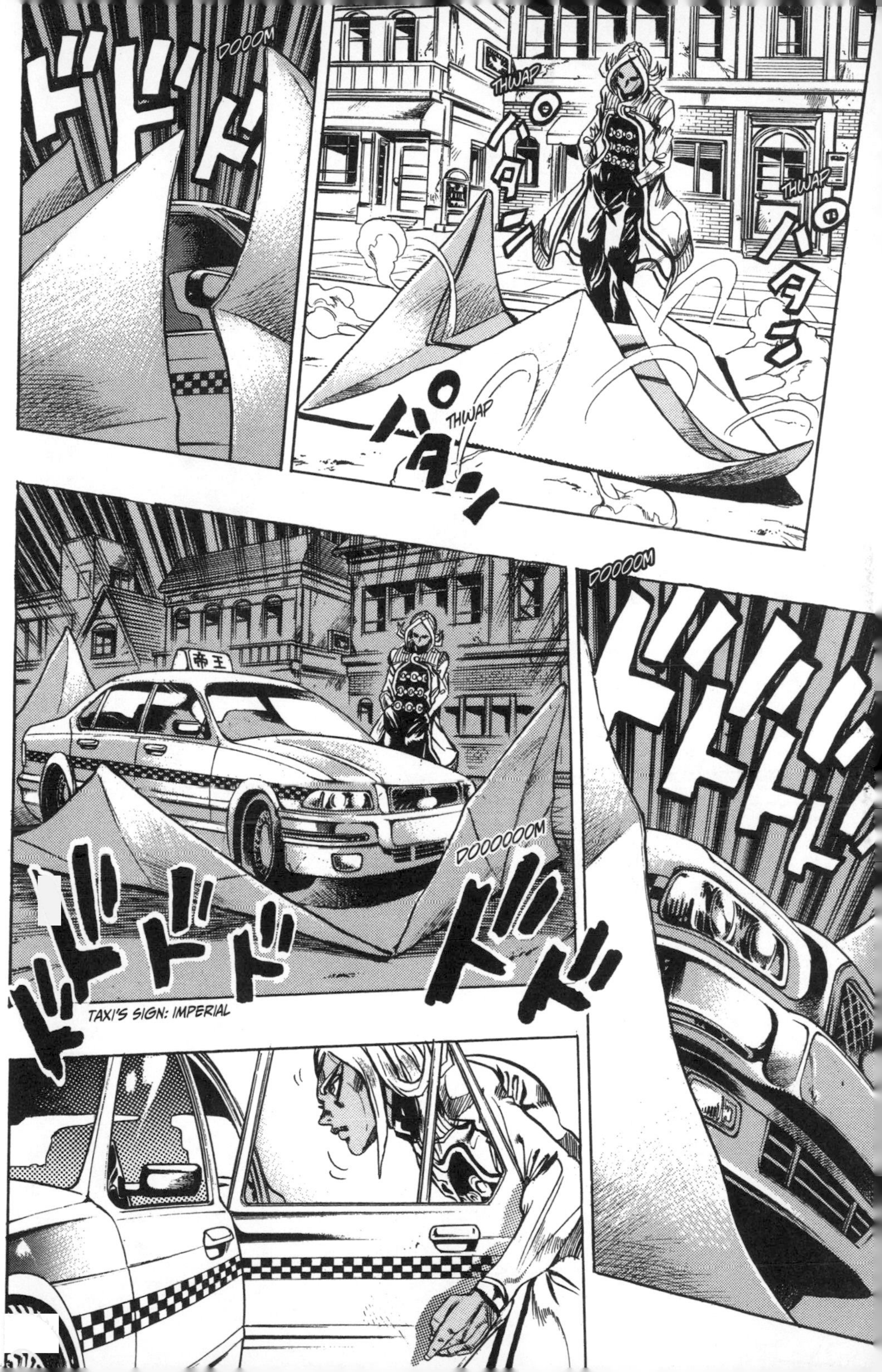
THWAP
THWAP
THWAP
DOOOM
DOOOOM
DOOOOOOM
TAXI'S SIGN: IMPERIAL

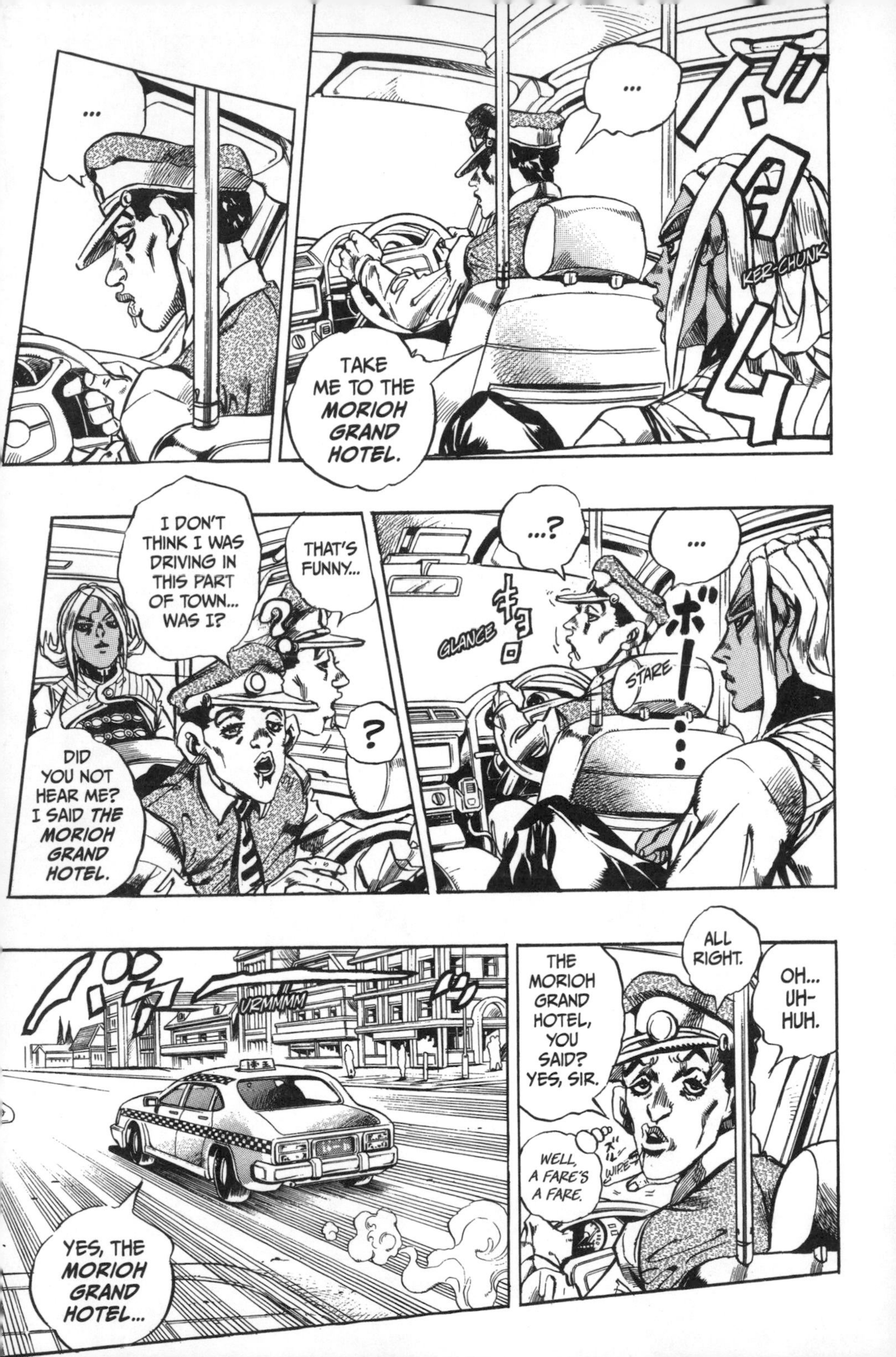
KER-CHUNK
...
TAKE ME TO THE MORIOH GRAND HOTEL.
...
...
...?
STARE
GLANCE
THAT'S FUNNY...
I DON'T THINK I WAS DRIVING IN THIS PART OF TOWN... WAS I?
?
DID YOU NOT HEAR ME? I SAID THE MORIOH GRAND HOTEL.
OH... UH-HUH.
ALL RIGHT.
THE MORIOH GRAND HOTEL, YOU SAID? YES, SIR.
WIPE
WELL, A FARE'S A FARE.
URMMMM
YES, THE MORIOH GRAND HOTEL...

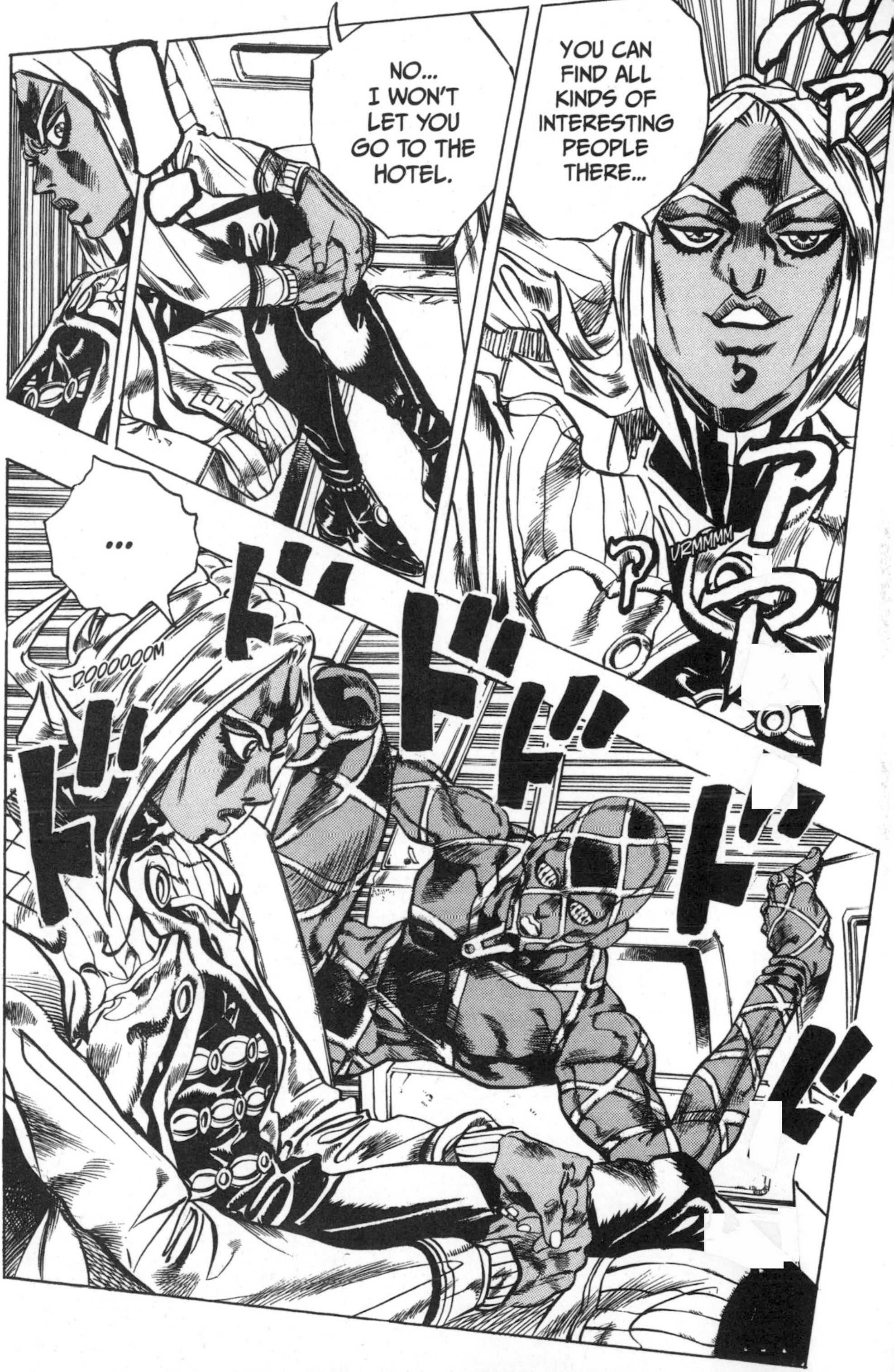
YOU CAN FIND ALL KINDS OF INTERESTING PEOPLE THERE...
URMMMM
NO... I WON'T LET YOU GO TO THE HOTEL.
...
DOOOOOOOM

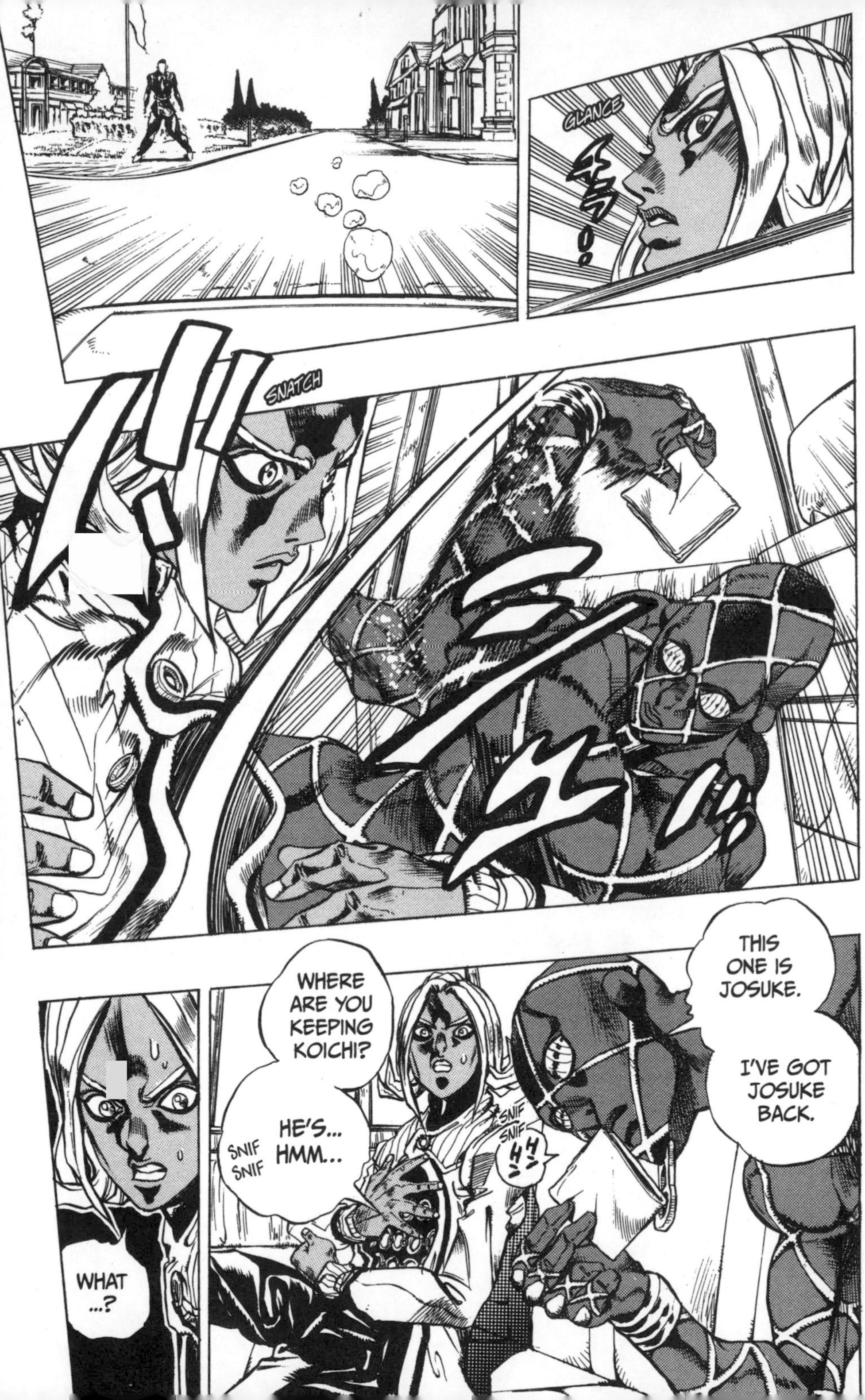
GLANCE
SNATCH
THIS ONE IS JOSUKE.
I'VE GOT JOSUKE BACK.
WHERE ARE YOU KEEPING KOICHI?
SNIF SNIF
HE'S... HMM...
SNIF SNIF
WHAT ...?

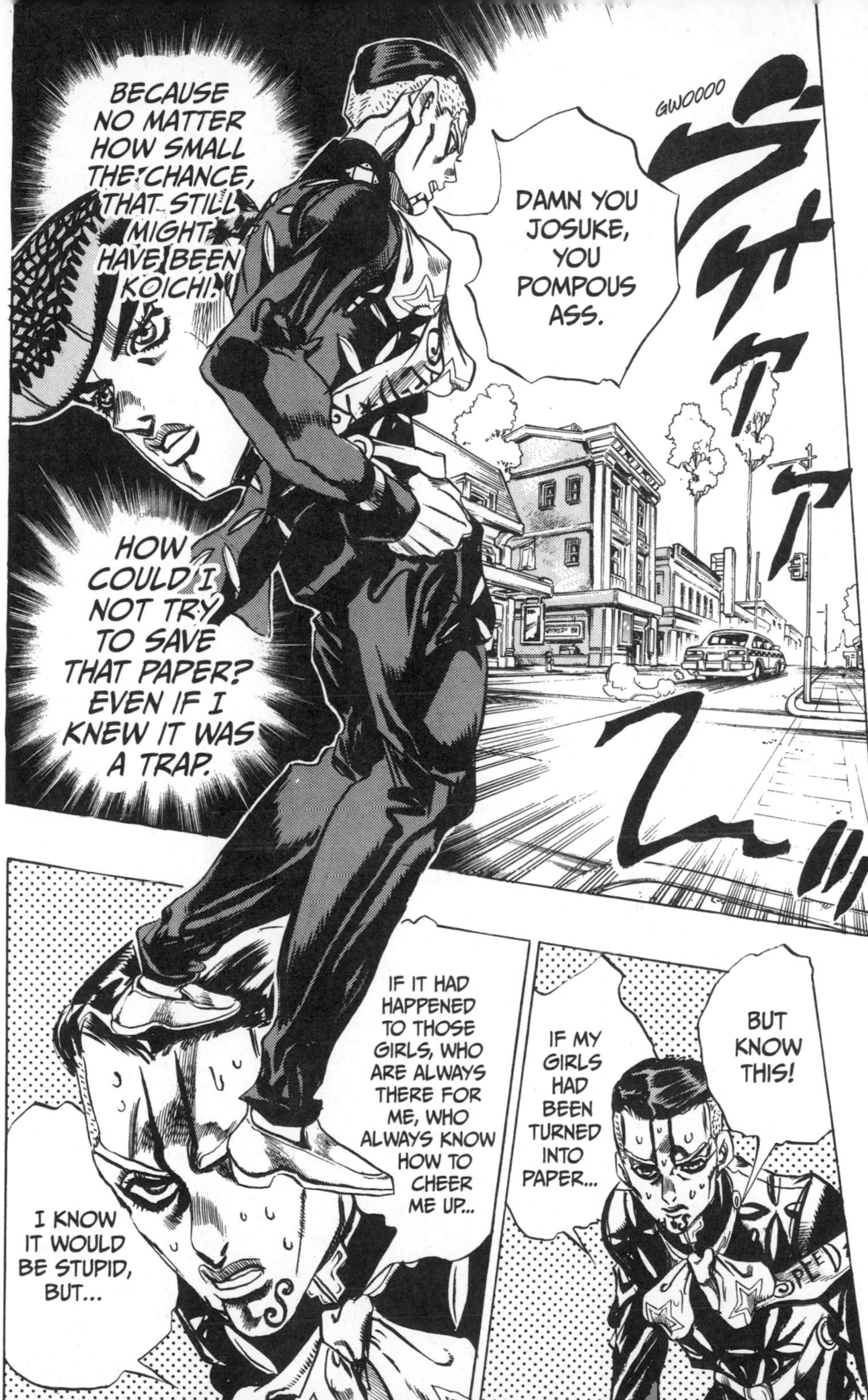
GWOOOO
DAMN YOU JOSUKE, YOU POMPOUS ASS.
BECAUSE NO MATTER HOW SMALL THE CHANCE, THAT STILL MIGHT HAVE BEEN KOICHI.
HOW COULD I NOT TRY TO SAVE THAT PAPER? EVEN IF I KNEW IT WAS A TRAP.
BUT KNOW THIS!
IF MY GIRLS HAD BEEN TURNED INTO PAPER...
IF IT HAD HAPPENED TO THOSE GIRLS, WHO ARE ALWAYS THERE FOR ME, WHO ALWAYS KNOW HOW TO CHEER ME UP...
I KNOW IT WOULD BE STUPID, BUT...

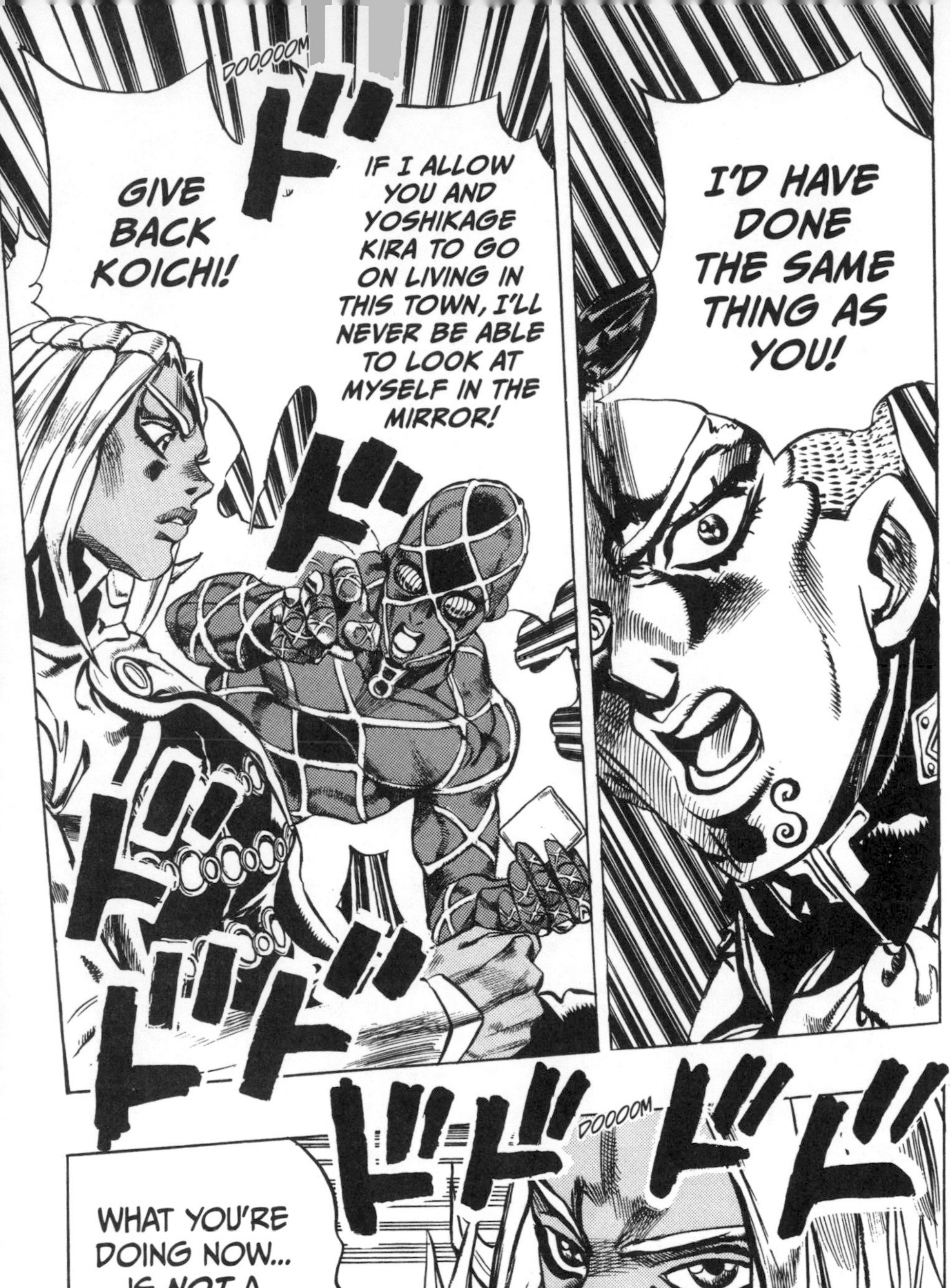
I'D HAVE DONE THE SAME THING AS YOU!
DOOOOOM
IF I ALLOW YOU AND YOSHIKAGE KIRA TO GO ON LIVING IN THIS TOWN, I'LL NEVER BE ABLE TO LOOK AT MYSELF IN THE MIRROR!
GIVE BACK KOICHI!
DOOOOM
WHAT YOU'RE DOING NOW... IS NOT A WISE MOVE.

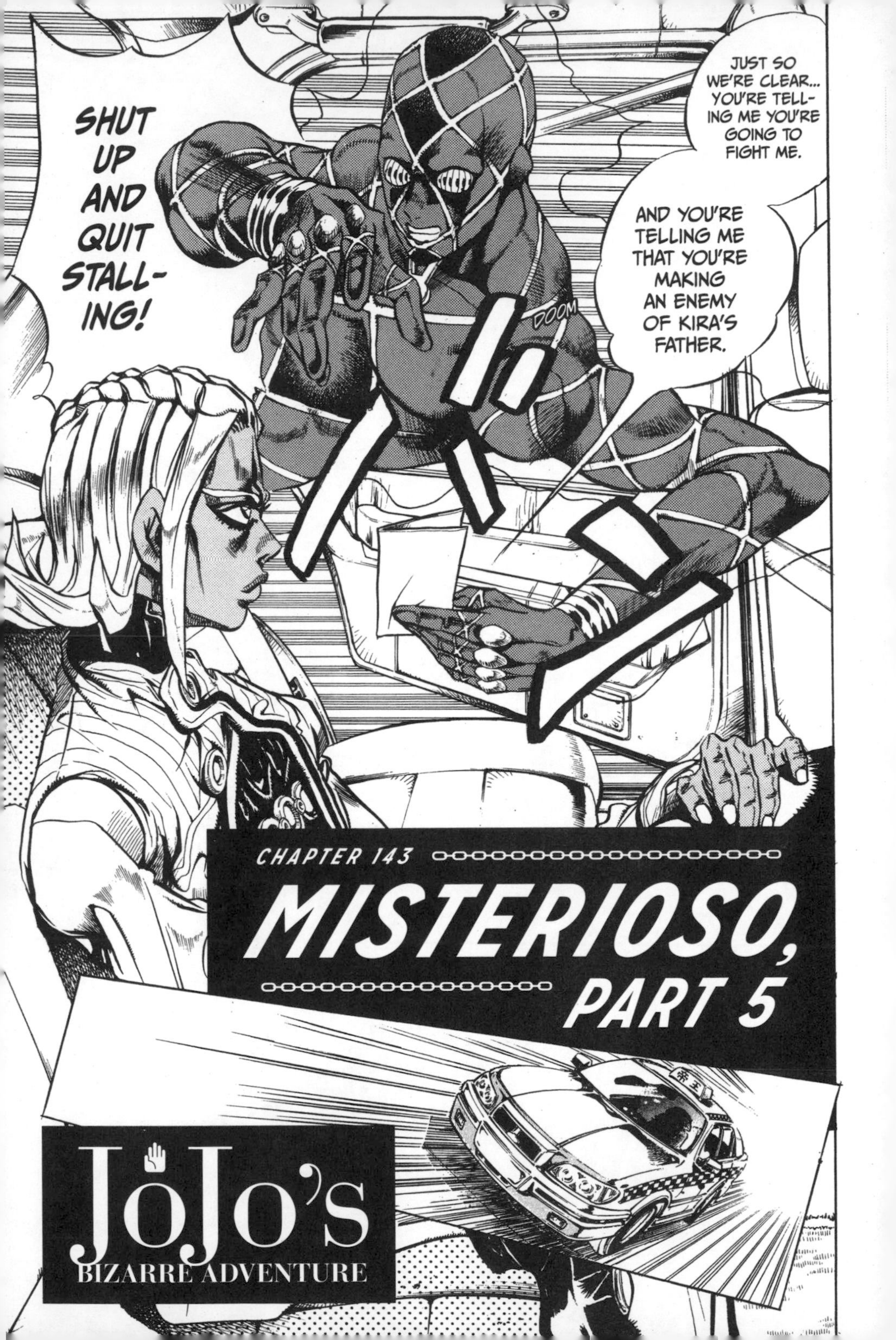
JUST SO WE'RE CLEAR... YOU'RE TELLING ME YOU'RE GOING TO FIGHT ME.
AND YOU'RE TELLING ME THAT YOU'RE MAKING AN ENEMY OF KIRA'S FATHER.
SHUT UP AND QUIT STALLING!
DOOM
CHAPTER 143
MISTERIOSO, PART 5
JoJo's BIZARRE ADVENTURE

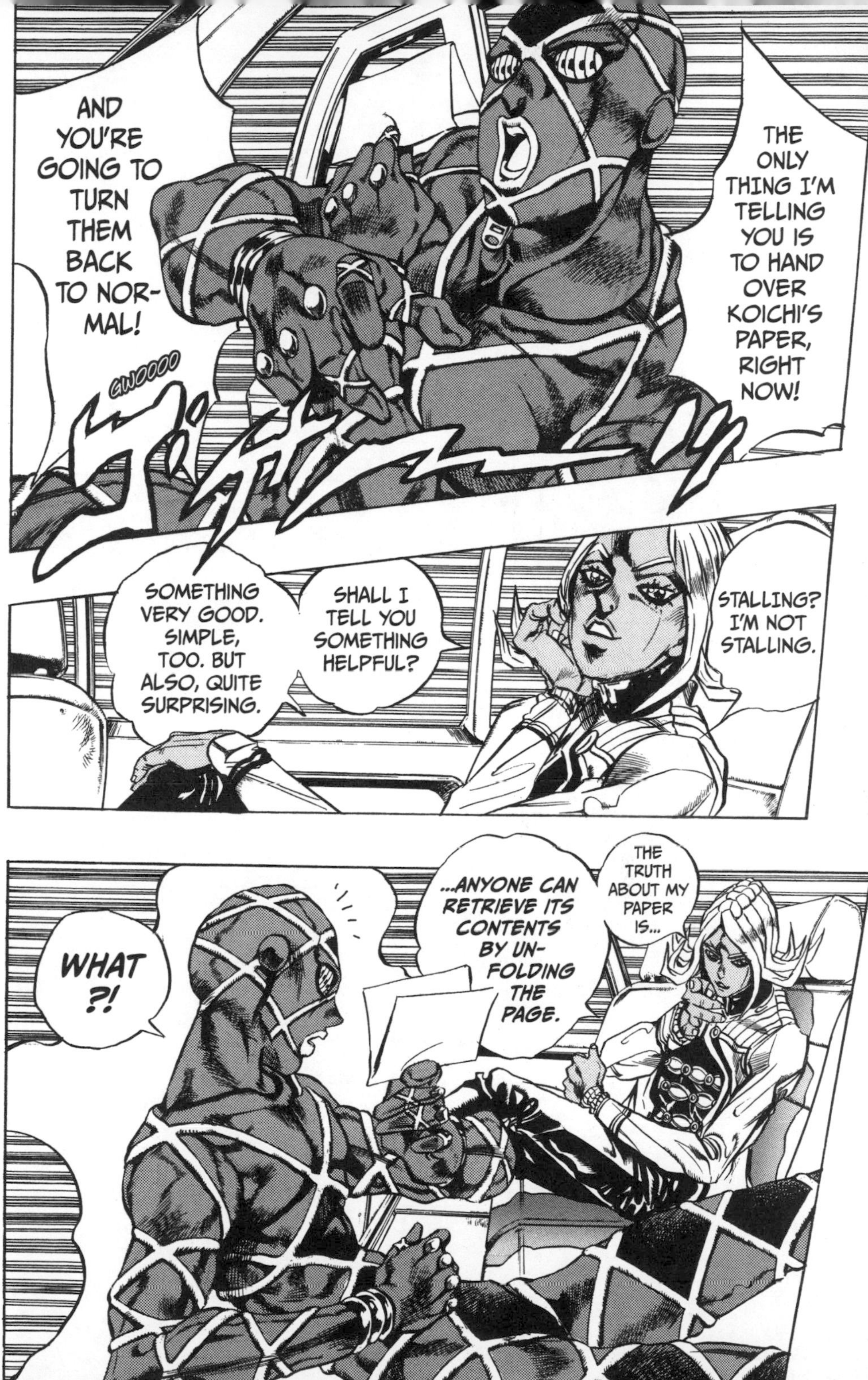
THE ONLY THING I'M TELLING YOU IS TO HAND OVER KOICHI'S PAPER, RIGHT NOW!
AND YOU'RE GOING TO TURN THEM BACK TO NOR-MAL!
GWOOOO
STALLING? I'M NOT STALLING.
SHALL I TELL YOU SOMETHING HELPFUL?
SOMETHING VERY GOOD. SIMPLE, TOO. BUT ALSO, QUITE SURPRISING.
THE TRUTH ABOUT MY PAPER IS...
...ANYONE CAN RETRIEVE ITS CONTENTS BY UN-FOLDING THE PAGE.
WHAT?!

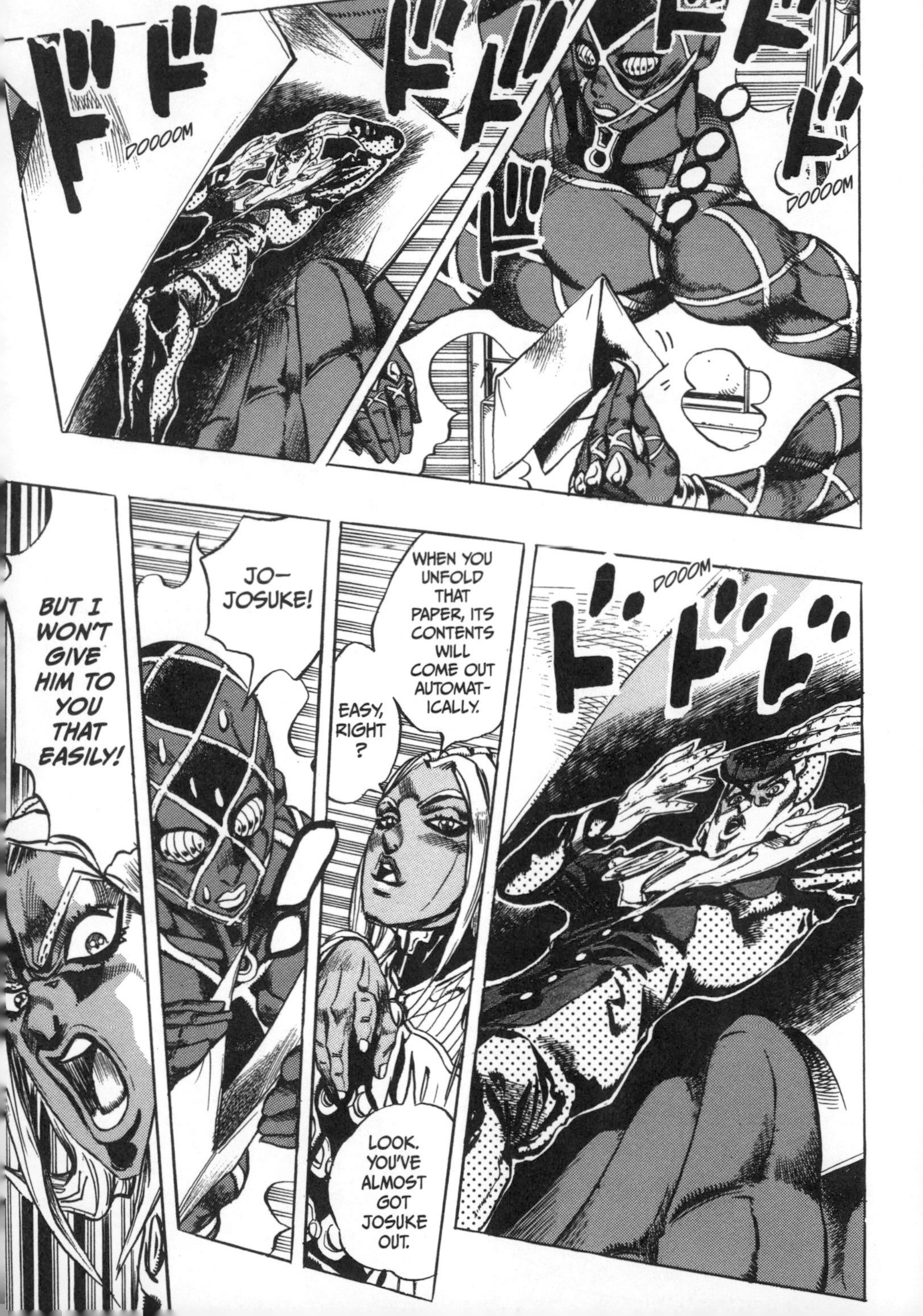
DOOOOM
DOOOOM
DOOOM
WHEN YOU UNFOLD THAT PAPER, ITS CONTENTS WILL COME OUT AUTOMAT-ICALLY.
EASY, RIGHT?
LOOK. YOU'VE ALMOST GOT JOSUKE OUT.
JO-JOSUKE!
BUT I WON'T GIVE HIM TO YOU THAT EASILY!

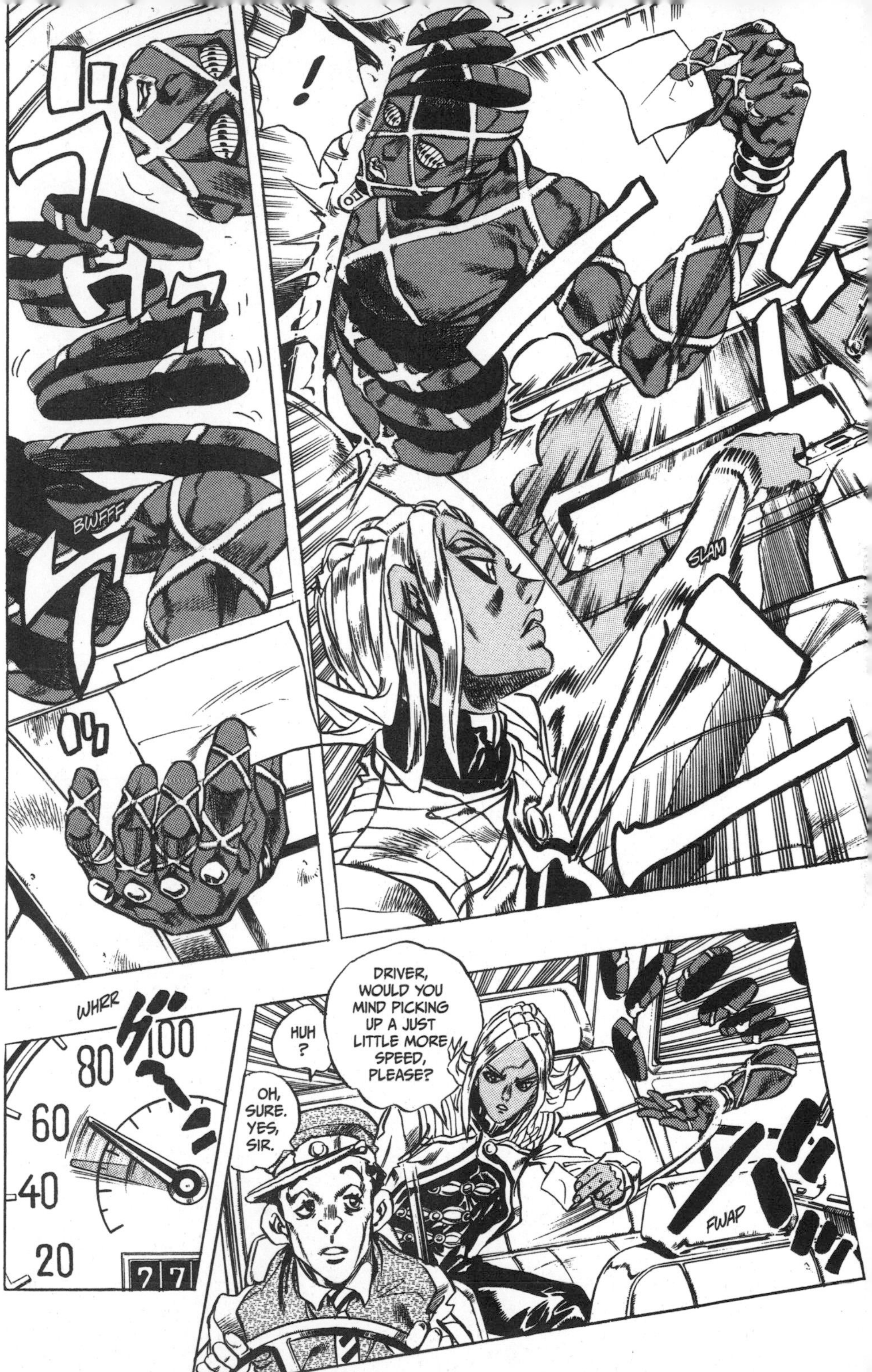

!
SLAM
BWFFF
DRIVER, WOULD YOU MIND PICKING UP A JUST LITTLE MORE SPEED, PLEASE?
HUH ?
OH, SURE. YES, SIR.
FWAP
WHRR
100
80
60
40
20
77

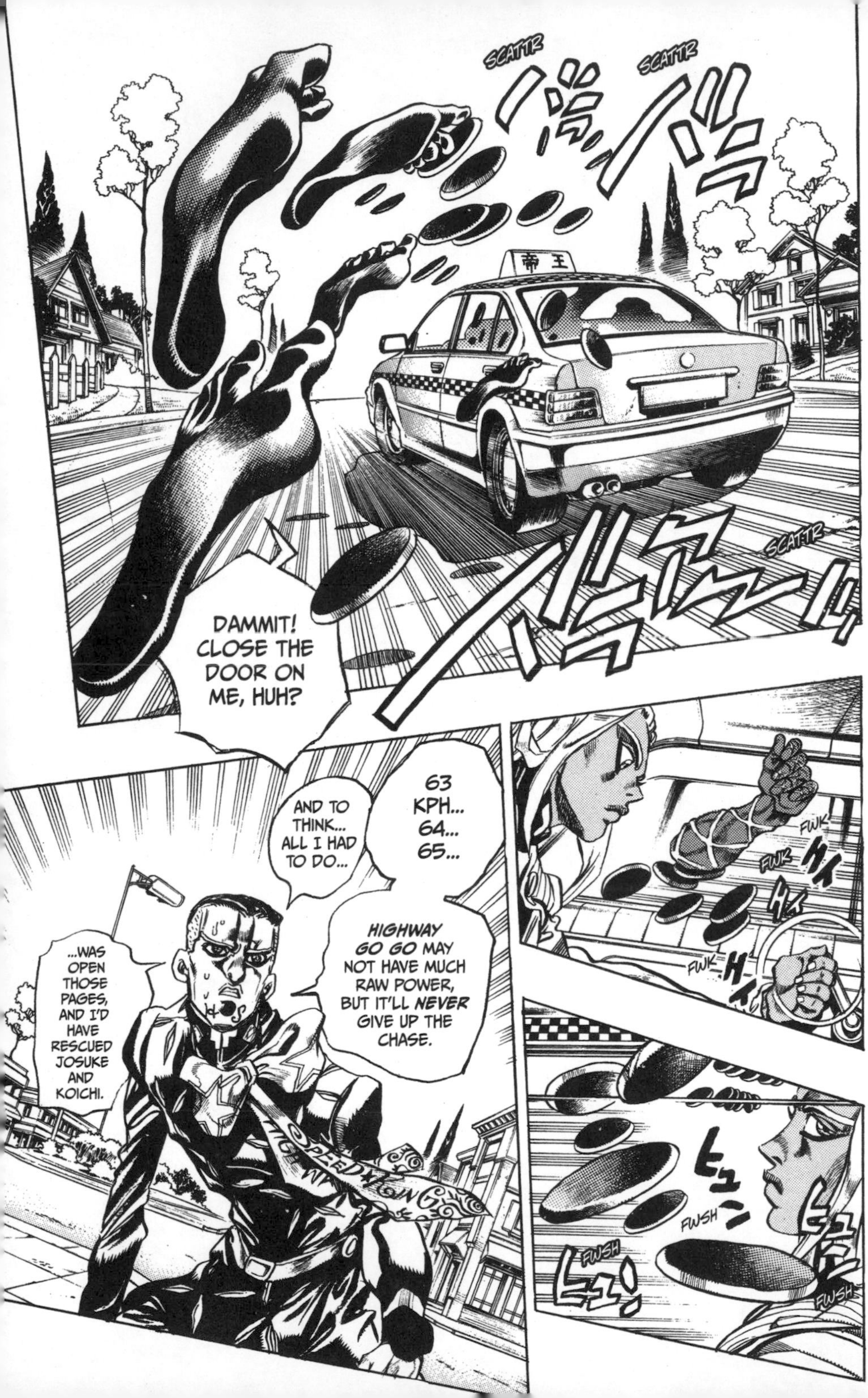
SCATTR
SCATTR
帝王
SCATTR
DAMMIT! CLOSE THE DOOR ON ME, HUH?
FWK
FWK
FWK
FWSH
FWSH
FWSH
63 KPH... 64... 65...
AND TO THINK... ALL I HAD TO DO...
HIGHWAY GO GO MAY NOT HAVE MUCH RAW POWER, BUT IT'LL NEVER GIVE UP THE CHASE.
...WAS OPEN THOSE PAGES, AND I'D HAVE RESCUED JOSUKE AND KOICHI.

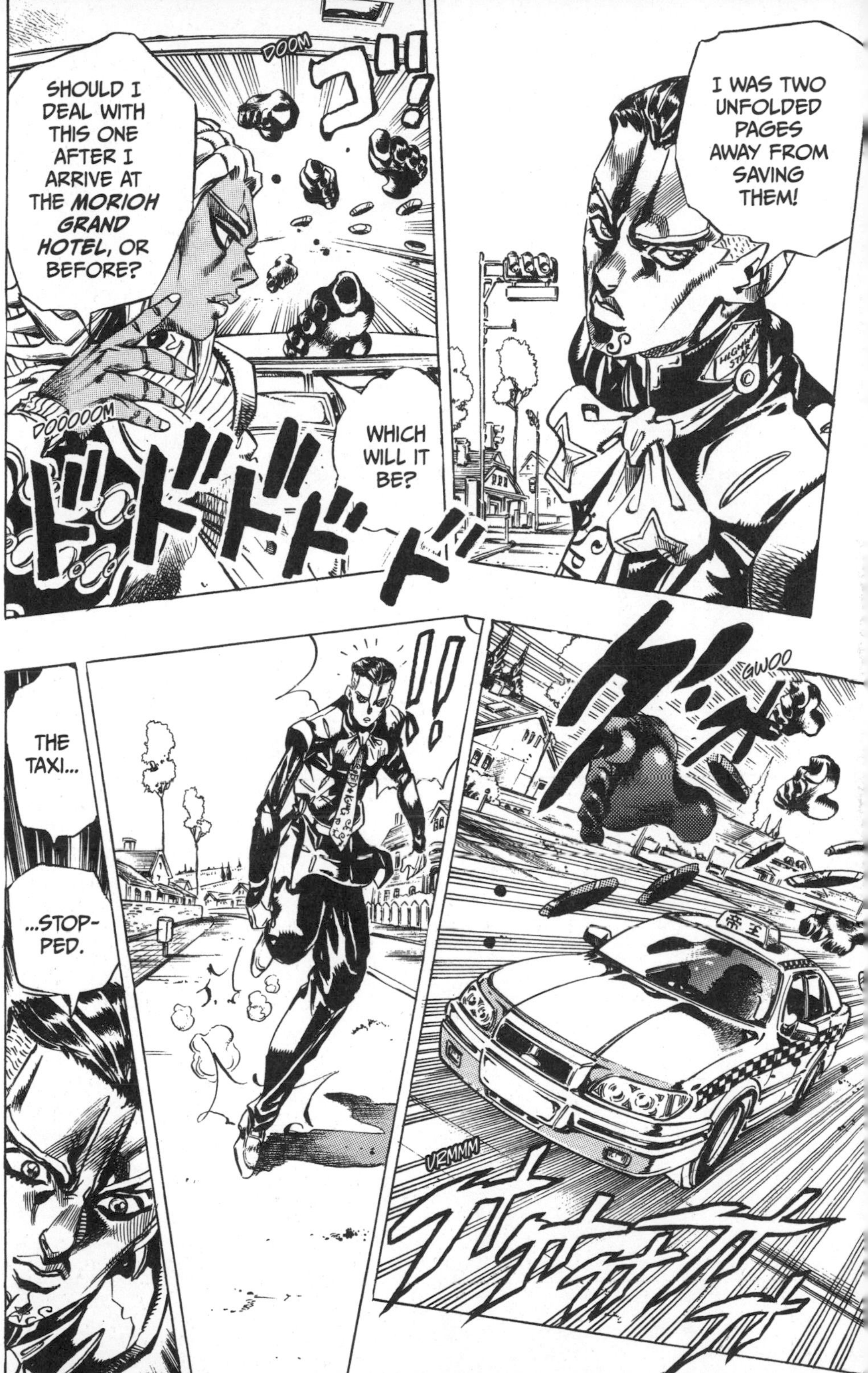
I WAS TWO UNFOLDED PAGES AWAY FROM SAVING THEM!
DOOM
SHOULD I DEAL WITH THIS ONE AFTER I ARRIVE AT THE *MORIOH GRAND HOTEL*, OR BEFORE?
WHICH WILL IT BE?
DOOOOOM
GWOO
URMMM
THE TAXI...
...STOP-PED.

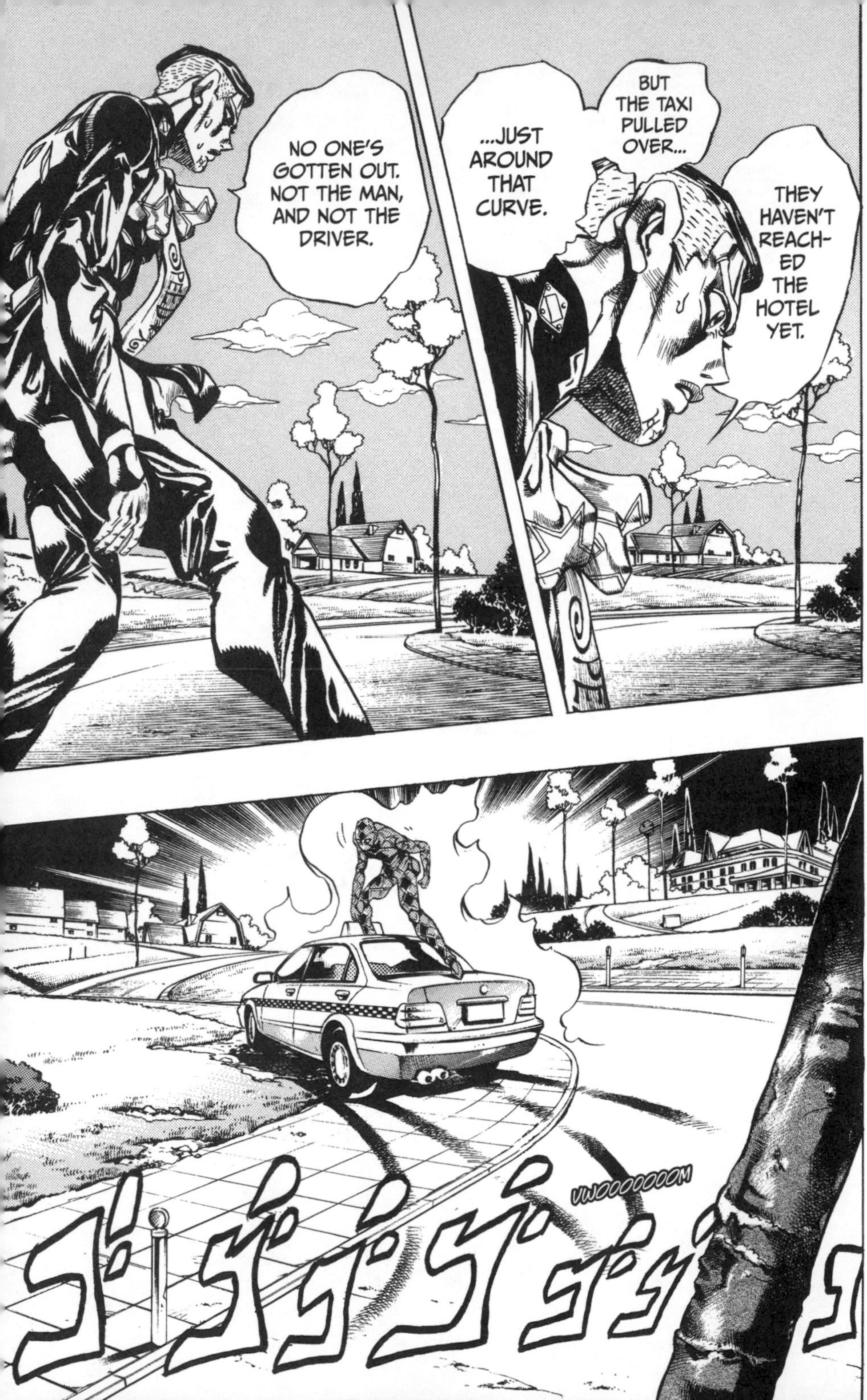
THEY HAVEN'T REACHED THE HOTEL YET.
BUT THE TAXI PULLED OVER...
...JUST AROUND THAT CURVE.
NO ONE'S GOTTEN OUT. NOT THE MAN, AND NOT THE DRIVER.
VWOOOOOOOM

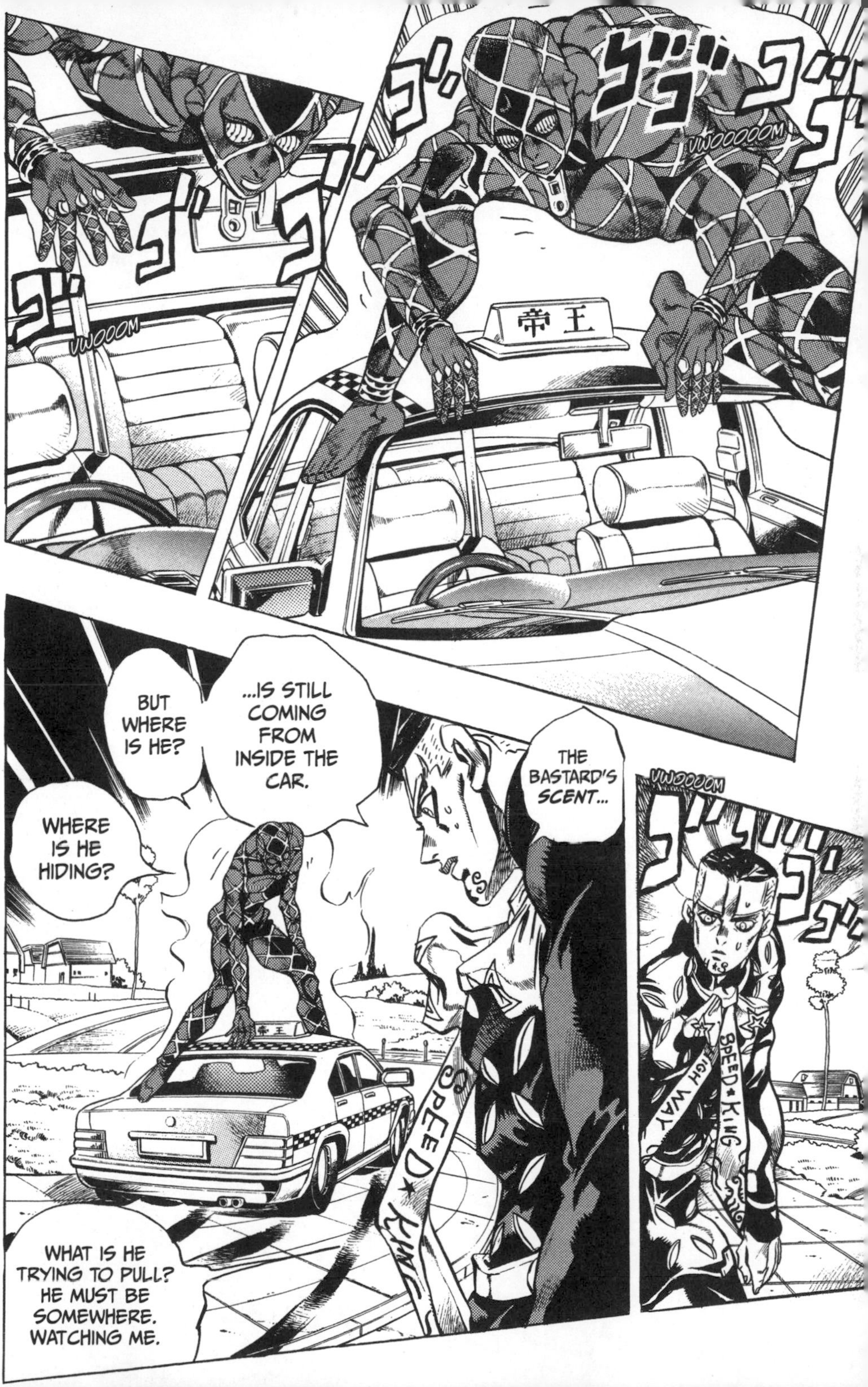

VWOOOOOM
帝王
VWOOOM
VWOOOOM
THE BASTARD'S SCENT...
...IS STILL COMING FROM INSIDE THE CAR.
BUT WHERE IS HE?
WHERE IS HE HIDING?
WHAT IS HE TRYING TO PULL? HE MUST BE SOMEWHERE. WATCHING ME.

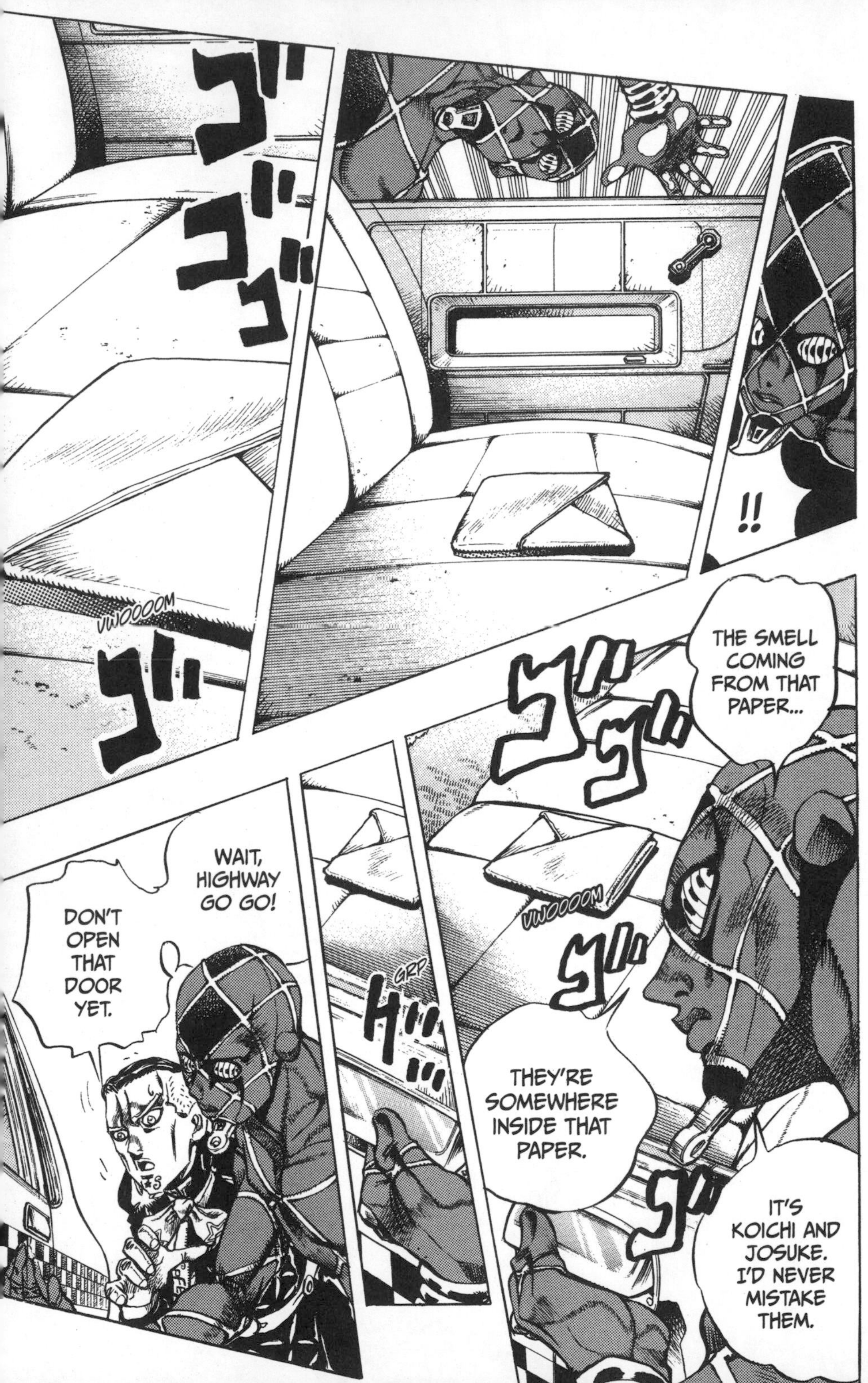
!!
VWOOOOM
THE SMELL COMING FROM THAT PAPER...
VWOOOOM
THEY'RE SOMEWHERE INSIDE THAT PAPER.
IT'S KOICHI AND JOSUKE. I'D NEVER MISTAKE THEM.
GRP
WAIT, HIGHWAY GO GO!
DON'T OPEN THAT DOOR YET.

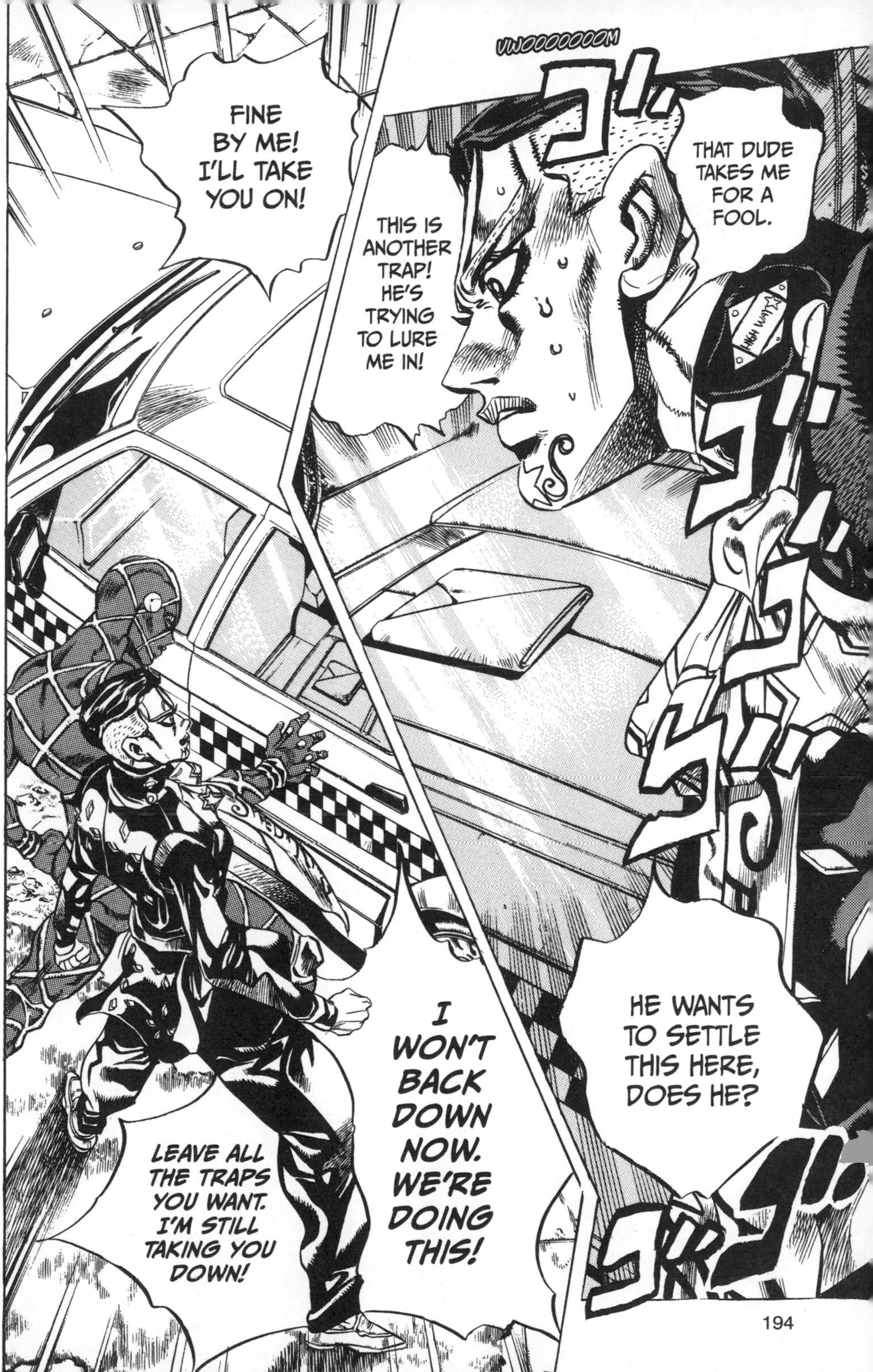
VWOOOOOOOM
THAT DUDE TAKES ME FOR A FOOL.
THIS IS ANOTHER TRAP! HE'S TRYING TO LURE ME IN!
HE WANTS TO SETTLE THIS HERE, DOES HE?
SKR
FINE BY ME! I'LL TAKE YOU ON!
I WON'T BACK DOWN NOW. WE'RE DOING THIS!
LEAVE ALL THE TRAPS YOU WANT. I'M STILL TAKING YOU DOWN!

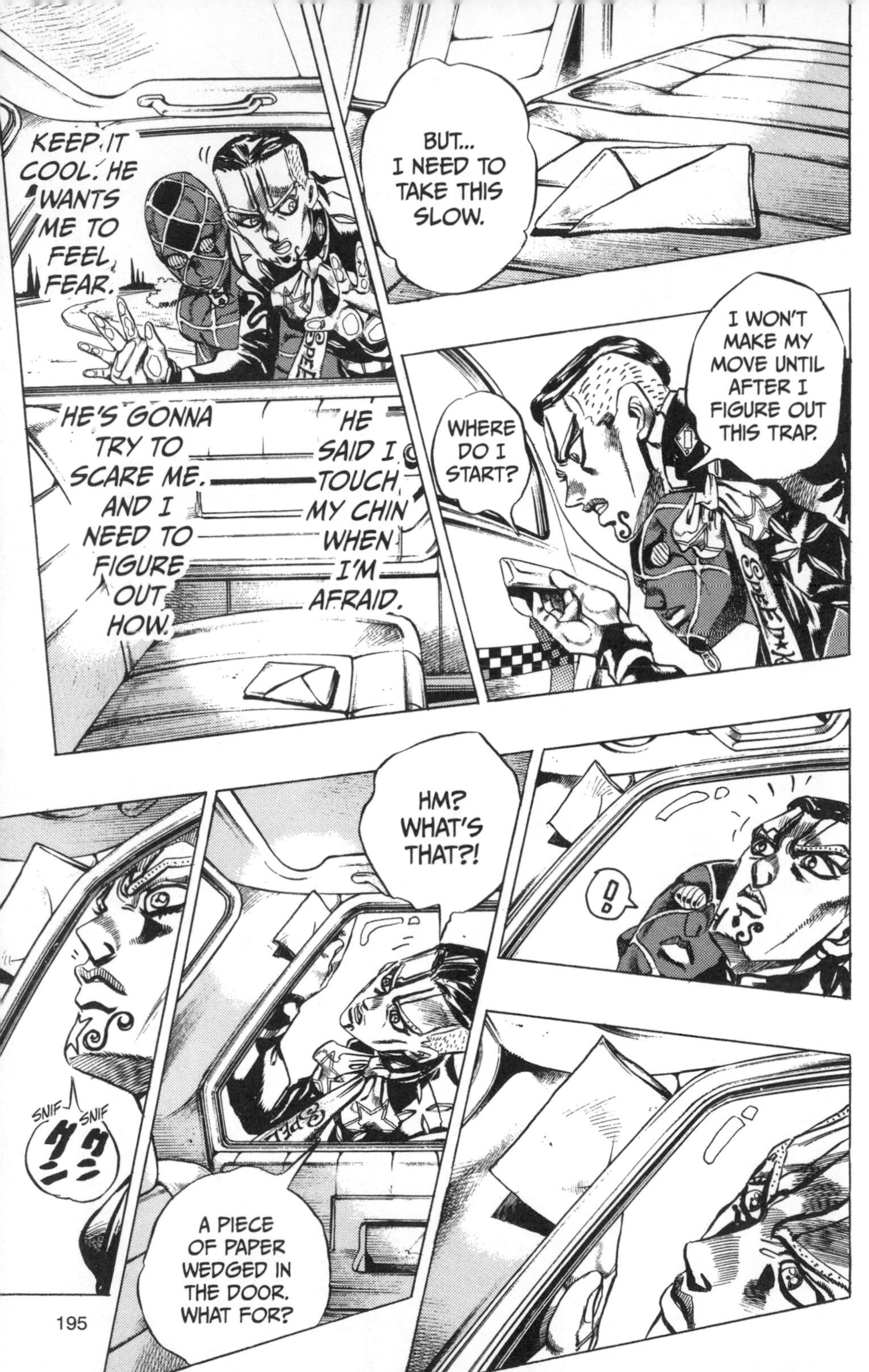
BUT... I NEED TO TAKE THIS SLOW.
KEEP IT COOL. HE WANTS ME TO FEEL FEAR.
I WON'T MAKE MY MOVE UNTIL AFTER I FIGURE OUT THIS TRAP.
WHERE DO I START?
HE SAID I TOUCH MY CHIN WHEN I'M AFRAID.
HE'S GONNA TRY TO SCARE ME. AND I NEED TO FIGURE OUT HOW.
!?
HM? WHAT'S THAT?!
A PIECE OF PAPER WEDGED IN THE DOOR. WHAT FOR?
SNIF SNIF

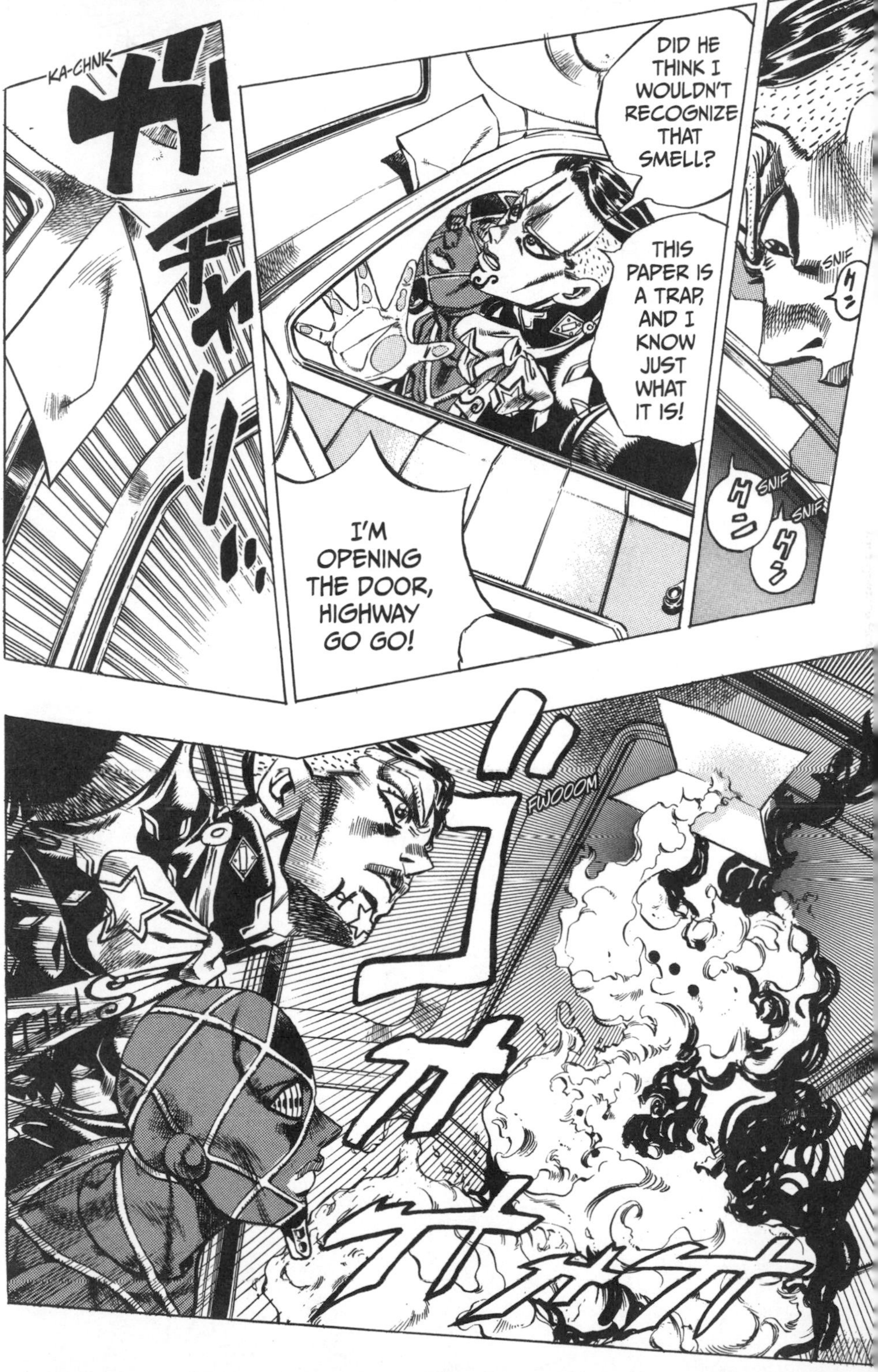
SNIF
SNIF
SNIF
DID HE THINK I WOULDN'T RECOGNIZE THAT SMELL?
THIS PAPER IS A TRAP, AND I KNOW JUST WHAT IT IS!
I'M OPENING THE DOOR, HIGHWAY GO GO!
KA-CHNK
FWOOOM

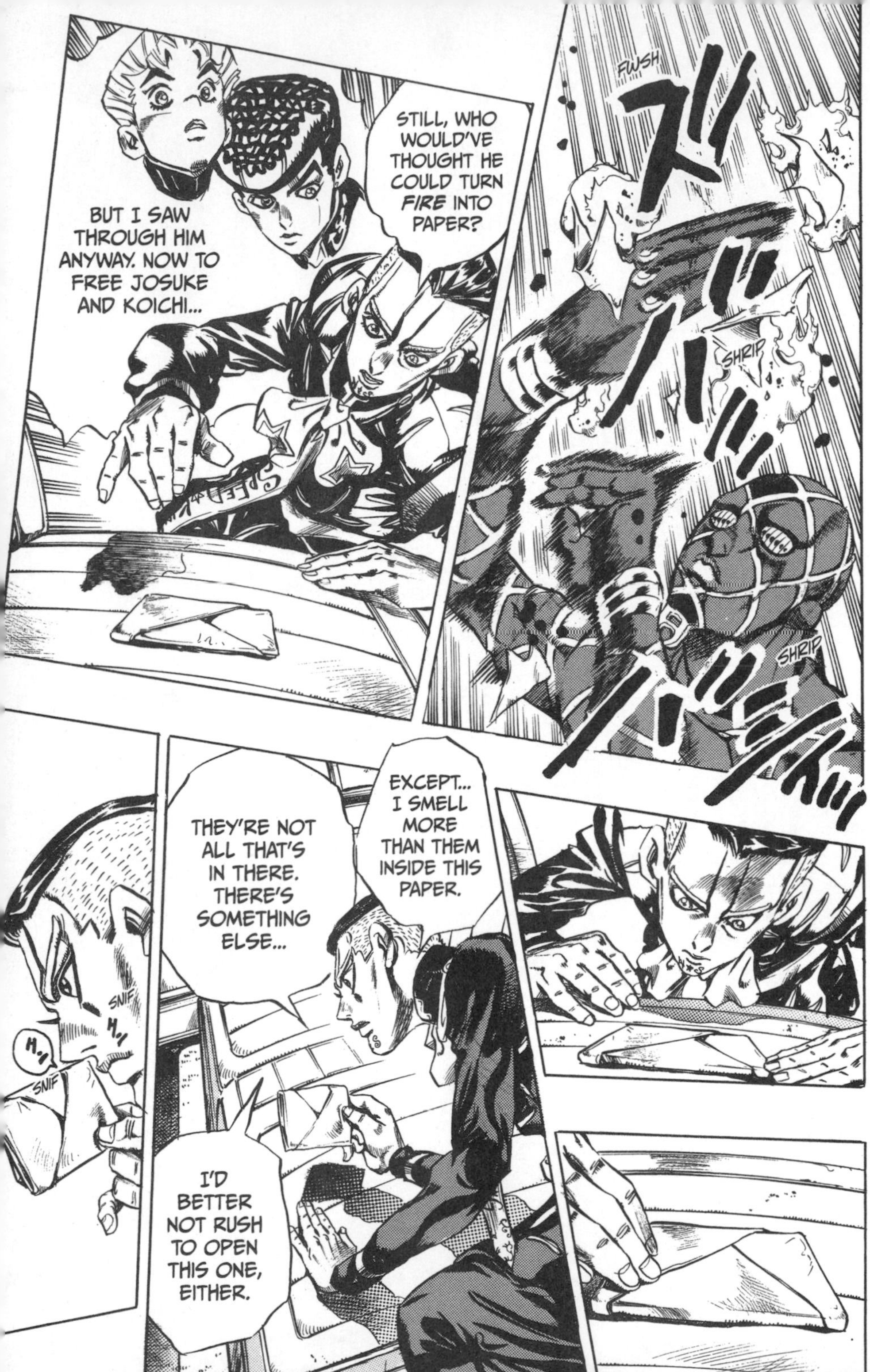
FWSH
SHRIP
SHRIP
STILL, WHO WOULD'VE THOUGHT HE COULD TURN *FIRE* INTO PAPER?
BUT I SAW THROUGH HIM ANYWAY. NOW TO FREE JOSUKE AND KOICHI...
EXCEPT... I SMELL MORE THAN THEM INSIDE THIS PAPER.
THEY'RE NOT ALL THAT'S IN THERE. THERE'S SOMETHING ELSE...
I'D BETTER NOT RUSH TO OPEN THIS ONE, EITHER.
SNIF
SNIF

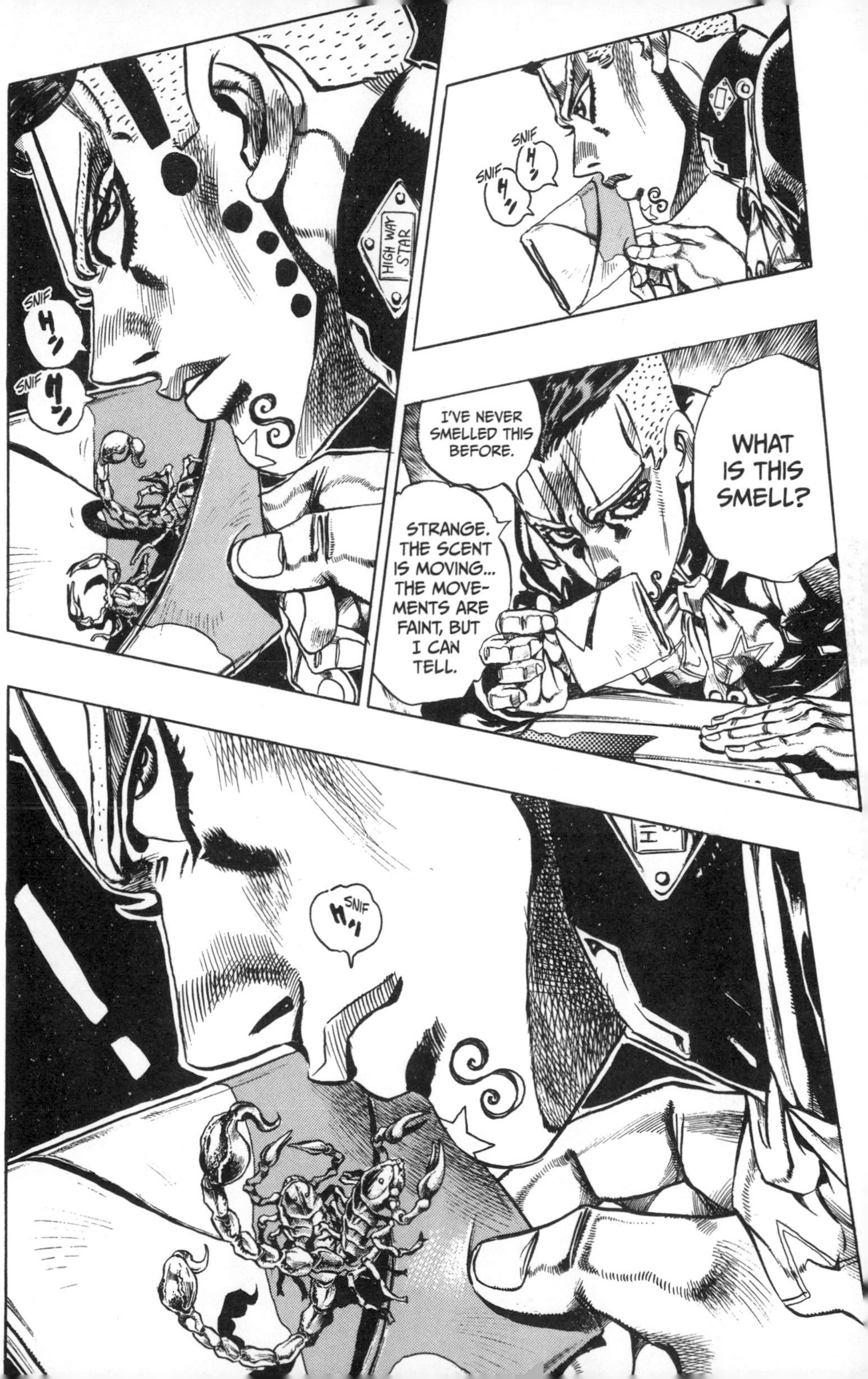
SNIF
SNIF
WHAT IS THIS SMELL?
I'VE NEVER SMELLED THIS BEFORE.
STRANGE. THE SCENT IS MOVING... THE MOVEMENTS ARE FAINT, BUT I CAN TELL.
HIGH WAY STAR
SNIF
SNIF
SNIF

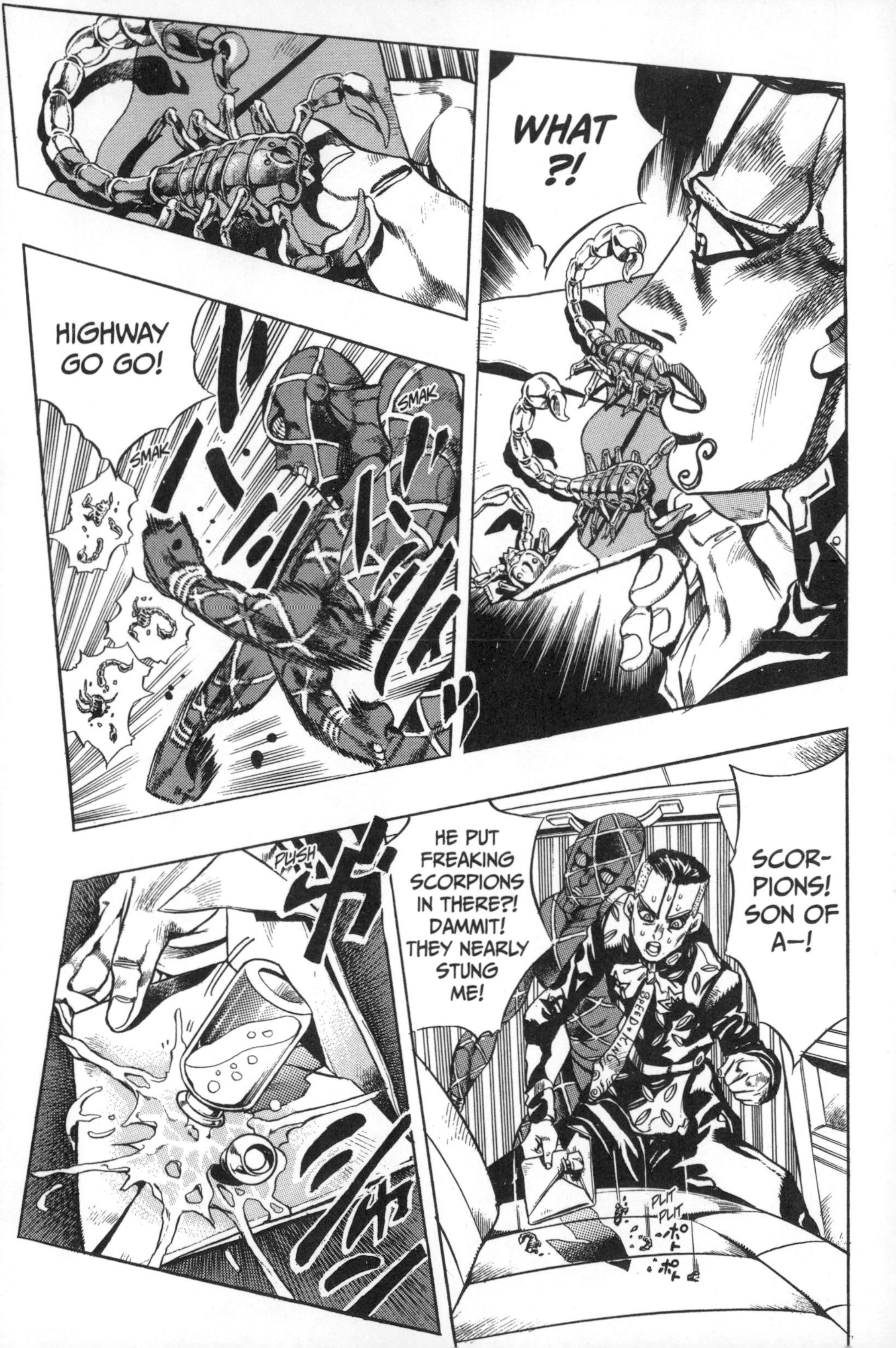
WHAT ?!
HIGHWAY GO GO!
SMAK
SMAK
SCOR-PIONS! SON OF A-!
HE PUT FREAKING SCORPIONS IN THERE?! DAMMIT! THEY NEARLY STUNG ME!
SPEED★KING
PLIT PLIT
PLISH

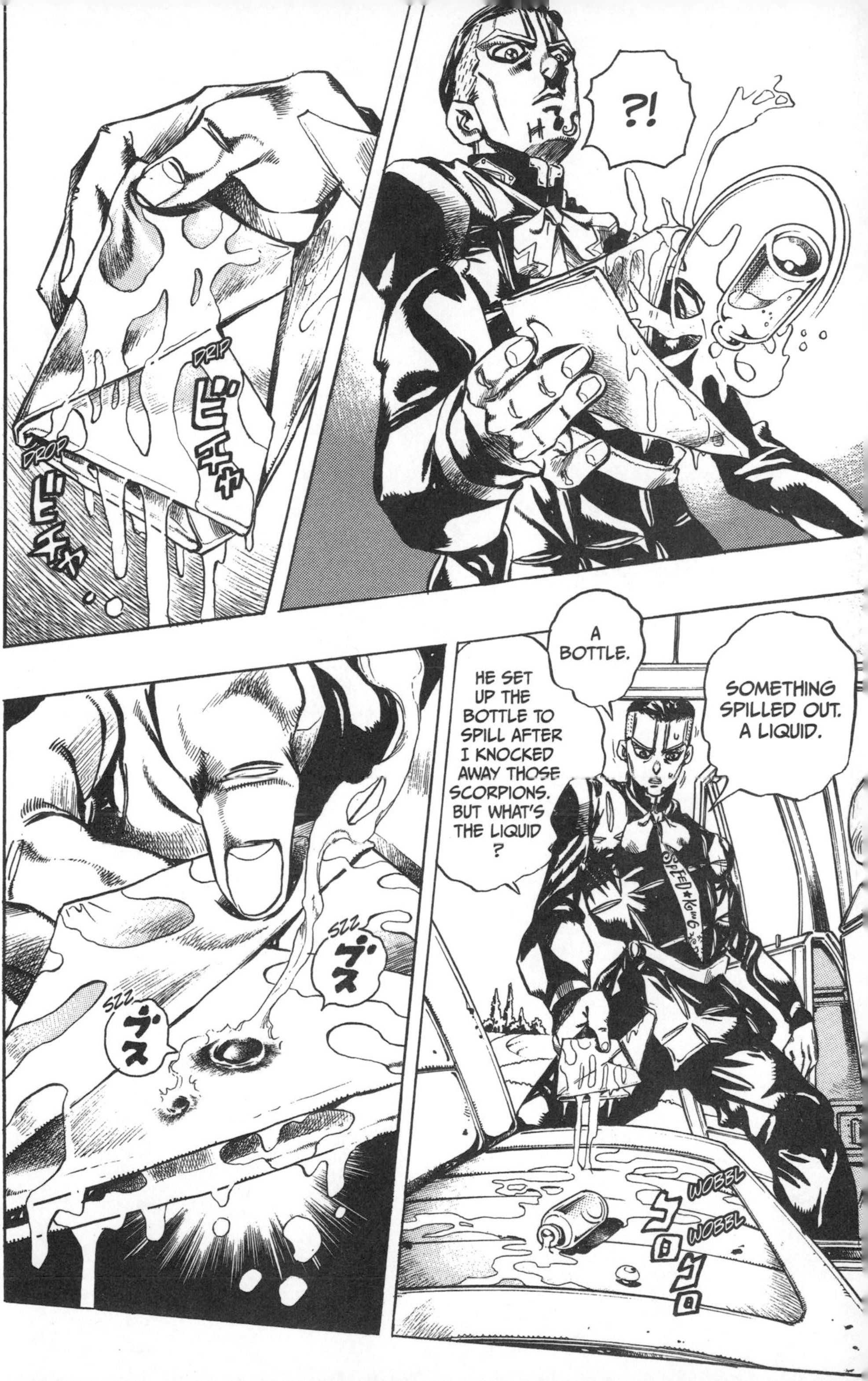
?!
DRIP
ビチャ
DROP
ビチャ
SOMETHING SPILLED OUT. A LIQUID.
A BOTTLE.
HE SET UP THE BOTTLE TO SPILL AFTER I KNOCKED AWAY THOSE SCORPIONS. BUT WHAT'S THE LIQUID ?
WOBBL
WOBBL
SZZ
プス
SZZ
プス

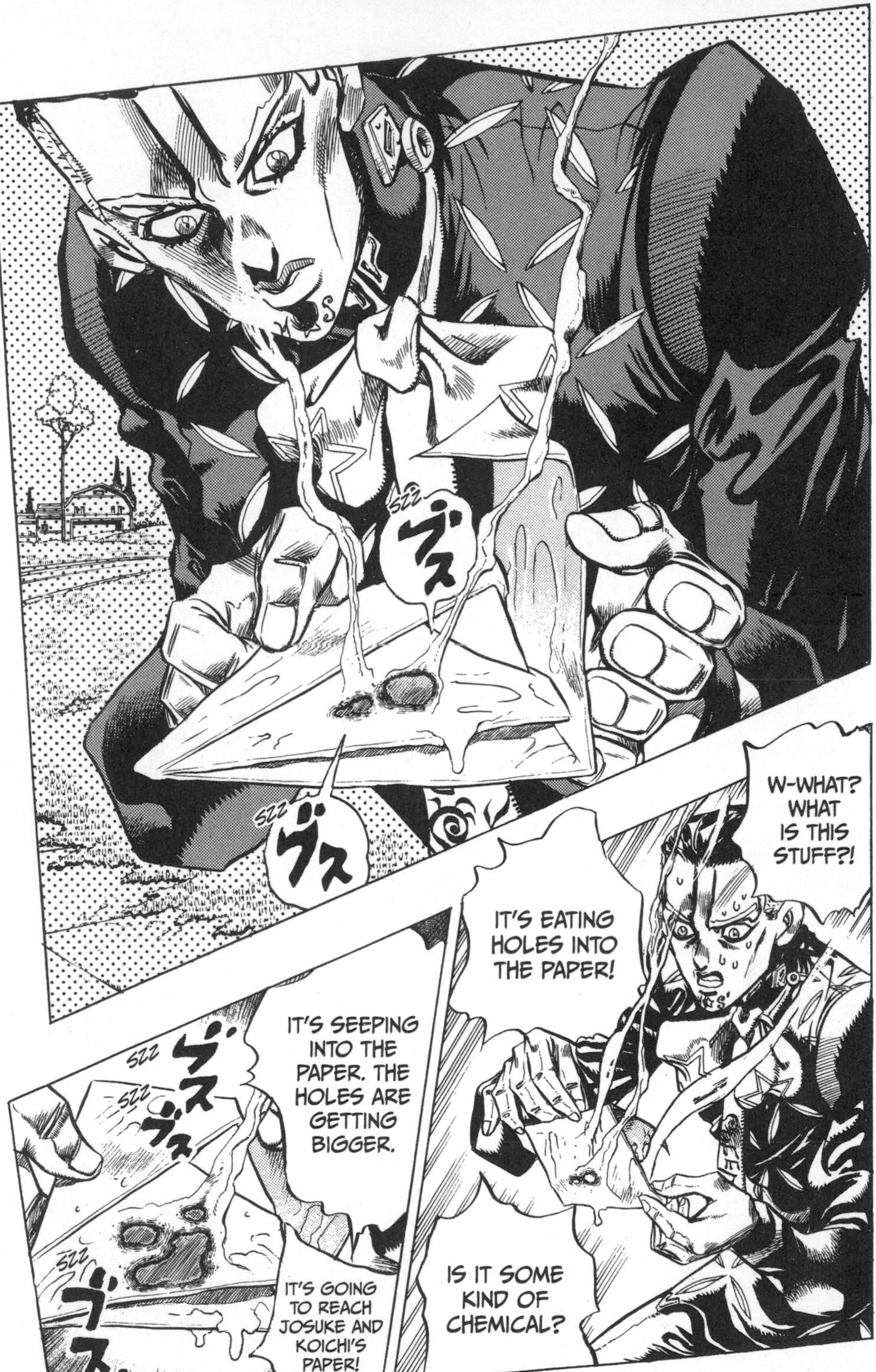
SZZ ブス
SZZ ブス
W-WHAT? WHAT IS THIS STUFF?!
IT'S EATING HOLES INTO THE PAPER!
IS IT SOME KIND OF CHEMICAL?
IT'S SEEPING INTO THE PAPER. THE HOLES ARE GETTING BIGGER.
SZZ ブス
SZZ ブス
SZZ ブスッ
IT'S GOING TO REACH JOSUKE AND KOICHI'S PAPER!

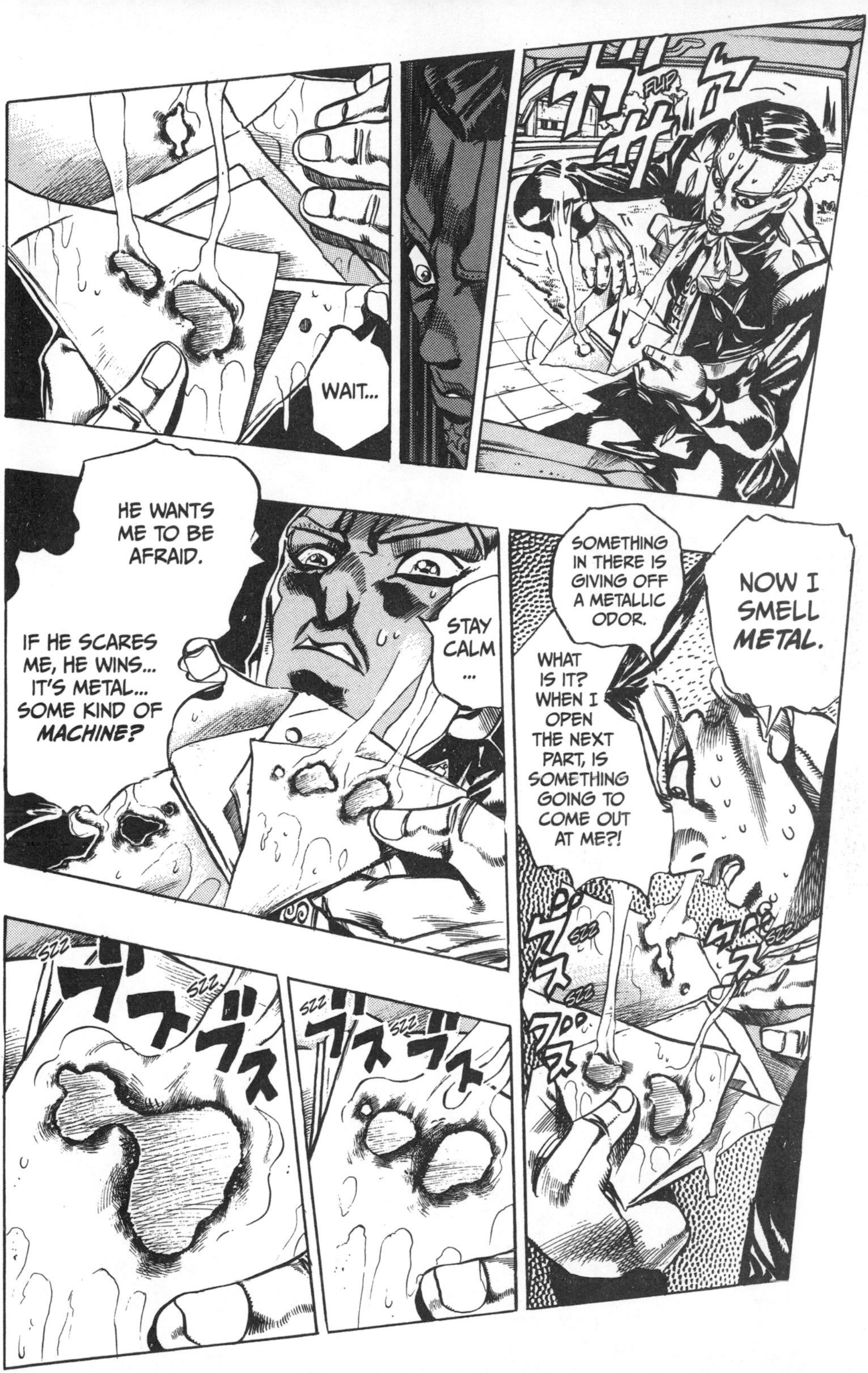
FLIP
WAIT...
NOW I SMELL *METAL.*
SOMETHING IN THERE IS GIVING OFF A METALLIC ODOR.
WHAT IS IT? WHEN I OPEN THE NEXT PART, IS SOMETHING GOING TO COME OUT AT ME?!
STAY CALM ...
HE WANTS ME TO BE AFRAID.
IF HE SCARES ME, HE WINS... IT'S METAL... SOME KIND OF *MACHINE?*
SZZ
SZZ
SZZ
SZZ
SZZ
SZZ
SZZ
SZZ

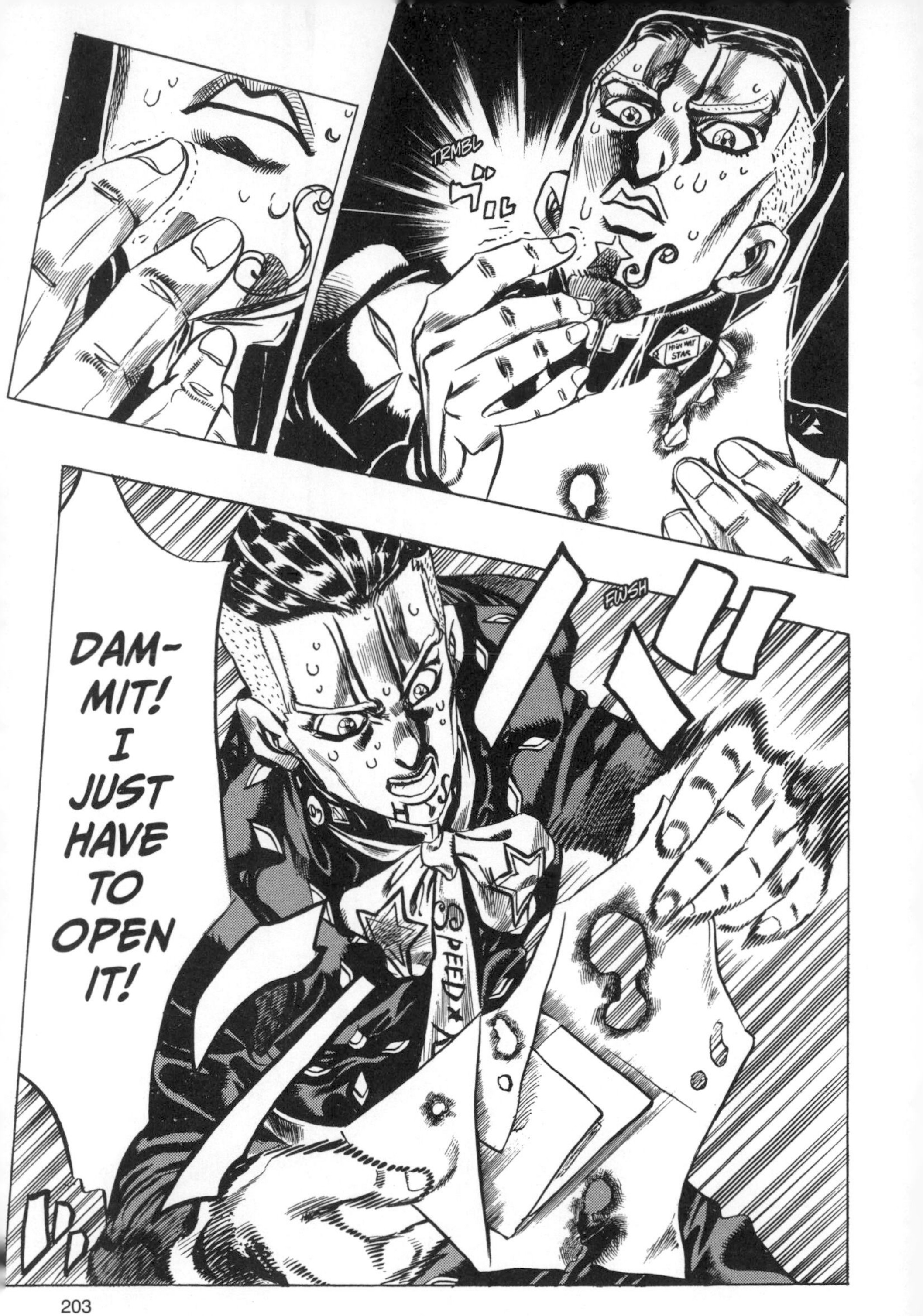
TRMBL
FWSH
DAM-MIT! I JUST HAVE TO OPEN IT!

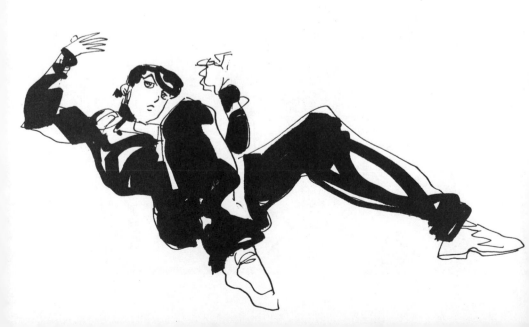

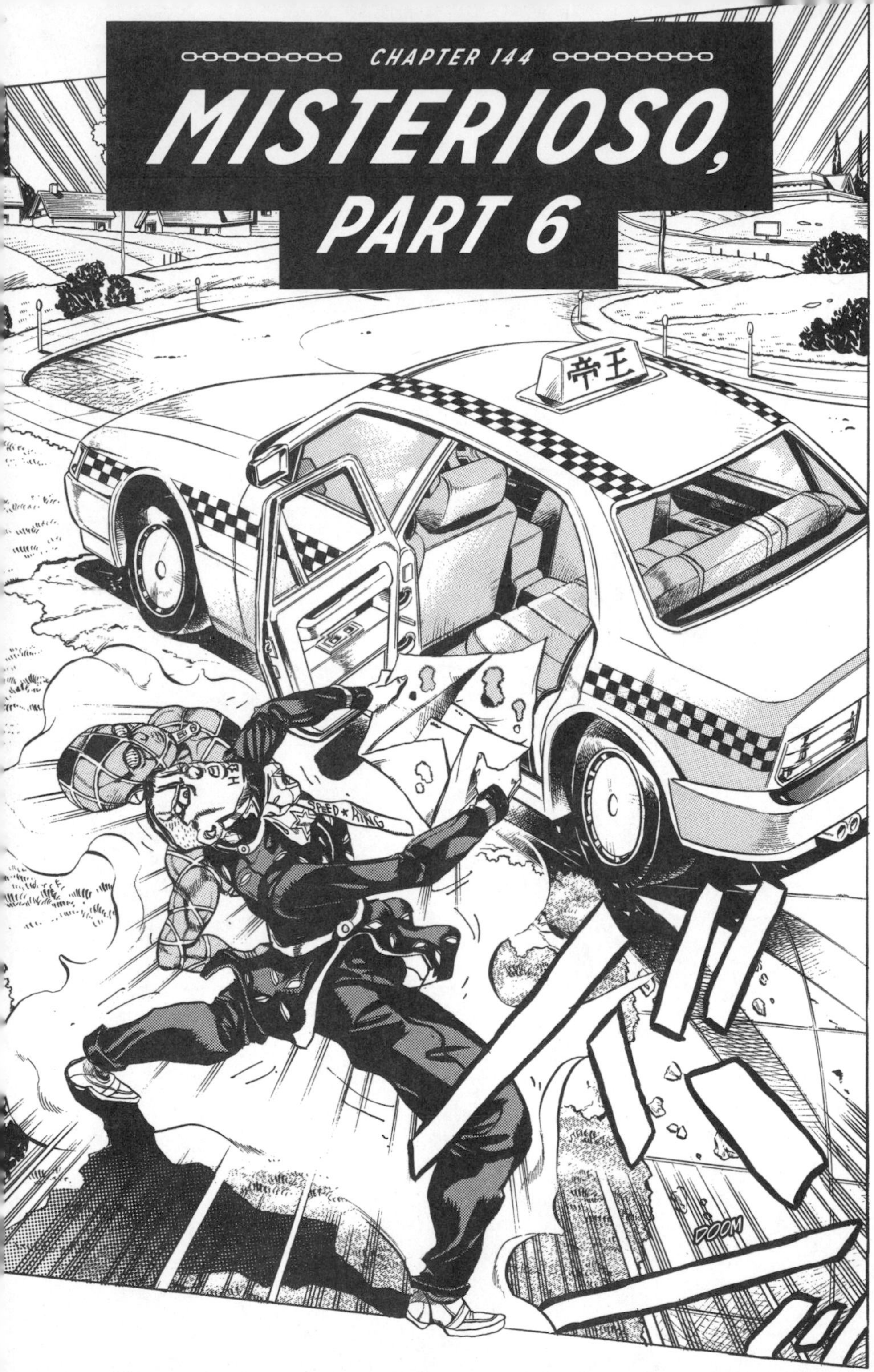
CHAPTER 144
MISTERIOSO, PART 6
帝王
SPEED★KING
DOOM

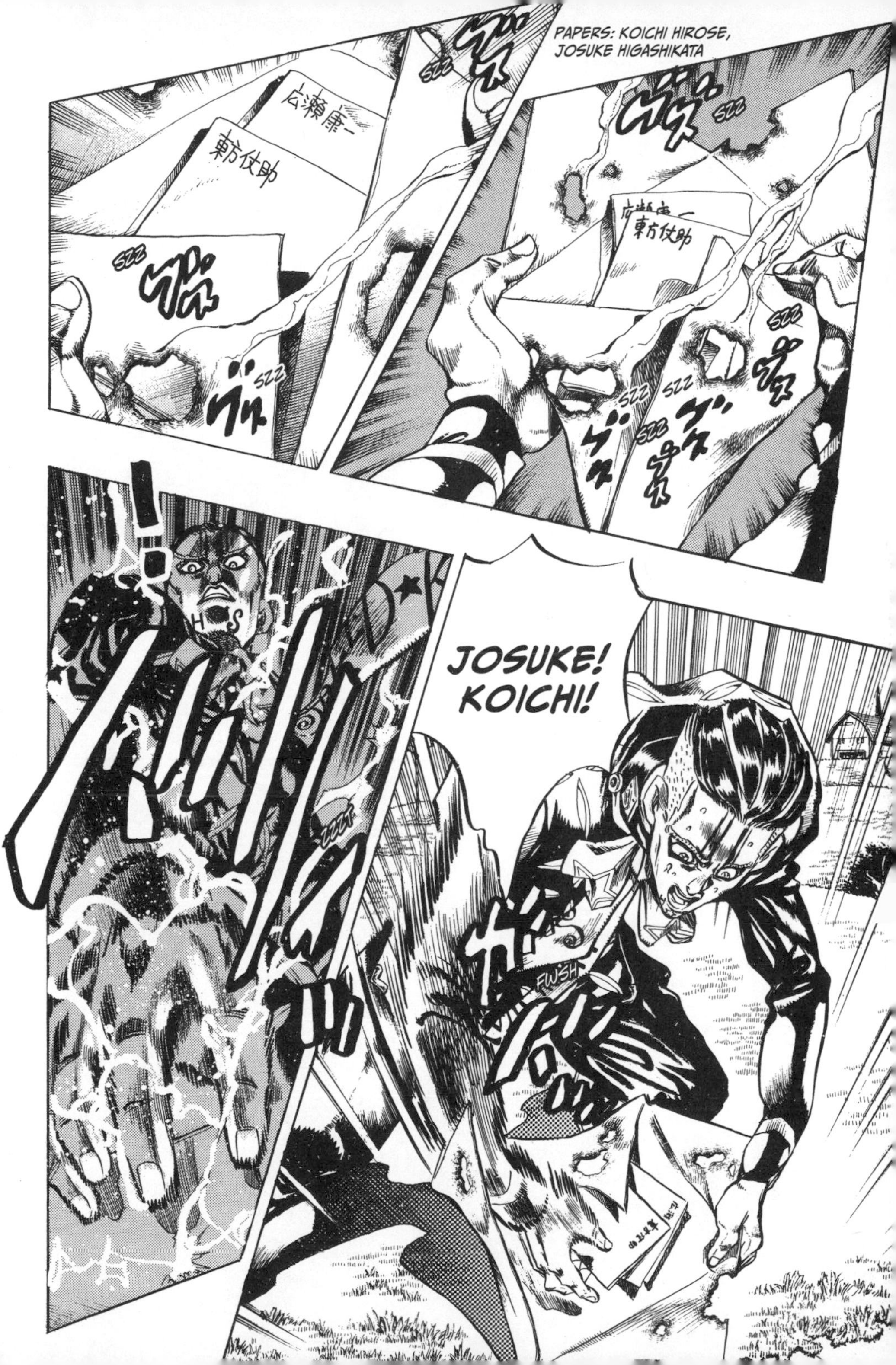
PAPERS: KOICHI HIROSE, JOSUKE HIGASHIKATA
SZZ
東方仗助
SZZ
SZZ
SZZ
SZZ
SZZ
広瀬康一
東方仗助
SZZ
SZZ
JOSUKE! KOICHI!
FWSH

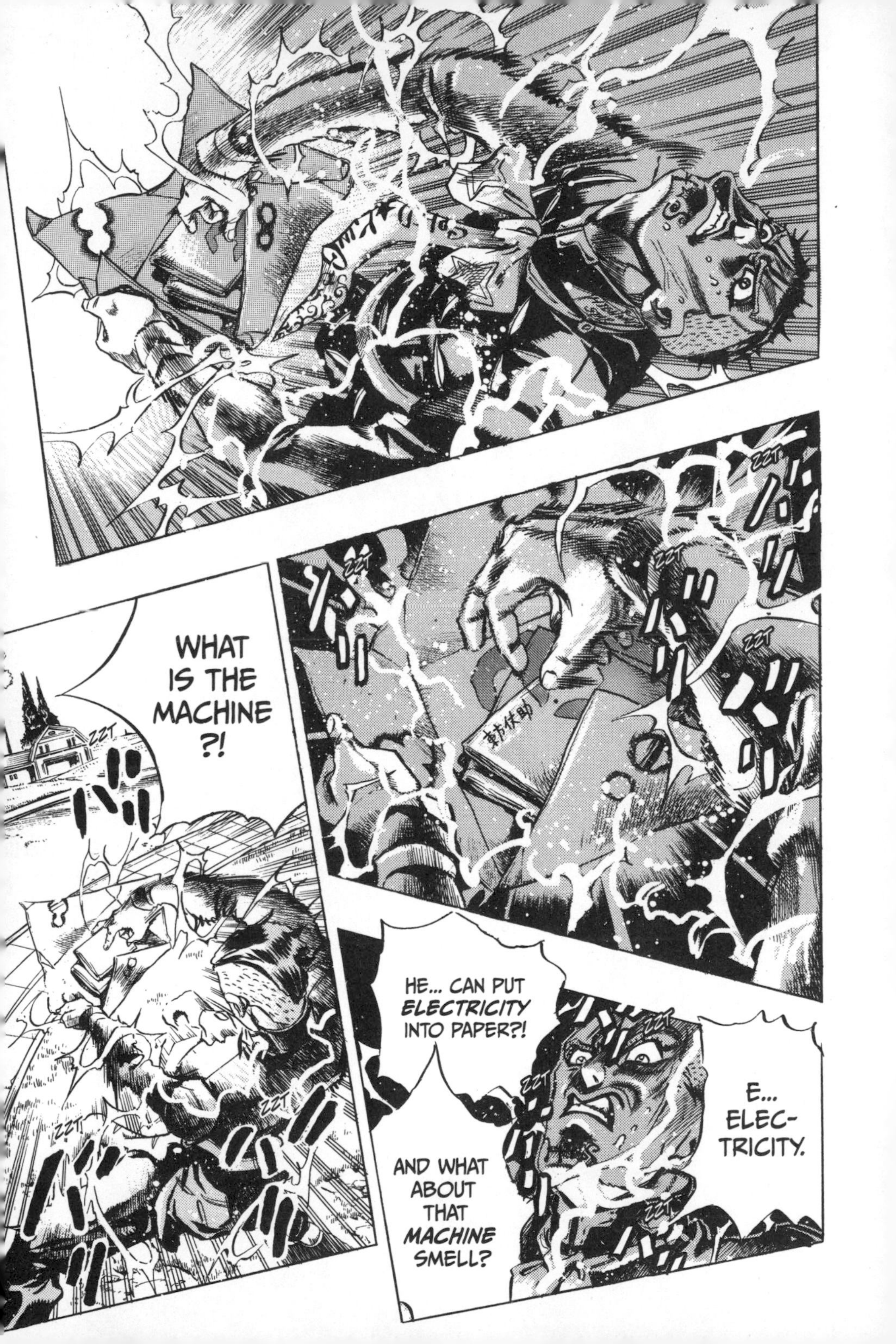
ZZT
ZZT
ZZT
ZZT
E... ELEC-TRICITY.
HE... CAN PUT ELECTRICITY INTO PAPER?!
ZZT
AND WHAT ABOUT THAT MACHINE SMELL?
WHAT IS THE MACHINE ?!
ZZT
ZZT
ZZT

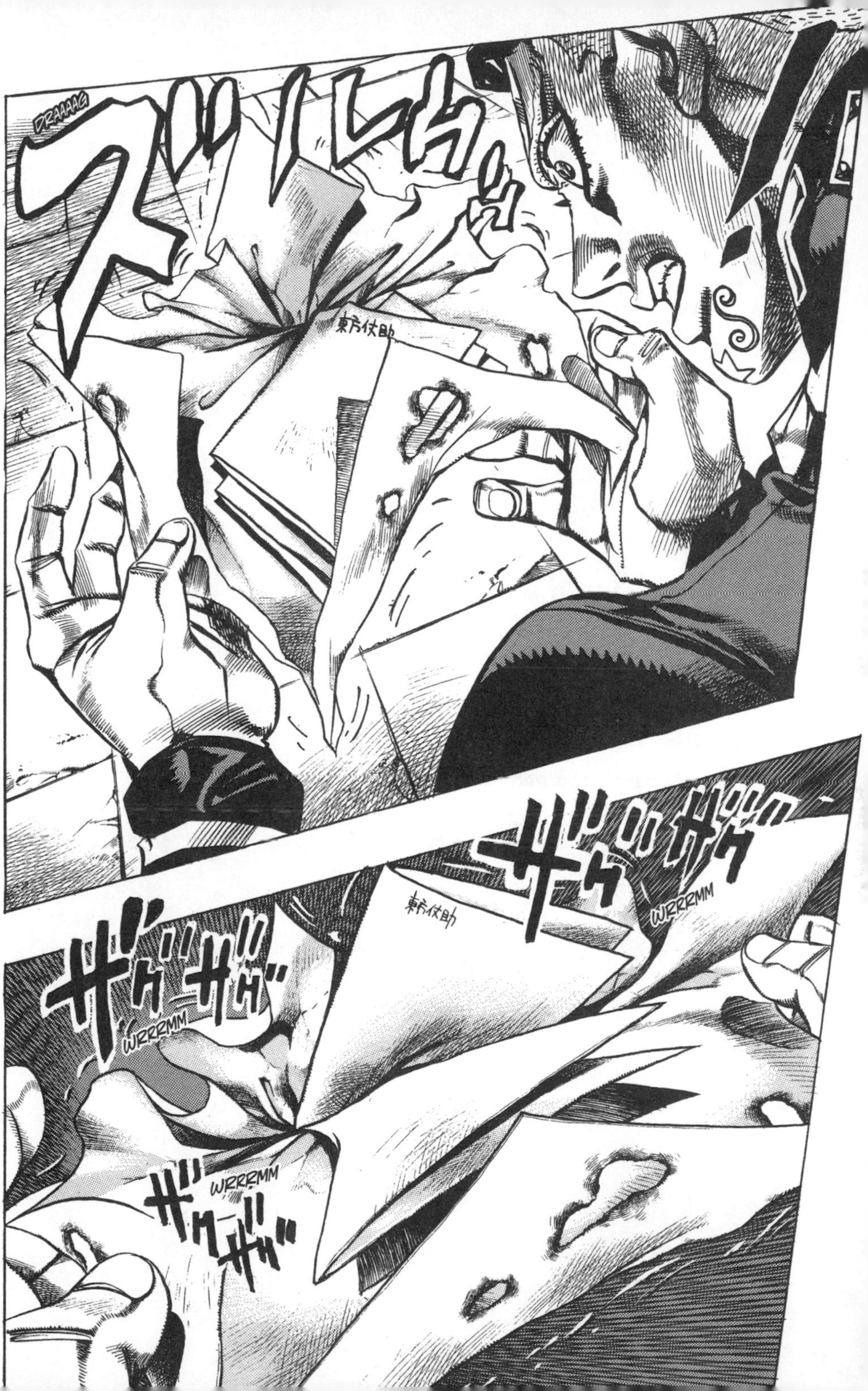
DRAAAAG
東方仗助
東方仗助
WRRRMM
WRRRMM
WRRRMM

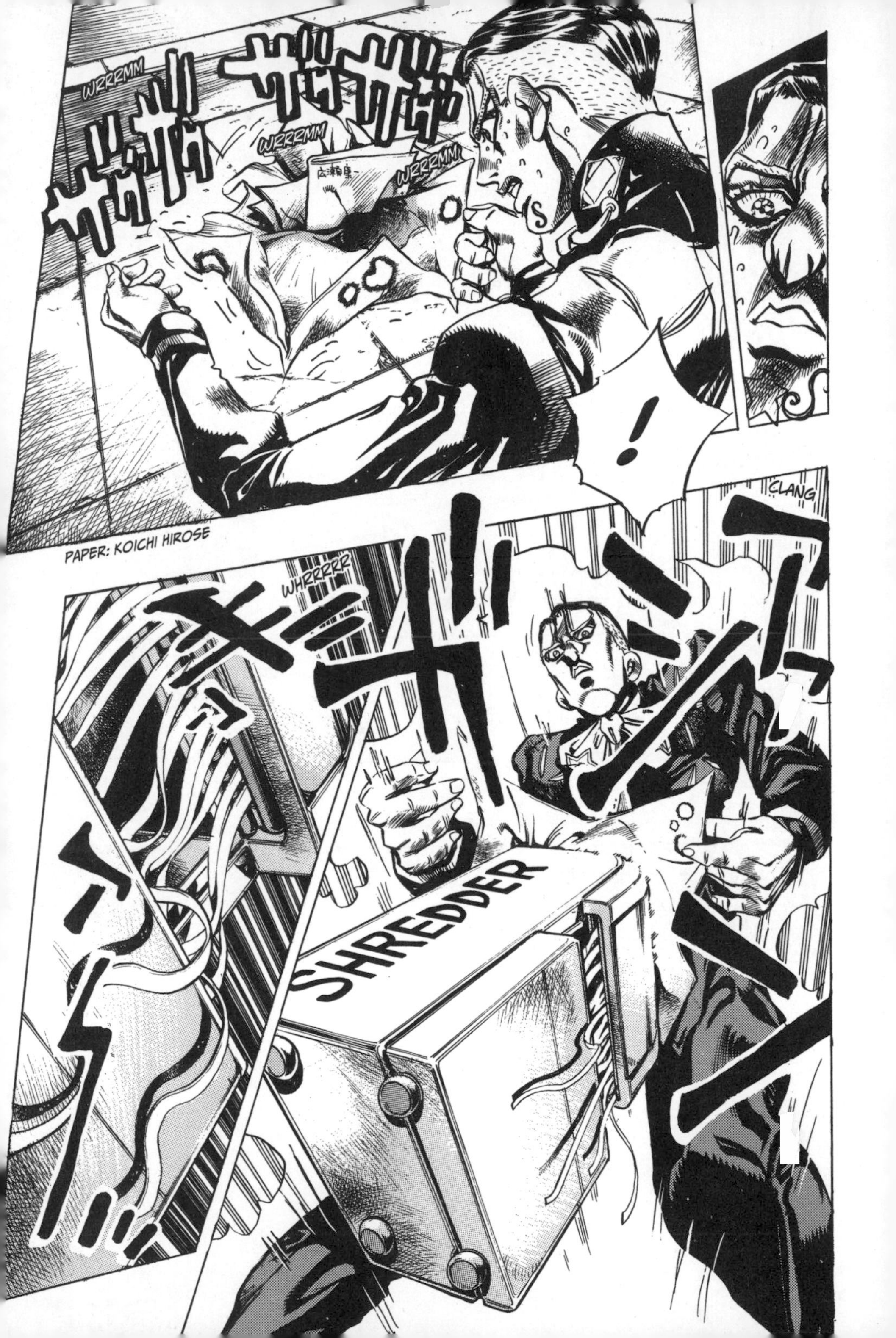
WRRRMM
WRRRMM
WRRRMM
!
PAPER: KOICHI HIROSE
CLANG
WHRRRRR
SHREDDER

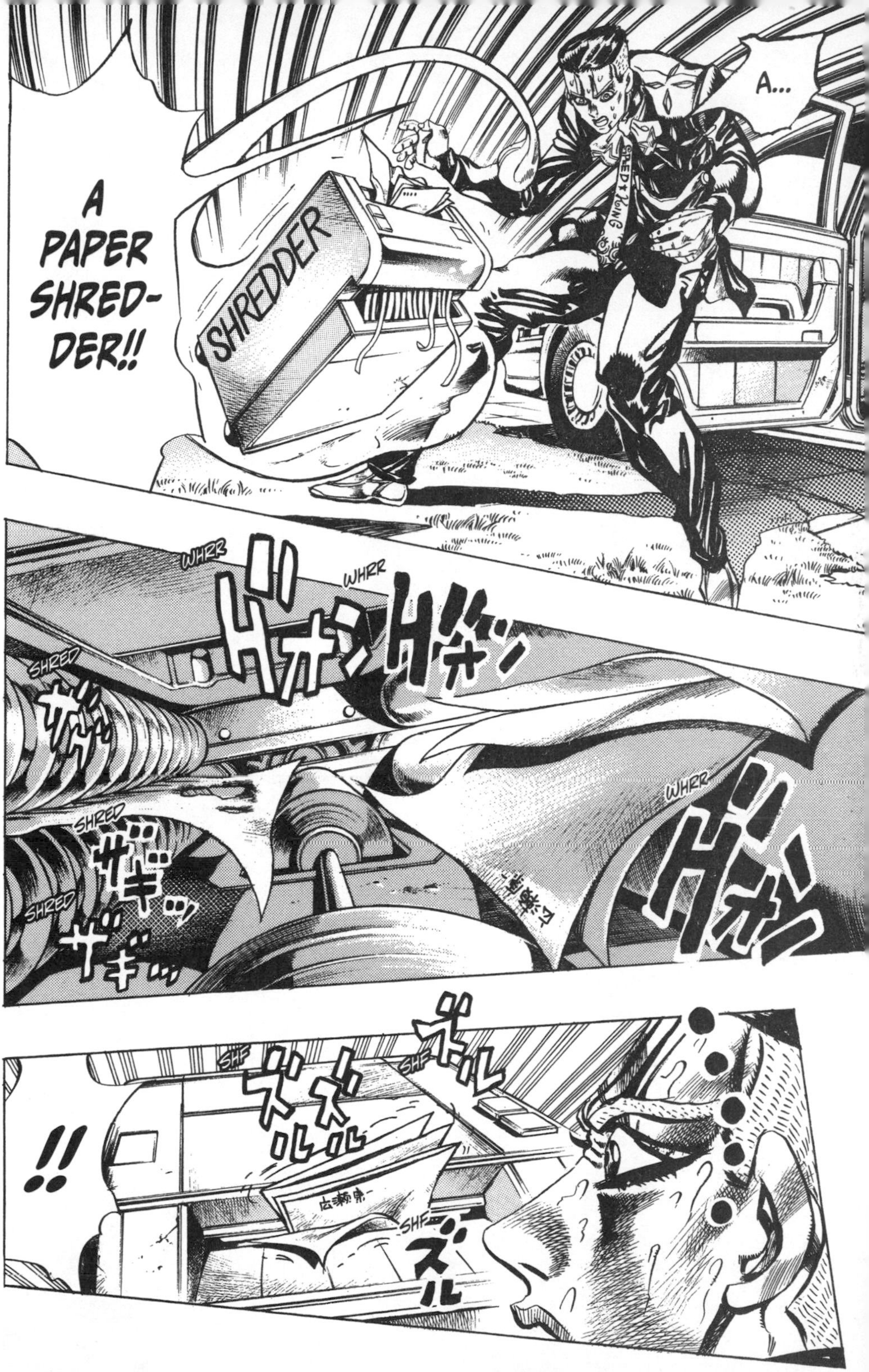
A...
A PAPER SHREDDER!!
SHREDDER
WHRR
WHRR
WHRR
SHRED
SHRED
SHRED
SHF
SHF
!!
SHF

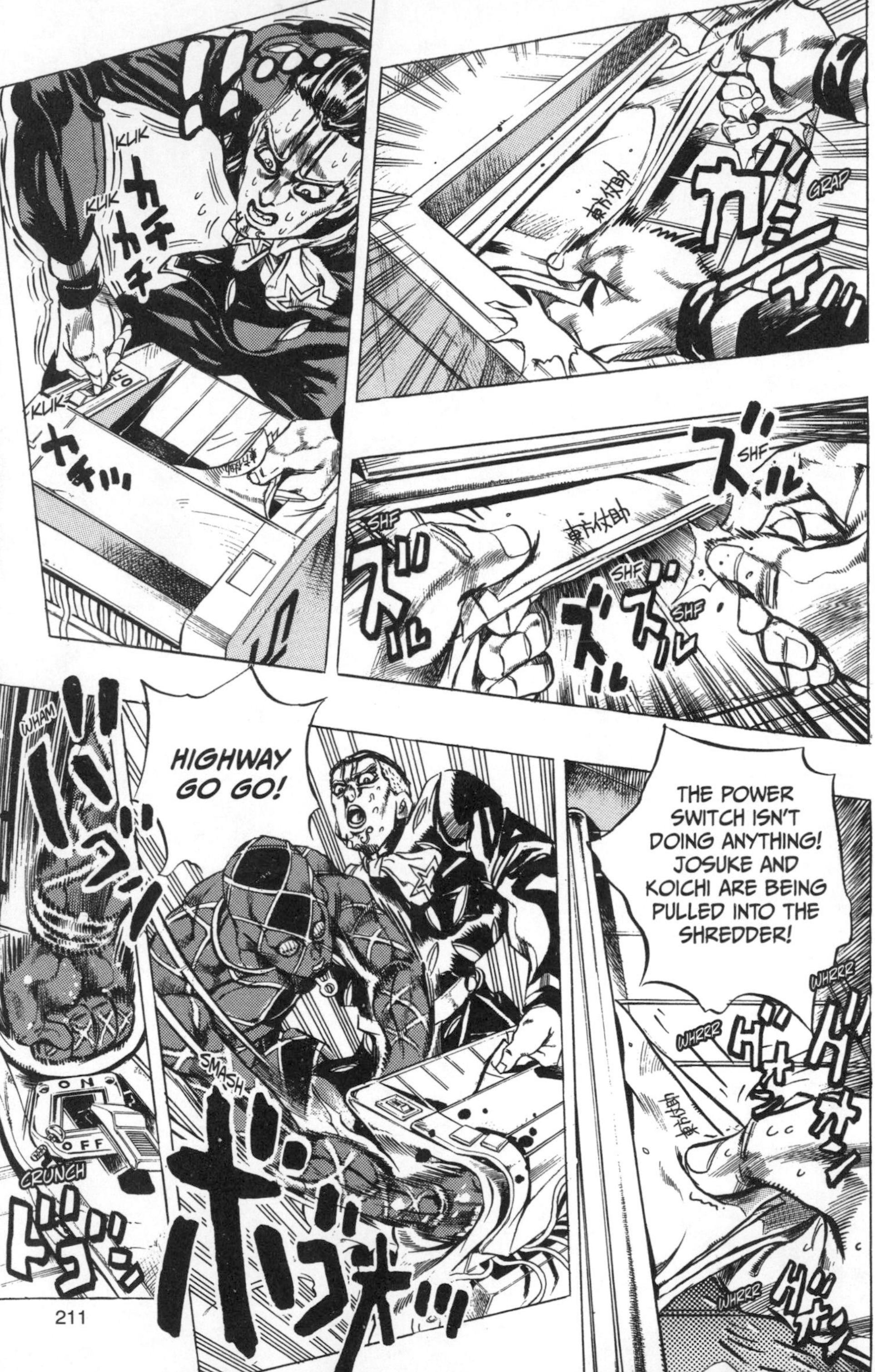
GRAP
SHF
SHF
SHF
SHF
KUK
KUK
KUK
THE POWER SWITCH ISN'T DOING ANYTHING! JOSUKE AND KOICHI ARE BEING PULLED INTO THE SHREDDER!
WHRRR
WHRRR
WHRRR
HIGHWAY GO GO!
WHAM
SMASH
ON
OFF
CRUNCH

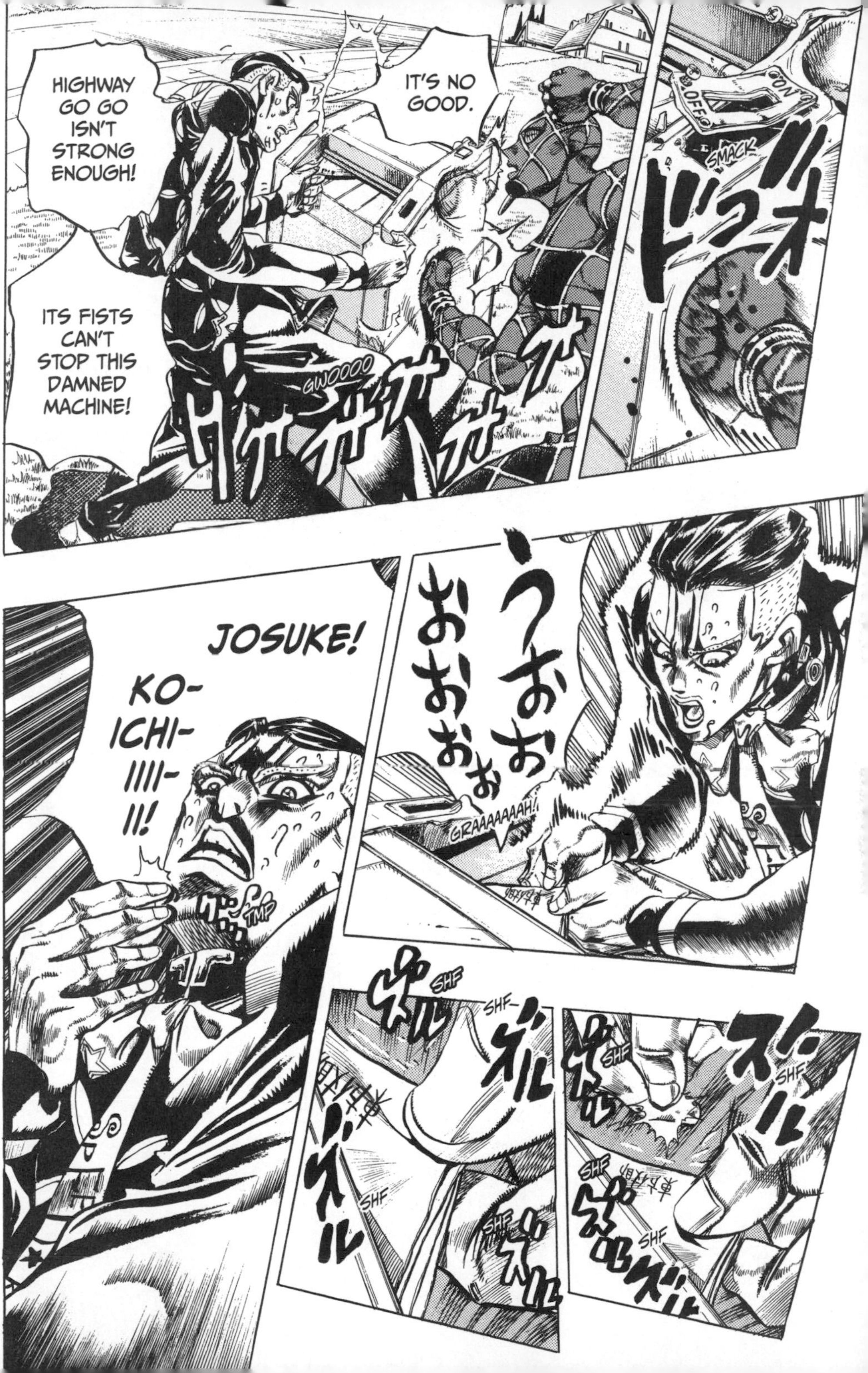
ON
OFF
SMACK
IT'S NO GOOD.
HIGHWAY GO GO ISN'T STRONG ENOUGH!
ITS FISTS CAN'T STOP THIS DAMNED MACHINE!
GWOOOO
うおおおおお
GRAAAAAAAH!
JOSUKE!
KO-ICHI-IIIII-II!
TMP
SHF
SHF
SHF
SHF
SHF-
SHF
SHF
SHF

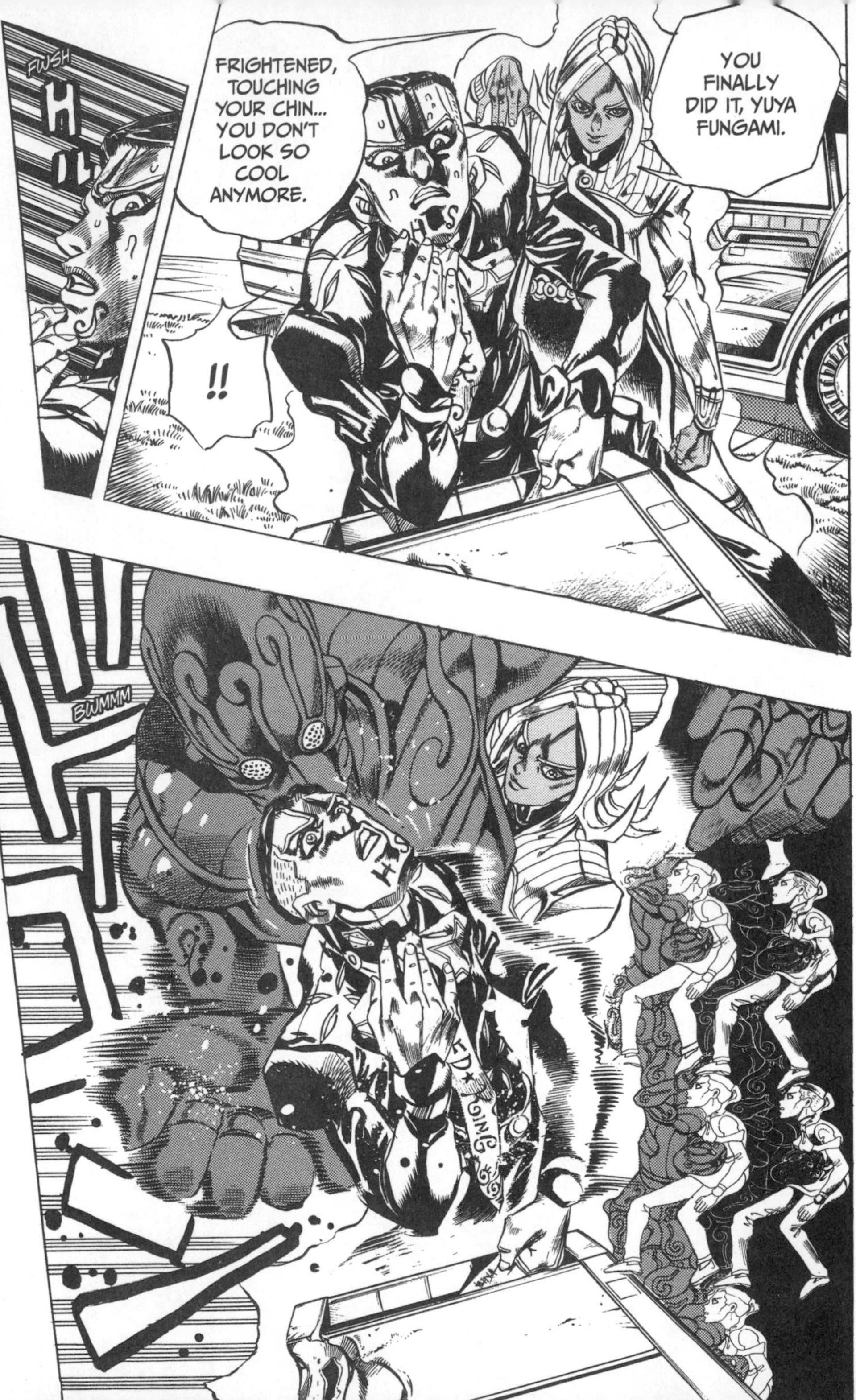
YOU FINALLY DID IT, YUYA FUNGAMI.
FRIGHTENED, TOUCHING YOUR CHIN... YOU DON'T LOOK SO COOL ANYMORE.
FWSH
!!
BWMMM

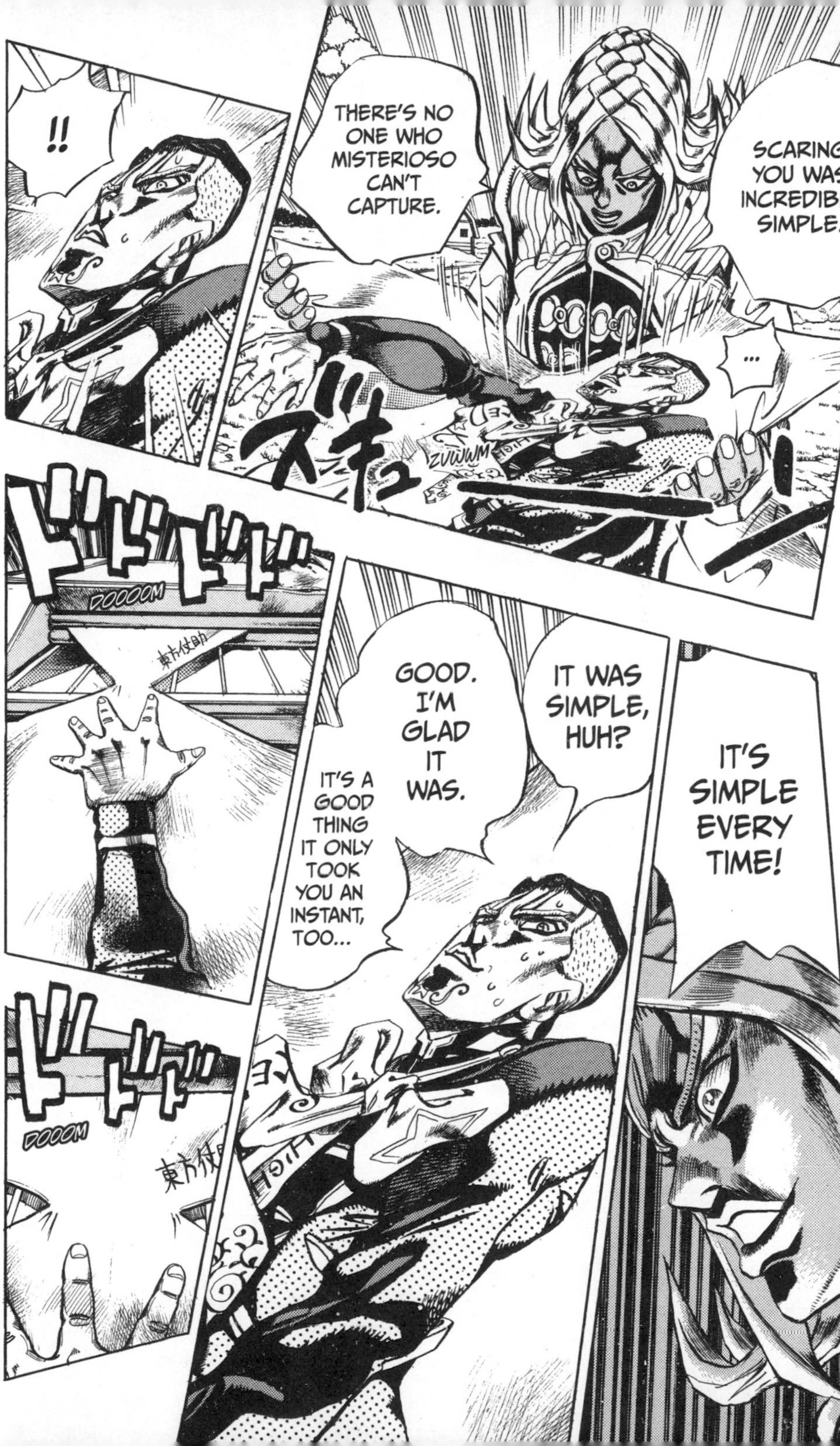
SCARING YOU WAS INCREDIBLY SIMPLE.
THERE'S NO ONE WHO MISTERIOSO CAN'T CAPTURE.
...
ズキュ
ZUWWM
!!
IT'S SIMPLE EVERY TIME!
IT WAS SIMPLE, HUH?
GOOD. I'M GLAD IT WAS.
IT'S A GOOD THING IT ONLY TOOK YOU AN INSTANT, TOO...
DOOOOM
東方仗助
DOOOM

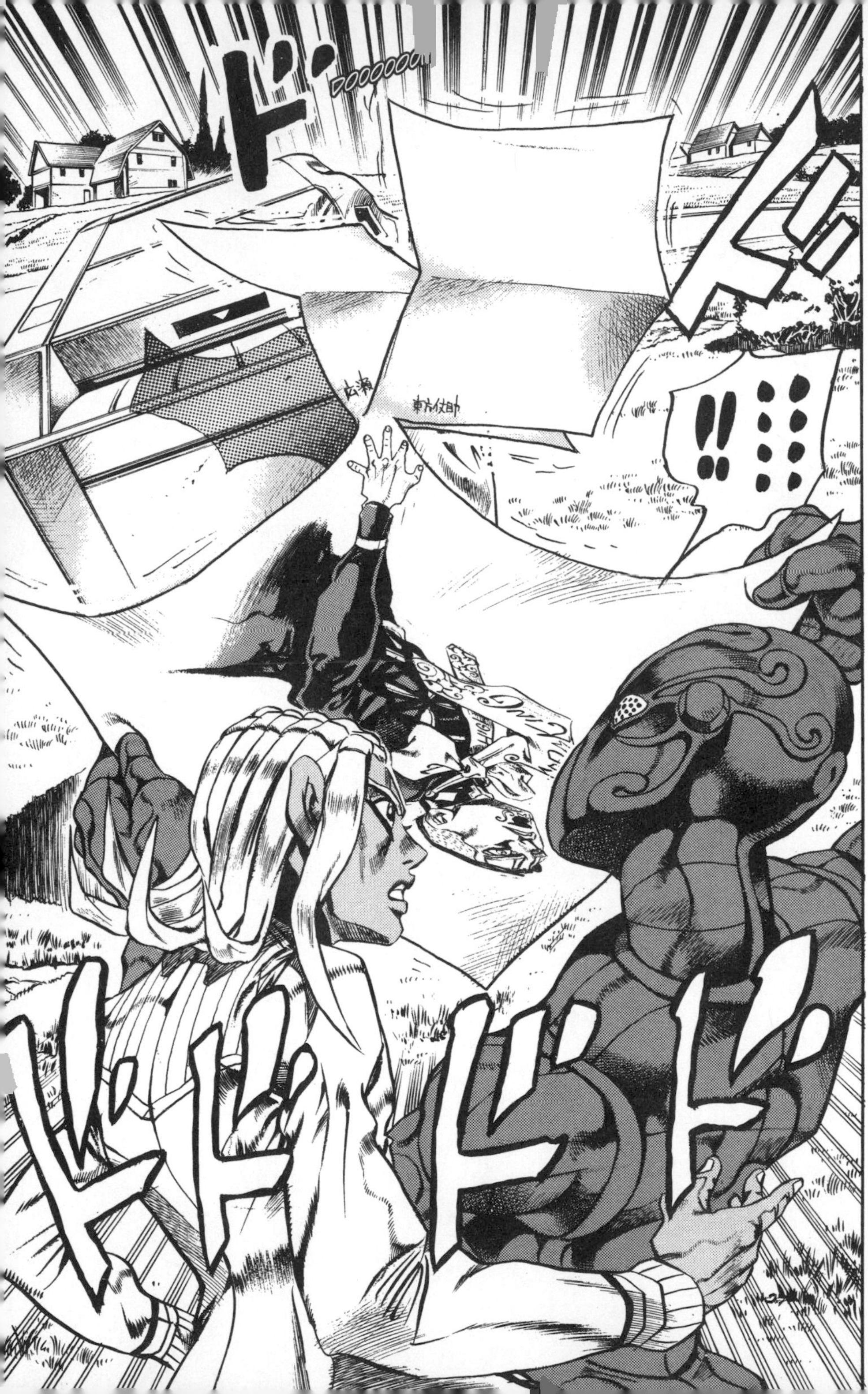
ドDOOOOOOO
ド
広瀬
東方仗助
!!......
ドドドド

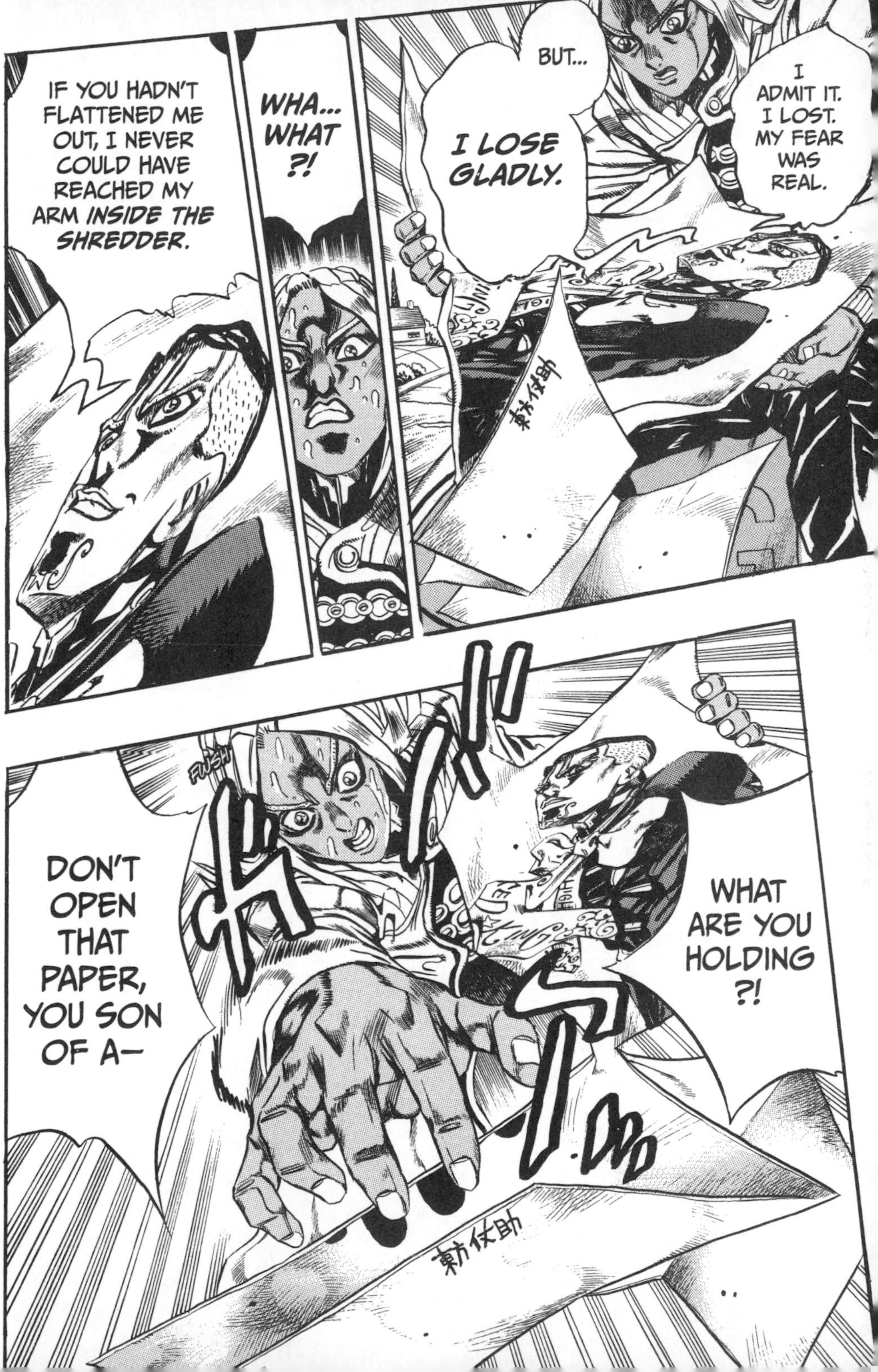
I ADMIT IT. I LOST. MY FEAR WAS REAL.
BUT...
I LOSE GLADLY.
東方仗助
WHA... WHAT ?!
IF YOU HADN'T FLATTENED ME OUT, I NEVER COULD HAVE REACHED MY ARM INSIDE THE SHREDDER.
WHAT ARE YOU HOLDING ?!
DON'T OPEN THAT PAPER, YOU SON OF A–
東方仗助

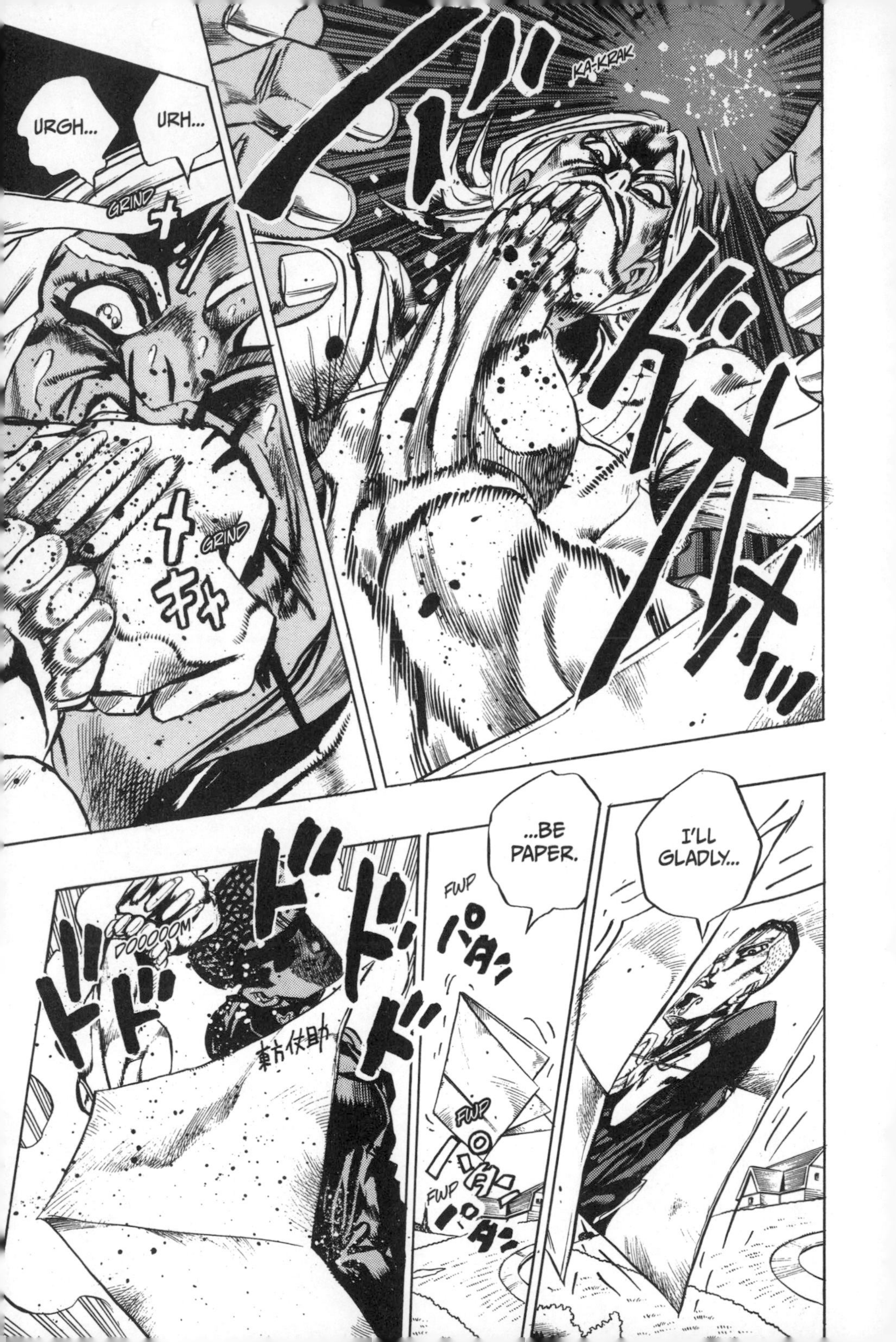
KA-KRAK
URGH...
URH...
GRIND
GRIND
I'LL GLADLY...
...BE PAPER.
FWP
FWP
FWP
DOOOOOM
東方仗助

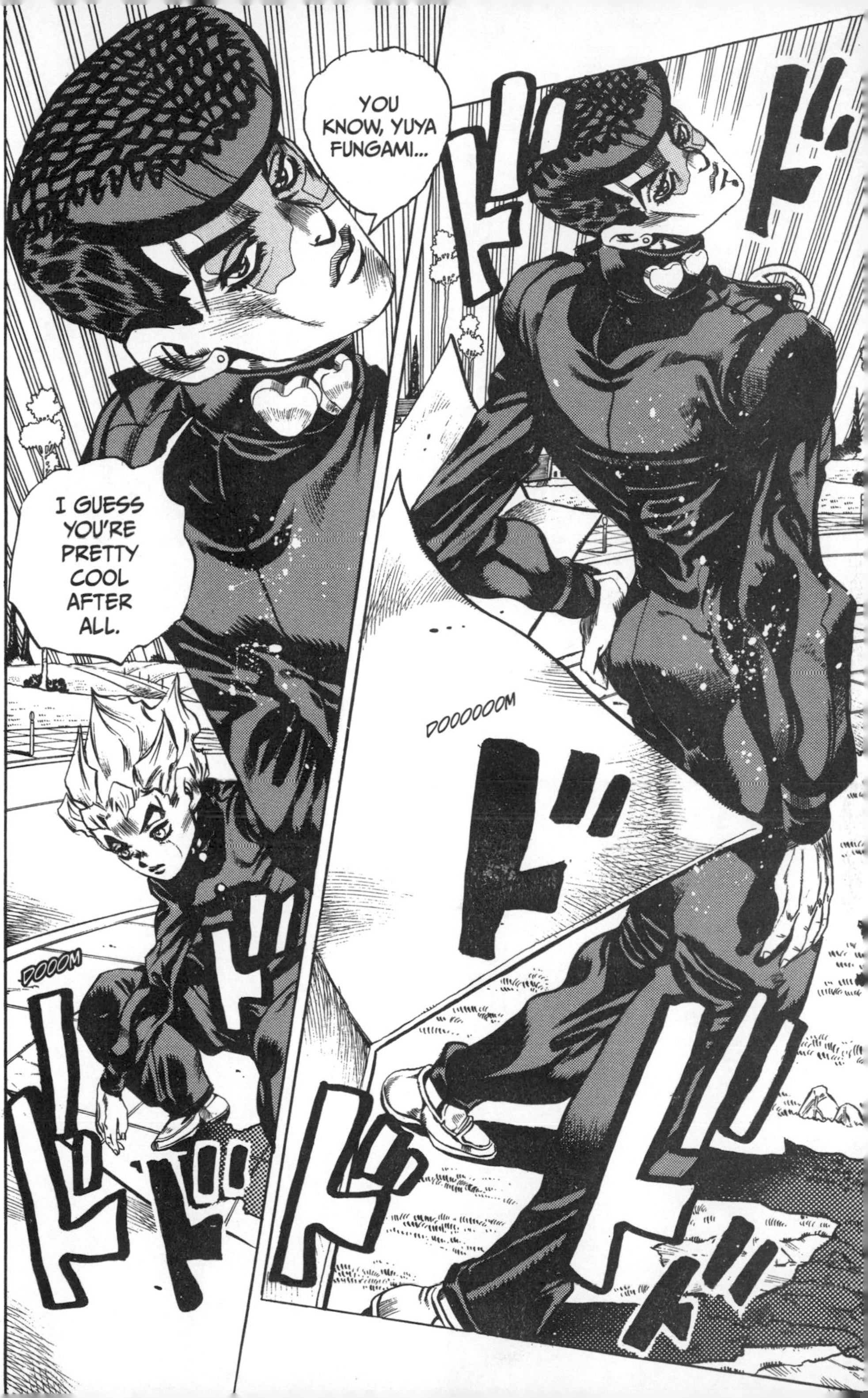
DOOOOOOM
YOU KNOW, YUYA FUNGAMI...
I GUESS YOU'RE PRETTY COOL AFTER ALL.
DOOOM

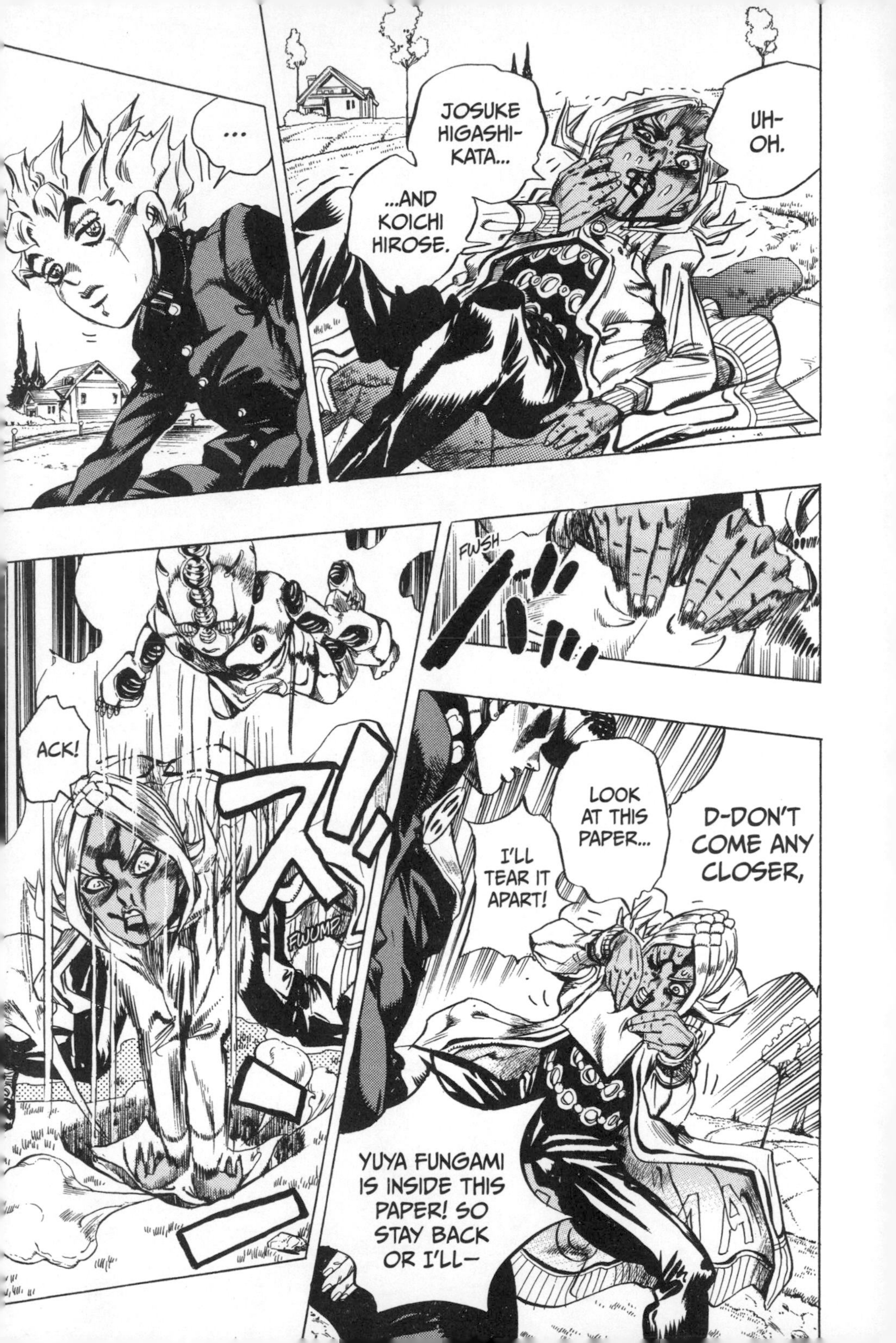
UH-OH.
JOSUKE HIGASHIKATA...
...AND KOICHI HIROSE.
...
FWSH
D-DON'T COME ANY CLOSER,
LOOK AT THIS PAPER...
I'LL TEAR IT APART!
YUYA FUNGAMI IS INSIDE THIS PAPER! SO STAY BACK OR I'LL—
ACK!
FWUMP

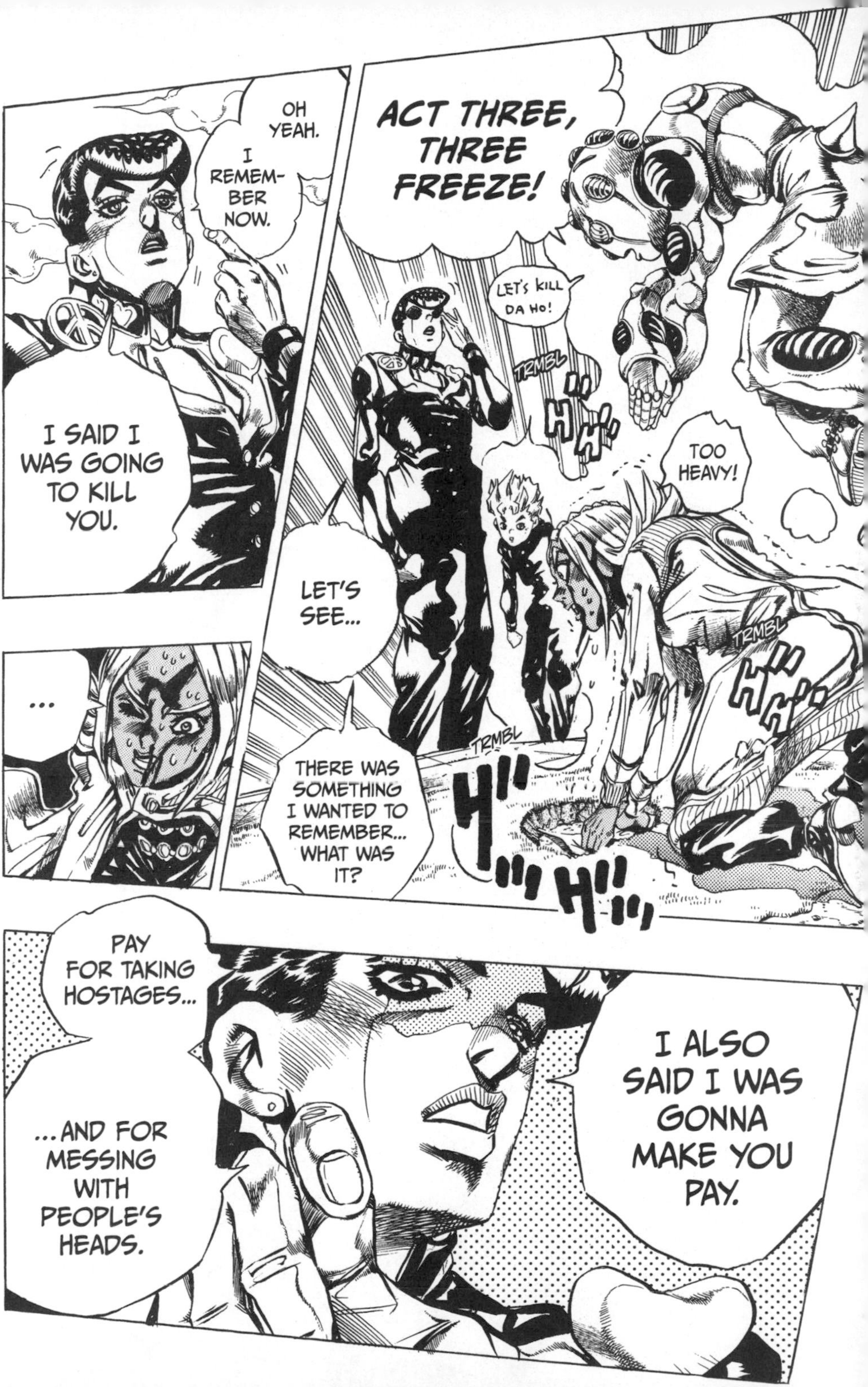
ACT THREE, THREE FREEZE!
LET'S KILL DA HO!
TRMBL
TOO HEAVY!
TRMBL
LET'S SEE...
THERE WAS SOMETHING I WANTED TO REMEMBER... WHAT WAS IT?
TRMBL
OH YEAH.
I REMEMBER NOW.
I SAID I WAS GOING TO KILL YOU.
...
I ALSO SAID I WAS GONNA MAKE YOU PAY.
PAY FOR TAKING HOSTAGES...
...AND FOR MESSING WITH PEOPLE'S HEADS.

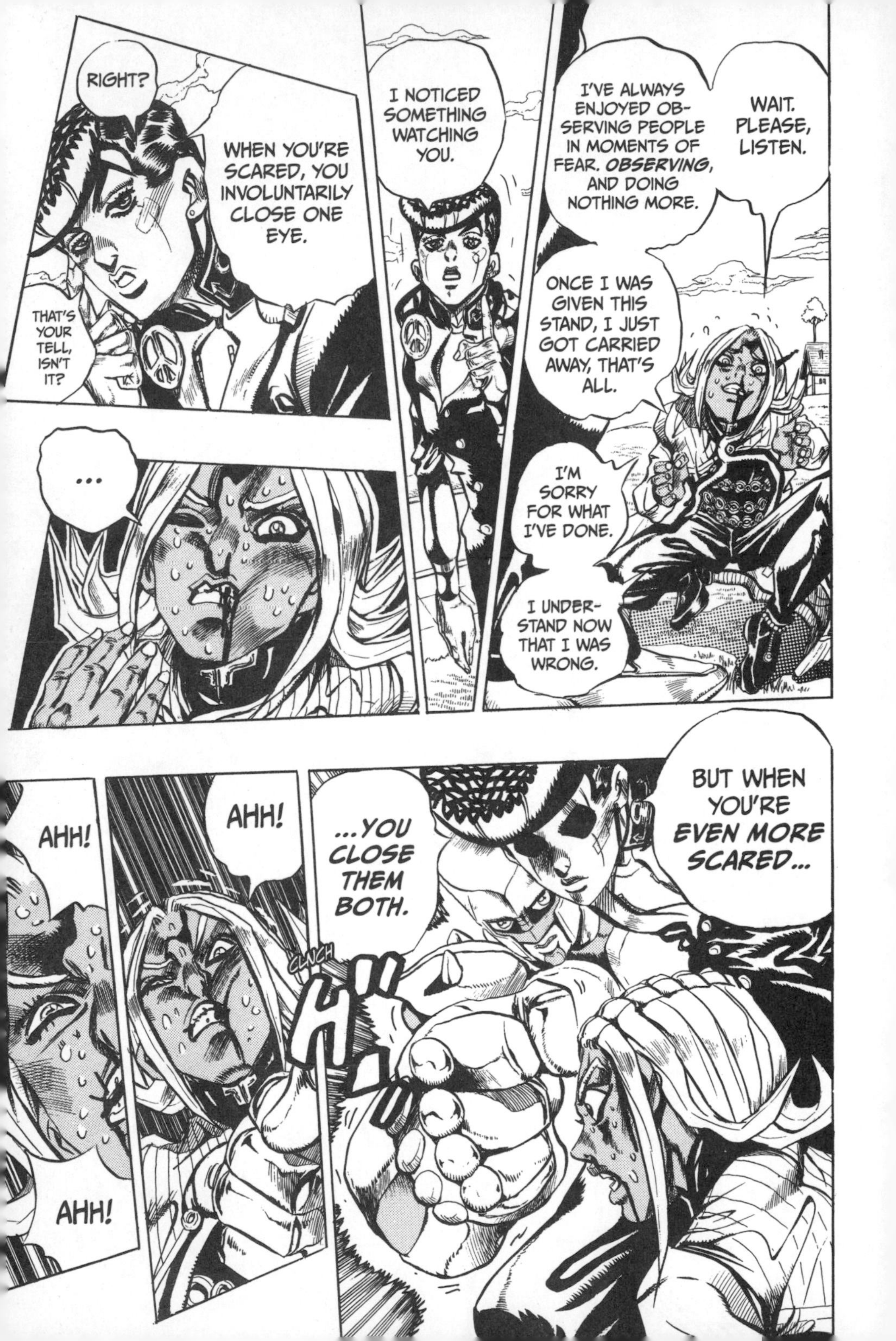
WAIT. PLEASE, LISTEN.
I'VE ALWAYS ENJOYED OB-SERVING PEOPLE IN MOMENTS OF FEAR. *OBSERVING*, AND DOING NOTHING MORE.
ONCE I WAS GIVEN THIS STAND, I JUST GOT CARRIED AWAY, THAT'S ALL.
I'M SORRY FOR WHAT I'VE DONE.
I UNDER-STAND NOW THAT I WAS WRONG.
I NOTICED SOMETHING WATCHING YOU.
WHEN YOU'RE SCARED, YOU INVOLUNTARILY CLOSE ONE EYE.
RIGHT?
THAT'S YOUR TELL, ISN'T IT?
...
BUT WHEN YOU'RE *EVEN MORE SCARED...*
...YOU CLOSE THEM BOTH.
CLNCH
AHH!
AHH!
AHH!

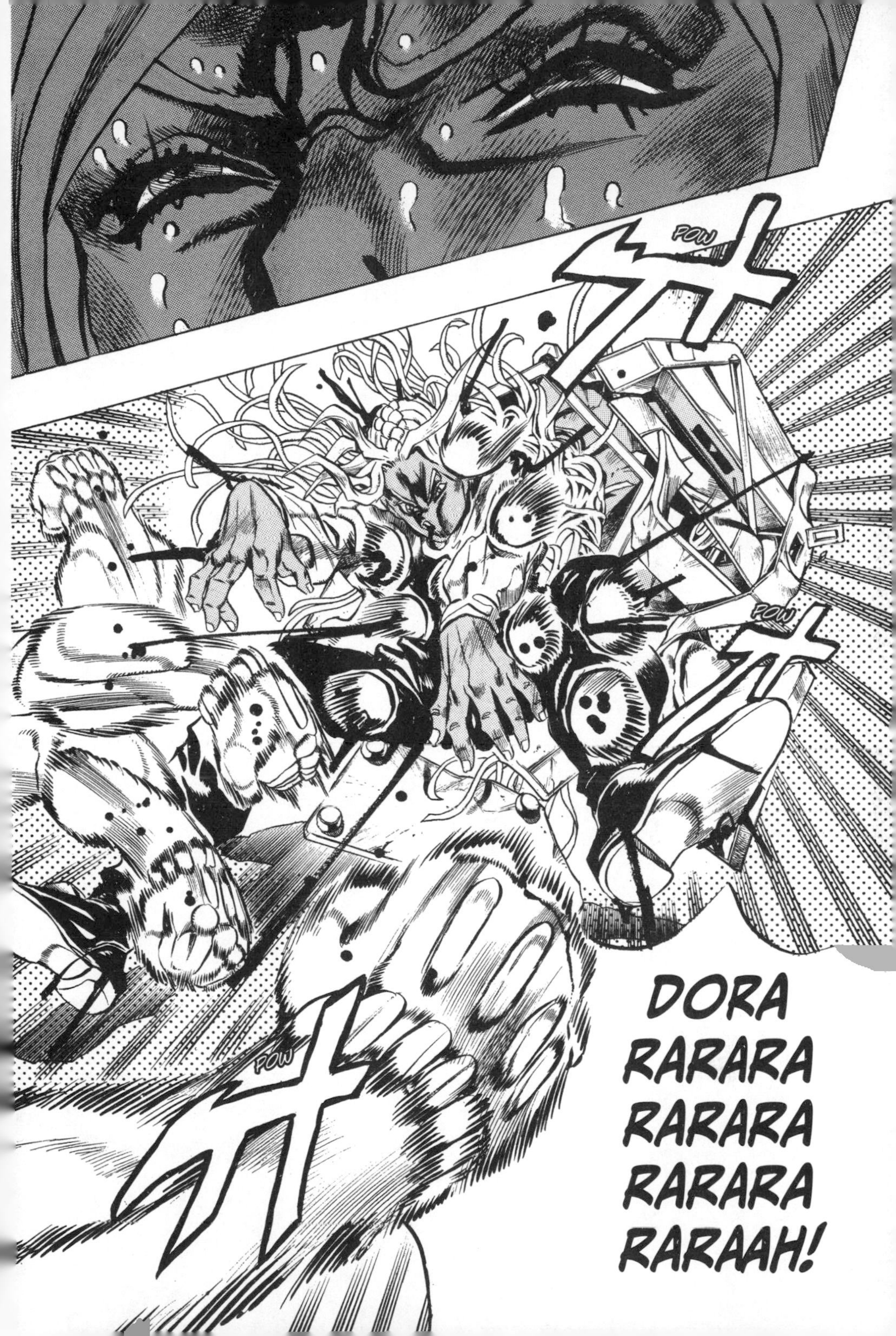
POW
POW
DORA
RARARA
RARARA
RARARA
RARAAH!
POW

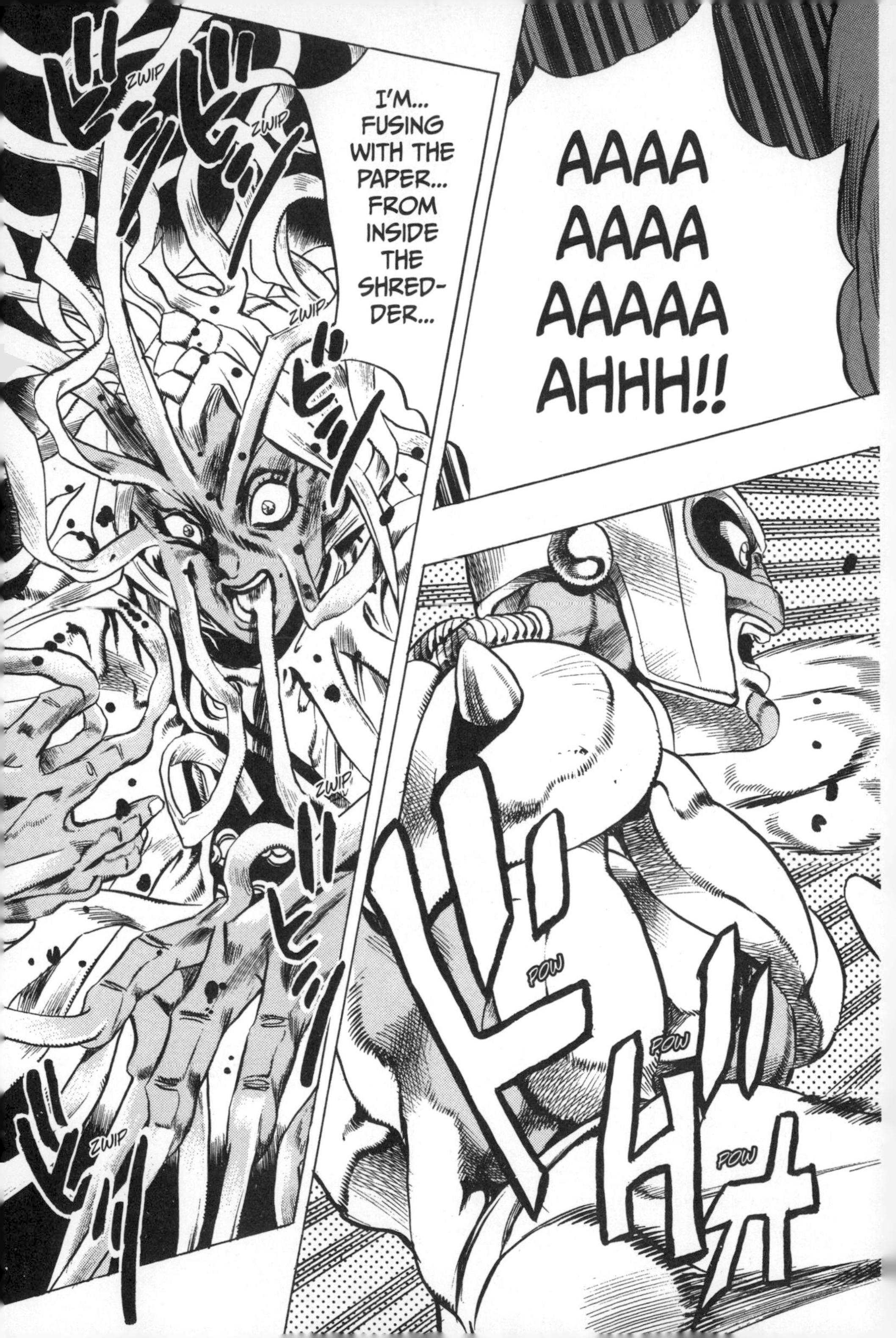
AAAA AAAA AAAAA AHHH!!
POW
POW
POW
ZWIP
ZWIP
I'M... FUSING WITH THE PAPER... FROM INSIDE THE SHRED-DER...
ZWIP
ZWIP
ZWIP

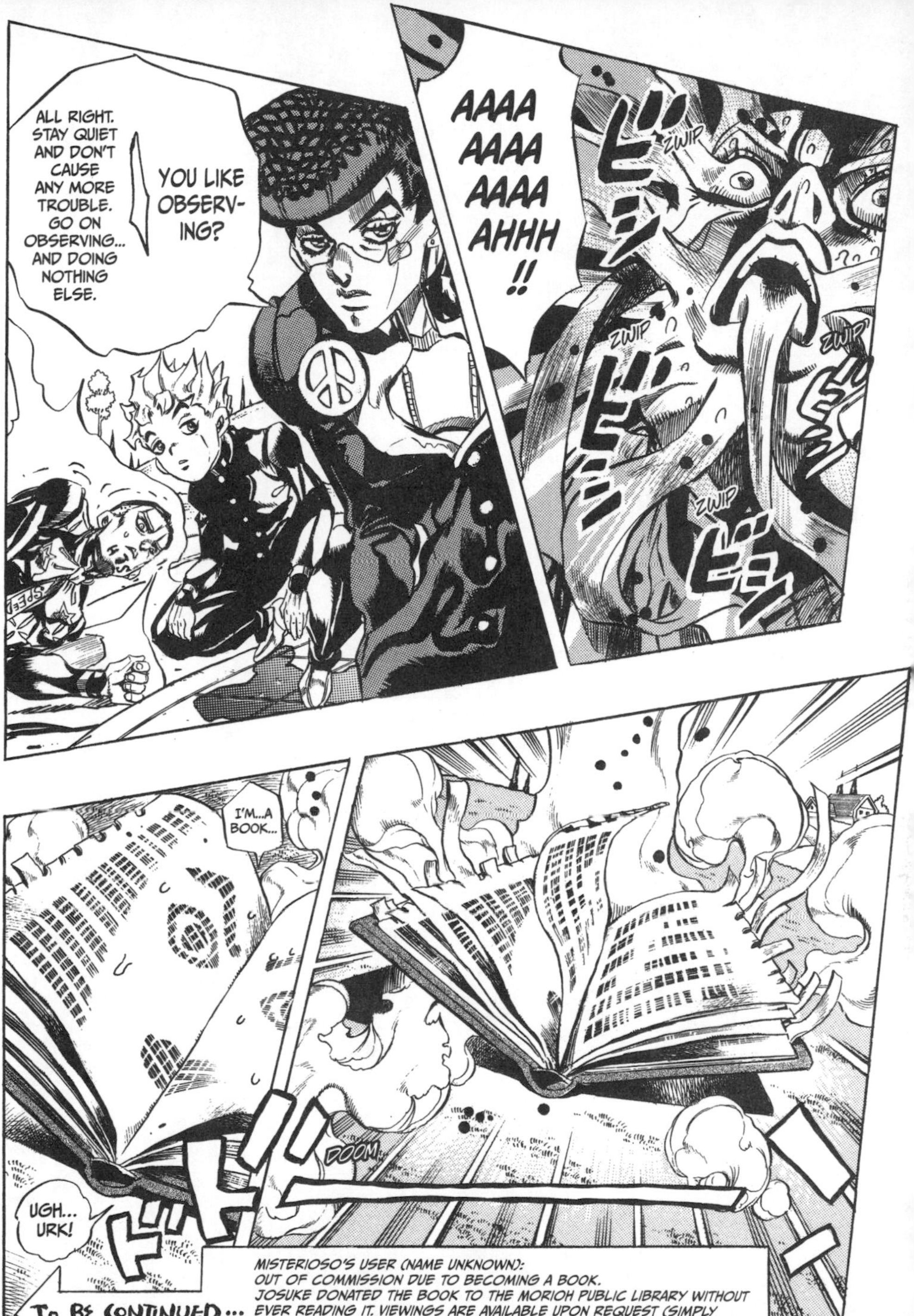
AAAA AAAA AAAA AHHH!!
ZWIP
ZWIP
ZWIP
ZWIP
YOU LIKE OBSERVING?
ALL RIGHT. STAY QUIET AND DON'T CAUSE ANY MORE TROUBLE. GO ON OBSERVING... AND DOING NOTHING ELSE.
DOOM
I'M...A BOOK...
UGH... URK!
MISTERIOSO'S USER (NAME UNKNOWN):
OUT OF COMMISSION DUE TO BECOMING A BOOK.
JOSUKE DONATED THE BOOK TO THE MORIOH PUBLIC LIBRARY WITHOUT EVER READING IT. VIEWINGS ARE AVAILABLE UPON REQUEST (SIMPLY MENTION "MISTERIOSO" TO A LIBRARIAN), BUT NO CHECKOUTS. READERS OF THE BOOK MAY OCCASIONALLY FEEL LIKE THEY HEAR A VOICE.
To Be Continued...

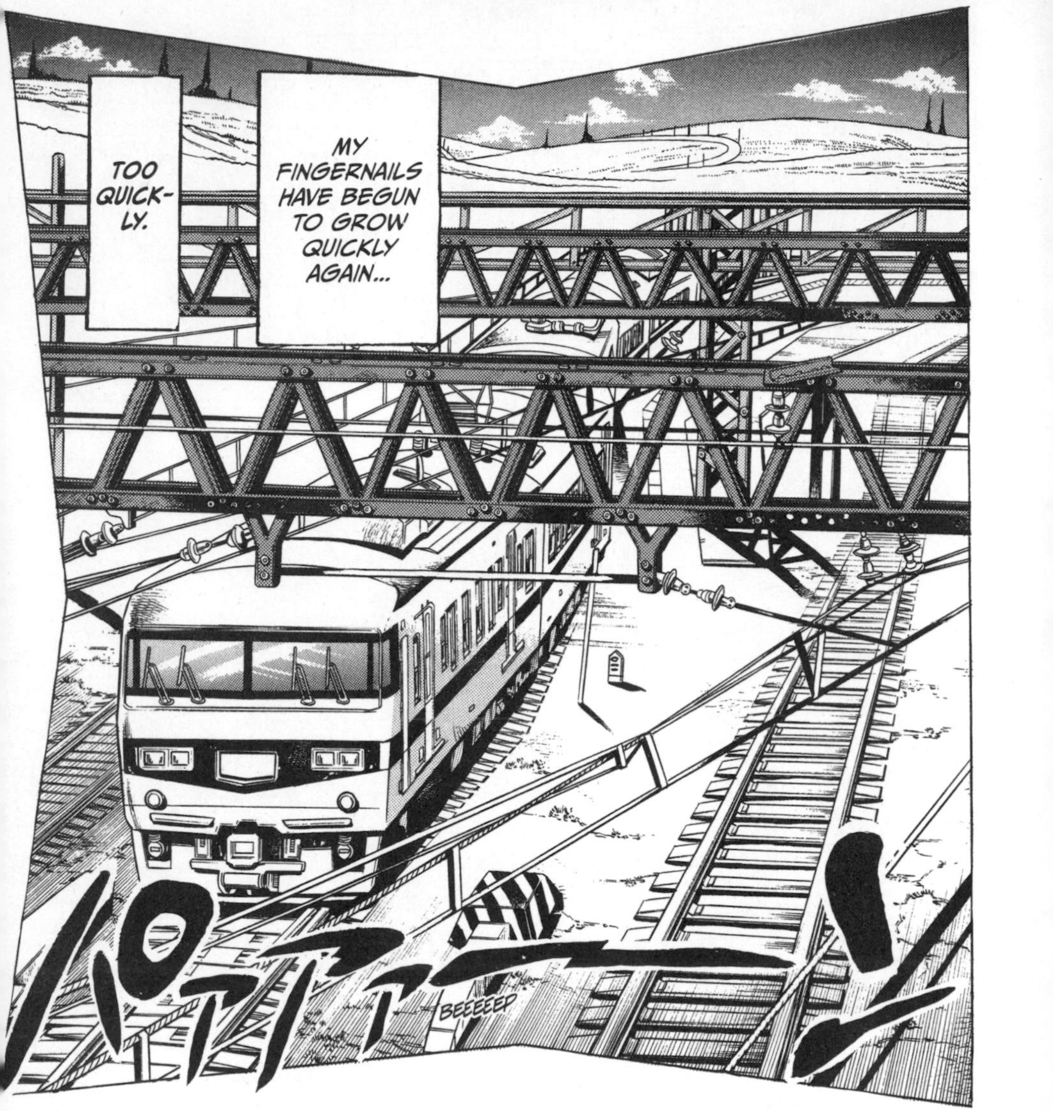
MY FINGERNAILS HAVE BEGUN TO GROW QUICKLY AGAIN...
TOO QUICK-LY.
BEEEEEP

CHAPTER 145

MY DAD IS NOT MY DAD, PART 1

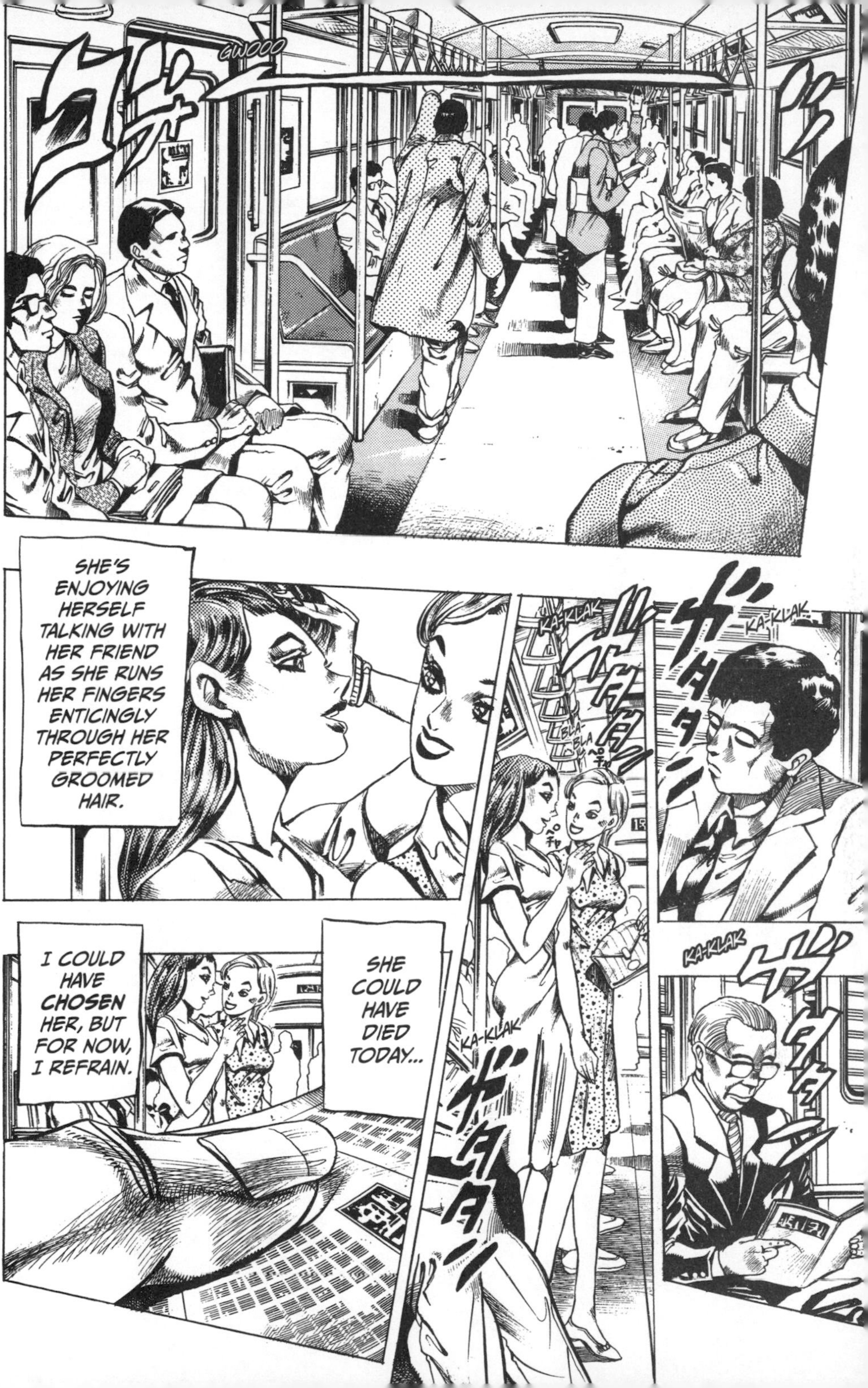
GWOOO
KA-KLAK
KA-KLAK
KA-KLAK
BLA BLA
KA-KLAK
SHE'S ENJOYING HERSELF TALKING WITH HER FRIEND AS SHE RUNS HER FINGERS ENTICINGLY THROUGH HER PERFECTLY GROOMED HAIR.
SHE COULD HAVE DIED TODAY...
I COULD HAVE CHOSEN HER, BUT FOR NOW, I REFRAIN.

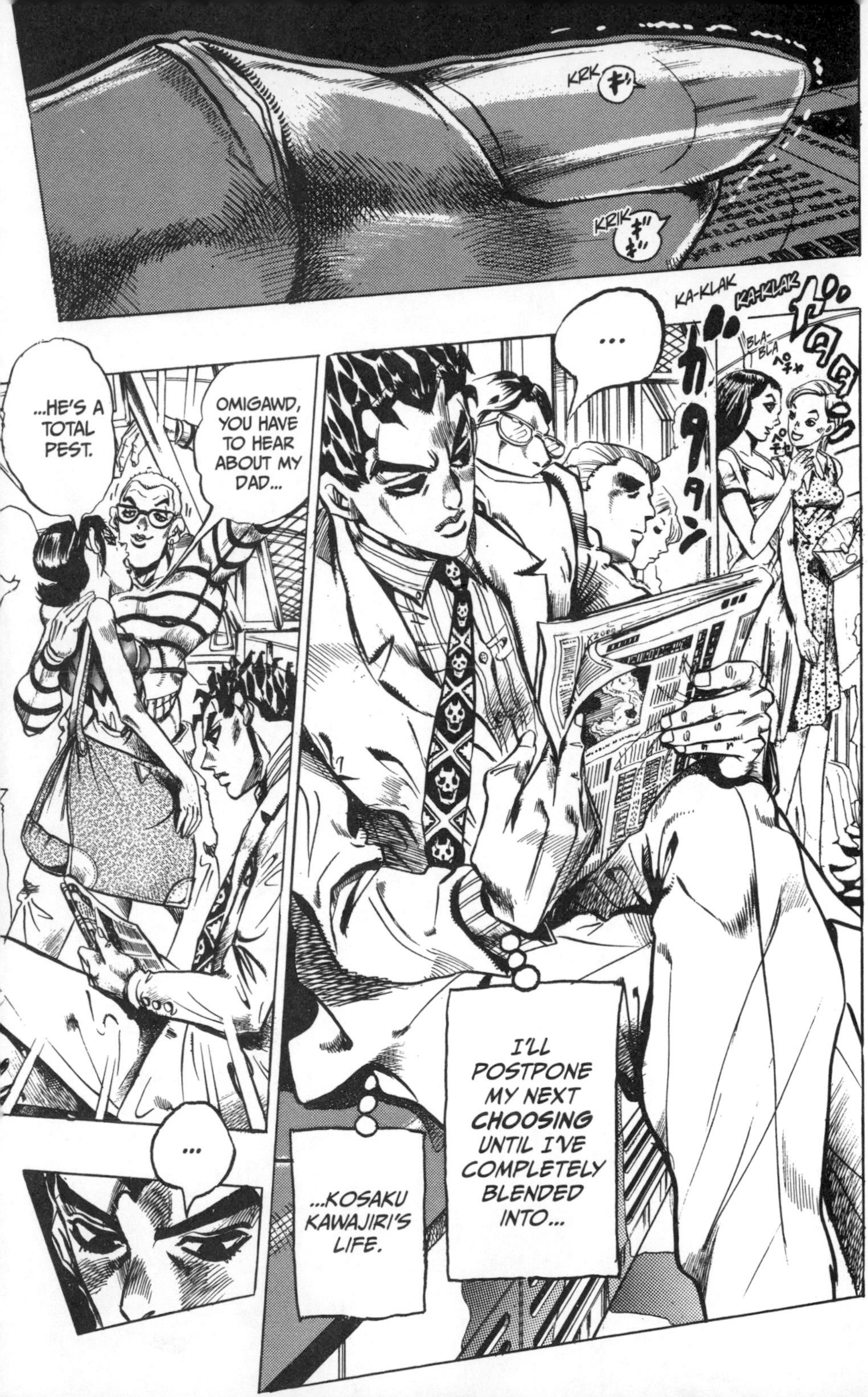
KRK
KRIK
KA-KLAK
KA-KLAK
...
BLA-BLA
I'LL POSTPONE MY NEXT CHOOSING UNTIL I'VE COMPLETELY BLENDED INTO...
...KOSAKU KAWAJIRI'S LIFE.
OMIGAWD, YOU HAVE TO HEAR ABOUT MY DAD...
...HE'S A TOTAL PEST.
...

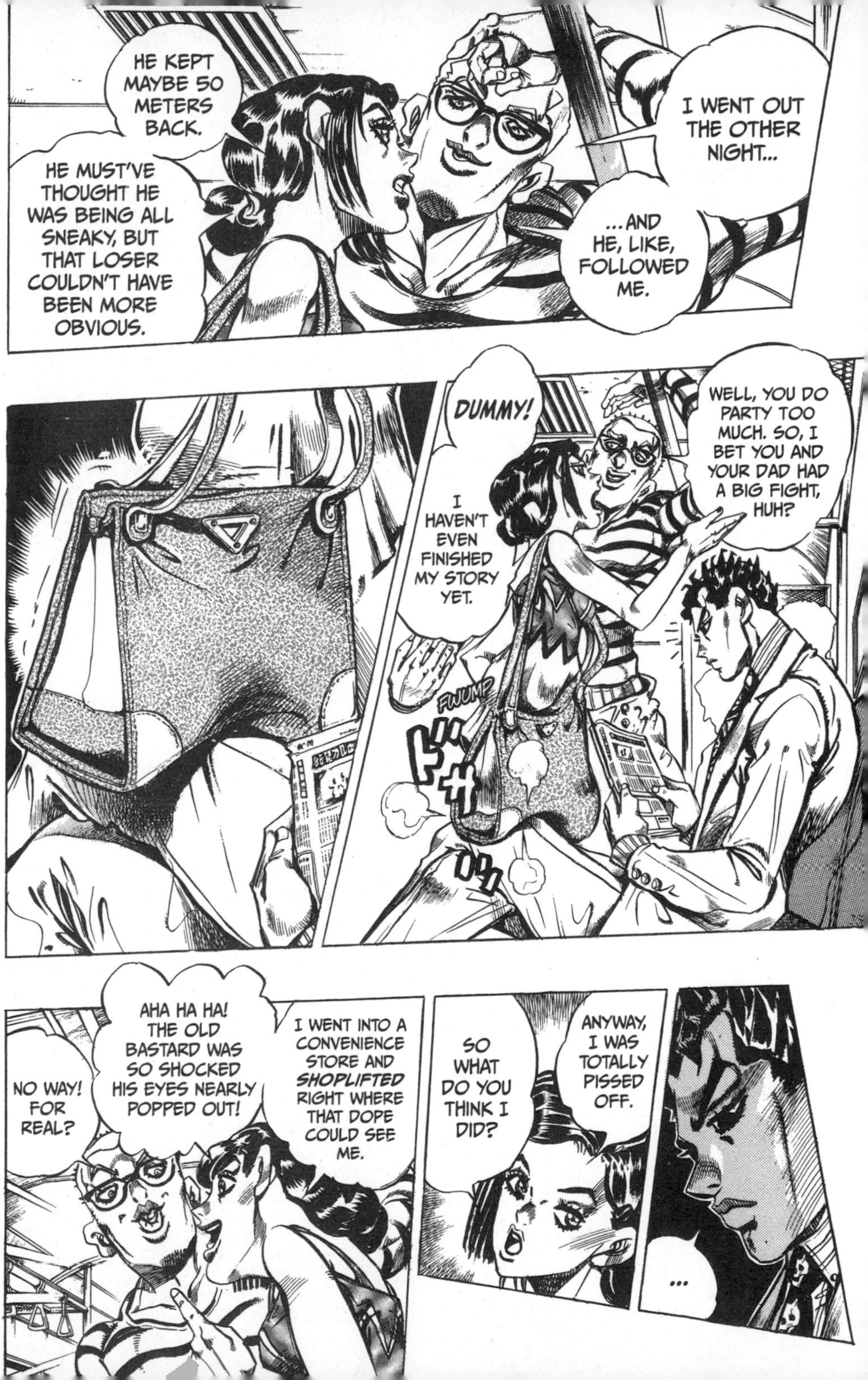
I WENT OUT THE OTHER NIGHT...
...AND HE, LIKE, FOLLOWED ME.
HE KEPT MAYBE 50 METERS BACK.
HE MUST'VE THOUGHT HE WAS BEING ALL SNEAKY, BUT THAT LOSER COULDN'T HAVE BEEN MORE OBVIOUS.
WELL, YOU DO PARTY TOO MUCH. SO, I BET YOU AND YOUR DAD HAD A BIG FIGHT, HUH?
DUMMY!
I HAVEN'T EVEN FINISHED MY STORY YET.
FWUMP
...
ANYWAY, I WAS TOTALLY PISSED OFF.
SO WHAT DO YOU THINK I DID?
I WENT INTO A CONVENIENCE STORE AND SHOPLIFTED RIGHT WHERE THAT DOPE COULD SEE ME.
AHA HA HA! THE OLD BASTARD WAS SO SHOCKED HIS EYES NEARLY POPPED OUT!
NO WAY! FOR REAL?

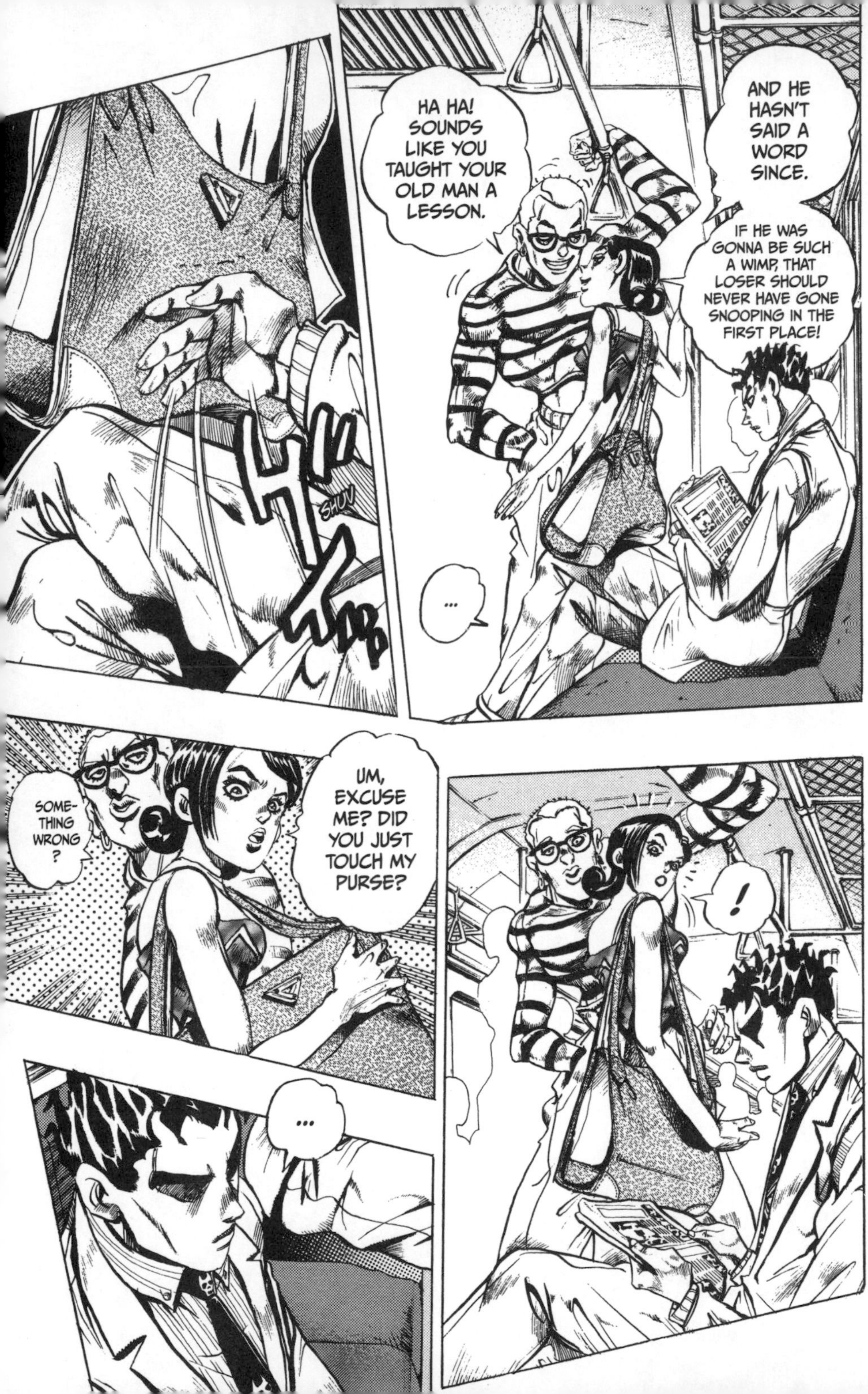
AND HE HASN'T SAID A WORD SINCE.
IF HE WAS GONNA BE SUCH A WIMP, THAT LOSER SHOULD NEVER HAVE GONE SNOOPING IN THE FIRST PLACE!
HA HA! SOUNDS LIKE YOU TAUGHT YOUR OLD MAN A LESSON.
...
SHUV
!
UM, EXCUSE ME? DID YOU JUST TOUCH MY PURSE?
SOME-THING WRONG?
...

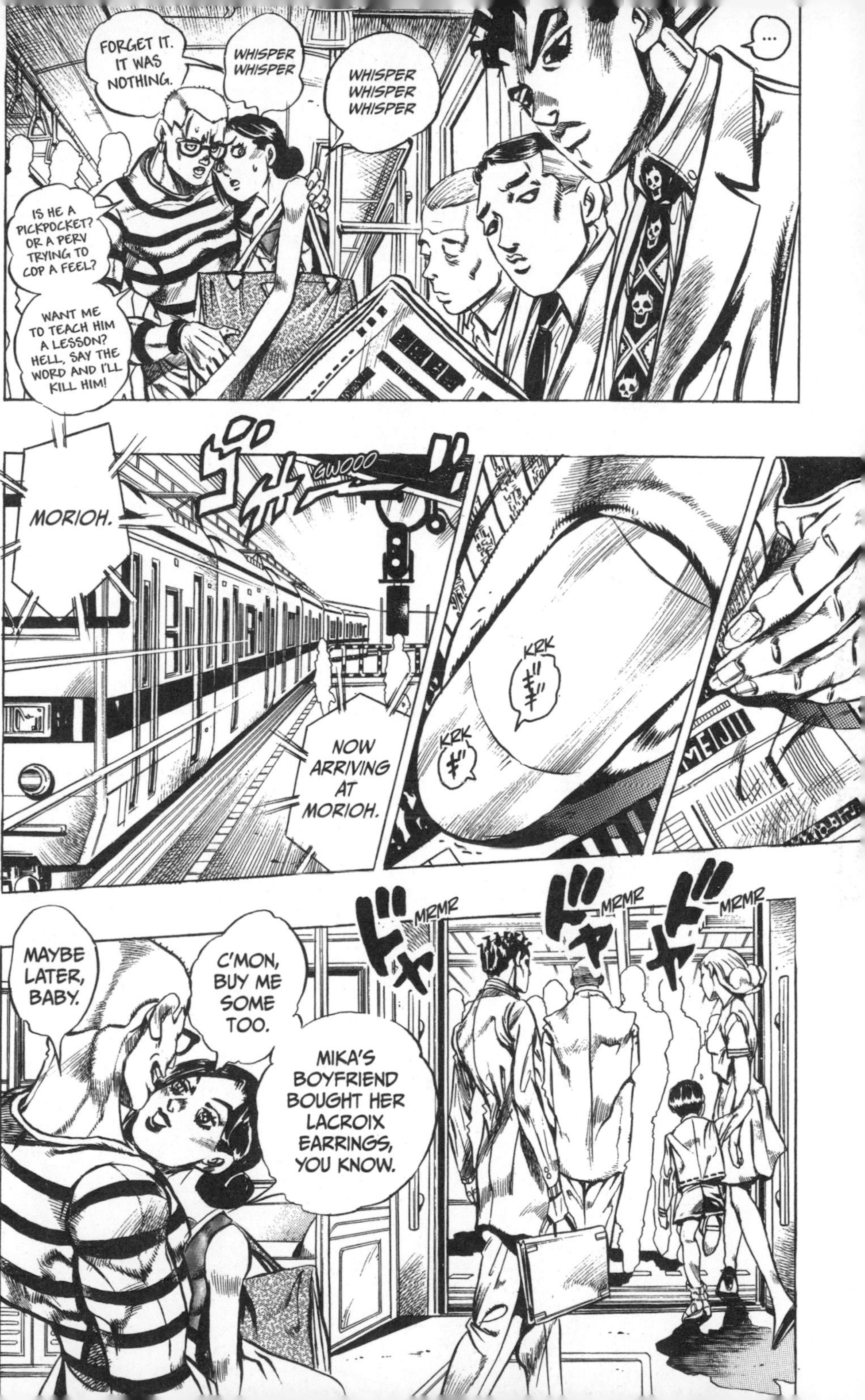
...
WHISPER WHISPER WHISPER
WHISPER WHISPER
FORGET IT. IT WAS NOTHING.
IS HE A PICKPOCKET? OR A PERV TRYING TO COP A FEEL?
WANT ME TO TEACH HIM A LESSON? HELL, SAY THE WORD AND I'LL KILL HIM!
KRK
KRK
GWOOO
MORIOH.
NOW ARRIVING AT MORIOH.
MRMR
MRMR
MRMR
MIKA'S BOYFRIEND BOUGHT HER LACROIX EARRINGS, YOU KNOW.
C'MON, BUY ME SOME TOO.
MAYBE LATER, BABY.

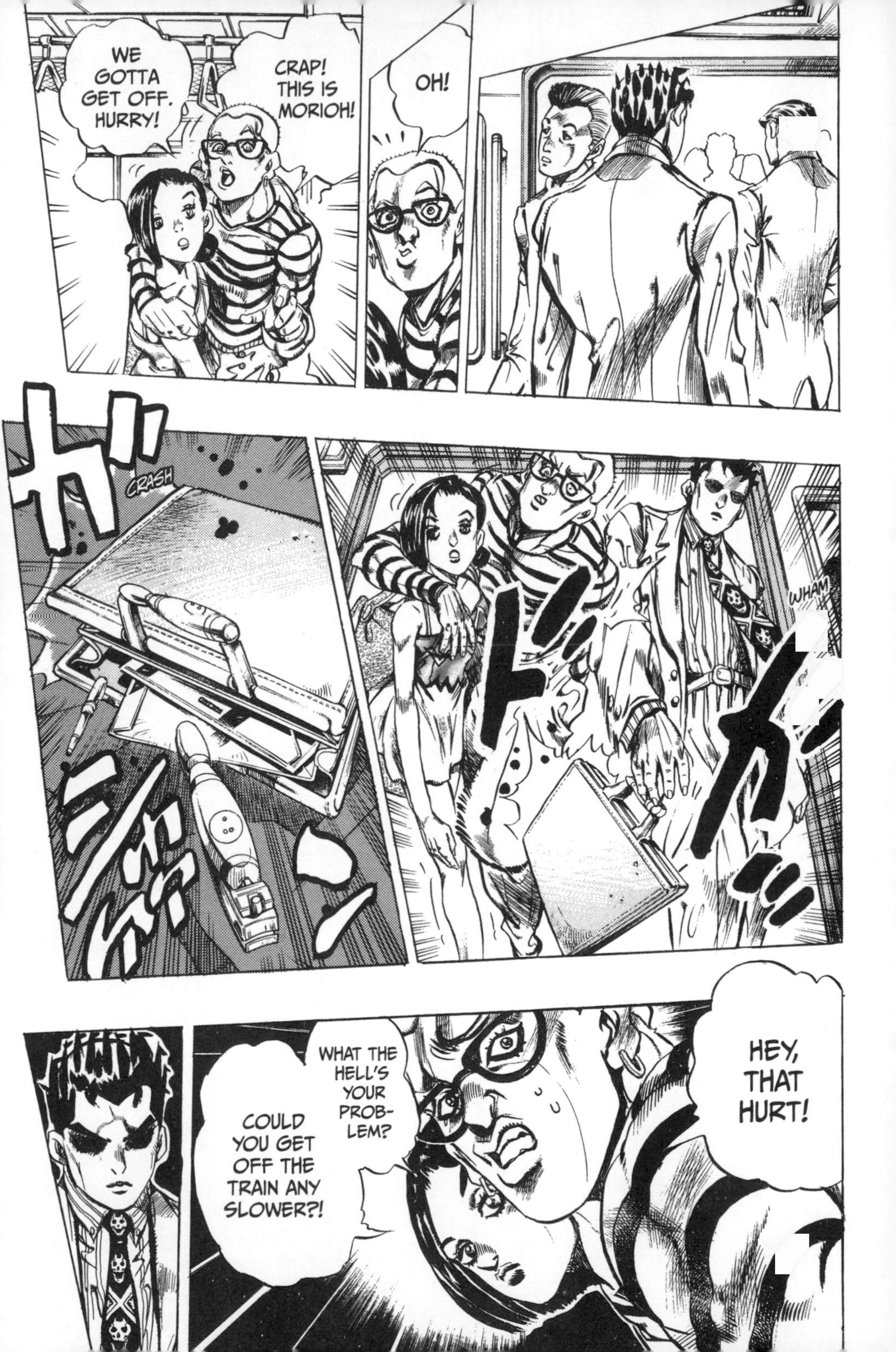
OH!
CRAP! THIS IS MORIOH!
WE GOTTA GET OFF. HURRY!
WHAM
CRASH
HEY, THAT HURT!
WHAT THE HELL'S YOUR PROB-LEM?
COULD YOU GET OFF THE TRAIN ANY SLOWER?!

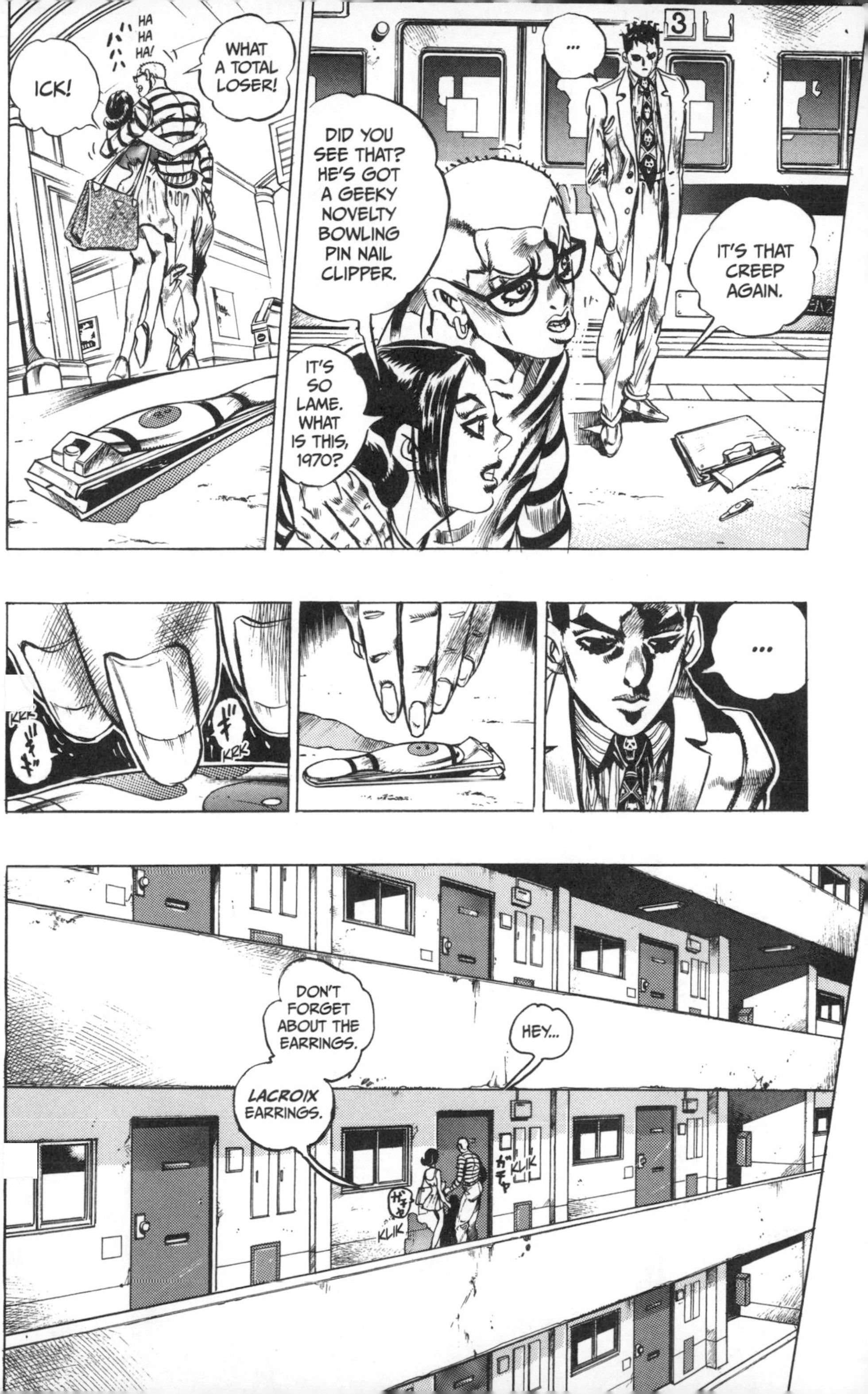
...
IT'S THAT CREEP AGAIN.
DID YOU SEE THAT? HE'S GOT A GEEKY NOVELTY BOWLING PIN NAIL CLIPPER.
IT'S SO LAME. WHAT IS THIS, 1970?
WHAT A TOTAL LOSER!
HA HA HA!
ICK!
...
KRK
KRK
HEY...
DON'T FORGET ABOUT THE EARRINGS.
LACROIX EARRINGS.
KLIK
KLIK

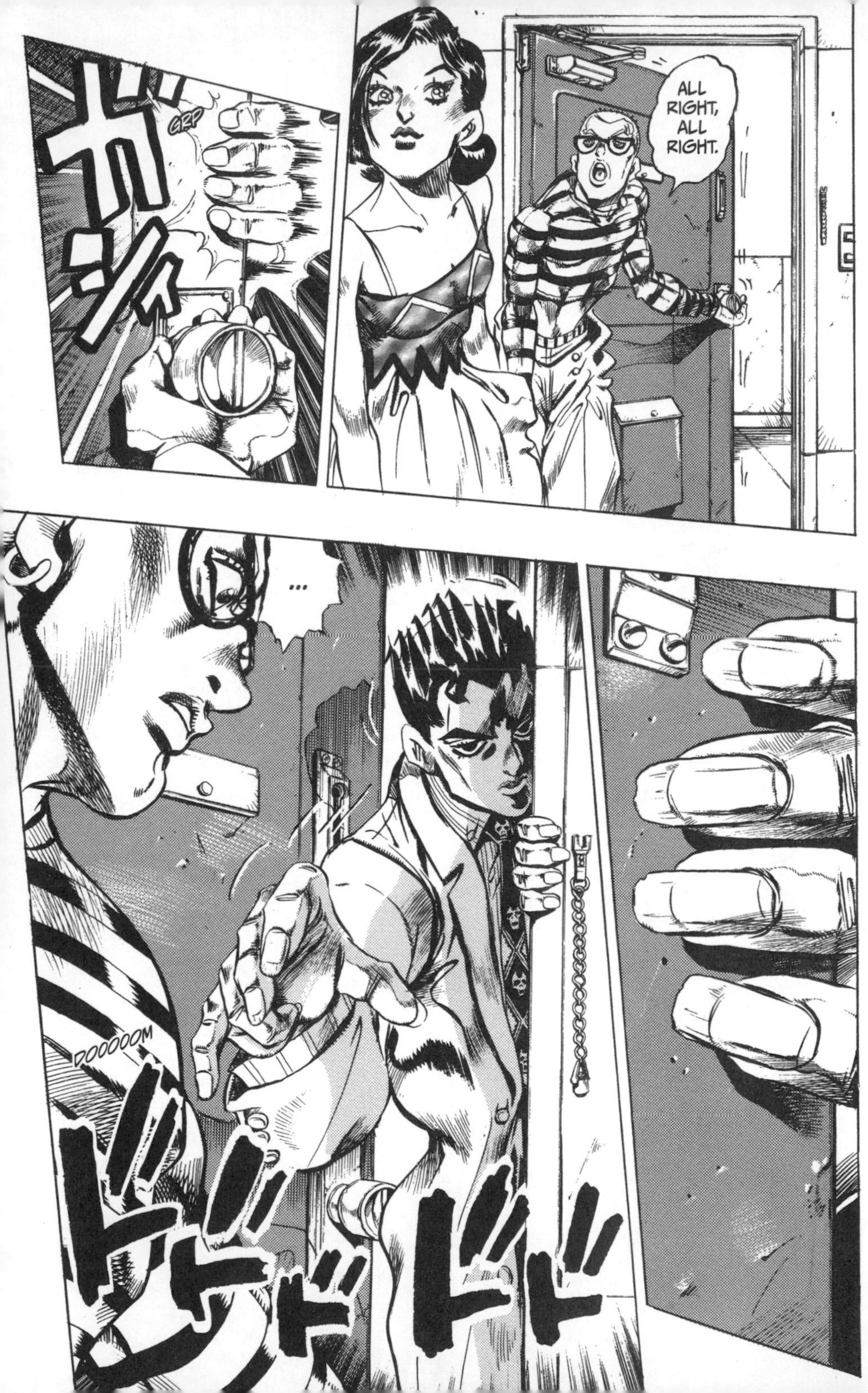
ALL RIGHT, ALL RIGHT.
GRP
ガシィ
...
DOOOOOM
ドドドドド

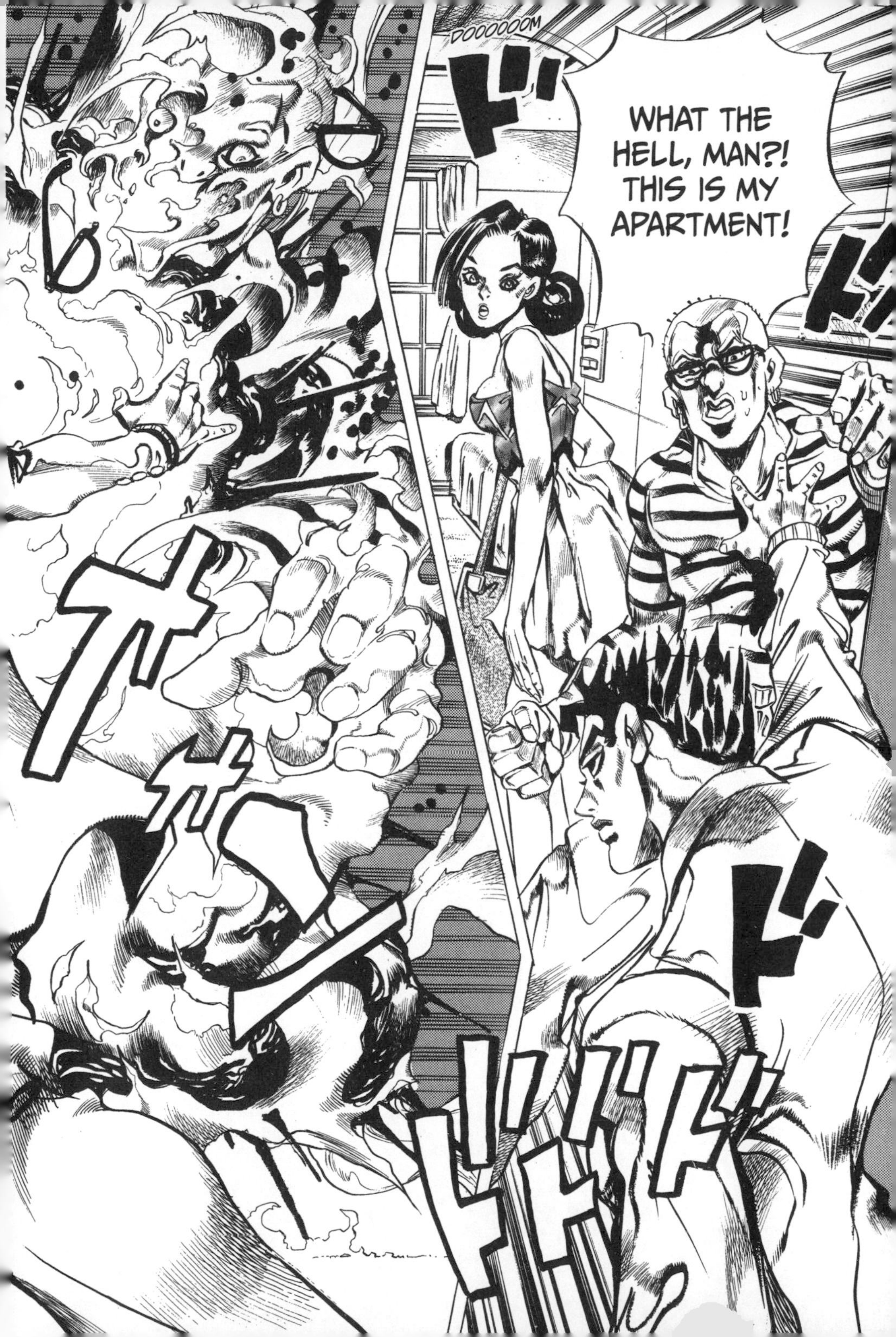
DOOOOOOM
WHAT THE HELL, MAN?! THIS IS MY APARTMENT!

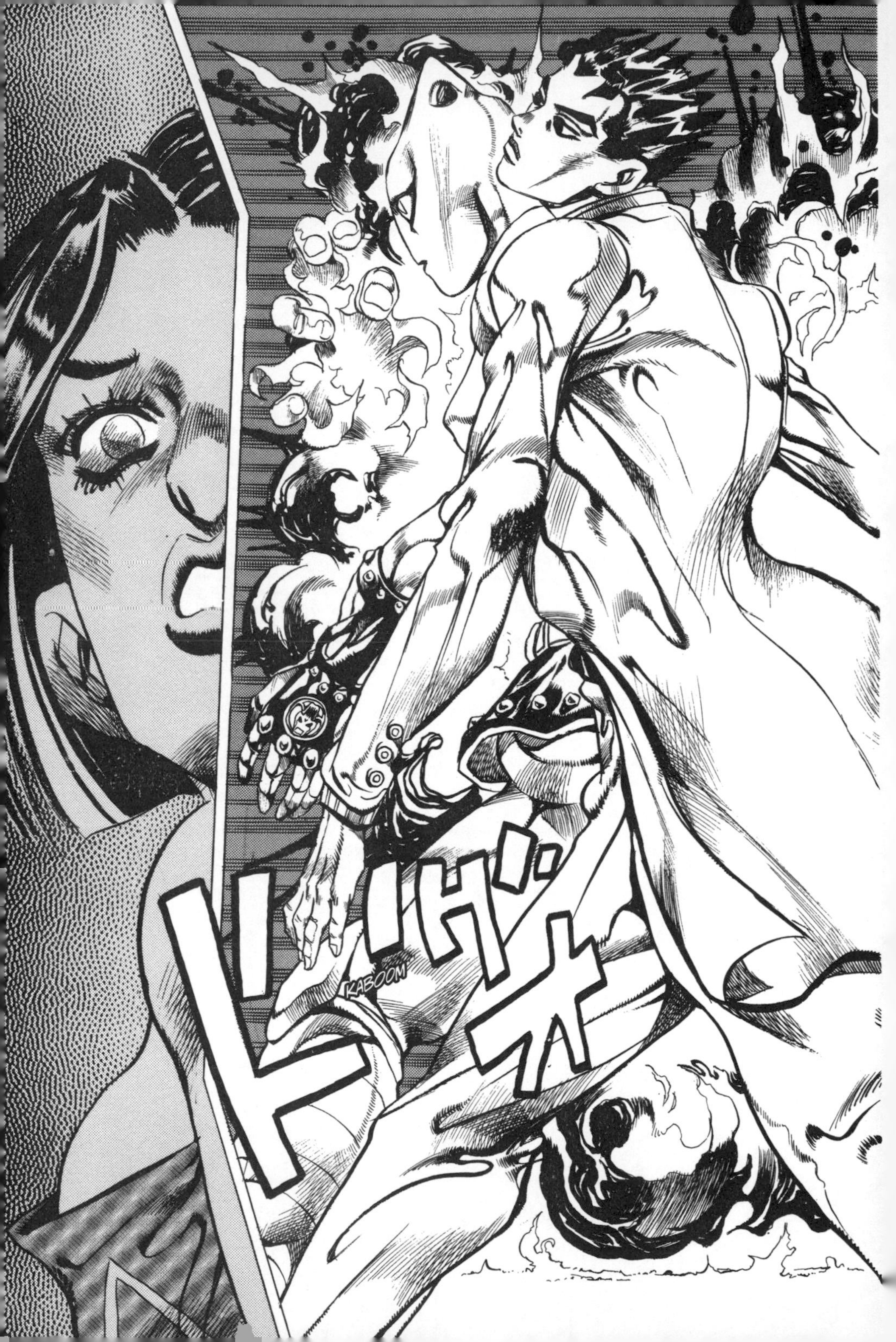
ドバオ
KABOOM

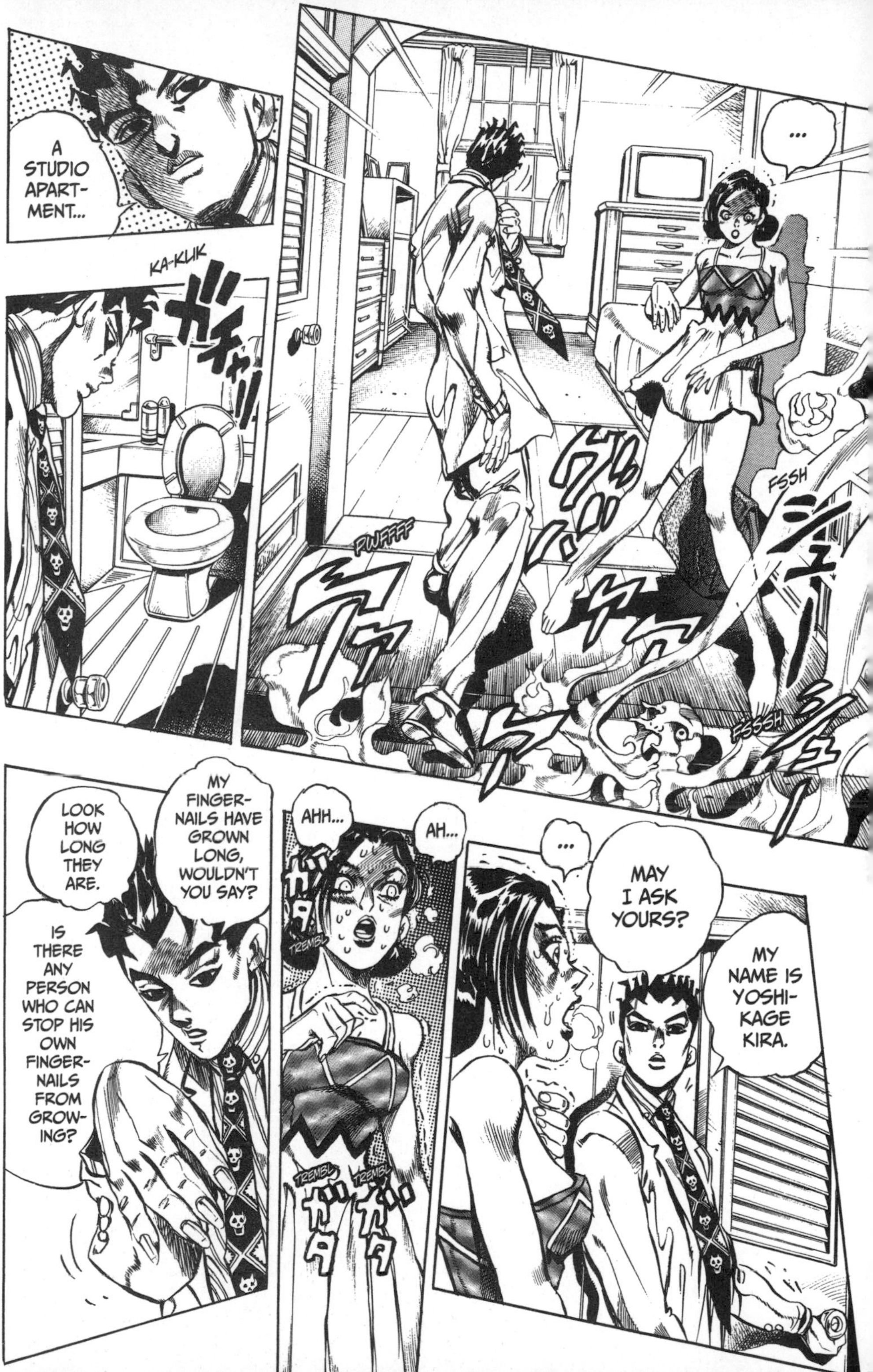
...
RWFFFF
FSSH
FSSSH
A STUDIO APARTMENT...
KA-KLIK
...
MAY I ASK YOURS?
MY NAME IS YOSHIKAGE KIRA.
AH...
AHH...
TREMBL
TREMBL
TREMBL
MY FINGERNAILS HAVE GROWN LONG, WOULDN'T YOU SAY?
LOOK HOW LONG THEY ARE.
IS THERE ANY PERSON WHO CAN STOP HIS OWN FINGERNAILS FROM GROWING?

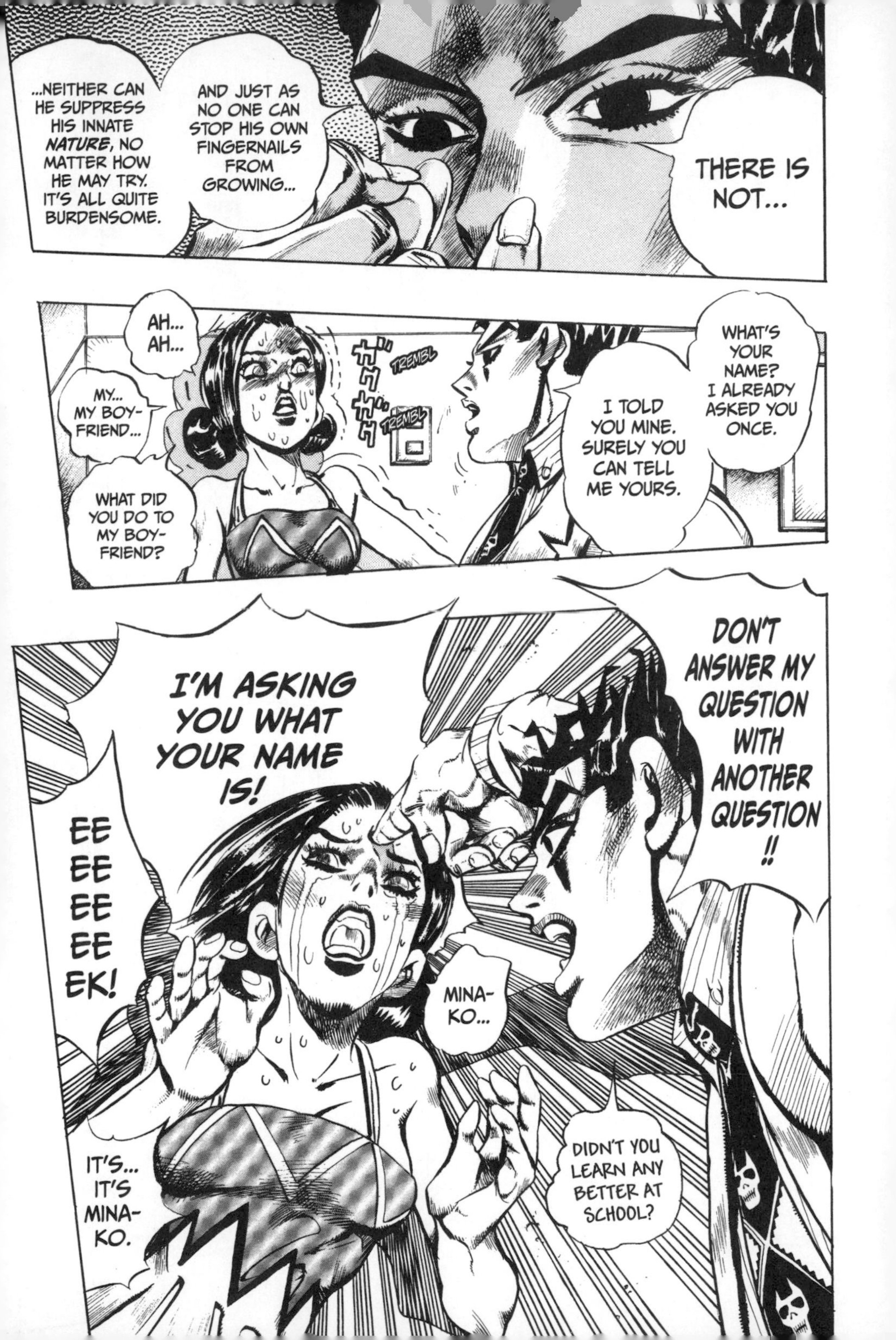
THERE IS NOT...
AND JUST AS NO ONE CAN STOP HIS OWN FINGERNAILS FROM GROWING...
...NEITHER CAN HE SUPPRESS HIS INNATE *NATURE*, NO MATTER HOW HE MAY TRY. IT'S ALL QUITE BURDENSOME.
WHAT'S YOUR NAME? I ALREADY ASKED YOU ONCE.
I TOLD YOU MINE. SURELY YOU CAN TELL ME YOURS.
TREMBL
TREMBL
AH... AH...
MY... MY BOY-FRIEND...
WHAT DID YOU DO TO MY BOY-FRIEND?
DON'T ANSWER MY QUESTION WITH ANOTHER QUESTION!!
I'M ASKING YOU WHAT YOUR NAME IS!
EEEEEEEEEK!
MINA-KO...
DIDN'T YOU LEARN ANY BETTER AT SCHOOL?
IT'S... IT'S MINA-KO.

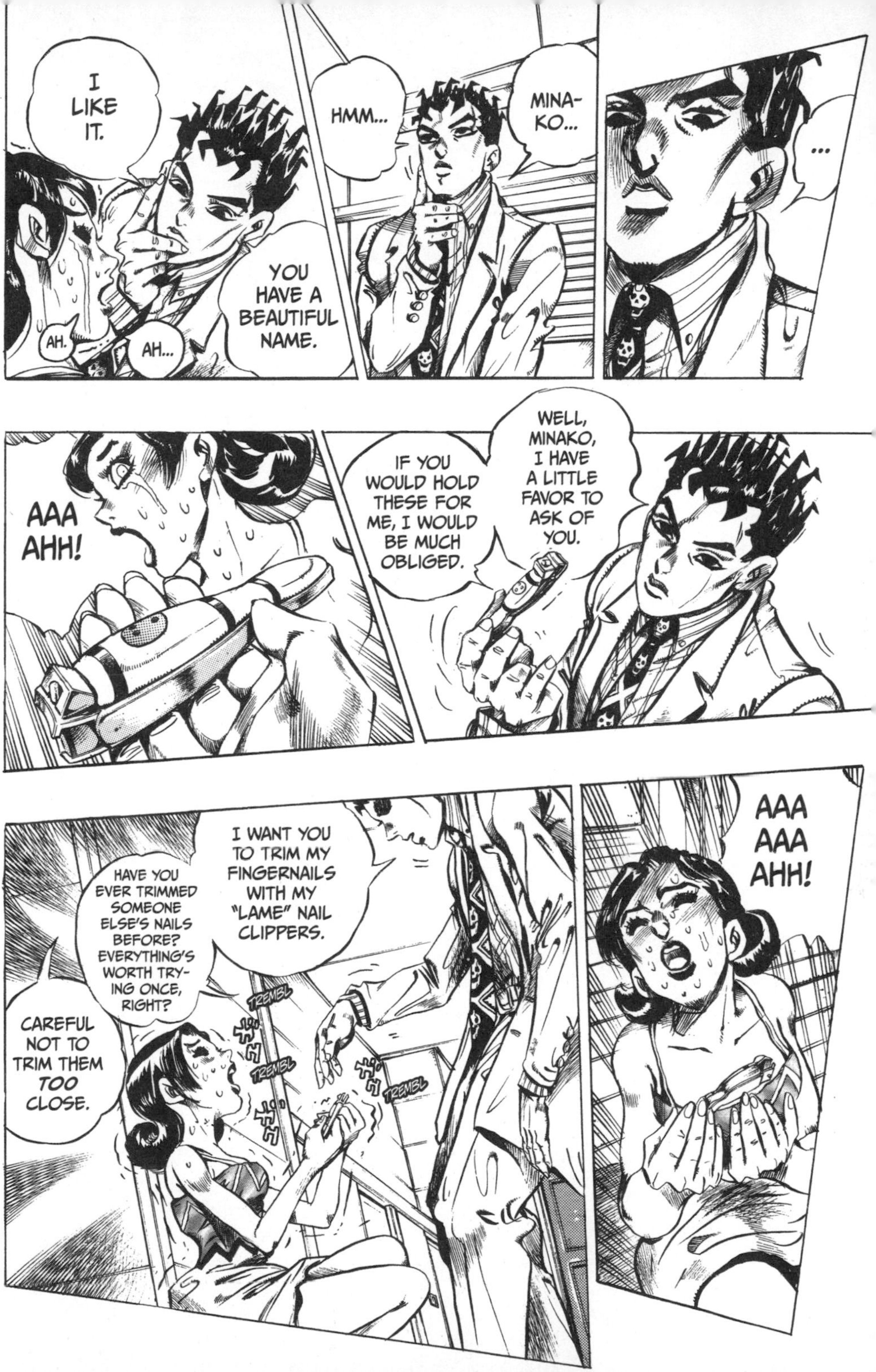
...
MINAKO...
HMM...
I LIKE IT.
YOU HAVE A BEAUTIFUL NAME.
AH...
AH.
WELL, MINAKO, I HAVE A LITTLE FAVOR TO ASK OF YOU.
IF YOU WOULD HOLD THESE FOR ME, I WOULD BE MUCH OBLIGED.
AAA AHH!
AAA AAA AHH!
I WANT YOU TO TRIM MY FINGERNAILS WITH MY "LAME" NAIL CLIPPERS.
HAVE YOU EVER TRIMMED SOMEONE ELSE'S NAILS BEFORE? EVERYTHING'S WORTH TRYING ONCE, RIGHT?
TREMBL
TREMBL
TREMBL
CAREFUL NOT TO TRIM THEM *TOO* CLOSE.

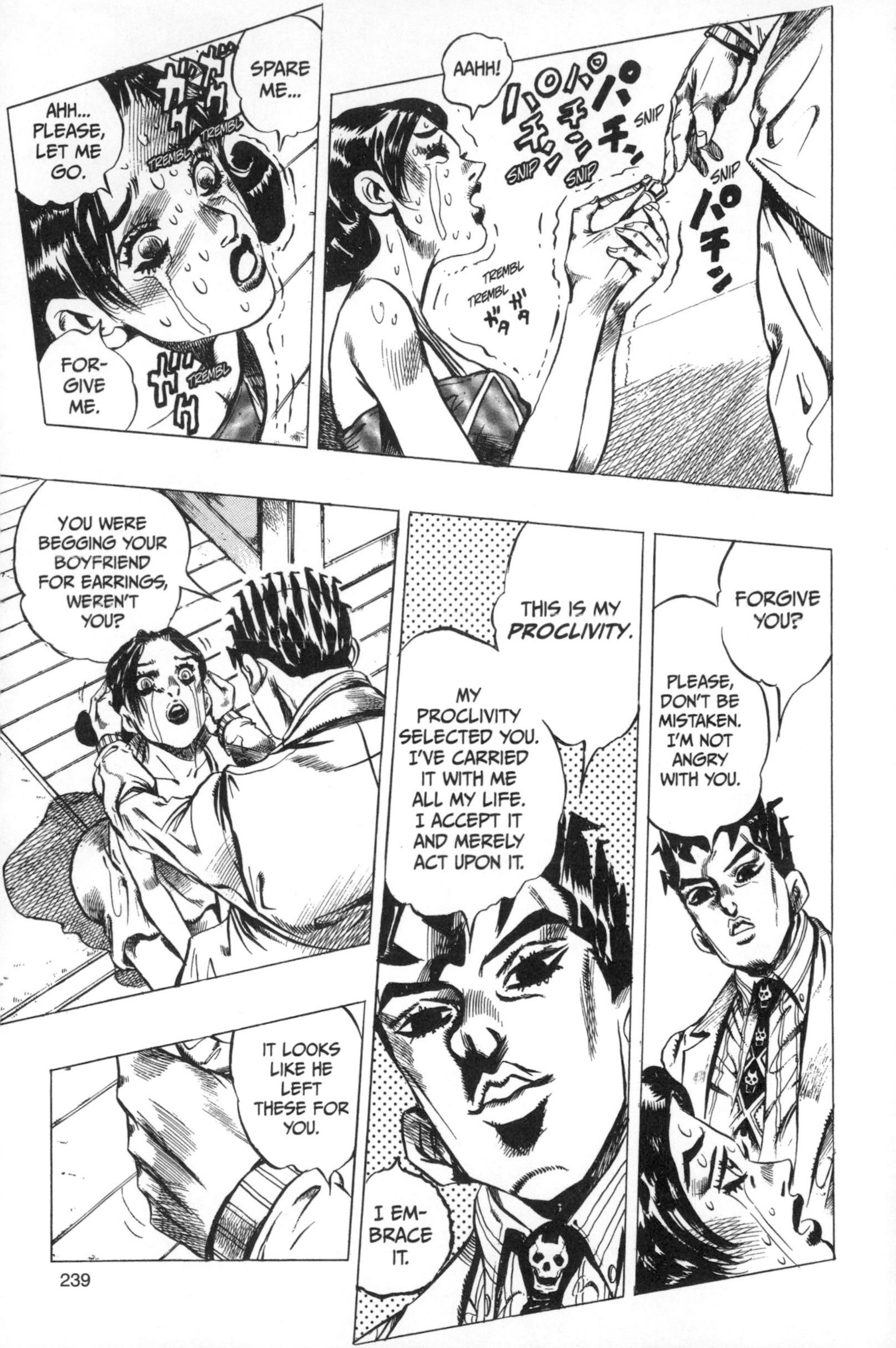
AAHH!
SNIP SNIP SNIP
SNIP
TREMBL TREMBL
SPARE ME...
AHH... PLEASE, LET ME GO.
TREMBL TREMBL
FOR-GIVE ME.
TREMBL
FORGIVE YOU?
PLEASE, DON'T BE MISTAKEN. I'M NOT ANGRY WITH YOU.
THIS IS MY *PROCLIVITY*.
MY PROCLIVITY SELECTED YOU. I'VE CARRIED IT WITH ME ALL MY LIFE. I ACCEPT IT AND MERELY ACT UPON IT.
I EM-BRACE IT.
YOU WERE BEGGING YOUR BOYFRIEND FOR EARRINGS, WEREN'T YOU?
IT LOOKS LIKE HE LEFT THESE FOR YOU.

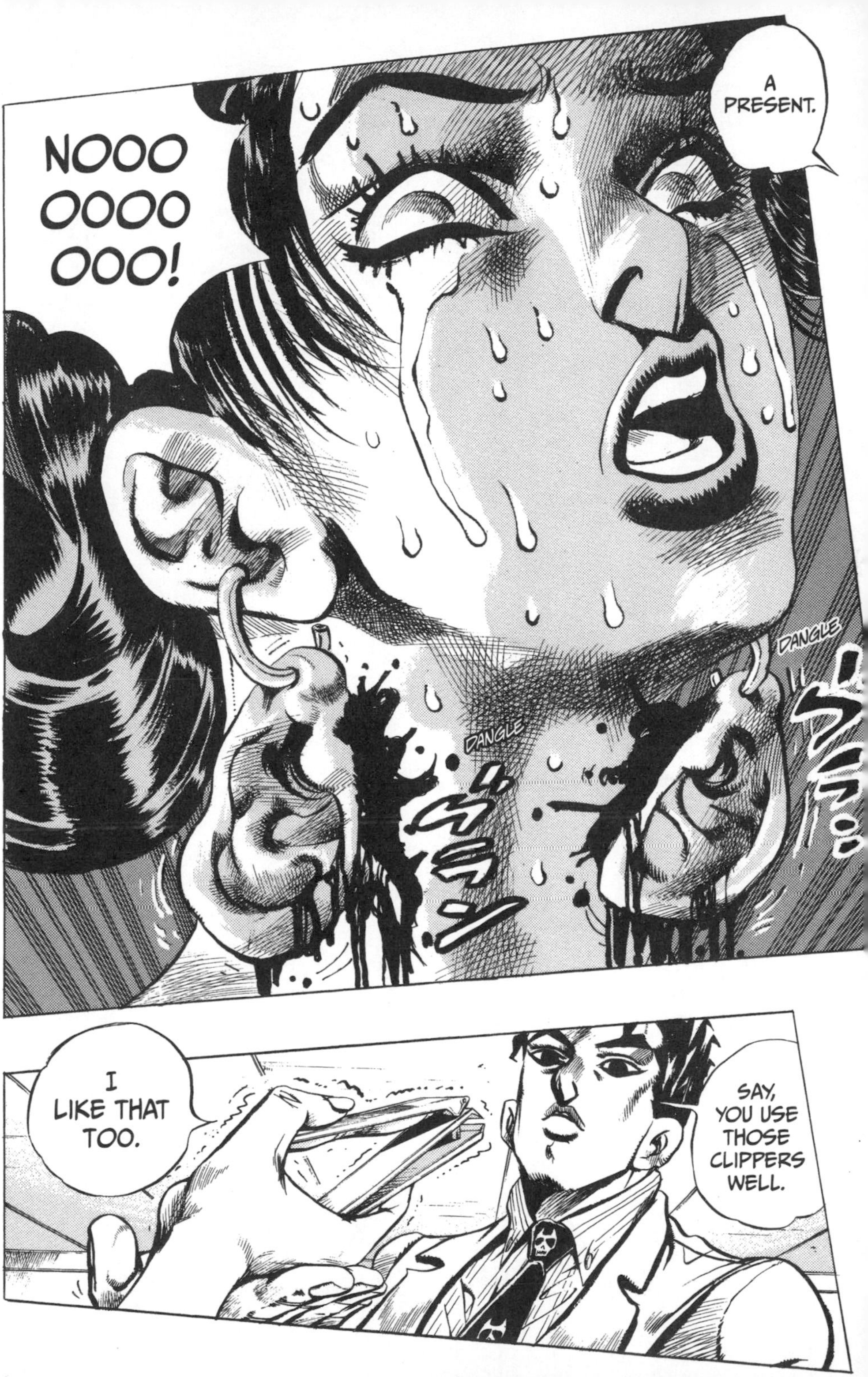
A PRESENT.
NOOO OOOO OOO!
DANGLE
DANGLE
SAY, YOU USE THOSE CLIPPERS WELL.
I LIKE THAT TOO.

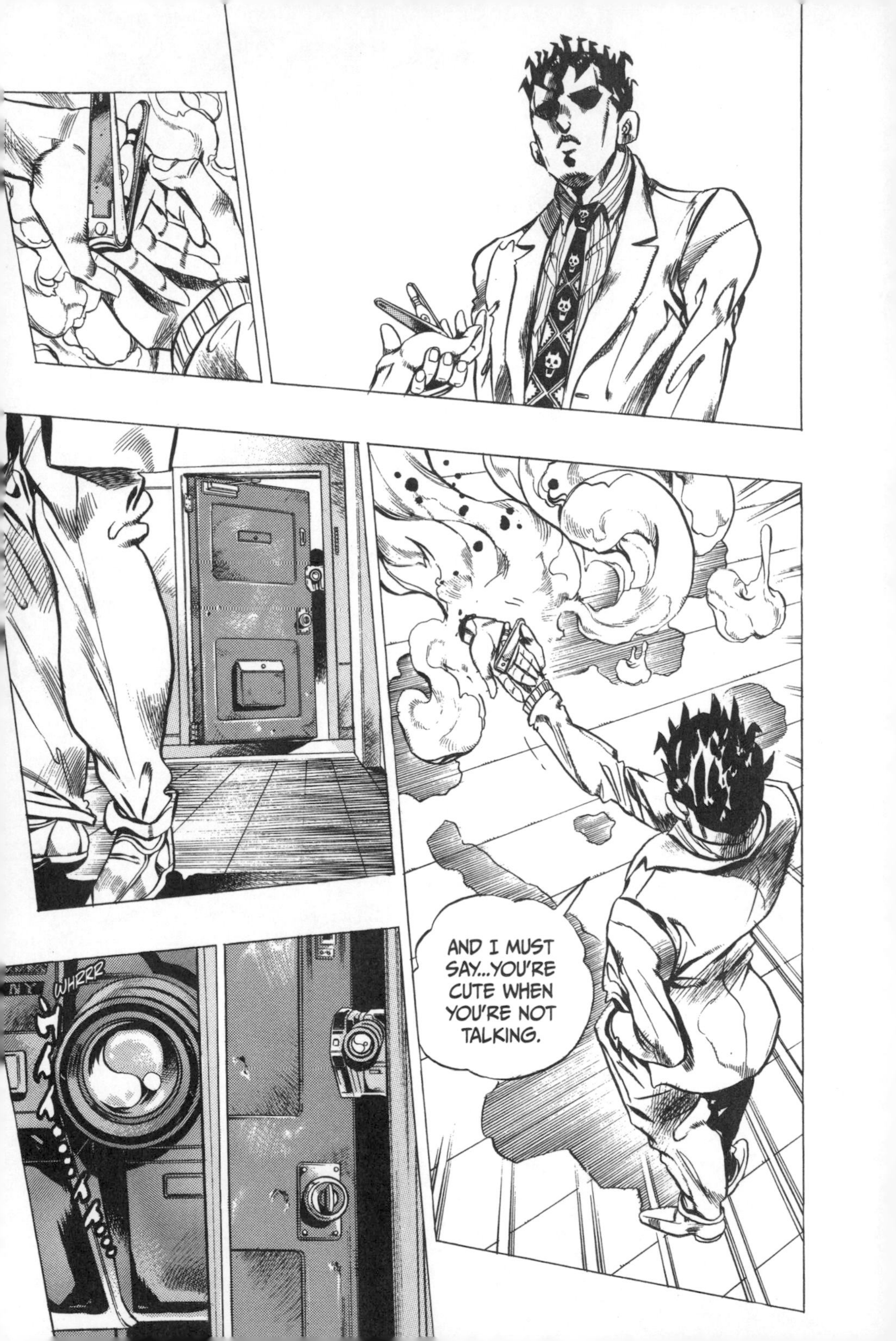
AND I MUST SAY...YOU'RE CUTE WHEN YOU'RE NOT TALKING.
WHRRR

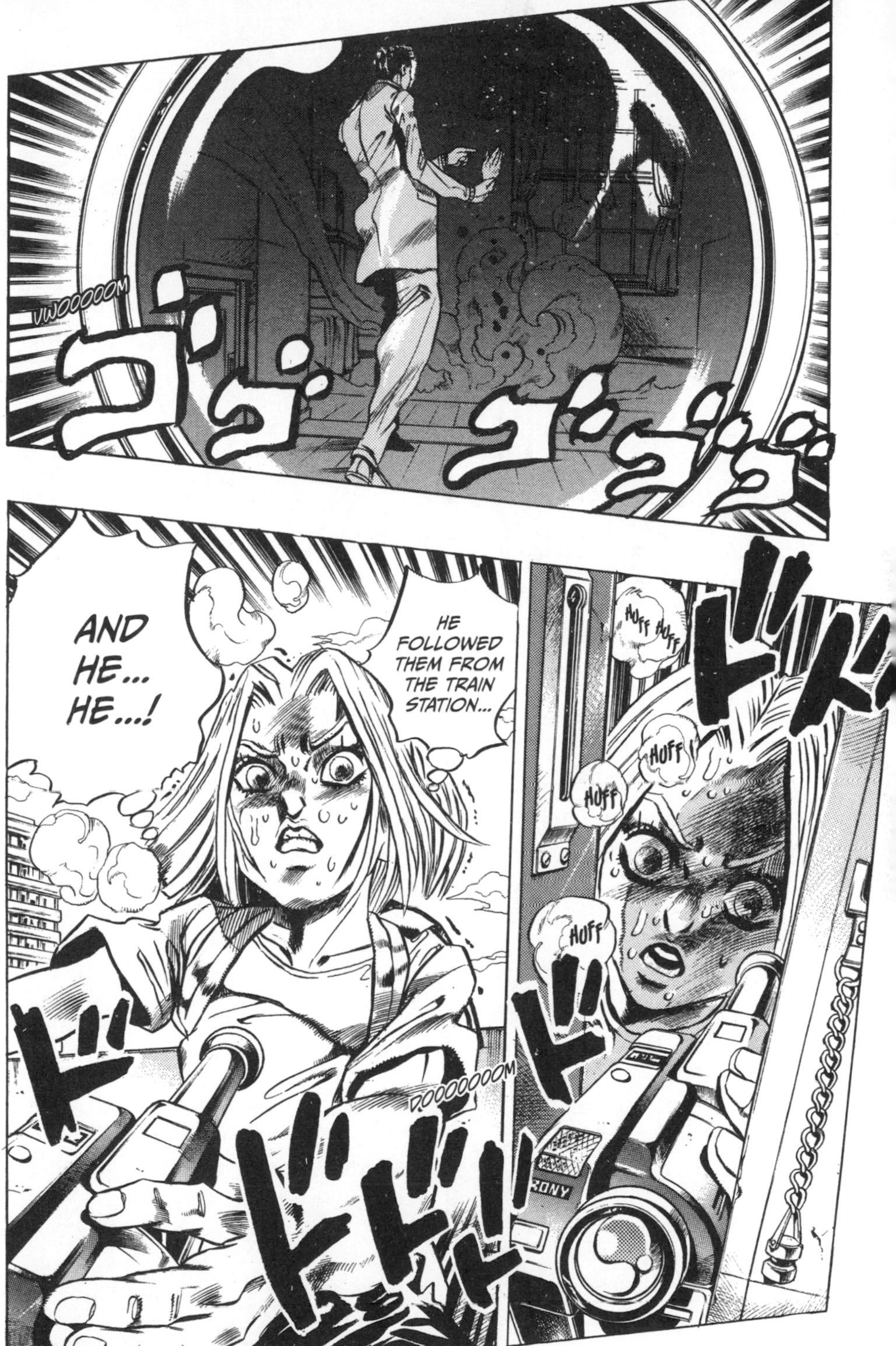
VWOOOOOM
HUFF HUFF
HUFF
HUFF
HUFF
HE FOLLOWED THEM FROM THE TRAIN STATION...
AND HE... HE...!
DOOOOOOOM

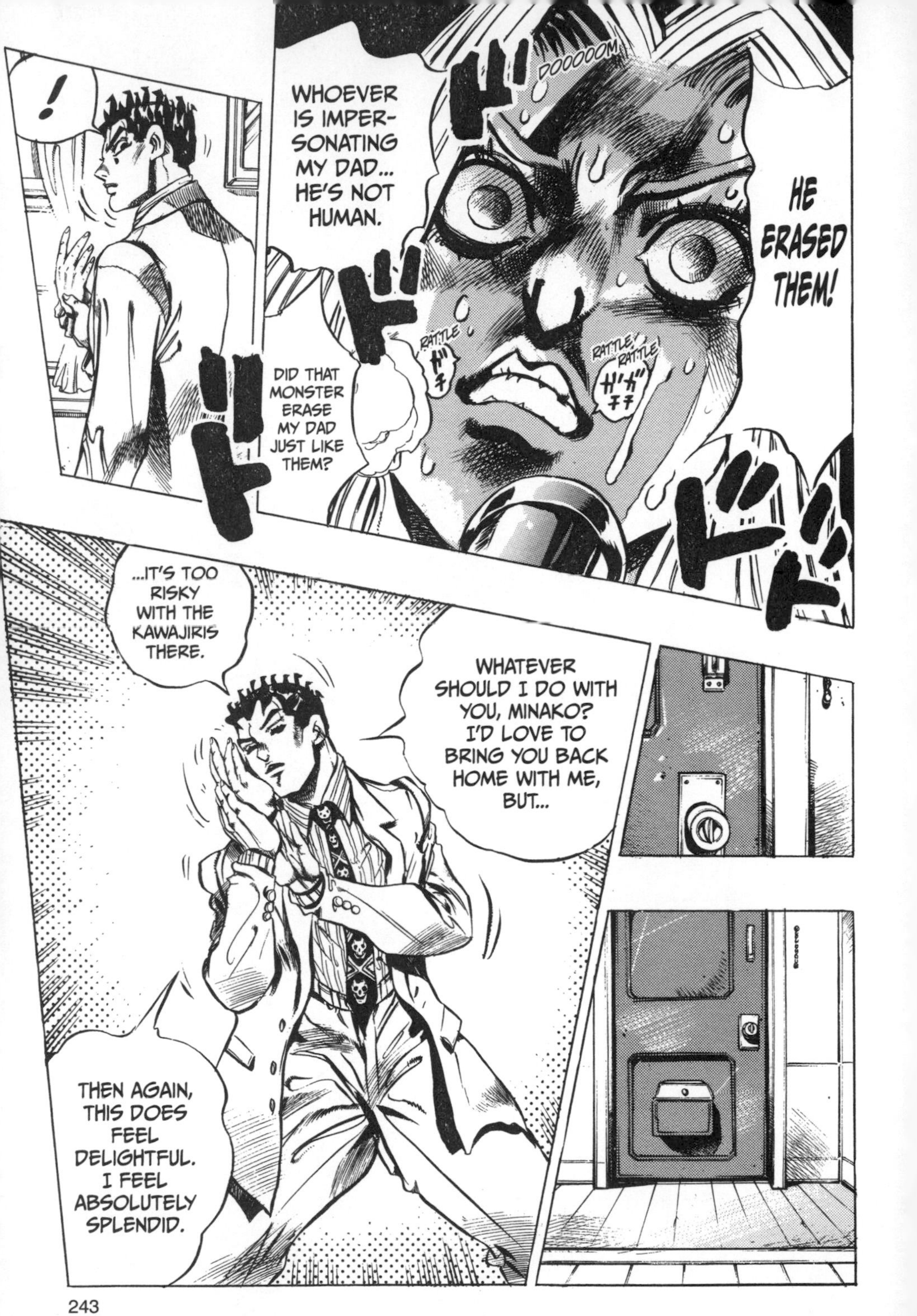
DOOOOOM
ドドド
HE ERASED THEM!
WHOEVER IS IMPER-SONATING MY DAD... HE'S NOT HUMAN.
RATTLE, RATTLE
ガガチチ
RATTLE
ガチ
DID THAT MONSTER ERASE MY DAD JUST LIKE THEM?
ドドド
!
WHATEVER SHOULD I DO WITH YOU, MINAKO? I'D LOVE TO BRING YOU BACK HOME WITH ME, BUT...
...IT'S TOO RISKY WITH THE KAWAJIRIS THERE.
THEN AGAIN, THIS DOES FEEL DELIGHTFUL. I FEEL ABSOLUTELY SPLENDID.

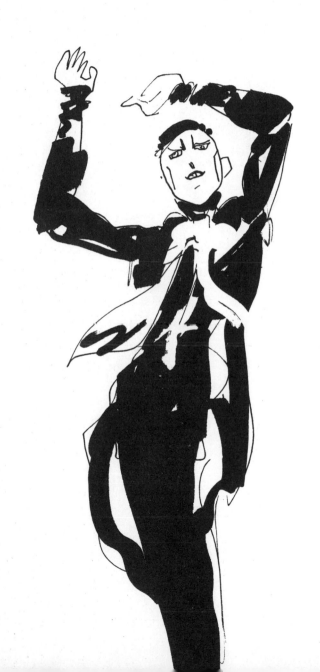

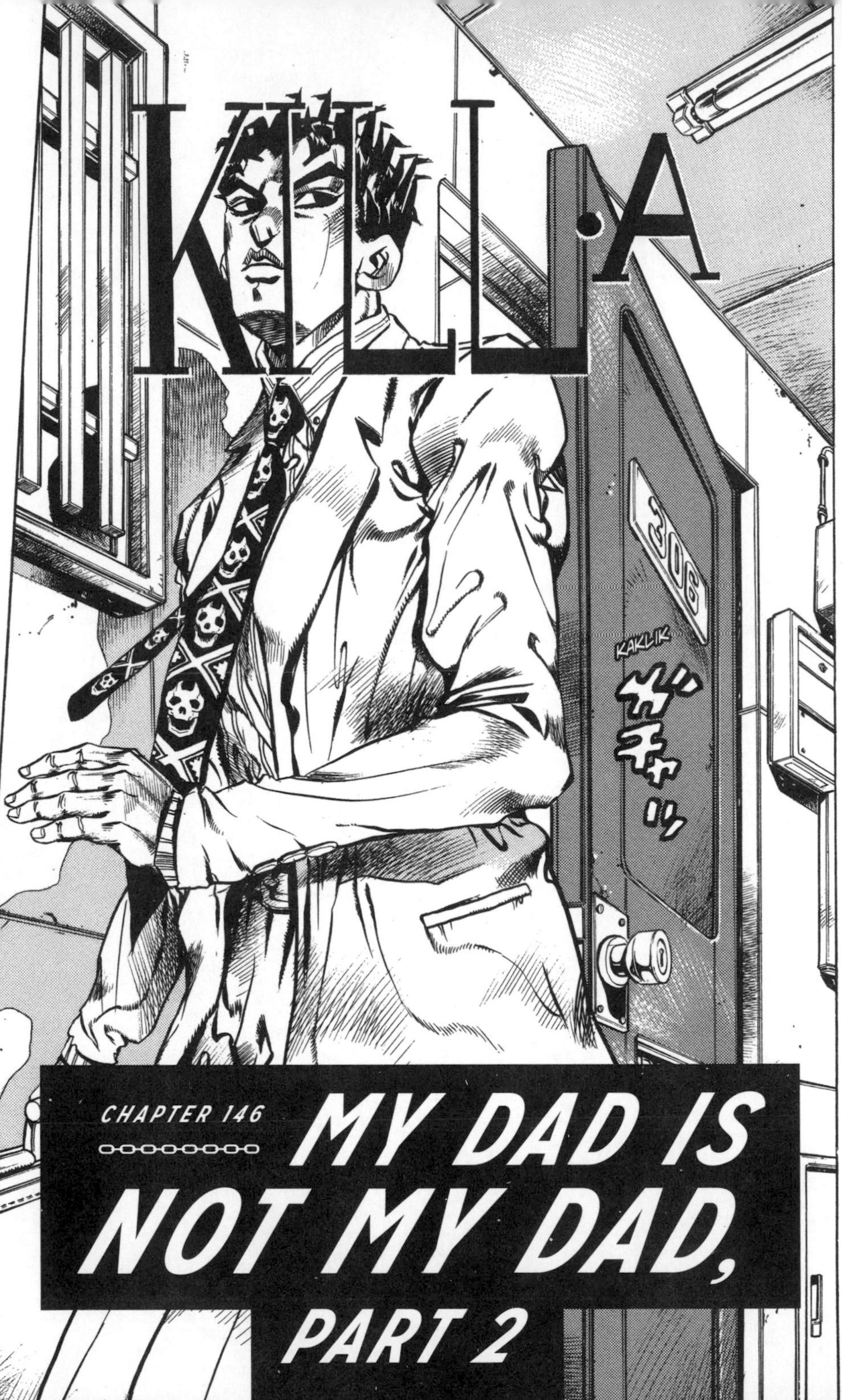
KILL A
306
KAKLIK
ガチャッ

CHAPTER 146 MY DAD IS NOT MY DAD, PART 2

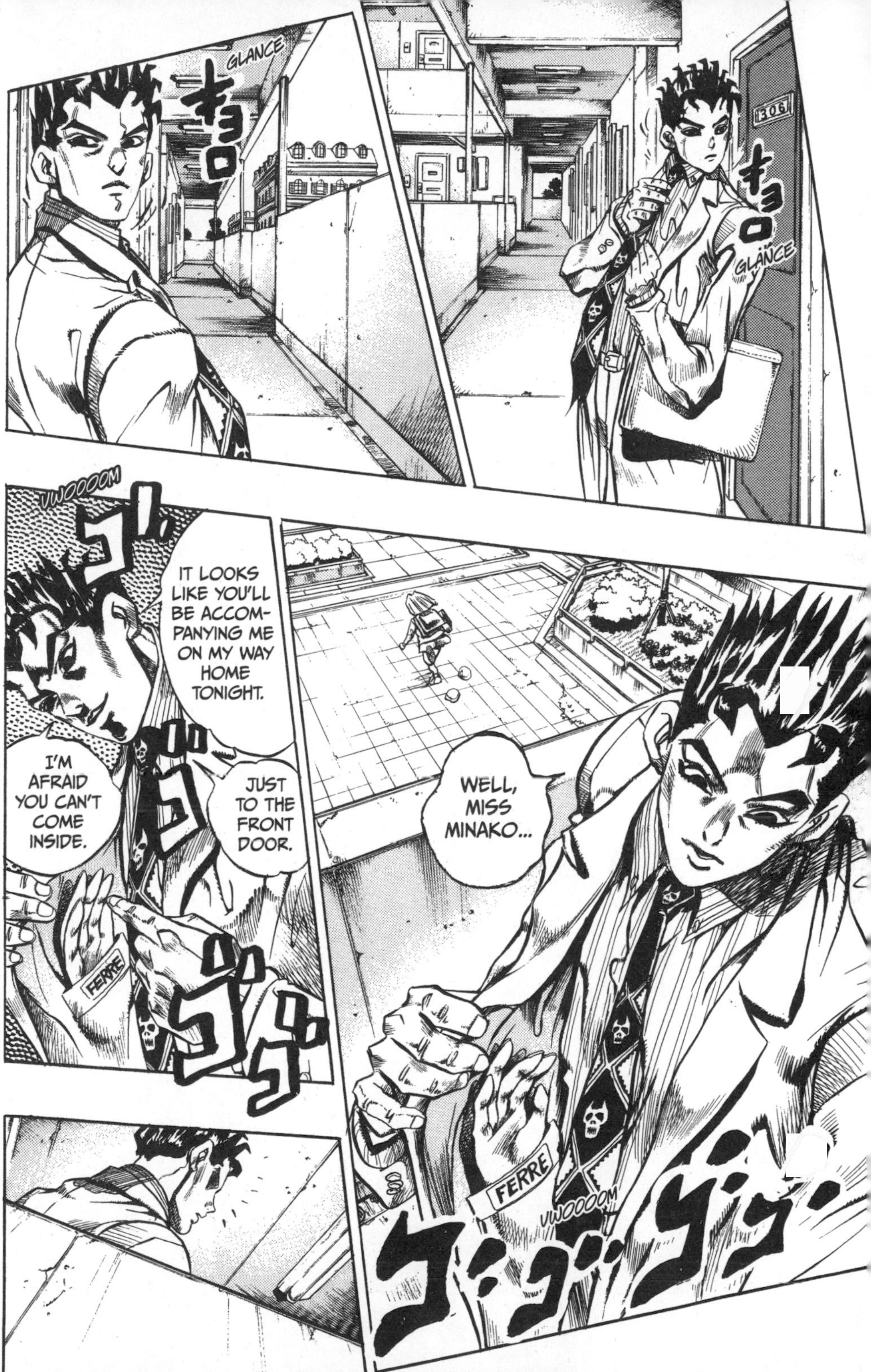
306
キョロ
GLANCE
GLANCE
キョロ
WELL, MISS MINAKO...
VWOOOOM
IT LOOKS LIKE YOU'LL BE ACCOMPANYING ME ON MY WAY HOME TONIGHT.
JUST TO THE FRONT DOOR.
I'M AFRAID YOU CAN'T COME INSIDE.
VWOOOOM
FERRE
FERRE

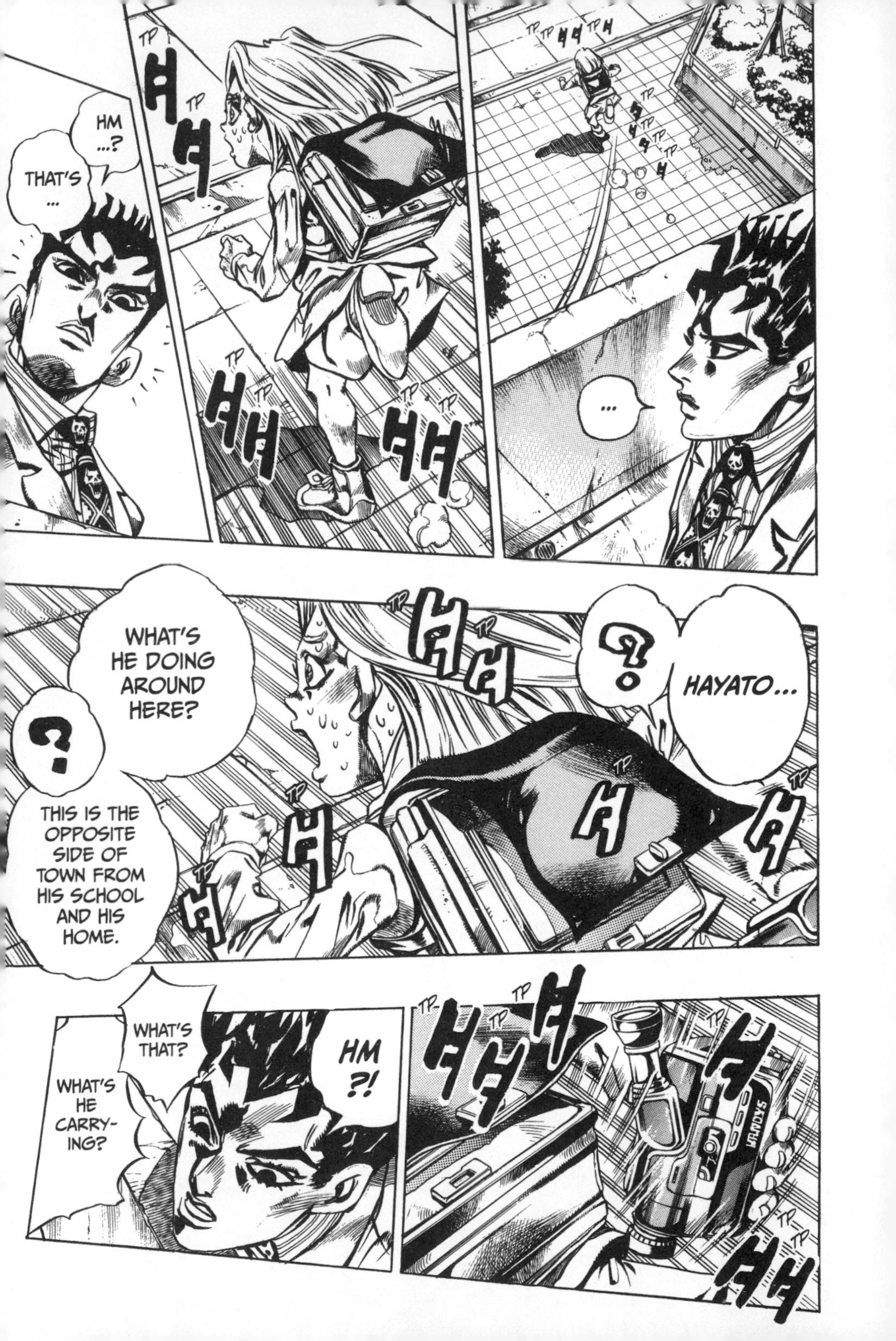
TP TP TP
...
TP TP TP
HM ...?
THAT'S ...
TP TP
HAYATO...
?
WHAT'S HE DOING AROUND HERE?
?
THIS IS THE OPPOSITE SIDE OF TOWN FROM HIS SCHOOL AND HIS HOME.
TP TP TP TP
HM ?!
WHAT'S THAT?
WHAT'S HE CARRYING?

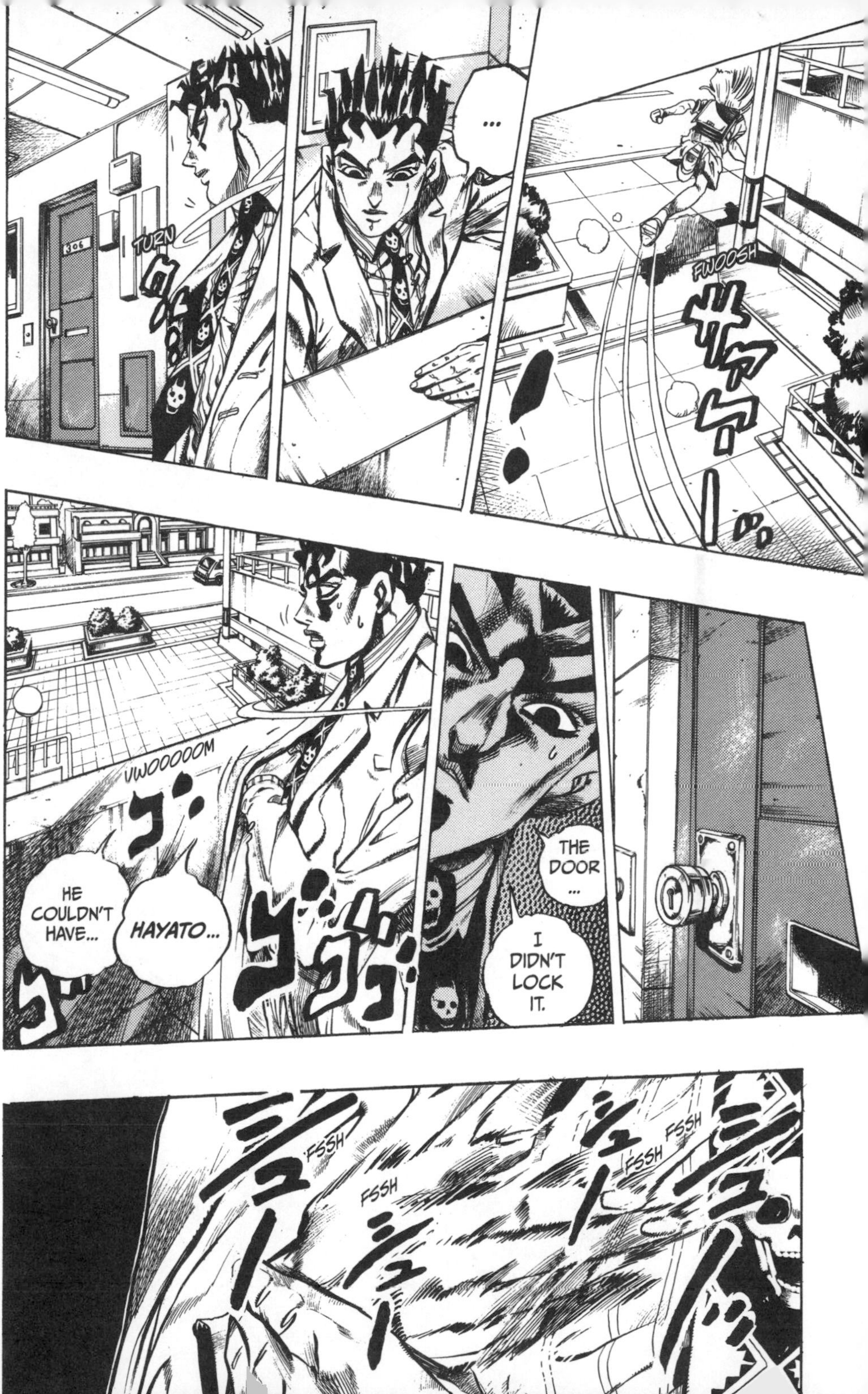
FWOOSH
...
TURN
THE DOOR ...
I DIDN'T LOCK IT.
VWOOOOOM
HAYATO...
HE COULDN'T HAVE...
FSSH
FSSH
FSSH
FSSH

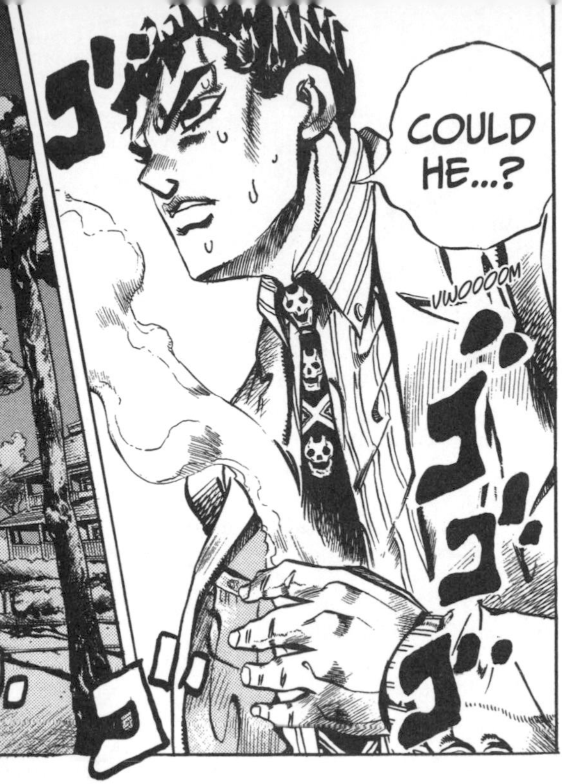
COULD HE...?
VWOOOOM

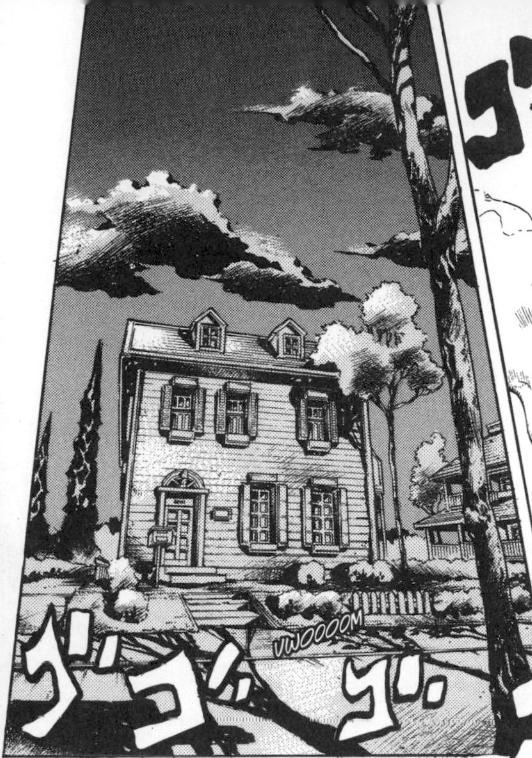
VWOOOOM

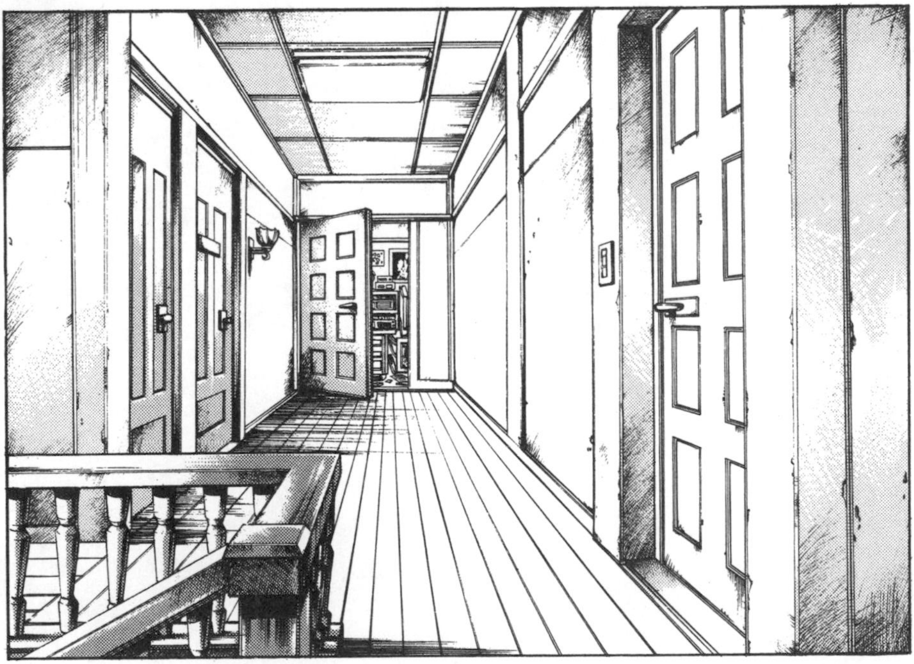

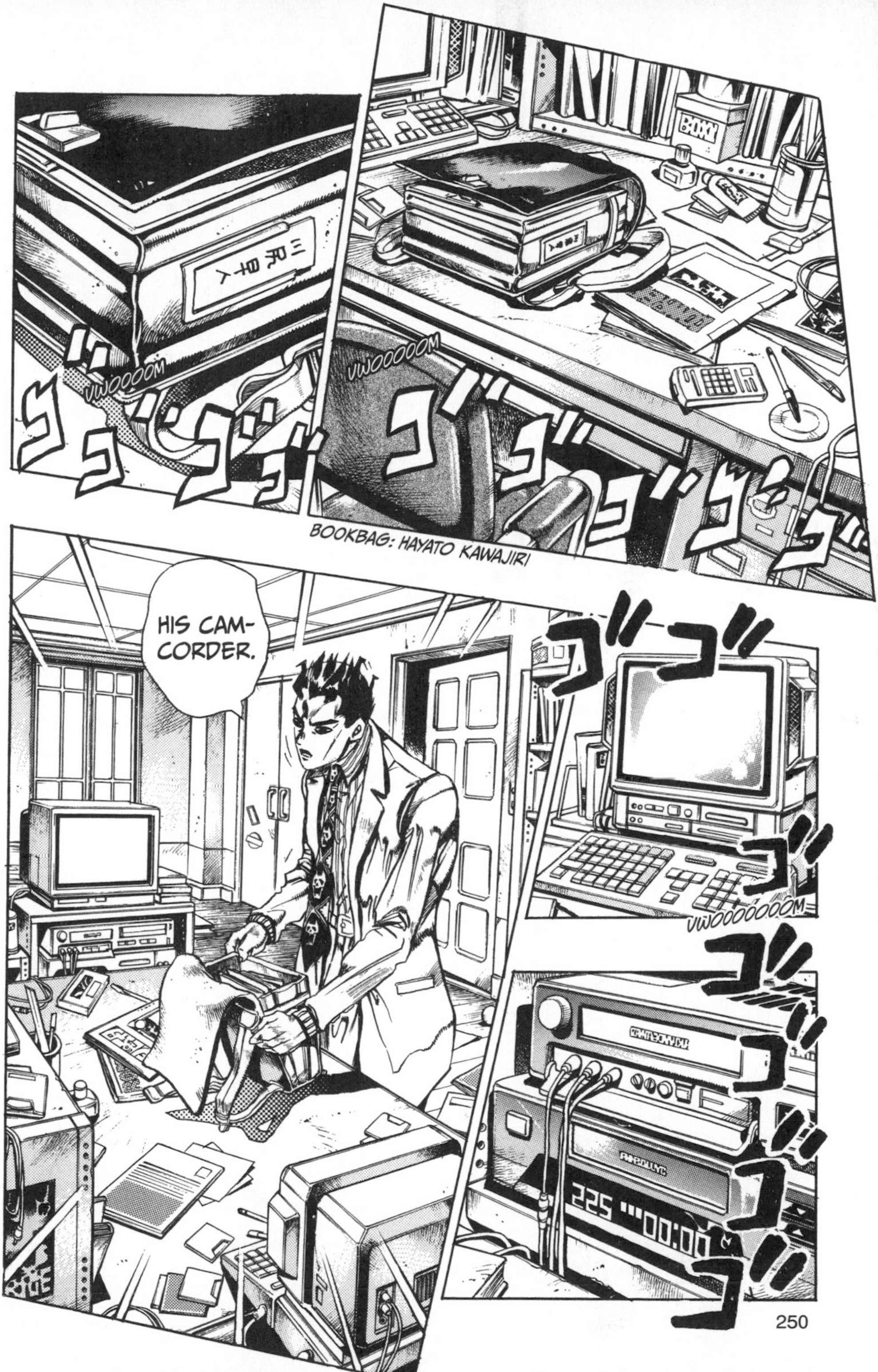

VWOOOOOM
BOOKBAG: HAYATO KAWAJIRI
VWOOOOM
VWOOOOOOOOM
HIS CAM-CORDER.

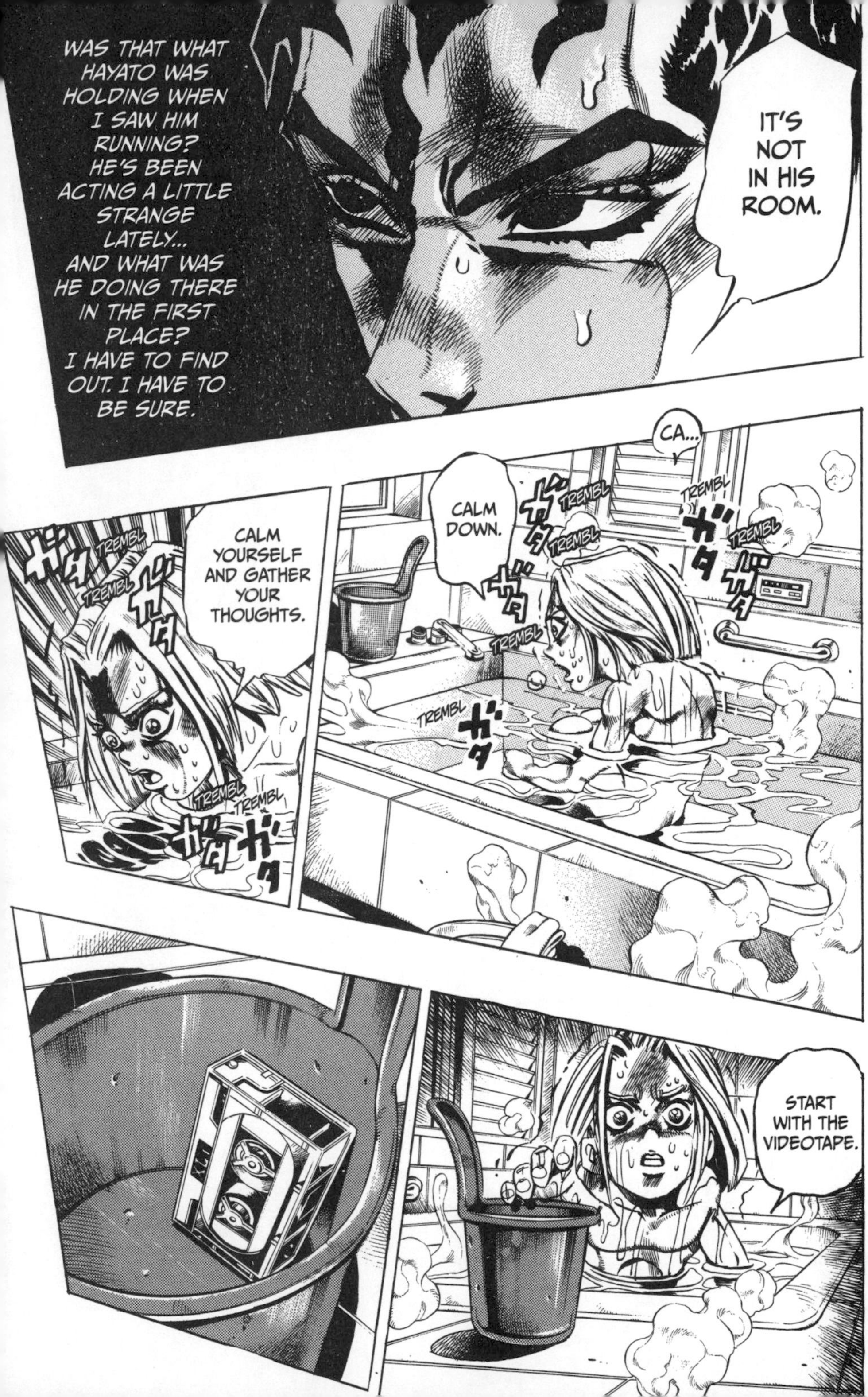
IT'S NOT IN HIS ROOM.
WAS THAT WHAT HAYATO WAS HOLDING WHEN I SAW HIM RUNNING? HE'S BEEN ACTING A LITTLE STRANGE LATELY... AND WHAT WAS HE DOING THERE IN THE FIRST PLACE? I HAVE TO FIND OUT. I HAVE TO BE SURE.
CA...
TREMBL TREMBL
CALM DOWN.
TREMBL TREMBL TREMBL TREMBL
TREMBL
CALM YOURSELF AND GATHER YOUR THOUGHTS.
TREMBL TREMBL
TREMBL TREMBL
START WITH THE VIDEOTAPE.

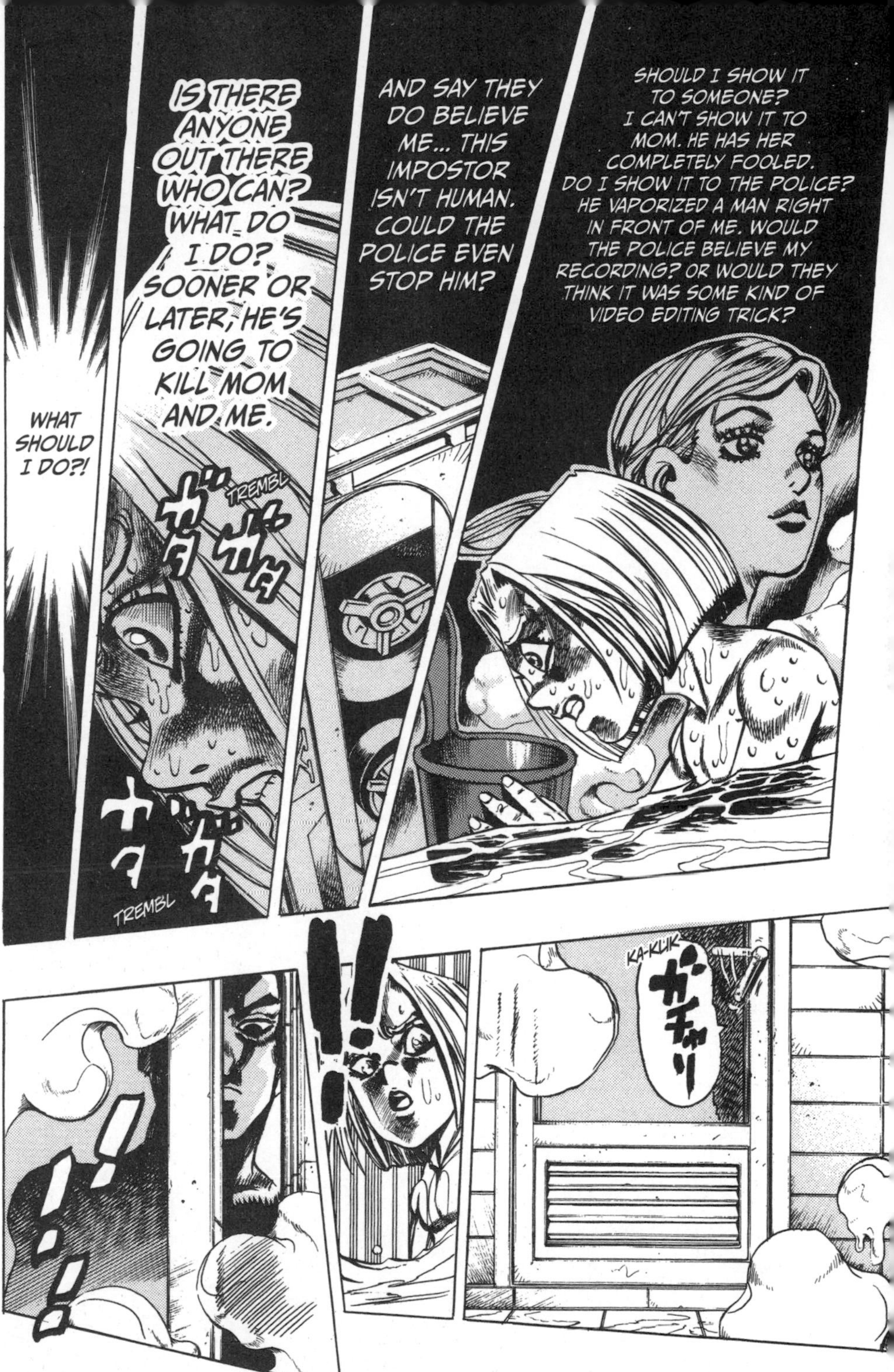
SHOULD I SHOW IT TO SOMEONE? I CAN'T SHOW IT TO MOM. HE HAS HER COMPLETELY FOOLED. DO I SHOW IT TO THE POLICE? HE VAPORIZED A MAN RIGHT IN FRONT OF ME. WOULD THE POLICE BELIEVE MY RECORDING? OR WOULD THEY THINK IT WAS SOME KIND OF VIDEO EDITING TRICK?
AND SAY THEY DO BELIEVE ME... THIS IMPOSTOR ISN'T HUMAN. COULD THE POLICE EVEN STOP HIM?
IS THERE ANYONE OUT THERE WHO CAN? WHAT DO I DO? SOONER OR LATER, HE'S GOING TO KILL MOM AND ME.
TREMBL
WHAT SHOULD I DO?!
TREMBL
KA-KLIK
!!
!!

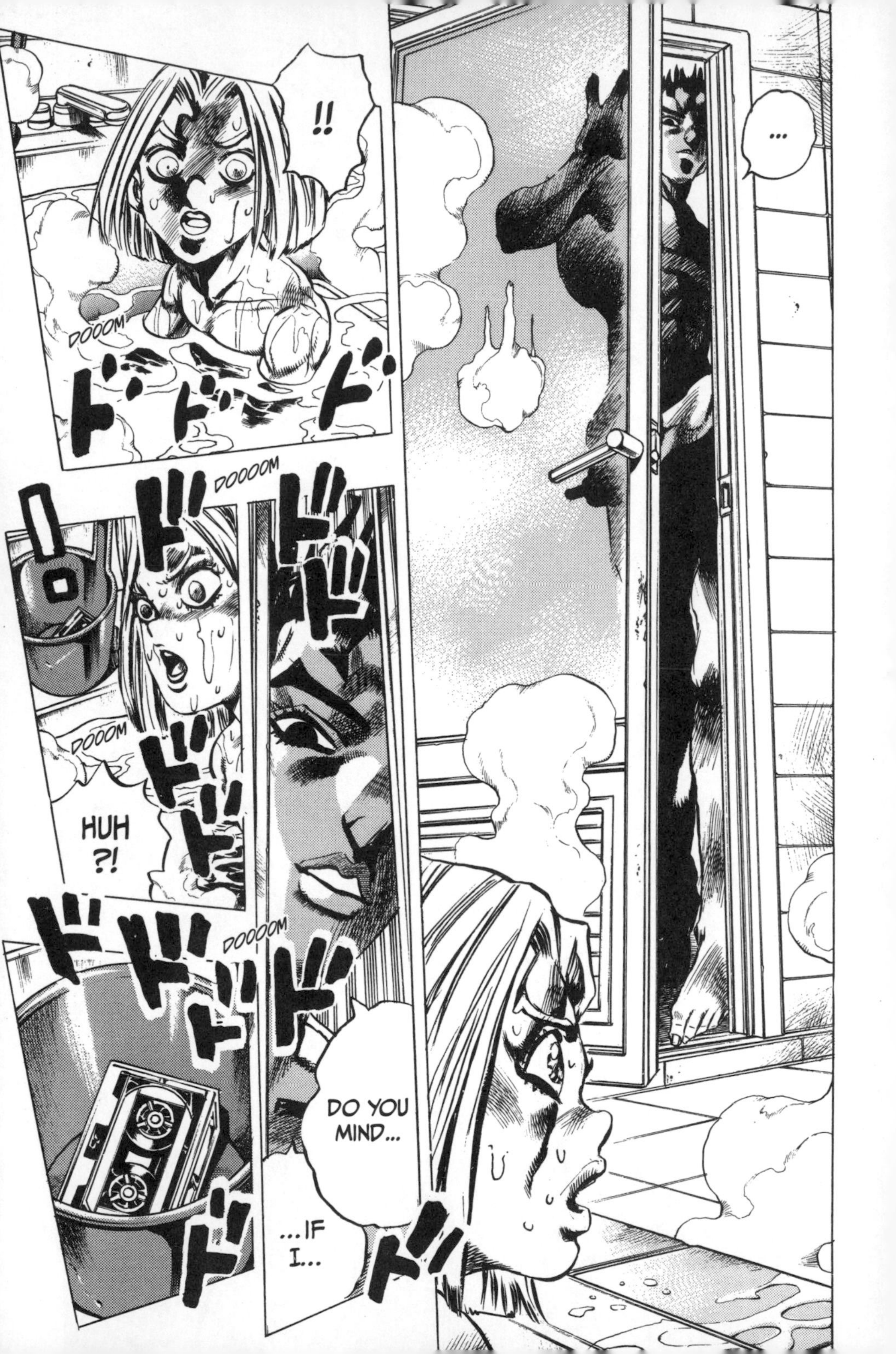
...
!!
DOOOM
ドドド
DOOOOM
ドドド
DOOOM
HUH ?!
ドドド
DOOOOM
ドドドド
DO YOU MIND...
...IF I...
ドド

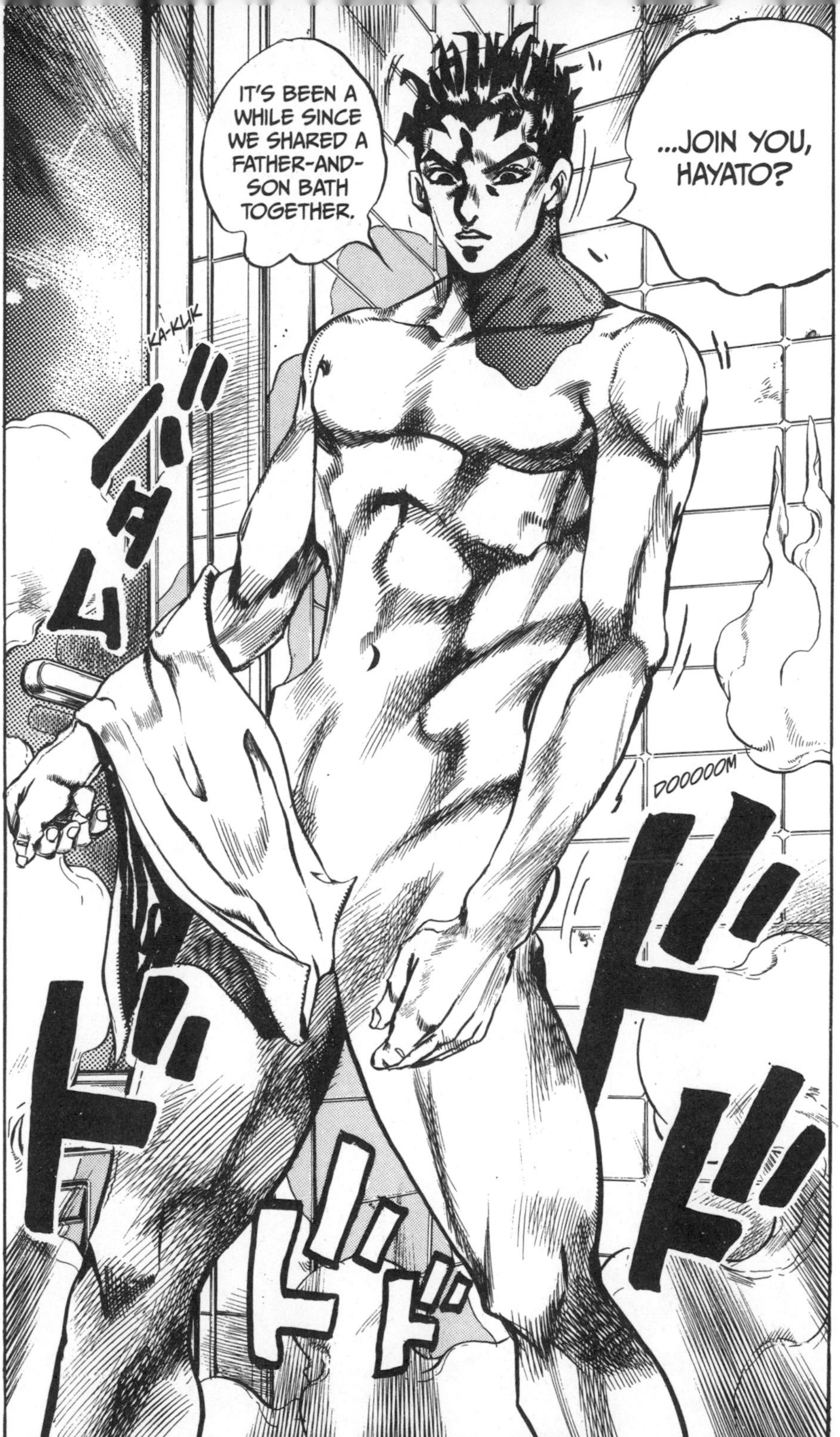
...JOIN YOU, HAYATO?
IT'S BEEN A WHILE SINCE WE SHARED A FATHER-AND-SON BATH TOGETHER.
KA-KLIK
DOOOOOM

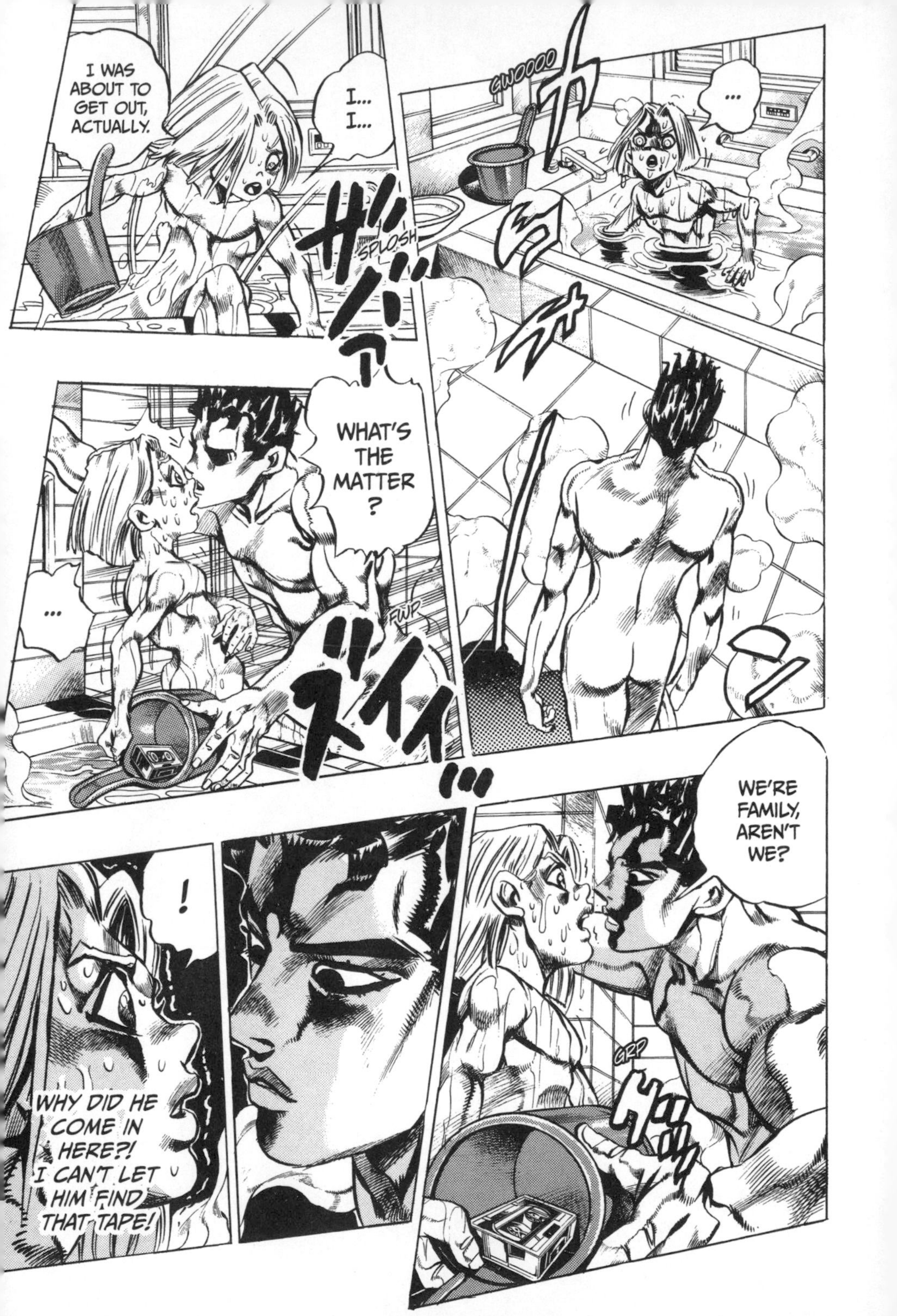
GWOOOO
...
I...
I...
I WAS ABOUT TO GET OUT, ACTUALLY.
SPLOSH
WHAT'S THE MATTER?
...
FWP
WE'RE FAMILY, AREN'T WE?
GRP
!
WHY DID HE COME IN HERE?! I CAN'T LET HIM FIND THAT TAPE!

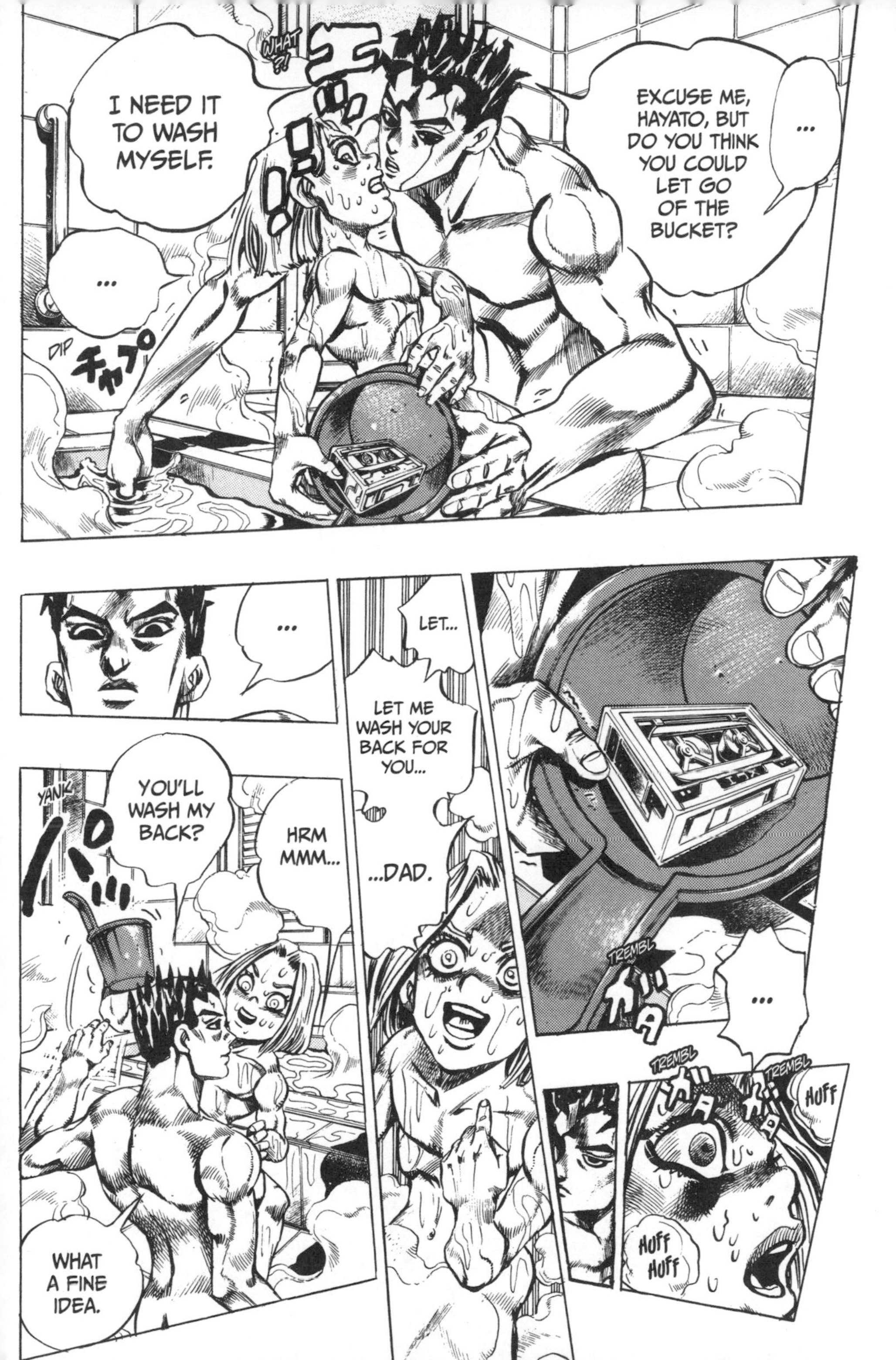
...
EXCUSE ME, HAYATO, BUT DO YOU THINK YOU COULD LET GO OF THE BUCKET?
WHAT?!
I NEED IT TO WASH MYSELF.
...
DIP
TREMBL
...
TREMBL
TREMBL
HUFF
HUFF HUFF
LET...
LET ME WASH YOUR BACK FOR YOU...
...DAD.
...
HRM MMM...
YOU'LL WASH MY BACK?
YANK
WHAT A FINE IDEA.

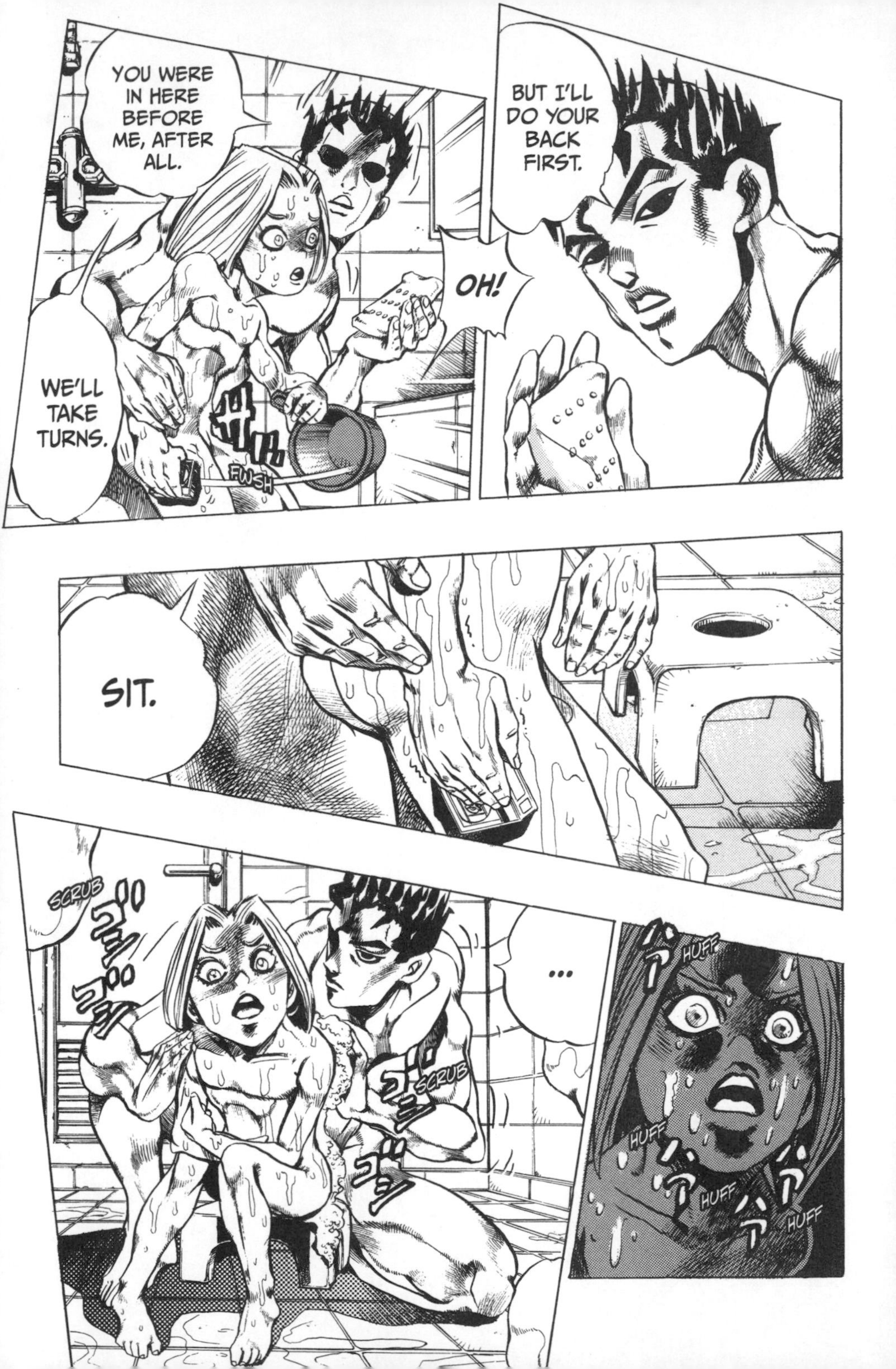
BUT I'LL DO YOUR BACK FIRST.
OH!
YOU WERE IN HERE BEFORE ME, AFTER ALL.
WE'LL TAKE TURNS.
FWSH
SIT.
HUFF
HUFF
HUFF
HUFF
...
SCRUB
SCRUB

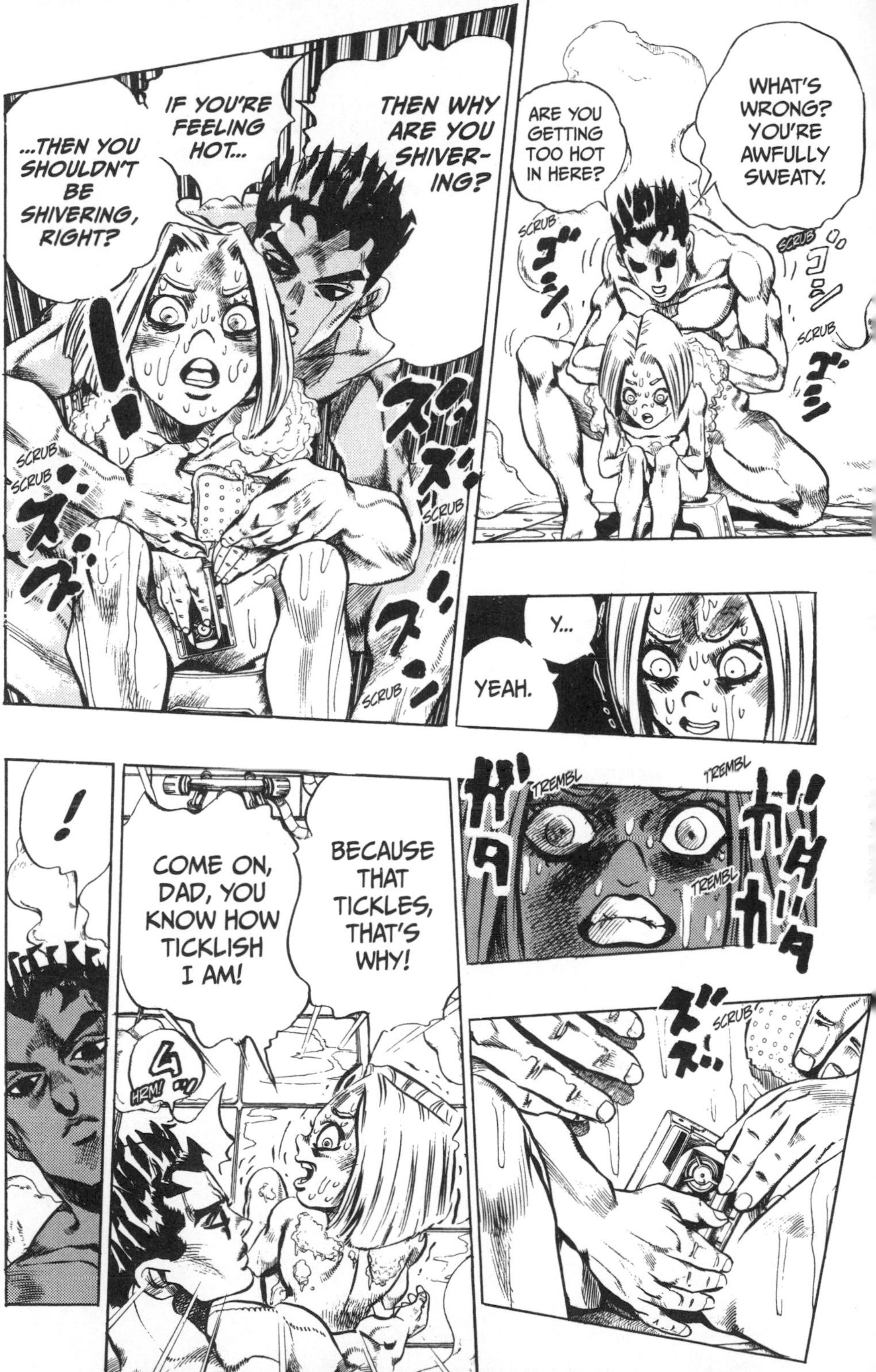
WHAT'S WRONG? YOU'RE AWFULLY SWEATY.
ARE YOU GETTING TOO HOT IN HERE?
SCRUB
SCRUB
SCRUB
Y...
YEAH.
IF YOU'RE FEELING HOT...
...THEN YOU SHOULDN'T BE SHIVERING, RIGHT?
THEN WHY ARE YOU SHIVER-ING?
SCRUB
SCRUB
SCRUB
SCRUB
TREMBL
TREMBL
TREMBL
SCRUB
BECAUSE THAT TICKLES, THAT'S WHY!
COME ON, DAD, YOU KNOW HOW TICKLISH I AM!
HRM!
!

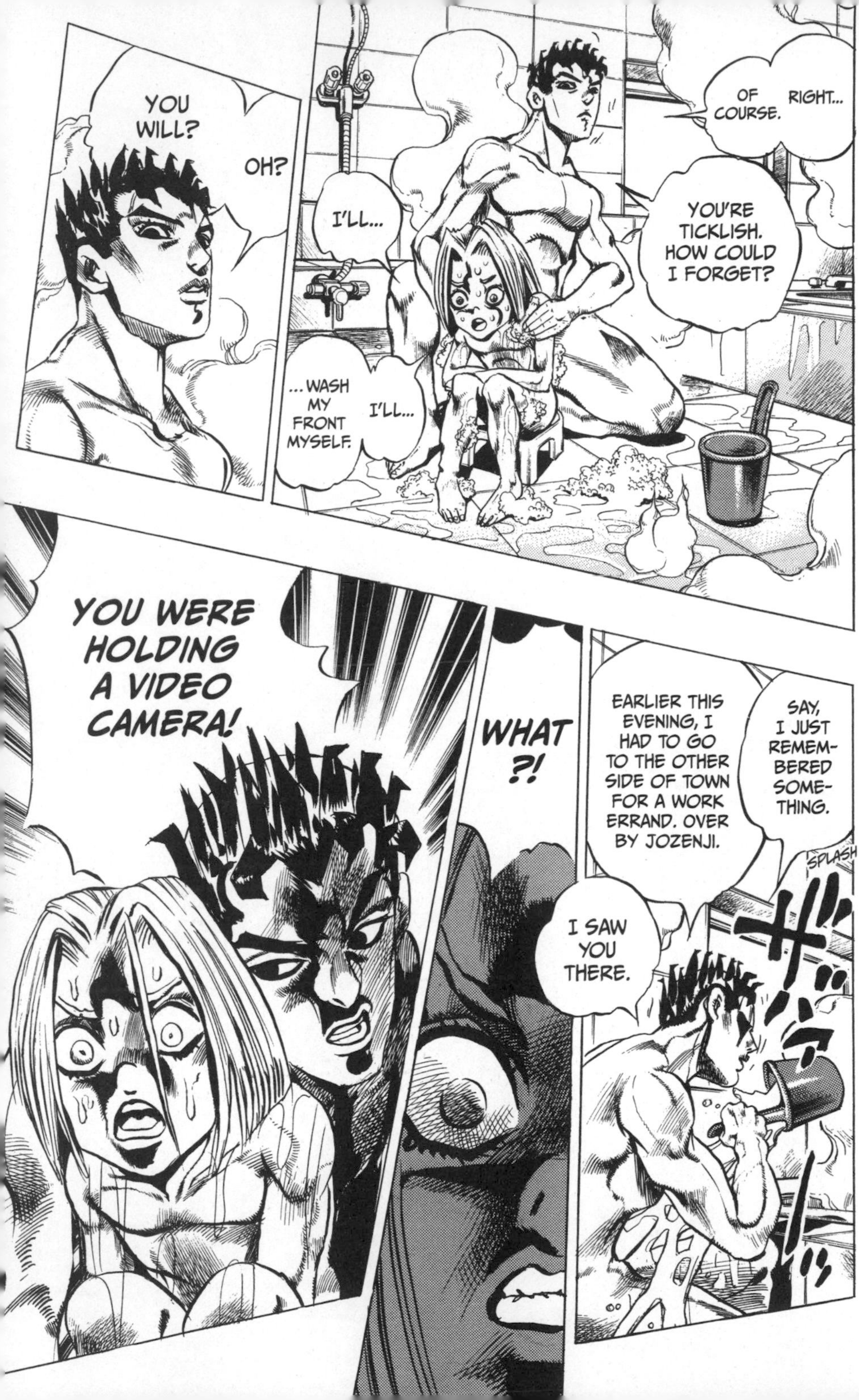

RIGHT... OF COURSE.
YOU'RE TICKLISH. HOW COULD I FORGET?
I'LL...
I'LL...
...WASH MY FRONT MYSELF.
OH?
YOU WILL?
SAY, I JUST REMEM-BERED SOME-THING.
SPLASH
EARLIER THIS EVENING, I HAD TO GO TO THE OTHER SIDE OF TOWN FOR A WORK ERRAND. OVER BY JOZENJI.
I SAW YOU THERE.
WHAT ?!
YOU WERE HOLDING A VIDEO CAMERA!

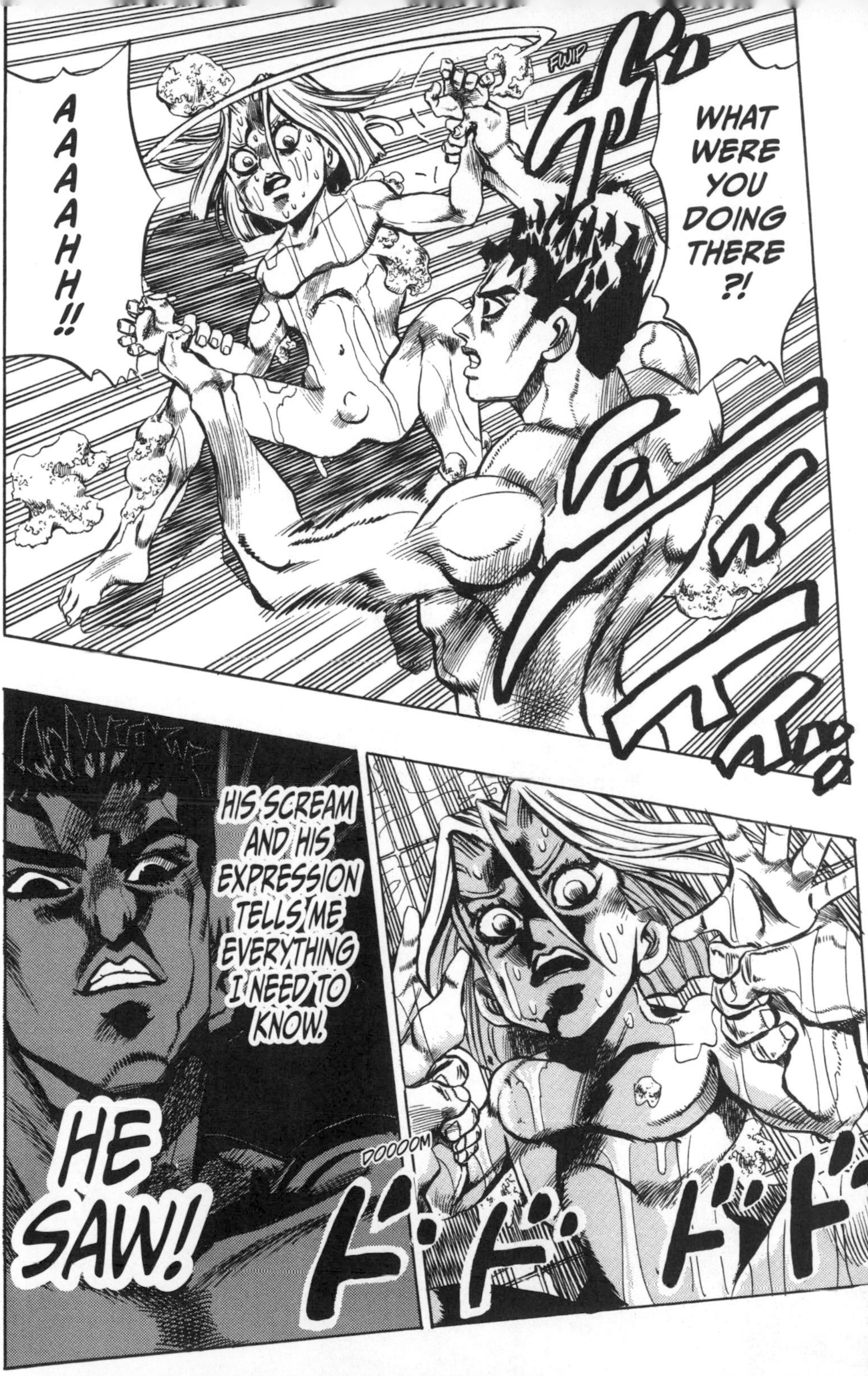
FWIP
WHAT WERE YOU DOING THERE?!
AAAAAHH!!
DOOOOM
HIS SCREAM AND HIS EXPRESSION TELLS ME EVERYTHING I NEED TO KNOW.
HE SAW!

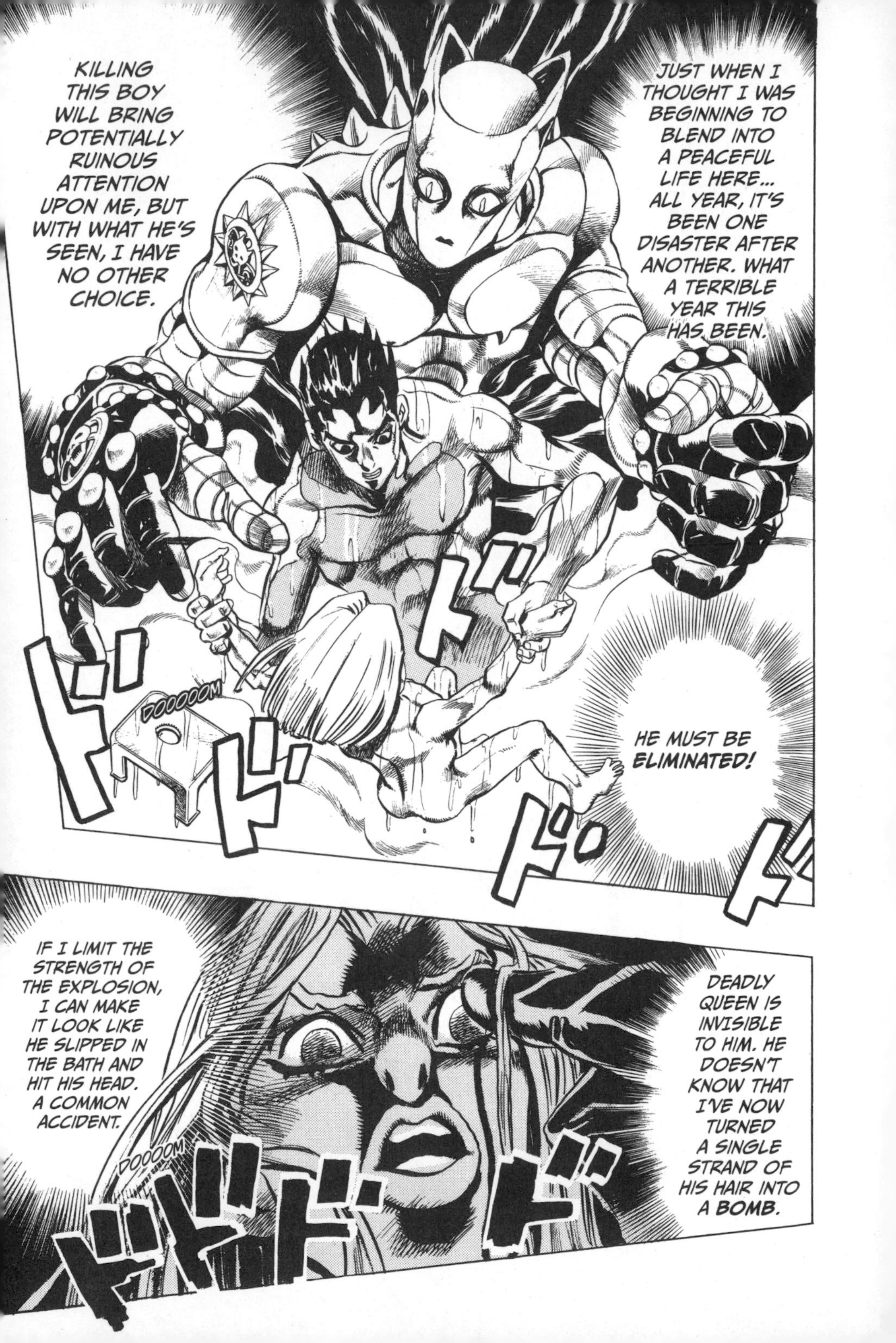
JUST WHEN I THOUGHT I WAS BEGINNING TO BLEND INTO A PEACEFUL LIFE HERE... ALL YEAR, IT'S BEEN ONE DISASTER AFTER ANOTHER. WHAT A TERRIBLE YEAR THIS HAS BEEN.
KILLING THIS BOY WILL BRING POTENTIALLY RUINOUS ATTENTION UPON ME, BUT WITH WHAT HE'S SEEN, I HAVE NO OTHER CHOICE.
HE MUST BE **ELIMINATED!**
DOOOOOM
DEADLY QUEEN IS INVISIBLE TO HIM. HE DOESN'T KNOW THAT I'VE NOW TURNED A SINGLE STRAND OF HIS HAIR INTO A **BOMB.**
IF I LIMIT THE STRENGTH OF THE EXPLOSION, I CAN MAKE IT LOOK LIKE HE SLIPPED IN THE BATH AND HIT HIS HEAD. A COMMON ACCIDENT.
DOOOOM

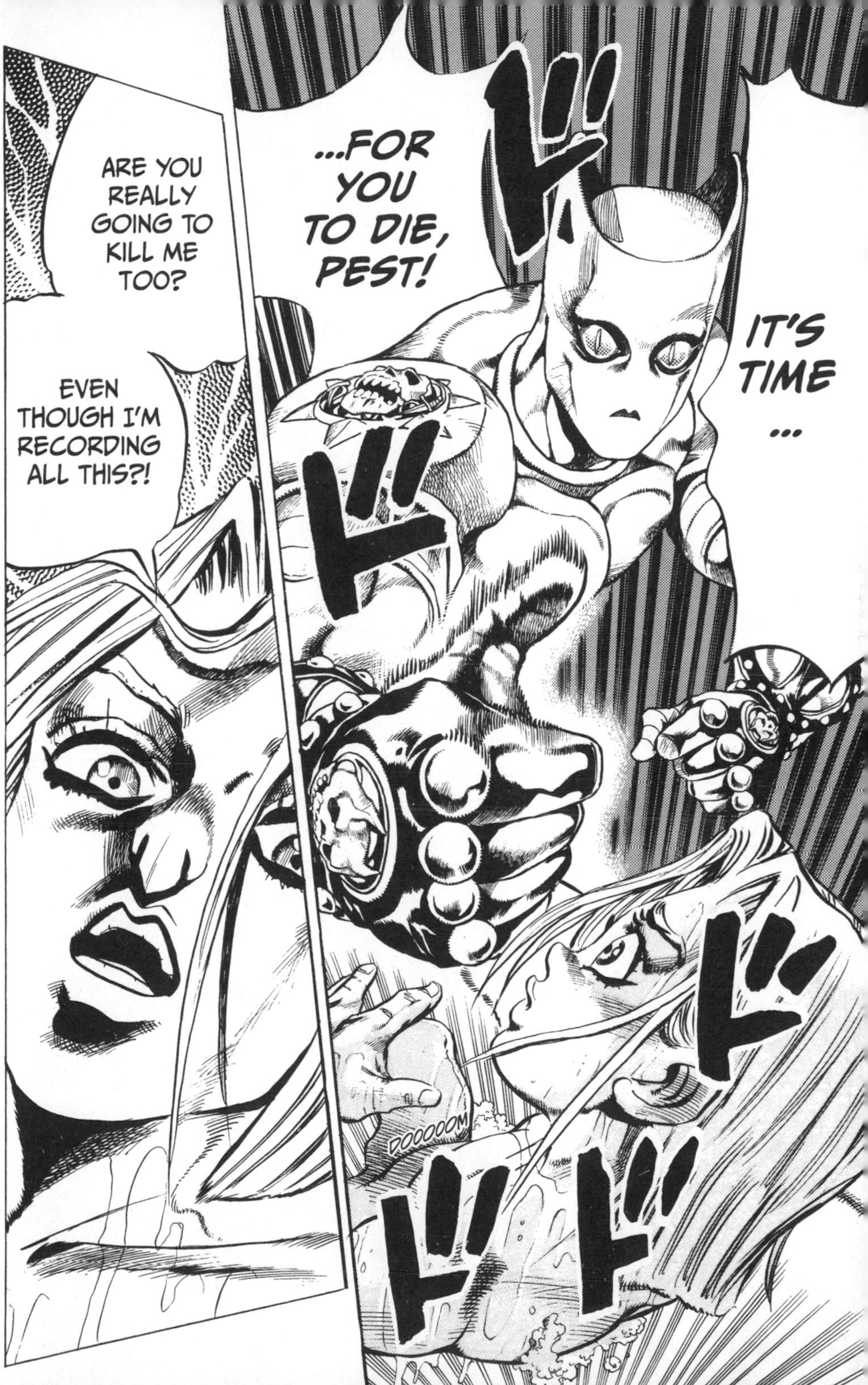
IT'S TIME ...
...FOR YOU TO DIE, PEST!
DOOOOOM
ARE YOU REALLY GOING TO KILL ME TOO?
EVEN THOUGH I'M RECORDING ALL THIS?!

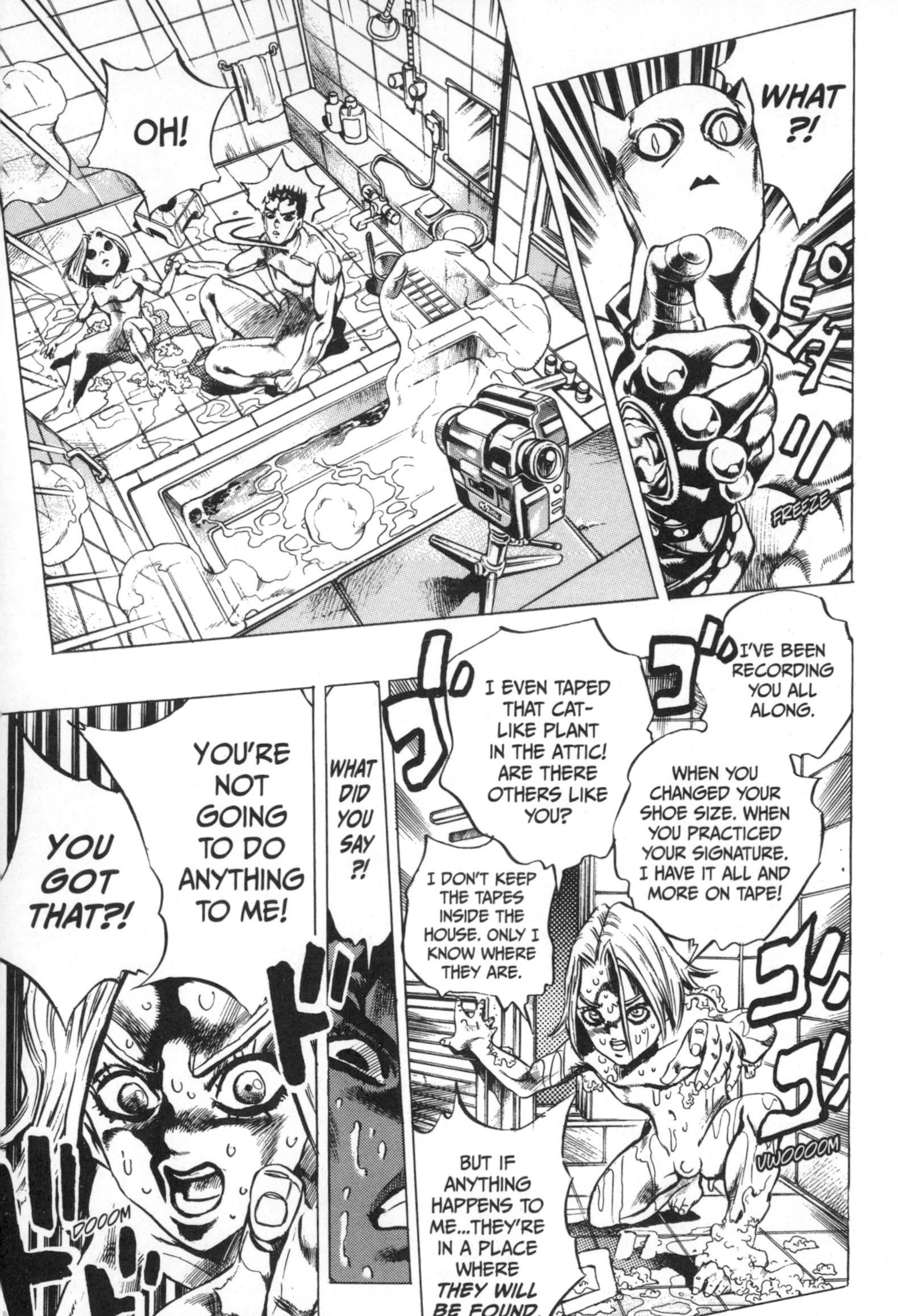
WHAT ?!
FREEZE
OH!
I'VE BEEN RECORDING YOU ALL ALONG.
I EVEN TAPED THAT CAT-LIKE PLANT IN THE ATTIC! ARE THERE OTHERS LIKE YOU?
WHEN YOU CHANGED YOUR SHOE SIZE. WHEN YOU PRACTICED YOUR SIGNATURE. I HAVE IT ALL AND MORE ON TAPE!
I DON'T KEEP THE TAPES INSIDE THE HOUSE. ONLY I KNOW WHERE THEY ARE.
VWOOOOM
BUT IF ANYTHING HAPPENS TO ME...THEY'RE IN A PLACE WHERE *THEY WILL BE FOUND*.
WHAT DID YOU SAY ?!
YOU'RE NOT GOING TO DO ANYTHING TO ME!
YOU GOT THAT?!
DOOOM

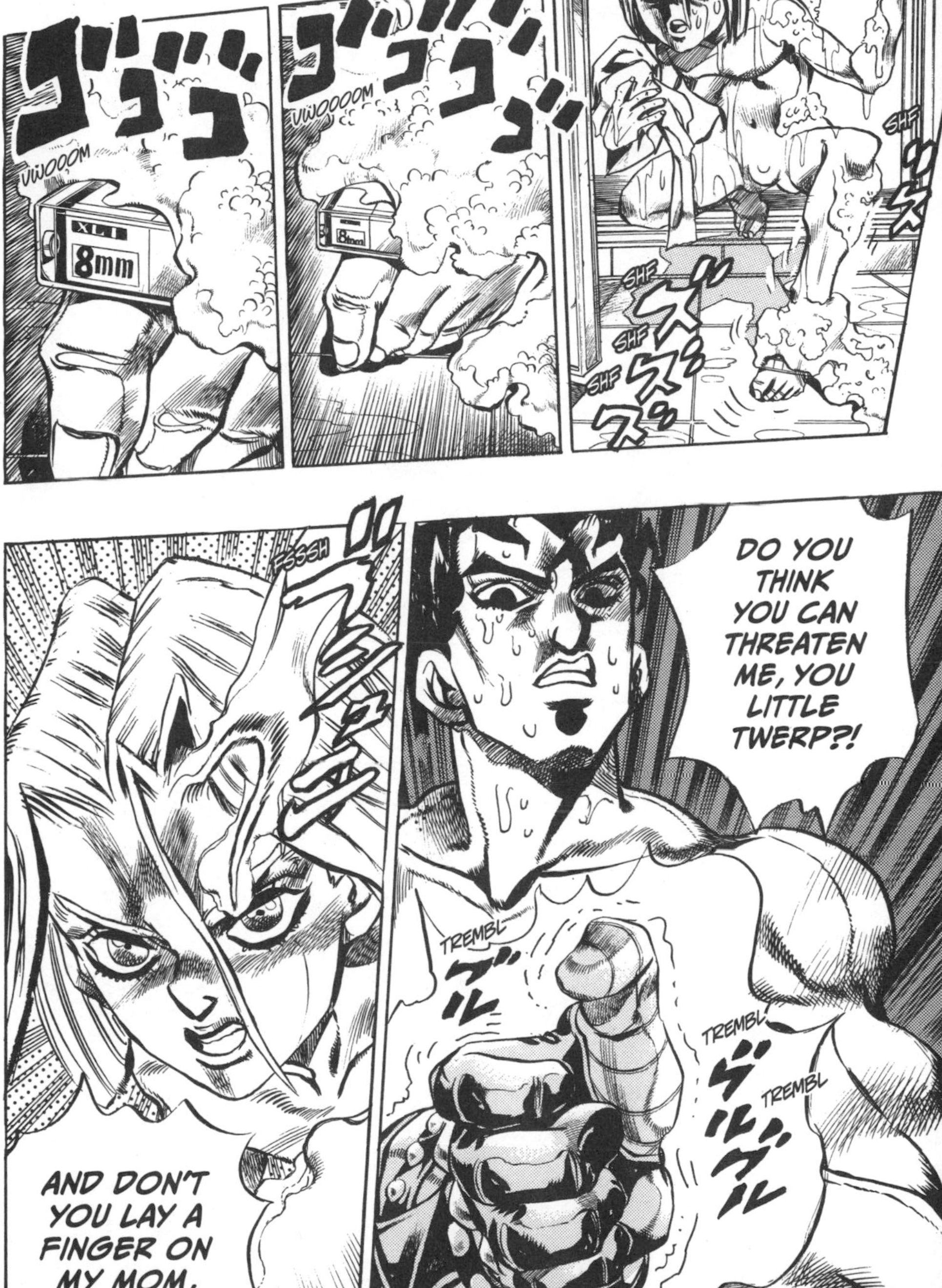
SHF
SHF
SHF
SHF
VWOOOOM
VWOOOM
DO YOU THINK YOU CAN THREATEN ME, YOU LITTLE TWERP?!
TREMBL
TREMBL
TREMBL
FSSSH
AND DON'T YOU LAY A FINGER ON MY MOM, EITHER!

CHAPTER 147

CHEAP TRAP, PART 1

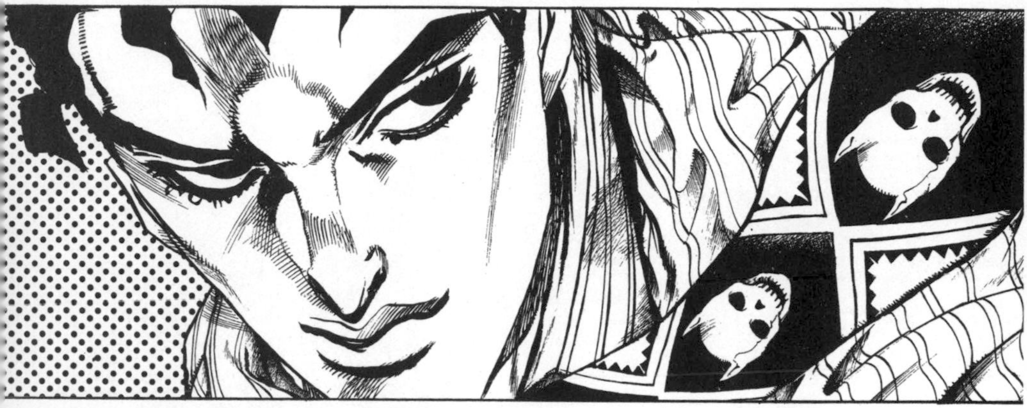

PROFILE

YOSHIKAGE KIRA

(currently has Kosaku Kawajiri's face and fingerprints)

• Birthdate: January 30, 1966 • Blood type: A • Birthplace: Morioh • Dominant Hand: Right

• Education: Graduate of D University, Department of Literature • Religious affiliation: None

• Personality: Maintains a mild-mannered demeanor that doesn't attract suspicion. At work, he situates himself in positions beneath his exceptional intellect and abilities. While his coworkers climb the corporate ladder, he shows no interest in getting a promotion. His only desire is to live a peaceful, inconspicuous life.

• Hobbies: He records the growth of his fingernails and has collected his trimmings since 1975, though he is currently unable to do so.

• Favorite movie: *The Remains of the Day* • Favorite designer: Gianfranco Ferré

• Feelings toward women: He doesn't have a particular type. Women tend to find him attractive, but on dates they quickly start looking for an excuse to leave. He finds hairy fingers unattractive.

• Killer's M.O.: Once every four or five years, his fingernails enter a period of rapid growth, during which he can no longer contain his murderous desires. He enjoys talking to the women he targets and asks them questions, including their name and interests, but loathes when a woman says anything self-centered or egotistical. He takes each victim's hand home as a trophy and finds pleasure in using it, sometimes playing with it or even using it to help wipe his bottom.

• Stand: **Deadly Queen**
He doesn't like to start a fight, but he will use his Stand to kill anyone who tries to uncover his true nature.

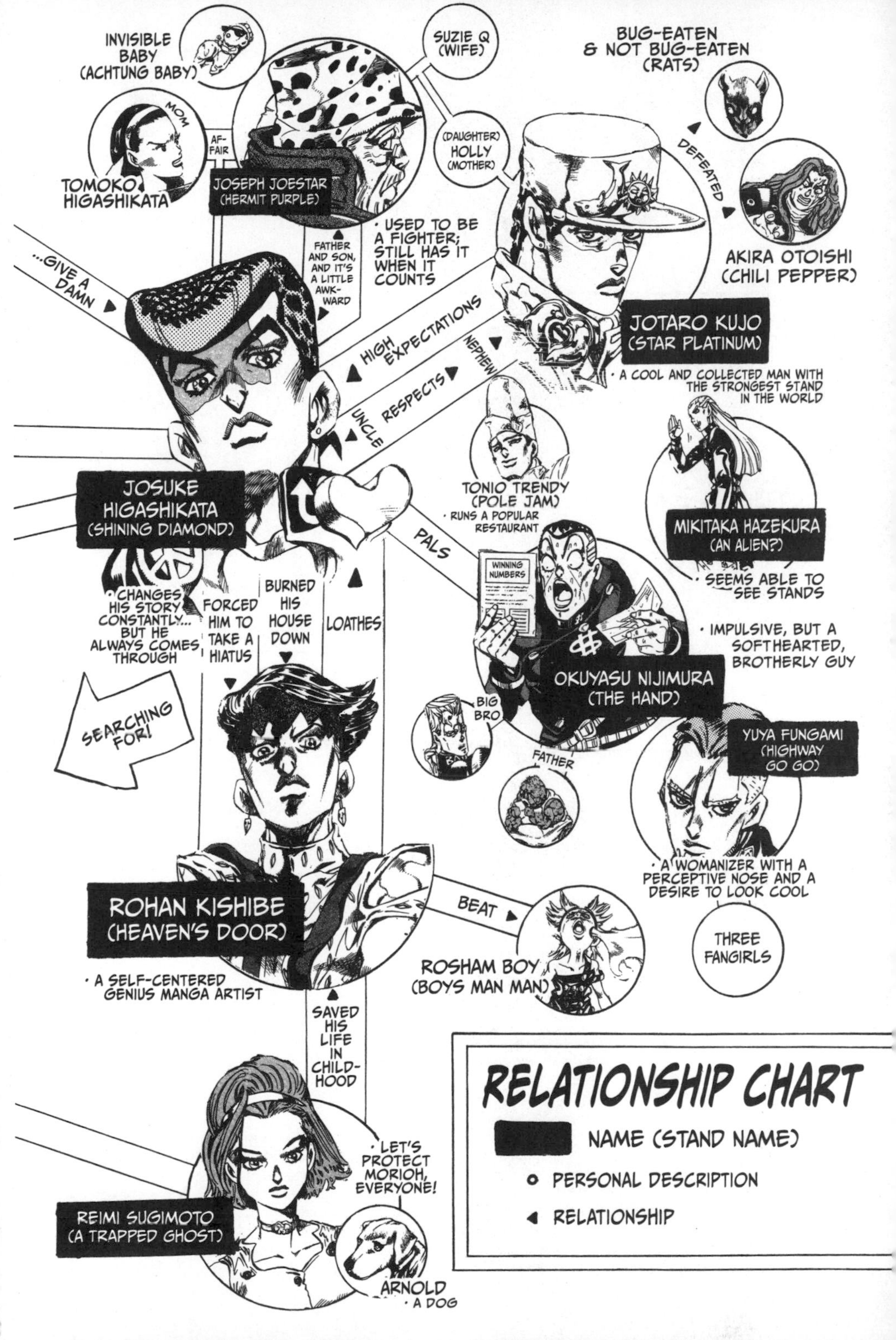

INVISIBLE BABY (ACHTUNG BABY)
SUZIE Q (WIFE)
BUG-EATEN & NOT BUG-EATEN (RATS)
MOM
AF-FAIR
TOMOKO HIGASHIKATA
JOSEPH JOESTAR (HERMIT PURPLE)
(DAUGHTER) HOLLY (MOTHER)
DEFEATED
AKIRA OTOISHI (CHILI PEPPER)
· USED TO BE A FIGHTER; STILL HAS IT WHEN IT COUNTS
FATHER AND SON, AND IT'S A LITTLE AWK-WARD
...GIVE A DAMN
HIGH EXPECTATIONS
NEPHEW
RESPECTS
UNCLE
JOTARO KUJO (STAR PLATINUM)
· A COOL AND COLLECTED MAN WITH THE STRONGEST STAND IN THE WORLD
TONIO TRENDY (POLE JAM)
· RUNS A POPULAR RESTAURANT
MIKITAKA HAZEKURA (AN ALIEN?)
· SEEMS ABLE TO SEE STANDS
JOSUKE HIGASHIKATA (SHINING DIAMOND)
PALS
WINNING NUMBERS
· CHANGES HIS STORY CONSTANTLY... BUT HE ALWAYS COMES THROUGH
FORCED HIM TO TAKE A HIATUS
BURNED HIS HOUSE DOWN
LOATHES
· IMPULSIVE, BUT A SOFTHEARTED, BROTHERLY GUY
OKUYASU NIJIMURA (THE HAND)
BIG BRO
FATHER
SEARCHING FOR!
YUYA FUNGAMI (HIGHWAY GO GO)
· A WOMANIZER WITH A PERCEPTIVE NOSE AND A DESIRE TO LOOK COOL
THREE FANGIRLS
BEAT
ROHAN KISHIBE (HEAVEN'S DOOR)
· A SELF-CENTERED GENIUS MANGA ARTIST
ROSHAM BOY (BOYS MAN MAN)
SAVED HIS LIFE IN CHILD-HOOD
RELATIONSHIP CHART
NAME (STAND NAME)
PERSONAL DESCRIPTION
RELATIONSHIP
· LET'S PROTECT MORIOH, EVERYONE!
REIMI SUGIMOTO (A TRAPPED GHOST)
ARNOLD
· A DOG

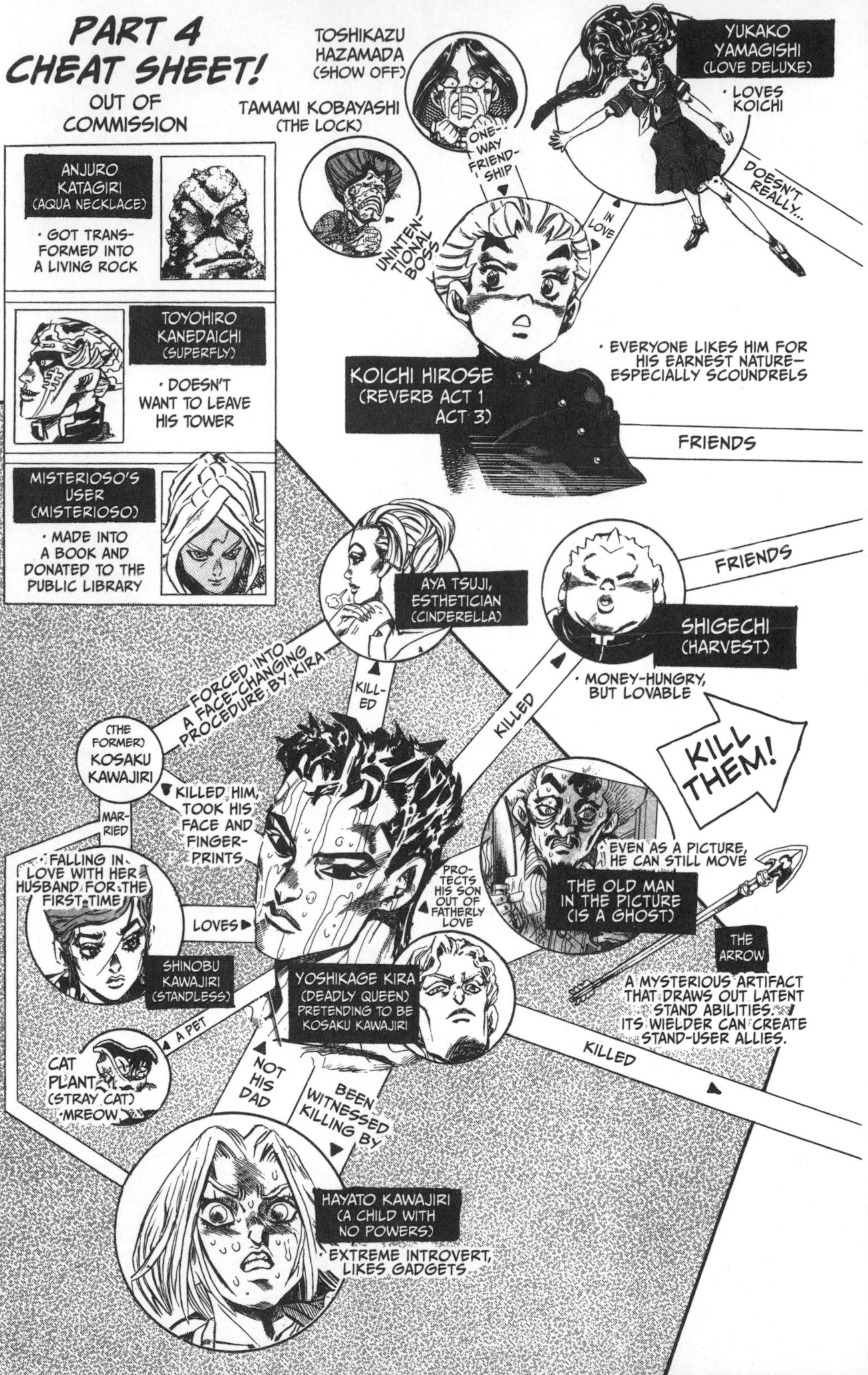
PART 4 CHEAT SHEET!
OUT OF COMMISSION
ANJURO KATAGIRI (AQUA NECKLACE)
· GOT TRANSFORMED INTO A LIVING ROCK
TOYOHIRO KANEDAICHI (SUPERFLY)
· DOESN'T WANT TO LEAVE HIS TOWER
MISTERIOSO'S USER (MISTERIOSO)
· MADE INTO A BOOK AND DONATED TO THE PUBLIC LIBRARY
TOSHIKAZU HAZAMADA (SHOW OFF)
TAMAMI KOBAYASHI (THE LOCK)
YUKAKO YAMAGISHI (LOVE DELUXE)
· LOVES KOICHI
ONE-WAY FRIENDSHIP
UNINTENTIONAL BOSS
IN LOVE
DOESN'T REALLY...
KOICHI HIROSE (REVERB ACT 1 ACT 3)
· EVERYONE LIKES HIM FOR HIS EARNEST NATURE—ESPECIALLY SCOUNDRELS
FRIENDS
AYA TSUJI, ESTHETICIAN (CINDERELLA)
FRIENDS
SHIGECHI (HARVEST)
· MONEY-HUNGRY, BUT LOVABLE
FORCED INTO A FACE-CHANGING PROCEDURE BY KIRA
KILLED
KILLED
KILL THEM!
(THE FORMER) KOSAKU KAWAJIRI
KILLED HIM, TOOK HIS FACE AND FINGERPRINTS
MARRIED
· FALLING IN LOVE WITH HER HUSBAND FOR THE FIRST TIME
LOVES
PROTECTS HIS SON OUT OF FATHERLY LOVE
· EVEN AS A PICTURE, HE CAN STILL MOVE
THE OLD MAN IN THE PICTURE (IS A GHOST)
THE ARROW
A MYSTERIOUS ARTIFACT THAT DRAWS OUT LATENT STAND ABILITIES. ITS WIELDER CAN CREATE STAND-USER ALLIES.
SHINOBU KAWAJIRI (STANDLESS)
YOSHIKAGE KIRA (DEADLY QUEEN) PRETENDING TO BE KOSAKU KAWAJIRI
A PET
CAT PLANT (STRAY CAT) ·MREOW
NOT HIS DAD
BEEN WITNESSED KILLING BY
KILLED
HAYATO KAWAJIRI (A CHILD WITH NO POWERS)
· EXTREME INTROVERT, LIKES GADGETS

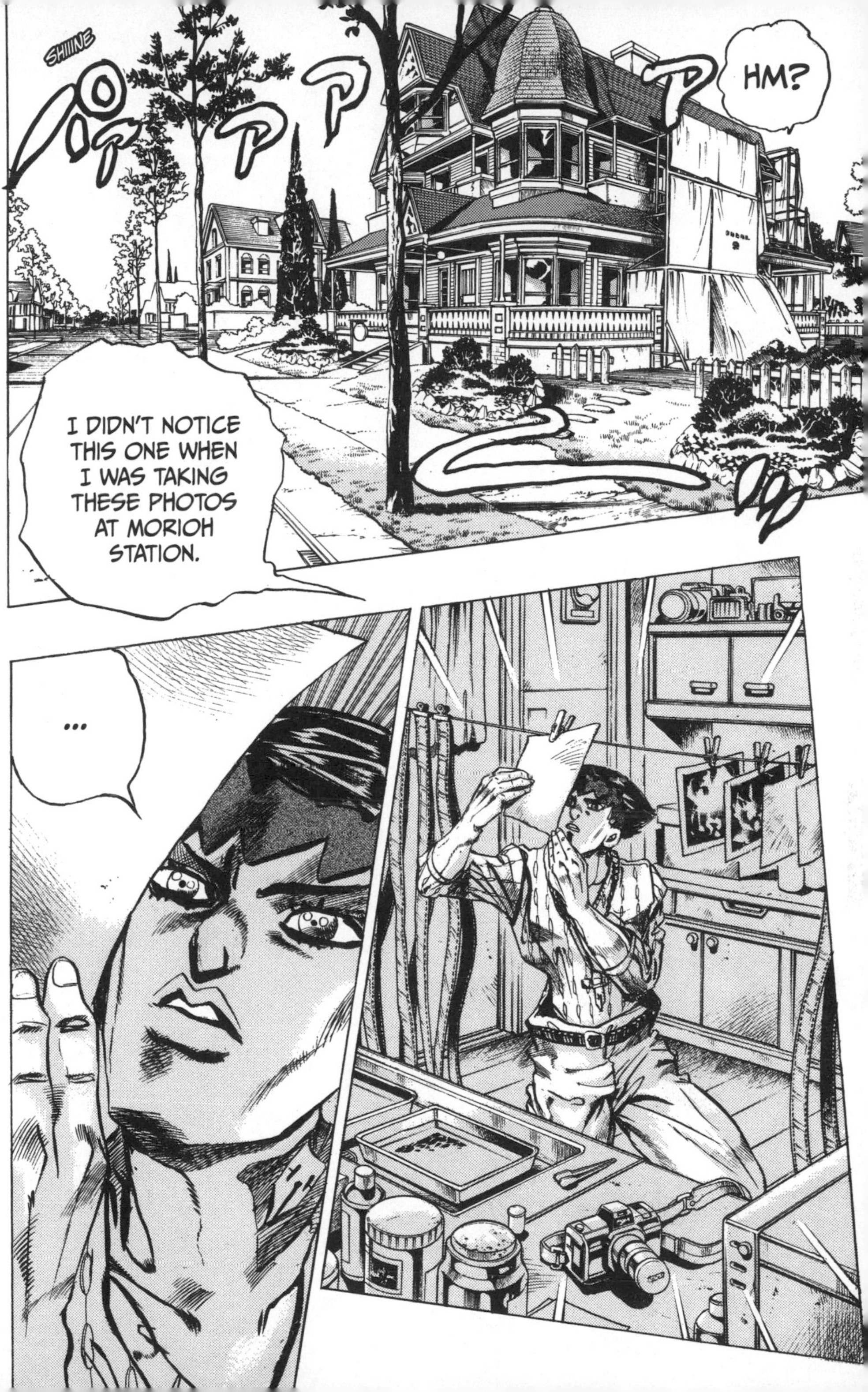
HM?
SHIIINE
I DIDN'T NOTICE THIS ONE WHEN I WAS TAKING THESE PHOTOS AT MORIOH STATION.
...

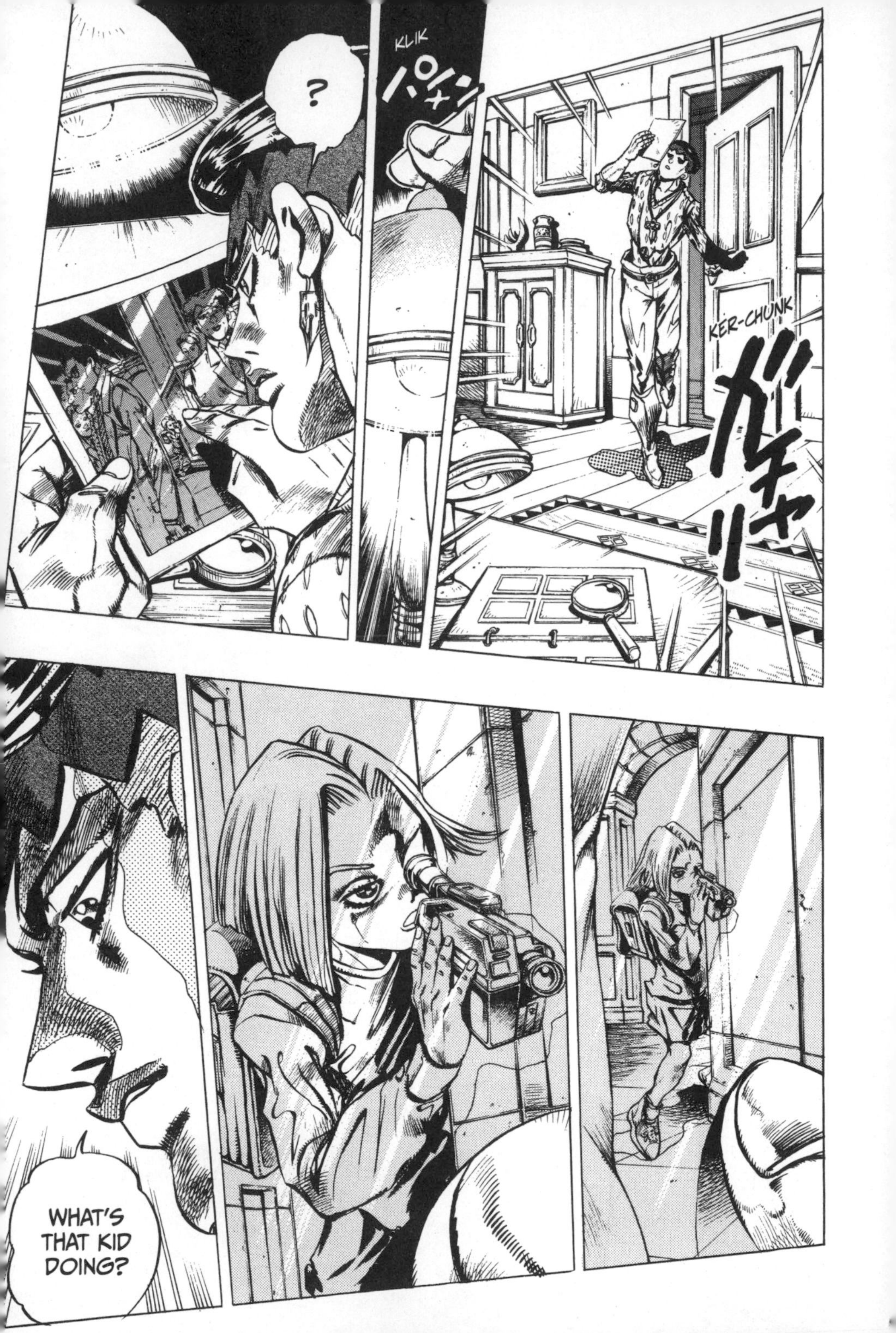
KER-CHUNK
ガチャリ
KLIK
?
WHAT'S THAT KID DOING?

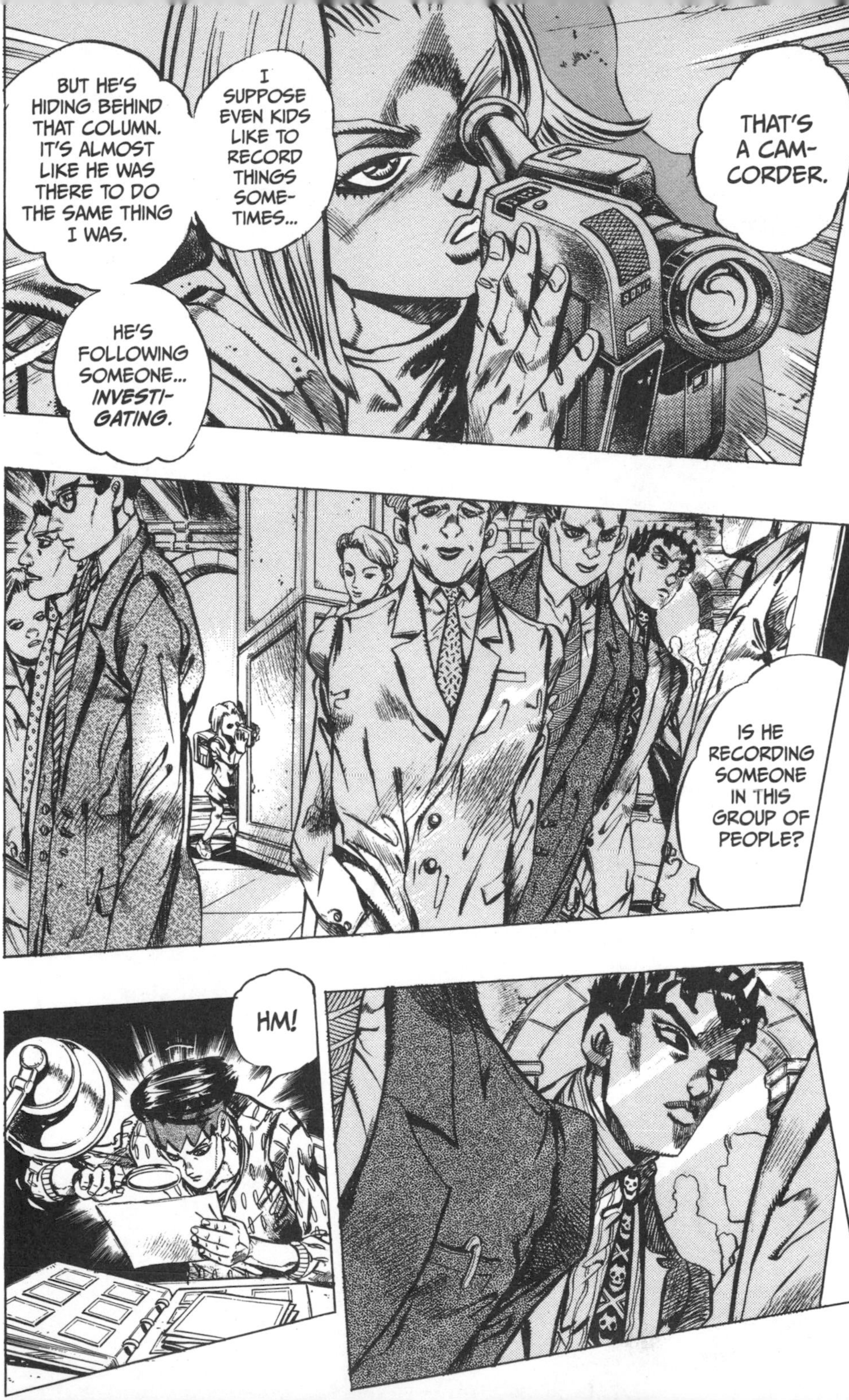
THAT'S A CAM-CORDER.
I SUPPOSE EVEN KIDS LIKE TO RECORD THINGS SOME-TIMES...
BUT HE'S HIDING BEHIND THAT COLUMN. IT'S ALMOST LIKE HE WAS THERE TO DO THE SAME THING I WAS.
HE'S FOLLOWING SOMEONE... *INVESTI-GATING.*
IS HE RECORDING SOMEONE IN THIS GROUP OF PEOPLE?
HM!

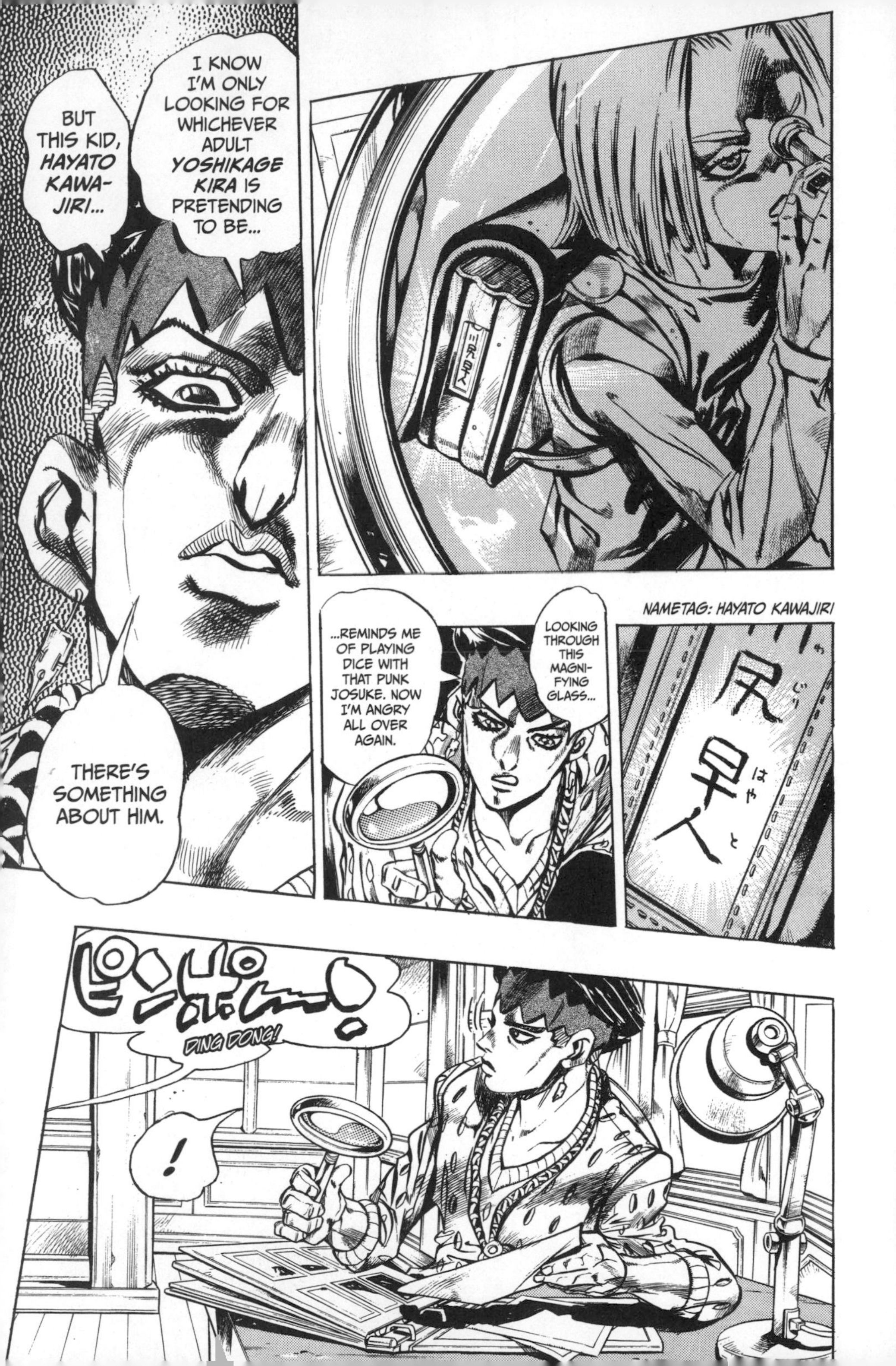
NAMETAG: HAYATO KAWAJIRI
LOOKING THROUGH THIS MAGNI-FYING GLASS...
...REMINDS ME OF PLAYING DICE WITH THAT PUNK JOSUKE. NOW I'M ANGRY ALL OVER AGAIN.
I KNOW I'M ONLY LOOKING FOR WHICHEVER ADULT YOSHIKAGE KIRA IS PRETENDING TO BE...
BUT THIS KID, HAYATO KAWA-JIRI...
THERE'S SOMETHING ABOUT HIM.
DING DONG!
!

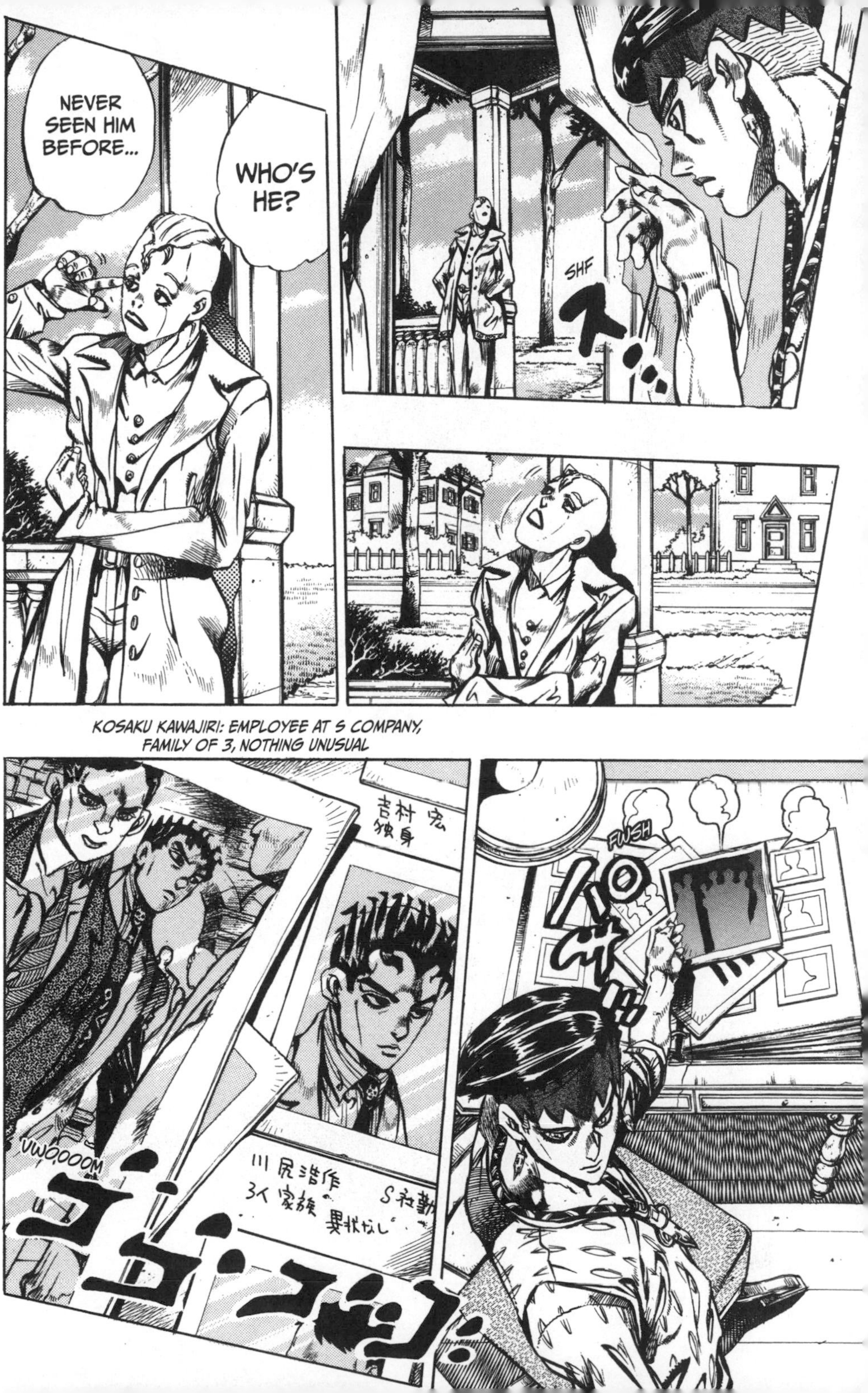
SHF
WHO'S HE?
NEVER SEEN HIM BEFORE...
KOSAKU KAWAJIRI: EMPLOYEE AT S COMPANY, FAMILY OF 3, NOTHING UNUSUAL
FWSH
吉村宏
独身
VWOOOOM
川尻浩作
3人家族
S社勤
異状なし

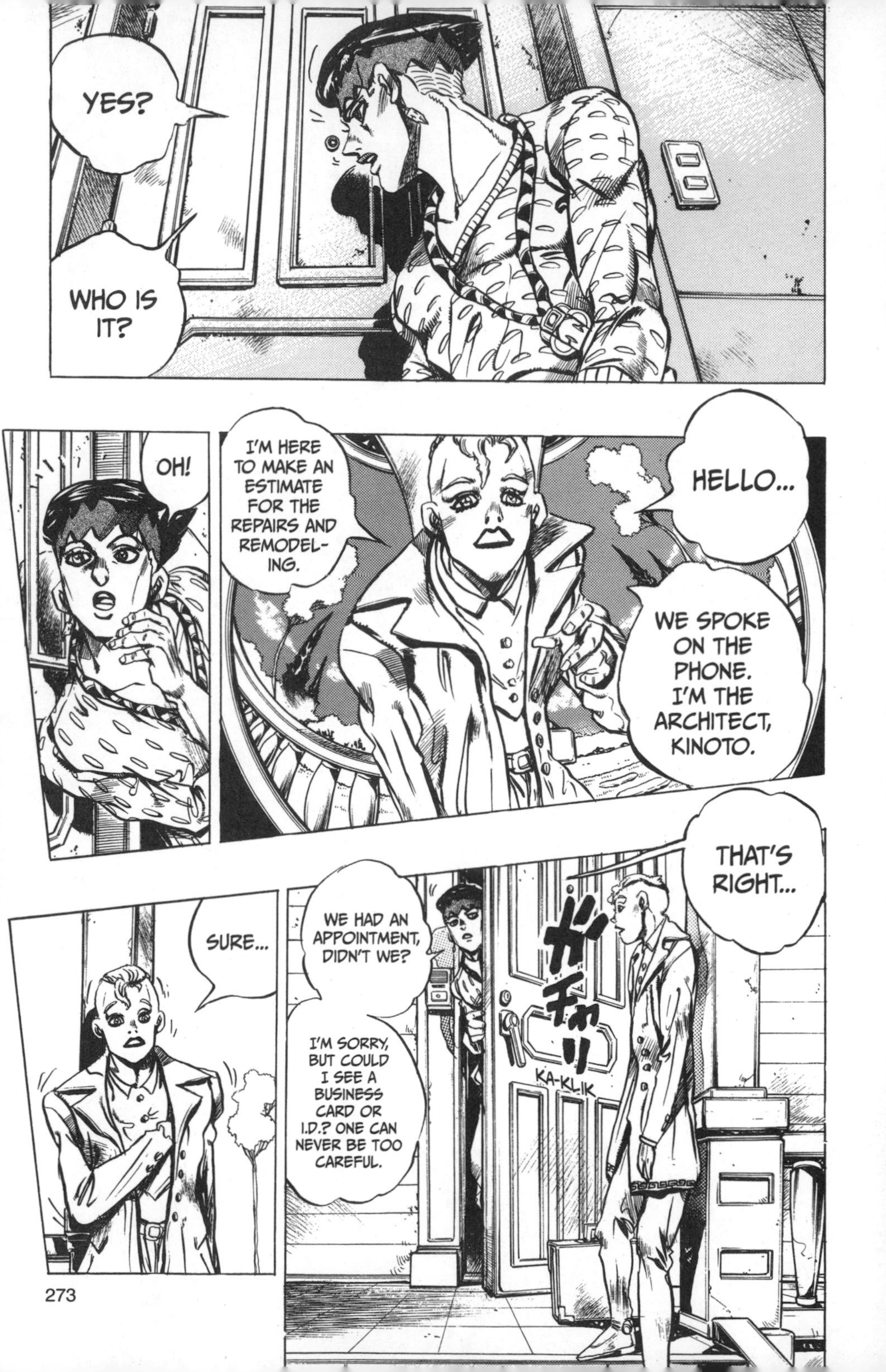
YES?
WHO IS IT?
HELLO...
I'M HERE TO MAKE AN ESTIMATE FOR THE REPAIRS AND REMODEL-ING.
WE SPOKE ON THE PHONE. I'M THE ARCHITECT, KINOTO.
OH!
THAT'S RIGHT...
WE HAD AN APPOINTMENT, DIDN'T WE?
ガチャリ
KA-KLIK
I'M SORRY, BUT COULD I SEE A BUSINESS CARD OR I.D.? ONE CAN NEVER BE TOO CAREFUL.
SURE...

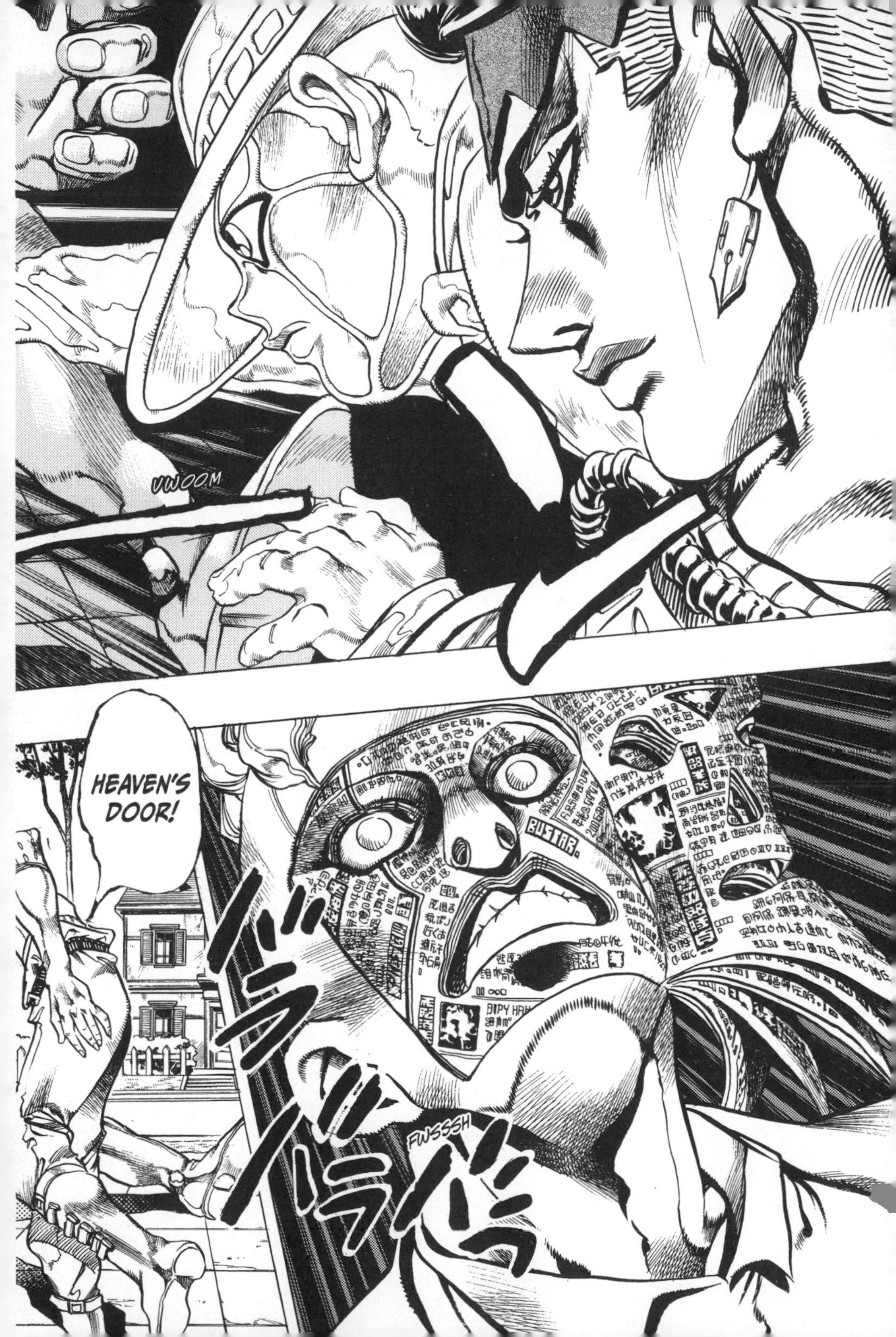
UWOOM
HEAVEN'S DOOR!
FWSSSH

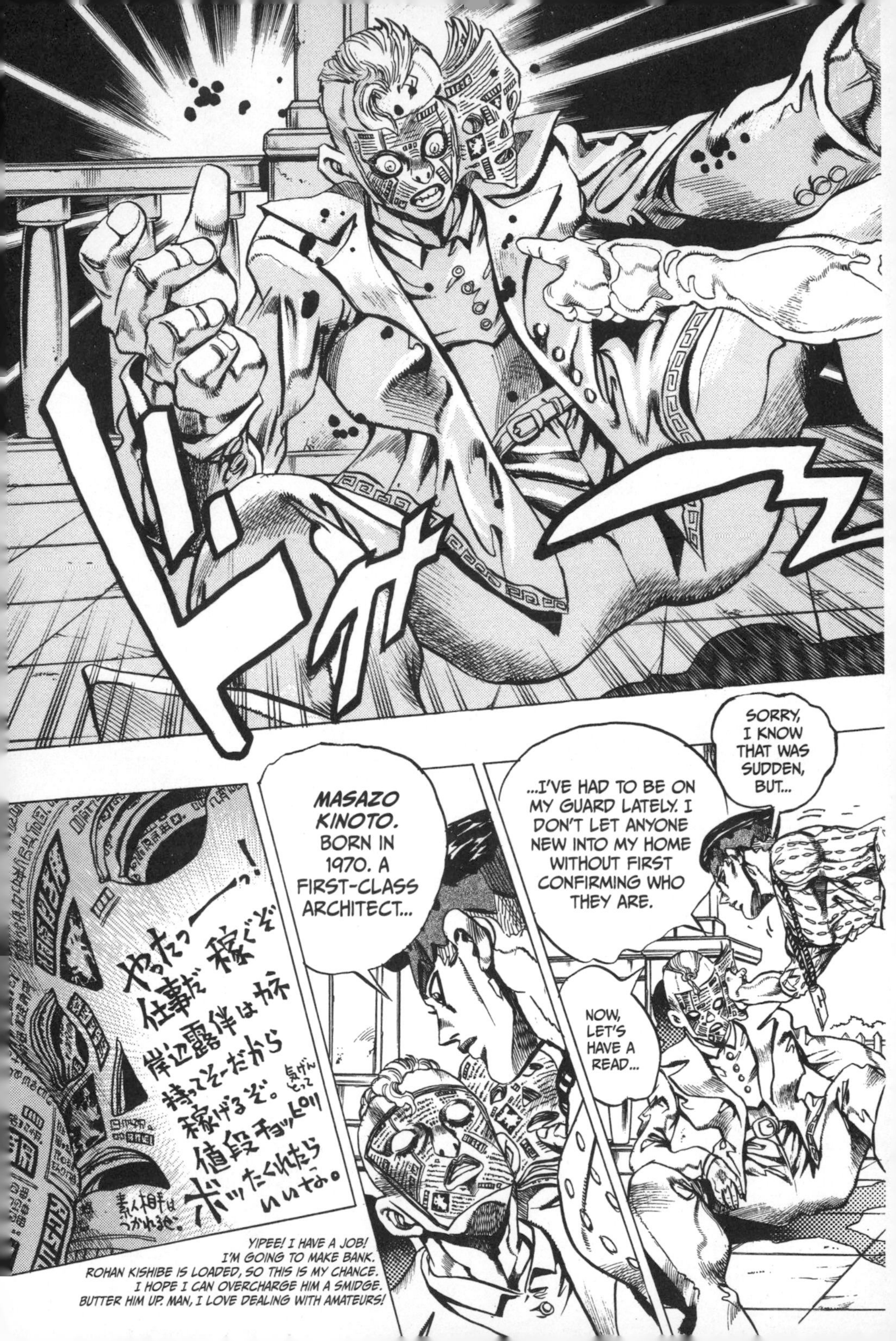
SORRY, I KNOW THAT WAS SUDDEN, BUT...
...I'VE HAD TO BE ON MY GUARD LATELY. I DON'T LET ANYONE NEW INTO MY HOME WITHOUT FIRST CONFIRMING WHO THEY ARE.
NOW, LET'S HAVE A READ...
MASAZO KINOTO. BORN IN 1970. A FIRST-CLASS ARCHITECT...
やったっーーっ! 仕事だ 稼ぐぞ 岸辺露伴はカネ持ってそーだから 稼げるぞ。気げんとって 値段チョッピリボッたくれたらいいな。
YIPEE! I HAVE A JOB! I'M GOING TO MAKE BANK. ROHAN KISHIBE IS LOADED, SO THIS IS MY CHANCE. I HOPE I CAN OVERCHARGE HIM A SMIDGE. BUTTER HIM UP. MAN, I LOVE DEALING WITH AMATEURS!

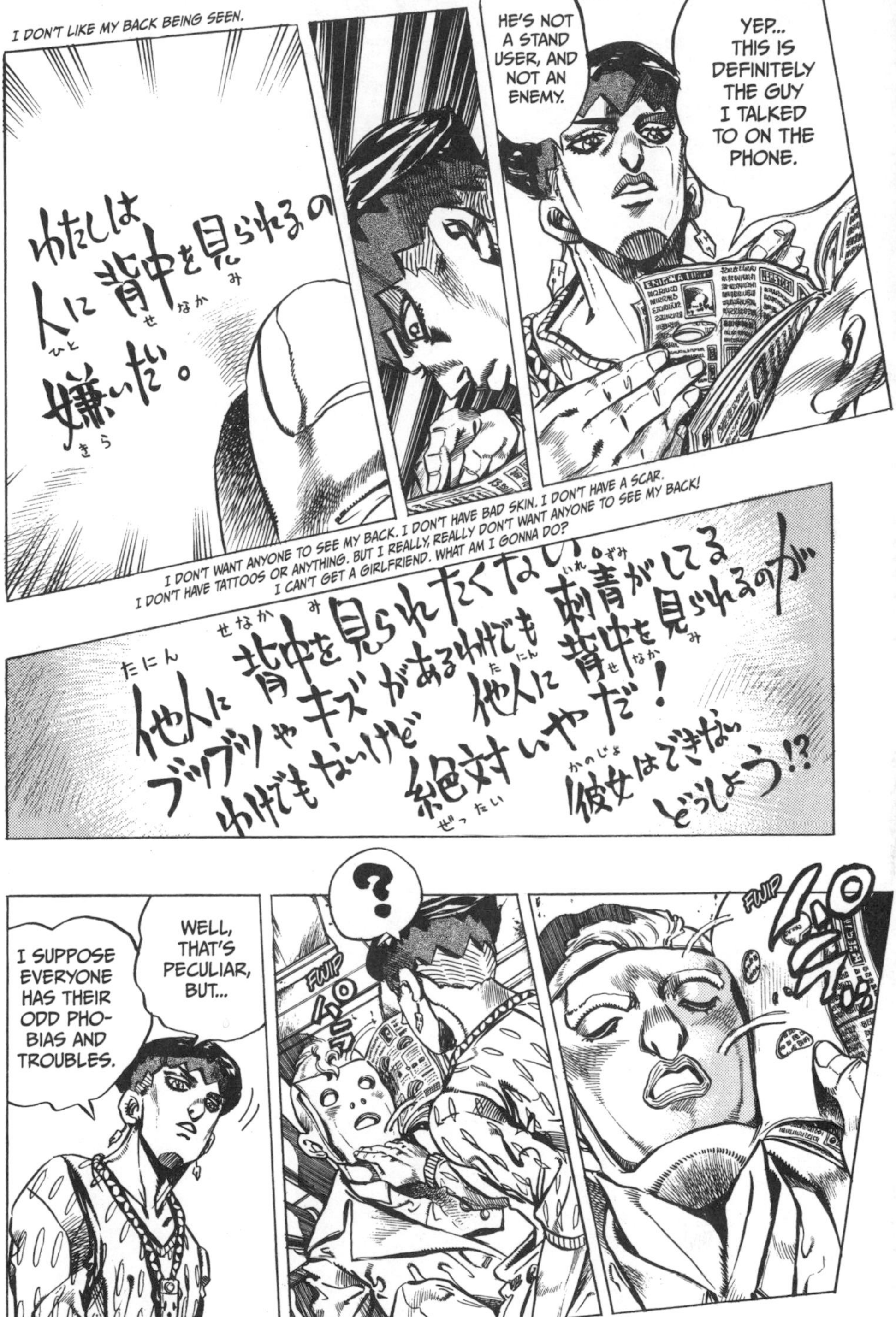
YEP... THIS IS DEFINITELY THE GUY I TALKED TO ON THE PHONE.
HE'S NOT A STAND USER, AND NOT AN ENEMY.
I DON'T LIKE MY BACK BEING SEEN.
わたしは人に背中を見られるの嫌いだ。
I DON'T WANT ANYONE TO SEE MY BACK. I DON'T HAVE BAD SKIN. I DON'T HAVE A SCAR. I DON'T HAVE TATTOOS OR ANYTHING. BUT I REALLY, REALLY DON'T WANT ANYONE TO SEE MY BACK! I CAN'T GET A GIRLFRIEND. WHAT AM I GONNA DO?
他人に背中を見られたくない。ブツブツやキズがあるわけでも刺青がしてるわけでもないけど 他人に背中を見られるのが絶対いやだ! 彼女はできない どうしよう!?
FWIP
?
FWIP
WELL, THAT'S PECULIAR, BUT...
I SUPPOSE EVERYONE HAS THEIR ODD PHO-BIAS AND TROUBLES.

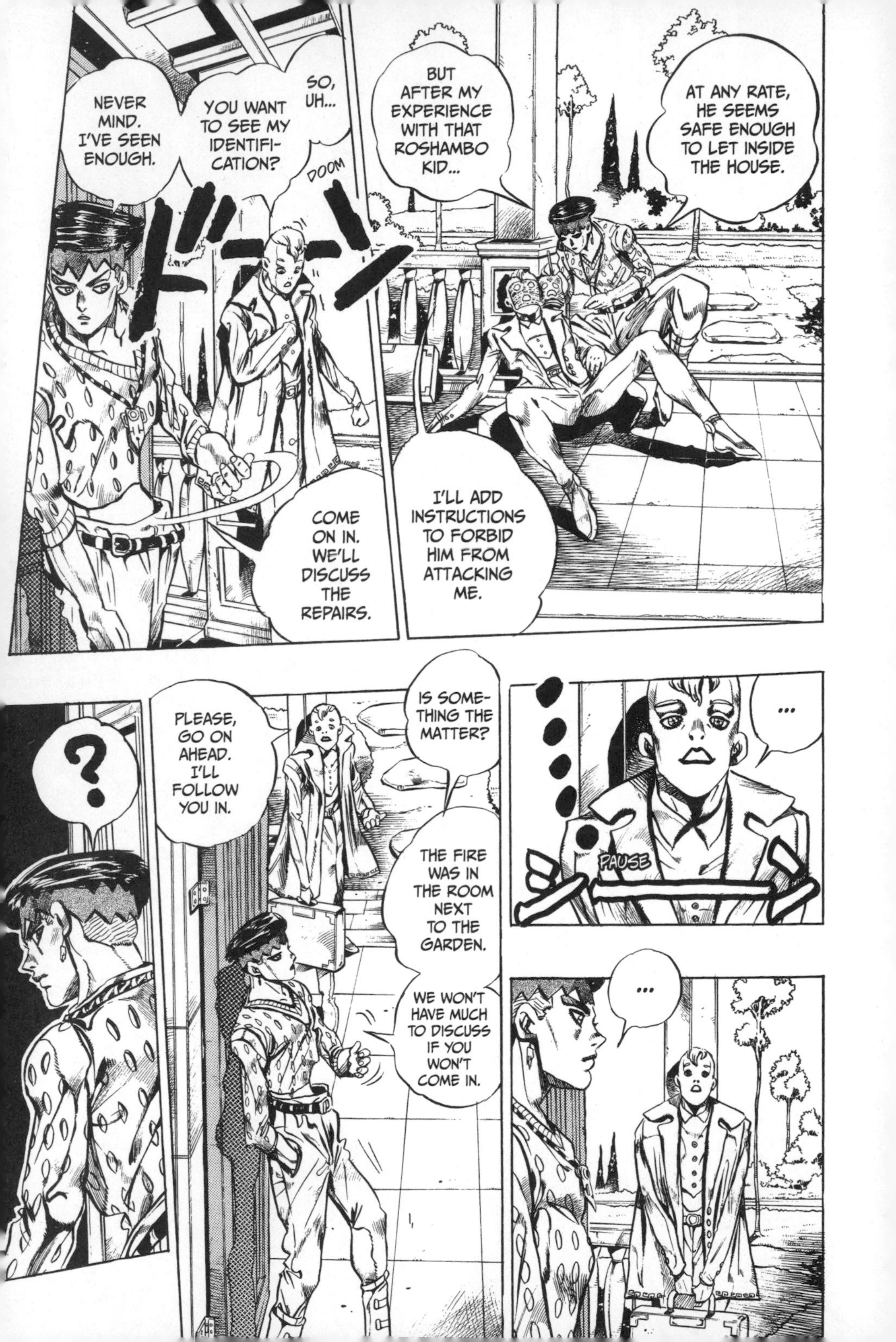
AT ANY RATE, HE SEEMS SAFE ENOUGH TO LET INSIDE THE HOUSE.
BUT AFTER MY EXPERIENCE WITH THAT ROSHAMBO KID...
I'LL ADD INSTRUCTIONS TO FORBID HIM FROM ATTACKING ME.
SO, UH...
YOU WANT TO SEE MY IDENTIFI-CATION?
NEVER MIND. I'VE SEEN ENOUGH.
DOOM
ドーン
COME ON IN. WE'LL DISCUSS THE REPAIRS.
...
PAUSE
...
IS SOME-THING THE MATTER?
THE FIRE WAS IN THE ROOM NEXT TO THE GARDEN.
WE WON'T HAVE MUCH TO DISCUSS IF YOU WON'T COME IN.
?
PLEASE, GO ON AHEAD. I'LL FOLLOW YOU IN.

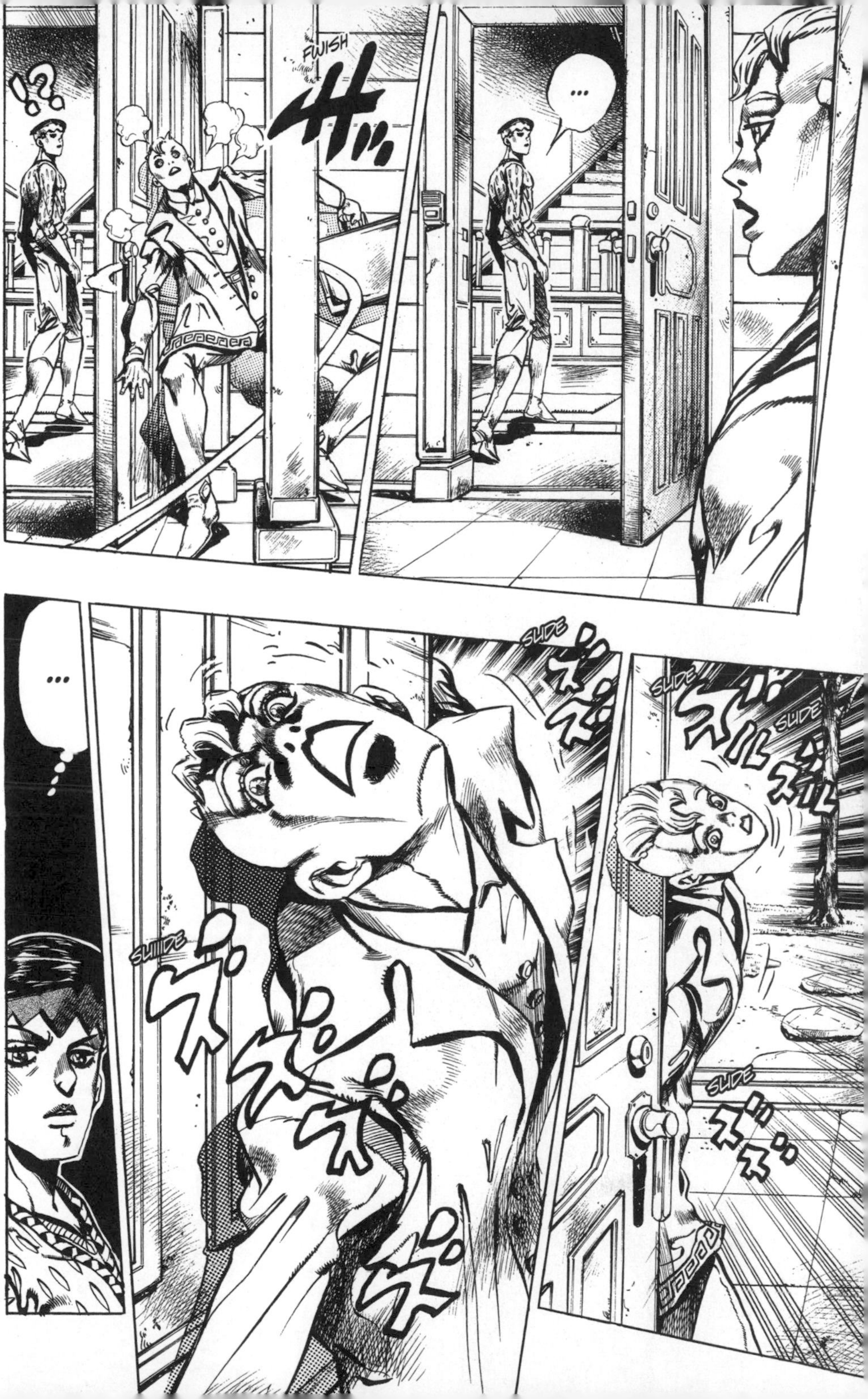
...
!?
FWISH
SLIDE
SLIDE
SLIDE
SLIDE
SLIIIDE
...

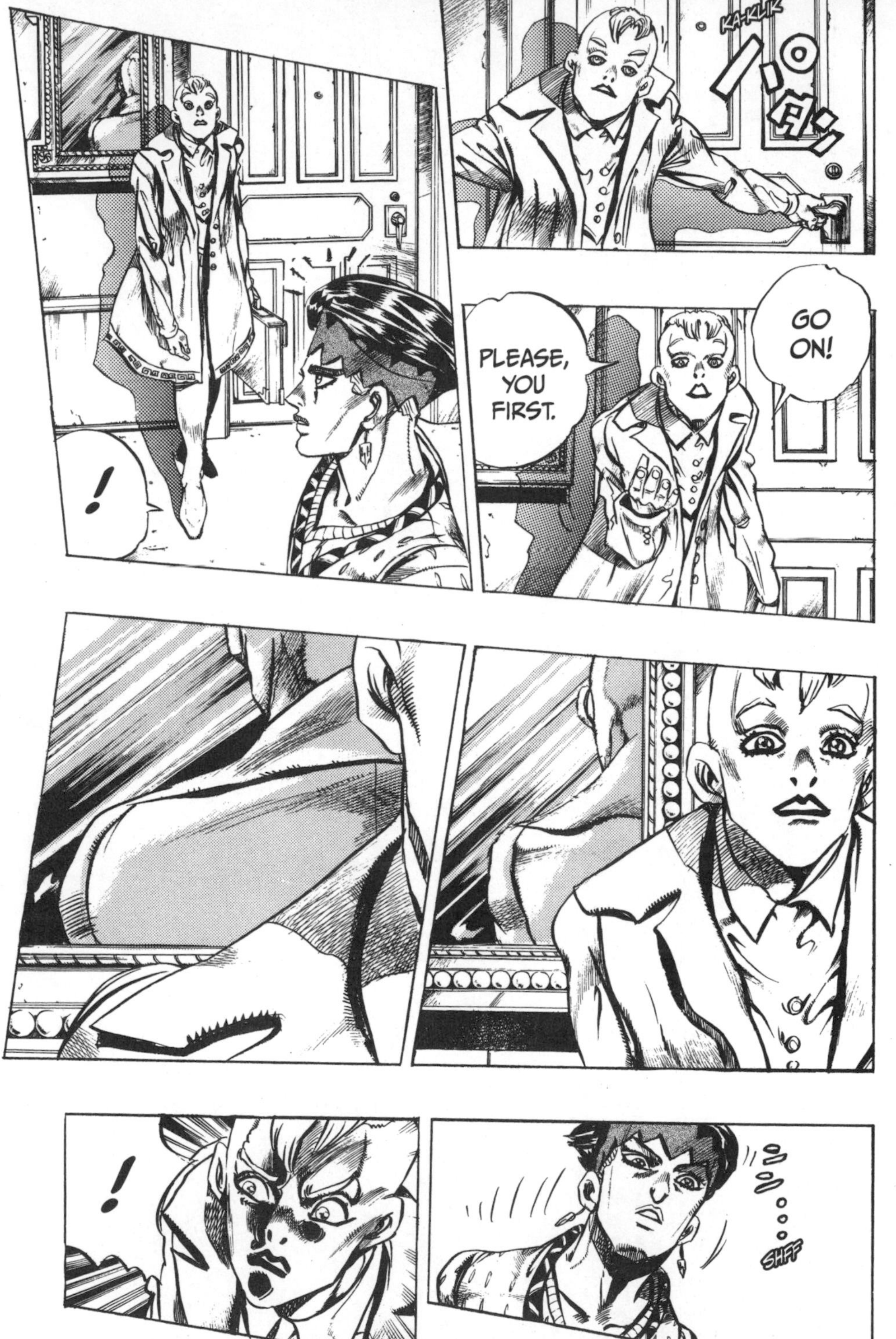
KA-KLIK
GO ON!
PLEASE, YOU FIRST.
!
SHFF
!

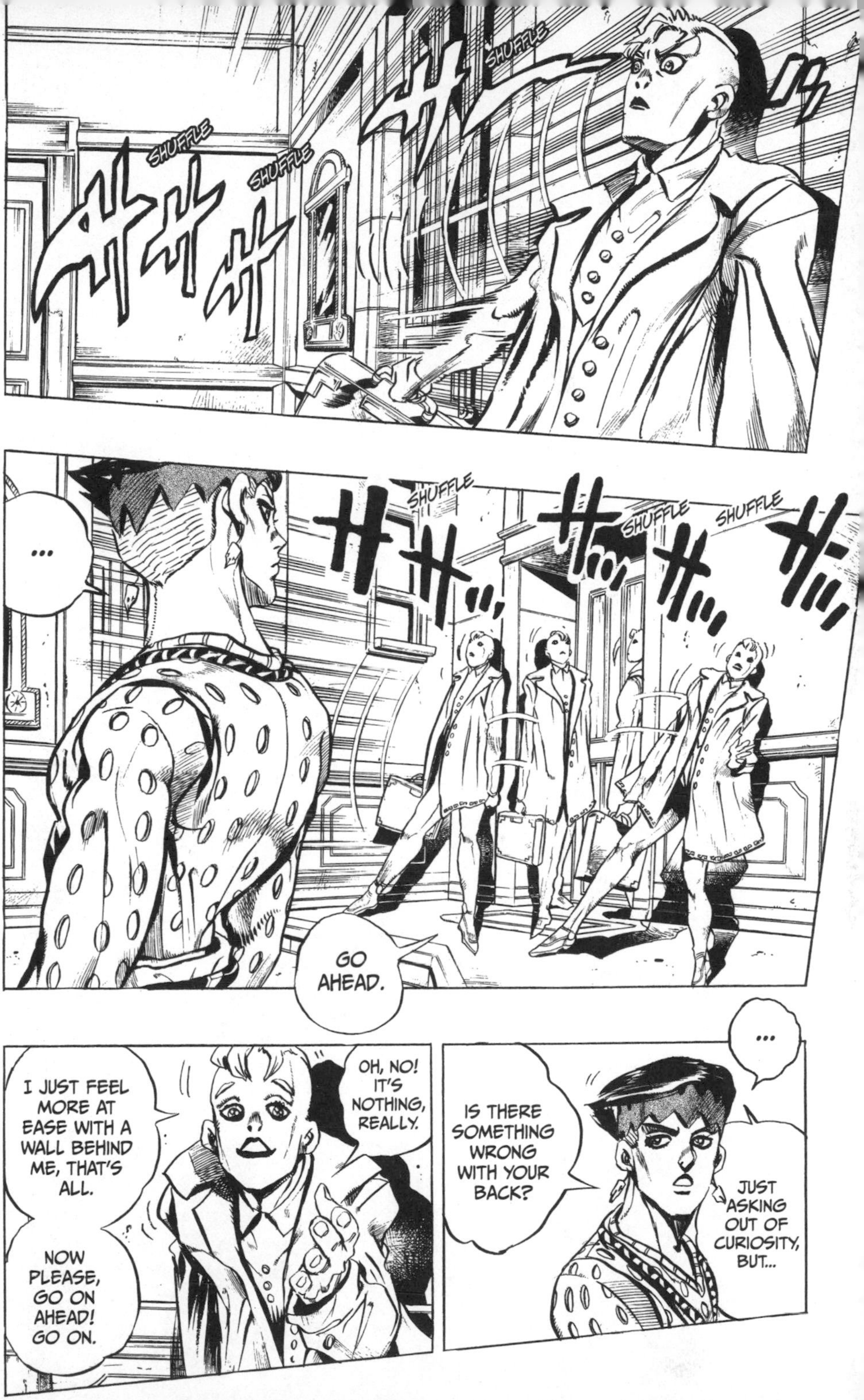
SHUFFLE
SHUFFLE
SHUFFLE
SHUFFLE
SHUFFLE
SHUFFLE
...
GO AHEAD.
...
IS THERE SOMETHING WRONG WITH YOUR BACK?
JUST ASKING OUT OF CURIOSITY, BUT...
OH, NO! IT'S NOTHING, REALLY.
I JUST FEEL MORE AT EASE WITH A WALL BEHIND ME, THAT'S ALL.
NOW PLEASE, GO ON AHEAD! GO ON.

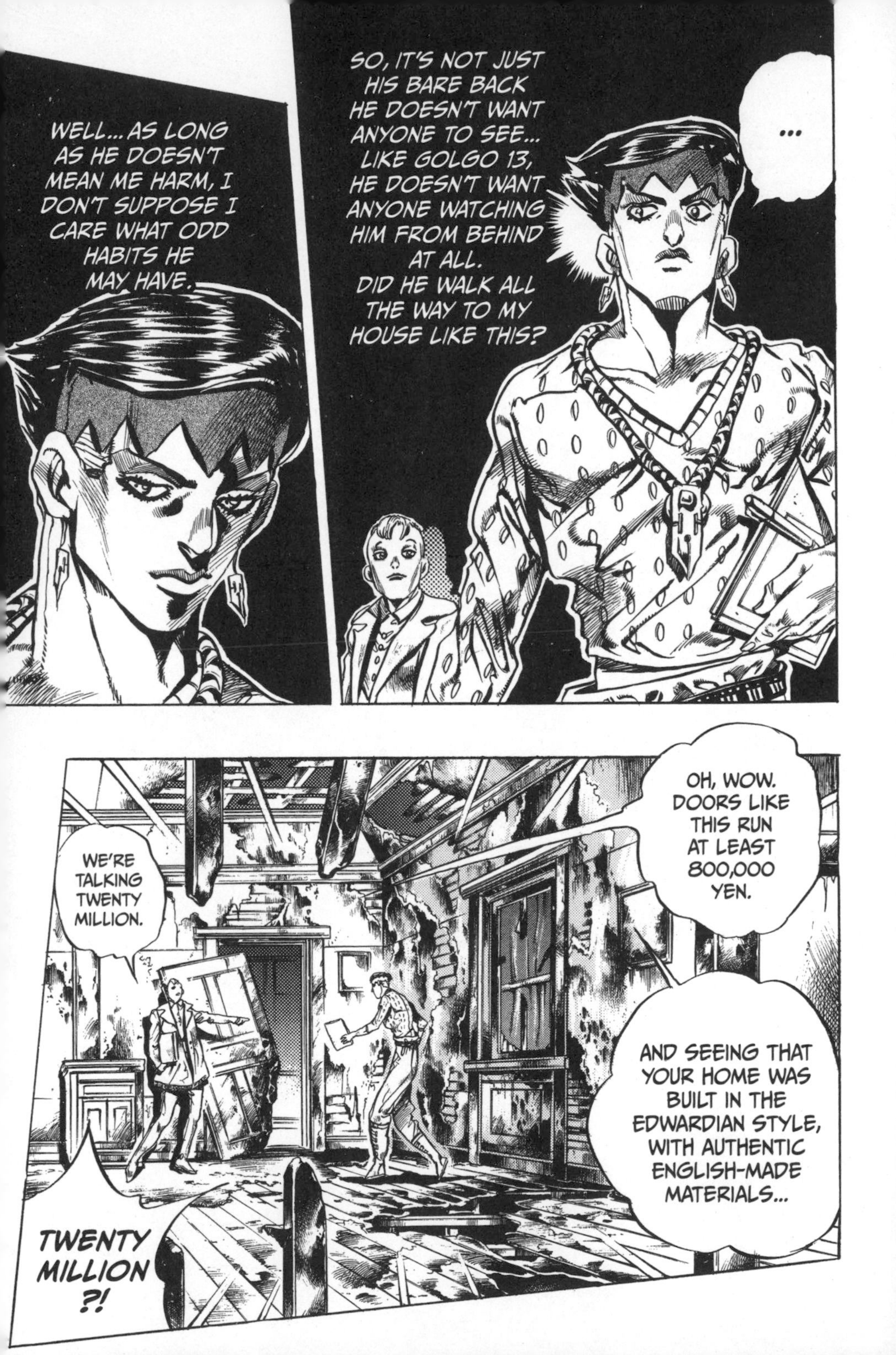
...
SO, IT'S NOT JUST HIS BARE BACK HE DOESN'T WANT ANYONE TO SEE... LIKE GOLGO 13, HE DOESN'T WANT ANYONE WATCHING HIM FROM BEHIND AT ALL. DID HE WALK ALL THE WAY TO MY HOUSE LIKE THIS?
WELL... AS LONG AS HE DOESN'T MEAN ME HARM, I DON'T SUPPOSE I CARE WHAT ODD HABITS HE MAY HAVE.
OH, WOW. DOORS LIKE THIS RUN AT LEAST 800,000 YEN.
WE'RE TALKING TWENTY MILLION.
AND SEEING THAT YOUR HOME WAS BUILT IN THE EDWARDIAN STYLE, WITH AUTHENTIC ENGLISH-MADE MATERIALS...
TWENTY MILLION ?!

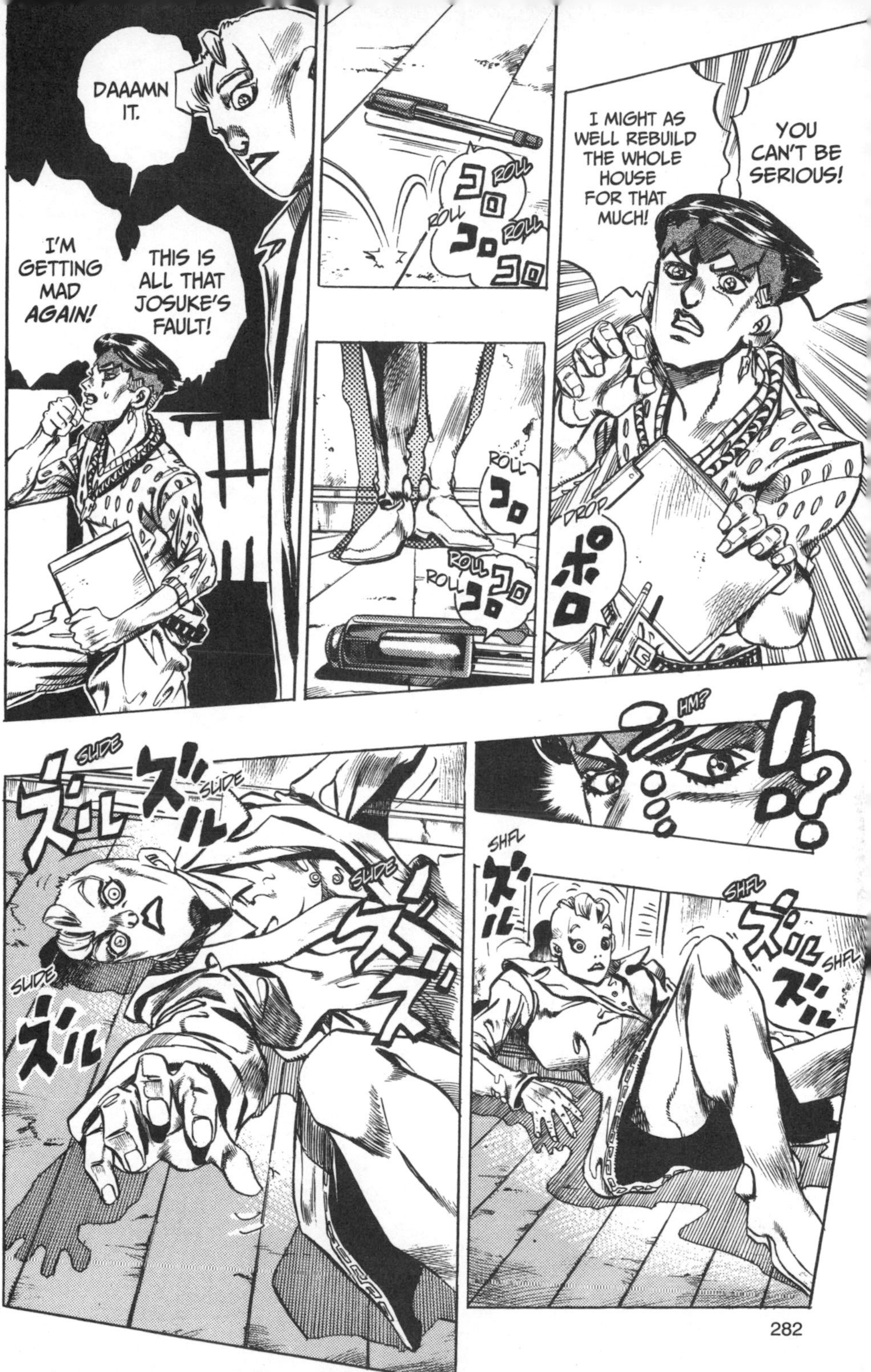
YOU CAN'T BE SERIOUS!
I MIGHT AS WELL REBUILD THE WHOLE HOUSE FOR THAT MUCH!
DROP
ポロ
ROLL
コロ
ROLL
コロ
ROLL
コロ
ROLL
コロ
ROLL
コロ
ROLL
コロ
DAAAMN IT.
THIS IS ALL THAT JOSUKE'S FAULT!
I'M GETTING MAD AGAIN!
HM?
!?
SHFL
ズル
SHFL
SHFL
ズル
SLIDE
ズル
SLIDE
ズル
SLIDE
SLIDE
ズル

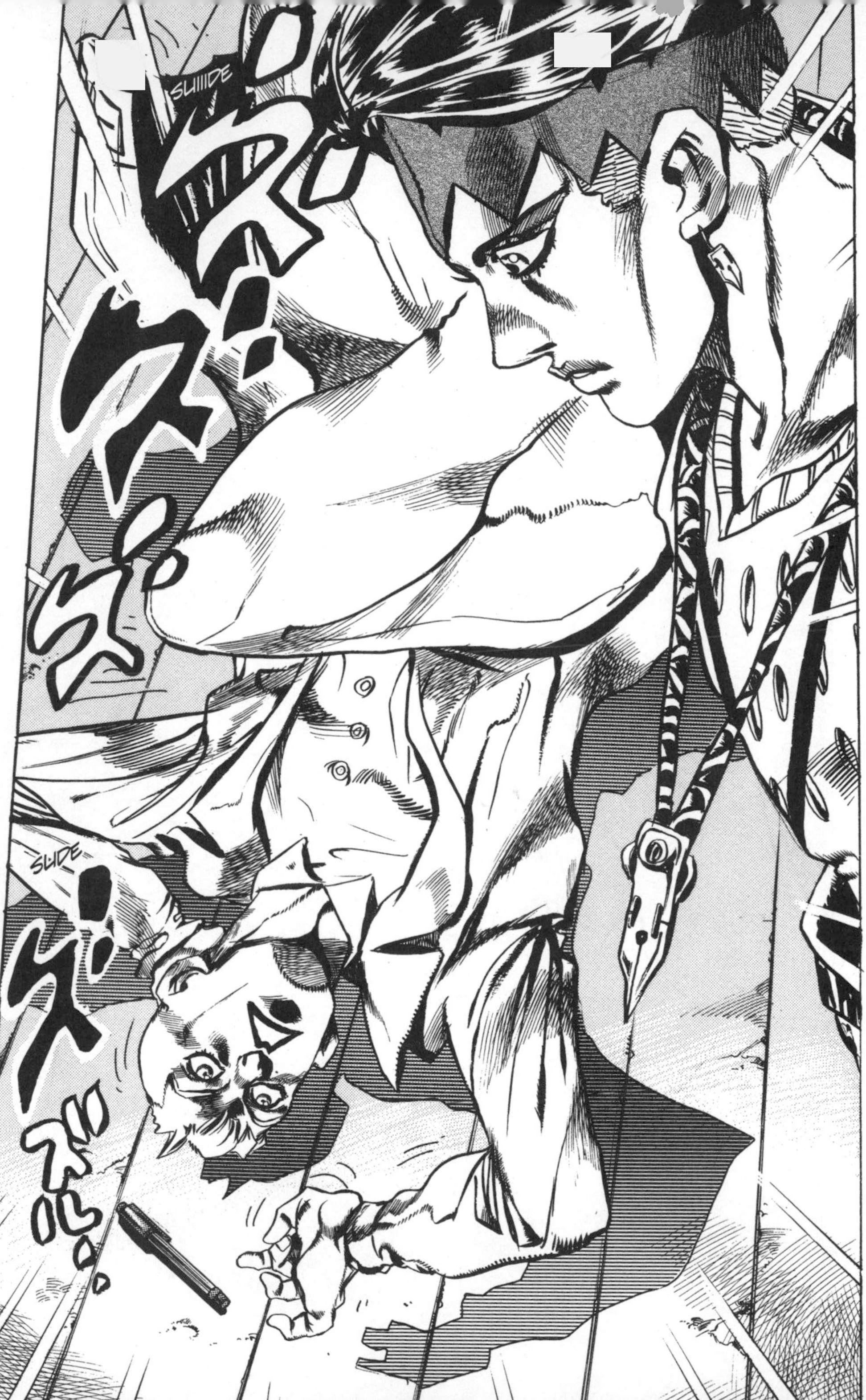
SLIIIDE
SLIDE

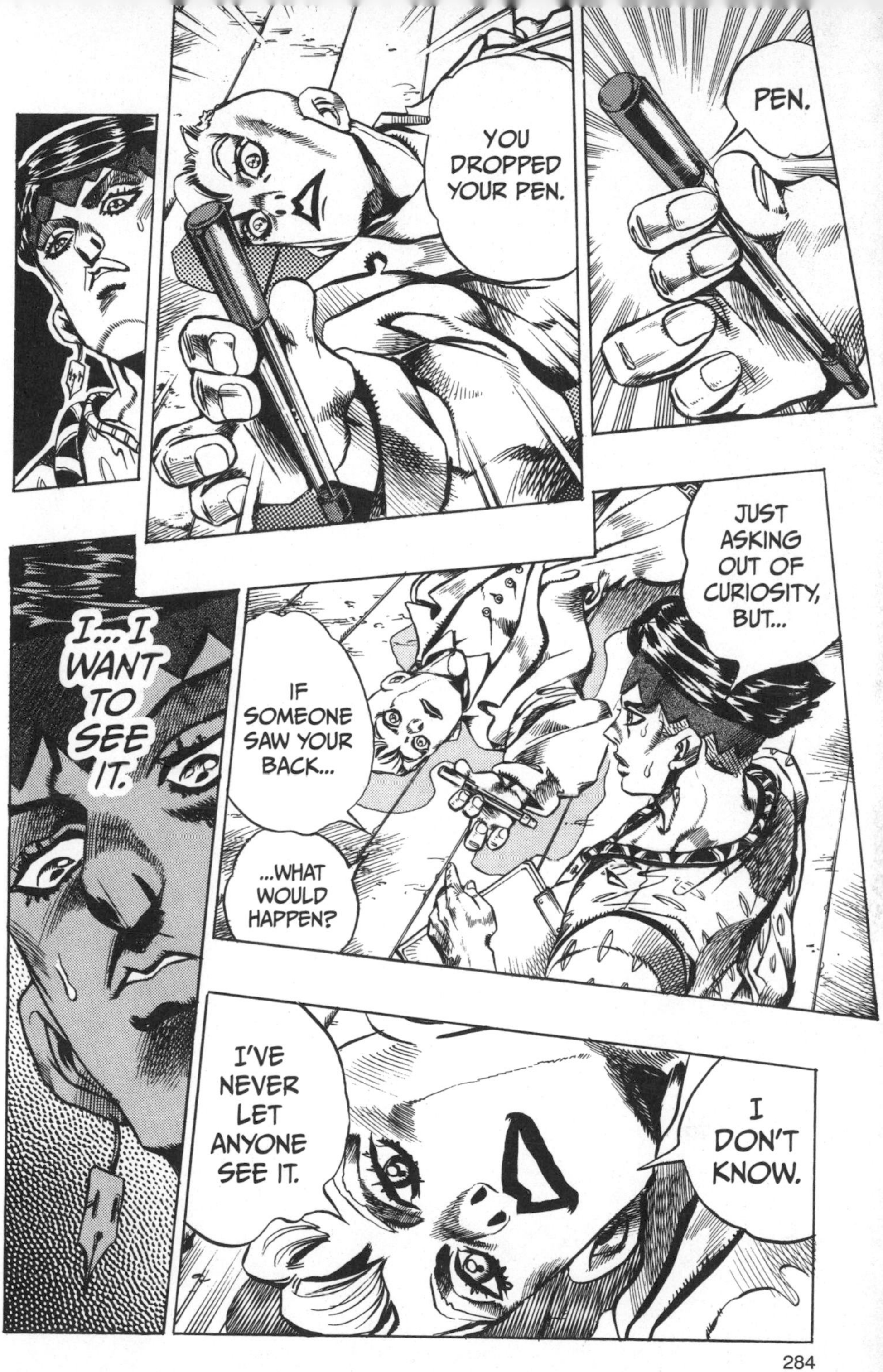

PEN.
YOU DROPPED YOUR PEN.
JUST ASKING OUT OF CURIOSITY, BUT...
IF SOMEONE SAW YOUR BACK...
...WHAT WOULD HAPPEN?
I DON'T KNOW.
I'VE NEVER LET ANYONE SEE IT.
I... I WANT TO SEE IT.

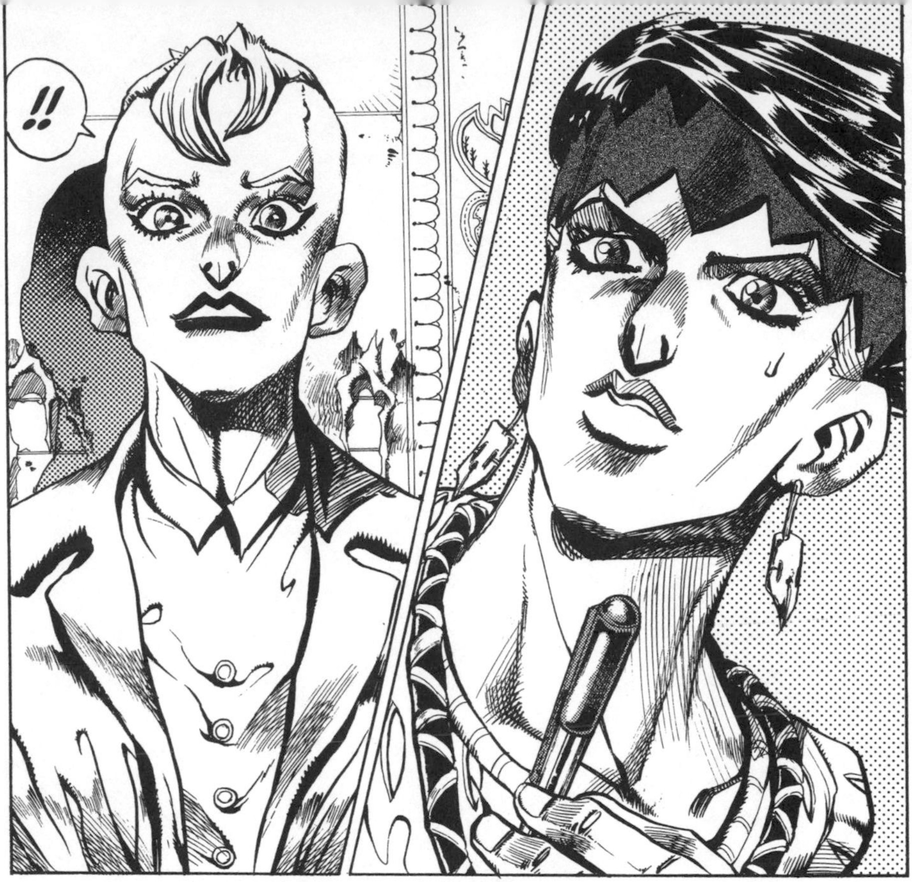
!!

CHAPTER 148 ★ CHEAP TRAP, PART 2

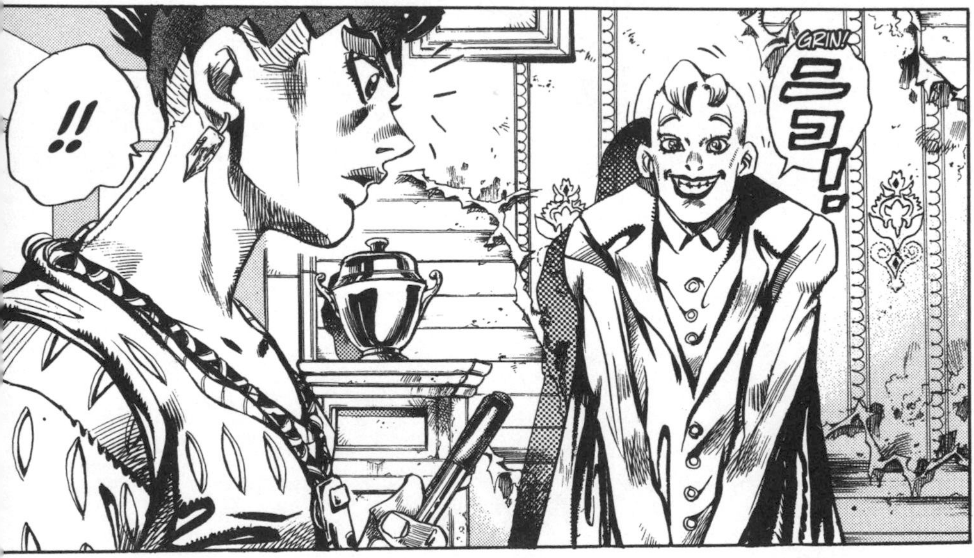
GRIN!
!!

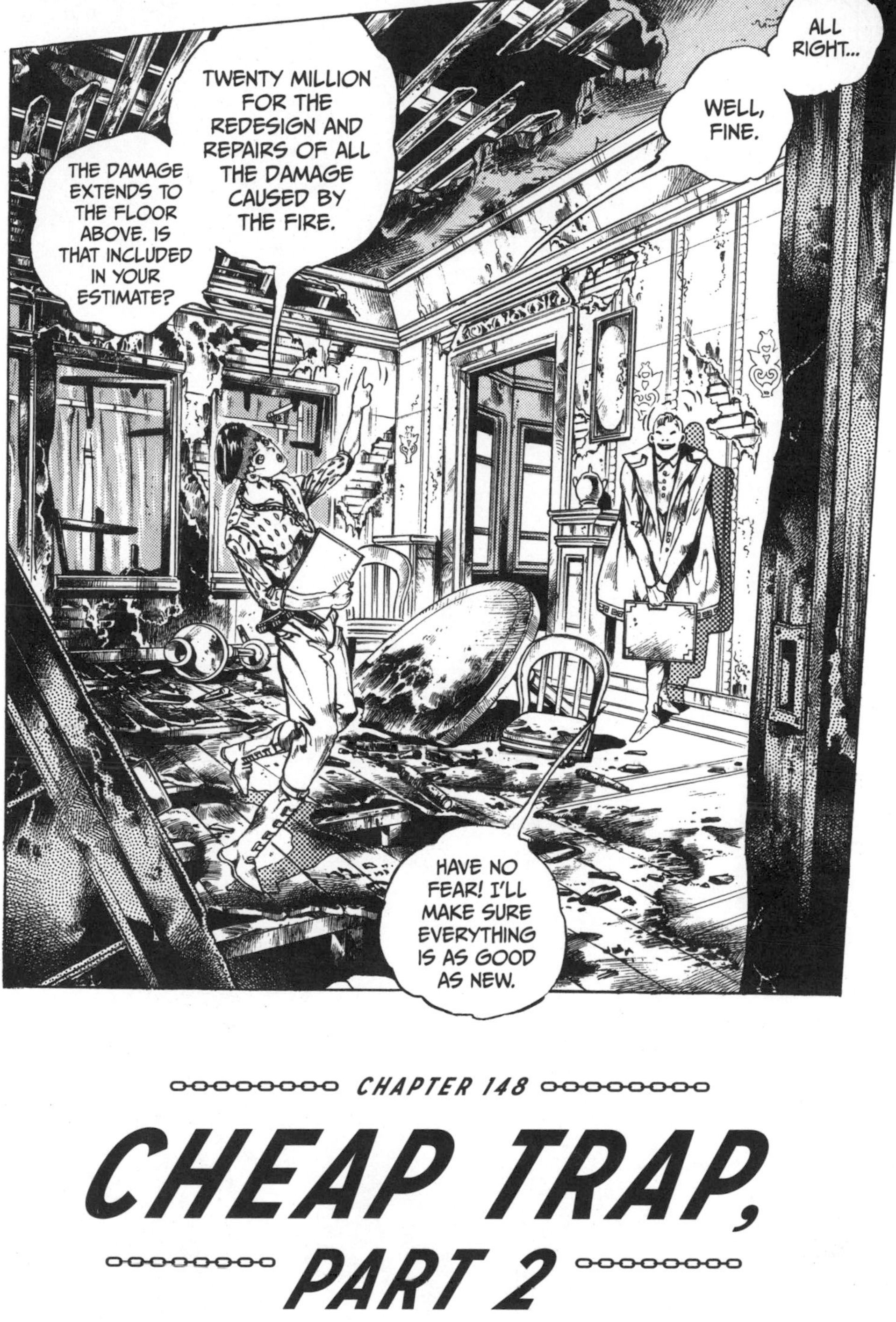
ALL RIGHT...
WELL, FINE.
TWENTY MILLION FOR THE REDESIGN AND REPAIRS OF ALL THE DAMAGE CAUSED BY THE FIRE.
THE DAMAGE EXTENDS TO THE FLOOR ABOVE. IS THAT INCLUDED IN YOUR ESTIMATE?
HAVE NO FEAR! I'LL MAKE SURE EVERYTHING IS AS GOOD AS NEW.

CHAPTER 148

CHEAP TRAP, PART 2

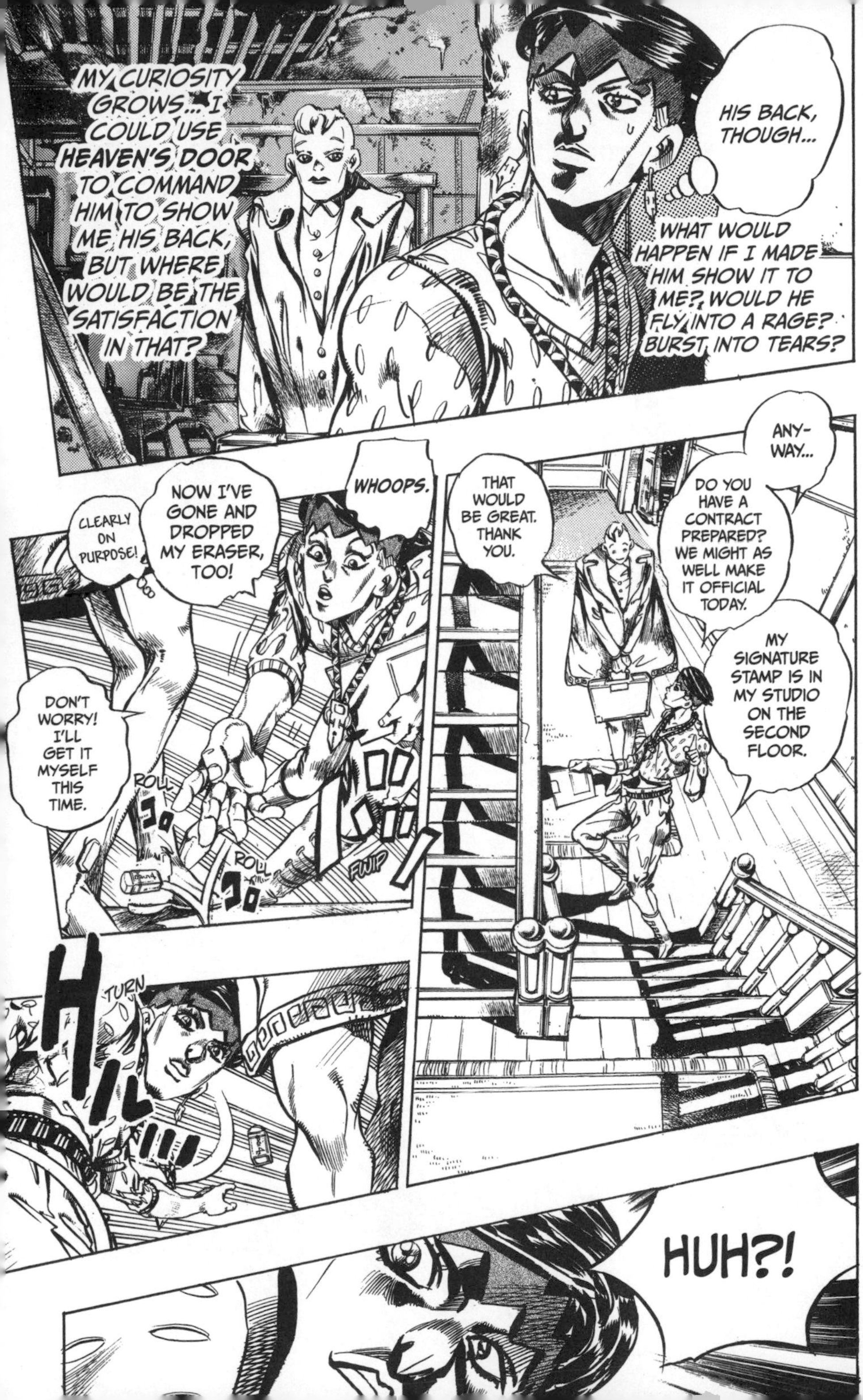
HIS BACK, THOUGH...
WHAT WOULD HAPPEN IF I MADE HIM SHOW IT TO ME? WOULD HE FLY INTO A RAGE? BURST INTO TEARS?
MY CURIOSITY GROWS... I COULD USE HEAVEN'S DOOR TO COMMAND HIM TO SHOW ME HIS BACK, BUT WHERE WOULD BE THE SATISFACTION IN THAT?
ANY-WAY...
DO YOU HAVE A CONTRACT PREPARED? WE MIGHT AS WELL MAKE IT OFFICIAL TODAY.
MY SIGNATURE STAMP IS IN MY STUDIO ON THE SECOND FLOOR.
THAT WOULD BE GREAT. THANK YOU.
WHOOPS.
NOW I'VE GONE AND DROPPED MY ERASER, TOO!
CLEARLY ON PURPOSE!
DON'T WORRY! I'LL GET IT MYSELF THIS TIME.
ROLL
FWIP
ROLL
TURN
HUH?!

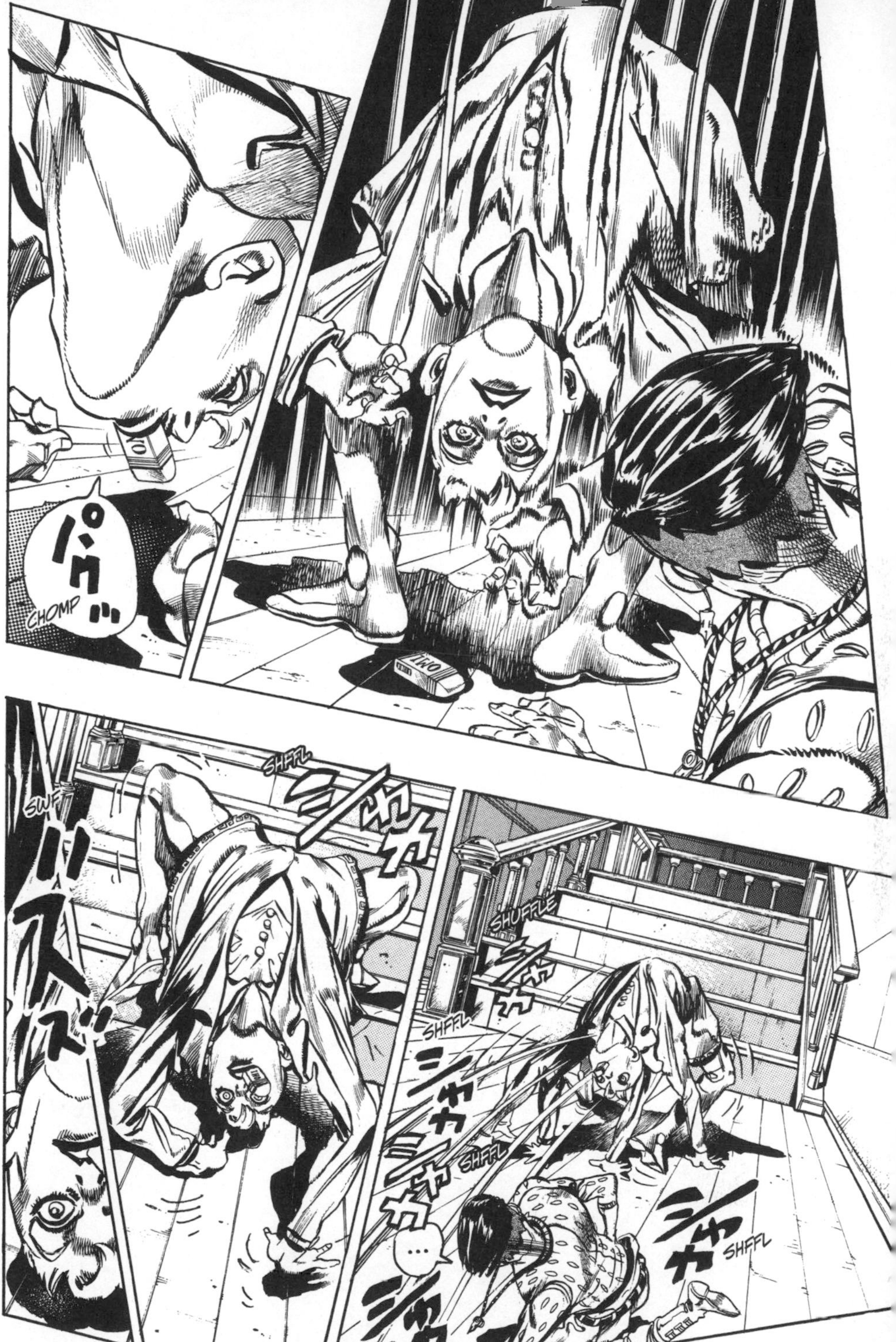
TWO
パクッ
CHOMP
SHUFFLE
SHFFL
SHFFL
…
シャカ
SHFFL
SHFFL
SHFFL
SWF

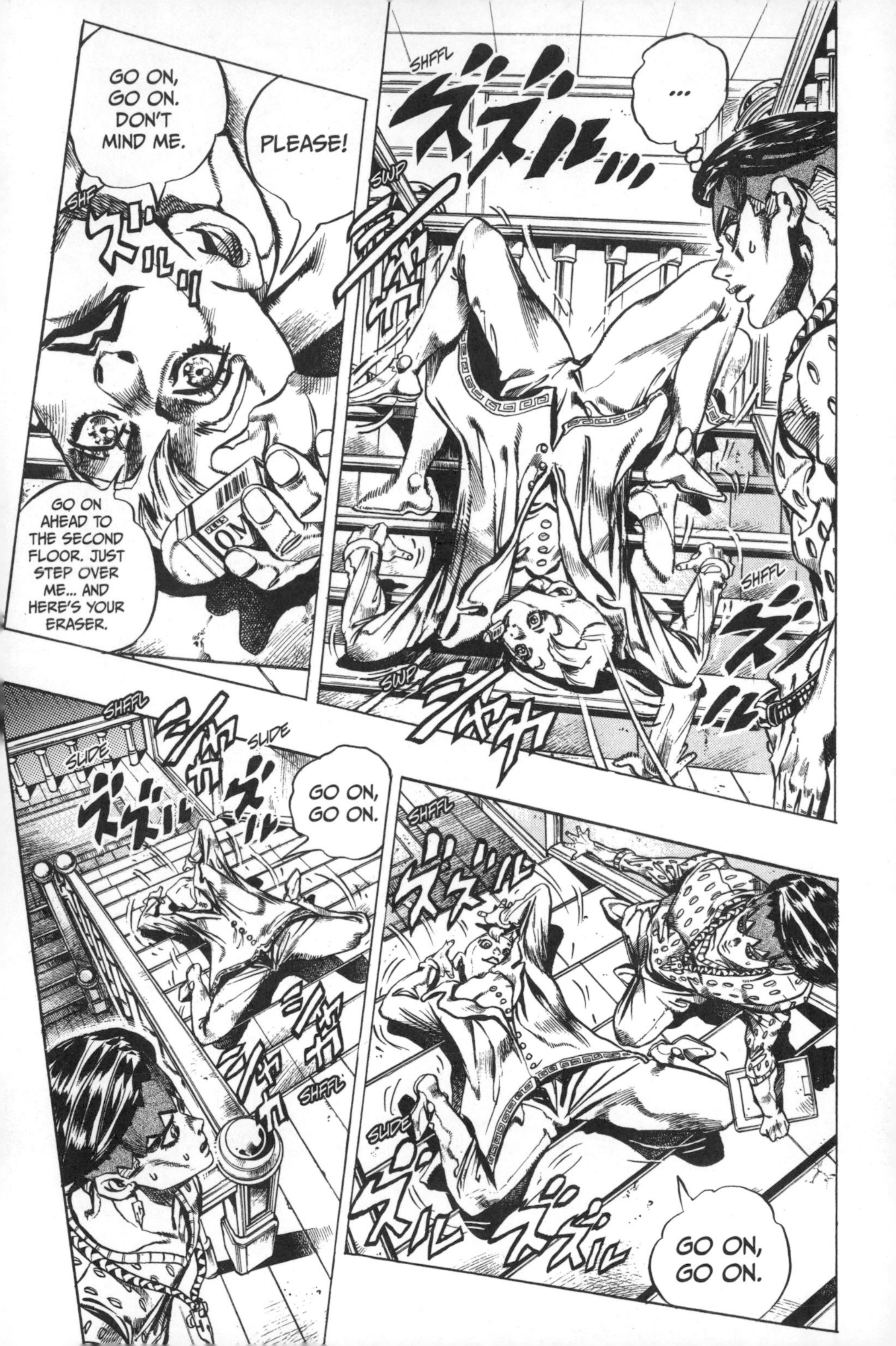
SHFFL
...
SWP
SHFFL
SWP
PLEASE!
GO ON, GO ON. DON'T MIND ME.
SHF
GO ON AHEAD TO THE SECOND FLOOR. JUST STEP OVER ME... AND HERE'S YOUR ERASER.
SHFFL
SLIDE
GO ON, GO ON.
SHFFL
SLIDE
SLIDE
GO ON, GO ON.
SHFFL

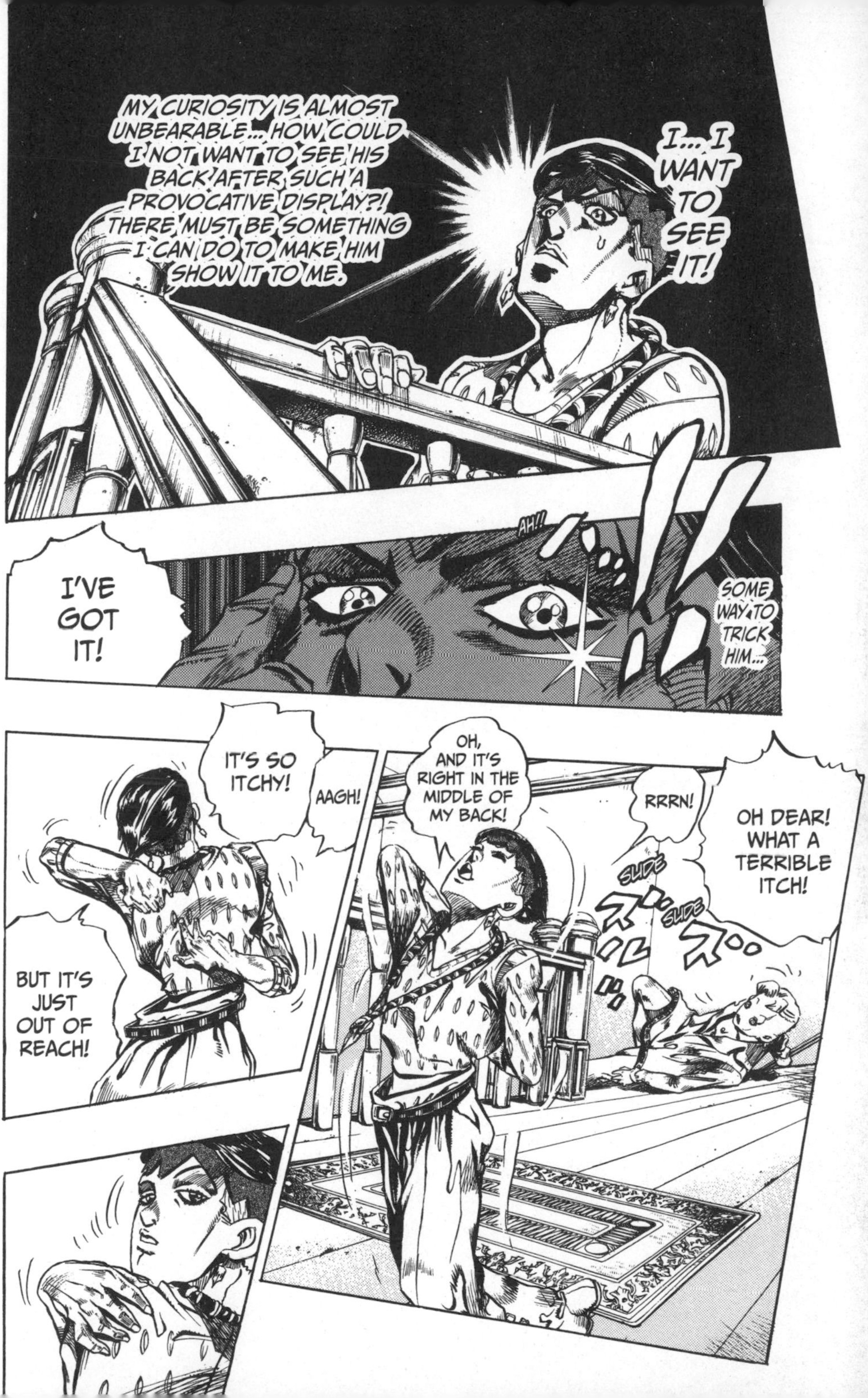
I... I WANT TO SEE IT!
MY CURIOSITY IS ALMOST UNBEARABLE... HOW COULD I NOT WANT TO SEE HIS BACK AFTER SUCH A PROVOCATIVE DISPLAY?! THERE MUST BE SOMETHING I CAN DO TO MAKE HIM SHOW IT TO ME.
AH!!
SOME WAY TO TRICK HIM...
I'VE GOT IT!
OH DEAR! WHAT A TERRIBLE ITCH!
RRRN!
SLIDE
SLIDE
OH, AND IT'S RIGHT IN THE MIDDLE OF MY BACK!
AAGH!
IT'S SO ITCHY!
BUT IT'S JUST OUT OF REACH!

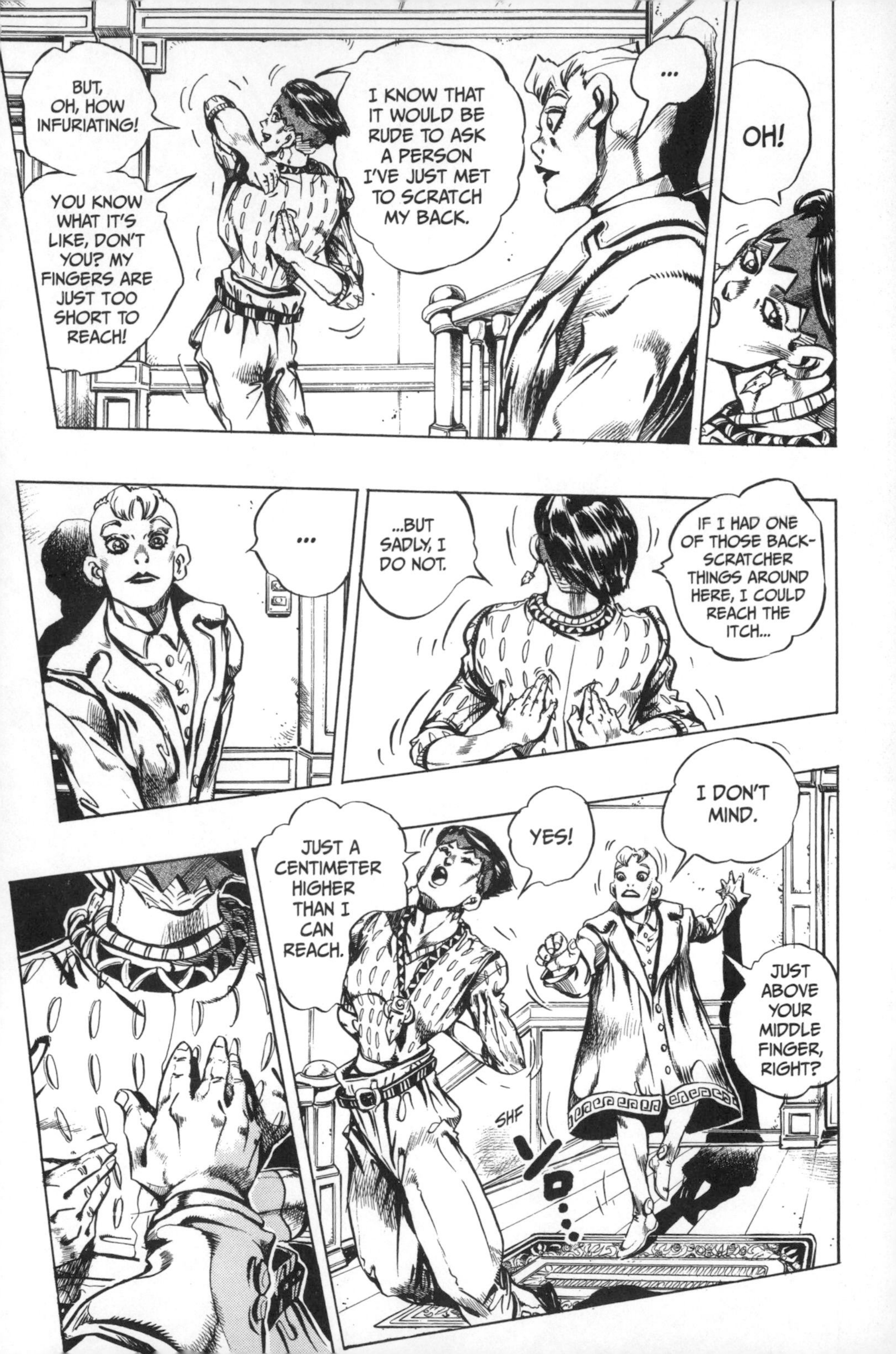
OH!
...
I KNOW THAT IT WOULD BE RUDE TO ASK A PERSON I'VE JUST MET TO SCRATCH MY BACK.
BUT, OH, HOW INFURIATING!
YOU KNOW WHAT IT'S LIKE, DON'T YOU? MY FINGERS ARE JUST TOO SHORT TO REACH!
IF I HAD ONE OF THOSE BACK-SCRATCHER THINGS AROUND HERE, I COULD REACH THE ITCH...
...BUT SADLY, I DO NOT.
...
I DON'T MIND.
YES!
JUST A CENTIMETER HIGHER THAN I CAN REACH.
JUST ABOVE YOUR MIDDLE FINGER, RIGHT?
SHF

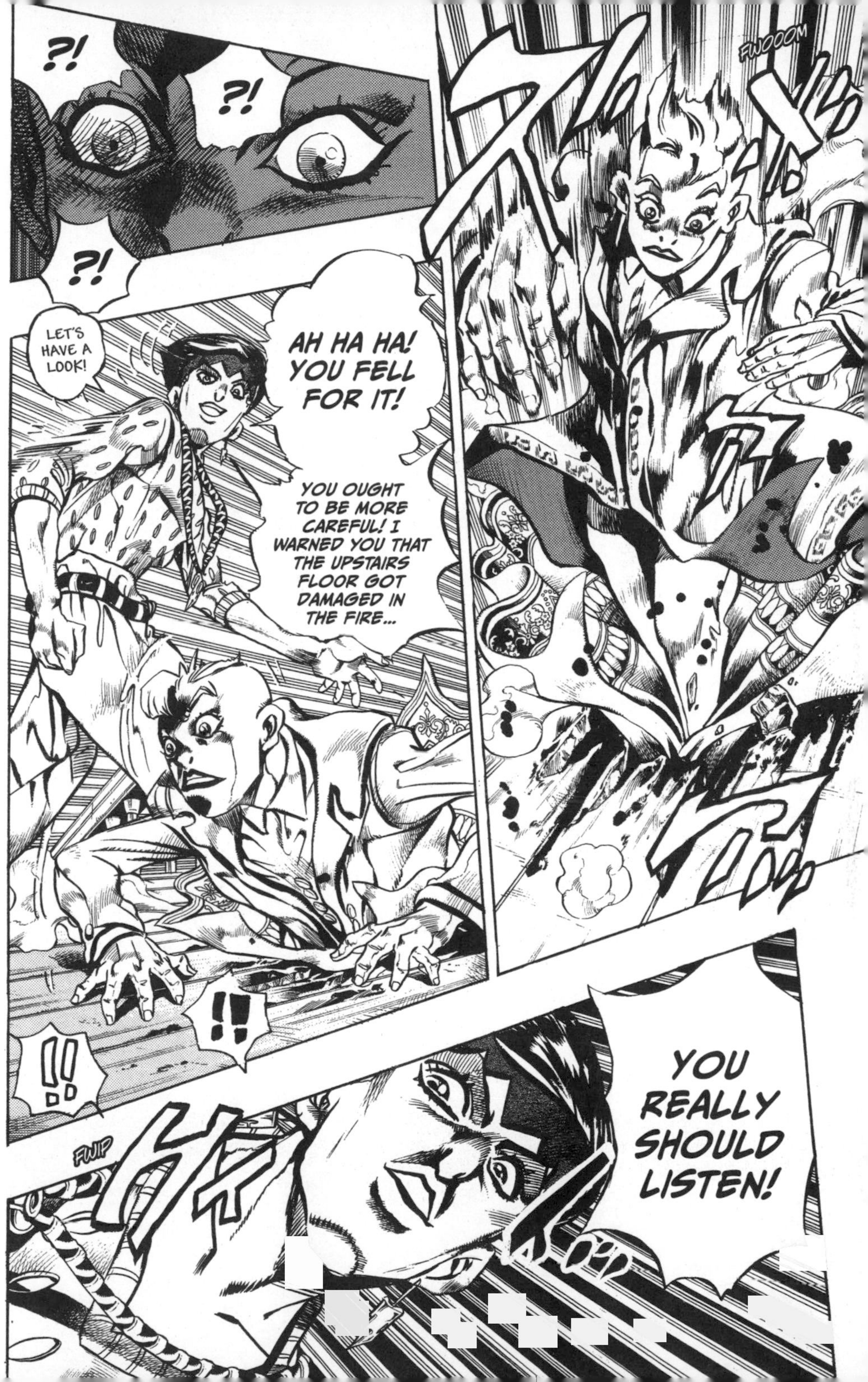
FWOOOM
?!
?!
?!
AH HA HA! YOU FELL FOR IT!
LET'S HAVE A LOOK!
YOU OUGHT TO BE MORE CAREFUL! I WARNED YOU THAT THE UPSTAIRS FLOOR GOT DAMAGED IN THE FIRE...
!!
!!
YOU REALLY SHOULD LISTEN!
FWIP

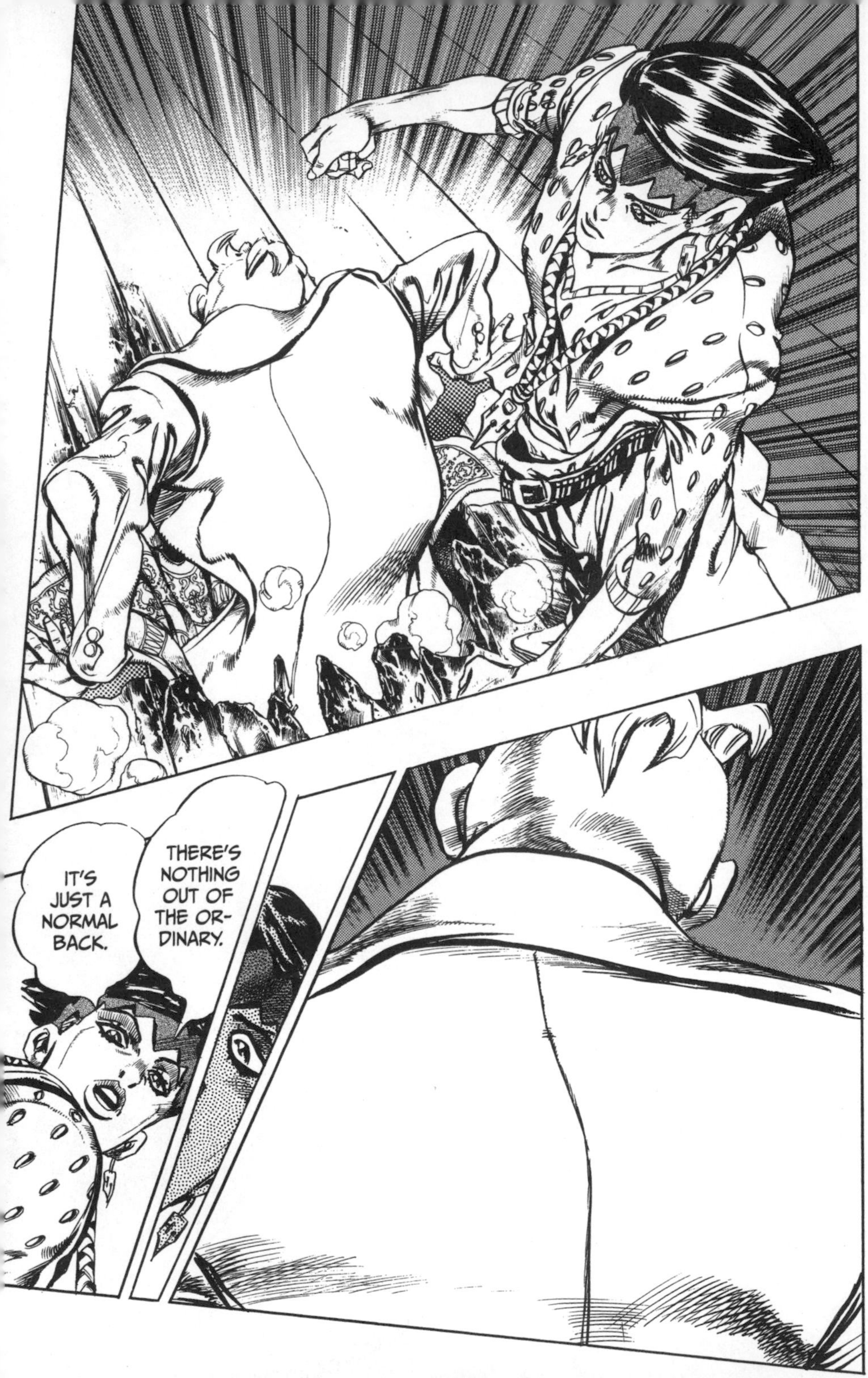
THERE'S NOTHING OUT OF THE OR-DINARY.
IT'S JUST A NORMAL BACK.

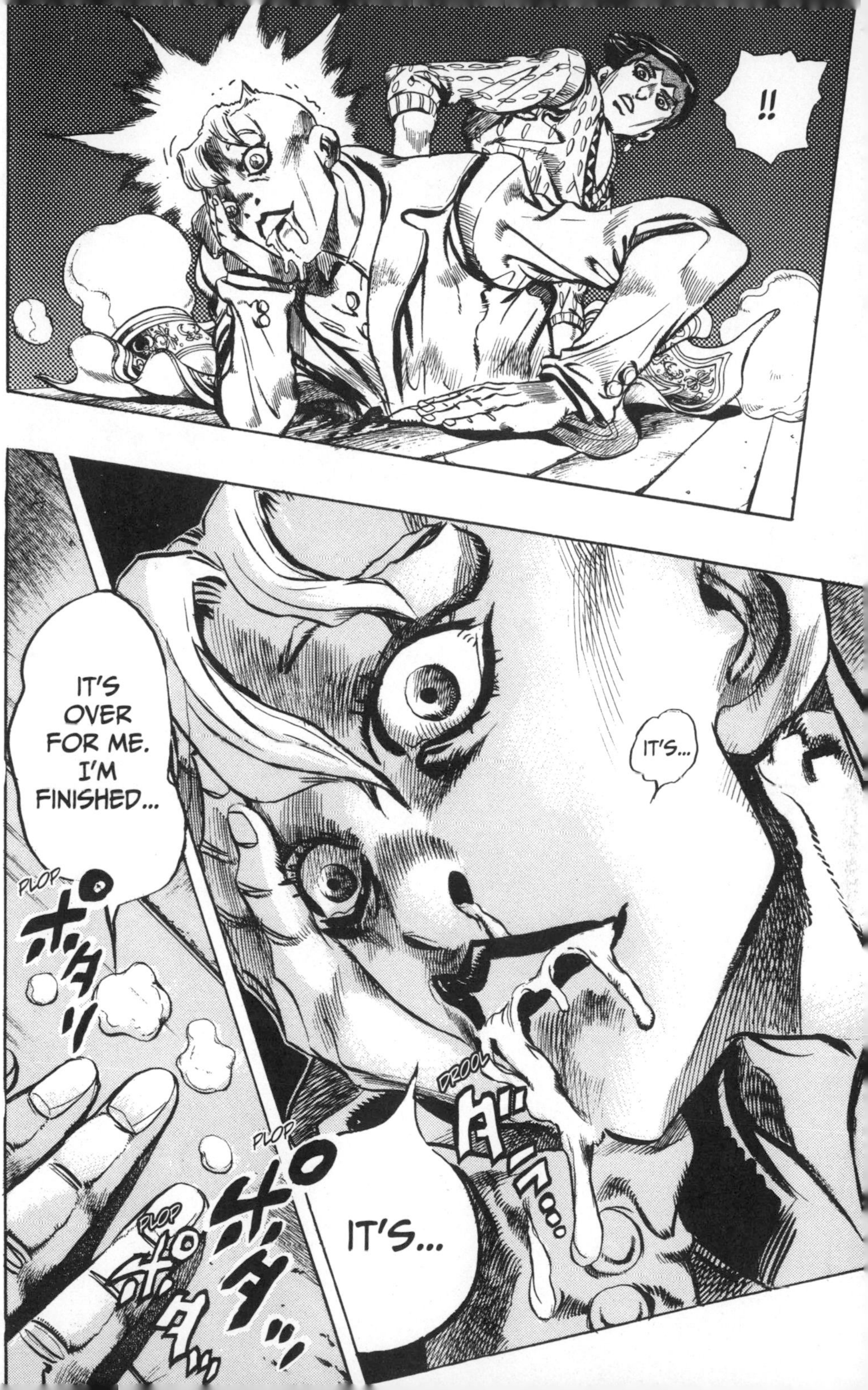
!!
IT'S...
IT'S OVER FOR ME. I'M FINISHED...
PLOP
DROOL
PLOP
IT'S...
PLOP

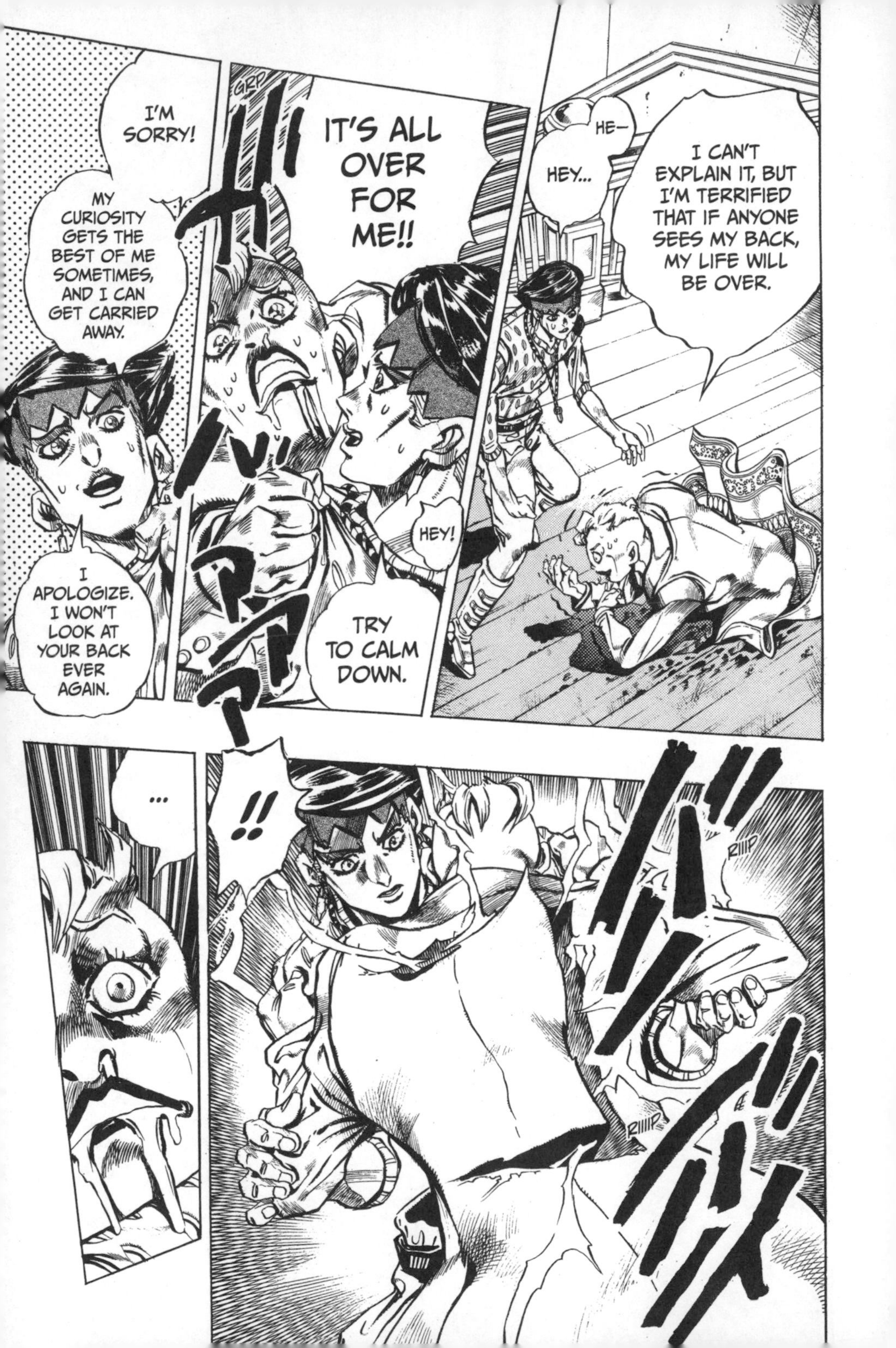
I CAN'T EXPLAIN IT, BUT I'M TERRIFIED THAT IF ANYONE SEES MY BACK, MY LIFE WILL BE OVER.
HE—
HEY...
IT'S ALL OVER FOR ME!!
GRP
HEY!
TRY TO CALM DOWN.
I'M SORRY!
MY CURIOSITY GETS THE BEST OF ME SOMETIMES, AND I CAN GET CARRIED AWAY.
I APOLOGIZE. I WON'T LOOK AT YOUR BACK EVER AGAIN.
!!
RIIIP
RIIIP
...

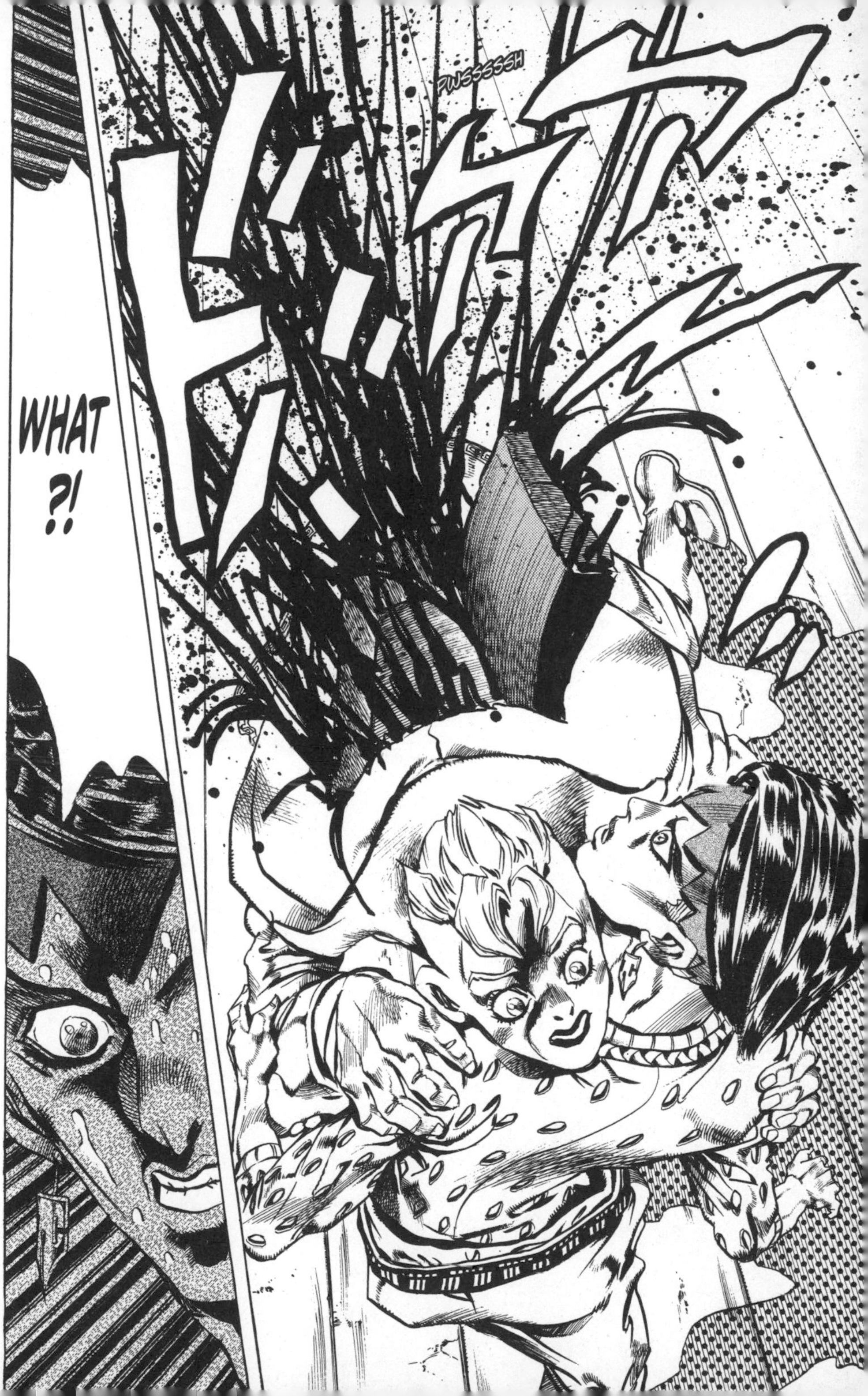
PWSSSSSH
WHAT ?!

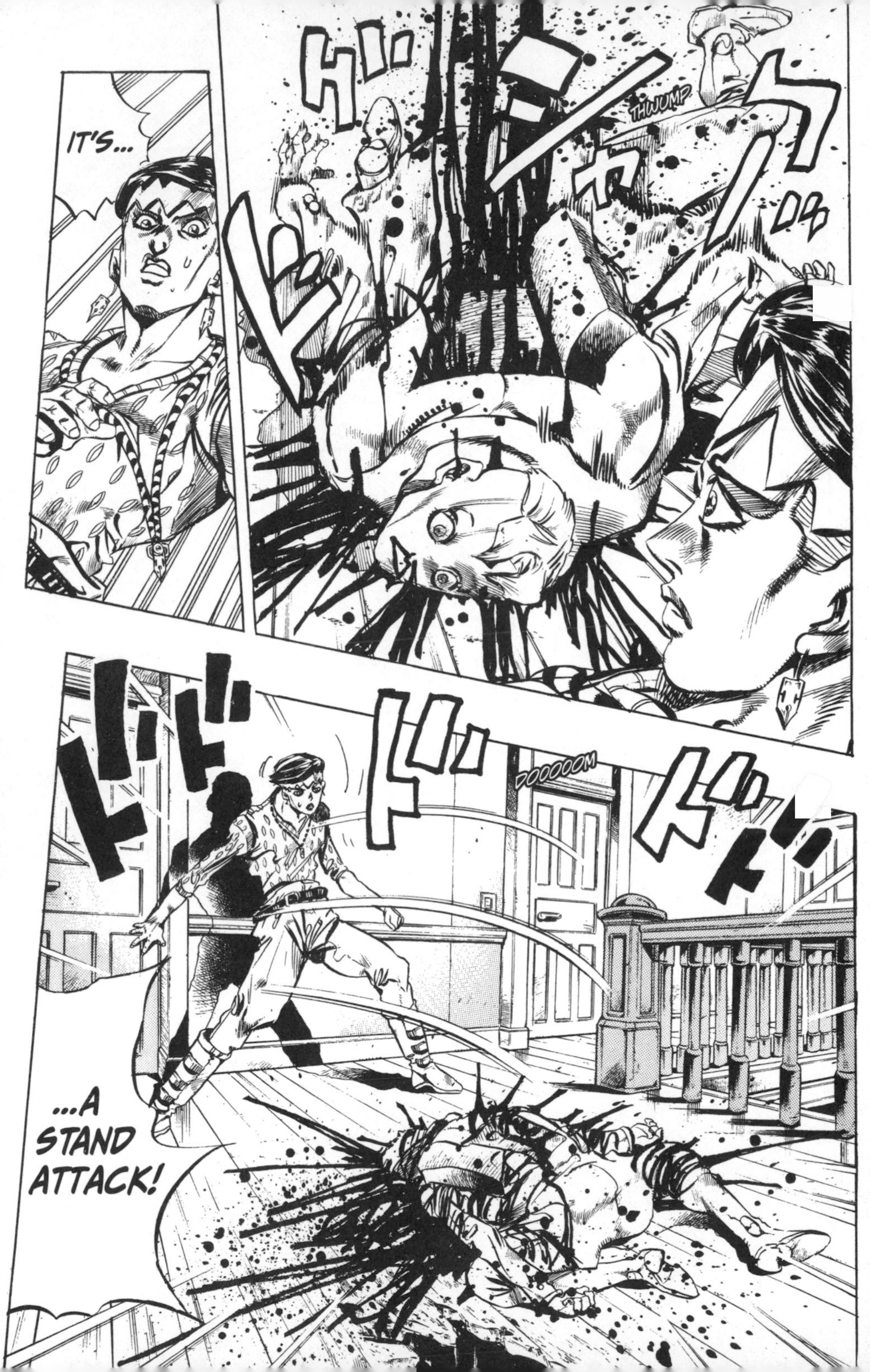
THWUMP
IT'S...
DOOOOOM
...A STAND ATTACK!

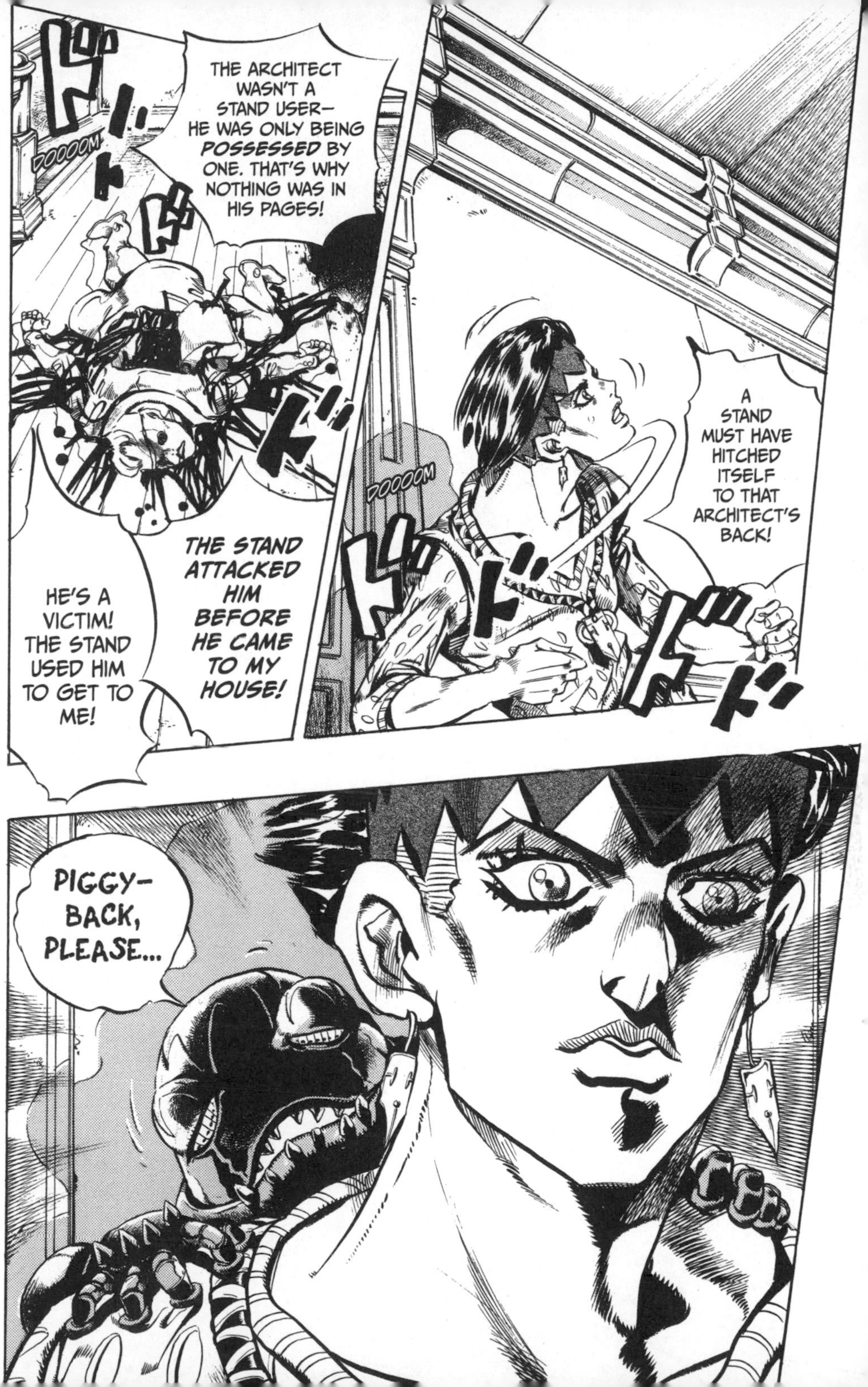
A STAND MUST HAVE HITCHED ITSELF TO THAT ARCHITECT'S BACK!
DOOOOM
THE ARCHITECT WASN'T A STAND USER— HE WAS ONLY BEING *POSSESSED* BY ONE. THAT'S WHY NOTHING WAS IN HIS PAGES!
DOOOOM
THE STAND ATTACKED HIM BEFORE HE CAME TO MY HOUSE!
HE'S A VICTIM! THE STAND USED HIM TO GET TO ME!
PIGGY-BACK, PLEASE...

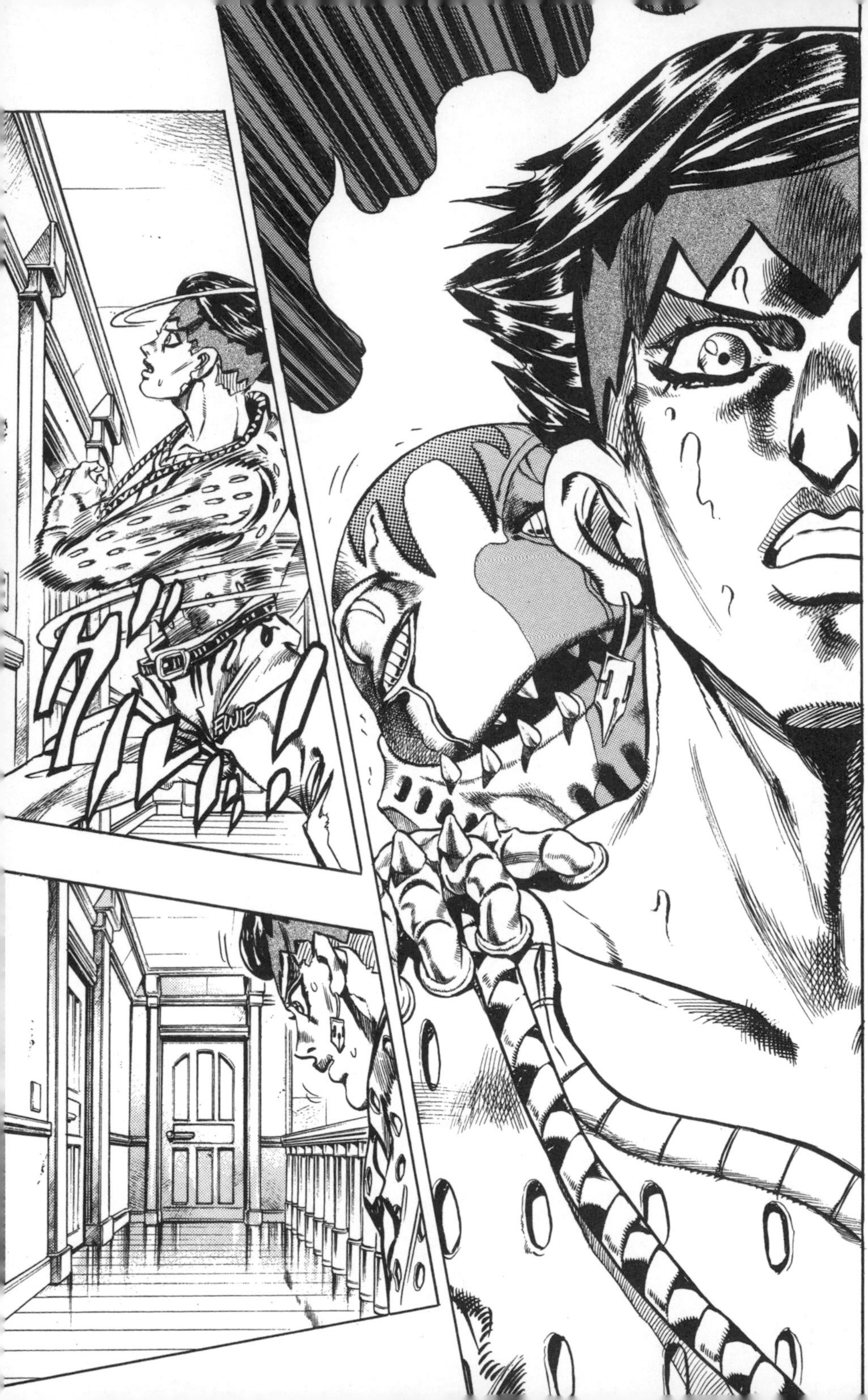
FWIP

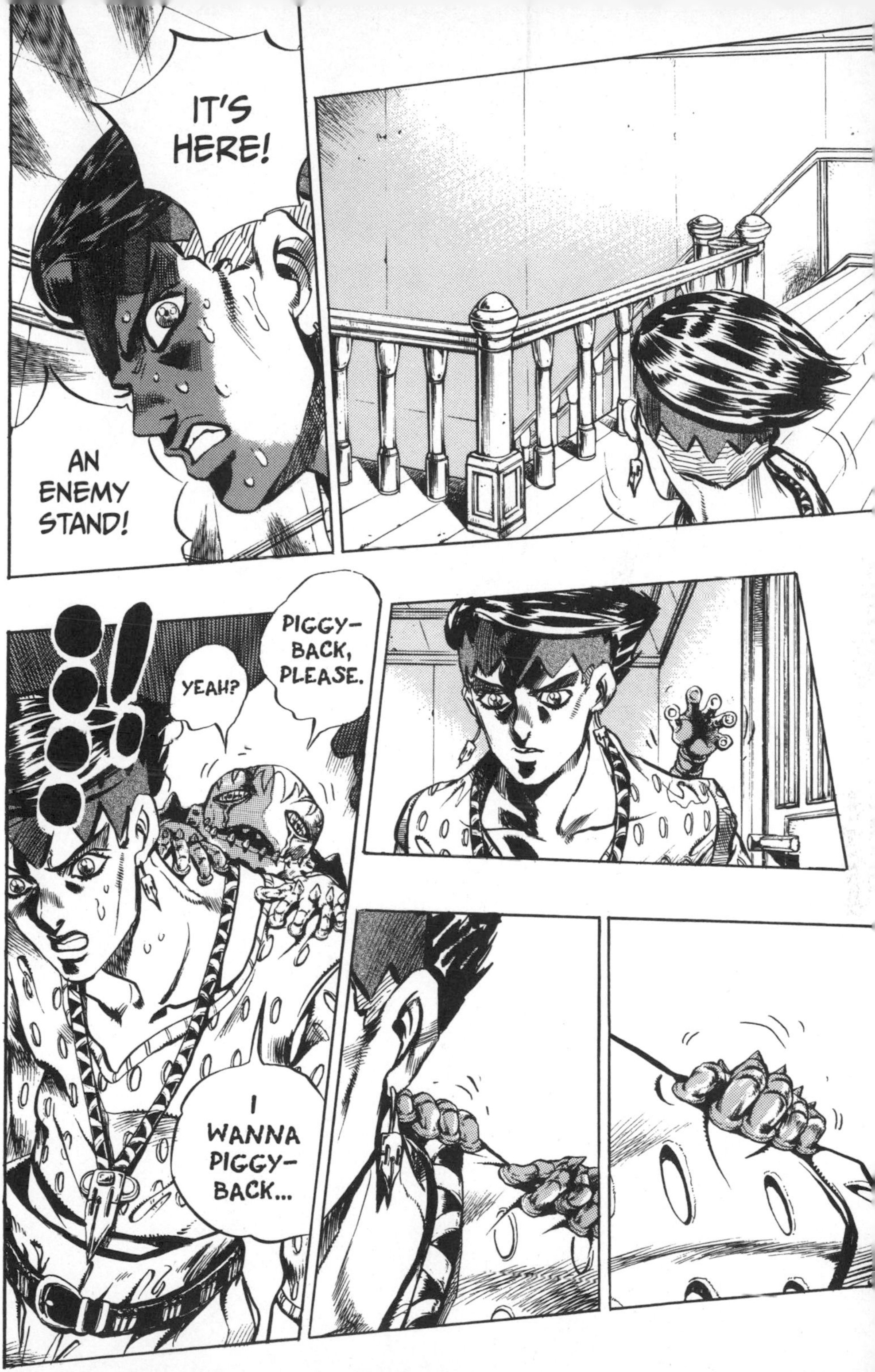
IT'S HERE!
AN ENEMY STAND!
PIGGY-BACK, PLEASE.
YEAH?
!!
I WANNA PIGGY-BACK...

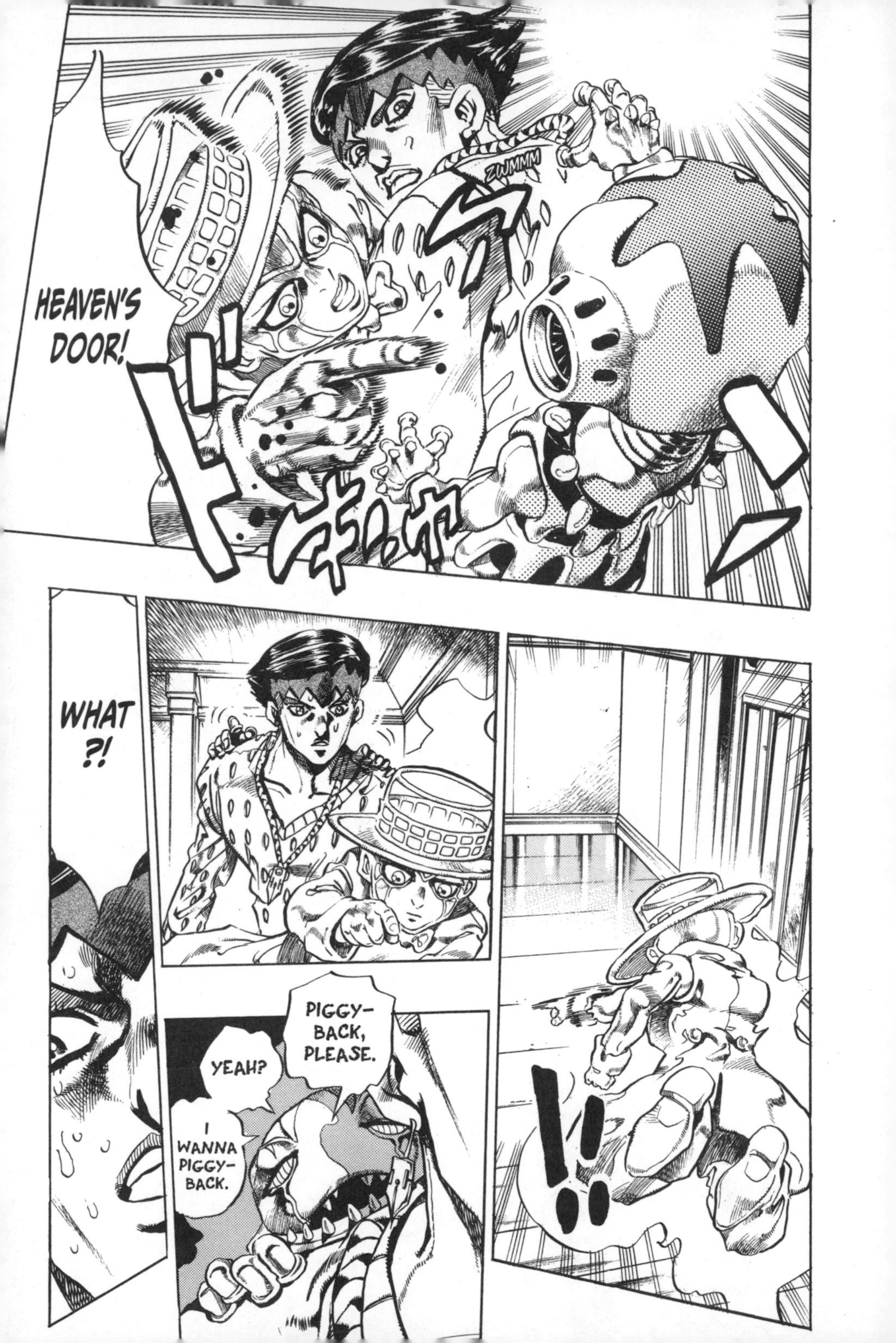
ZWMMM
HEAVEN'S DOOR!
!!
PIGGY-BACK, PLEASE.
YEAH?
I WANNA PIGGY-BACK.
WHAT ?!

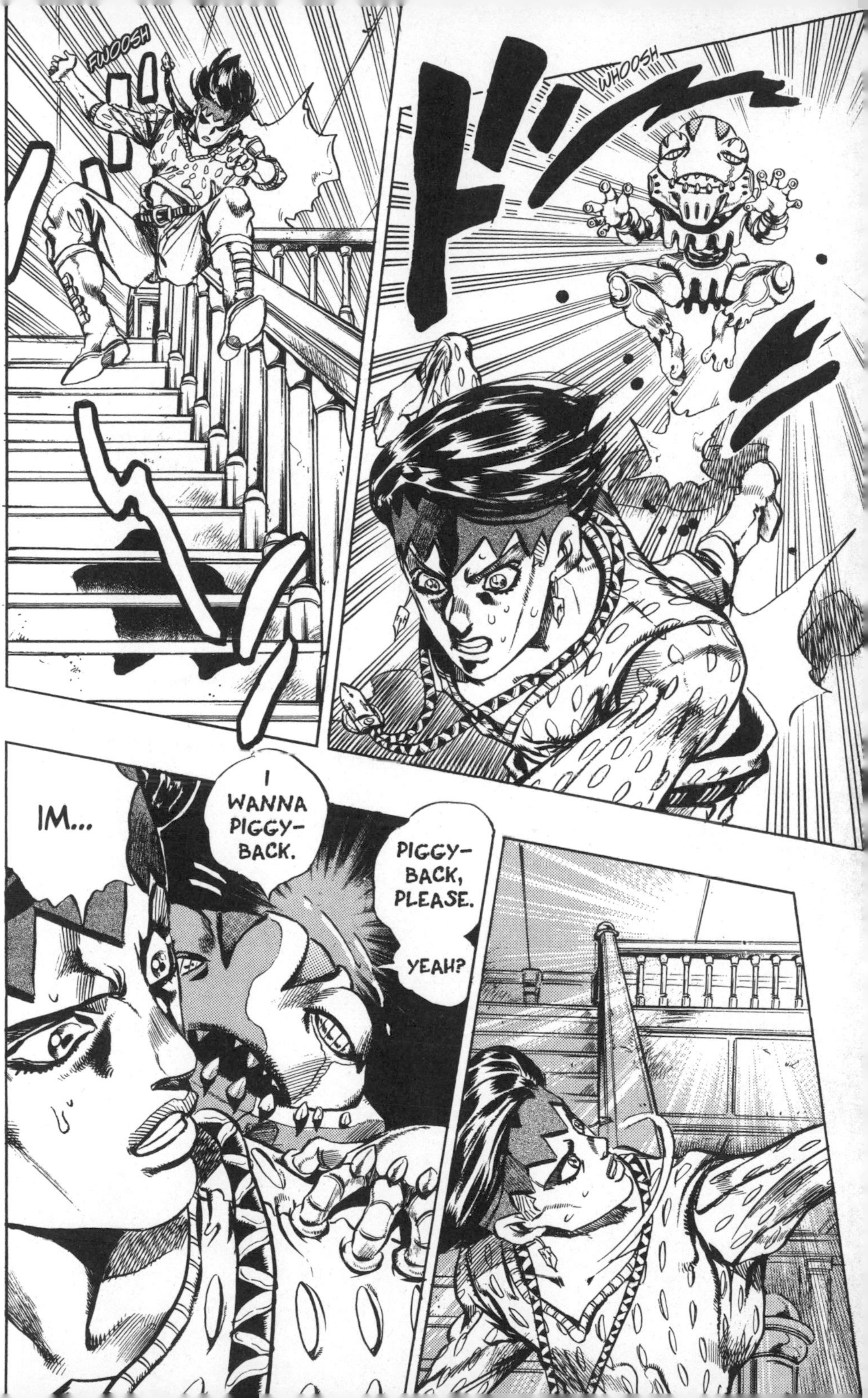
WHOOSH
FWOOSH
I WANNA PIGGY-BACK.
PIGGY-BACK, PLEASE.
YEAH?
IM...

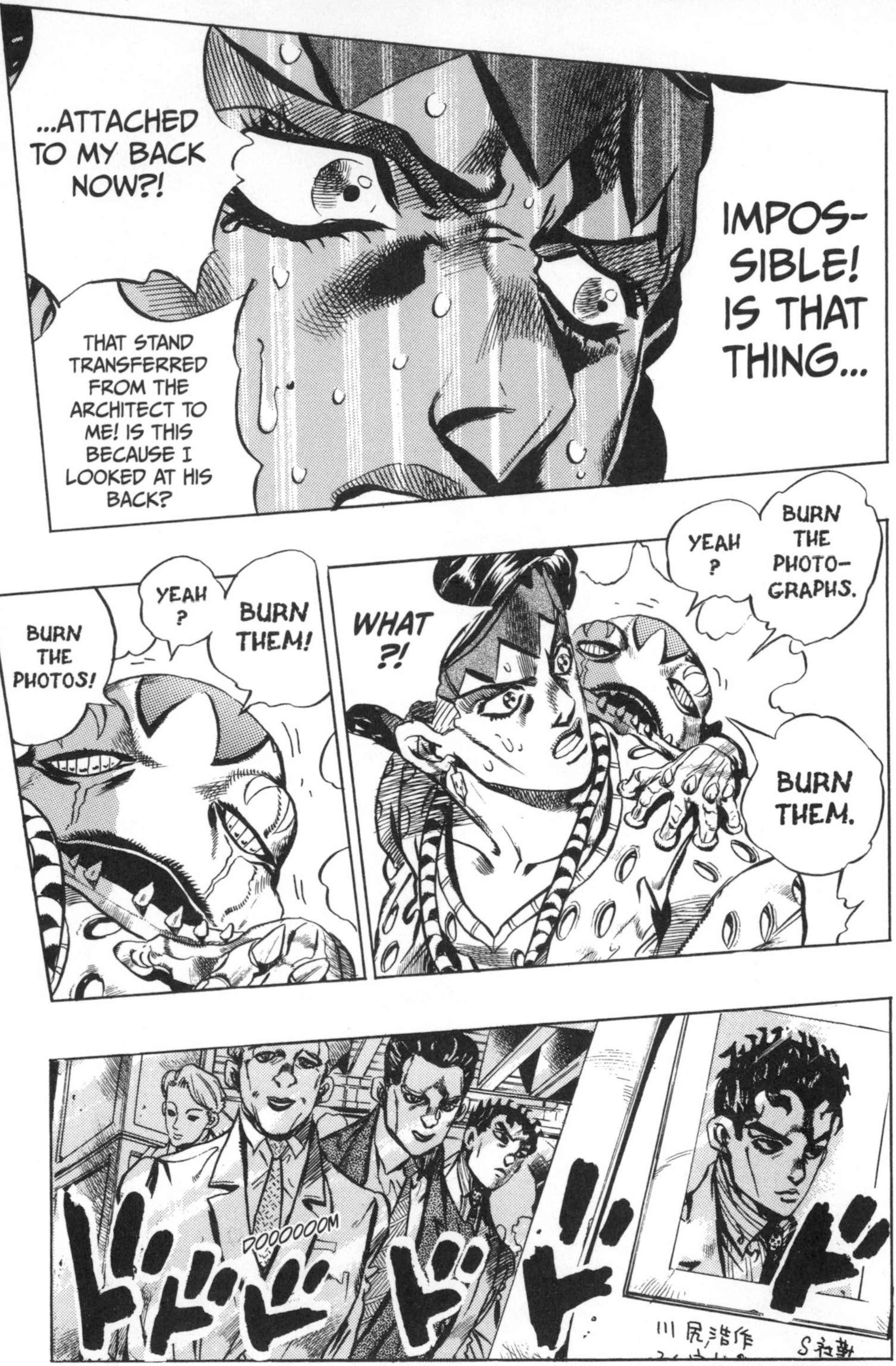

IMPOS-SIBLE! IS THAT THING...
...ATTACHED TO MY BACK NOW?!
THAT STAND TRANSFERRED FROM THE ARCHITECT TO ME! IS THIS BECAUSE I LOOKED AT HIS BACK?
BURN THE PHOTO-GRAPHS.
YEAH?
WHAT?!
BURN THEM.
BURN THEM!
YEAH?
BURN THE PHOTOS!
ドドドド
DOOOOOOOM
ドドド
川尻浩作
S社勤

KOSAKU KAWAJIRI EMPLOYEE AT S COMPANY
FAMILY OF 3

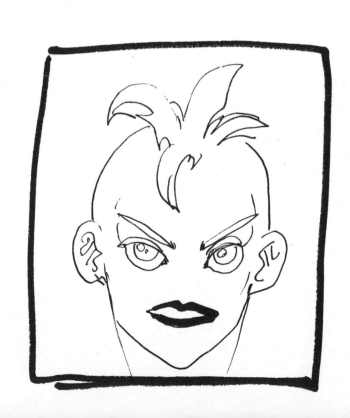

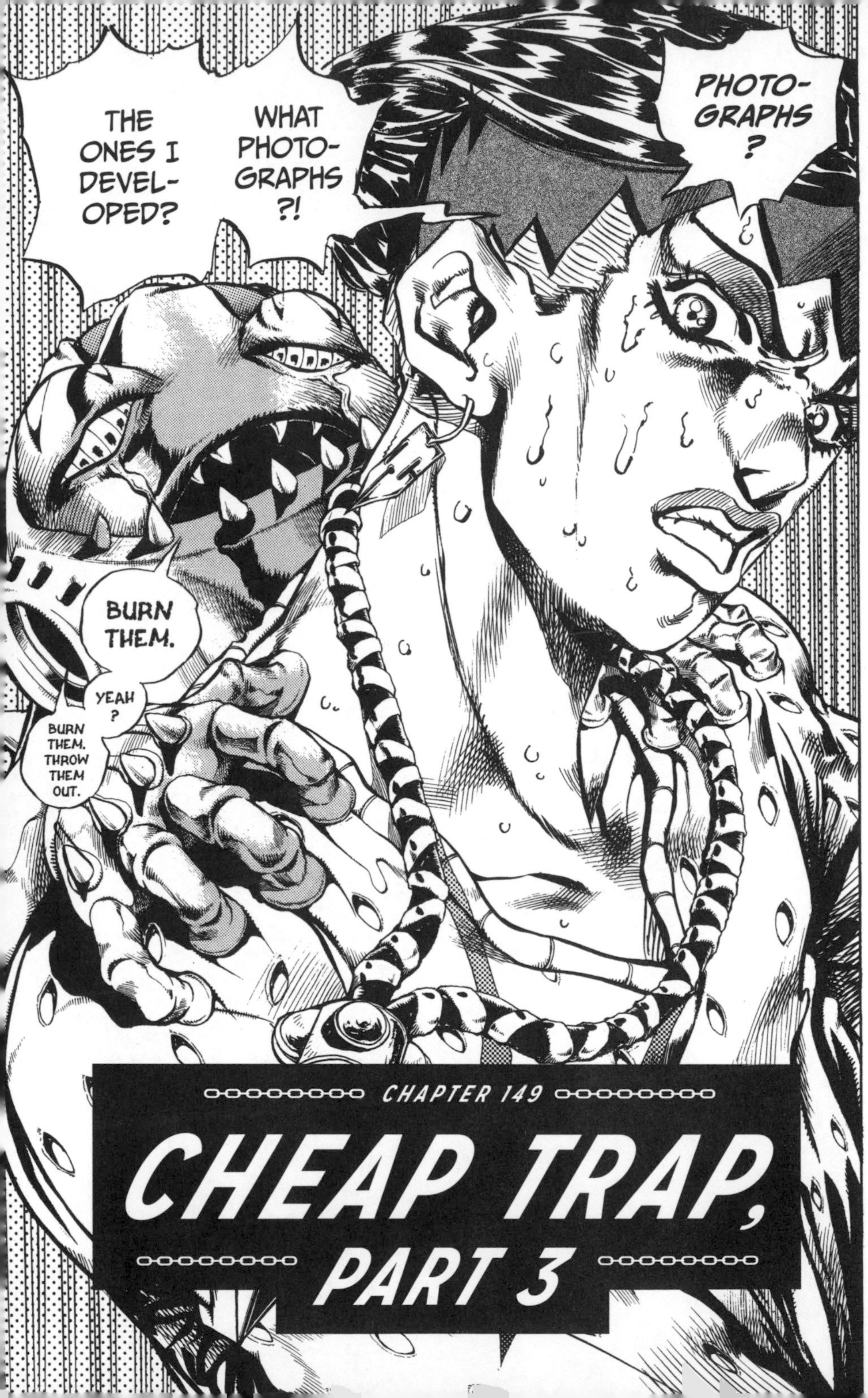
PHOTO-GRAPHS?
WHAT PHOTO-GRAPHS?!
THE ONES I DEVEL-OPED?
BURN THEM.
YEAH?
BURN THEM. THROW THEM OUT.
CHAPTER 149
CHEAP TRAP, PART 3

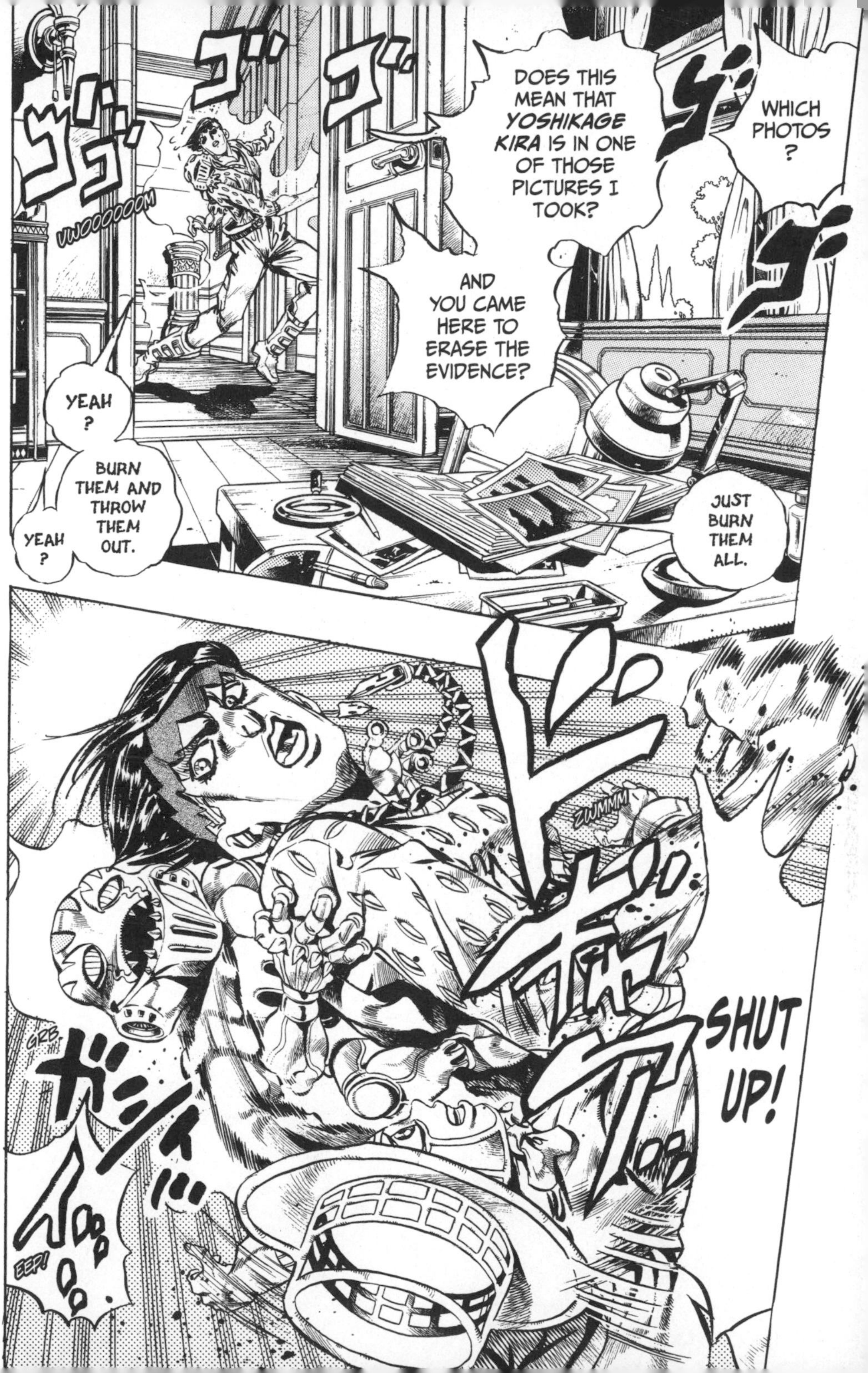
WHICH PHOTOS?
DOES THIS MEAN THAT YOSHIKAGE KIRA IS IN ONE OF THOSE PICTURES I TOOK?
AND YOU CAME HERE TO ERASE THE EVIDENCE?
UWOOOOOOOM
JUST BURN THEM ALL.
YEAH?
BURN THEM AND THROW THEM OUT.
YEAH?
ZWMMM
SHUT UP!
GRB
EEP!

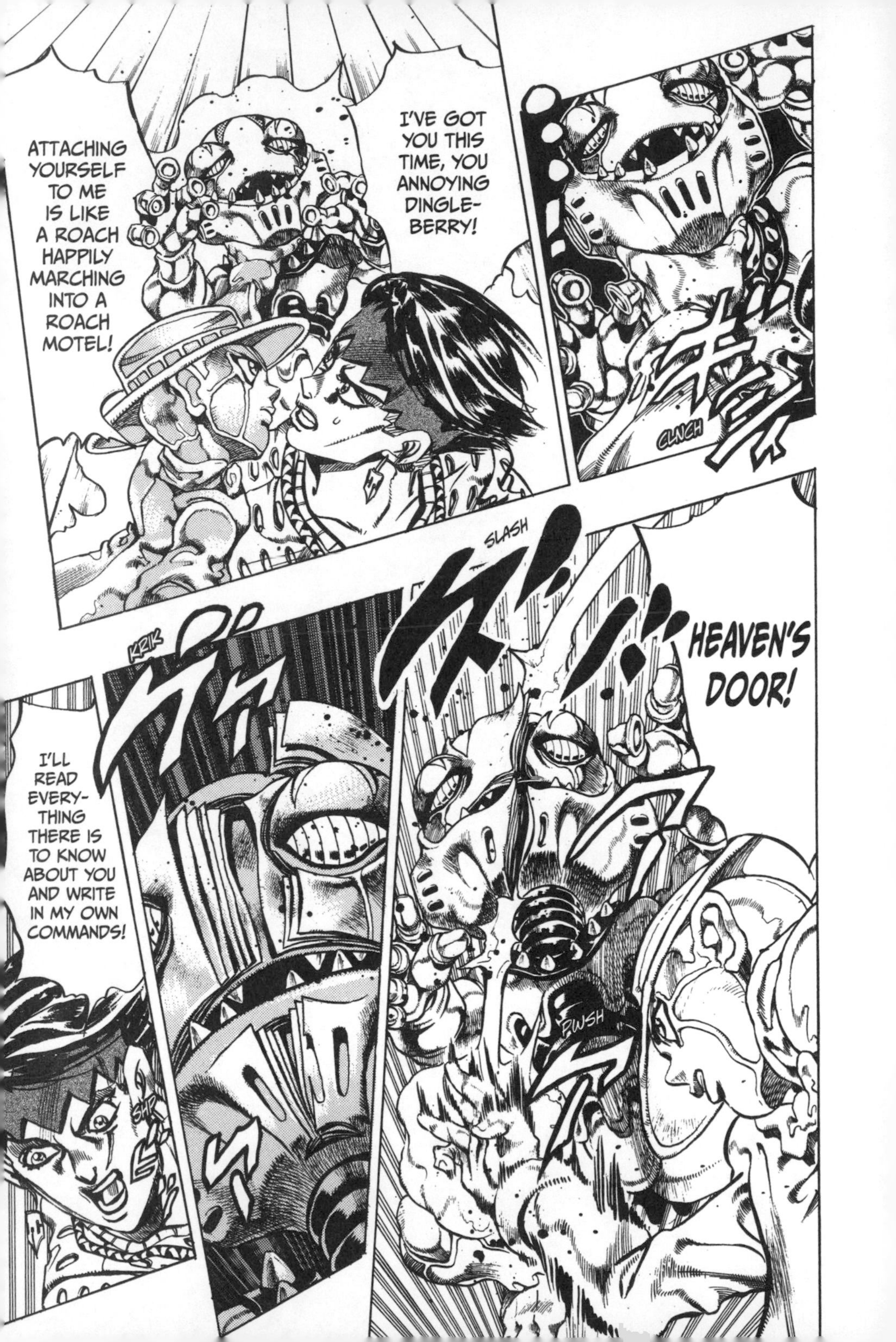
CLNCH
I'VE GOT YOU THIS TIME, YOU ANNOYING DINGLE-BERRY!
ATTACHING YOURSELF TO ME IS LIKE A ROACH HAPPILY MARCHING INTO A ROACH MOTEL!
SLASH
HEAVEN'S DOOR!
PWSH
KRIK
I'LL READ EVERY-THING THERE IS TO KNOW ABOUT YOU AND WRITE IN MY OWN COMMANDS!
SHP

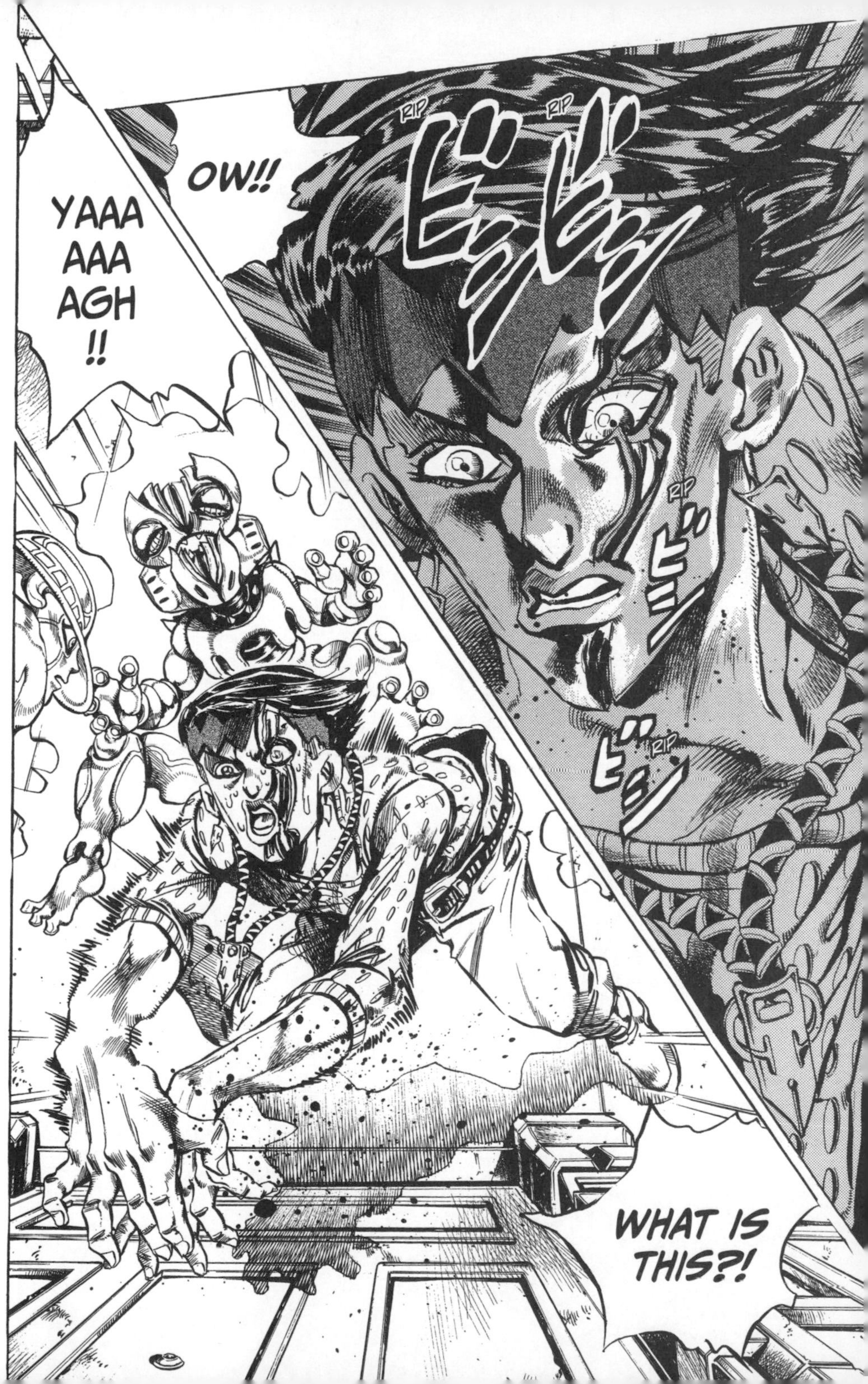
RIP
RIP
OW!!
RIP
RIP
YAAAAAAAGH!!
WHAT IS THIS?!

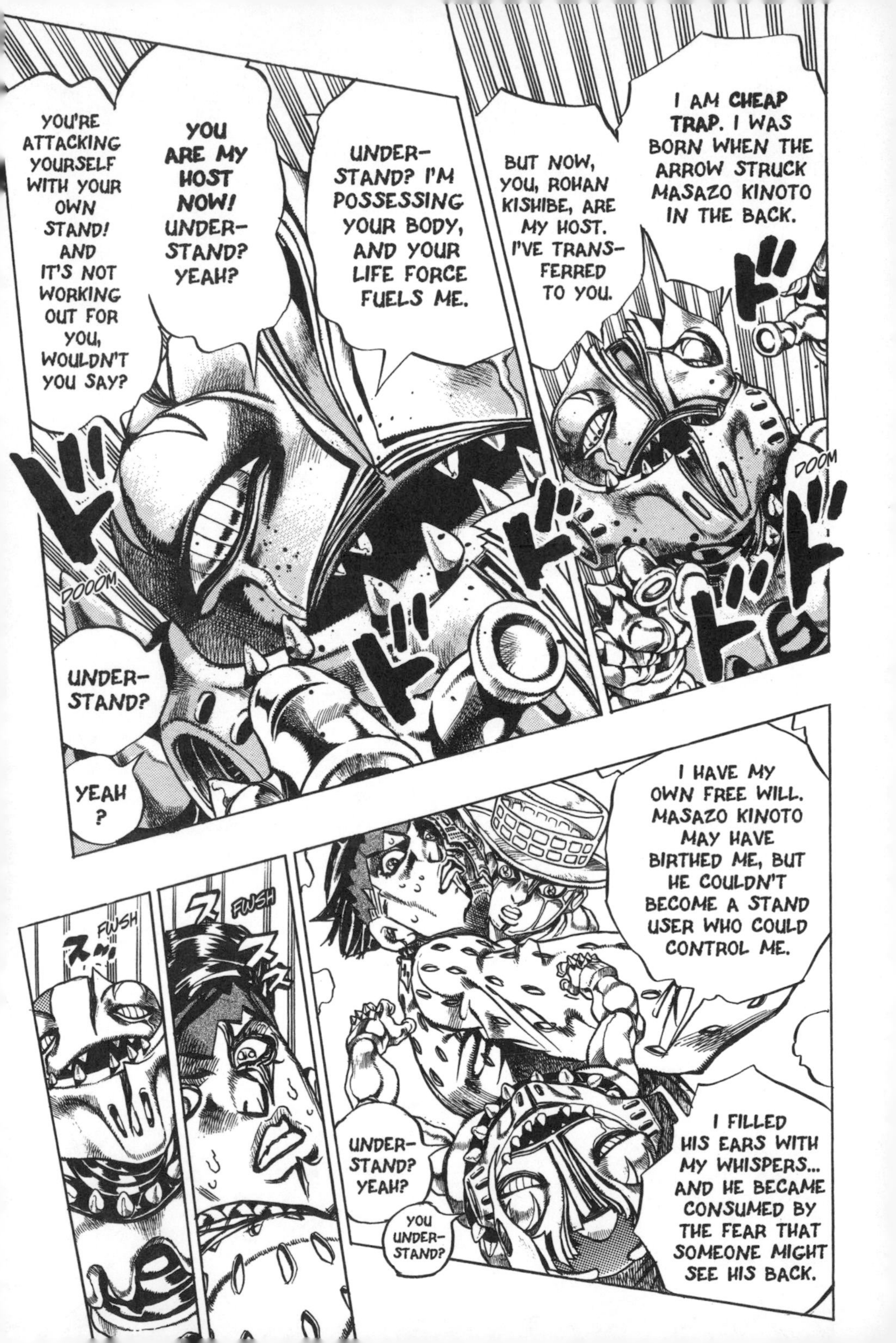
I AM CHEAP TRAP. I WAS BORN WHEN THE ARROW STRUCK MASAZO KINOTO IN THE BACK.
BUT NOW, YOU, ROHAN KISHIBE, ARE MY HOST. I'VE TRANS-FERRED TO YOU.
DOOM
UNDER-STAND? I'M POSSESSING YOUR BODY, AND YOUR LIFE FORCE FUELS ME.
YOU ARE MY HOST NOW! UNDER-STAND? YEAH?
YOU'RE ATTACKING YOURSELF WITH YOUR OWN STAND! AND IT'S NOT WORKING OUT FOR YOU, WOULDN'T YOU SAY?
DOOOM
UNDER-STAND?
YEAH ?
I HAVE MY OWN FREE WILL. MASAZO KINOTO MAY HAVE BIRTHED ME, BUT HE COULDN'T BECOME A STAND USER WHO COULD CONTROL ME.
I FILLED HIS EARS WITH MY WHISPERS... AND HE BECAME CONSUMED BY THE FEAR THAT SOMEONE MIGHT SEE HIS BACK.
UNDER-STAND? YEAH?
YOU UNDER-STAND?
FWSH
FWSH

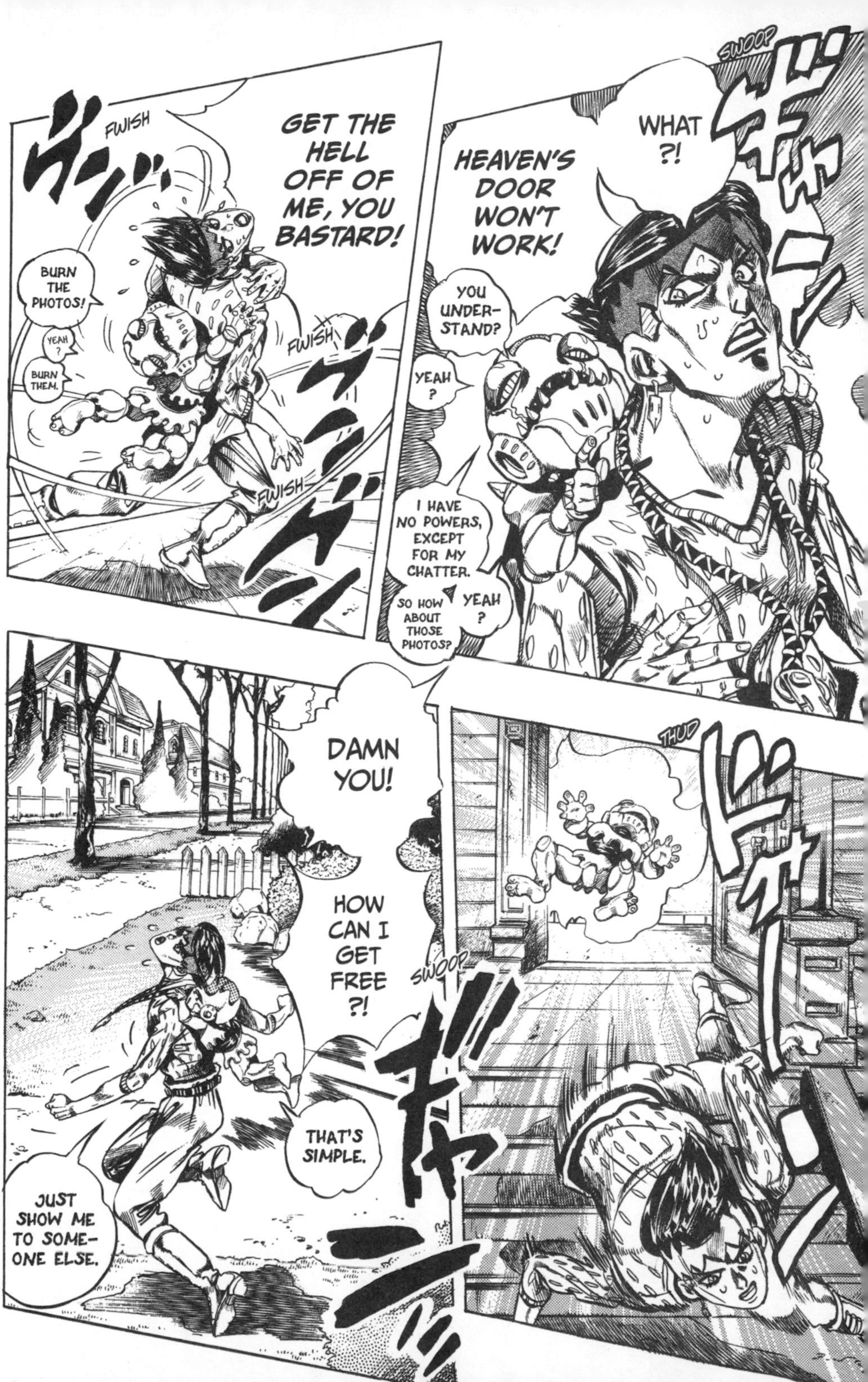
SWOOP
WHAT ?!
HEAVEN'S DOOR WON'T WORK!
YOU UNDER-STAND?
YEAH ?
I HAVE NO POWERS, EXCEPT FOR MY CHATTER.
YEAH ?
SO HOW ABOUT THOSE PHOTOS?
GET THE HELL OFF OF ME, YOU BASTARD!
FWISH
BURN THE PHOTOS!
YEAH ?
BURN THEM.
FWISH
FWISH
THUD
SWOOP
DAMN YOU!
HOW CAN I GET FREE ?!
THAT'S SIMPLE.
JUST SHOW ME TO SOME-ONE ELSE.

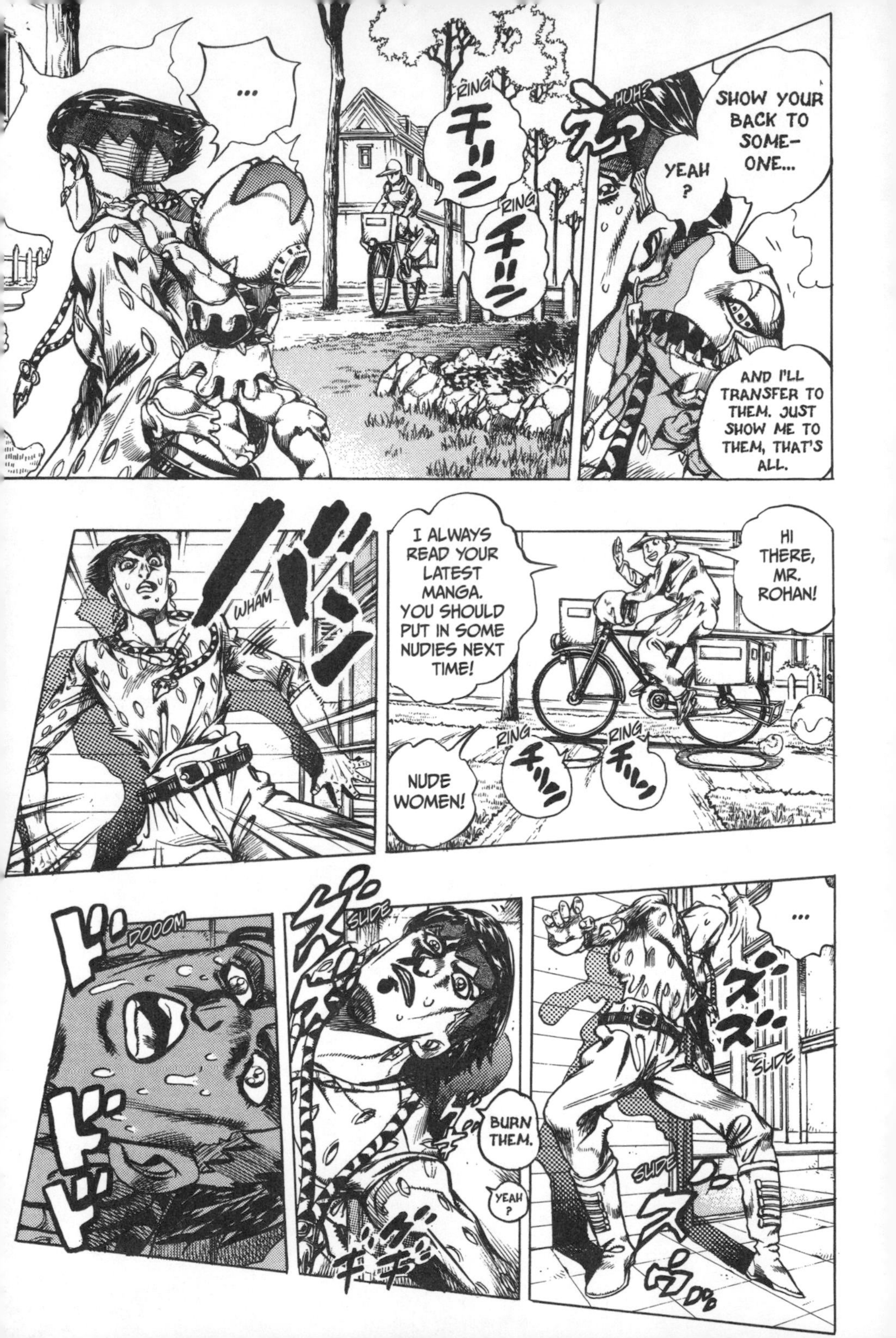
HUH?
えっ
SHOW YOUR BACK TO SOME-ONE...
YEAH?
AND I'LL TRANSFER TO THEM. JUST SHOW ME TO THEM, THAT'S ALL.
RING
チリン
RING
チリン
...
HI THERE, MR. ROHAN!
I ALWAYS READ YOUR LATEST MANGA. YOU SHOULD PUT IN SOME NUDIES NEXT TIME!
RING
RING
NUDE WOMEN!
WHAM
...
SLIDE
SLIDE
SLIDE
BURN THEM.
YEAH?
DOOOM

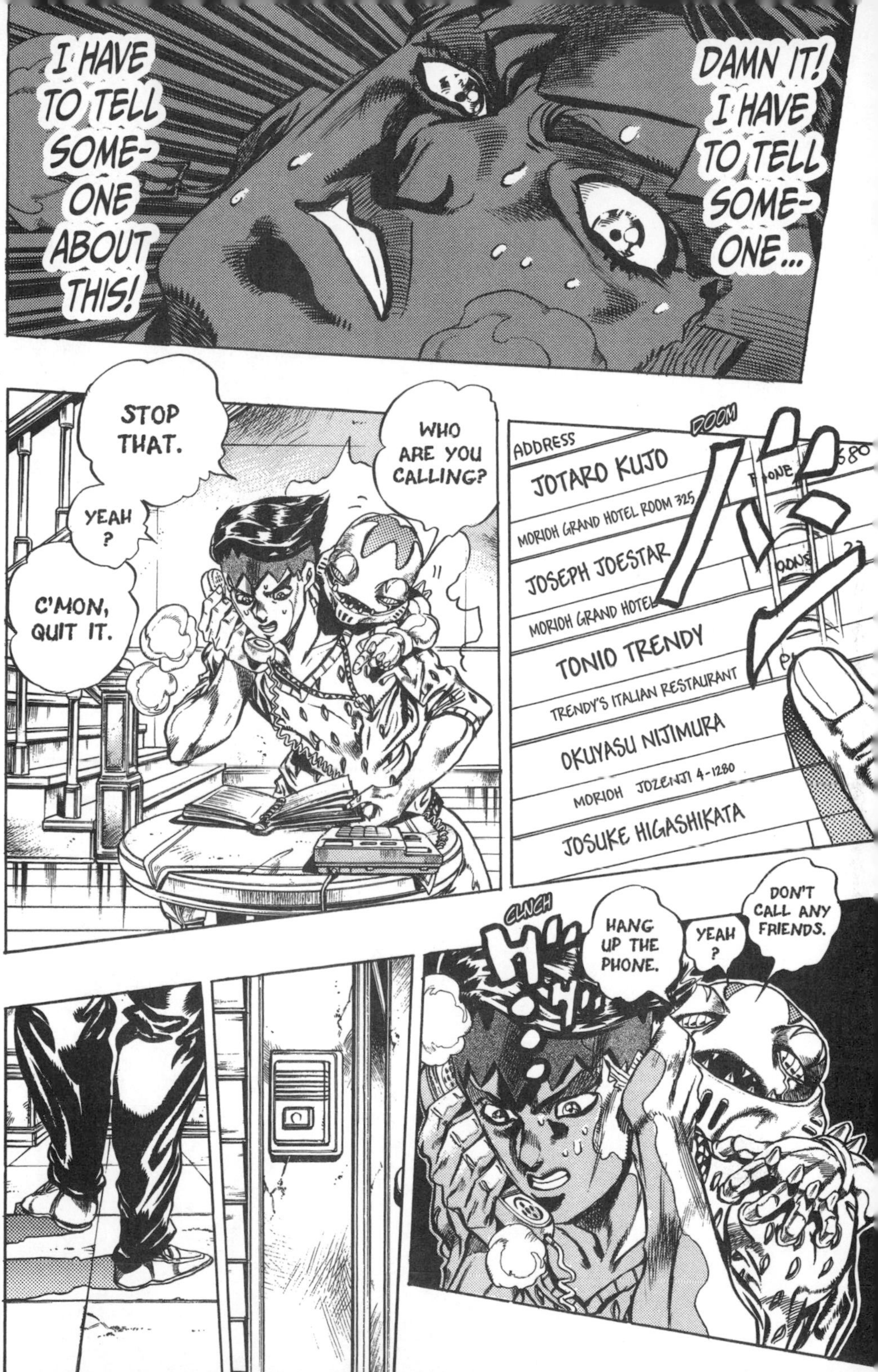
DAMN IT! I HAVE TO TELL SOME-ONE...
I HAVE TO TELL SOME-ONE ABOUT THIS!
DOOM
ADDRESS
JOTARO KUJO
MORIOH GRAND HOTEL ROOM 325
JOSEPH JOESTAR
MORIOH GRAND HOTEL
TONIO TRENDY
TRENDY'S ITALIAN RESTAURANT
OKUYASU NIJIMURA
MORIOH JOZENJI 4-1280
JOSUKE HIGASHIKATA
WHO ARE YOU CALLING?
STOP THAT.
YEAH?
C'MON, QUIT IT.
CLNCH
DON'T CALL ANY FRIENDS.
YEAH?
HANG UP THE PHONE.

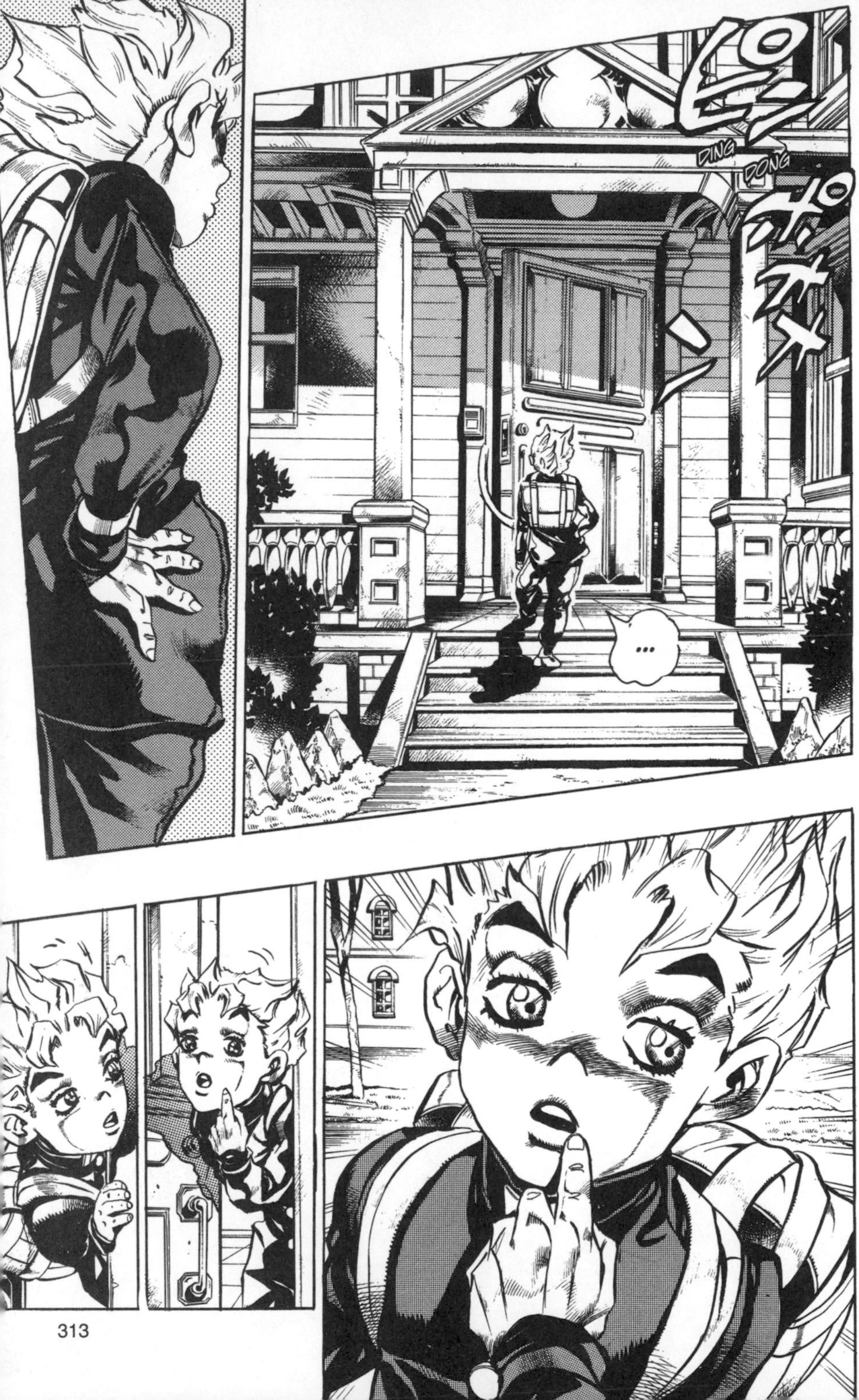
DING DONG
...

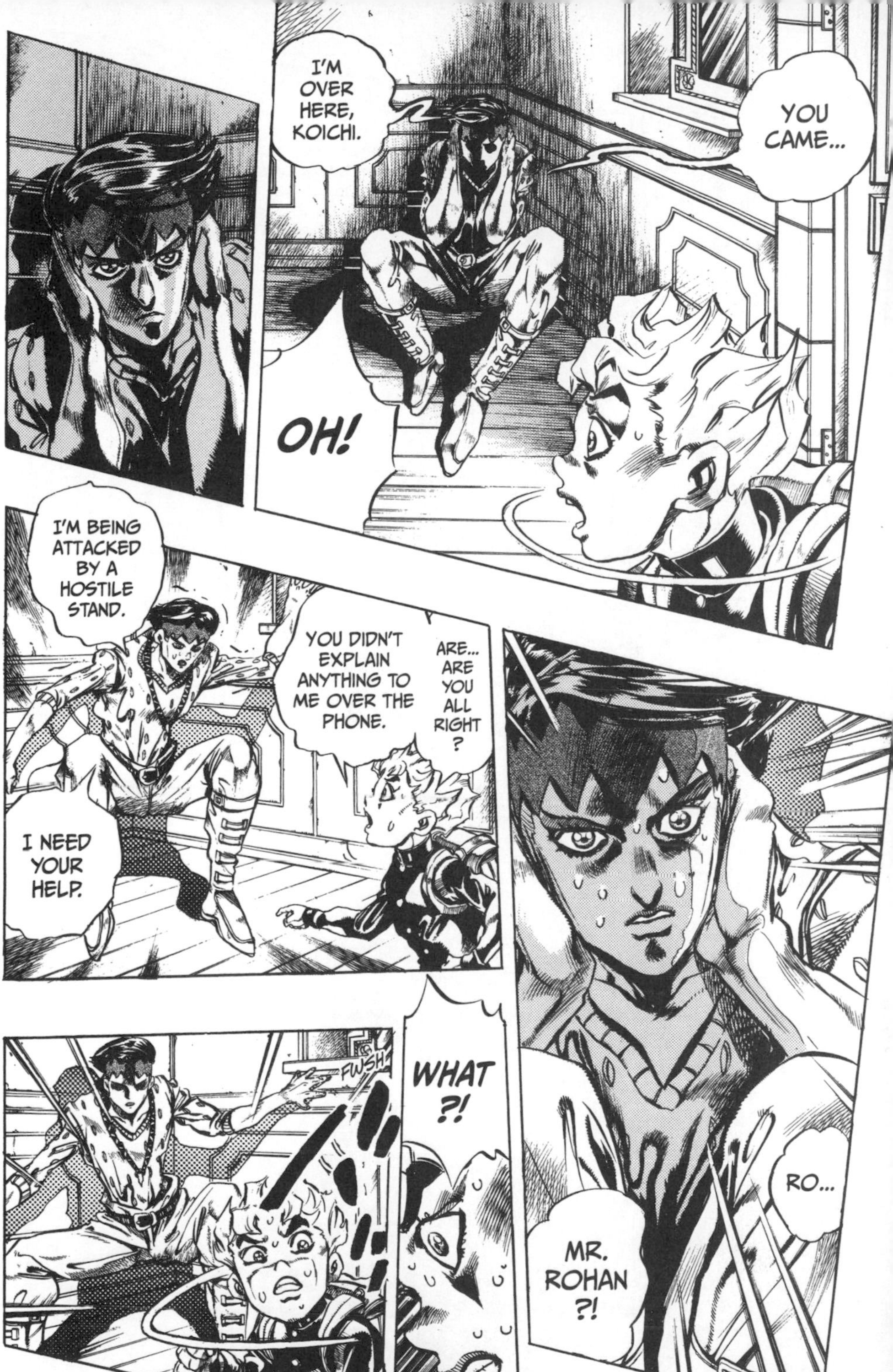
YOU CAME...
I'M OVER HERE, KOICHI.
OH!
RO...
MR. ROHAN ?!
ARE... ARE YOU ALL RIGHT ?
YOU DIDN'T EXPLAIN ANYTHING TO ME OVER THE PHONE.
I'M BEING ATTACKED BY A HOSTILE STAND.
I NEED YOUR HELP.
WHAT ?!
FWSH

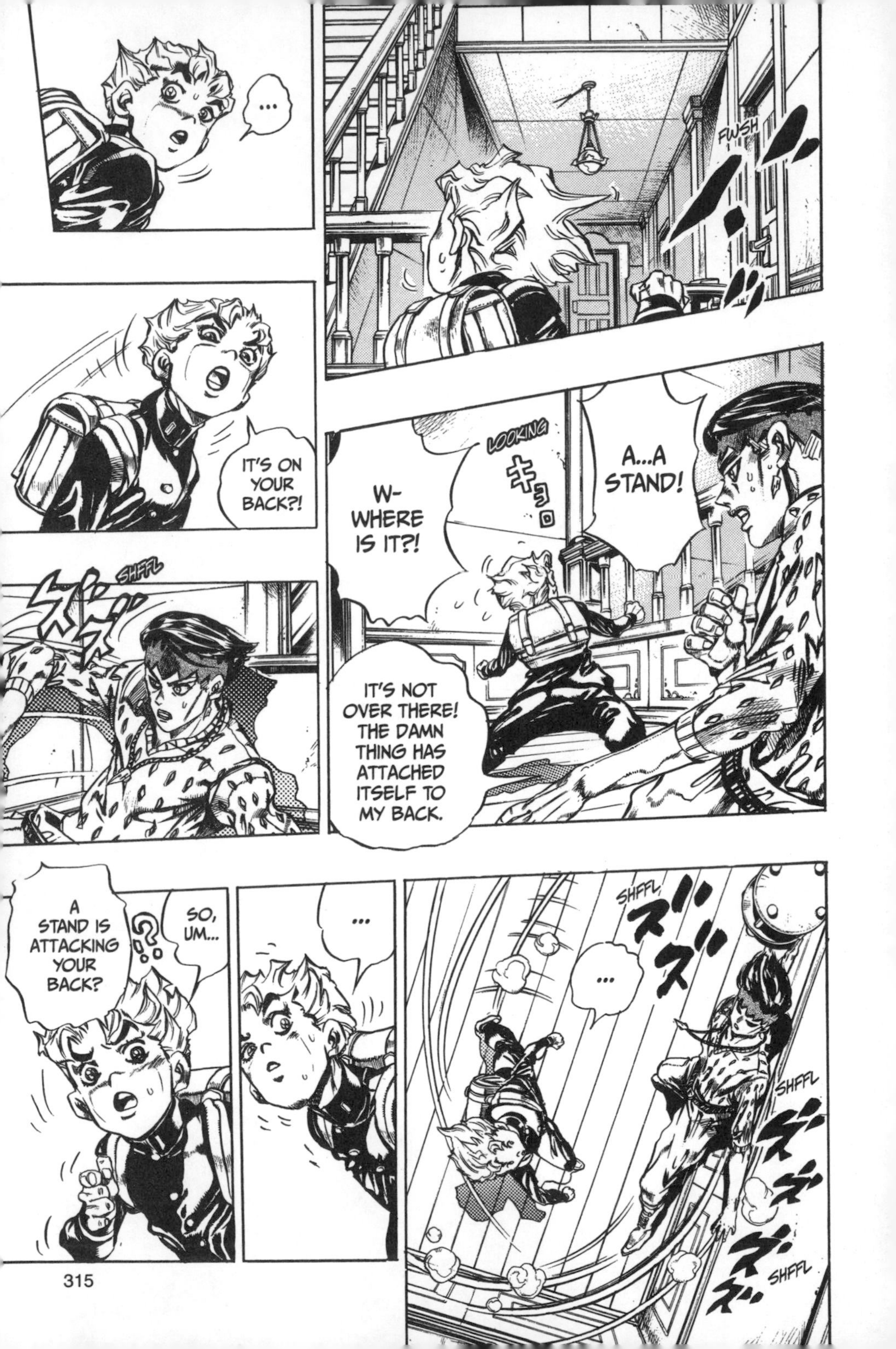

FWSH
...
LOOKING
キョロ
A...A STAND!
W-WHERE IS IT?!
IT'S NOT OVER THERE! THE DAMN THING HAS ATTACHED ITSELF TO MY BACK.
IT'S ON YOUR BACK?!
SHFFL
SHFFL
...
SHFFL
SHFFL
...
SO, UM...
A STAND IS ATTACKING YOUR BACK?

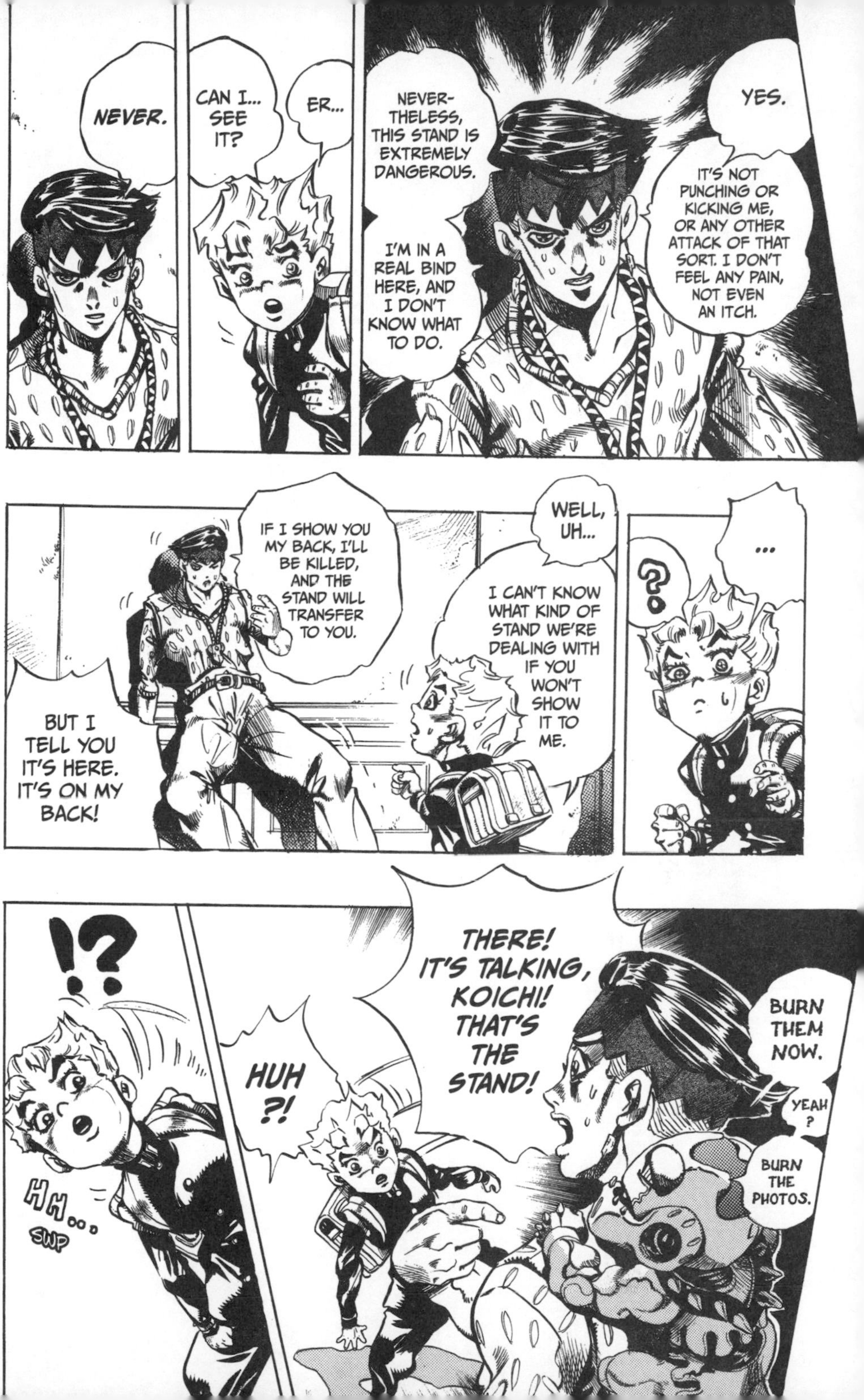
YES.
IT'S NOT PUNCHING OR KICKING ME, OR ANY OTHER ATTACK OF THAT SORT. I DON'T FEEL ANY PAIN, NOT EVEN AN ITCH.
NEVER-THELESS, THIS STAND IS EXTREMELY DANGEROUS.
I'M IN A REAL BIND HERE, AND I DON'T KNOW WHAT TO DO.
ER...
CAN I... SEE IT?
NEVER.
...
?
WELL, UH...
I CAN'T KNOW WHAT KIND OF STAND WE'RE DEALING WITH IF YOU WON'T SHOW IT TO ME.
IF I SHOW YOU MY BACK, I'LL BE KILLED, AND THE STAND WILL TRANSFER TO YOU.
BUT I TELL YOU IT'S HERE. IT'S ON MY BACK!
BURN THEM NOW.
YEAH?
BURN THE PHOTOS.
THERE! IT'S TALKING, KOICHI! THAT'S THE STAND!
HUH ?!
!?
HH...
SWP

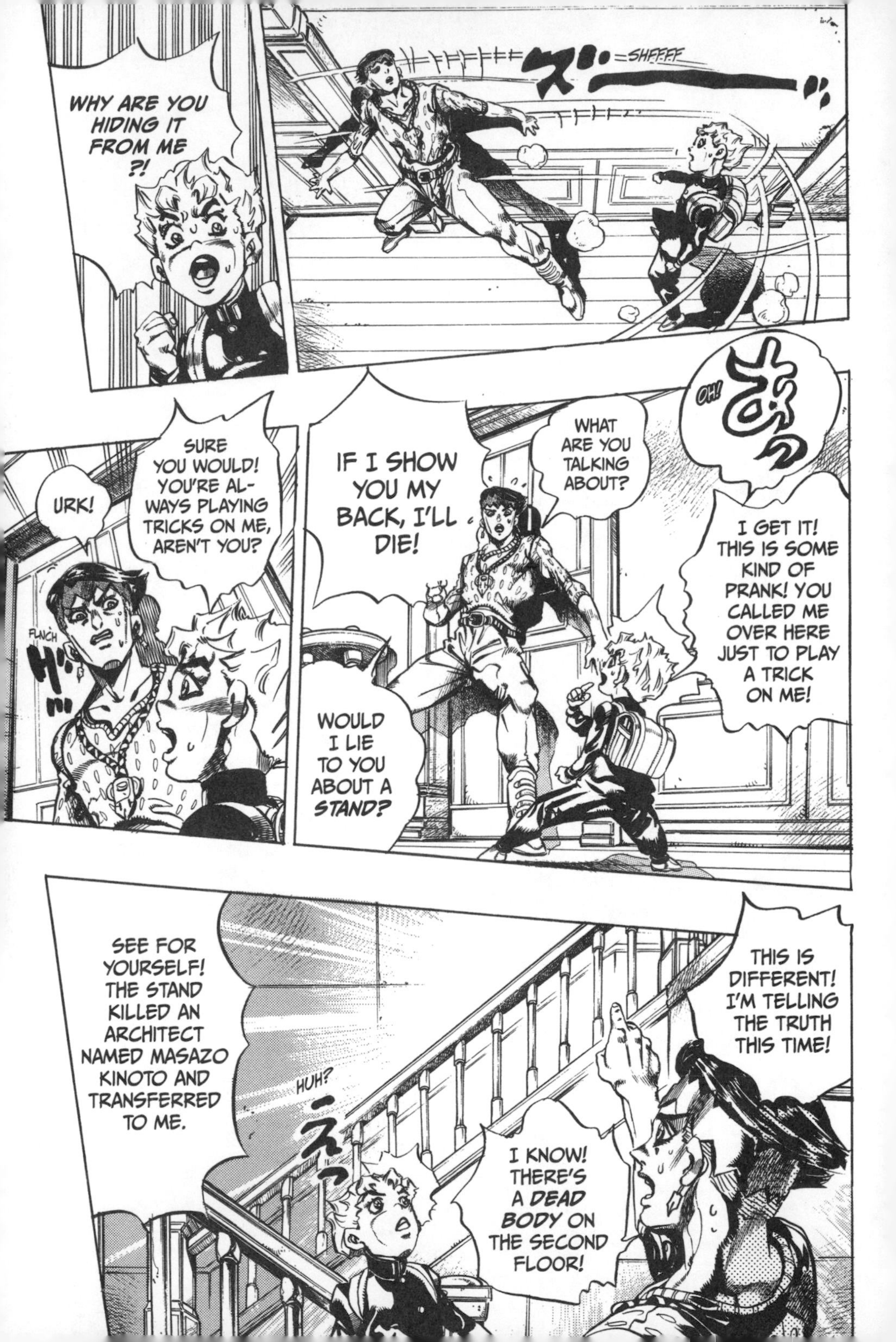
SHFFFF
WHY ARE YOU HIDING IT FROM ME ?!
OH!
WHAT ARE YOU TALKING ABOUT?
I GET IT! THIS IS SOME KIND OF PRANK! YOU CALLED ME OVER HERE JUST TO PLAY A TRICK ON ME!
IF I SHOW YOU MY BACK, I'LL DIE!
WOULD I LIE TO YOU ABOUT A *STAND?*
SURE YOU WOULD! YOU'RE AL- WAYS PLAYING TRICKS ON ME, AREN'T YOU?
URK!
FLINCH
THIS IS DIFFERENT! I'M TELLING THE TRUTH THIS TIME!
SEE FOR YOURSELF! THE STAND KILLED AN ARCHITECT NAMED MASAZO KINOTO AND TRANSFERRED TO ME.
HUH?
I KNOW! THERE'S A *DEAD BODY* ON THE SECOND FLOOR!

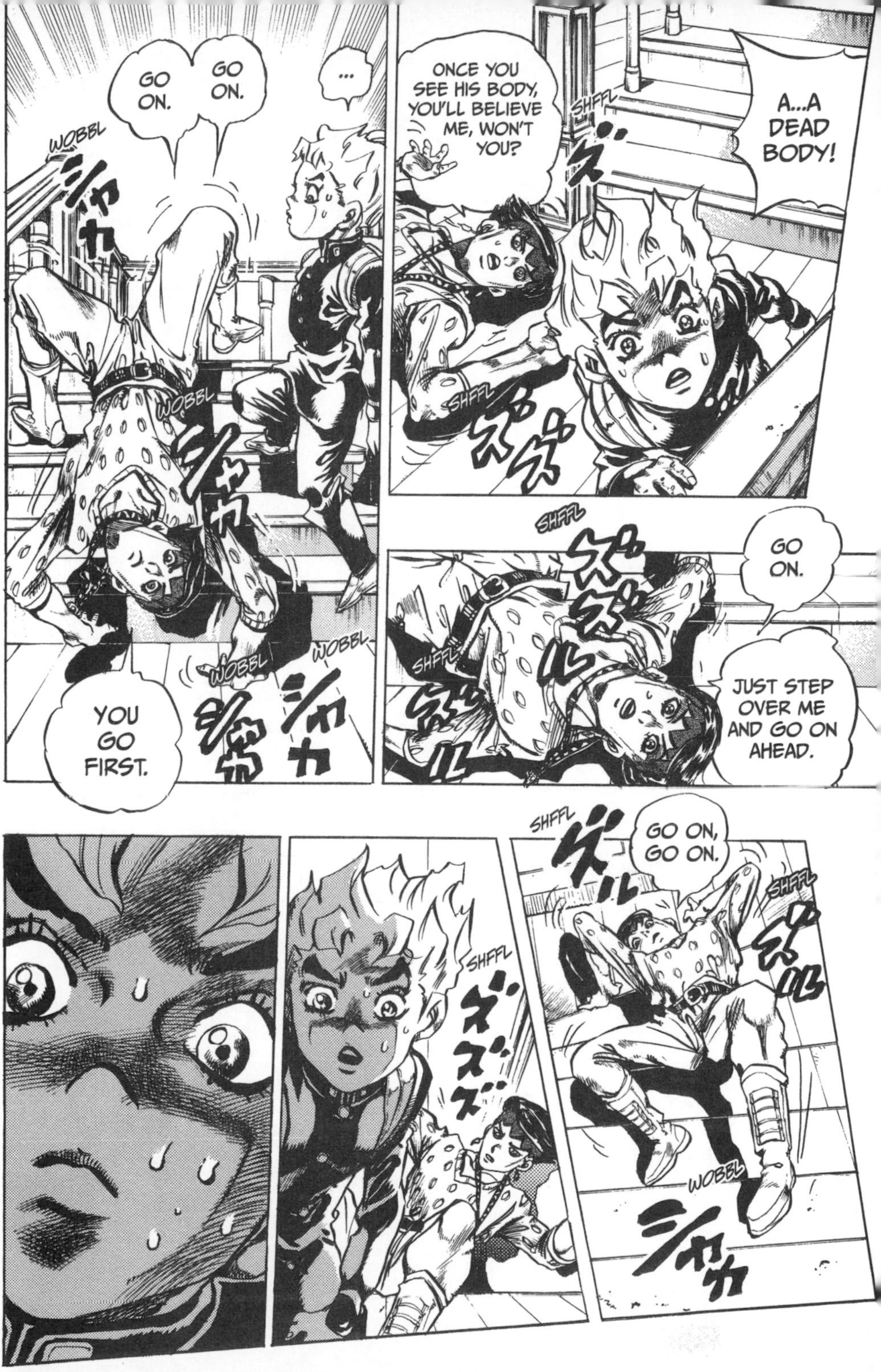
A...A DEAD BODY!
SHFFL
ONCE YOU SEE HIS BODY, YOU'LL BELIEVE ME, WON'T YOU?
SHFFL
GO ON.
SHFFL
JUST STEP OVER ME AND GO ON AHEAD.
SHFFL
GO ON.
GO ON.
...
WOBBL
WOBBL
WOBBL
WOBBL
YOU GO FIRST.
GO ON, GO ON.
SHFFL
SHFFL
WOBBL
SHFFL

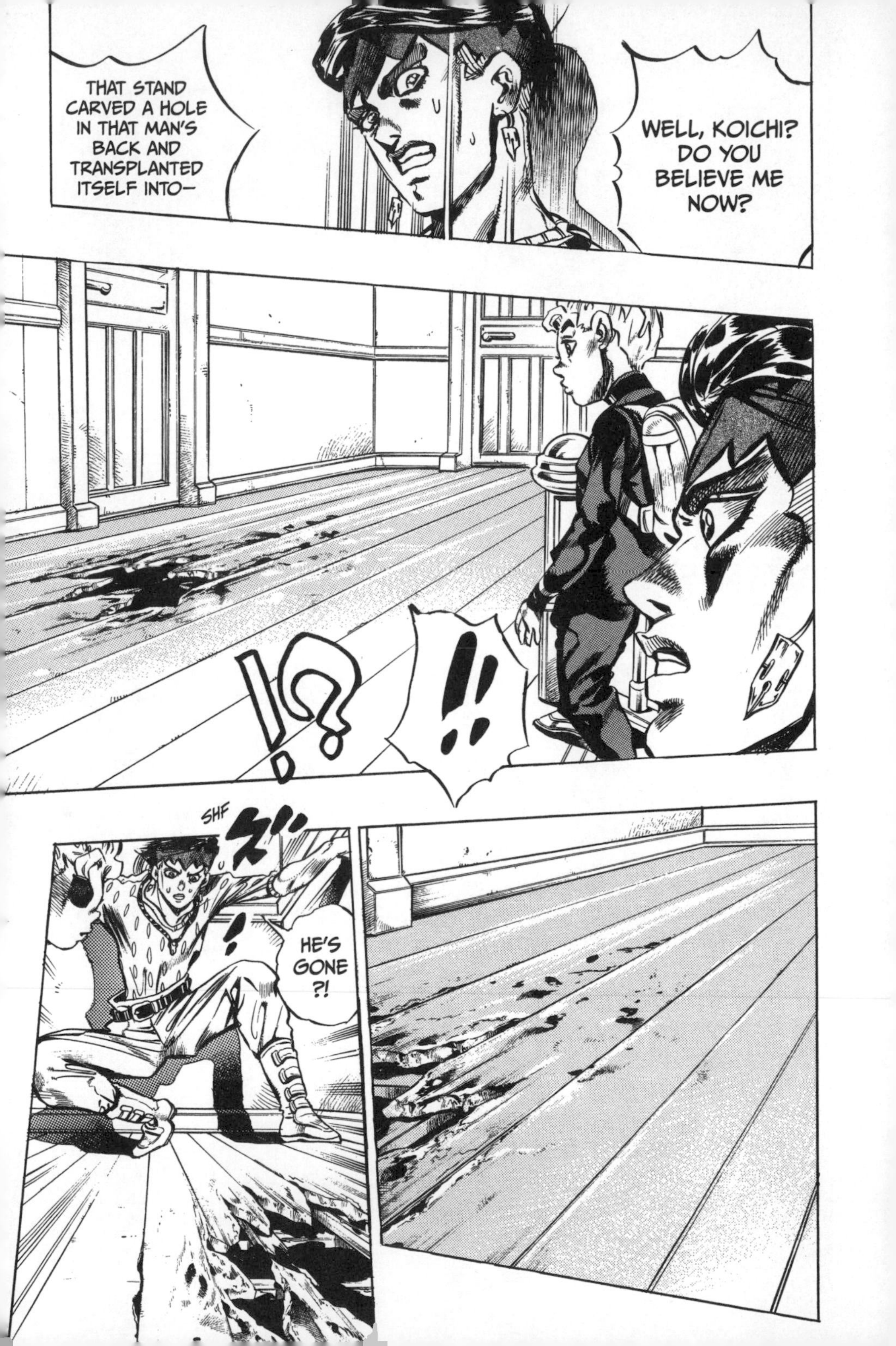
WELL, KOICHI? DO YOU BELIEVE ME NOW?
THAT STAND CARVED A HOLE IN THAT MAN'S BACK AND TRANSPLANTED ITSELF INTO—
!!
!?
SHF
HE'S GONE ?!

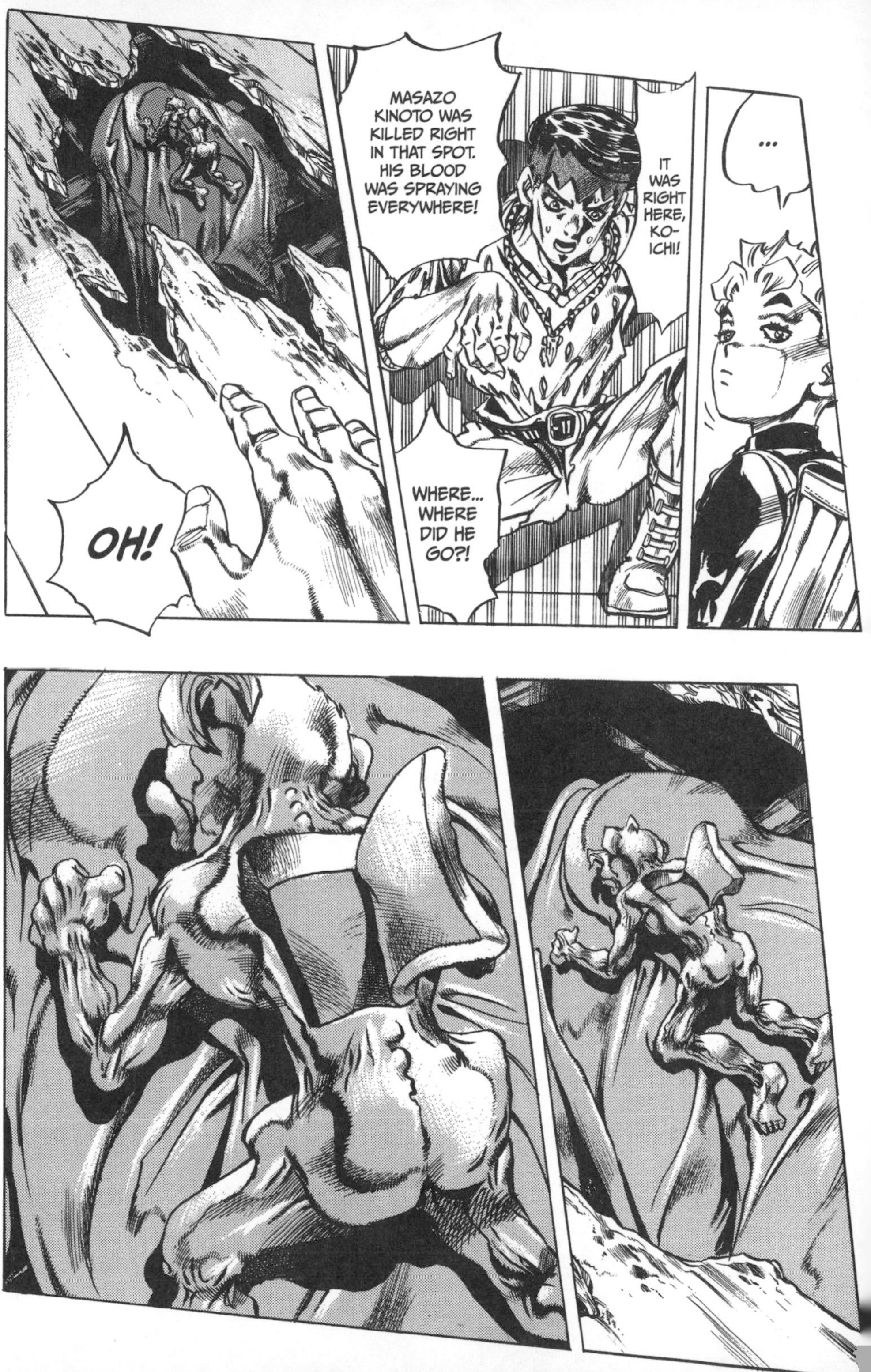
...
IT WAS RIGHT HERE, KO-ICHI!
MASAZO KINOTO WAS KILLED RIGHT IN THAT SPOT. HIS BLOOD WAS SPRAYING EVERYWHERE!
WHERE... WHERE DID HE GO?!
OH!

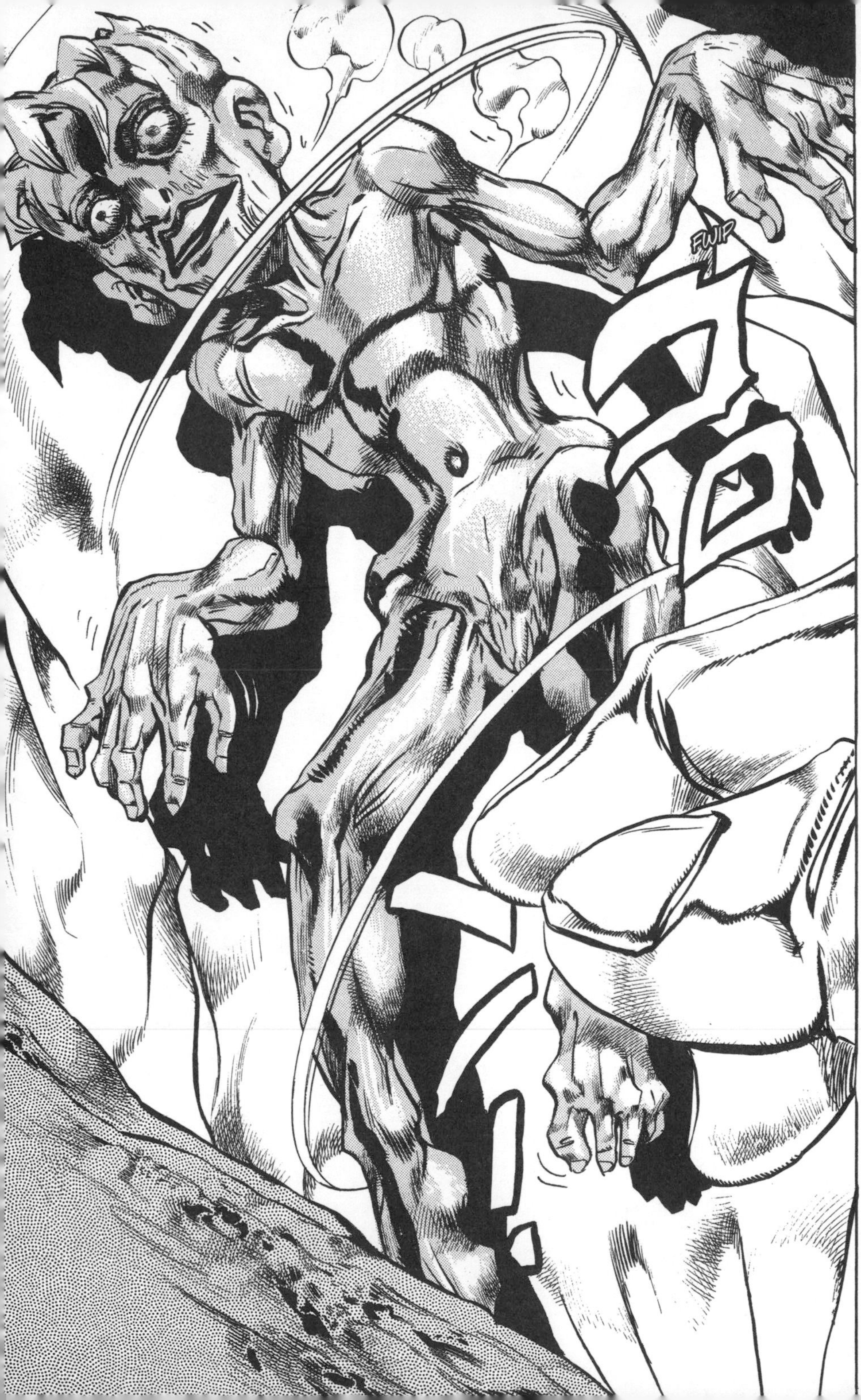
FWIP

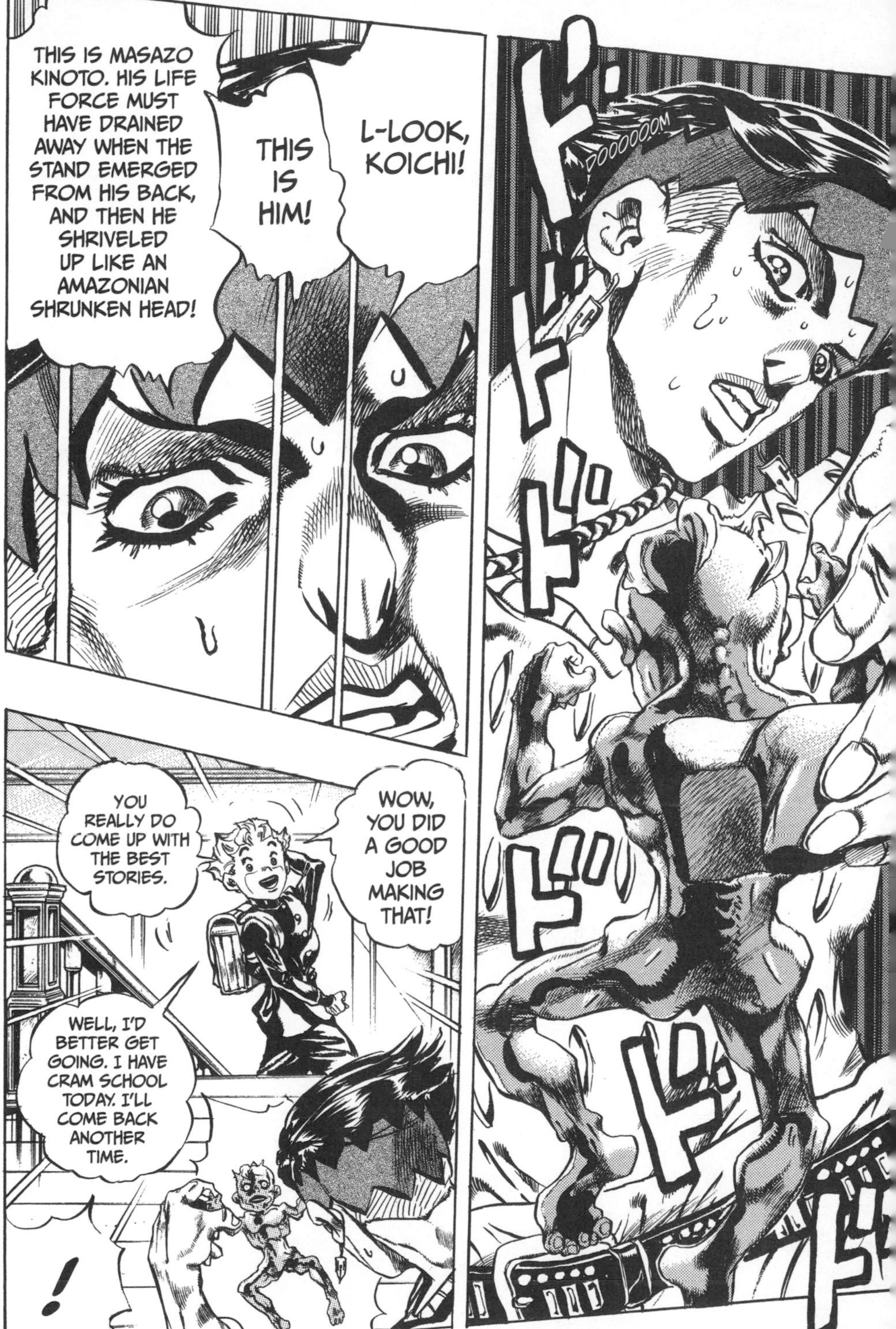
DOOOOOOOM
L-LOOK, KOICHI!
THIS IS HIM!
THIS IS MASAZO KINOTO. HIS LIFE FORCE MUST HAVE DRAINED AWAY WHEN THE STAND EMERGED FROM HIS BACK, AND THEN HE SHRIVELED UP LIKE AN AMAZONIAN SHRUNKEN HEAD!
WOW, YOU DID A GOOD JOB MAKING THAT!
YOU REALLY DO COME UP WITH THE BEST STORIES.
WELL, I'D BETTER GET GOING. I HAVE CRAM SCHOOL TODAY. I'LL COME BACK ANOTHER TIME.
!

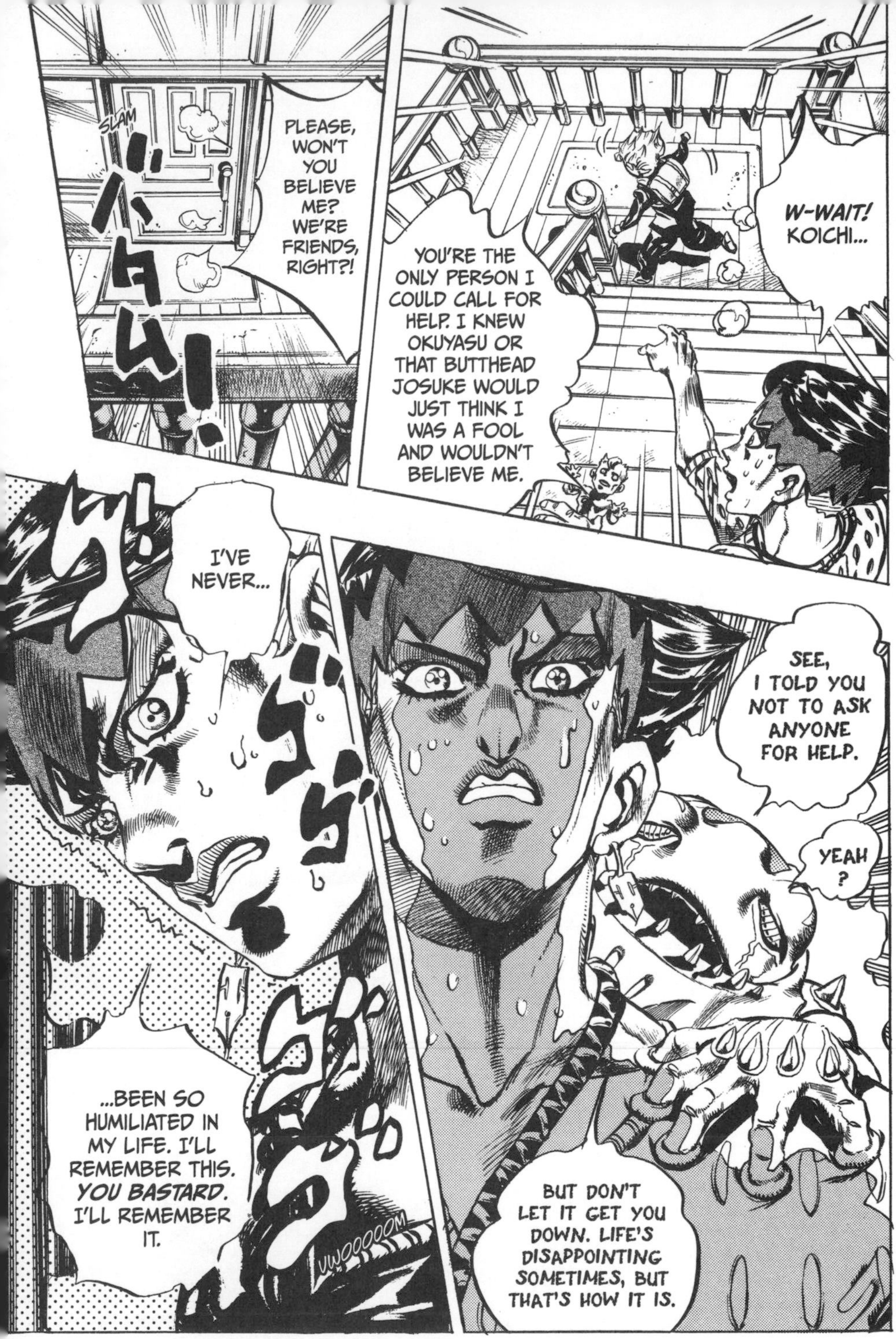
W-WAIT! KOICHI...
YOU'RE THE ONLY PERSON I COULD CALL FOR HELP. I KNEW OKUYASU OR THAT BUTTHEAD JOSUKE WOULD JUST THINK I WAS A FOOL AND WOULDN'T BELIEVE ME.
SLAM
PLEASE, WON'T YOU BELIEVE ME? WE'RE FRIENDS, RIGHT?!
SEE, I TOLD YOU NOT TO ASK ANYONE FOR HELP.
YEAH ?
BUT DON'T LET IT GET YOU DOWN. LIFE'S DISAPPOINTING SOMETIMES, BUT THAT'S HOW IT IS.
UWOOOOOM
I'VE NEVER...
...BEEN SO HUMILIATED IN MY LIFE. I'LL REMEMBER THIS. *YOU BASTARD.* I'LL REMEMBER IT.

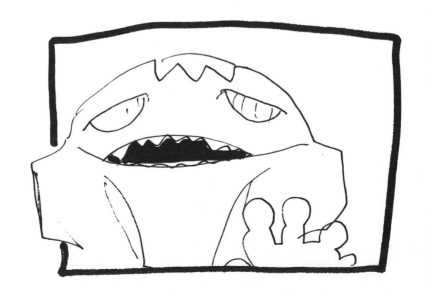

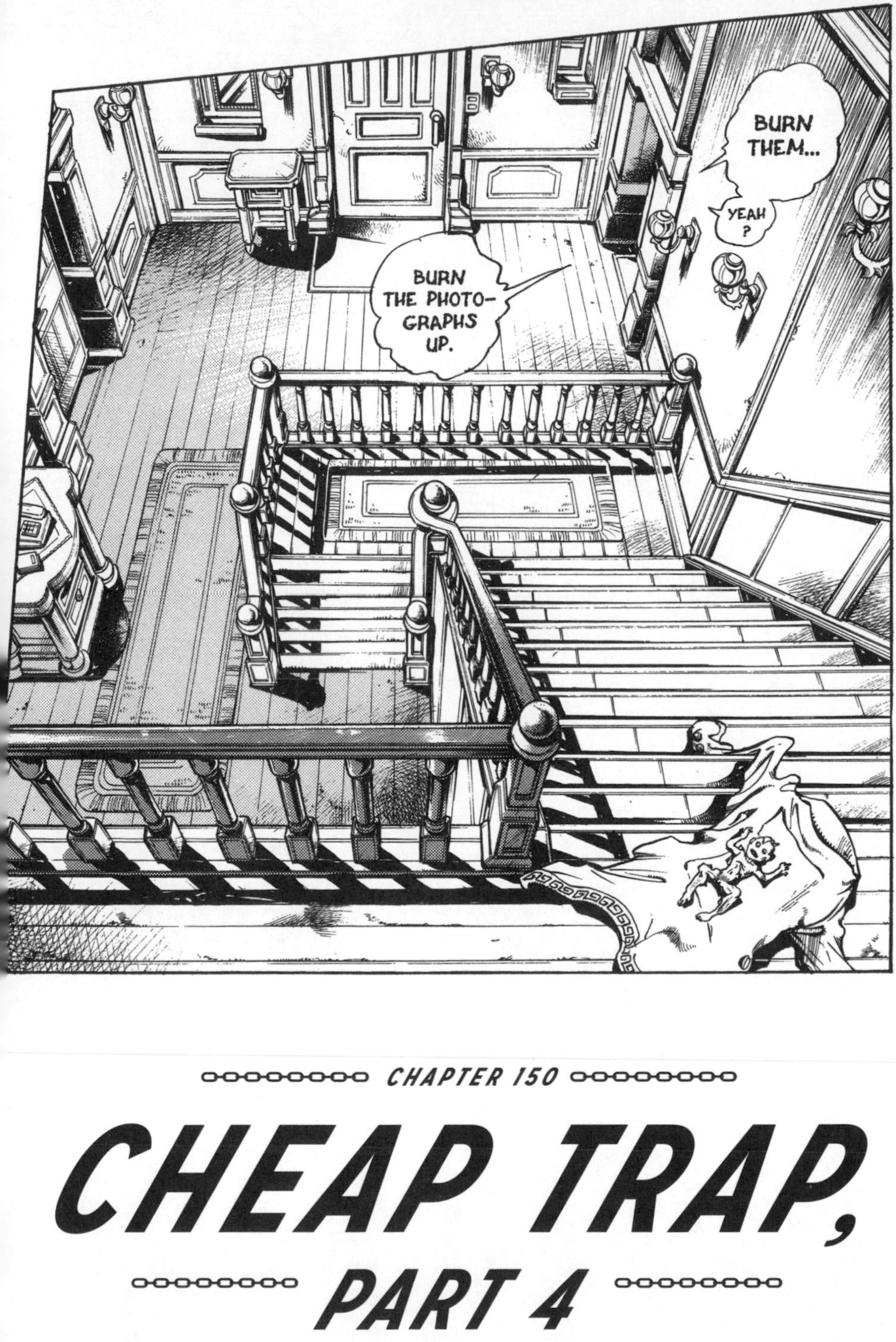
BURN THEM...
YEAH ?
BURN THE PHOTO-GRAPHS UP.

CHAPTER 150

CHEAP TRAP, PART 4

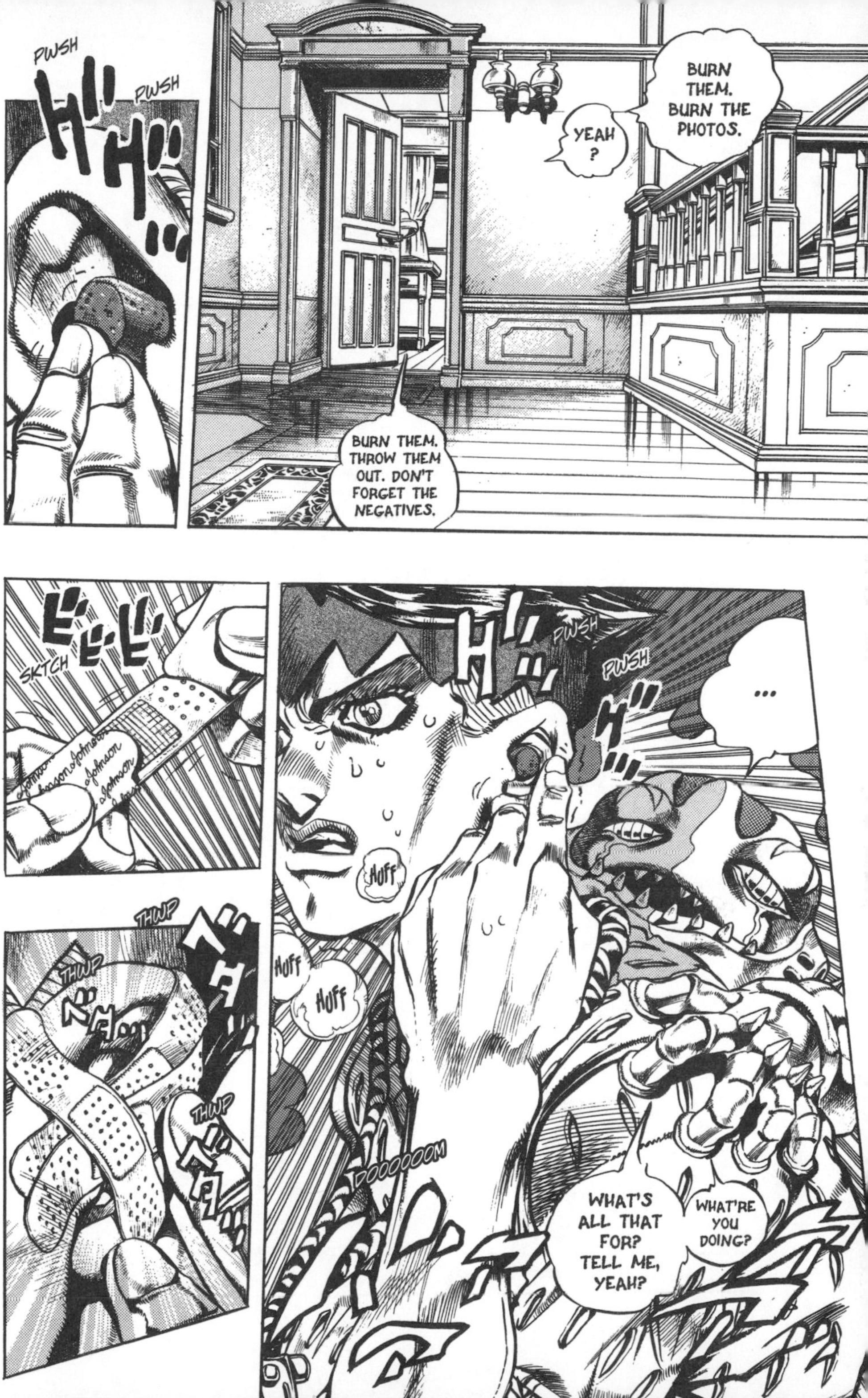
BURN THEM. BURN THE PHOTOS.
YEAH ?
BURN THEM. THROW THEM OUT. DON'T FORGET THE NEGATIVES.
PWSH
PWSH
PWSH
PWSH
...
HUFF
HUFF
HUFF
DOOOOOOOM
WHAT'RE YOU DOING?
WHAT'S ALL THAT FOR? TELL ME, YEAH?
ビビビ
SKTCH
Johnson Johnson Johnson Johnson
THWP
THWP
THWP

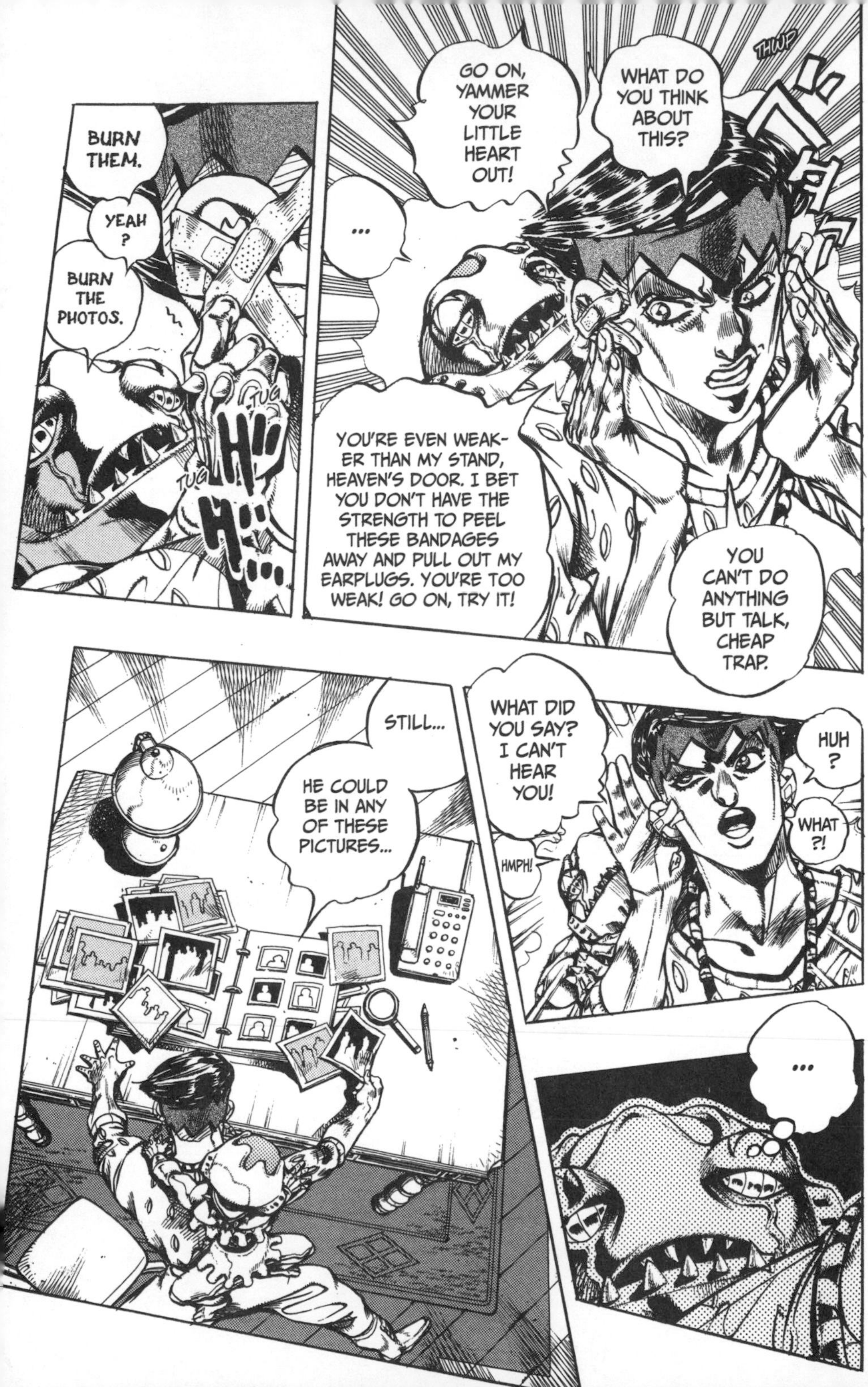
THWP
WHAT DO YOU THINK ABOUT THIS?
GO ON, YAMMER YOUR LITTLE HEART OUT!
...
YOU'RE EVEN WEAKER THAN MY STAND, HEAVEN'S DOOR. I BET YOU DON'T HAVE THE STRENGTH TO PEEL THESE BANDAGES AWAY AND PULL OUT MY EARPLUGS. YOU'RE TOO WEAK! GO ON, TRY IT!
YOU CAN'T DO ANYTHING BUT TALK, CHEAP TRAP.
BURN THEM.
YEAH?
BURN THE PHOTOS.
TUG
TUG
WHAT DID YOU SAY? I CAN'T HEAR YOU!
HUH?
WHAT?!
HMPH!
...
STILL...
HE COULD BE IN ANY OF THESE PICTURES...

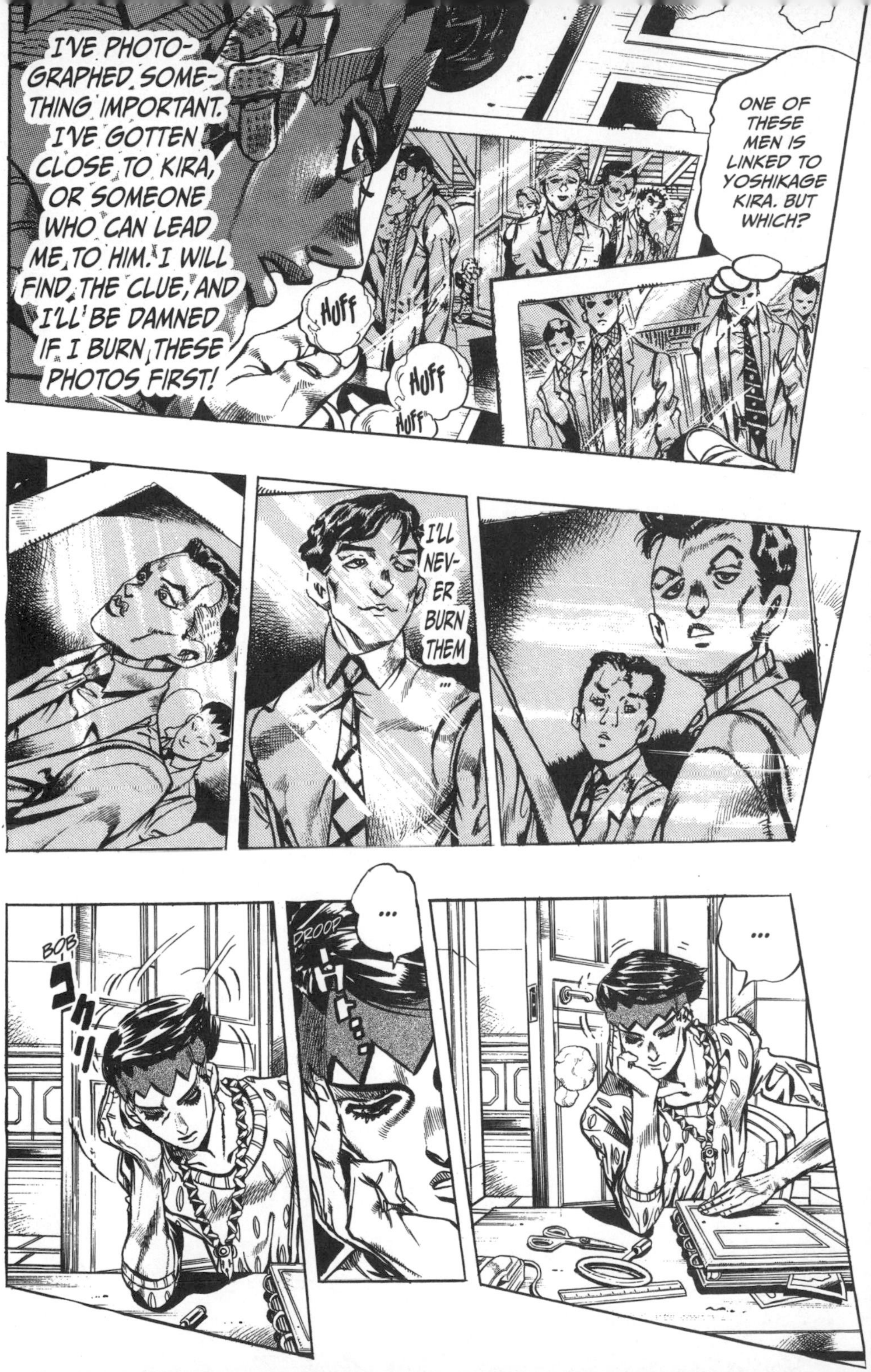
ONE OF THESE MEN IS LINKED TO YOSHIKAGE KIRA. BUT WHICH?
I'VE PHOTOGRAPHED SOMETHING IMPORTANT. I'VE GOTTEN CLOSE TO KIRA, OR SOMEONE WHO CAN LEAD ME TO HIM. I WILL FIND THE CLUE, AND I'LL BE DAMNED IF I BURN THESE PHOTOS FIRST!
HUFF
HUFF
HUFF
I'LL NEVER BURN THEM ...
...
DROOP
...
BOB

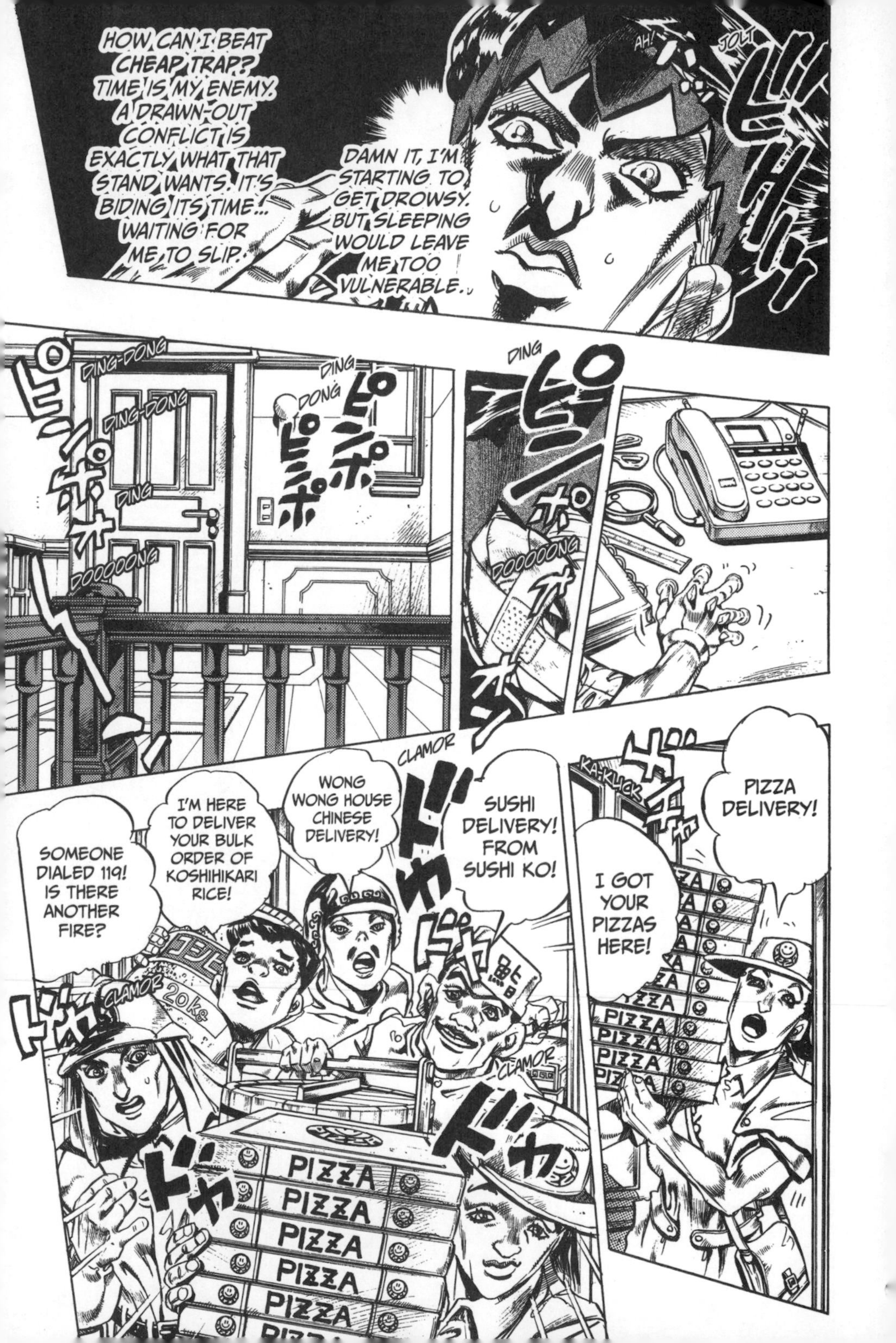
JOLT
AH!
HOW CAN I BEAT CHEAP TRAP? TIME IS MY ENEMY. A DRAWN-OUT CONFLICT IS EXACTLY WHAT THAT STAND WANTS. IT'S BIDING ITS TIME... WAITING FOR ME TO SLIP.
DAMN IT, I'M STARTING TO GET DROWSY. BUT SLEEPING WOULD LEAVE ME TOO VULNERABLE...
DING
DOOOOONG
DING-DONG
DING
DONG
DING-DONG
DING
DOOOOONG
KA-KLICK
PIZZA DELIVERY!
I GOT YOUR PIZZAS HERE!
CLAMOR
SUSHI DELIVERY! FROM SUSHI KO!
WONG WONG HOUSE CHINESE DELIVERY!
I'M HERE TO DELIVER YOUR BULK ORDER OF KOSHIHIKARI RICE!
SOMEONE DIALED 119! IS THERE ANOTHER FIRE?
CLAMOR
20kg
CLAMOR
PIZZA
PIZZA
PIZZA
PIZZA
PIZZA

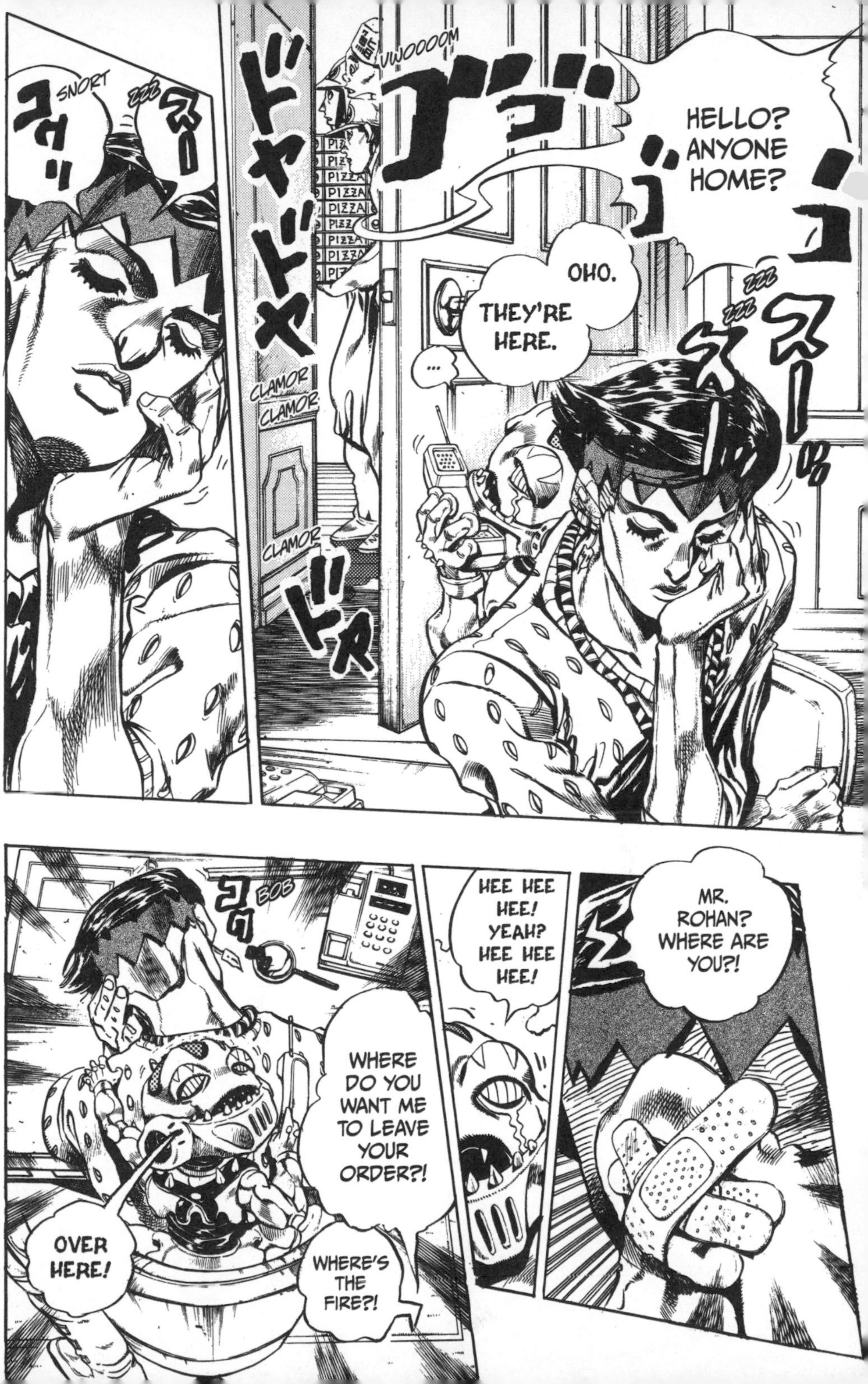

HELLO? ANYONE HOME?
ZZZ
ZZZ
OHO. THEY'RE HERE.
...
VWOOOOOM
PIZZA
CLAMOR
CLAMOR
CLAMOR
SNORT
ZZZ
MR. ROHAN? WHERE ARE YOU?!
HEE HEE HEE! YEAH? HEE HEE HEE!
BOB
WHERE DO YOU WANT ME TO LEAVE YOUR ORDER?!
WHERE'S THE FIRE?!
OVER HERE!

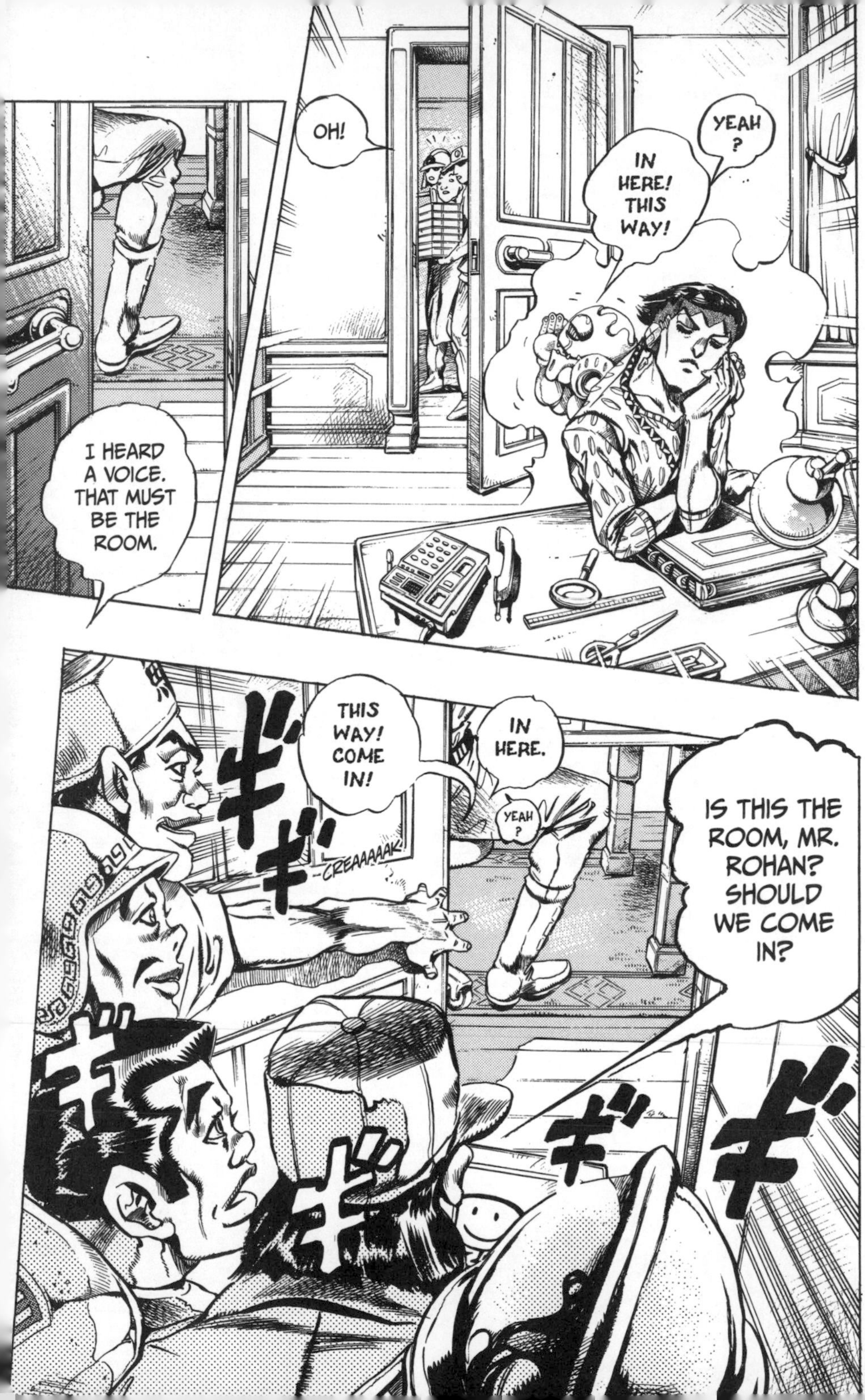
YEAH?
IN HERE! THIS WAY!
OH!
I HEARD A VOICE. THAT MUST BE THE ROOM.
IS THIS THE ROOM, MR. ROHAN? SHOULD WE COME IN?
IN HERE.
YEAH?
THIS WAY! COME IN!
ギギ
-CREAAAAAK
ギギ
ギギ

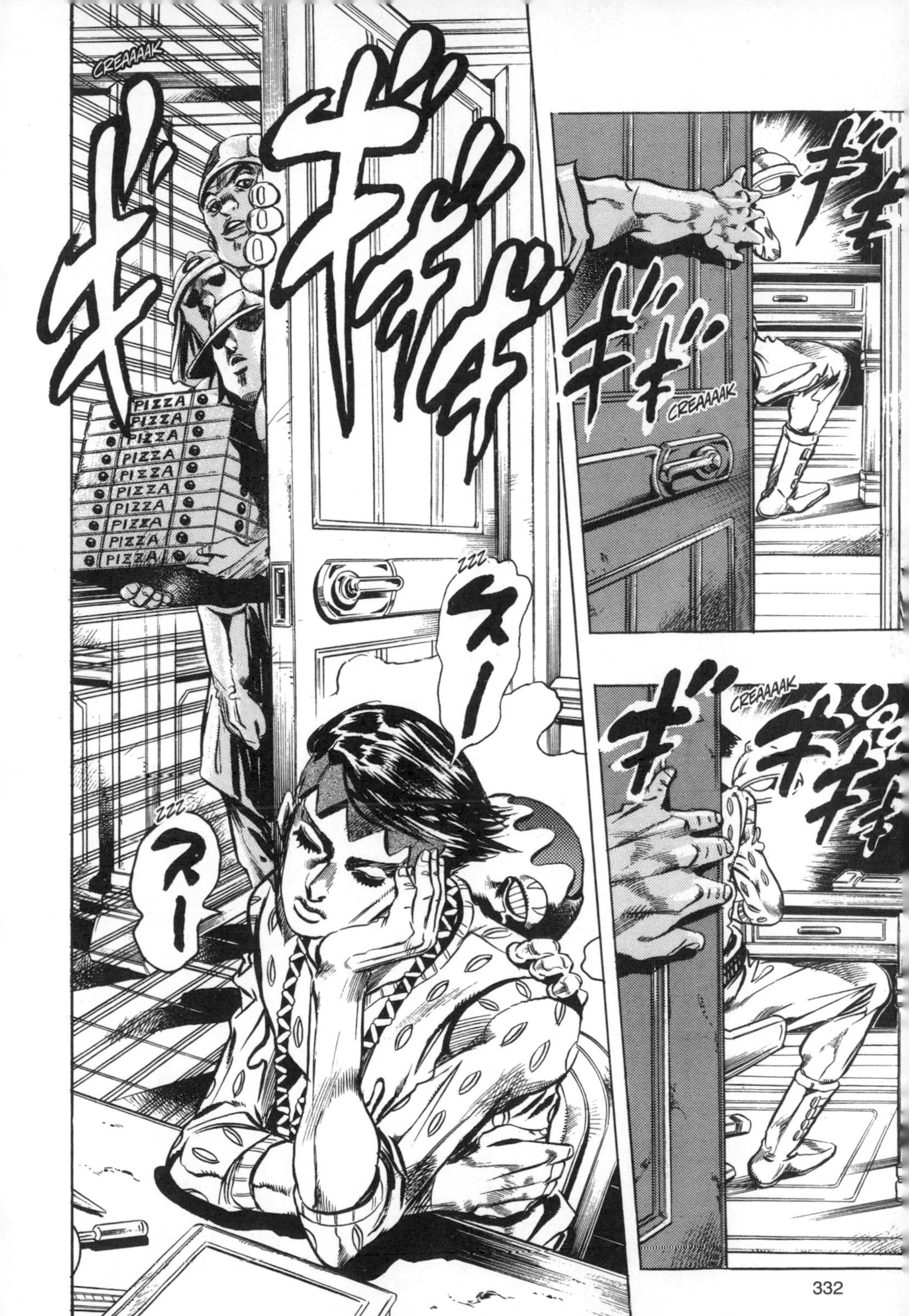
ギギ
CREAAAAK
ギギギ
CREAAAAK
CREAAAAK
ギギギギ
ZZZ
スー
ZZZ
スー

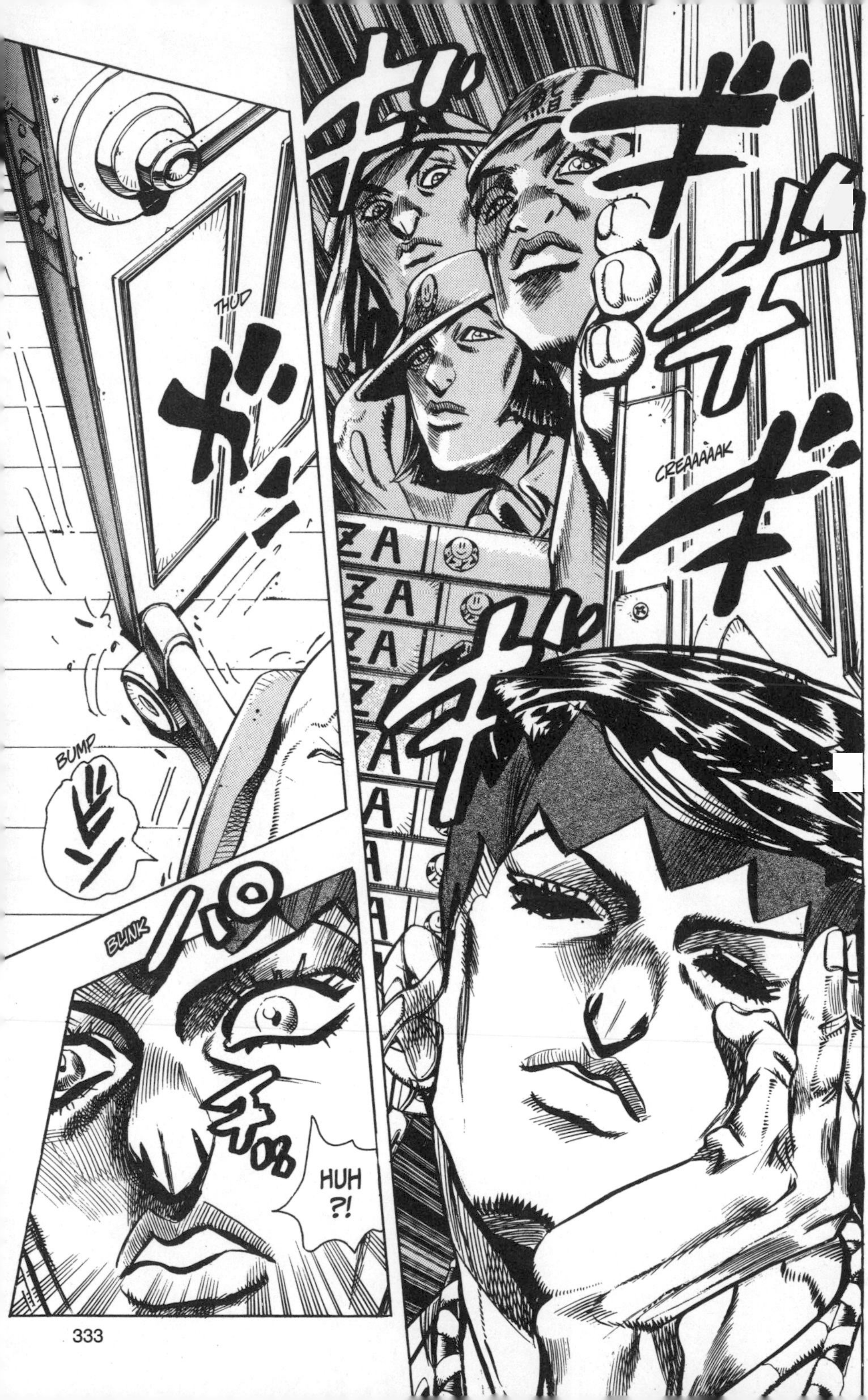
CREAAAAAK
THUD
BUMP
BLINK
HUH ?!

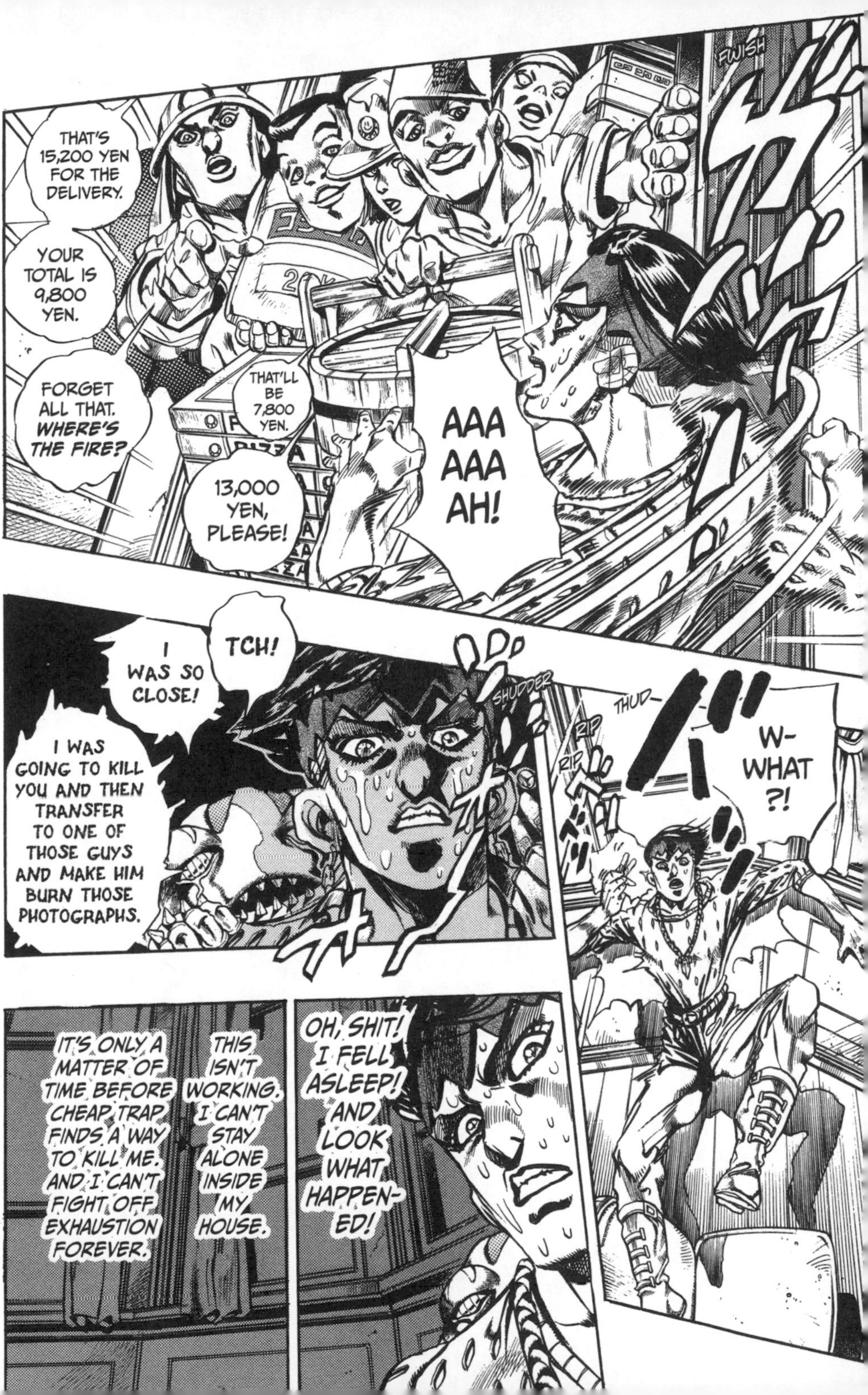
FWISH
AAA AAA AH!
THAT'S 15,200 YEN FOR THE DELIVERY.
YOUR TOTAL IS 9,800 YEN.
THAT'LL BE 7,800 YEN.
FORGET ALL THAT. *WHERE'S THE FIRE?*
13,000 YEN, PLEASE!
THUD
RIP
RIP
W-WHAT?!
SHUDDER
TCH!
I WAS SO CLOSE!
I WAS GOING TO KILL YOU AND THEN TRANSFER TO ONE OF THOSE GUYS AND MAKE HIM BURN THOSE PHOTOGRAPHS.
OH, SHIT! I FELL ASLEEP! AND LOOK WHAT HAPPEN-ED!
THIS ISN'T WORKING. I CAN'T STAY ALONE INSIDE MY HOUSE.
IT'S ONLY A MATTER OF TIME BEFORE CHEAP TRAP FINDS A WAY TO KILL ME. AND I CAN'T FIGHT OFF EXHAUSTION FOREVER.

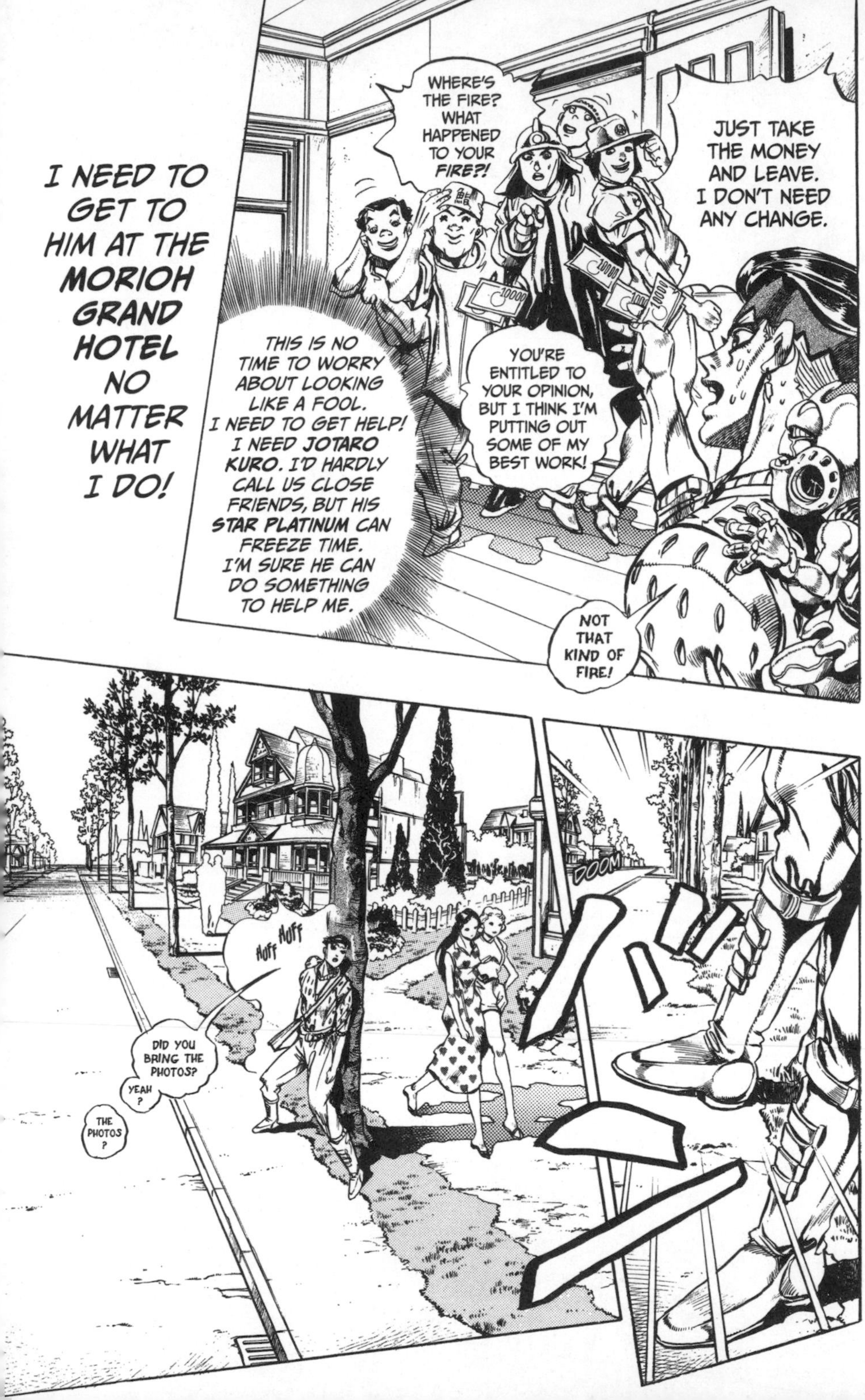
JUST TAKE THE MONEY AND LEAVE. I DON'T NEED ANY CHANGE.
WHERE'S THE FIRE? WHAT HAPPENED TO YOUR FIRE?!
YOU'RE ENTITLED TO YOUR OPINION, BUT I THINK I'M PUTTING OUT SOME OF MY BEST WORK!
THIS IS NO TIME TO WORRY ABOUT LOOKING LIKE A FOOL. I NEED TO GET HELP! I NEED JOTARO KURO. I'D HARDLY CALL US CLOSE FRIENDS, BUT HIS STAR PLATINUM CAN FREEZE TIME. I'M SURE HE CAN DO SOMETHING TO HELP ME.
NOT THAT KIND OF FIRE!
I NEED TO GET TO HIM AT THE MORIOH GRAND HOTEL NO MATTER WHAT I DO!
DOOM
HUFF HUFF
DID YOU BRING THE PHOTOS?
YEAH?
THE PHOTOS?

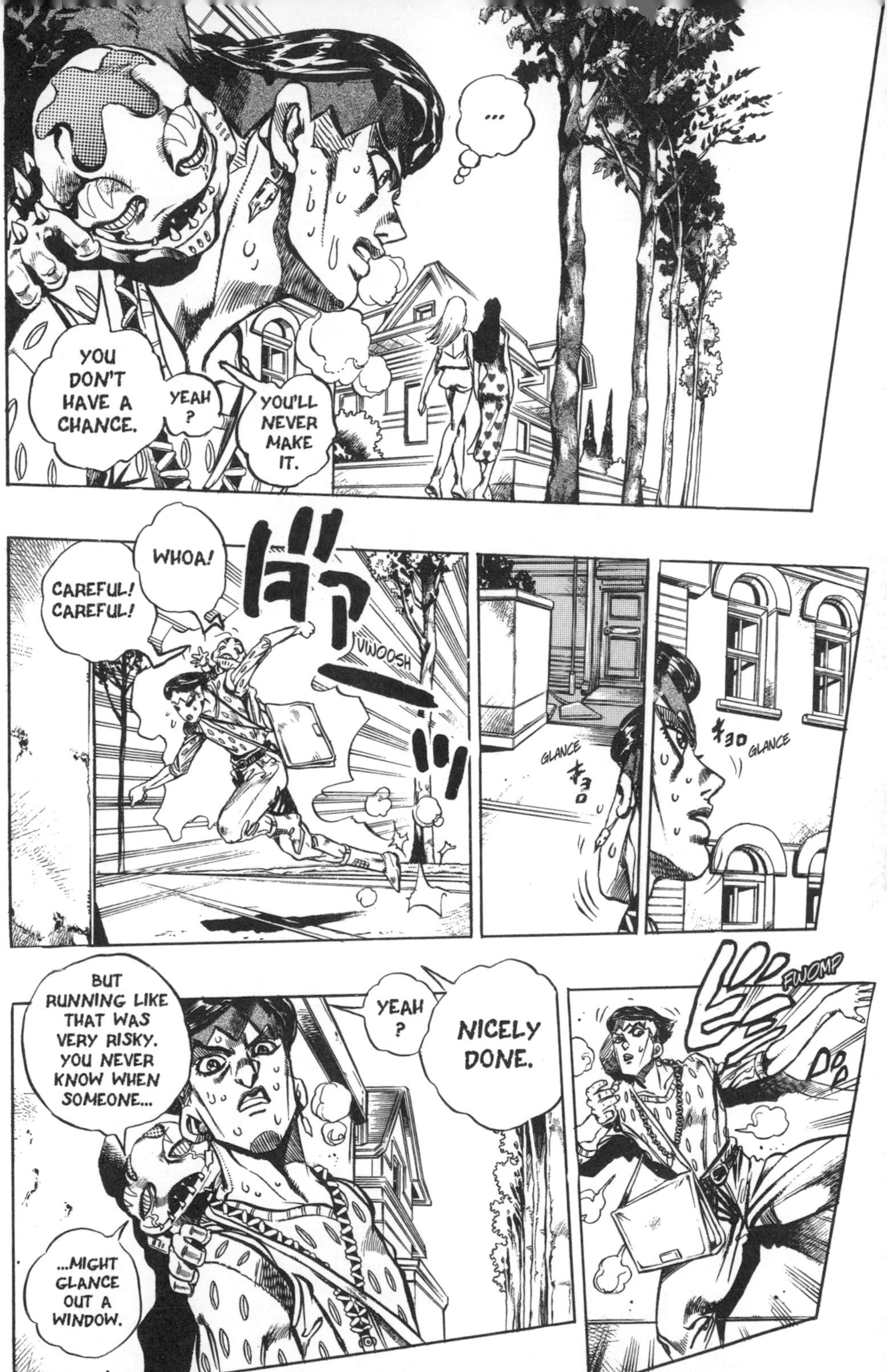
...
YOU'LL NEVER MAKE IT.
YEAH ?
YOU DON'T HAVE A CHANCE.
キョロ GLANCE
GLANCE キョロ
WHOA!
ダァーッ
VWOOSH
CAREFUL! CAREFUL!
FWOMP
NICELY DONE.
YEAH ?
BUT RUNNING LIKE THAT WAS VERY RISKY. YOU NEVER KNOW WHEN SOMEONE...
...MIGHT GLANCE OUT A WINDOW.

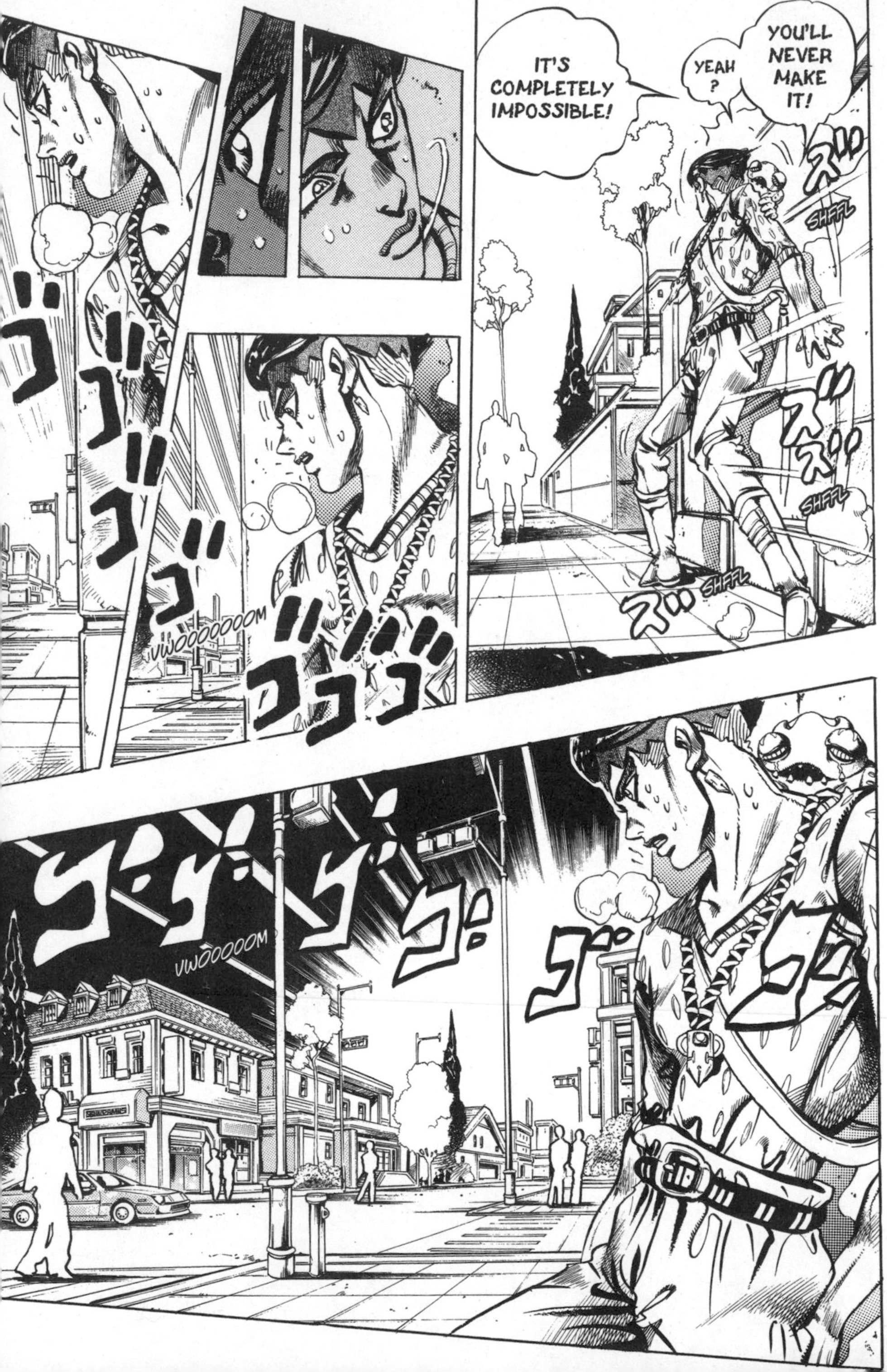
YOU'LL NEVER MAKE IT!
YEAH ?
IT'S COMPLETELY IMPOSSIBLE!
SHFFL
SHFFL
SHFFL
VWOOOOOOOM
VWOOOOOM

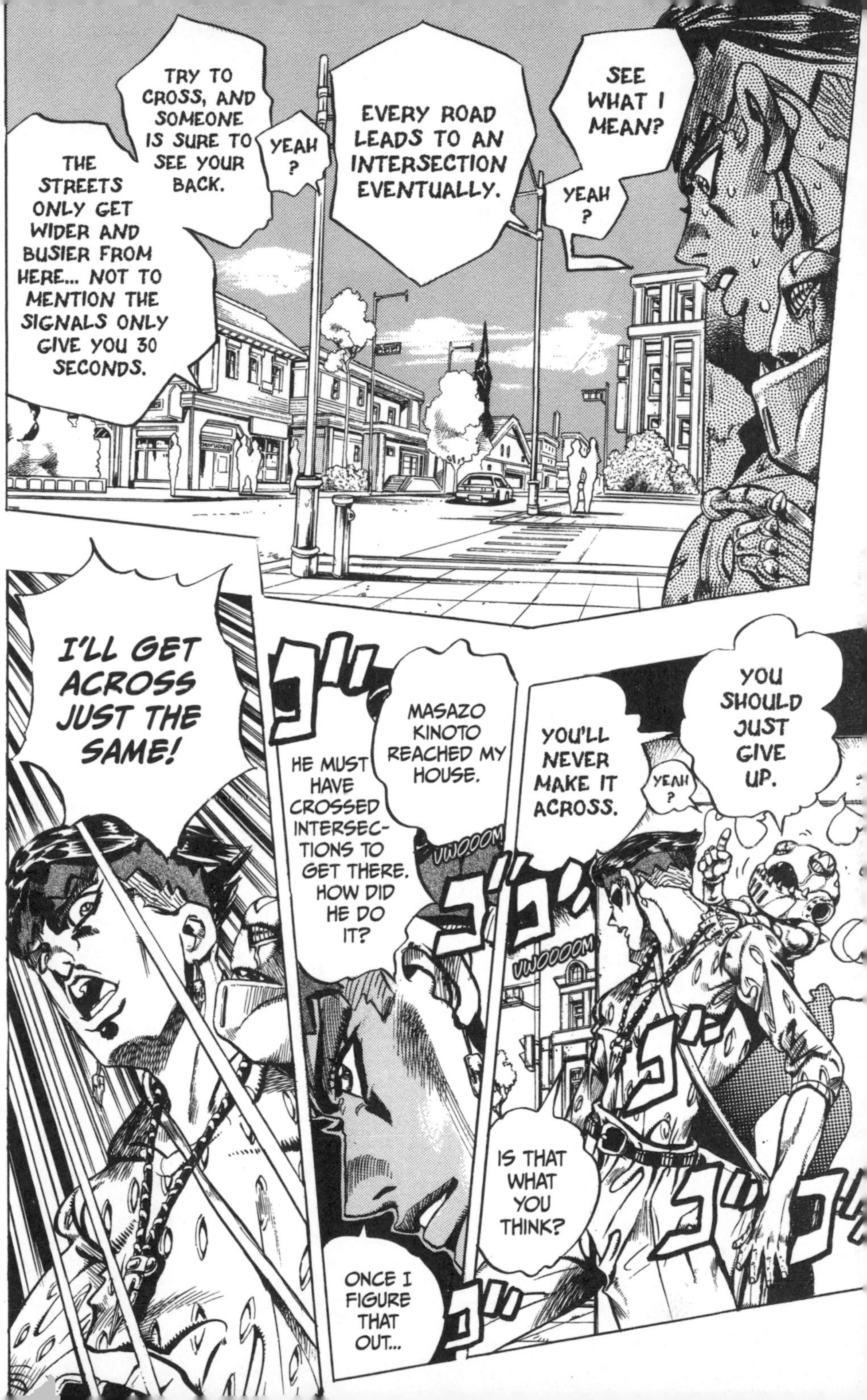
SEE WHAT I MEAN?
YEAH ?
EVERY ROAD LEADS TO AN INTERSECTION EVENTUALLY.
YEAH ?
TRY TO CROSS, AND SOMEONE IS SURE TO SEE YOUR BACK.
THE STREETS ONLY GET WIDER AND BUSIER FROM HERE... NOT TO MENTION THE SIGNALS ONLY GIVE YOU 30 SECONDS.
YOU SHOULD JUST GIVE UP.
YEAH ?
YOU'LL NEVER MAKE IT ACROSS.
VWOOOOM
IS THAT WHAT YOU THINK?
MASAZO KINOTO REACHED MY HOUSE.
HE MUST HAVE CROSSED INTERSEC-TIONS TO GET THERE. HOW DID HE DO IT?
VWOOOM
ONCE I FIGURE THAT OUT...
I'LL GET ACROSS JUST THE SAME!

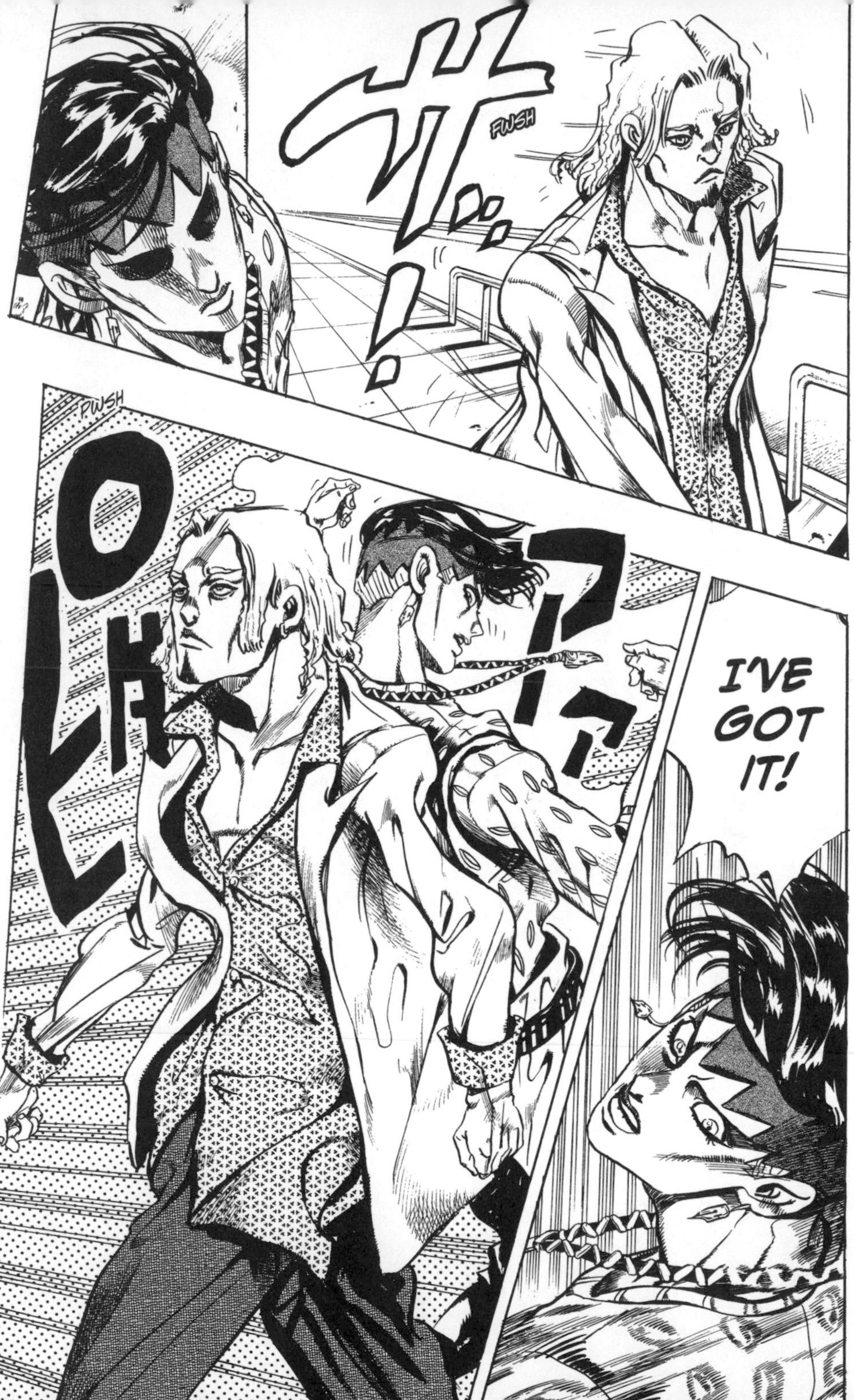
FWSH
I'VE GOT IT!
PWSH

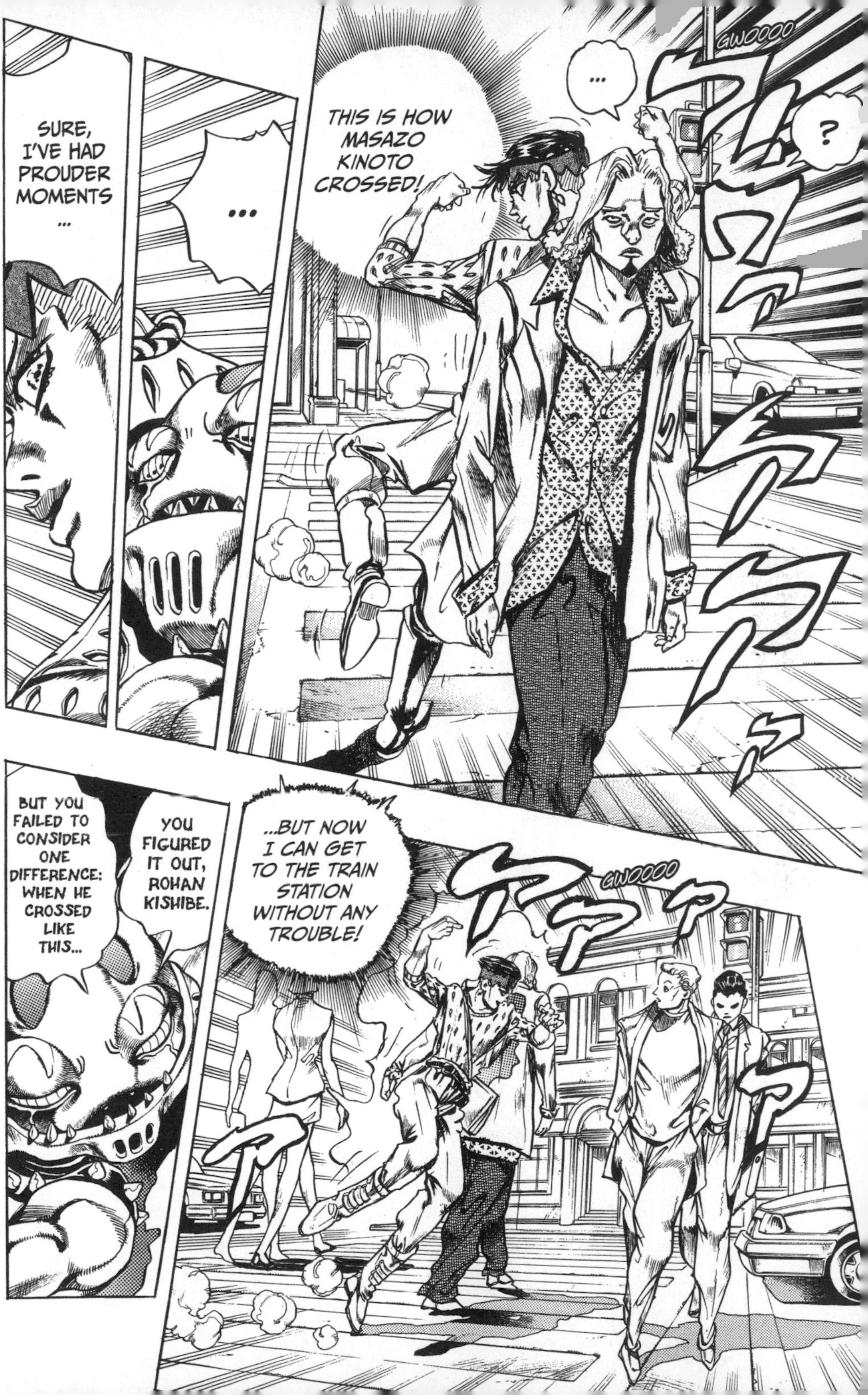
GWOOOO
?
...
THIS IS HOW MASAZO KINOTO CROSSED!
...
SURE, I'VE HAD PROUDER MOMENTS ...
...BUT NOW I CAN GET TO THE TRAIN STATION WITHOUT ANY TROUBLE!
GWOOOO
YOU FIGURED IT OUT, ROHAN KISHIBE.
BUT YOU FAILED TO CONSIDER ONE DIFFERENCE: WHEN HE CROSSED LIKE THIS...

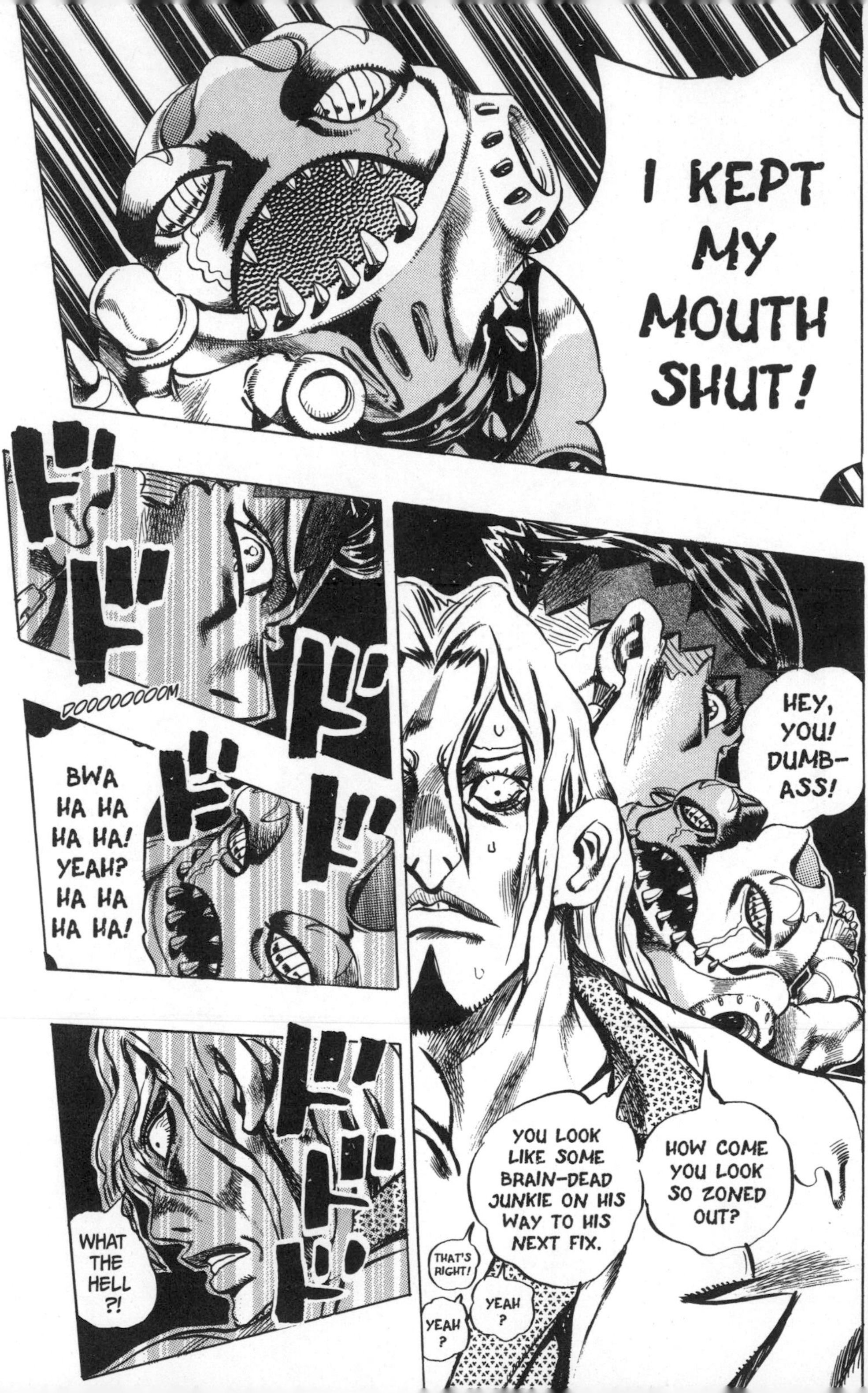
I KEPT MY MOUTH SHUT!
HEY, YOU! DUMB-ASS!
HOW COME YOU LOOK SO ZONED OUT?
YOU LOOK LIKE SOME BRAIN-DEAD JUNKIE ON HIS WAY TO HIS NEXT FIX.
THAT'S RIGHT!
YEAH ?
YEAH ?
DOOOOOOOOM
BWA HA HA HA HA! YEAH? HA HA HA HA!
WHAT THE HELL ?!

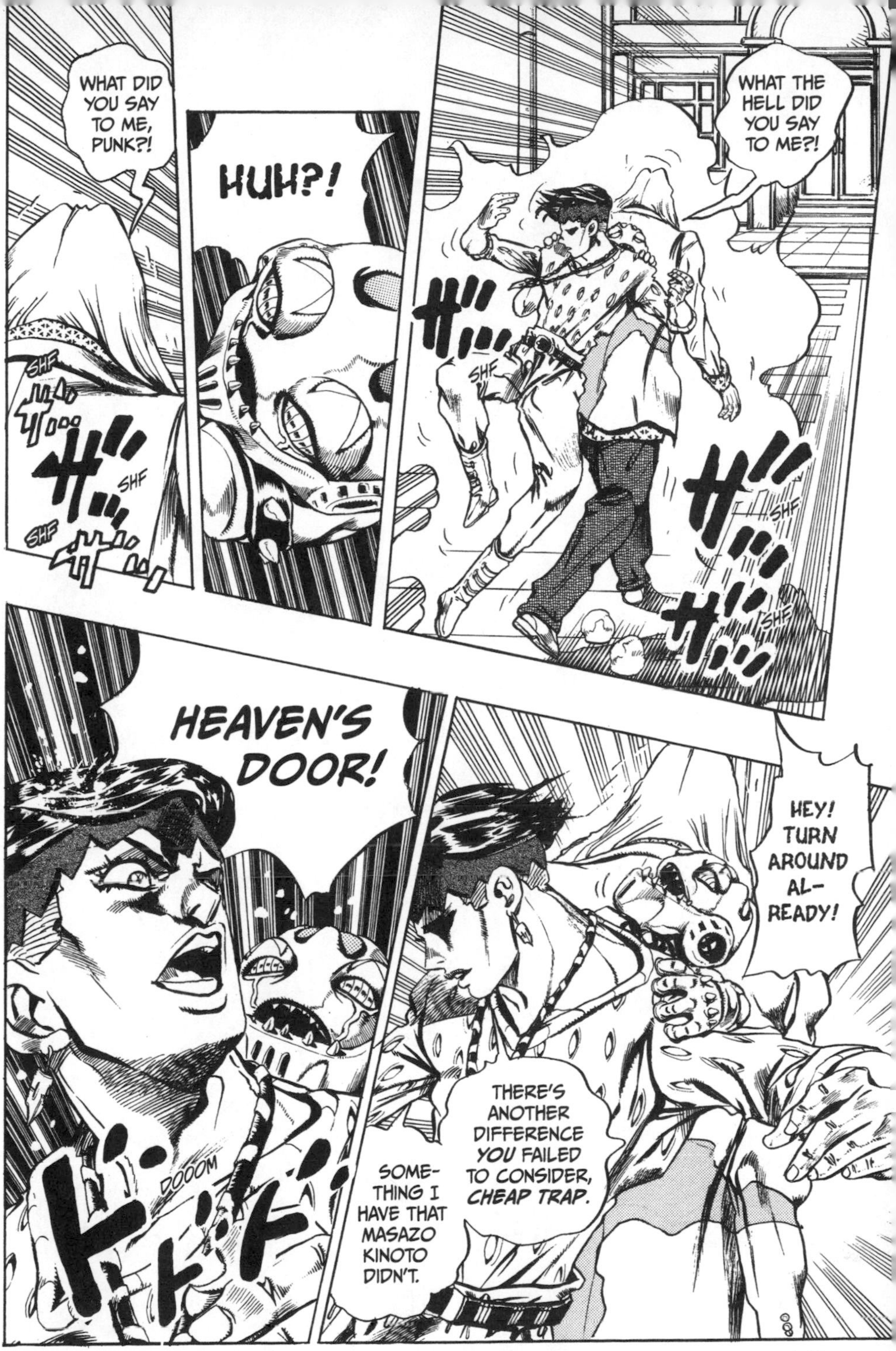
WHAT THE HELL DID YOU SAY TO ME?!
SHF
SHF
SHF
HUH?!
WHAT DID YOU SAY TO ME, PUNK?!
SHF
SHF
SHF
HEY! TURN AROUND AL-READY!
THERE'S ANOTHER DIFFERENCE *YOU* FAILED TO CONSIDER, *CHEAP TRAP.*
SOME-THING I HAVE THAT MASAZO KINOTO DIDN'T.
HEAVEN'S DOOR!
DOOOM

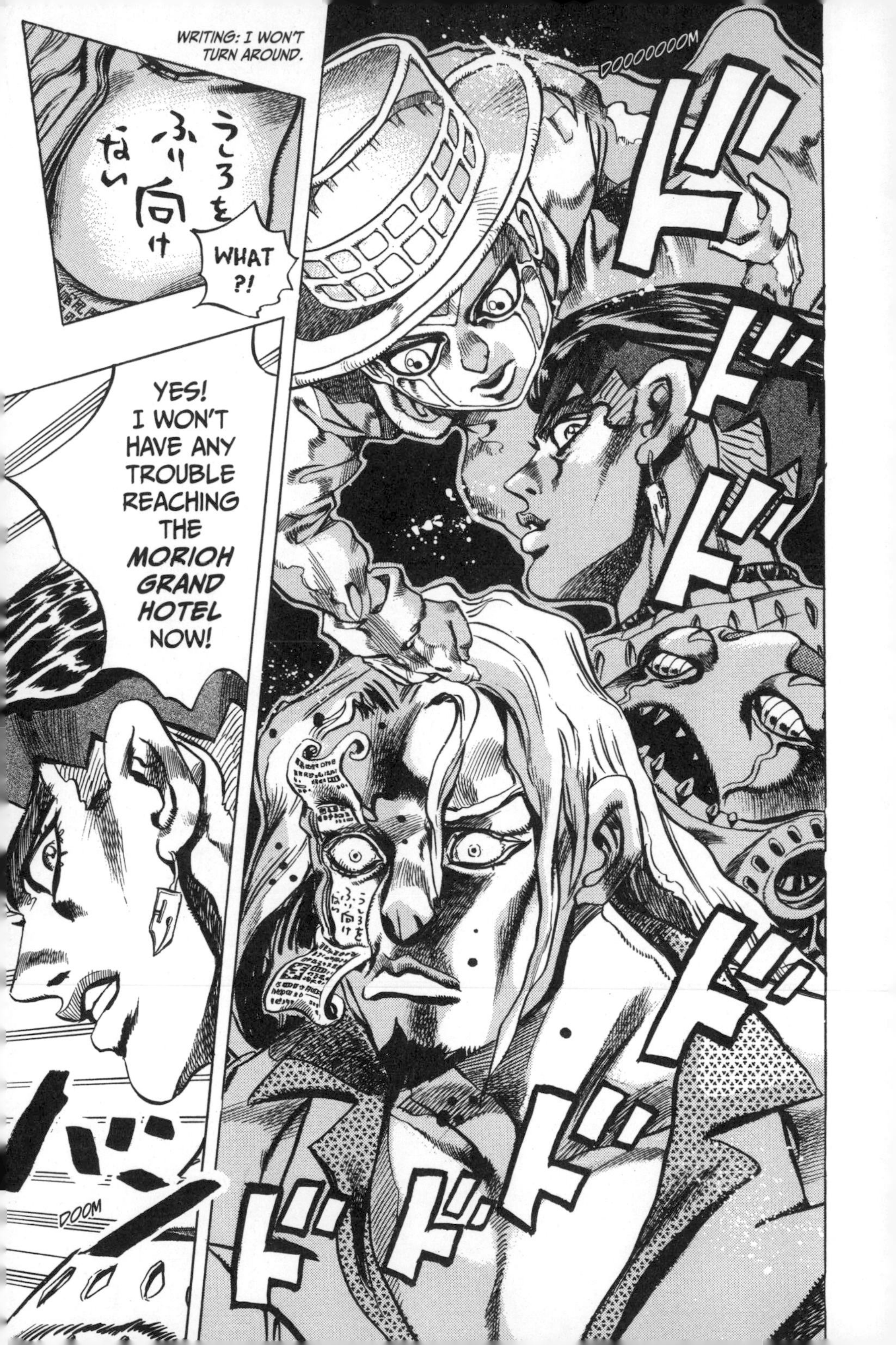
DOOOOOOOM
WRITING: I WON'T TURN AROUND.
うしろをふり向けない
WHAT?!
YES! I WON'T HAVE ANY TROUBLE REACHING THE *MORIOH GRAND HOTEL* NOW!
DOOM

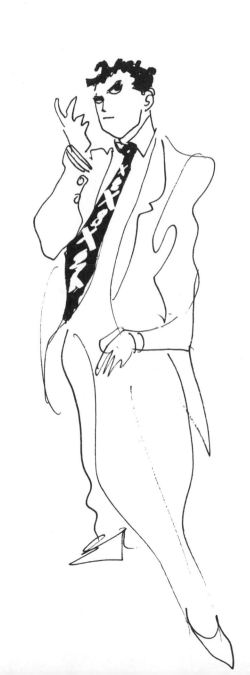

CHAPTER 151

CHEAP TRAP, PART 5

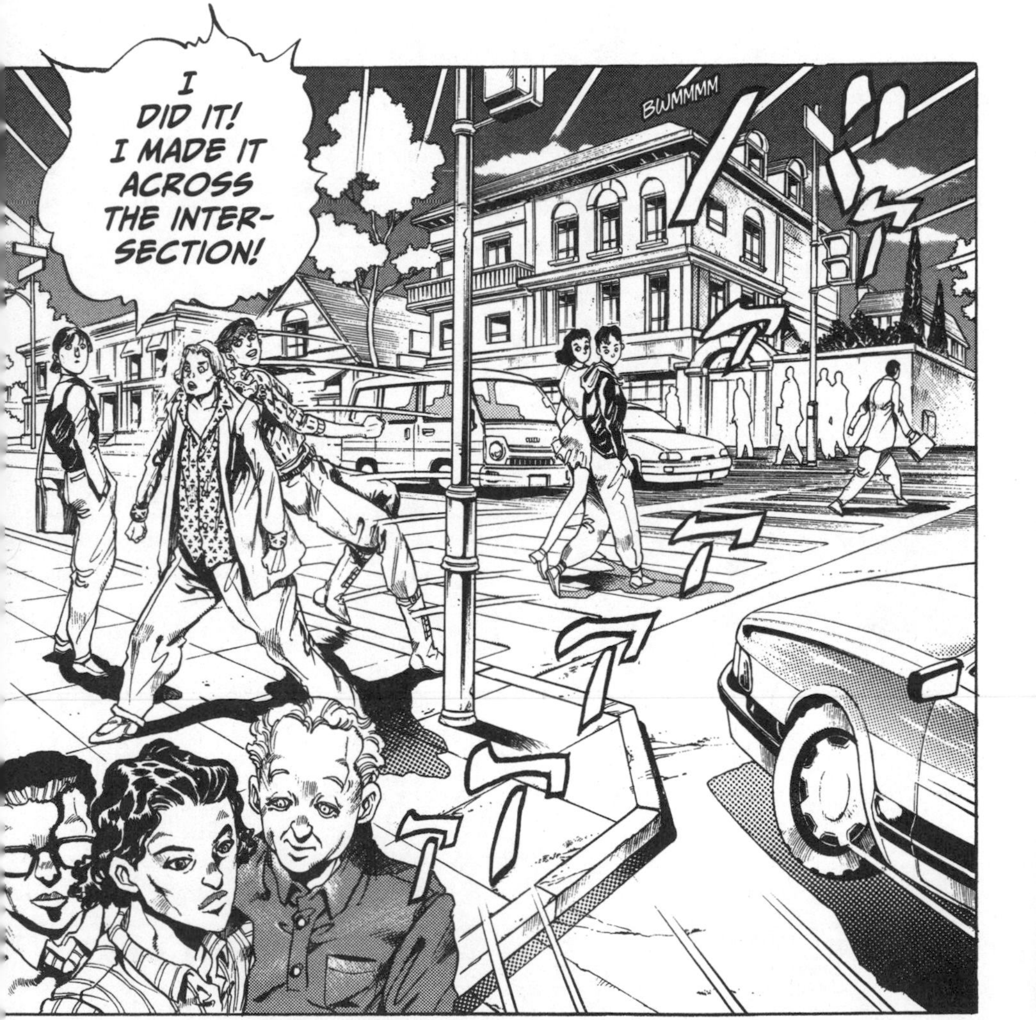
I DID IT! I MADE IT ACROSS THE INTER-SECTION!
BWMMMM

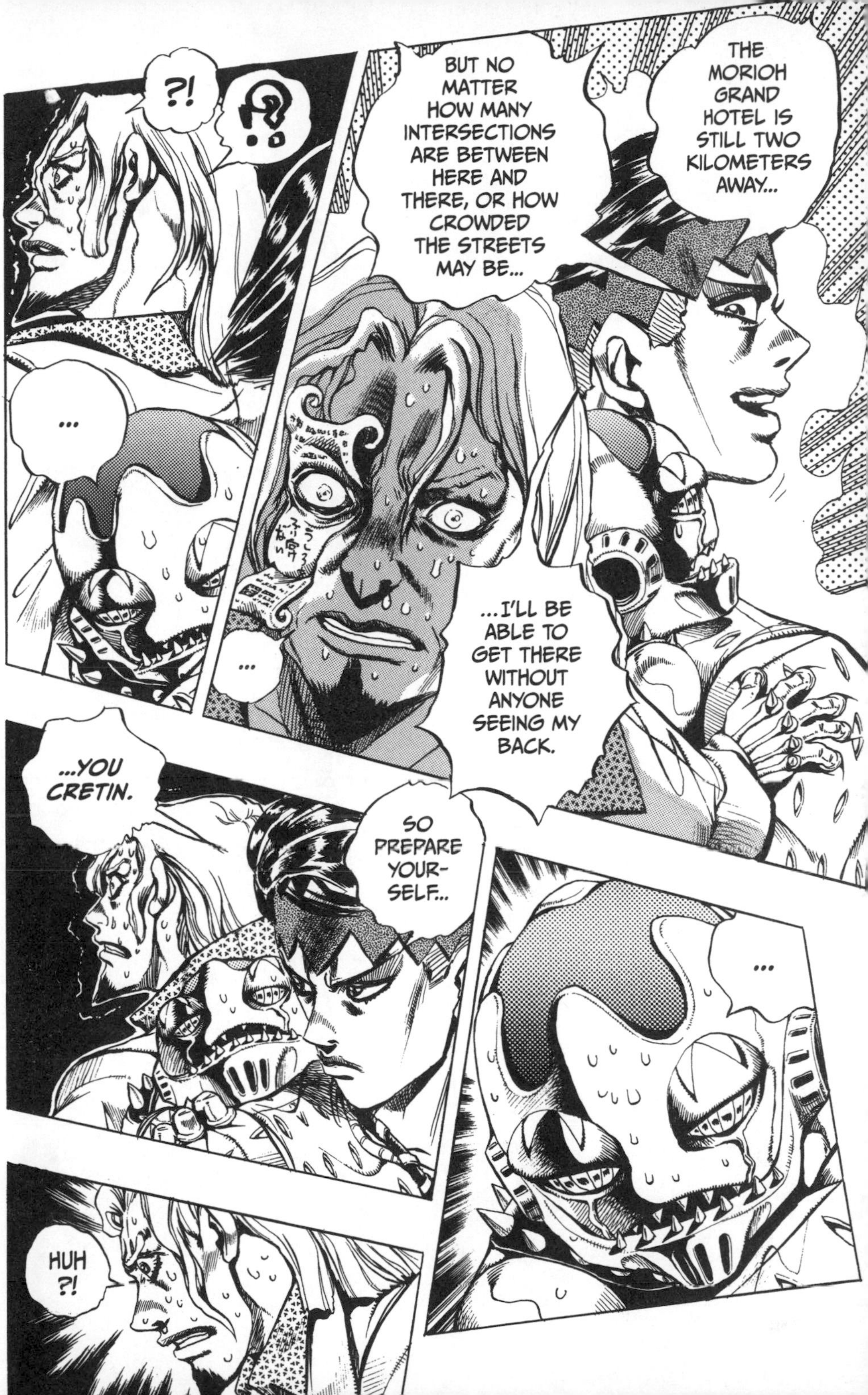
THE MORIOH GRAND HOTEL IS STILL TWO KILOMETERS AWAY...
BUT NO MATTER HOW MANY INTERSECTIONS ARE BETWEEN HERE AND THERE, OR HOW CROWDED THE STREETS MAY BE...
...I'LL BE ABLE TO GET THERE WITHOUT ANYONE SEEING MY BACK.
...
!?
?!
...
...
SO PREPARE YOUR-SELF...
...YOU CRETIN.
HUH ?!

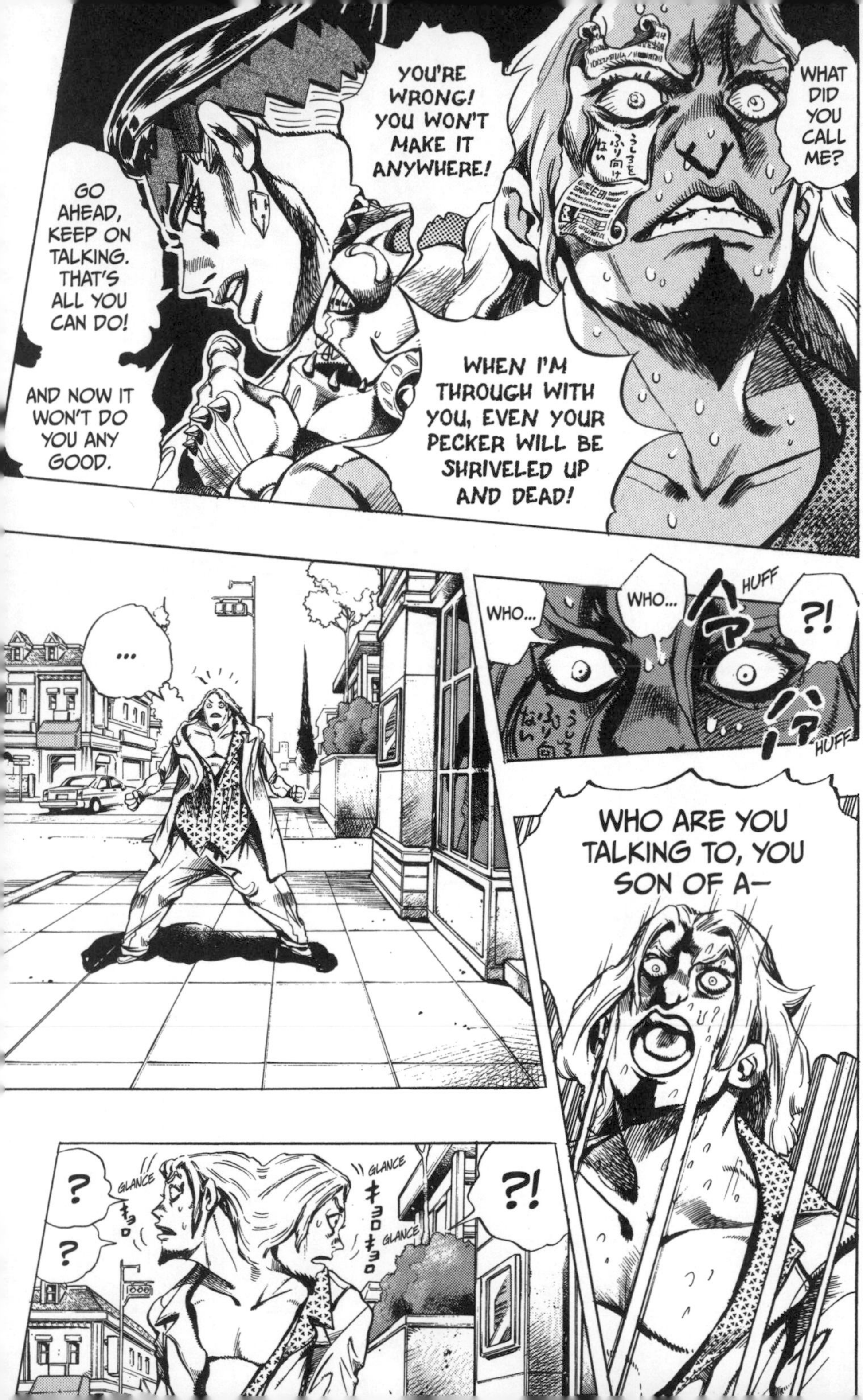
WHAT DID YOU CALL ME?
YOU'RE WRONG! YOU WON'T MAKE IT ANYWHERE!
GO AHEAD, KEEP ON TALKING. THAT'S ALL YOU CAN DO!
WHEN I'M THROUGH WITH YOU, EVEN YOUR PECKER WILL BE SHRIVELED UP AND DEAD!
AND NOW IT WON'T DO YOU ANY GOOD.
?!
HUFF
WHO...
WHO...
HUFF
...
WHO ARE YOU TALKING TO, YOU SON OF A—
?!
GLANCE
GLANCE
GLANCE
?
?

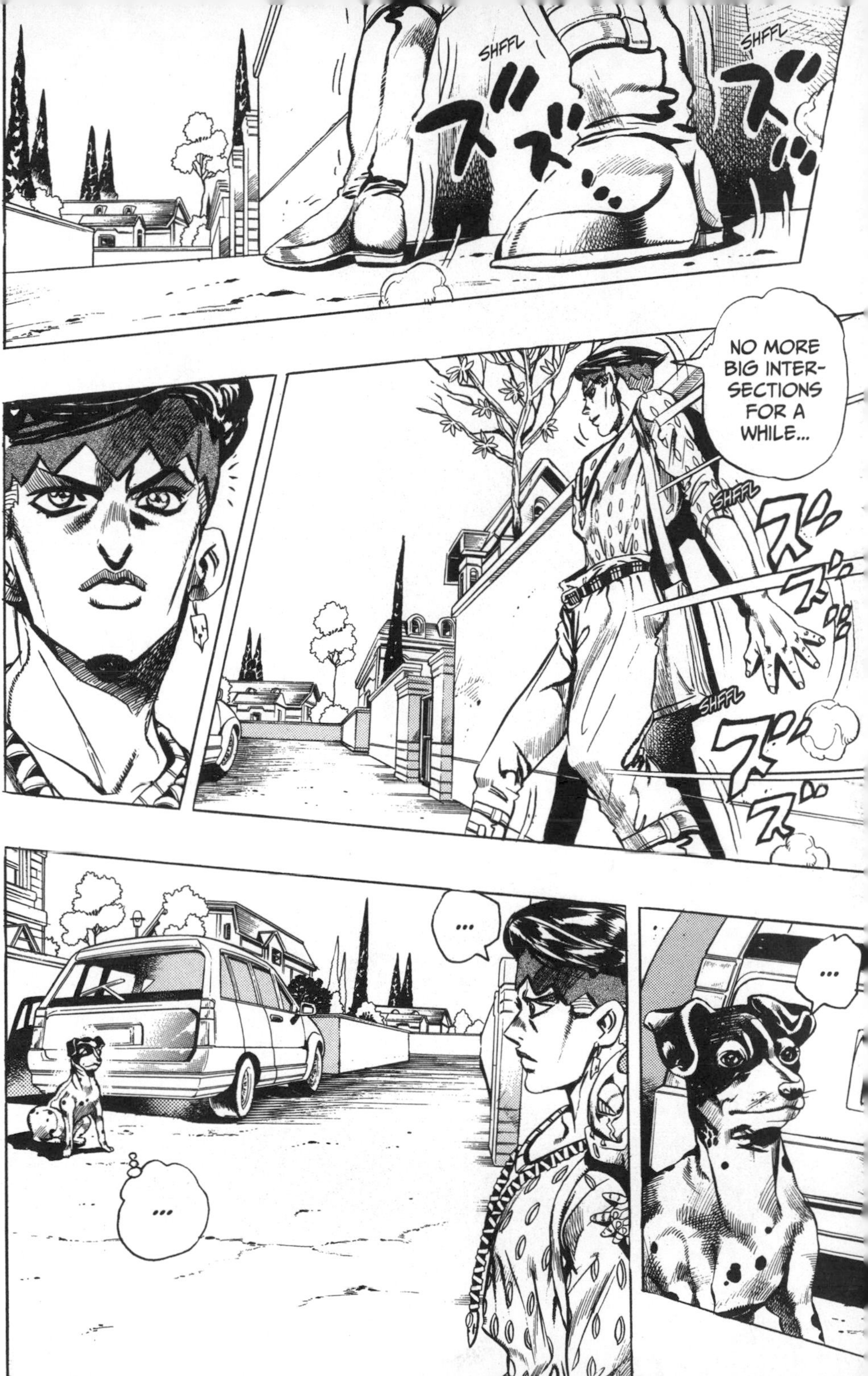
SHFFL
SHFFL
NO MORE BIG INTER-SECTIONS FOR A WHILE...
SHFFL
SHFFL
...
...
...
...

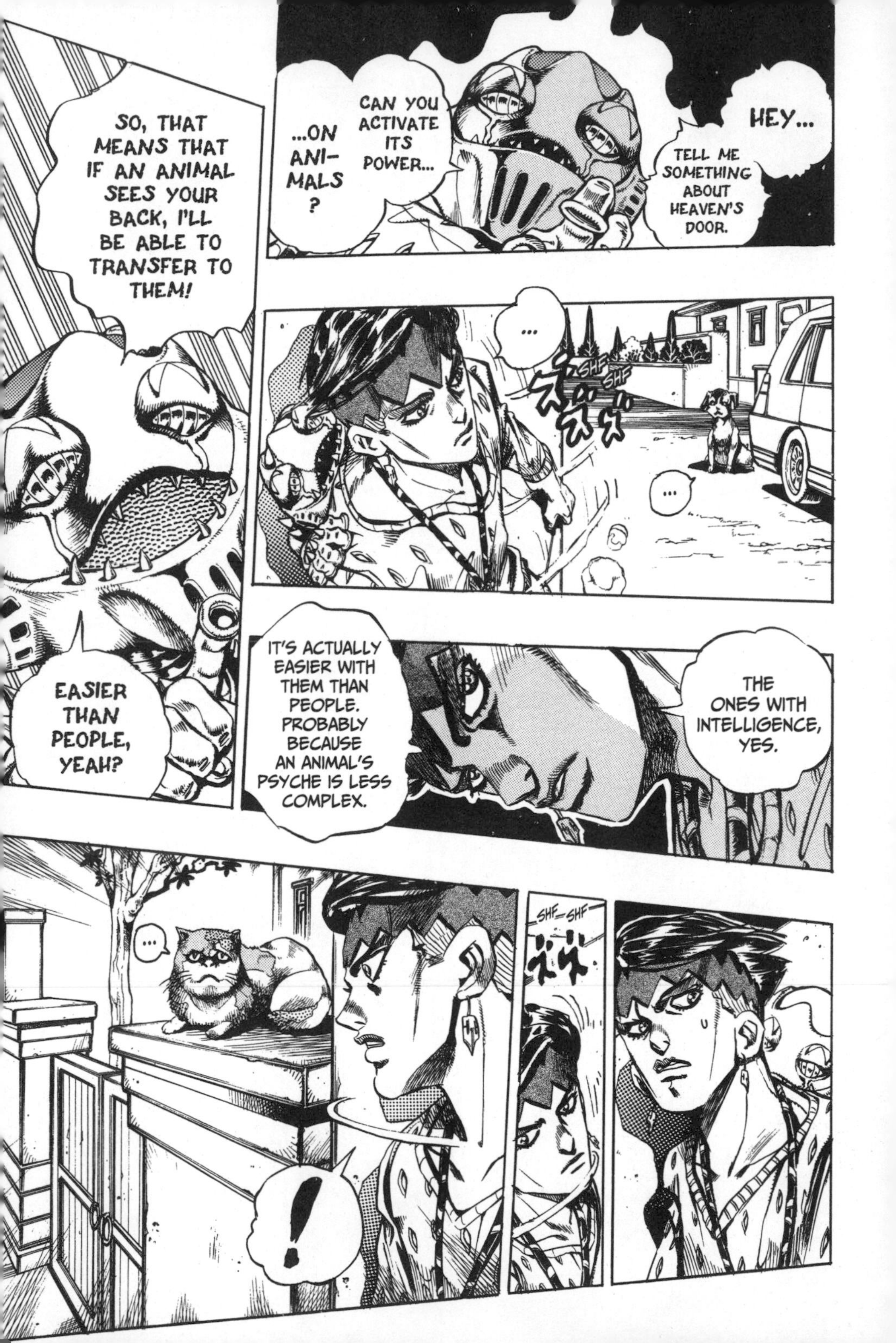
HEY...
TELL ME SOMETHING ABOUT HEAVEN'S DOOR.
CAN YOU ACTIVATE ITS POWER...
...ON ANIMALS?
...
SHF SHF
...
THE ONES WITH INTELLIGENCE, YES.
IT'S ACTUALLY EASIER WITH THEM THAN PEOPLE. PROBABLY BECAUSE AN ANIMAL'S PSYCHE IS LESS COMPLEX.
SO, THAT MEANS THAT IF AN ANIMAL SEES YOUR BACK, I'LL BE ABLE TO TRANSFER TO THEM!
EASIER THAN PEOPLE, YEAH?
SHF SHF
...
!

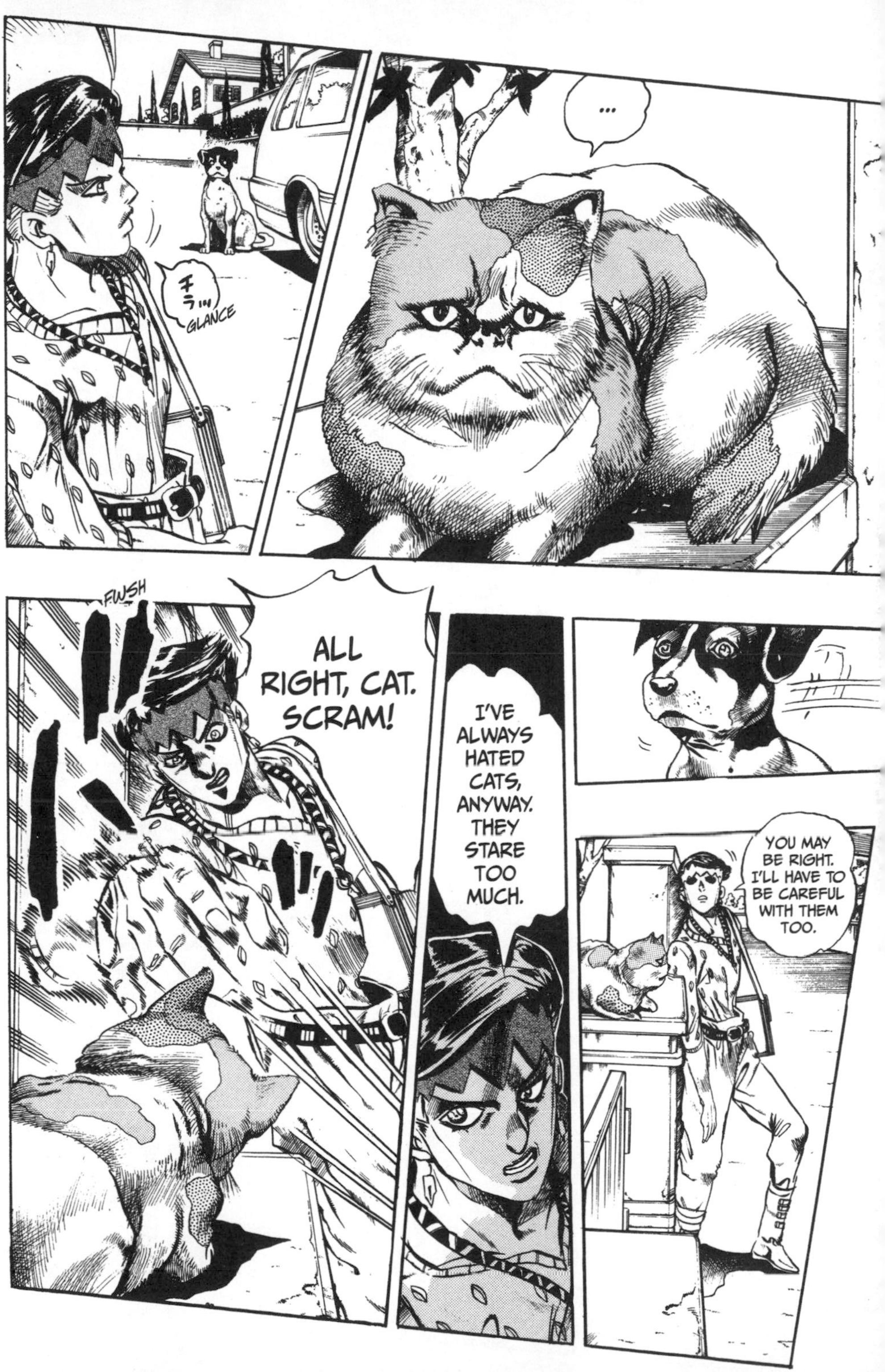
...
チラッ
GLANCE
YOU MAY BE RIGHT. I'LL HAVE TO BE CAREFUL WITH THEM TOO.
I'VE ALWAYS HATED CATS, ANYWAY. THEY STARE TOO MUCH.
FWSH
ALL RIGHT, CAT. SCRAM!

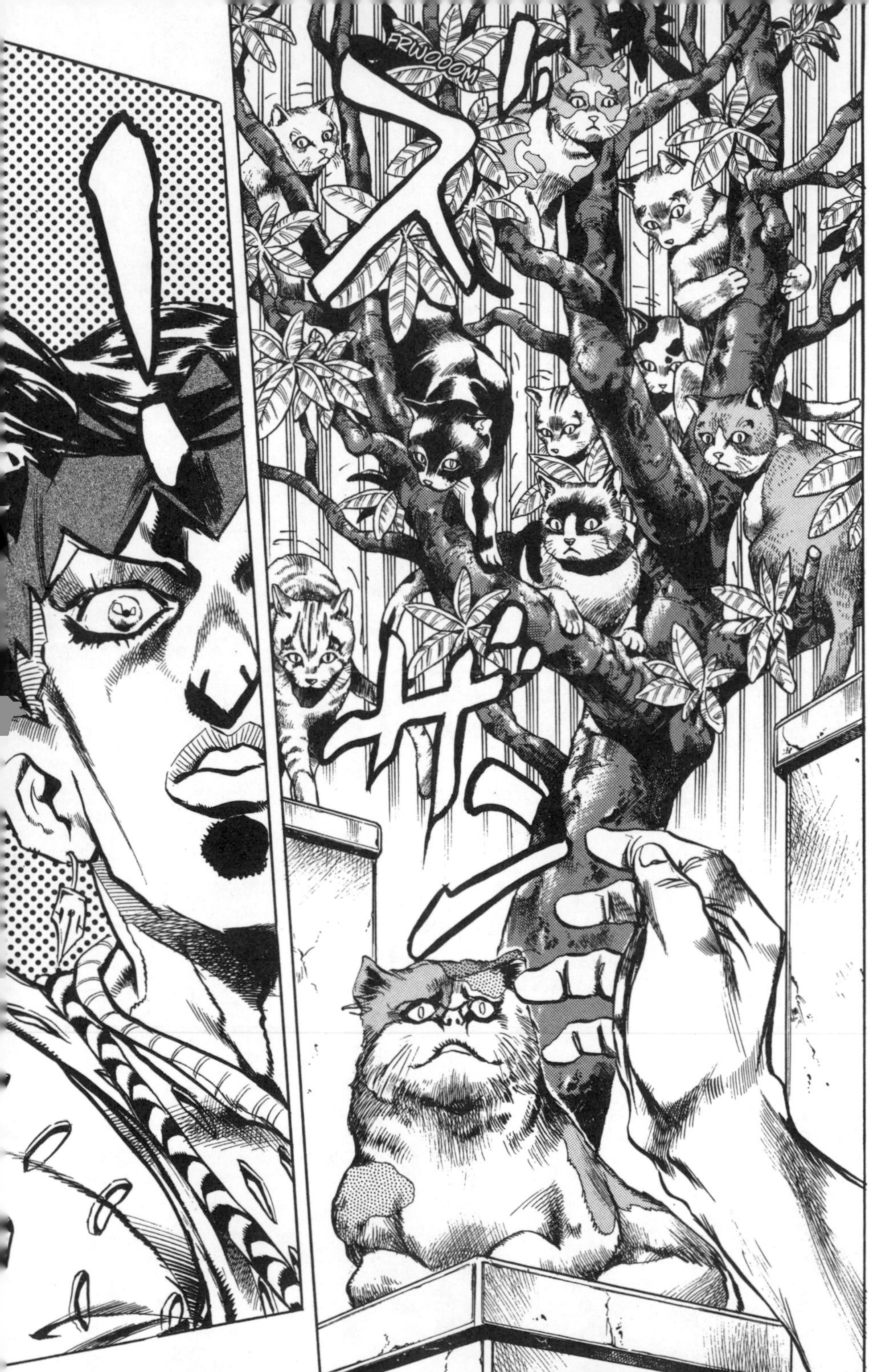
FRWOOOM

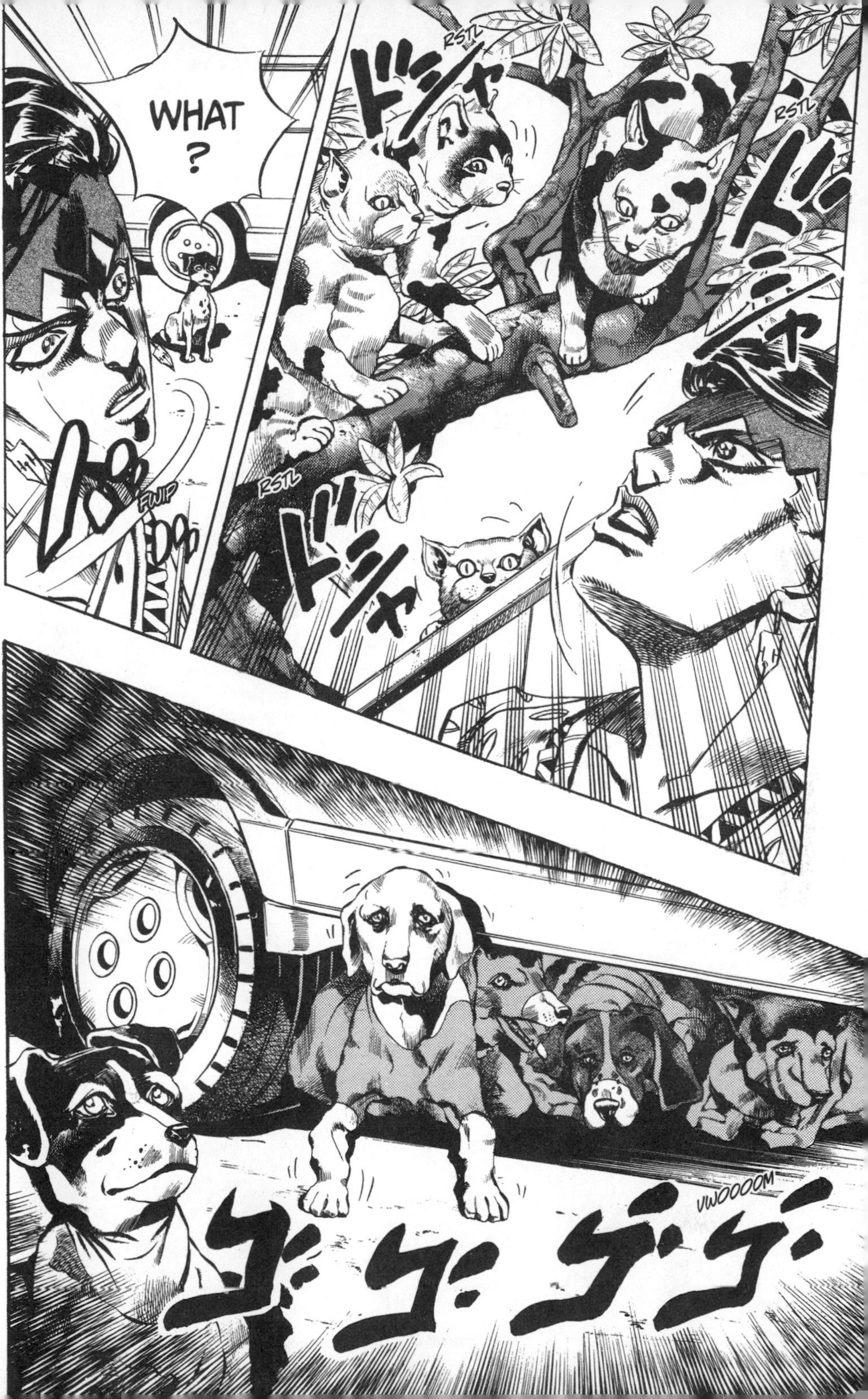

RSTL
ドシャ
RSTL
ドシャ
RSTL
ドシャ
WHAT
?
FWIP
VWOOOOM
ゴゴゴゴ

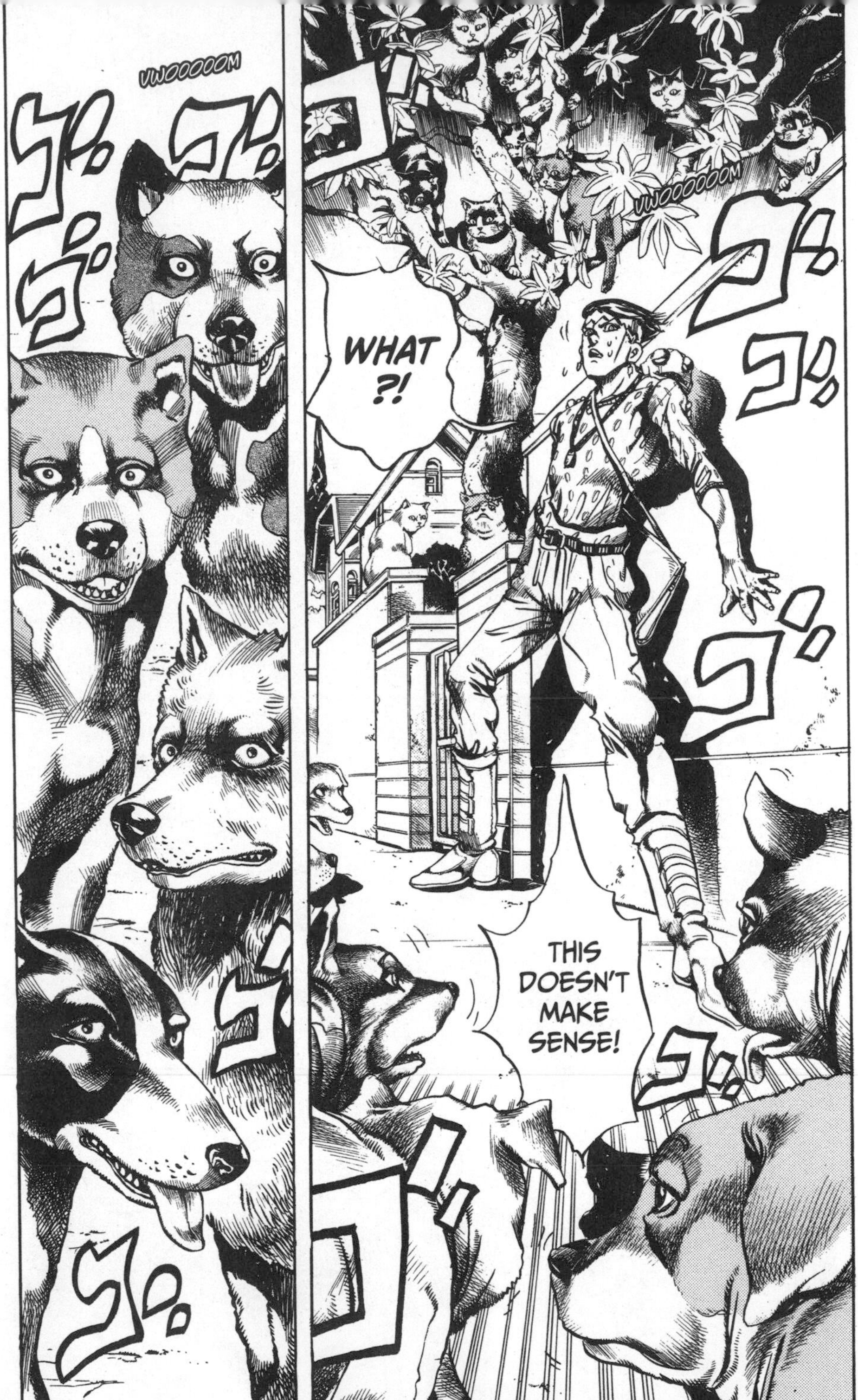
VWOOOOOOM
WHAT ?!
THIS DOESN'T MAKE SENSE!
VWOOOOOM

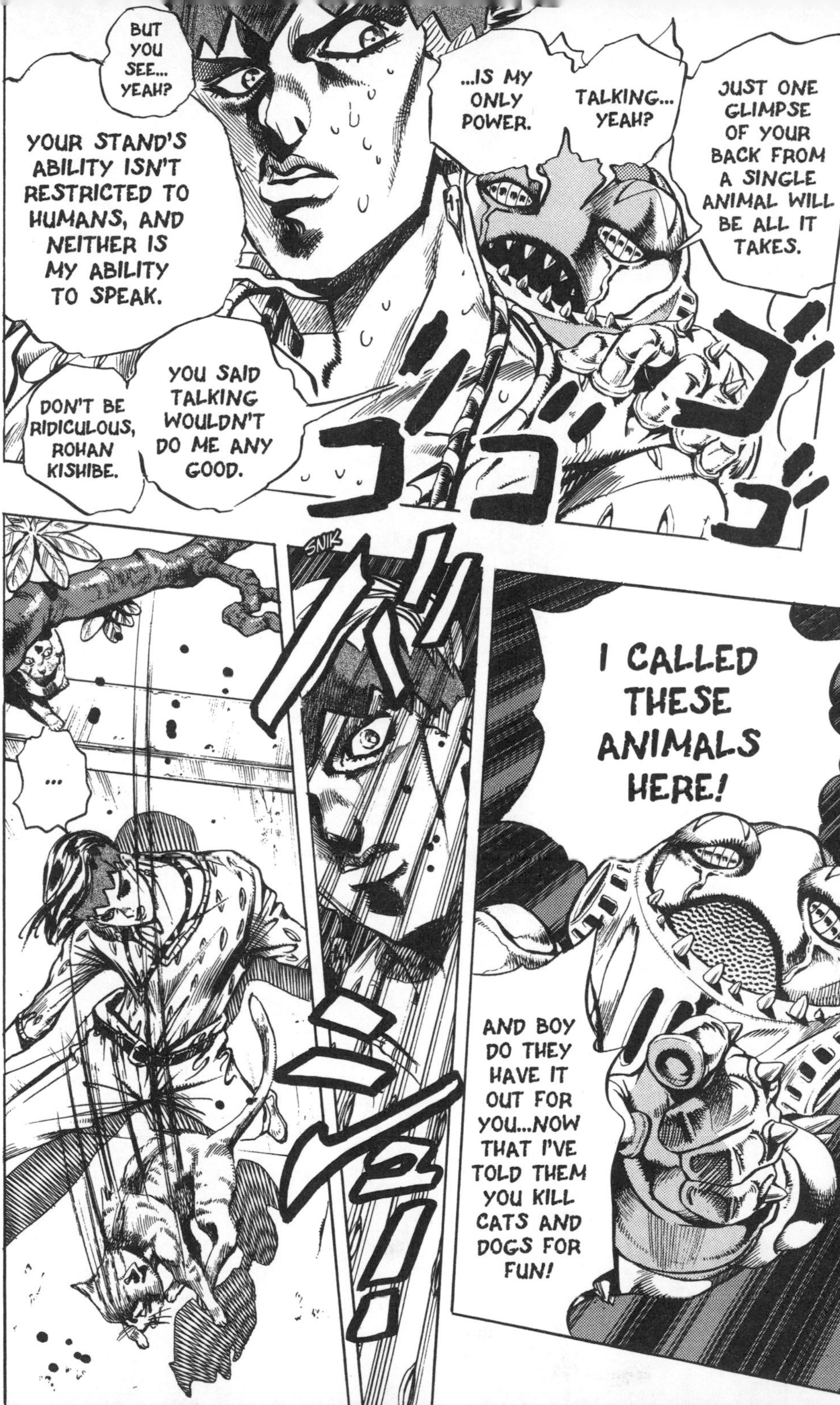
DON'T BE RIDICULOUS, ROHAN KISHIBE.
YOU SAID TALKING WOULDN'T DO ME ANY GOOD.
YOUR STAND'S ABILITY ISN'T RESTRICTED TO HUMANS, AND NEITHER IS MY ABILITY TO SPEAK.
BUT YOU SEE... YEAH?
TALKING... YEAH?
...IS MY ONLY POWER.
JUST ONE GLIMPSE OF YOUR BACK FROM A SINGLE ANIMAL WILL BE ALL IT TAKES.
I CALLED THESE ANIMALS HERE!
AND BOY DO THEY HAVE IT OUT FOR YOU...NOW THAT I'VE TOLD THEM YOU KILL CATS AND DOGS FOR FUN!
SNIK
...

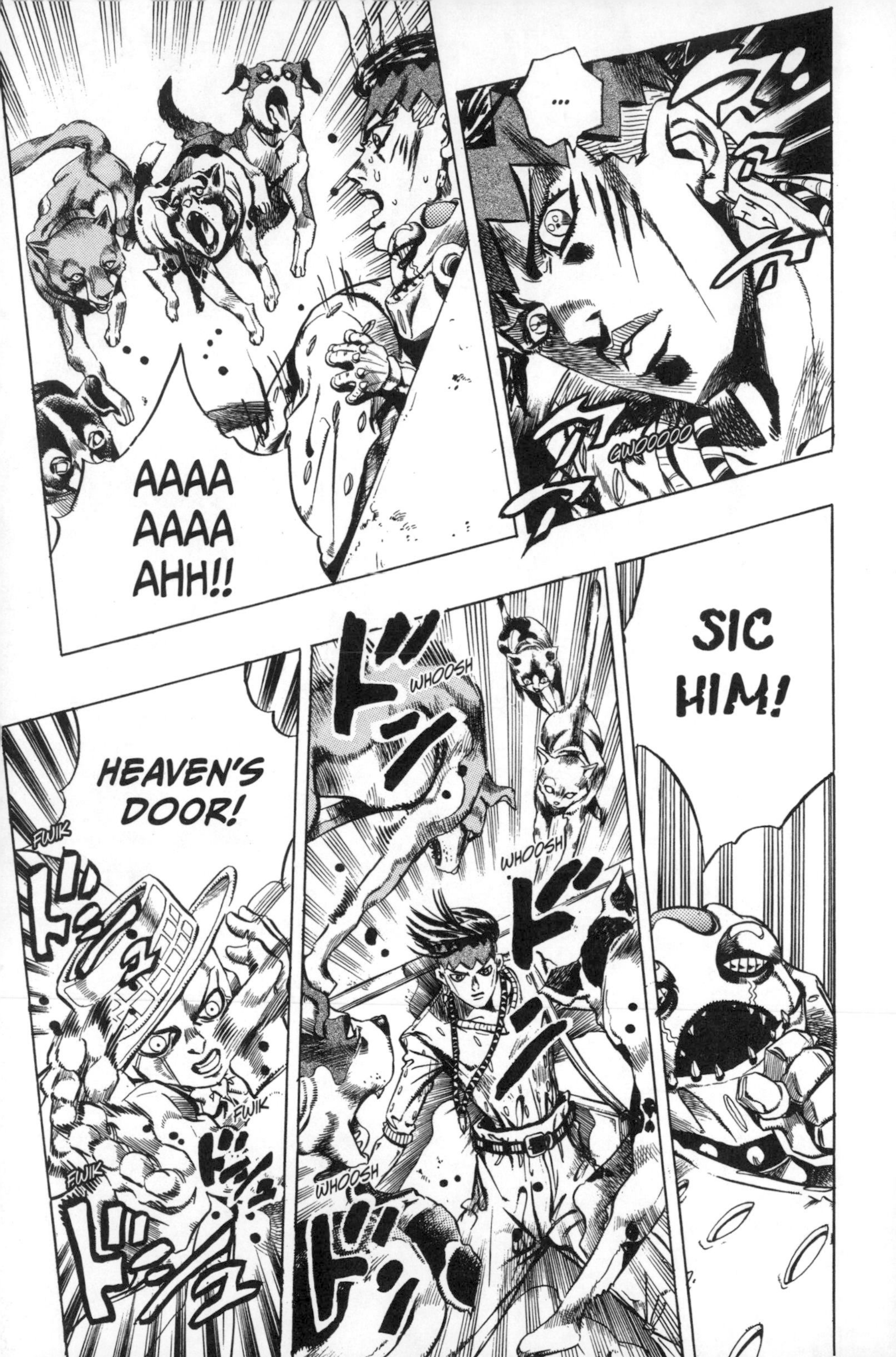
...
GWOOOOO
AAAA AAAA AHH!!
SIC HIM!
WHOOSH
WHOOSH
WHOOSH
HEAVEN'S DOOR!
FWIK
FWIK
FWIK

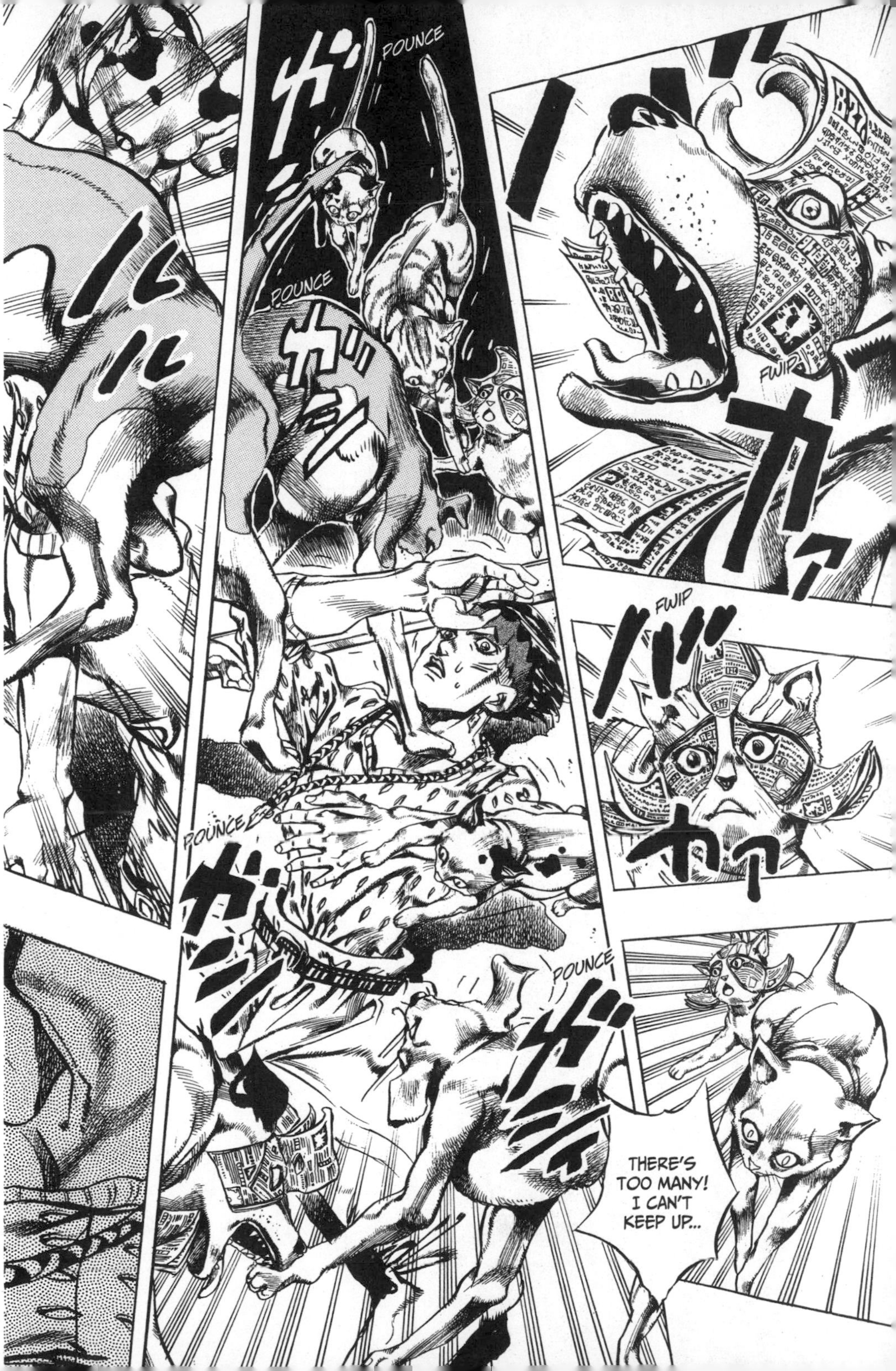

FWIP
FWIP
THERE'S TOO MANY! I CAN'T KEEP UP...
POUNCE
POUNCE
POUNCE
POUNCE

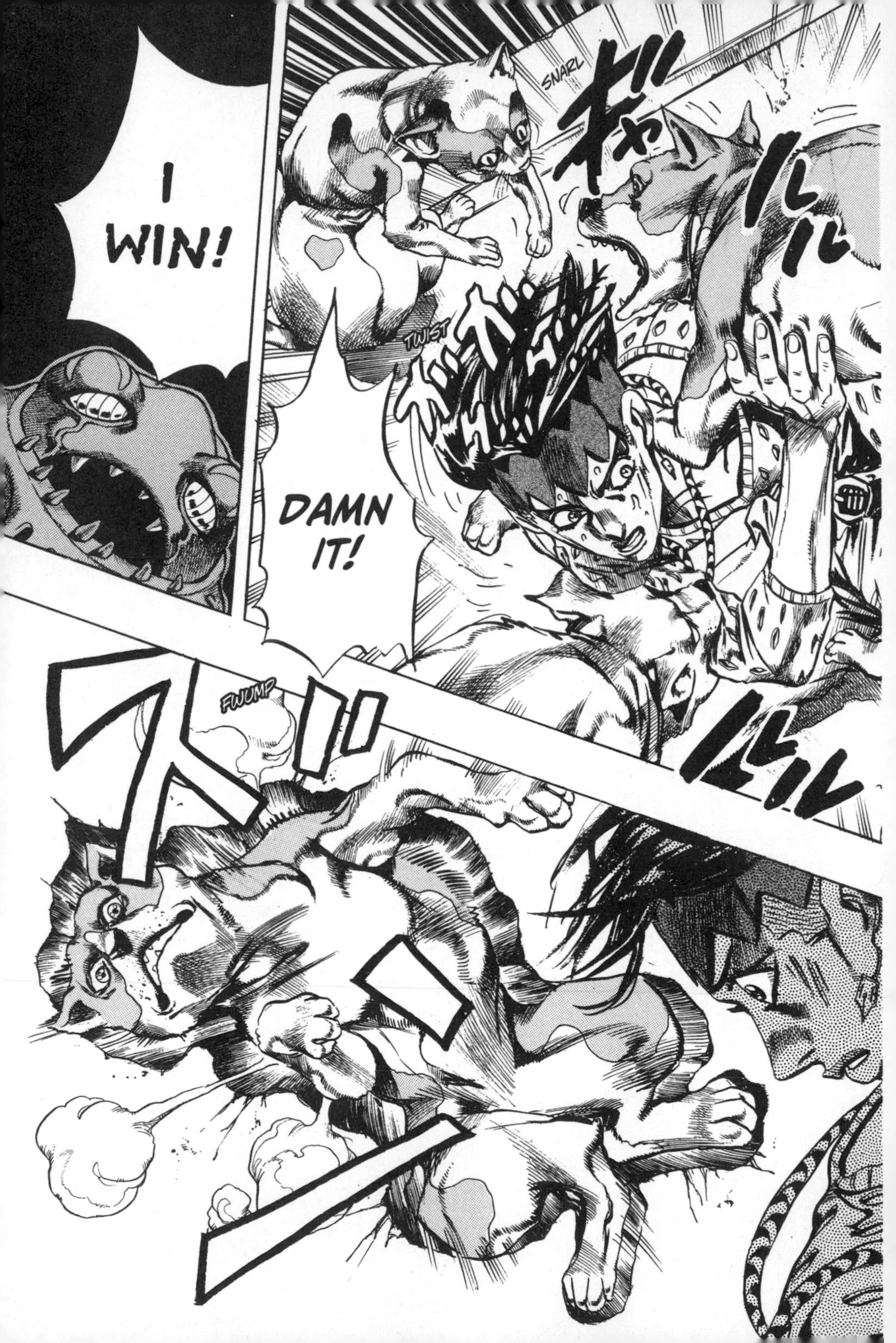
SNARL
TWIST
DAMN IT!
I WIN!
FWUMP

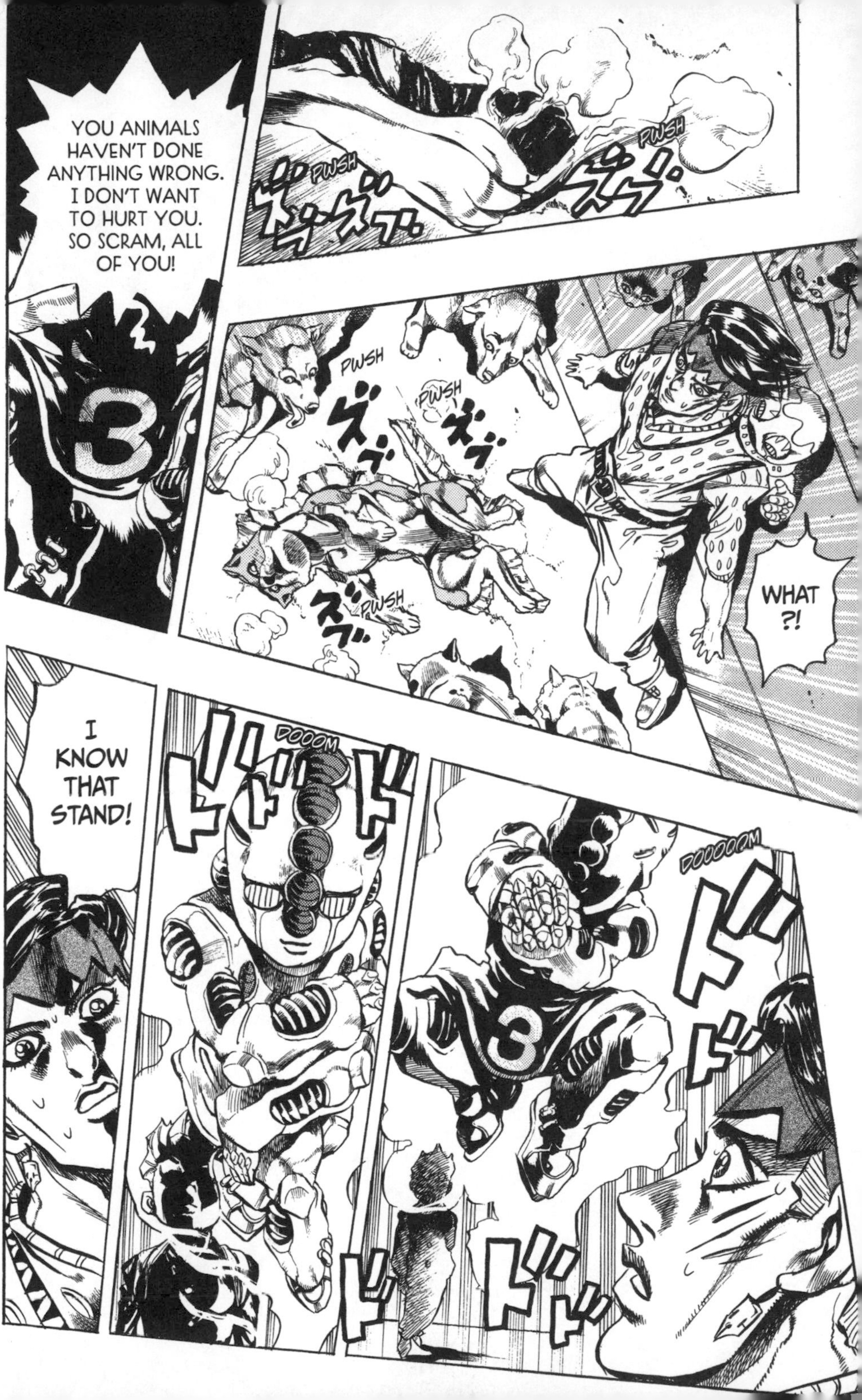
PWSH
PWSH
PWSH
PWSH
PWSH
WHAT ?!
YOU ANIMALS HAVEN'T DONE ANYTHING WRONG. I DON'T WANT TO HURT YOU. SO SCRAM, ALL OF YOU!
DOOOOOM
DOOOM
I KNOW THAT STAND!

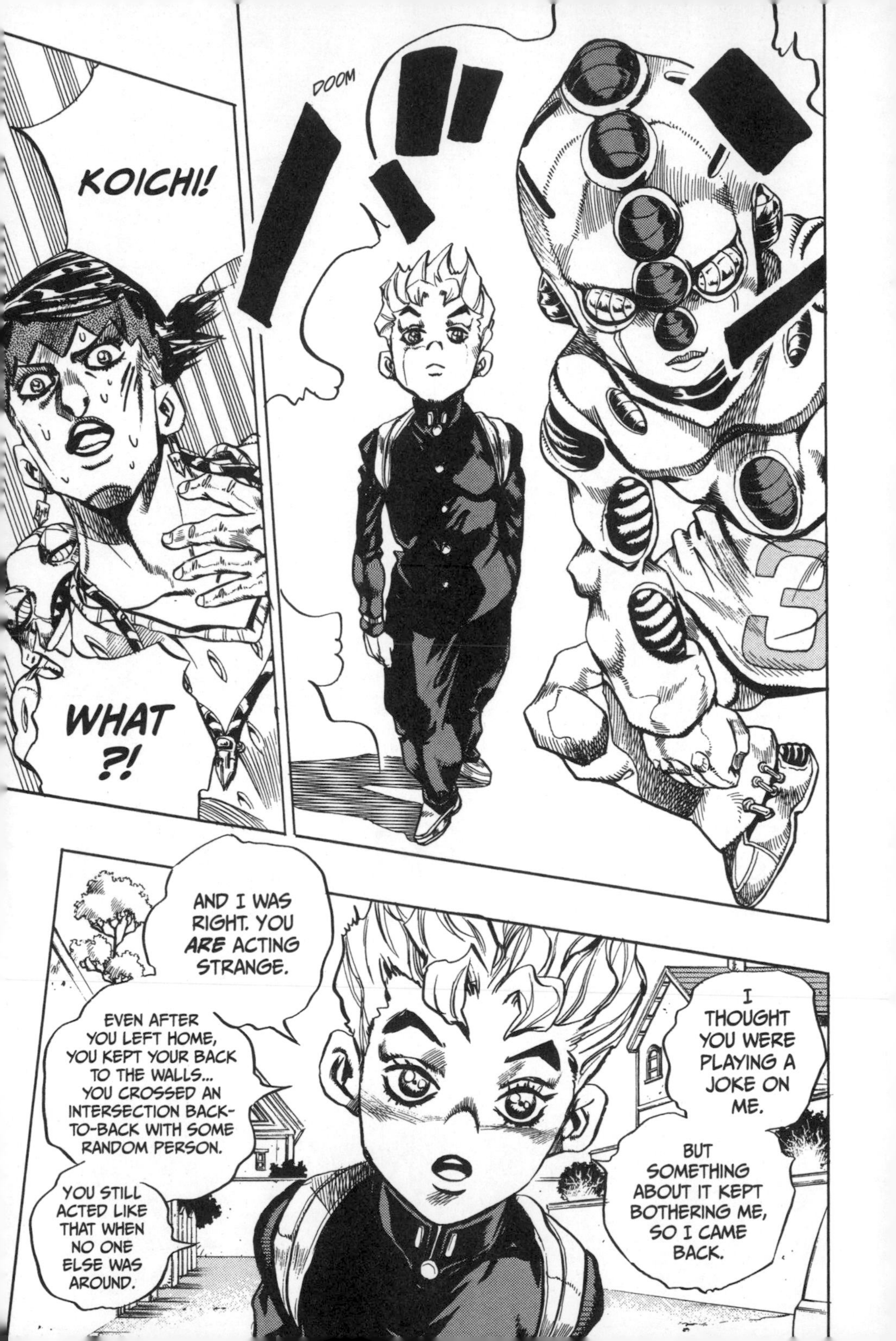
DOOM
KOICHI!
WHAT ?!
I THOUGHT YOU WERE PLAYING A JOKE ON ME.
BUT SOMETHING ABOUT IT KEPT BOTHERING ME, SO I CAME BACK.
AND I WAS RIGHT. YOU ARE ACTING STRANGE.
EVEN AFTER YOU LEFT HOME, YOU KEPT YOUR BACK TO THE WALLS... YOU CROSSED AN INTERSECTION BACK-TO-BACK WITH SOME RANDOM PERSON.
YOU STILL ACTED LIKE THAT WHEN NO ONE ELSE WAS AROUND.

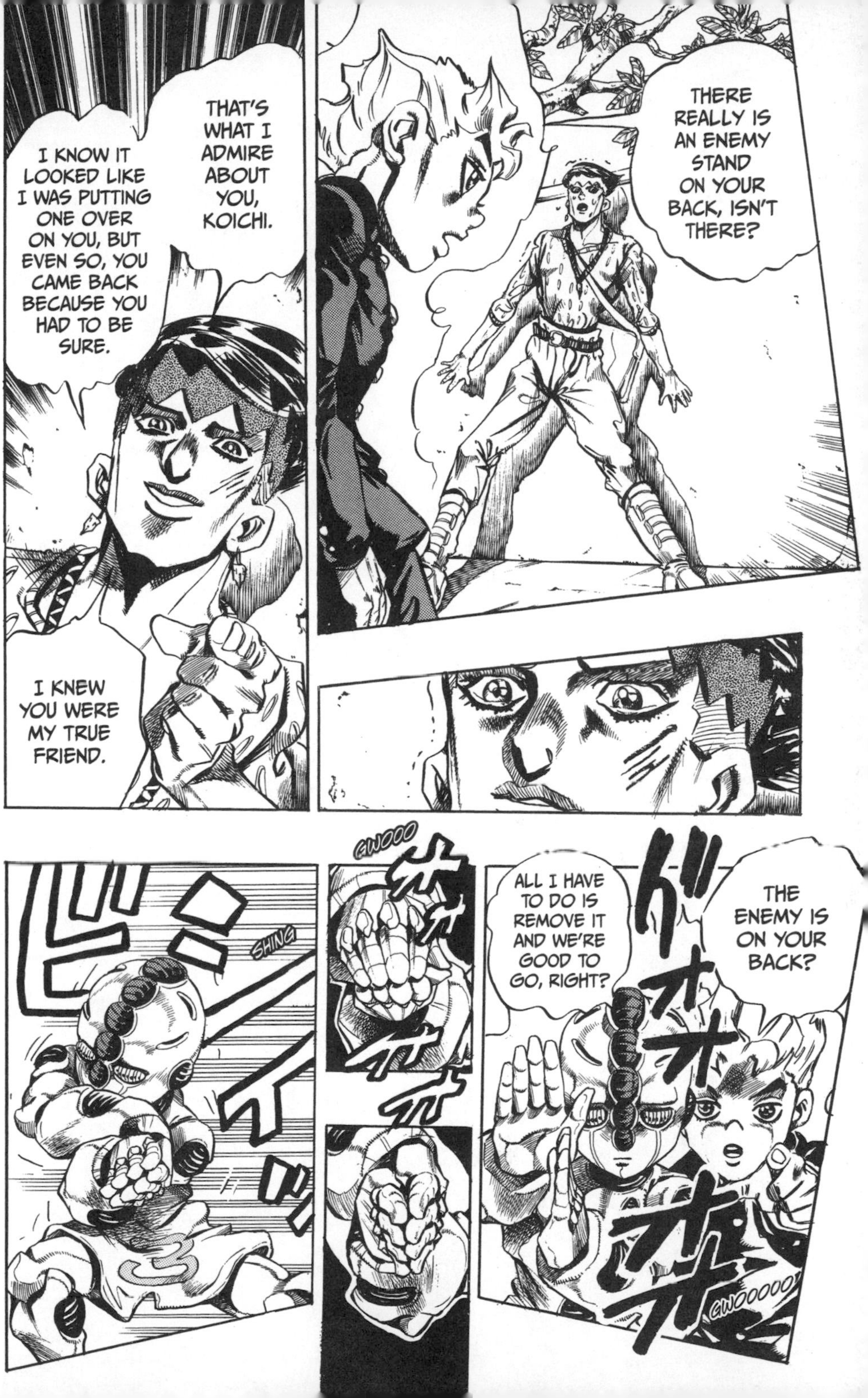
THERE REALLY IS AN ENEMY STAND ON YOUR BACK, ISN'T THERE?
THAT'S WHAT I ADMIRE ABOUT YOU, KOICHI.
I KNOW IT LOOKED LIKE I WAS PUTTING ONE OVER ON YOU, BUT EVEN SO, YOU CAME BACK BECAUSE YOU HAD TO BE SURE.
I KNEW YOU WERE MY TRUE FRIEND.
THE ENEMY IS ON YOUR BACK?
ALL I HAVE TO DO IS REMOVE IT AND WE'RE GOOD TO GO, RIGHT?
GWOOOOO
GWOOO
SHING

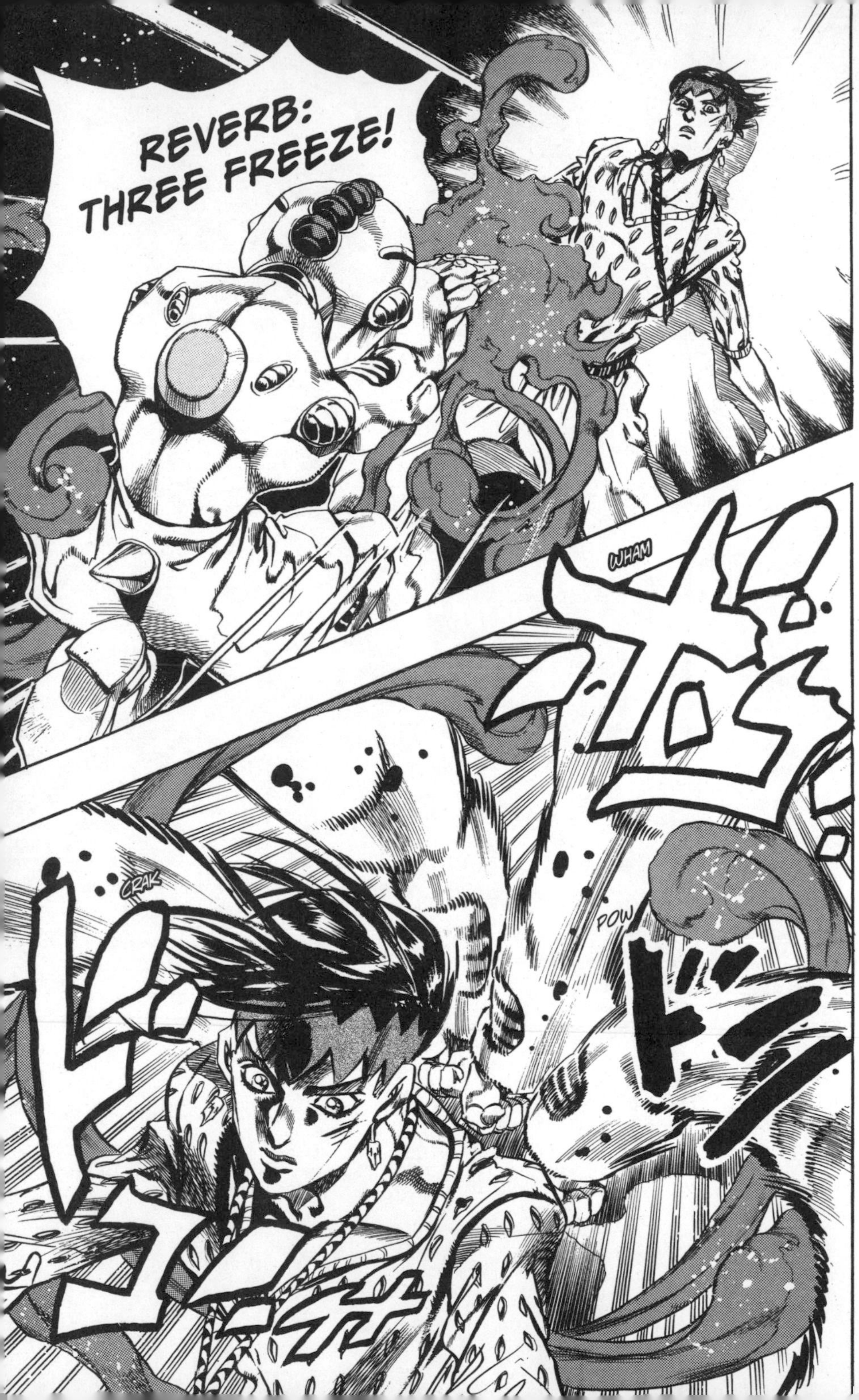
REVERB: THREE FREEZE!
WHAM
POW
CRAK

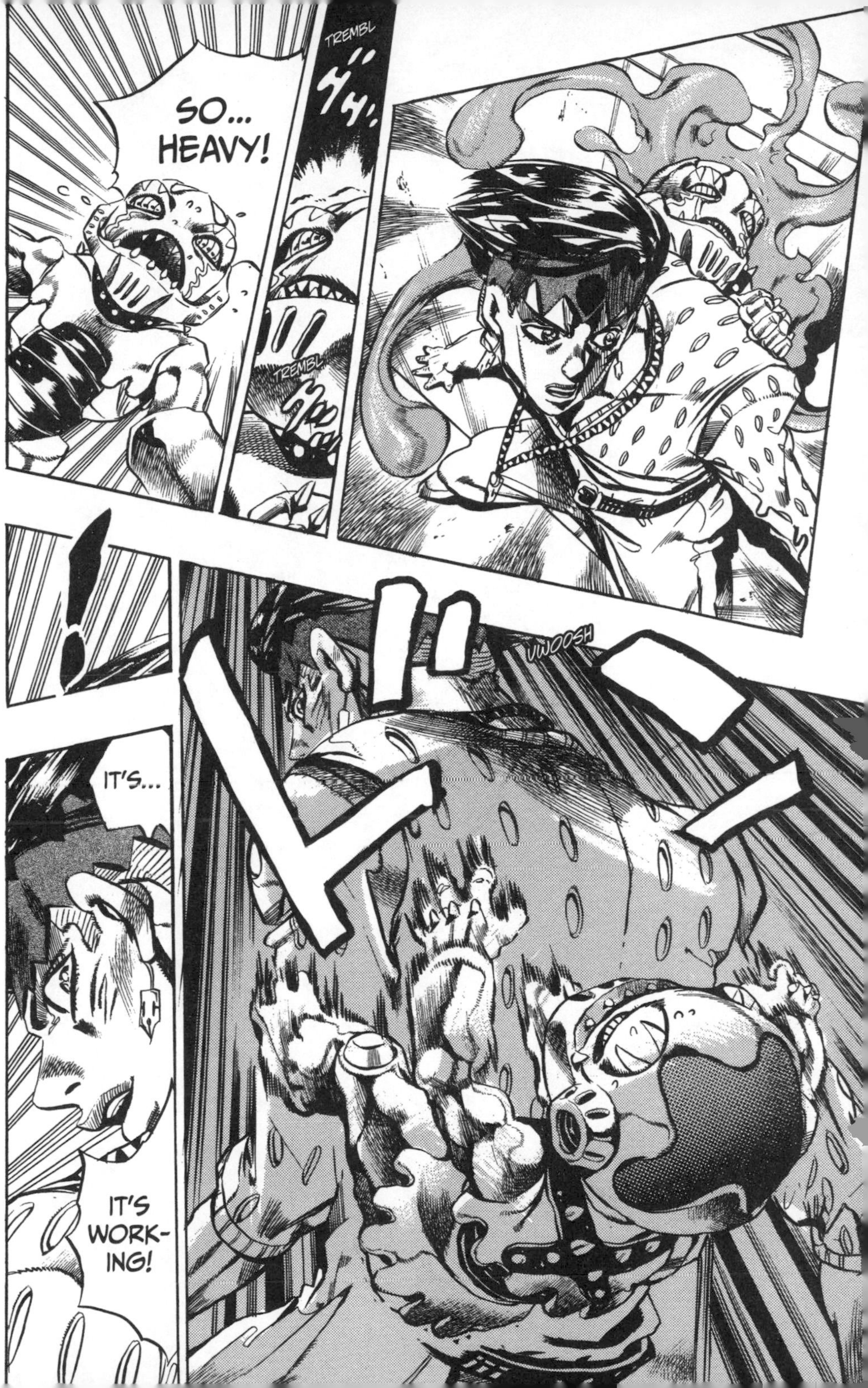

TREMBL
TREMBL
SO... HEAVY!
UWOOSH
!
IT'S...
IT'S WORKING!

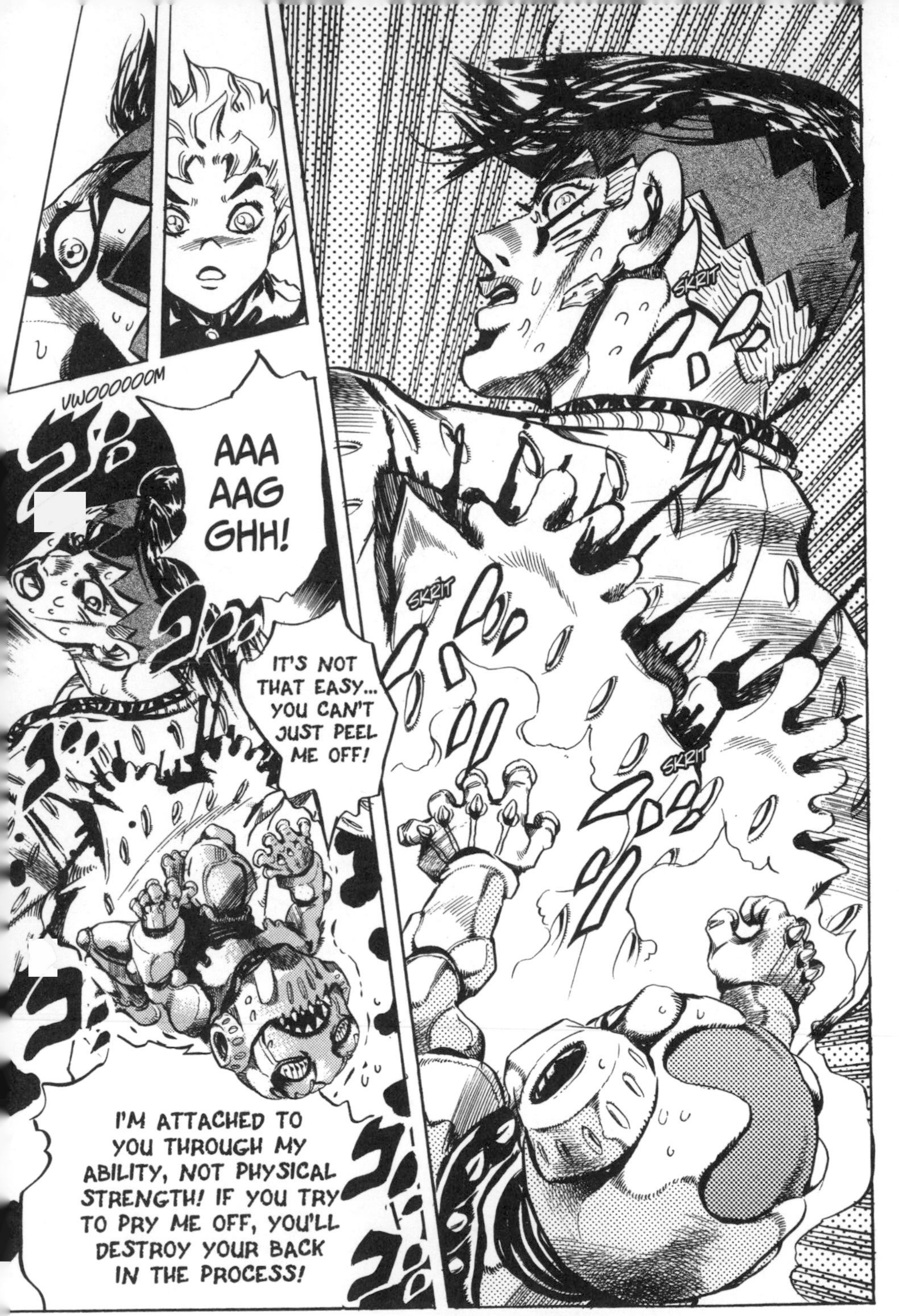
SKRIT
SKRIT
SKRIT
VWOOOOOOM
AAA AAG GHH!
IT'S NOT THAT EASY... YOU CAN'T JUST PEEL ME OFF!
I'M ATTACHED TO YOU THROUGH MY ABILITY, NOT PHYSICAL STRENGTH! IF YOU TRY TO PRY ME OFF, YOU'LL DESTROY YOUR BACK IN THE PROCESS!

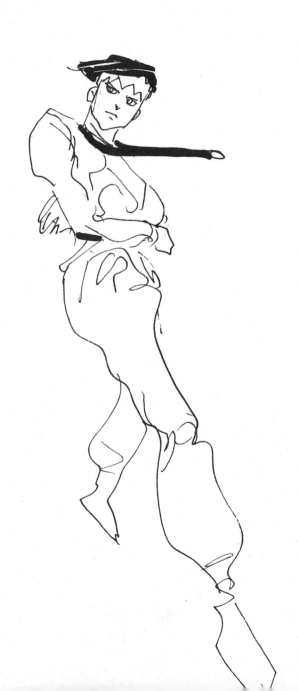

CHAPTER 152
CHEAP TRAP, PART 6

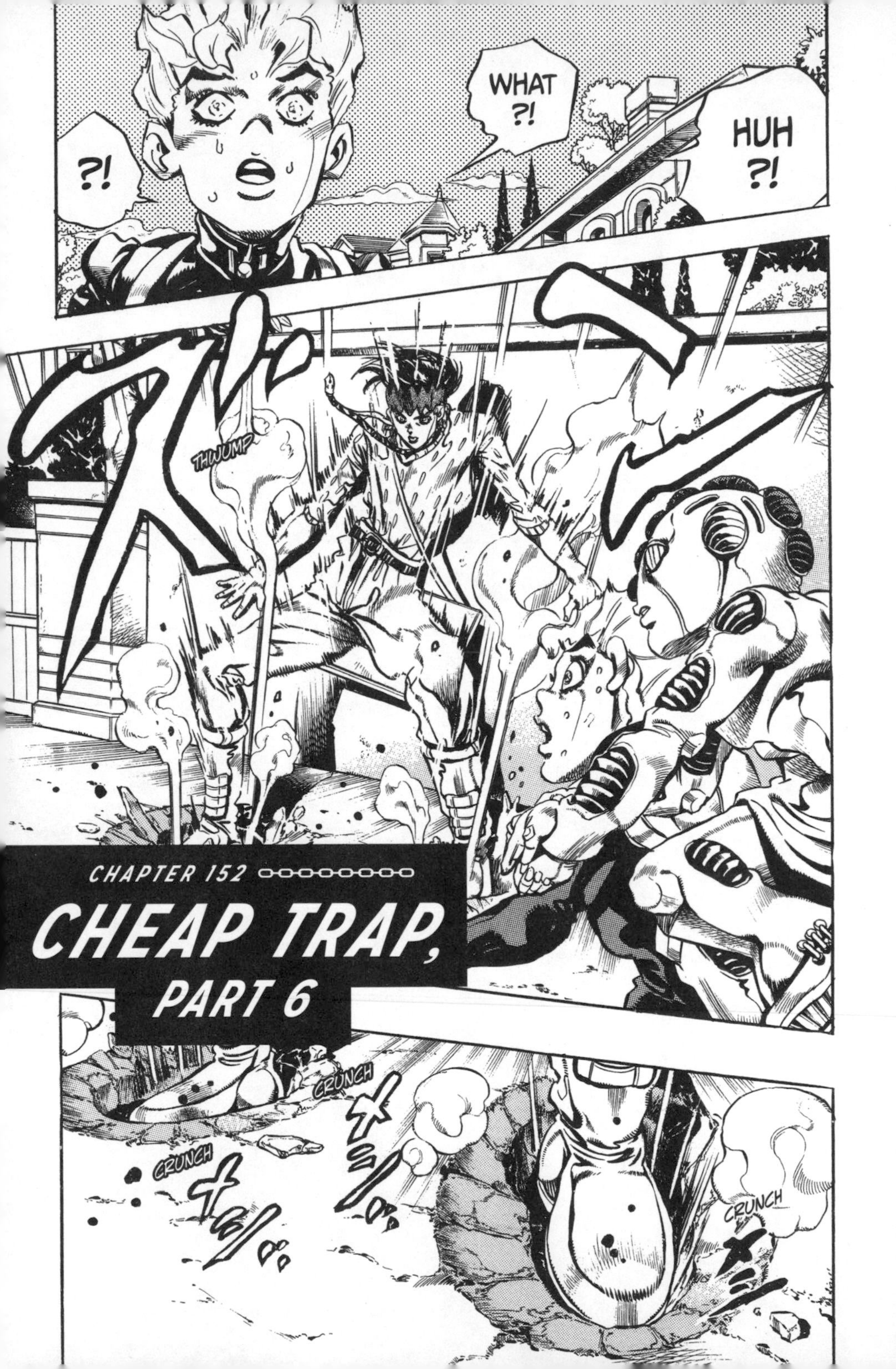
HUH ?!
WHAT ?!
?!
THWUMP
CRUNCH
CRUNCH
CRUNCH

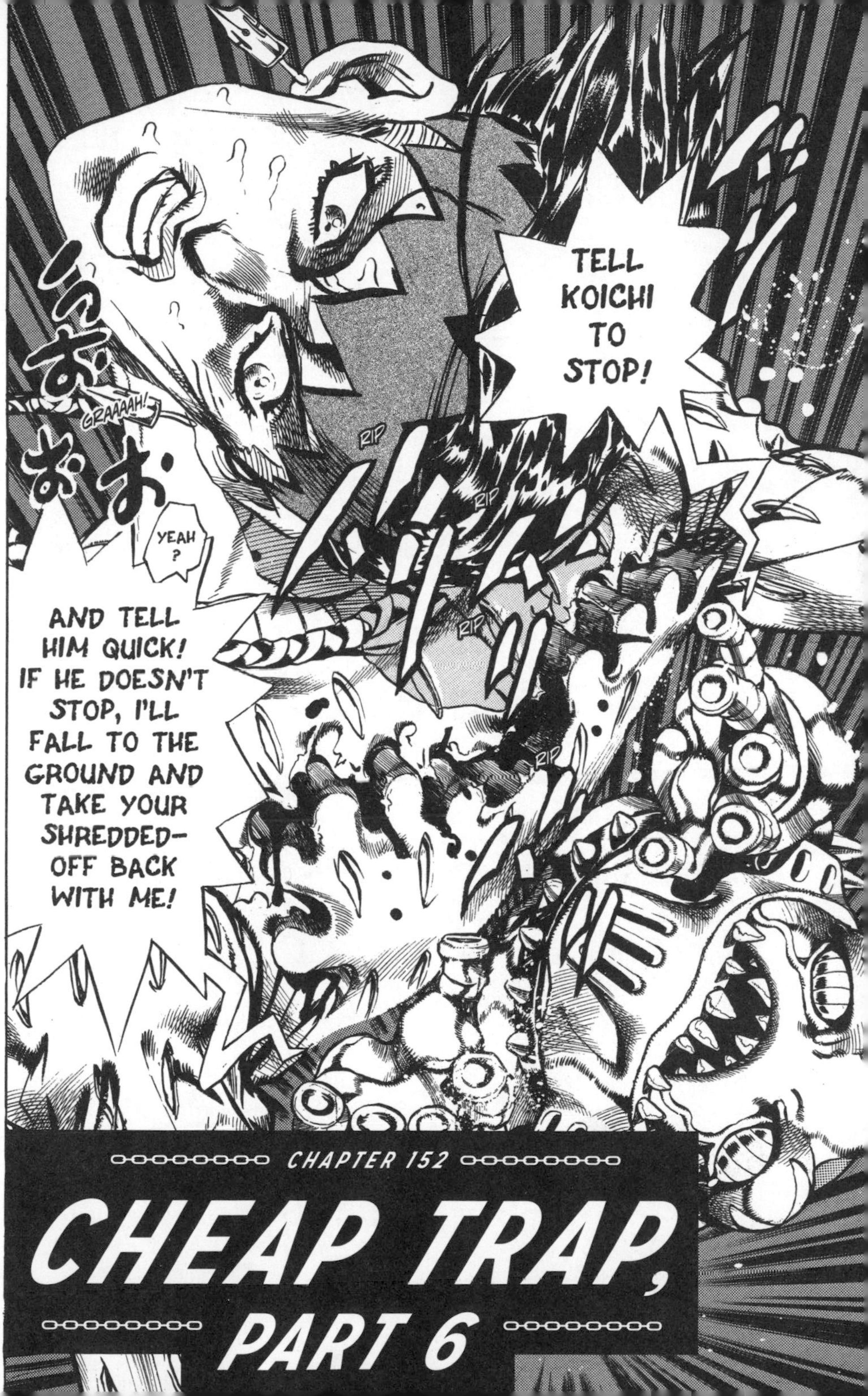
TELL KOICHI TO STOP!
RIP
RIP
RIP
RIP
GRAAAAH!
YEAH ?
AND TELL HIM QUICK! IF HE DOESN'T STOP, I'LL FALL TO THE GROUND AND TAKE YOUR SHREDDED-OFF BACK WITH ME!

CHAPTER 152

CHEAP TRAP, PART 6

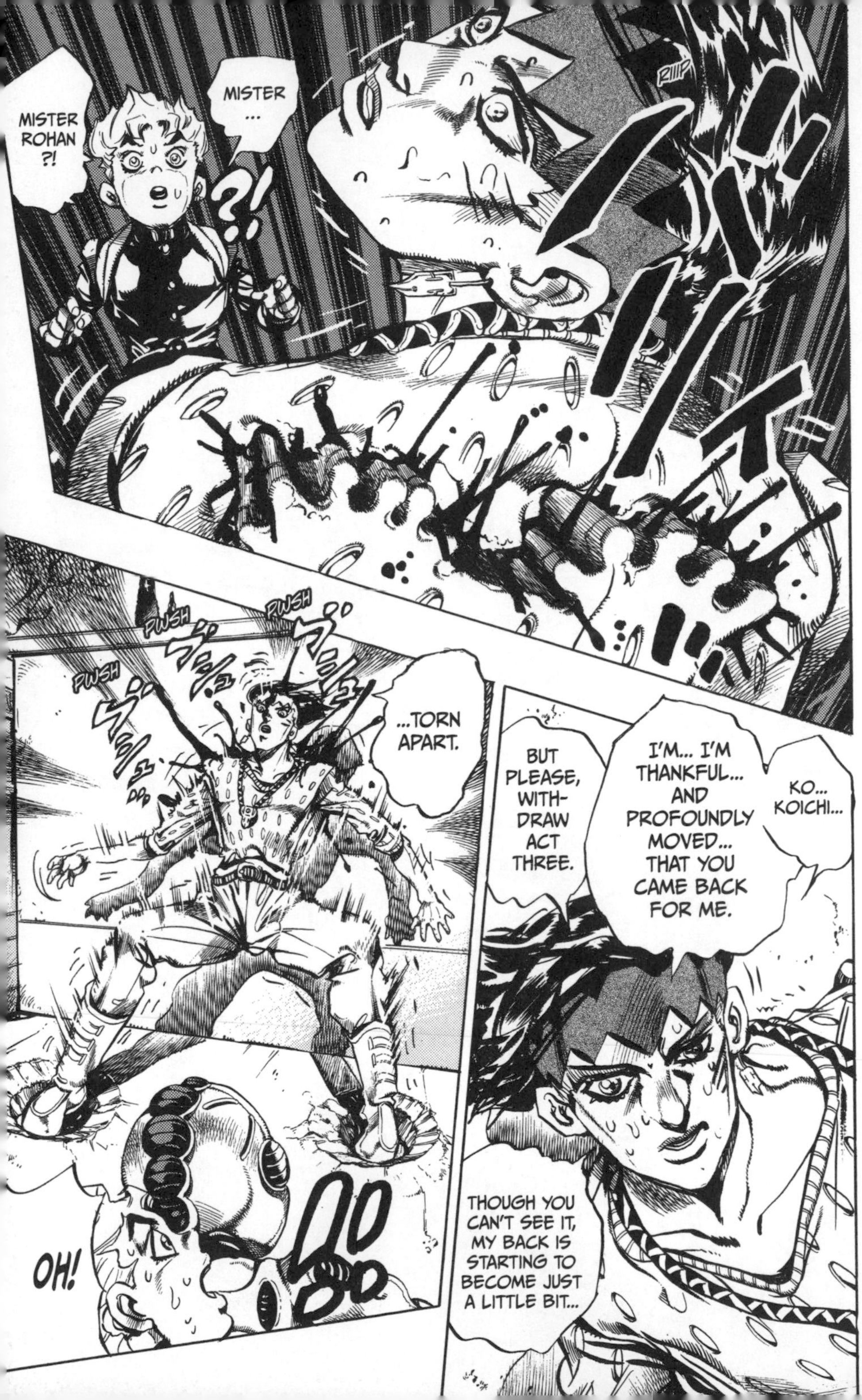
RIIP
MISTER ...
MISTER ROHAN ?!
?!
KO... KOICHI...
I'M... I'M THANKFUL... AND PROFOUNDLY MOVED... THAT YOU CAME BACK FOR ME.
BUT PLEASE, WITH-DRAW ACT THREE.
THOUGH YOU CAN'T SEE IT, MY BACK IS STARTING TO BECOME JUST A LITTLE BIT...
...TORN APART.
PWSH
PWSH
PWSH
OH!

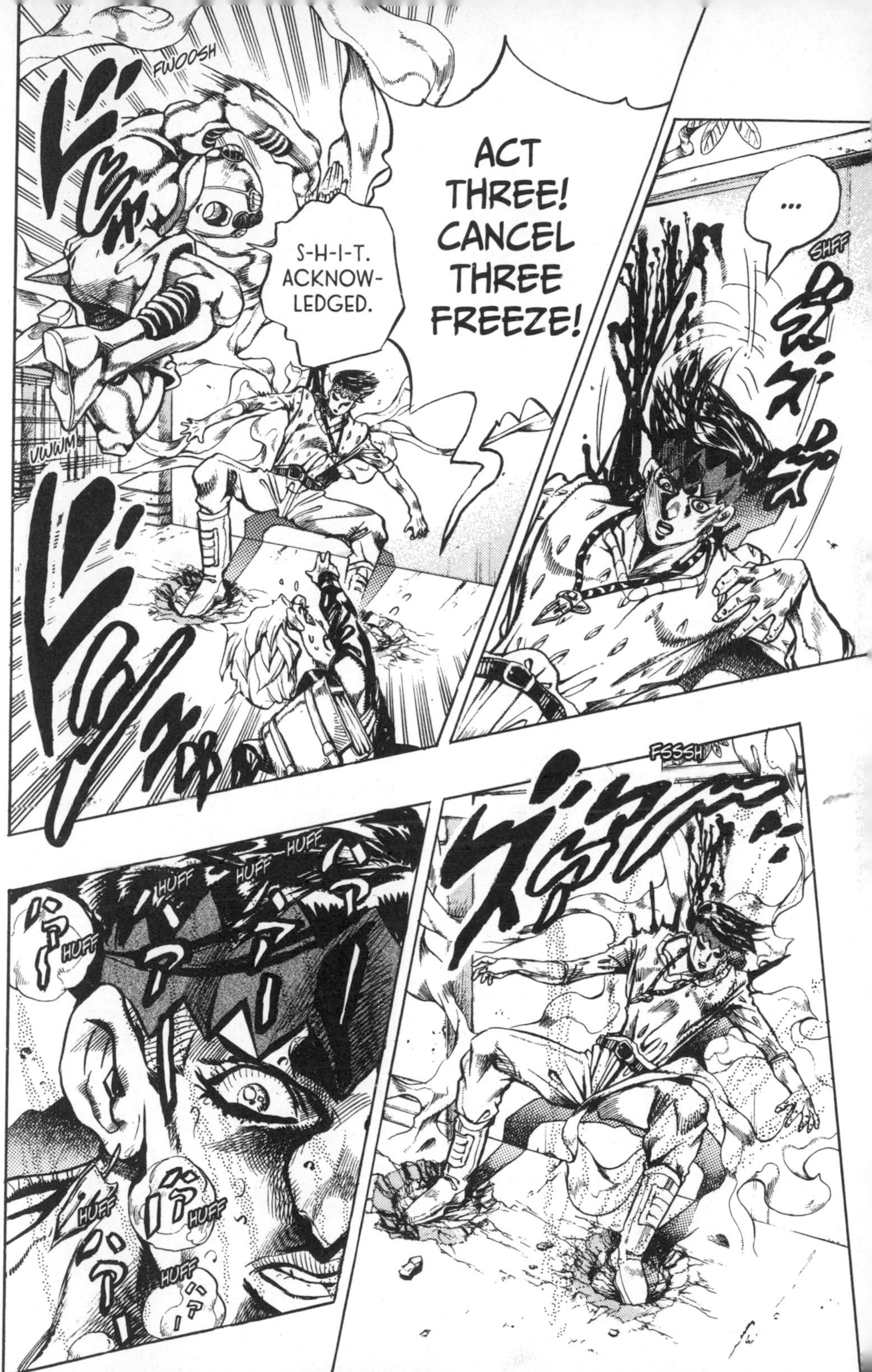
...
SHFF
FWOOSH
ACT THREE! CANCEL THREE FREEZE!
S-H-I-T. ACKNOW-LEDGED.
VWWM
FSSSH
HUFF
HUFF
HUFF
HUFF
HUFF
HUFF
HUFF

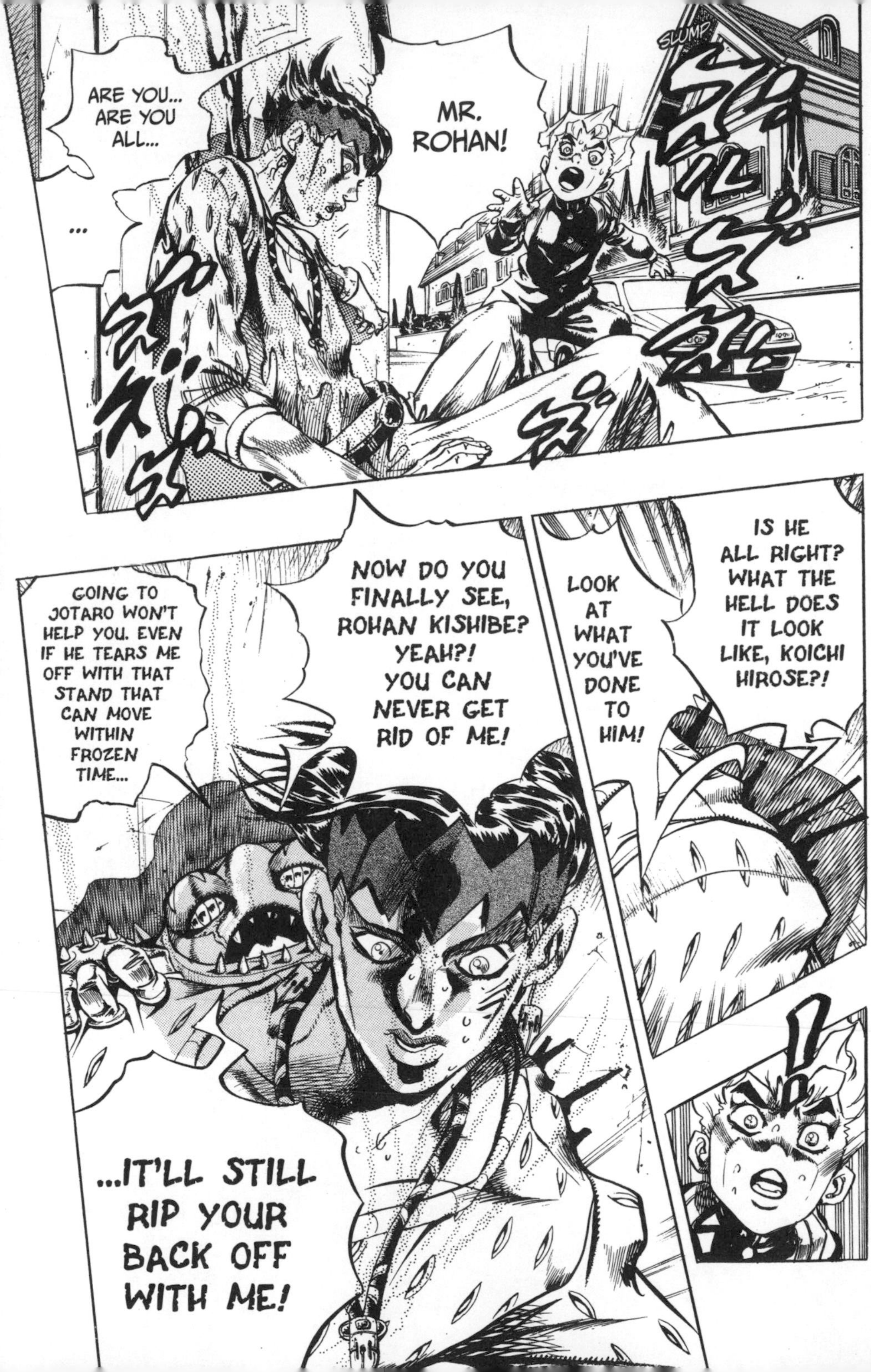
SLUMP
MR. ROHAN!
ARE YOU... ARE YOU ALL...
...
IS HE ALL RIGHT? WHAT THE HELL DOES IT LOOK LIKE, KOICHI HIROSE?!
LOOK AT WHAT YOU'VE DONE TO HIM!
NOW DO YOU FINALLY SEE, ROHAN KISHIBE? YEAH?! YOU CAN NEVER GET RID OF ME!
GOING TO JOTARO WON'T HELP YOU. EVEN IF HE TEARS ME OFF WITH THAT STAND THAT CAN MOVE WITHIN FROZEN TIME...
...IT'LL STILL RIP YOUR BACK OFF WITH ME!
!

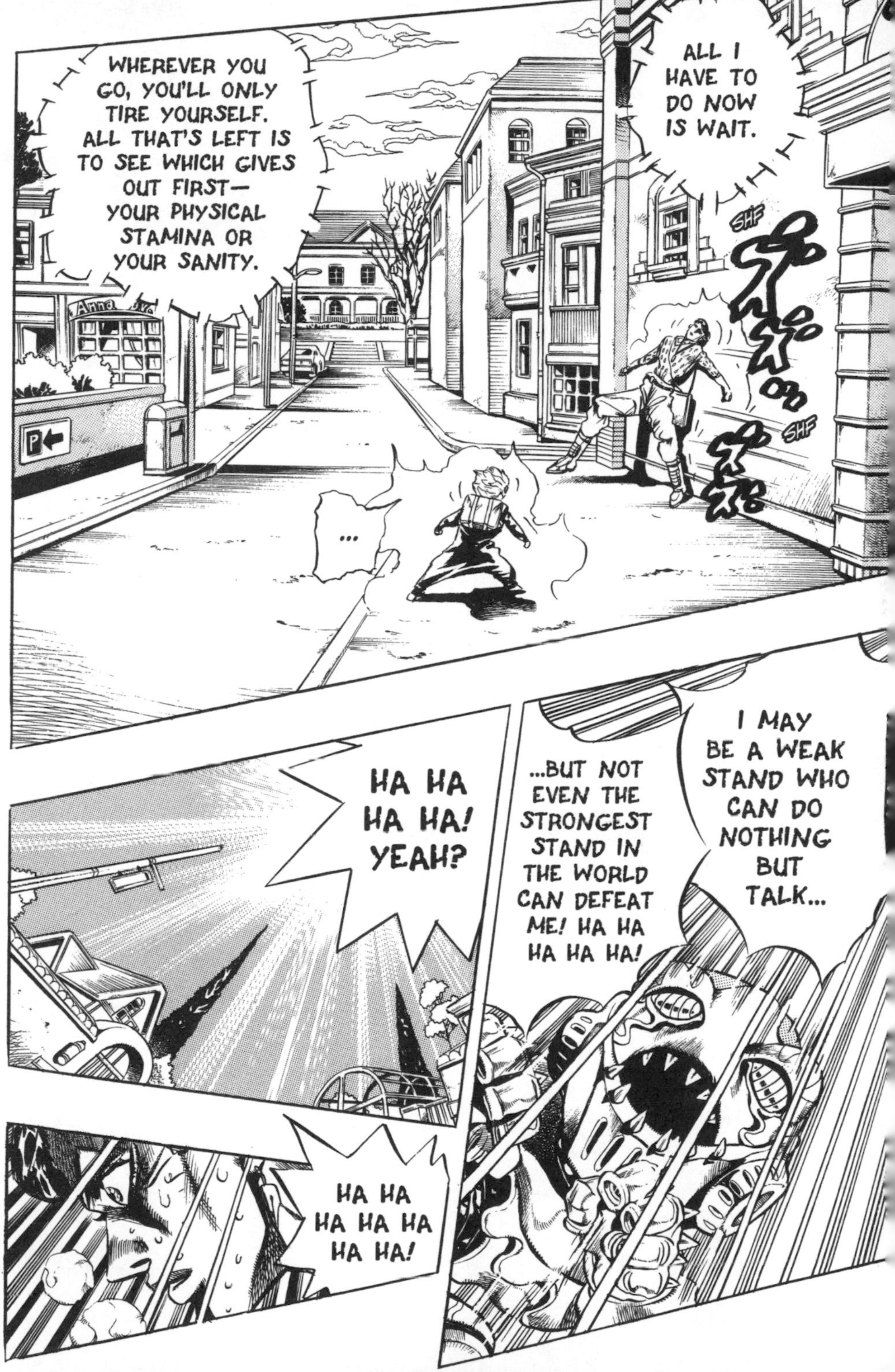
ALL I HAVE TO DO NOW IS WAIT.
WHEREVER YOU GO, YOU'LL ONLY TIRE YOURSELF. ALL THAT'S LEFT IS TO SEE WHICH GIVES OUT FIRST— YOUR PHYSICAL STAMINA OR YOUR SANITY.
SHF
SHF
...
I MAY BE A WEAK STAND WHO CAN DO NOTHING BUT TALK...
...BUT NOT EVEN THE STRONGEST STAND IN THE WORLD CAN DEFEAT ME! HA HA HA HA HA!
HA HA HA HA! YEAH?
HA HA HA HA HA HA HA!

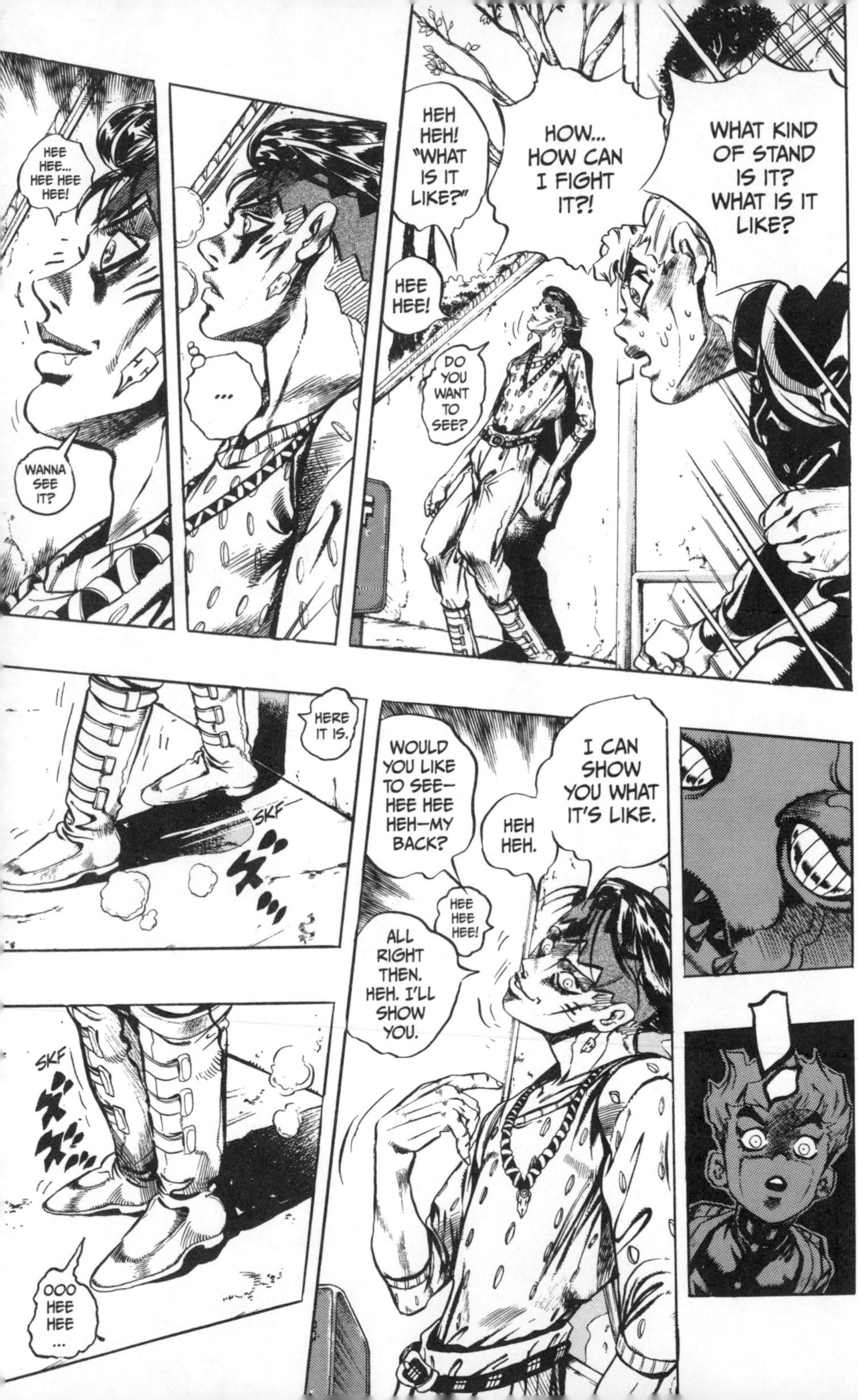
WHAT KIND OF STAND IS IT? WHAT IS IT LIKE?
HOW... HOW CAN I FIGHT IT?!
HEH HEH! "WHAT IS IT LIKE?"
HEE HEE!
DO YOU WANT TO SEE?
...
HEE HEE... HEE HEE HEE!
WANNA SEE IT?
I CAN SHOW YOU WHAT IT'S LIKE.
HEH HEH.
WOULD YOU LIKE TO SEE—HEE HEE HEH—MY BACK?
HEE HEE HEE!
ALL RIGHT THEN. HEH. I'LL SHOW YOU.
HERE IT IS.
SKF
SKF
OOO HEE HEE ...

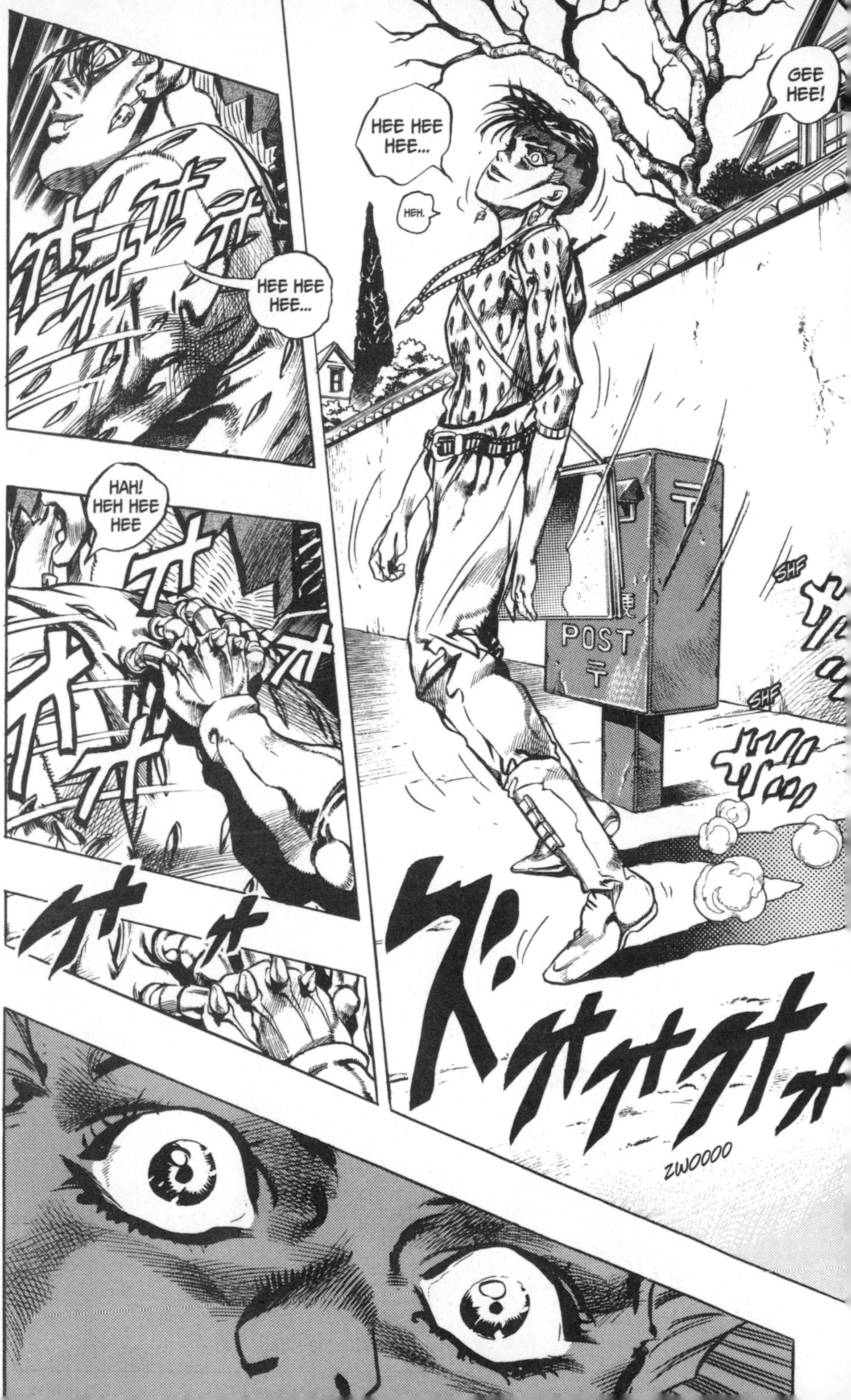
GEE HEE!
HEE HEE HEE...
HEH.
SHF
SHF
ZWOOOO
HEE HEE HEE...
HAH! HEH HEE HEE

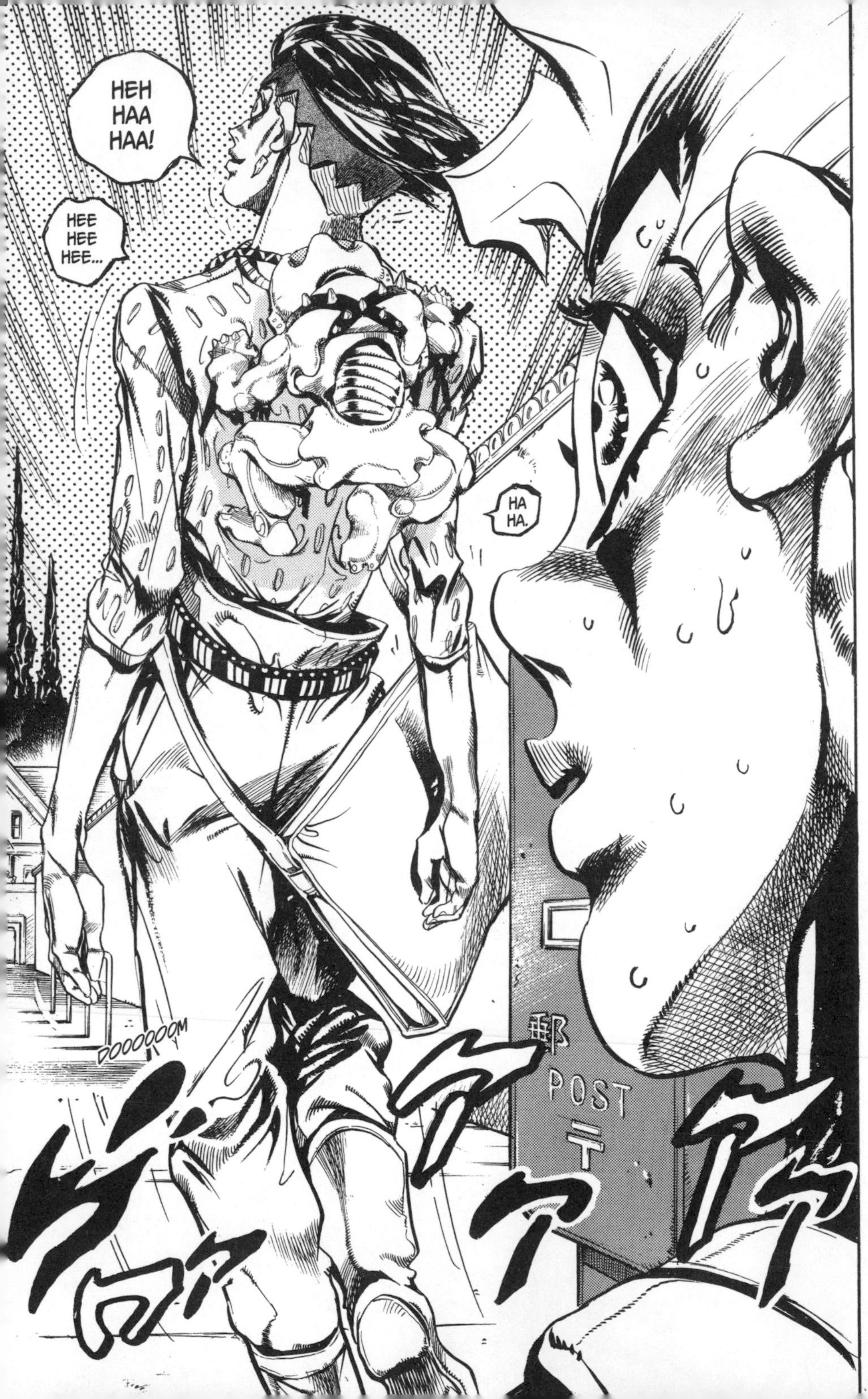
HEH HAA HAA!
HEE HEE HEE...
HA HA.
POST
DOOOOOOM

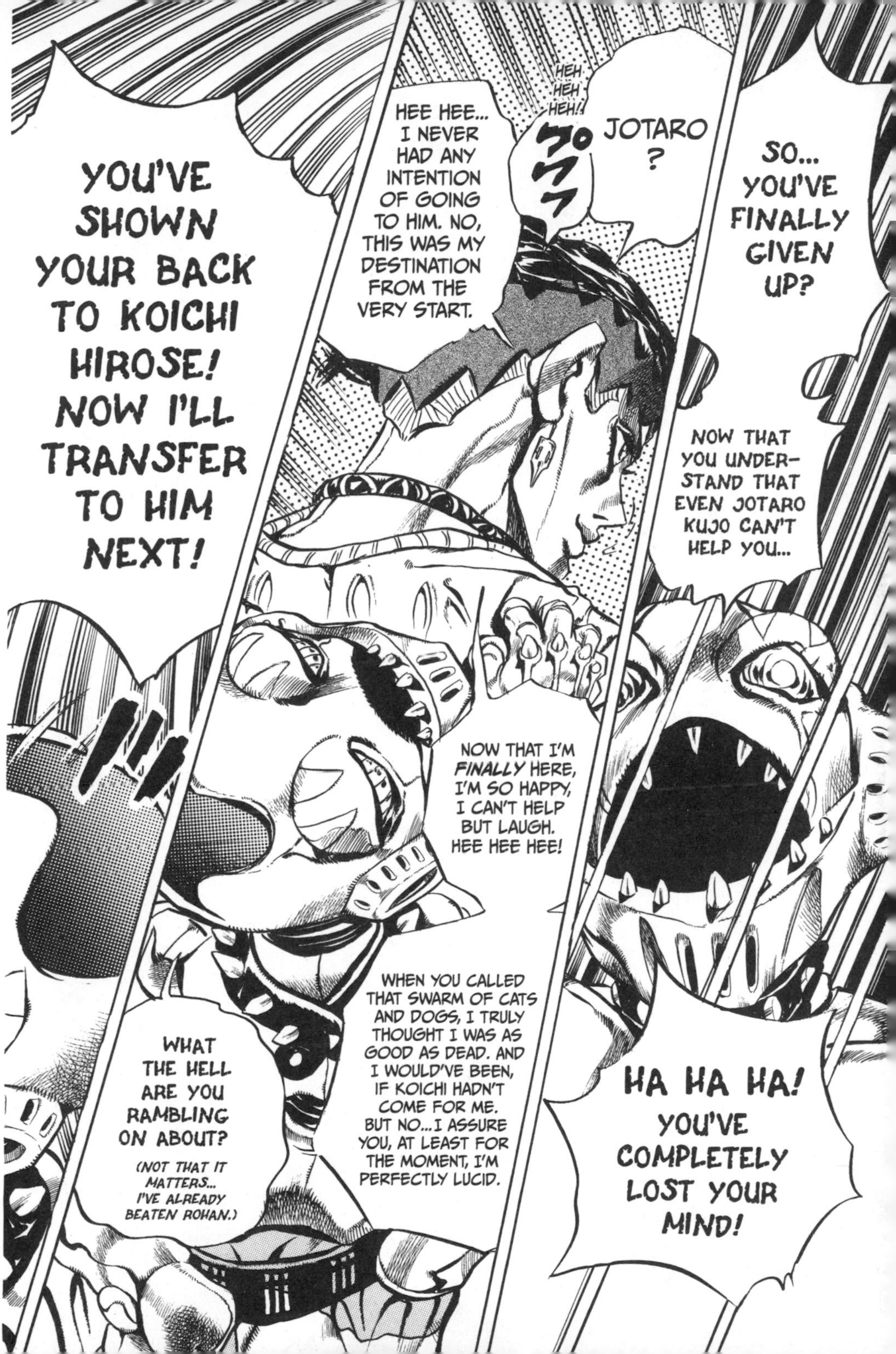
SO... YOU'VE FINALLY GIVEN UP?
NOW THAT YOU UNDER-STAND THAT EVEN JOTARO KUJO CAN'T HELP YOU...
JOTARO?
HEH HEH HEH!
HEE HEE... I NEVER HAD ANY INTENTION OF GOING TO HIM. NO, THIS WAS MY DESTINATION FROM THE VERY START.
NOW THAT I'M *FINALLY* HERE, I'M SO HAPPY, I CAN'T HELP BUT LAUGH. HEE HEE HEE!
WHEN YOU CALLED THAT SWARM OF CATS AND DOGS, I TRULY THOUGHT I WAS AS GOOD AS DEAD. AND I WOULD'VE BEEN, IF KOICHI HADN'T COME FOR ME. BUT NO...I ASSURE YOU, AT LEAST FOR THE MOMENT, I'M PERFECTLY LUCID.
HA HA HA! YOU'VE COMPLETELY LOST YOUR MIND!
YOU'VE SHOWN YOUR BACK TO KOICHI HIROSE! NOW I'LL TRANSFER TO HIM NEXT!
WHAT THE HELL ARE YOU RAMBLING ON ABOUT?
(NOT THAT IT MATTERS... I'VE ALREADY BEATEN ROHAN.)

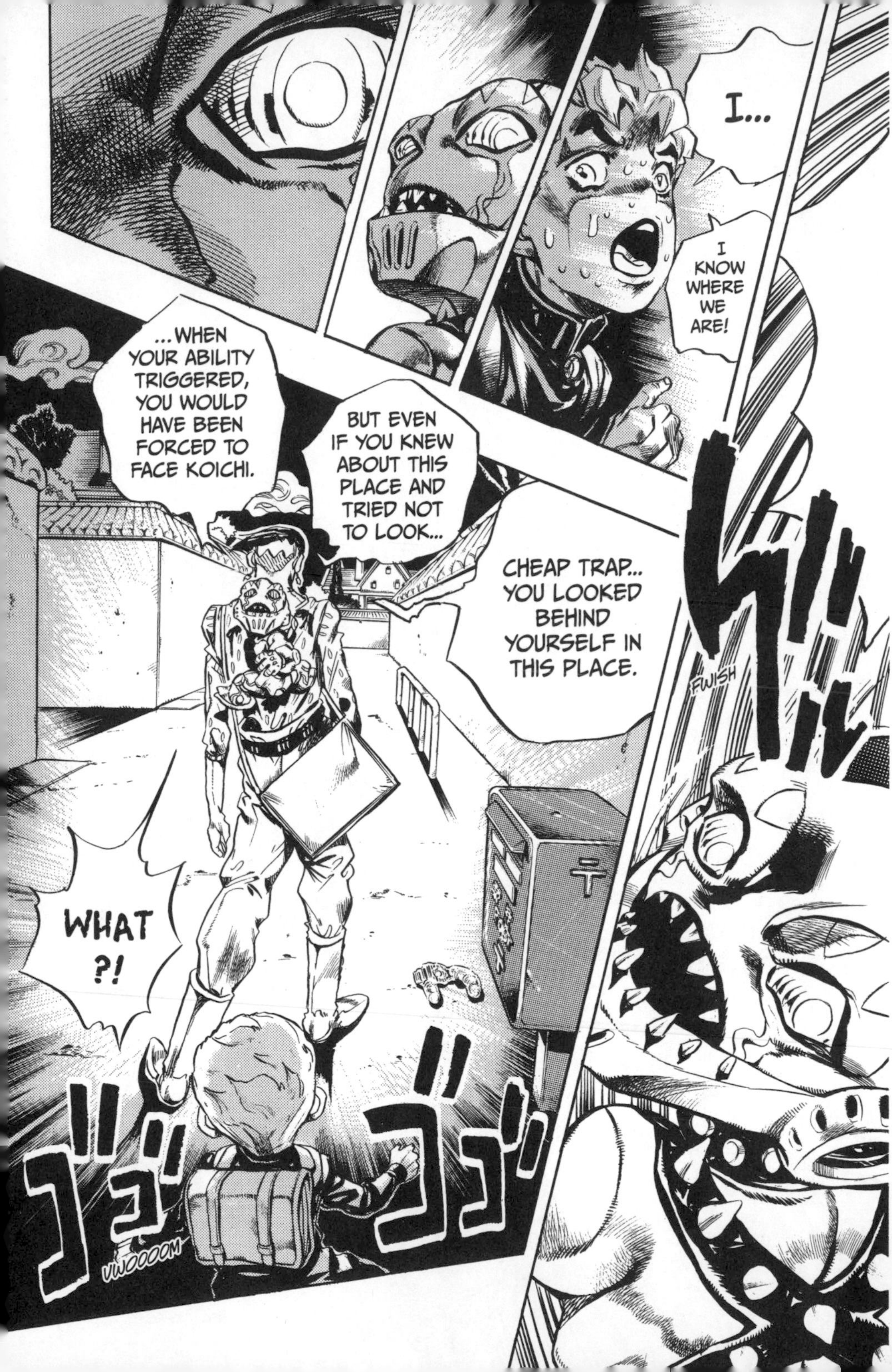
I...
I KNOW WHERE WE ARE!
FWISH
CHEAP TRAP... YOU LOOKED BEHIND YOURSELF IN THIS PLACE.
BUT EVEN IF YOU KNEW ABOUT THIS PLACE AND TRIED NOT TO LOOK...
...WHEN YOUR ABILITY TRIGGERED, YOU WOULD HAVE BEEN FORCED TO FACE KOICHI.
WHAT ?!
ゴゴゴゴ
VWOOOOM

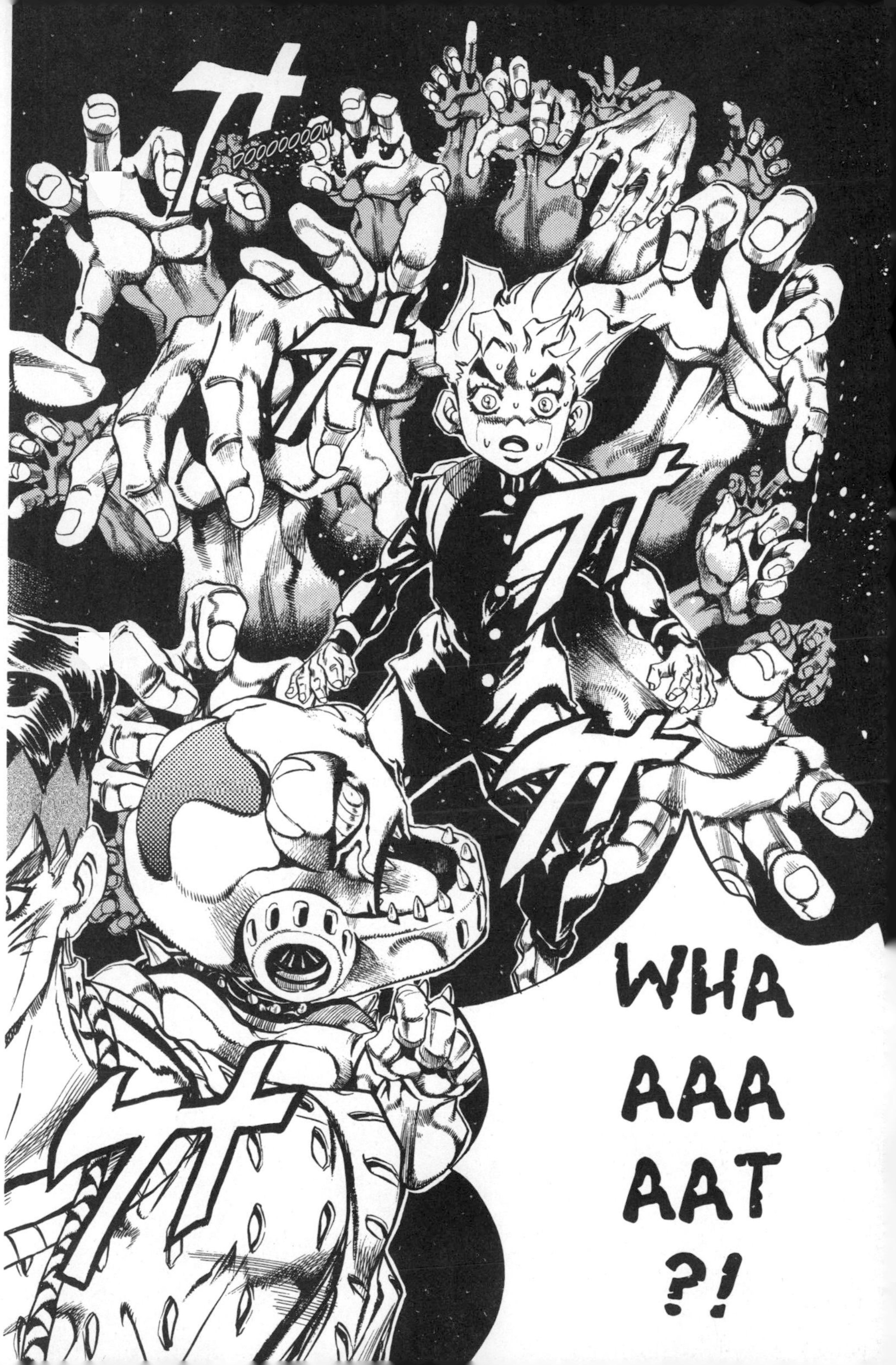
DOOOOOOOOM
WHA AAA AAT ?!

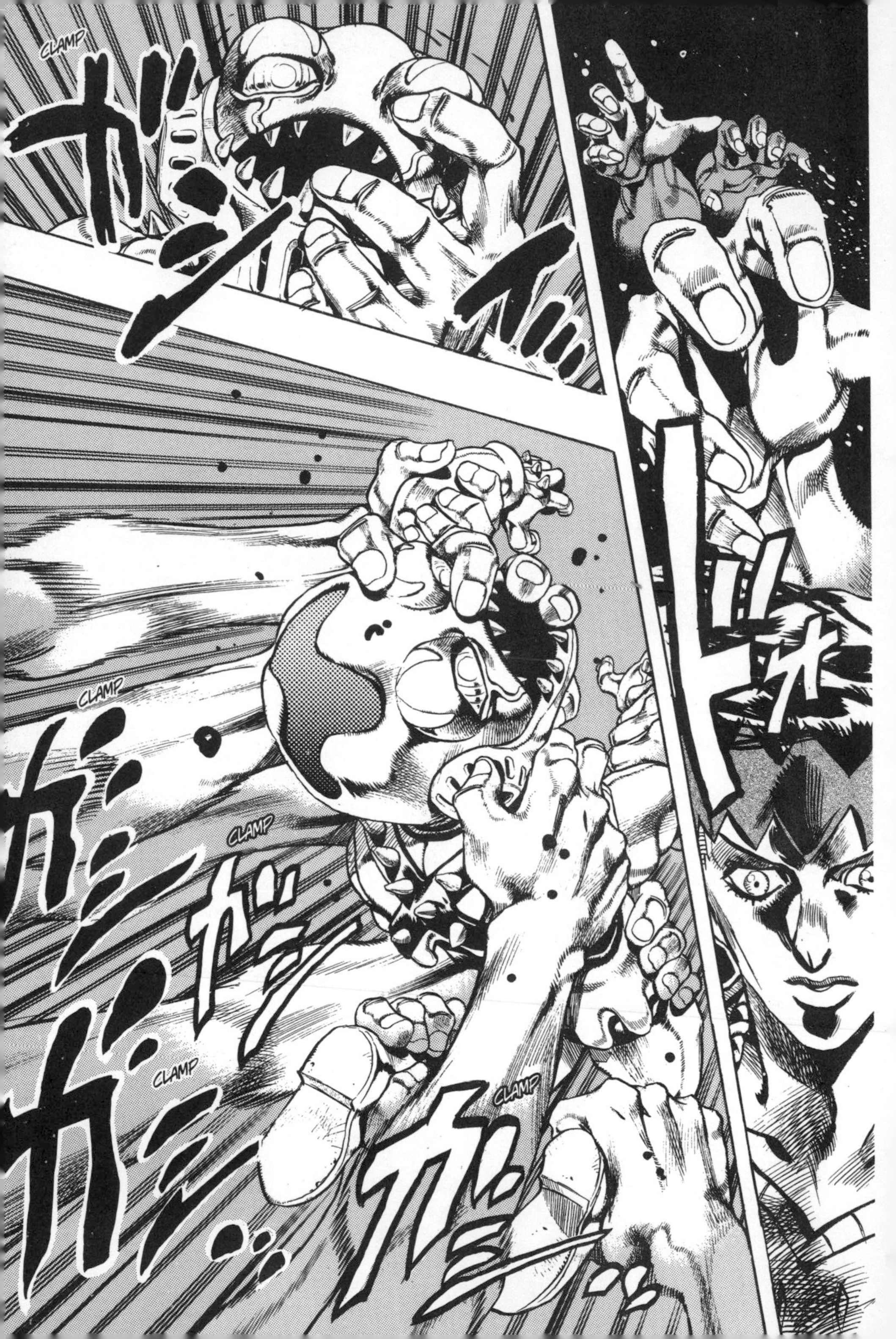
CLAMP
CLAMP
CLAMP
CLAMP
CLAMP

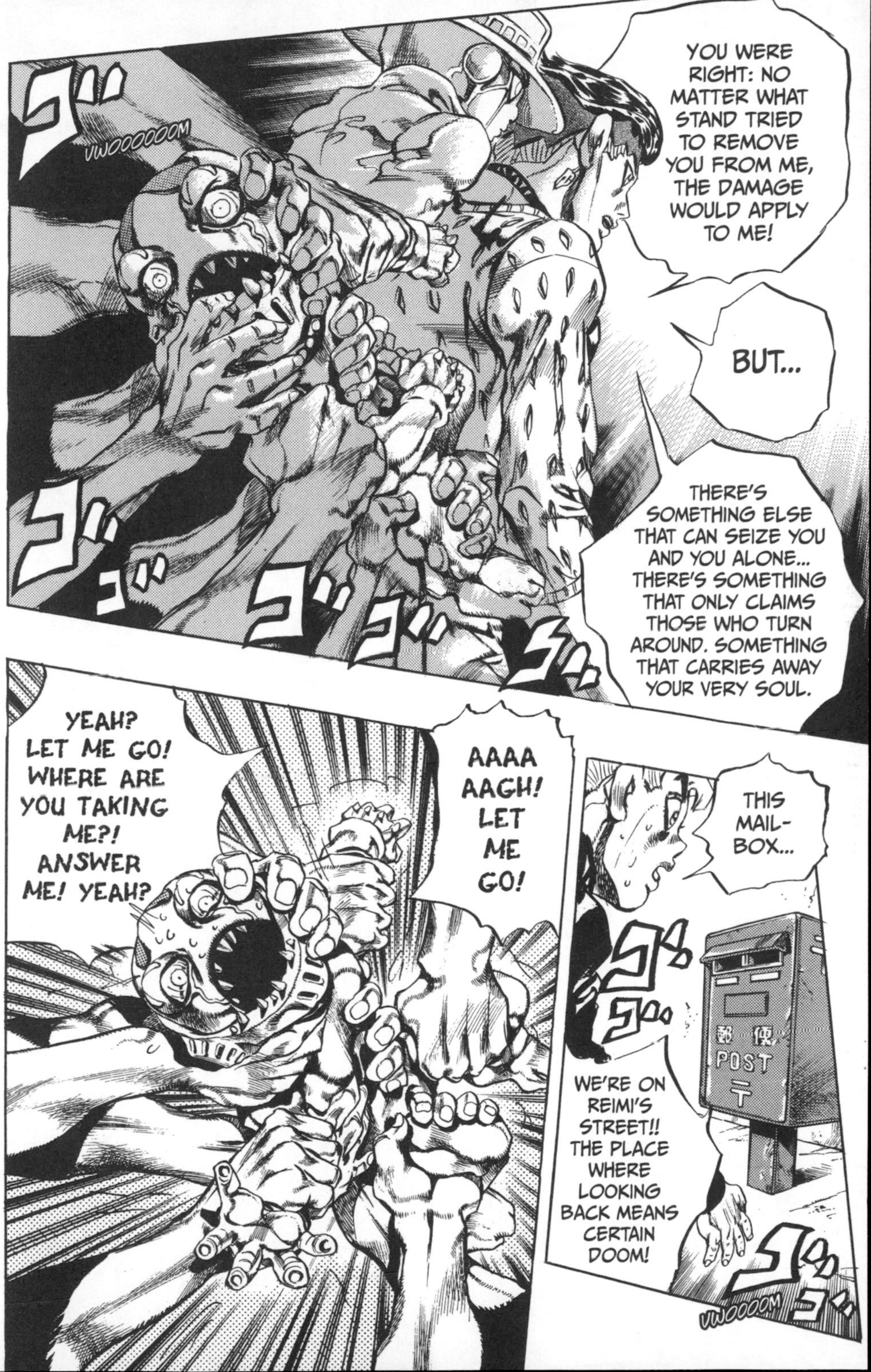

VWOOOOOOM
YOU WERE RIGHT: NO MATTER WHAT STAND TRIED TO REMOVE YOU FROM ME, THE DAMAGE WOULD APPLY TO ME!
BUT...
THERE'S SOMETHING ELSE THAT CAN SEIZE YOU AND YOU ALONE... THERE'S SOMETHING THAT ONLY CLAIMS THOSE WHO TURN AROUND. SOMETHING THAT CARRIES AWAY YOUR VERY SOUL.
THIS MAIL-BOX...
WE'RE ON REIMI'S STREET!! THE PLACE WHERE LOOKING BACK MEANS CERTAIN DOOM!
POST
VWOOOOM
AAAA AAGH! LET ME GO!
YEAH? LET ME GO! WHERE ARE YOU TAKING ME?! ANSWER ME! YEAH?

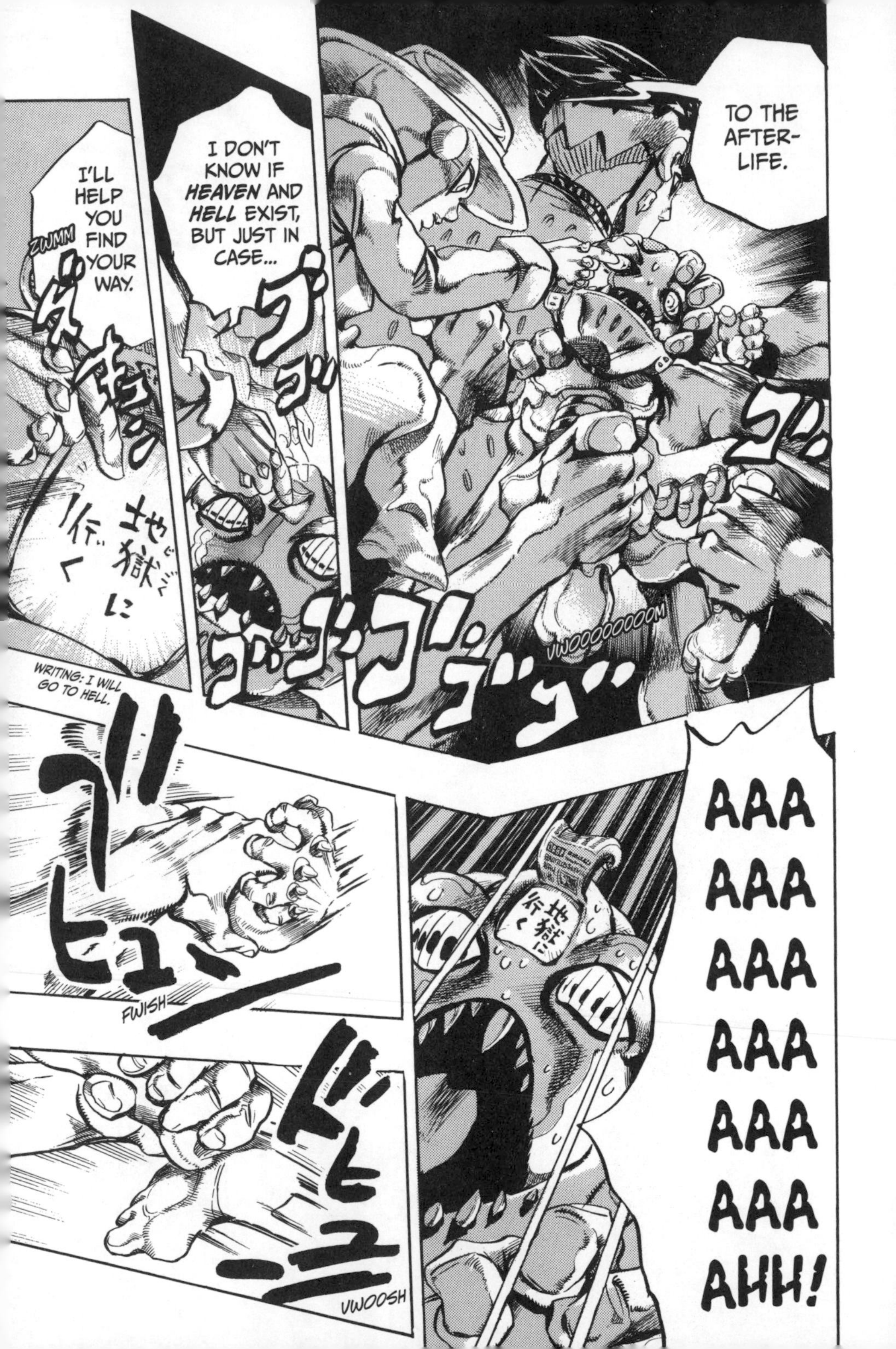
TO THE AFTER-LIFE.
VWOOOOOOOOM
I DON'T KNOW IF *HEAVEN* AND *HELL* EXIST, BUT JUST IN CASE...
I'LL HELP YOU FIND YOUR WAY.
ZWMM
地獄に行く
WRITING: I WILL GO TO HELL.
AAA AAA AAA AAA AAA AAA AHH!
地獄に行く
FWISH
VWOOSH

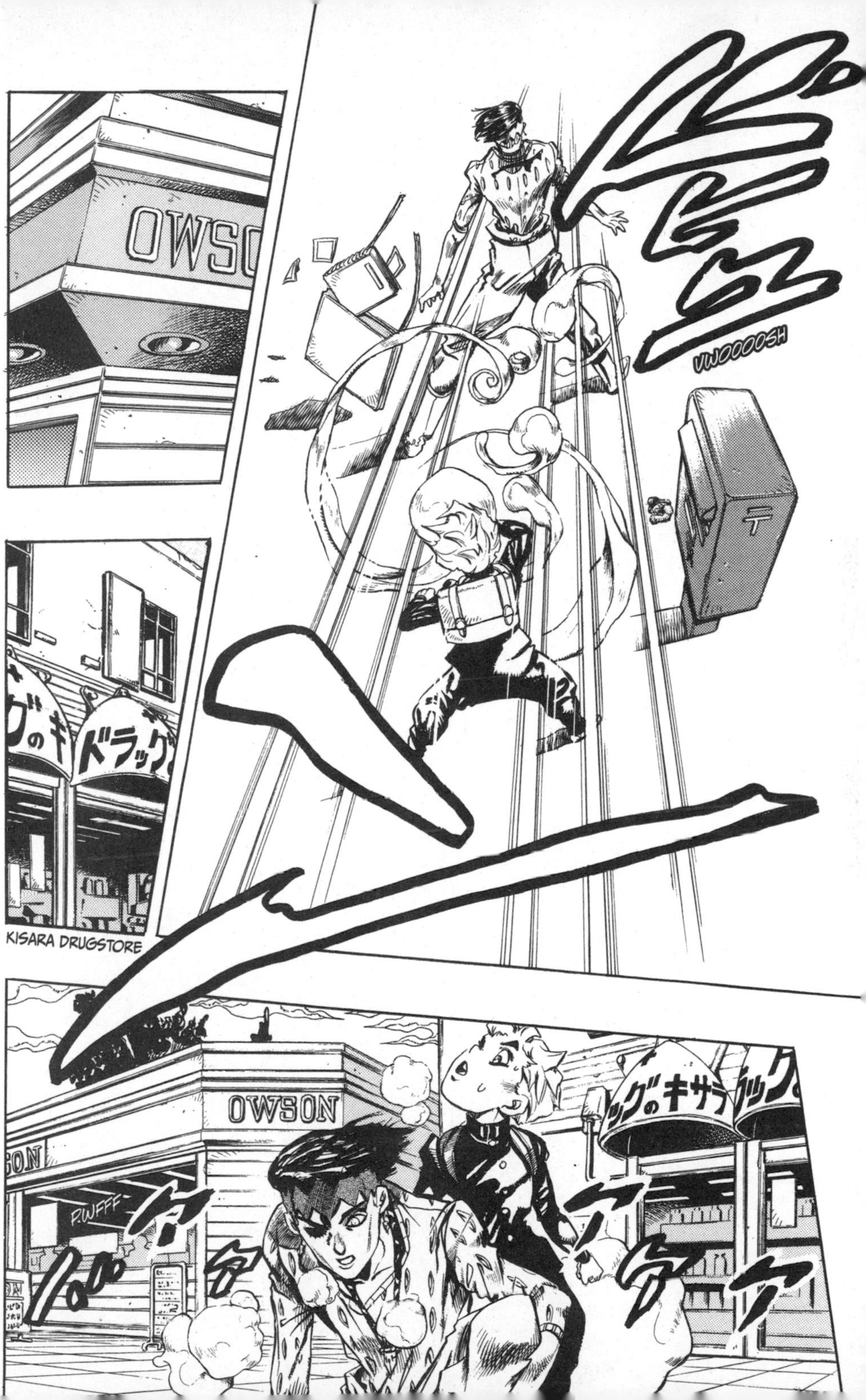
VWOOOOSH
OWSON
KISARA DRUGSTORE
OWSON
PWFFF

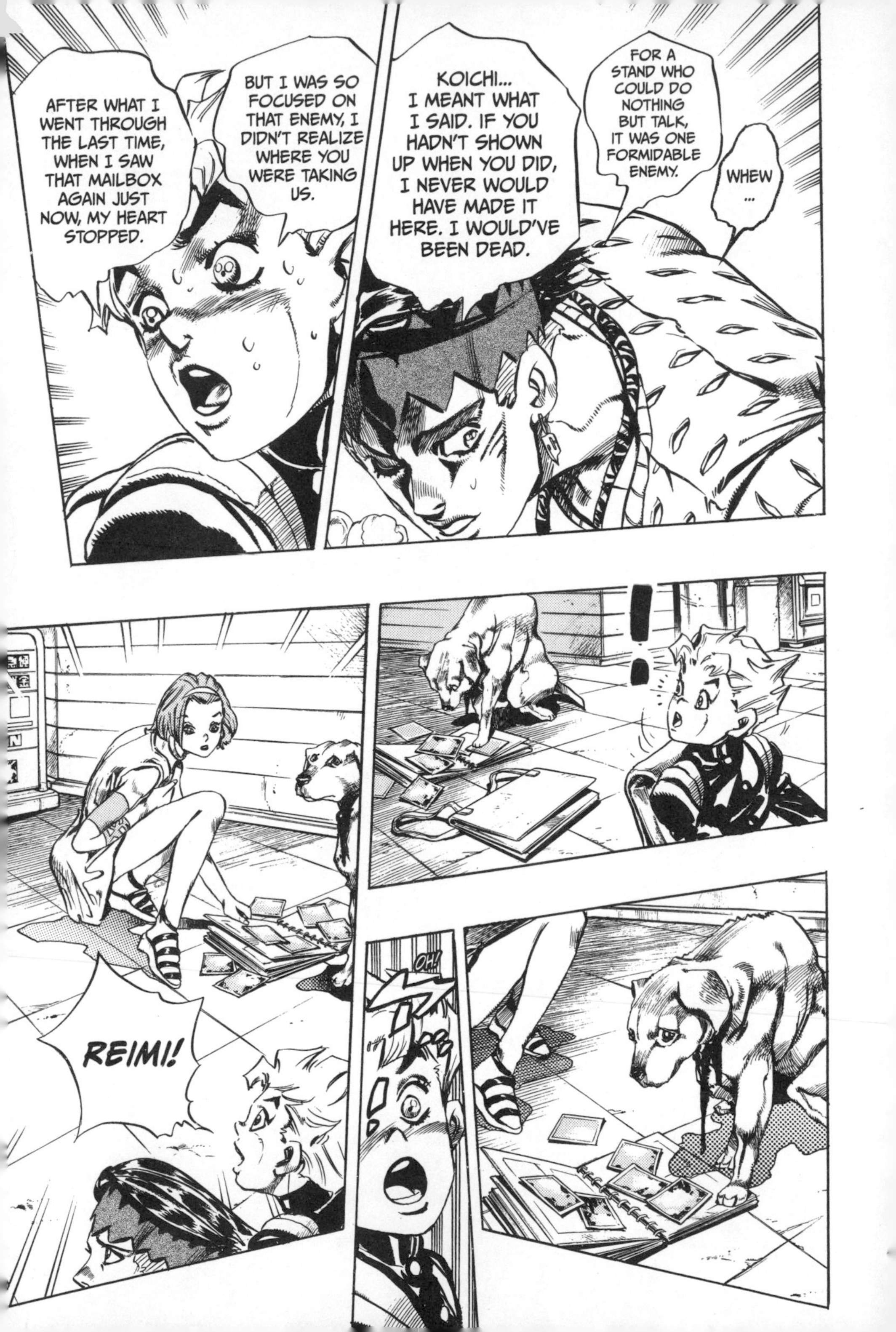
WHEW ...
FOR A STAND WHO COULD DO NOTHING BUT TALK, IT WAS ONE FORMIDABLE ENEMY.
KOICHI... I MEANT WHAT I SAID. IF YOU HADN'T SHOWN UP WHEN YOU DID, I NEVER WOULD HAVE MADE IT HERE. I WOULD'VE BEEN DEAD.
AFTER WHAT I WENT THROUGH THE LAST TIME, WHEN I SAW THAT MAILBOX AGAIN JUST NOW, MY HEART STOPPED.
BUT I WAS SO FOCUSED ON THAT ENEMY, I DIDN'T REALIZE WHERE YOU WERE TAKING US.
!
OH!
REIMI!

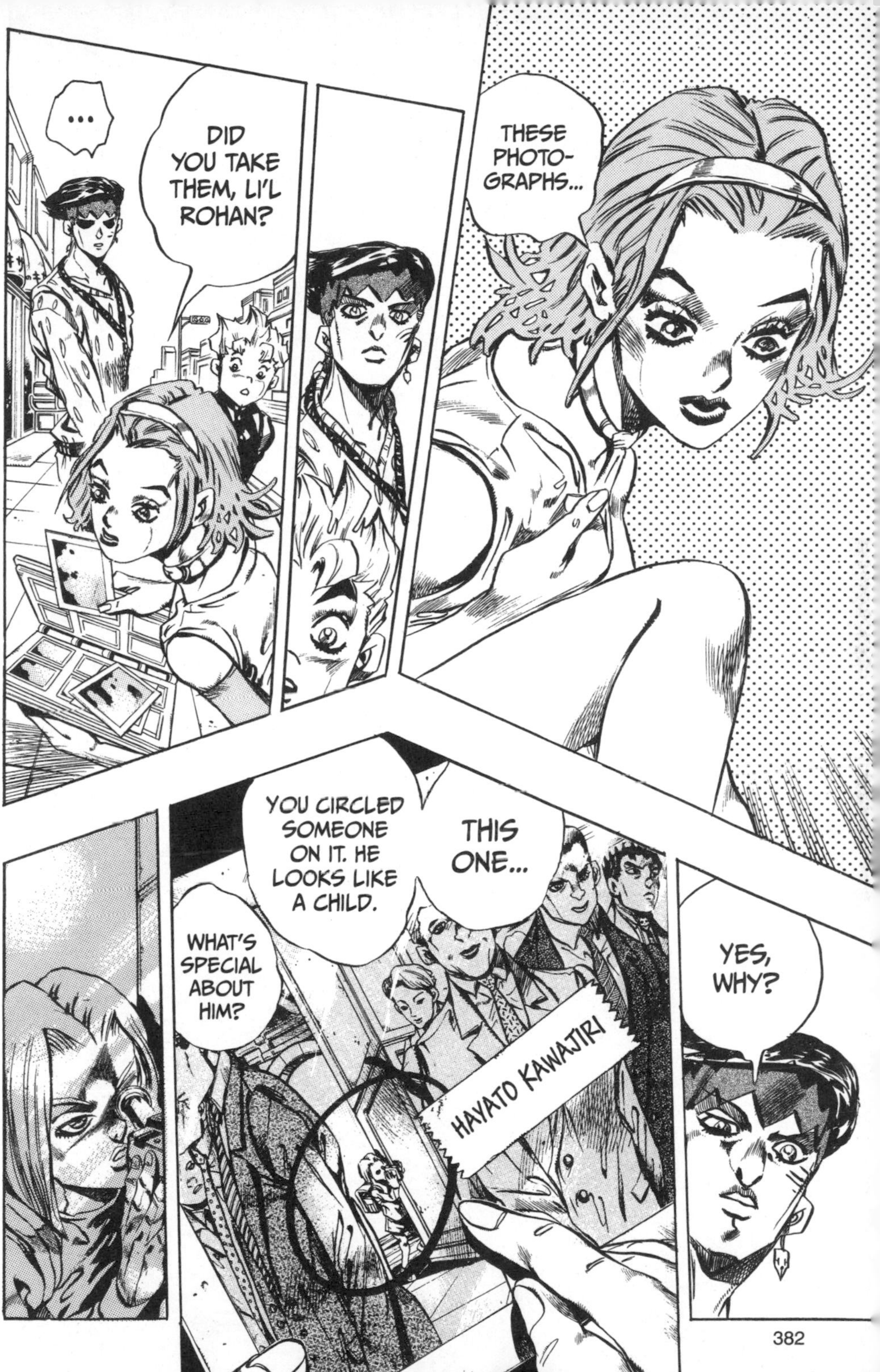
THESE PHOTO-GRAPHS...
DID YOU TAKE THEM, LI'L ROHAN?
...
YES, WHY?
THIS ONE...
YOU CIRCLED SOMEONE ON IT. HE LOOKS LIKE A CHILD.
HAYATO KAWAJIRI
WHAT'S SPECIAL ABOUT HIM?

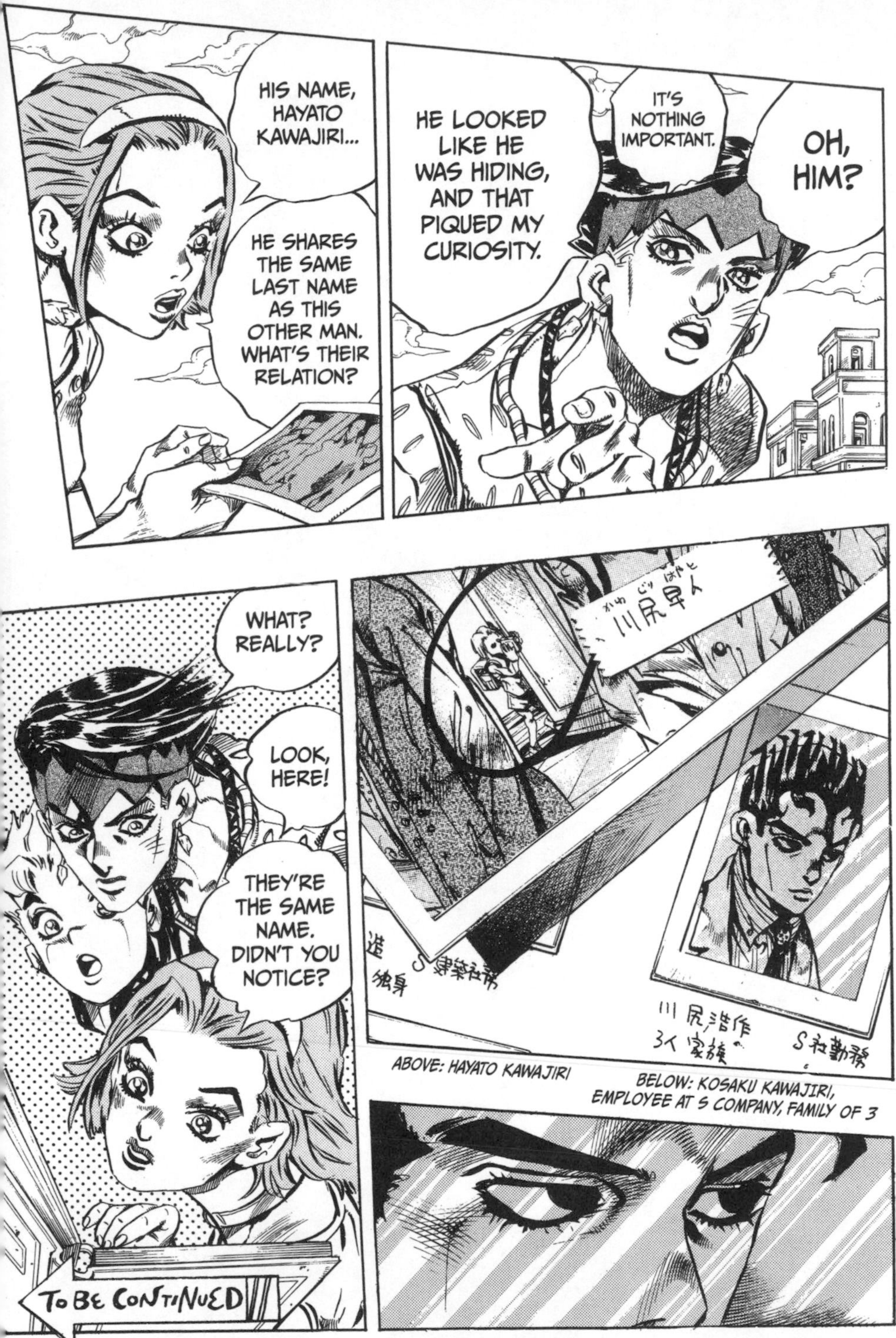
OH, HIM?
IT'S NOTHING IMPORTANT.
HE LOOKED LIKE HE WAS HIDING, AND THAT PIQUED MY CURIOSITY.
HIS NAME, HAYATO KAWAJIRI...
HE SHARES THE SAME LAST NAME AS THIS OTHER MAN. WHAT'S THEIR RELATION?
川尻早人
川尻浩作
3人家族
S社勤務
ABOVE: HAYATO KAWAJIRI
BELOW: KOSAKU KAWAJIRI, EMPLOYEE AT S COMPANY, FAMILY OF 3
WHAT? REALLY?
LOOK, HERE!
THEY'RE THE SAME NAME. DIDN'T YOU NOTICE?
TO BE CONTINUED

PART 4, VOLUME 8 / END

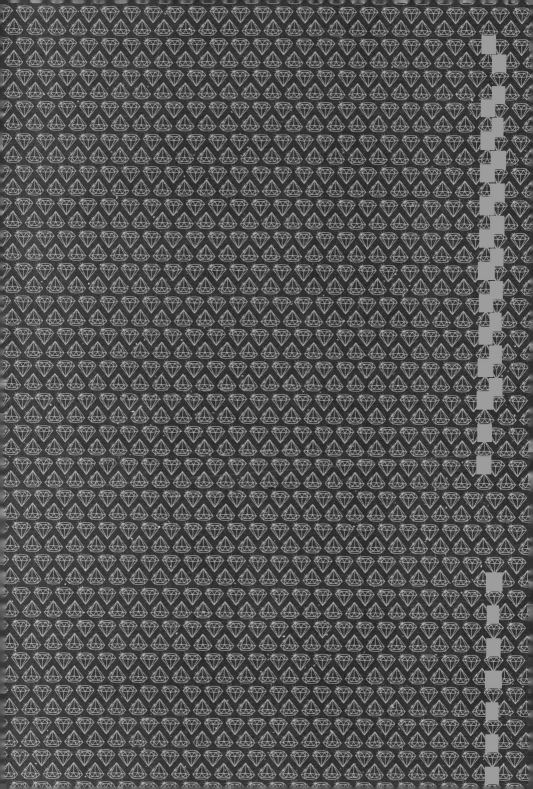

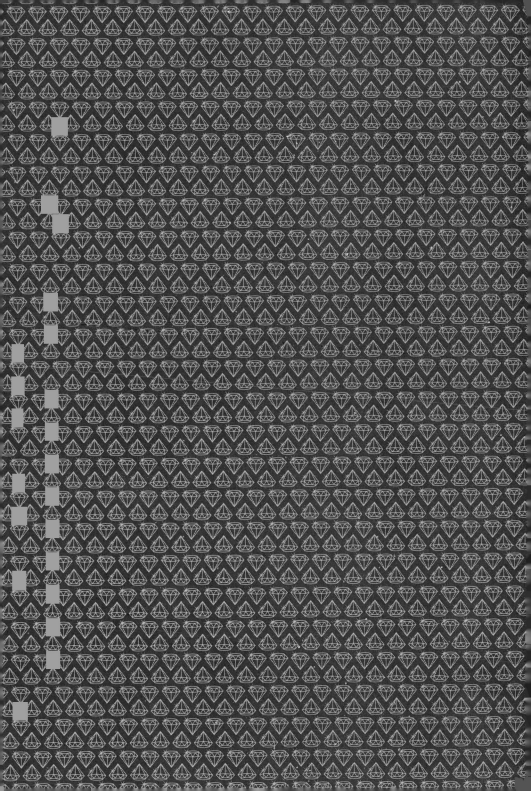

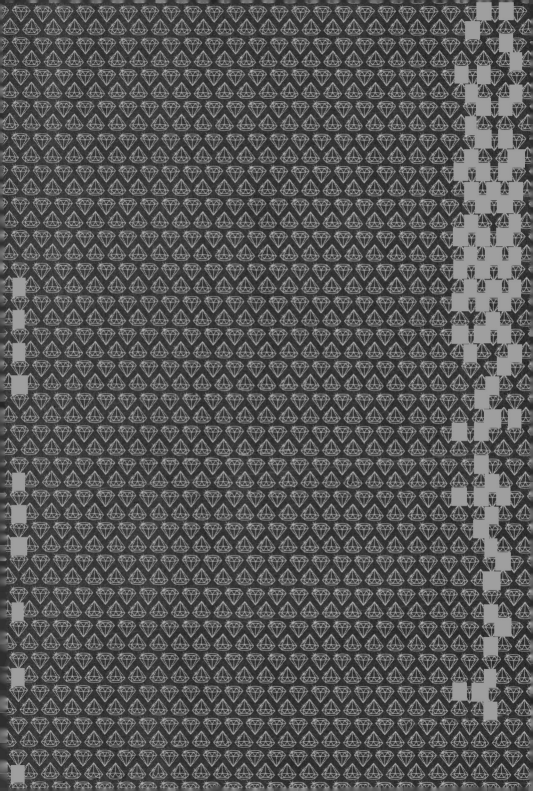

AUTHOR'S COMMENTS

STUDIO WILDLIFE OBSERVATIONS (PART 1)

The most common insect that infiltrates my studio is the lady-bug. Window screens are nothing to that bug. When they land on a surface, they tend to climb upward.

And when ladybugs land on the window screen, they climb up to the top rail—where a three-millimeter-wide gap is all they need to get inside.

Ladybugs aren't harmful, so when one comes in, we catch the insect and release it outside, and the same one will find its way back in again.

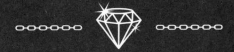

STUDIO WILDLIFE OBSERVATIONS (PART 2)

We keep a small flower garden on our balcony, but then some cats started to come and poop among the plants. Oh, come on! One of us heard that cats don't like weed killer, so we scattered some in the garden. Afterward, this old woman showed up at our door out of nowhere and told me, "Please don't put out weed killer. Think of those poor cats."

How did she know what we did? Our balcony is on the second floor!

Was she some kind of old cat lady that can talk to cats? She creeped me out.

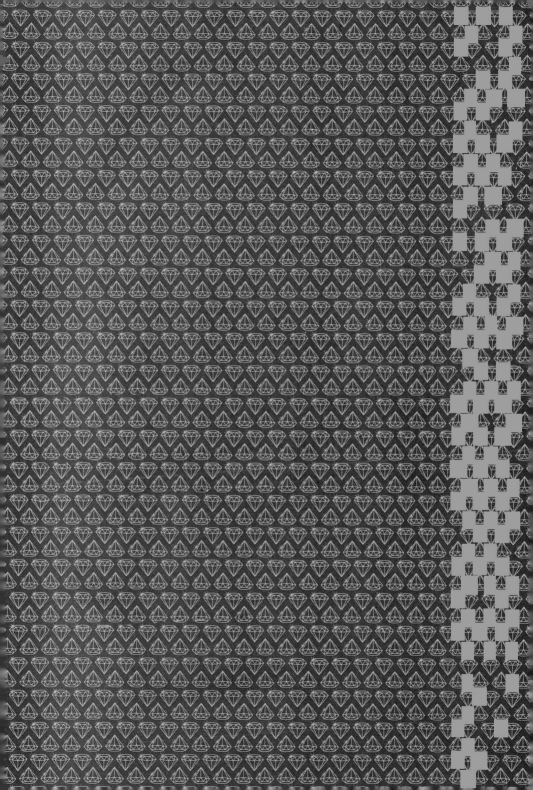

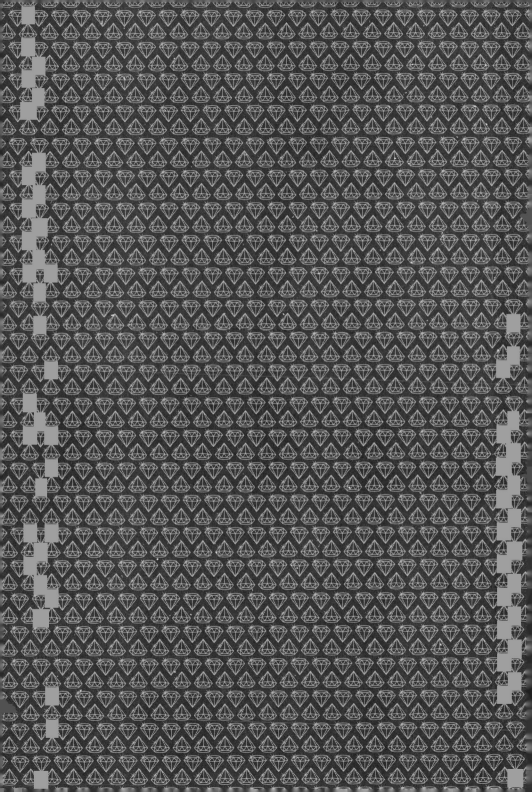

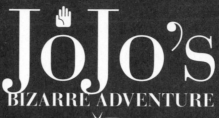

JoJo's

BIZARRE ADVENTURE

PART 4: DIAMOND IS UNBREAKABLE
VOLUME 8
BY HIROHIKO ARAKI

DELUXE HARDCOVER EDITION
Translation: Nathan A Collins
Touch-Up Art & Lettering: Mark McMurray
Design: Adam Grano
Editor: David Brothers

Printed in the U.S.A.

Published by VIZ Media, LLC
P.O. Box 77010
San Francisco, CA 94107

10 9 8 7 6 5 4 3 2 1
First printing, February 2021

VIZ MEDIA   SHONEN JUMP
viz.com

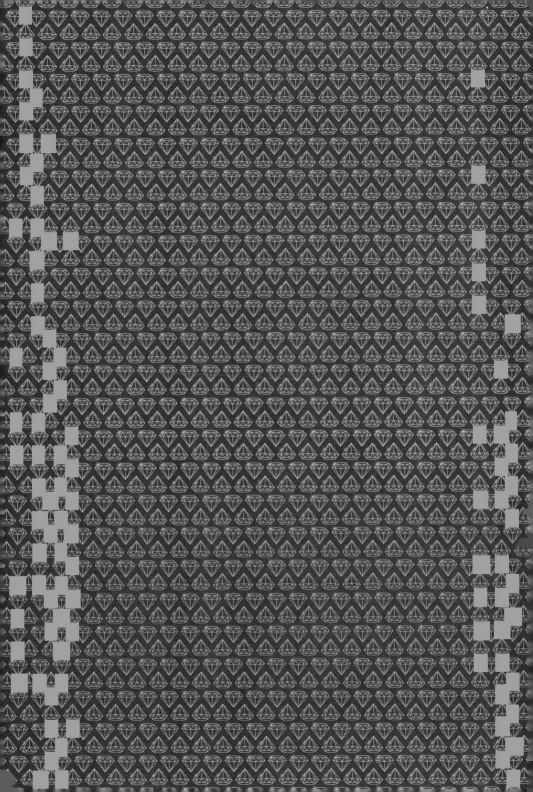

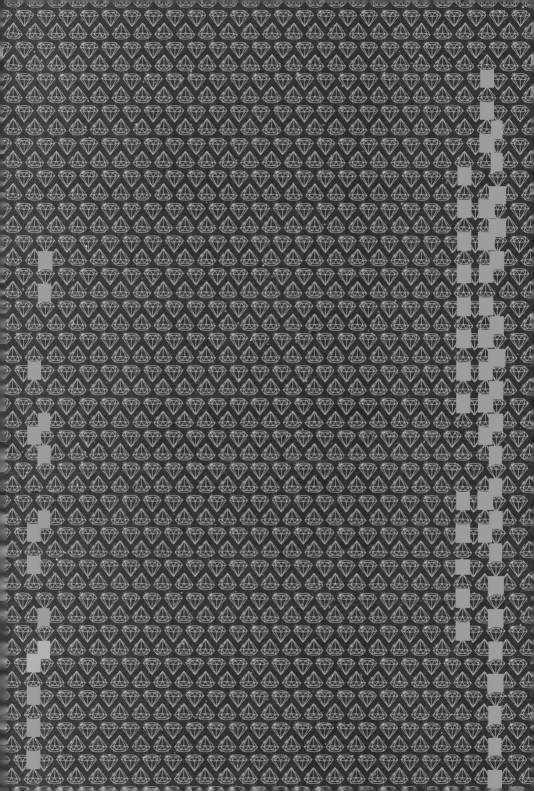

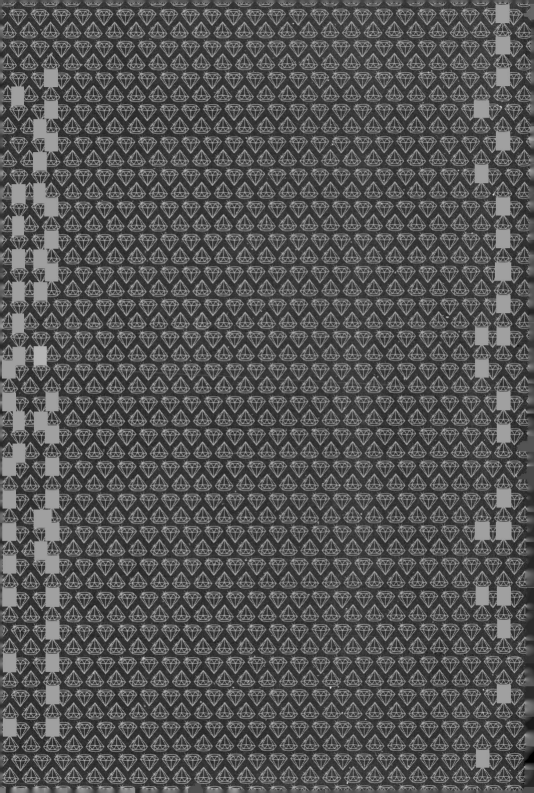

THIS IS THE LAST PAGE

JoJo's
BIZARRE ADVENTURE

has been printed in the original
Japanese format in order to preserve
the orientation of the original artwork.

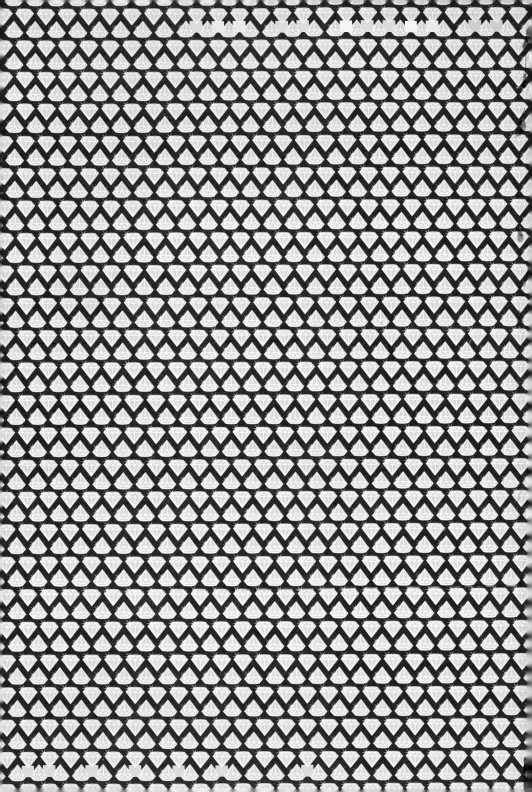